HOW THEY WON
THE WAR
IN THE PACIFIC

MORE MILITARY TITLES BY EDWIN P. HOYT

HOW THEY WON
THE WAR
IN THE PACIFIC

NIMITZ
AND HIS ADMIRALS

Edwin P. Hoyt

THE LYONS PRESS

Printed in The United States of America

Originally published by Weybright and Talley, 1970

10   9   8   7   6   5   4   3   2   1

The Library of Congress Cataloging-in-Publication Data
is available on file.

CONTENTS

v

INTRODUCTION

A nation is blessed indeed if it has leaders who add integrity, dedication, and unselfish patriotism to ability and courage. These are the Washingtons, Lincolns, Lees, Decaturs, Farraguts, and Nimitzes who have illumined the United States' course. One therefore welcomes this study of Nimitz and his admirals covering leadership in the Pacific through the greatest naval war of all time. An assiduous and skilled writer, Mr. Hoyt has contributed a unique book on World War II in this study of some of the key leaders who saved America in the Pacific.

Having served most of the war on Admiral Nimitz's staff, primarily in gunnery and training, and for the first year writing on the side the reports of operations, I find it fascinating now to see these seniors I knew and respected move again across the vast canvas of the Pacific, as viewed by an objective author.

They were men of varying talents and resilience under adversity or victory; they often had widely differing concepts on strategy and, as strong men should, fought to enforce their views. They could react differently on divergent courses to the same problem; yet all were dedicated Americans. All strove for her welfare; all were patriots. As human beings they had foibles, but remarkably few on the whole. The United States was fortunate in the breed of men she had, from the top down to the most junior rating.

Happy for America and the world that from earliest days an increasing number of Americans have risen to the challenge to serve the nation in leadership of freedom—as they did in World War II.

Mr. Hoyt plowed through seas of manuscripts in our Archives, he obtained, first-hand, the recollections of scores of leaders still living who had varying degrees of responsibility in the Pacific war. This useful book covers, at length or briefly, many leaders including the top fighting ones afloat and ashore like Spruance, Halsey, and Turner, each of unique ability.

Yet as one reads these thought-filled pages, a single man emerges like a mountain steadily rising over the horizon to a ship approaching from far at sea. This book shows Admiral Chester W. Nimitz as history will record him—the wise, calm tower of strength in adversity and success, the principal architect of victory in the Pacific in World War II. Many traits entered into Admiral Nimitz's strength. Not the least of them appears in his words that moved many listeners in Hawaii, on October 21, 1942:

> I am convinced that there comes a time when every leader entrusted with the safety of his country finds faith in God the ultimate inspiration for victory.

May the wisdom and strength that come from such faith continue to guide our leaders today as they guided those who voyage across these pages.

I am glad to participate in a small way in this book. May it help bring Americans to better knowledge of what so many sacrificed and achieved for our country in the Pacific in World War II.

In reading Mr. Hoyt's absorbing manuscript I could not help

comparing the events he unfolds with those we may face tomorrow —and will surely face if we are not wise, strong, and united.

This book shows that supremacy at sea was fundamental in all operations.

REAR ADMIRAL E. M. ELLER
USN (ret)
Director of Naval History

Washington, D.C.
January, 1970

PRELUDE

Early on the morning of December 7, 1941, ninety-four ships stood in Pearl Harbor. Half their crews had enjoyed the usual peacetime shore leave granted in port the night before. Since it was Sunday, most officers and men on shore and ship were preparing for a day of leisure or minimum duty. Pearl Harbor was quiet.

Suddenly through the morning air came squadrons of airplanes. At first the Americans thought the planes were their own—what else could they be? But in a moment some could make out the round red sun insignia of the Japanese Imperial Navy. Fighters, dive bombers, torpedo bombers, and horizontal bombers came down. They dove with remarkable accuracy, aiming for the big capital ships, the eight battleships tied up around Ford Island. Soon Arizona was burning and wrecked; Oklahoma had capsized, trapping many men below decks; West Virginia was sunk, California was

*sinking; Maryland, Tennessee, Nevada, and Utah were badly dam-
aged—Utah was beginning to capsize; and Pennsylvania, the flagship
of the fleet, was smashed in drydock.*

*Coming into Pearl Harbor a week later, not having been present
at the attack, Rear Admiral John H. Newton was aghast at what he
saw, even though by the time he arrived some of the damage had
already been repaired, some ships had moved toward the west coast
for major repairs. Newton, Commander of Cruisers in the Scouting
Force, issued a message to the officers and men of his cruisers, not
knowing yet fully what had happened to the fleet.*

*"Today I saw the destruction wrought upon the Navy in Pearl
Harbor by the Japanese on December 7, 1941," he wrote. "The
sight was not a pleasant one. It was a sight that must arouse the
wrath of every American. Turrets of stricken battleships, trained
fore and aft, gave mute testimony to the stealthy swiftness with which
the yellow serpents struck. They struck while their government's
representatives were being received in good faith by our President.
They struck in accordance with a diabolical plan conceived in crafty
minds, treacherous and cunning beyond our conception. In the
planning and execution of the dastardly attack they were aided
undoubtedly by their no less diabolical Nazi allies and certainly by
the incomparably low form of animal life, the fifth columnist.*

*"This heinous crime against the navy and the marine corps, our
country and the decency and integrity of the civilized world, must be
avenged. I assign this task to these heavy cruisers. Let every officer
and man be ever alert to detect the enemy's stealthy approach in the
air, on the water, and beneath the seas. Let every officer and man
work to the utmost of his ability to the end that whenever the enemy
is brought to battle he will be sunk swiftly and surely.*

"Let REMEMBER PEARL HARBOR *be our battle cry."*

*Admiral Newton's emotional message is repeated here, although
it is likely to draw shouts of disdain from young cynics born after
the event. "It reminds me of True War Magazine, or some such,"
wrote one young student of the new school of history, one of the
Americans of the 1970's who has no concept, obviously, of the impact with which these words struck the nation, or the fact that
"Remember Pearl Harbor" was celebrated in song and story for the*

next few months, as a badly hurt America struggled to strike a blow of its own in vengeance for the sneak attack. It is reminiscent of True War Magazine, "or some such," as are most of the stories that were likely to come out of such a war. The narrative of the war has been written a number of times, from Samuel Eliot Morison's exhaustive multivolume History of United States Naval Operations in World War II, *to single-volume histories and even juvenile books and books for young adults. But what has never been told before is the inside story of the decisions of the admirals—the naval high command who conducted the war in the Pacific—and the reasons for their actions, actions sometimes totally incomprehensible from the bridge of a destroyer or the cockpit of an F-6-F. What follows is the study of Nimitz and his admirals in the making of the Central Pacific victory that meant the defeat of the Japanese.*

EDWIN P. HOYT

January 3, 1970
Annapolis

ACKNOWLEDGMENTS

In this book on Nimitz and his admirals, I have tried not to retell the history of the Pacific war, but to give a picture of the principal commanders of the Central Pacific campaign and above all to show how and why the war was fought as it was. The official biography of Admiral Nimitz is being written by Professor E. B. Potter of the U.S. Naval Academy and will be published by the United States Naval Institute. My book is not primarily a biography, although there is biography in it, or a history, although it deals with the stuff of history—but the study of commands and commanders, and how they related to one another.

I was extremely fortunate in having the help of many people who "were there" at Pearl Harbor and in the Pacific theater in positions of authority and competence or who are closely related to the war in the Pacific. Some of them are, approximately in the order in which I was in touch with them: Rear Admiral Ernest M. Eller, Director of Naval History and former assistant gunnery officer of Cincpac; Rear Admiral Mell A. Peterson; Captain W. B. Goulett; E. B. Potter, of the U.S. Naval Academy faculty; Mrs. John Towers; Katherine Fleming Shea; Captain Thomas K. Kimmell; Mrs. Joan East; Dr. Clark G. Reynolds; General Robert E. Hogaboom, USMC; Vice Admiral John R. Redman; Admiral George W. Anderson, Jr.; Mrs. Raymond A. Spruance; Rear Admiral Chester W. Nimitz, Jr.; Rear Admiral C. L. C. Atkeson; Vice Admiral Charles P. Mason; Vice Admiral Carl F. Espe; Rear Admiral Earl L. Sackett; Captain Harold Hopkins; Mrs. Daniel Barbey; Rear Admiral Howard L. Collins; Captain R. C. Bourne; Vice Admiral W. M. Callaghan; Vice Admiral Charles A. Pownall; Captain F. Kent Loomis; Rear Admiral Preston Mercer; Rear Admiral W. H. Organ; John P. Cady; Rear Admiral Charles Johnes Moore; M. M. Marshall, Ministry of Defense, Whitehall, London; Harry Schwartz, U.S. National Archives; Captain P. C. Crosley; James E. Bassett; Captain Howell Arthur Lamar (for use of his reminiscences in the Department of Naval History files); Commander Carl J. Pritchard; Rear Admiral Milo Draemel; Rear Admiral Waldo Drake; Admiral Thomas Hart; Kenneth W. McArdle; Admiral Cato D. Glover; Admiral Aubrey W. Fitch; Vice Admiral James Fife; Rear Admiral Richard W. Bates; Admiral Arthur W. Radford; Admiral Harold B. Sallada; Ward H. Oehmann; R. B. McCann, Dr. Gerald Wheeler; Admiral John Hoover.

I am particularly grateful to a number of archivists at the Classified Archives of the Naval History Division in Washington, and specifically to Dr. Dean Allard of the Naval History Division and Mrs. Kathy Lloyd. Artemus Gates, former Assistant Secretary of the Navy for Air, was most helpful. So was R. A. Winnacker, historian in the office of the Secretary of Defense, and so were so many other persons that I cannot possibly name them all. Specific quotations and attributions, from conversations and documents, will be found to annotate the text.

As to bibliography, the author consulted every book he could find dealing with the Pacific war. More valuable, of course, was Morison's semi-official history of operations. Other very useful books were *The War at Sea*, by E. B. Potter and Admiral Nimitz, and Clark Reynolds' *The Fast Carriers*, but of the hundreds of books examined each produced a point of view or a bit of description that was valuable. Still, most of the book relies on specific conversations, documents, and notes such as those taken by permission of Mrs. Towers from the very extensive diaries Admiral John Towers kept during the war.

Lastly, I am very much indebted to various people who have read portions or all of this book in manuscript or proof—including Rear Admiral E. M. Eller, Vice Admiral B. L. Austin, Vice Admiral Andrew McB. Jackson, Admiral Harry W. Hill, Rear Admiral Charles Johnes Moore, Vice Admiral George Dyer, Professor E. B. Potter, Chairman of the Department of History, U.S. Naval Academy, and Dr. Gerald Wheeler, Chairman of the Department of History at San Jose State College.

Most of the information comes from the U.S. Naval Archives in the Washington Navy Yard, from documents and the papers of the men involved. References to these sources are to be found in the notes at the end of the book.

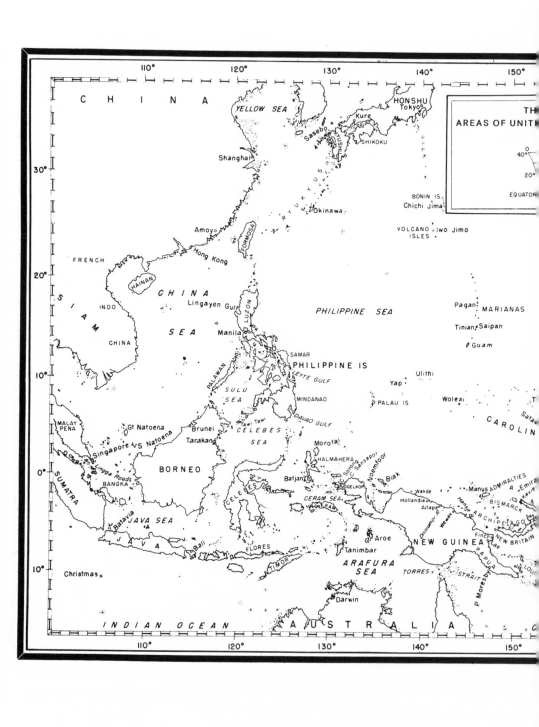

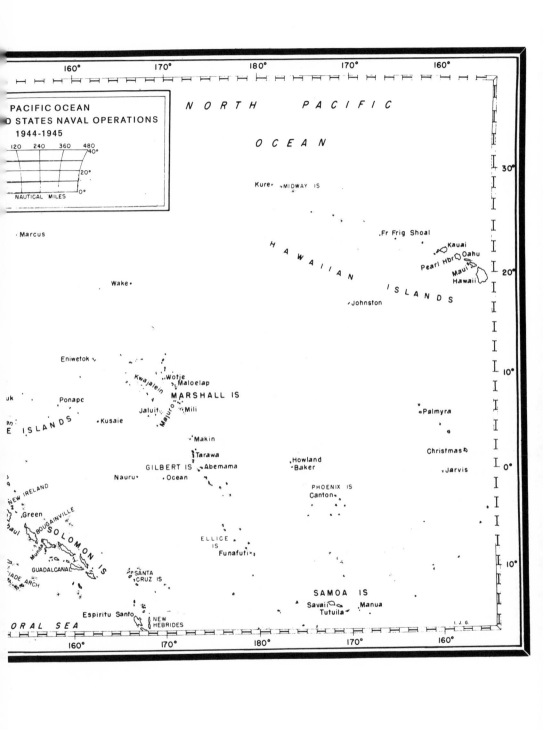

PACIFIC OCEAN
O STATES NAVAL OPERATIONS
1944-1945

120   240   360   480
40°
20°
0°
NAUTICAL MILES

N O R T H   P A C I F I C

O C E A N

Kure· ·MIDWAY IS

·Marcus

·Fr Frig Shoal
Kauai
Pearl Hbr Oahu
Maui
Hawaii

30°

20°

H A W A I I A N   I S L A N D S

Wake·

·Johnston

Eniwetok·

·Wotje
Kwajalein Maloelap
MARSHALL IS

uk·   Ponape·

ISLANDS   ·Kusaie

Jaluit·   Mili
Majuro·

·Makin

·Palmyra

10°

an·

·Tarawa
GILBERT IS ·Abemama

·Howland
·Baker

Christmas

Nauru·   ·Ocean

PHOENIX IS
Canton·

·Jarvis

0°

9·
·NEW IRELAND
·Green
BOUGAINVILLE
S O L O M O N IS
Munda·
·GUADALCANAL
ADE ARCH·

·SANTA
·CRUZ IS

ELLICE
IS
Funafuti·

SAMOA IS
·Savaii ·Manua
Tutuila

10°

Espiritu Santo·
·NEW
HEBRIDES

O R A L   S E A

I. J. G.

Chapter
One

CONFUSION

December 7–December 21, 1941

By mid-morning it was all over. Some officers said the last attack had come at 0920; some believed it arrived twenty minutes later. The ships were still firing at 1100, but by noon the shock was wearing off and Admiral Husband E. Kimmel's staff was beginning to pull itself together for retaliatory action against an enemy that had suddenly disappeared.

Smoke rose above Ford Island and the surrounding installations at Pearl Harbor. The battleship *Arizona* at mooring F-7 had been struck repeatedly and had settled atop the twelve-inch main that provided fresh water for Ford Island, crushing the pipe. A six-inch temporary line running to the south end of the island had been broken on the Navy Yard side by Japanese bombs. But already the Fourteenth Naval District's public works officers and men were repairing the lines, placing a new sixteen-inch main from Hospital Point to the island.

This rebound symbolized the spirit at Pearl Harbor on that frightful December 7, 1941, as Captain H. F. Bruns symbolized the Navy. Well before noon the captain had organized the workers in the yard to get the gantry crane clear of the fire that burned between drydocks, and the new drydock was put in shape for service. As anyone could see by casting an eye about the wreckage of the battleships in the harbor, drydocks aplenty would be needed.

Captain Bruns and his men symbolized the Navy spirit but they did not symbolize American naval policy of that moment, for if one flat statement about Pearl Harbor could be made it must be that America's naval leaders, from the President–Commander in Chief down to the commander in chief of the Pacific Fleet, were surprised. The extent of the surprise, the reasons for it, are matters for limitless debate among naval historians. But there is no question about the surprise. It was an old Japanese technique—one that had worked very well at Port Arthur nearly half a century earlier. At that time the Japanese had been talking with the Russian czar's government in Saint Petersburg, while the Japanese fleet went to war. Now it was happening again; one problem was that this time the techniques of naval warfare had so changed that the victims of the surprise attack were allowed no leeway at all. Even if the United States Army Air Corps—charged with the defense of Hawaiian air—had been thoroughly alert, some of the damage would still have been done. The battleships were caught in harbor that day—but not because the Pacific Fleet was totally napping. The big ships were moored because they were too slow to keep up with the carrier task forces that were on almost constant patrol in the Pacific.

Vice Admiral Wilson Brown, then commanding the Scouting Force, had worked out a program with Admiral Kimmel, which called for one task force to be in Pearl Harbor on the weekend, while two were at work, guarding.

The state of mind of the officers of the fleet could only be regarded as negative. For four long years the fleet had been on the alert. The war scares had begun in 1937 and 1938. The newspapers would run "scare" headlines, the rumors would spread across the country, and soon there would be an official report of a threat. Three such frights, beginning early in 1938, put the wind up in the whole fleet. Typical was one report of an impending Japanese attack on the battleships lying in San Pedro harbor. The Battle Force came to general quarters on this occasion. All liberty was canceled. Officers were called back to their ships. The whaleboats of the battleships were run over the side and they circled their ships all night long, to keep invaders away. A division of destroyers was called up from San Diego to patrol, and the planes of the Battle Force, the carriers, and the patrol force flew missions all over that area of the Pacific.

On such occasions the tension was replaced by a flood of relief. But the relief-tension-relief pattern brought with it a certain anesthetic reaction among the officers of the fleet, like the reaction of the towns-people in the fable of the little boy who cried wolf. As an officer of the Pacific Fleet in those days said, "All those scares got to be ridiculous and people thought, 'Oh, Thunder, here's another one of these . . . we won't pay any attention . . . .'"

By 1940 there was also a good deal of defeatism in high places. One day that year, Captain Harry W. Hill of the War Plans Division in Washington was called upon to make a presentation of the Orange Plan—the war plan against Japan—before a number of the senior officers of the Navy. His latest assignment had been as fleet war plans officer to Admiral Block and Admiral Richardson.

Hill made a vigorous presentation, and was dismayed to discover that the admirals looked upon the plan as totally impractical.

Hill argued that the plan had to be made with the assumption that in time of war the material would be made available to the Navy, but the admirals, having seen Congress cut down their budget year after year, were uniformly gloomy, including Admiral Harold R. Stark, the Chief of Naval Operations.

The single exception was Admiral Ernest J. King, commander in chief of the Atlantic Fleet. King, furious with his brother admirals, berated them that day for their lack of aggressive spirit. Right there, he made a follower of Harry Hill.

Not all the admirals were convinced, and the fleet continued to be divided between incautious optimism on the one hand and over-cautious pessimism on the other. And yet that is an oversimplification.

The fact that the carriers were not caught at Pearl Harbor in the Japanese attack was not simply a matter of luck, it was part of a careful plan. For two years the fleet had been based at Pearl Harbor; for many more years than that the fleet had practiced carrier task force attacks on the big base, attacks that in reality could only come from one source—Japan.

On Pearl Harbor day, Vice Admiral William F. Halsey was on his way to port with Task Force 8 and the carrier *Enterprise*. His guns were armed and his torpedoes carried warheads. Rear Admiral Milo Draemel, his second in command, had taken off, on orders, to form Task Force 2 while at sea, and had come back to port. Draemel's principal assignment was as commander of destroyers, Pacific, and his destroyers had live ammunition in the ready boxes, depth charges in the racks, and warheads on torpedoes.

Draemel gives an indication of the quality of surprise in his story of those days. He had brought his destroyers, the cruisers, and the three battleships of Halsey's force back to Pearl Harbor on Friday, nursing the seventeen-knot battleships into port with the faster ships. The smell of war was in the air. On that Friday, Admiral Draemel had gone to fleet headquarters for a talk with Captain W. W. Smith, Admiral Kimmel's chief of staff. Smith had informed him that in Washington the Japanese had burned their diplomatic code books.

That word meant war to Draemel, and he said as much.

Then he went back to his flagship, the cruiser *Detroit*, to await developments.

Rear Admiral Draemel was hesitant to give shore leave to his destroyer men, for in his opinion the world situation was critical. That day, however, the cruiser sailors and the men of the battleships had shore leave, so he granted leave. Admiral Kimmel, he said to himself, must have information that a destroyer commander would not have.

Draemel was aboard the *Detroit* when the Japanese attacked. Before 1030 his little ships had steam, and he was ready to go to sea. He was designated as commander Special Task Force One and directed to reinforce Admiral Halsey's force returning from landing planes on Wake Island. The order was revoked and about one half hour later he was directed to proceed, which indicates a measure of the confusion that existed at Pearl Harbor that morning.

In Washington the confusion was as it was at Pearl Harbor. War was expected, or half expected, but the coming of it had caught all America unawares. Secretary of the Navy Frank Knox was relaxing that day, quite a usual thing to do on a Sunday. Undersecretary James Forrestal was off in Long Island for the weekend. Assistant Secretary for Air Artemus Gates had flown down to Pensacola, and was playing golf there with Captain A. C. Read, commander of the naval air station. Gates, Read, a young commander named Arthur Radford, and several other officers were teeing off when the word of attack came. Gates did not believe it, and it was only when messages were brought to the course that the game was canceled and the officers went to Read's headquarters.

One message had ordered Captain Read to execute the current war plan, Rainbow, against Orange, which meant the Japanese. Gates was extremely interested in seeing that plan, then and there. They went to the safe, and discovered that it was closed by a time lock, and could not be opened until Monday morning. There was an indication of the readiness of all America on that December 7.

Once the attack came, those charged with the defense of the Unted States moved. Artemus Gates flew back to Washington. Forrestal came back from Long Island. Before they got there, the admirals on duty in the Navy Department had begun filing into the office of Admiral Stark, Chief of Naval Operations, to wait for word of the damage and the situation. The messages were coming, one after another, and each was more portentous of loss than the one before it.

The very existence of the job that Artemus Gates held indicated part of the change that had begun in naval thinking in the very recent past. Gates had been appointed Assistant Secretary for Air in the summer of 1941, and when he came to Washington, Secretary Knox had explained that he was giving Gates all his authority in the field of naval air, because he recognized the need for air power, but was not himself air-oriented. Gates was a Forrestal protégé, both were old-time naval aviators, and their presence together showed the change.

The meetings began, then, as the officers filed into Main Navy, the old building of the fleet forces. Rear Admiral Chester W. Nimitz was one of the early arrivals that day. He was chief of the Bureau of Navigation, the Navy's personnel department, and was regarded as one of the rising young stars of the fleet. A few months earlier, at Bremerton on the west coast, Rear Admiral E. B. Fenner, one of the old admirals, had asked Nimitz if he was ready to take command when the war began. Nimitz, who was then commander of a cruiser division, had stopped off on his way to California from Alaska. In his shy, controlled way, Nimitz had smiled and said nothing, passed it off. But for the past five years the seniors of the Navy had been keeping their eyes on Nimitz, along with Kimmel and Ghormley. In his important post, the white-haired, smiling Nimitz had maintained an almost unbelievable gentleness and equilibrium, whatever the request from his seniors, the commanders of the fleets, and the administrators above him. He had been chief of the Bureau of Navigation since 1939. It was not a job to make an admiral popular, but Nimitz had become extremely popular. As always in his career, men above and below him had been impressed by him— those above with his dedication and quiet competence, those below with his sense of compassion, his feeling for justice, and a humility that was not too usual among those who achieved flag rank.

Another admiral who filed into Stark's office that morning was Rear Admiral John H. Towers, Chief of the Navy's Bureau of Aeronautics. He and Nimitz were old acquaintances. Most recently, they had been fighting a battle for control of the naval air forces, with Towers pushing to secure air training for the Bureau of Aeronautics, and Nimitz standing steadfast for the traditional Navy way, whereby air training fell under the Bureau of Navigation. Towers was a brilliant aviator, Naval Aviator No. 2 as a matter of record, who had come up to achieve flag rank in an arm of the naval service that the aviators felt had first been viewed with deep suspicion, and then with cordial dislike by the old-fashioned admirals of the past, despite the successes of Admirals Moffet, Yarnell, and Reeves. To Towers, Nimitz represented the past—the best of it perhaps, because Towers respected Nimitz for his abilities. But to Towers, Nimitz was a battleship admiral, while, he, Towers, had the airman's independence and contempt for the old way of thinking.

The admirals and the civilian chieftains met in Washington on December 8, and that same day the joint board of the Army and

Navy convened to talk of the war. The only senior officer absent was General Arnold, the Army Air Corps commander. He had gone fishing in those happy days just before December 7, and had not yet returned.

The admirals and generals met again on December 9 for two hours, and by that time the picture was becoming clear. After the Pearl Harbor attack, off in London, Captain Charles A. Lockwood, the U.S. naval attaché to the embassy, had cursed and scribbled furiously in his diary on learning of the destruction dealt among the battleships.

"Who is responsible?" he had asked angrily, if rhetorically. It seemed all the more insane and infuriating to Lockwood, because on the night of December 6, the British admiralty had notified him of the movement of a large part of the Japanese fleet. But the British were watching the movement in terms of their own territories, and when nothing appeared to menace them the alert had been canceled and Britain had relaxed as much as a nation at war might.

But if Captain Lockwood's question was rhetorical, Secretary Knox was in anything but a rhetorical state of mind as he pondered the same question. On December 9 the Secretary set out for Pearl Harbor to discover precisely what had gone wrong, and who was responsible.

At Pearl Harbor the activity was intense and had been since midday on December 7. If there was momentary confusion in the headquarters of the Pacific Fleet, it was no more than that. When the attack began that morning, the staff duty officer and his assistants scurried about the officers' quarters above the base, and much further afield. Admiral Kimmel lived in a big house on Makalapa Drive, and he was one of the first to be notified. But his flag secretary, for example, lived beyond Diamond Head, and so did many officers. The fleet was not on a real war status, it was as simple as that. There was part of the confusion, for many of the attributes of war status were apparent. For example, Admiral Kimmel had ordered the ships to have ammunition at the guns, and thus they were able to get away antiaircraft fire in a minute or so after the bombs and torpedoes began falling.

The activity had intensified all morning, and all afternoon. By

1445 the *Lexington's* task force was proceeding at 27 knots to intercept the enemy "carrier" (someone thought there was only one),
on the assumption that the Japanese had sent their planes from a
point 200 miles south of Pearl Harbor and had then departed back
southward toward Jaluit. In fact, the Japanese had come in from
the north, and had retired to the north. Yet if the assumption was
wrong, the effort was not lacking. The *Enterprise* task force was out
searching too, as far as 700 miles out of Pearl Harbor. PBY's, patrol
bombers, were spaced 50 miles apart and were searching. Army aircraft were alerted for search, and the available ships were out on
patrol. The *Saratoga*, which arrived at San Diego just as the Japanese
struck Pearl Harbor, loaded munition, stores, and planes all night
and sailed for Oahu Monday morning.

Army and Navy were now fully alert, so alert that in mid-afternoon the Army warned the Navy to look out for parachute troops
when five unidentified planes were reported over Honolulu. That
afternoon the fleet prepared for an air raid at dawn, and all heavy
ships were warned to stay away from Pearl Harbor after dark.

On December 8 the confusion seemed to be lessening. There
were reports of attacks: enemy planes were "sighted" over Oahu early
in the afternoon, an unidentified submarine was spotted off Diamond
Head, and two more were seen south of Hickam towers. But to match
these fears came the reassuring word from the Army information
center that the Army was reasonably sure there were no enemy
planes within 200 miles. By the next morning calm was restored, so
that all concerned were reminded that the Pan American Clipper
would fly over Oahu shortly after 1100 on its way from Midway to
Hilo, and should not be shot down. Admiral Halsey's Task Force
8 was told to return to Pearl at moderate speed with one destroyer
squadron. When the *Enterprise* entered the harbor, the squadron
was to report to the commandant of the Fourteenth Naval District
for antisubmarine warfare. As for the rest of the task force, it was to
operate fifty miles north of the Kauai-Oahu line until relieved.

Kimmel was ordering ships' plates and parts, the liner *Lurline*
was chartered to bring repair and salvage experts from the mainland, and all efforts were being made at Pearl Harbor to do what
could be done with the materials at hand. Hawaii and its bases were

on real war status now. The base went to general quarters a half hour before sunrise from total blackout, remained alert all day, and went back to general quarters. The Pacific Fleet and its commanders were ready. Ships moved in and out of the harbor, but most of those available for patrol were out constantly, searching for the Japanese, their crews angry and looking for a fight.

The confusion of these first days was not confined to Pearl Harbor: on December 9 San Francisco Radio Station KNX broadcast a report that sixty Japanese planes had flown to within a few miles of the Golden Gate before being driven off by Army and Navy fighters. There had, of course, been no such attack.

The schizophrenia that had marked the past was still present, too. From Washington came this disheartening advice, originated in the office of the Chief of Naval Operations, Admiral Stark:

. . . Because of the great success of the Japanese raid on the seventh it is expected to be promptly followed up by additional attacks in order to render Hawaii untenable as a naval and air base, in which eventuality it is believed the Japanese have suitable forces for the initial occupation of the islands other than Oahu, including Midway, Maui, and Hawaii. Under present circumstances it seems questionable that Midway can be retained but it is hoped that Johnson, Palmyra, and Samoa may be. In expectation of further air raids and the inadequacy of defenses of Oahu, the chief of naval operations considers it essential that wounded vessels able to proceed under their own power should be sent to the west coast as soon as possible with due regard to safety from current raiding forces and very great importance of effective counter attacks on these raiders by you. Until defenses are increased it is doubtful if Pearl should be used as a base, except for patrol craft, naval aircraft, and submarines, or for short periods when it is reasonably certain Japanese attacks will not be made. Consider it especially important that submarines and tenders not suffer losses . . . .

Admiral Kimmel was dismayed to receive this message. To be sure, the Japanese were on the move. He had received messages

telling of attacks on Midway and Wake Island on December 8. The
next day Guam was attacked, and Wake was struck again. He had
been out of contact with Guam and Wake part of the time, and
when the news came, it was not encouraging. Still, Kimmel had no
intention of giving up. The Navy yard was asking Washington for
5000 cots, 10,000 blankets, 2000 scoop shovels; for wrenches, automatic pistols, belts, and holsters; for 10,000 steel helmets and
2000 more Springfield rifles. Kimmel and his men wanted to fight,
not talk about retreat. On December 11 Kimmel replied to Stark:

> Since the appearance of enemy in this area, all tactical
> efforts with all available forces have been vigorously prosecuted
> toward locating and destroying the enemy forces, primarily
> carriers. Our heavy losses have not seriously depleted our fast
> striking forces nor reduced morale and determination. Pearl must
> be used for essential supply and overhaul facilities and must be
> provided with additional aircraft, both army and navy, also
> relief pilots and maintenance personnel. Pearl channels are
> clear, the industrial establishment is intact and doing excellent
> work. Otherwise your suggestions being carried out.

This forthright attitude, even if particularly unresponsive to
the Chief of Naval Operations, quite fitted a young admiral who
had been regarded as one of the Navy's "comers" in recent years.
Kimmel was a Kentucky boy who had entered the Naval Academy in
1900 and graduated in 1904. He had served in destroyers, battleships,
and cruisers, and was Franklin D. Roosevelt's naval aide when Roosevelt was Assistant Secretary of the Navy in World War I. He had
seen action in the pacification of Cuba and at Vera Cruz, then was
executive officer of the USS *Arkansas* at the time of the German
surrender. He was noted for his gunnery and his innovations in the
field. He had served with distinction ashore at the U.S. Naval Gun
Factory in Washington, and as captain of the naval yard at Cavite in
the Philippines. He had commanded a division of destroyers in the
Asiatic Fleet during the Chinese revolution. He had been a battleship commander, a cruiser divisional commander, and chief of staff
to the commander of the Battle Force in the Pacific. Kimmel had

gone to the Naval War College. He had served a hitch as assistant director of fleet training, and another in the office of the Chief of Naval Operations. He had been naval budget officer for a time, and had gone on a goodwill mission as a sort of ambassador. Early in 1941 he was commander of cruisers in the Pacific Fleet Battle Force, a very responsible position, when suddenly President Roosevelt decided to remove Admiral James O. Richardson as commander of the fleet. Although Kimmel was very distinctly a junior admiral at the time, he was advanced past many others (Wilson Brown included) and jumped into the job of commander in chief, Pacific fleet.

He had been advanced thus because in the eyes of the senior naval officers and the civilians who ultimately controlled selection he was an outstanding officer. His predecessor, Admiral Richardson, had once spoken out about the Navy way in promotions, giving an idea of what it took to make admiral:

> Only the officer who is intelligent, thoroughly capable, and energetic will reach the commander's grade, and only the officer who is brilliant, resourceful, thoroughly capable, and energetic and has good health will reach the captain's grade—and the rank of flag officer is reserved for those few officers who combine outstanding personality and good fortune, with the other characteristics listed . . . .

Kimmel had been bright, diligent, healthy, and lucky until December 7, 1941. On that day he was still bright, diligent, and healthy.

On December 11 Kimmel was trying to fight a war, with very little help. The day before, he and his staff had prepared an estimate of the military situation. Because of the loss of the battleship force to the fleet, the United States in the Pacific was committed to the strategic defensive for the time being. "However," said the report, "a very powerful striking force of carriers, cruisers, and destroyers survive. These forces must be operated boldly and vigorously on the tactical offensive in order to retrieve our initial disaster."

The task of the fleet, for the moment, was to protect sea communications of the United States and her allies, to support the Army in defense of Hawaii, Samoa, Midway, Johnson, and Palmyra; to raid the enemy at sea, and to defend Wake Island. The fleet was also to protect the area east of 180 degrees longitude and prevent extension of the Japanese into the western hemisphere.

Considering the enemy courses of action, Kimmel and his staff concluded that the Japanese would make more raids on Hawaii, Midway, and perhaps the Aleutian Islands. Kimmel expected more raids on Wake and perhaps a landing attempt. He foresaw the concentration of Japanese submarines between Oahu and the mainland, and submarine and surface raids on communications between the islands and the west coast.

The American course of action would be to keep the naval forces at sea, anticipating these raids, to fight off the raids and keep the fleet forces north and west of Oahu to intercept any force moving toward or away from the west coast. The bases, such as Wake and Samoa, must be protected.

He proposed to send the battleships back to the Pacific coast, and use searching and striking groups of carriers, cruisers, and destroyers—supplied largely at sea—to support bases and intercept the Japanese.

Kimmel would have three task forces, each consisting of one fleet carrier, two or three cruisers, and six to nine destroyers. One task force would operate near Midway, one would operate north of Oahu, and the third would be en route or being supplied at Pearl Harbor. On arrival of a fourth carrier, an additional force would be organized.

Besides this, battleships and destroyers would convoy ships between the west coast and Hawaii. Shipping would be kept to a minimum as far as Australia and New Zealand were concerned. Submarines would patrol Japanese waters and protect Midway and Wake islands.

On December 11 Admiral Kimmel was trying to follow this plan. Task Force 12, commanded by Admiral Wilson Brown, was 230 miles west of Oahu and having trouble fueling. Early in the morning the tanker *Neosho* had come alongside the *Lexington*. The wind was blowing about 30 knots, and the seas were rough. Four times the tow lines were passed, and four times they dropped away; three times the messenger line parted, and on the fourth throw, the towing block tumbled and could not be righted.

By 1140 everyone, including Admiral Brown, was disgusted and discouraged. He gave orders to postpone the attempt to fuel; the ships moved apart and took course toward Midway.

Admiral Halsey, in Task Force 8, was patrolling to the north, and Admiral Fitch in the *Saratoga* was coming out from San Diego. In the headquarters at Pearl Harbor, Admiral Kimmel and his staff were making plans for the relief of Wake Island, which was under attack. There were a number of civilians on Wake—construction workers—and they should be retrieved and sent home. The island needed more air support, and could receive it from a squadron that was coming in aboard the *Saratoga*.

So far, so good.

But December 11 was also the day on which Secretary Knox arrived at Pearl Harbor.

The Secretary's first question was typical and brusque: "Did you receive my message on Saturday night?"

The message had been a warning against a surprise Japanese attack, but searches of the fleet files failed to disclose that it had ever arrived.

The Secretary wanted to know what had happened, why, and what Kimmel proposed to do. While they were talking, Kimmel's operations officer, Captain C. A. McMorris, came into the room to present a proposal that Kimmel dispatch forces to relieve Wake Island. Knox liked the cut of this officer's jib, and what he had to say pleased the Secretary more. He proposed to defend the island.

In these hours Kimmel was listening to many proposals from members of his staff. McMorris spoke strongly against evacuation of the island, and Secretary Knox, misreading Kimmel's quiet reaction as negative, was further convinced that Kimmel was not a fighting man.

By day's end, Admiral Kimmel had definitely decided on the reinforcement of Wake Island, but Knox was not aware of this decision. The Secretary was busy taking in the extent of the disaster around Ford Island, and was so horrified to see the wreckage of the great battleship fleet that he was not really listening to his admiral. He left the very next day for the west coast.

Kimmel knew that the Secretary had not been pleased with what he saw, but Kimmel also knew that he had a war to fight, and after seeing Knox off, he began laying his plans. Wilson Brown's Task Force 12 was still struggling with the fuel problem. At 0930 on December 12 the cruiser *Portland* was refueling from the *Neosho*, moving on a northerly course. At 1210 the *Chicago* was fueling when the *Portland* reported a submarine, bearing 200 degrees, just off the *Lexington's* side. The men of the *Chicago* cast off, but in such a hurry that they pulled the fueling nipples right out of the *Neosho* and made it impossible for the tanker to fuel another ship without repairs.

So it was back to Pearl, with a distinct flaw showing up in Admiral Kimmel's plan to keep the carrier task forces at sea. *Lexington* was still not fueled when Kimmel ordered the force back to Pearl to do the job.

On December 13 Task Force 12 entered Pearl Harbor, to receive Kimmel's orders changing the name of the force to Task Force 11, and sending it to raid Jaluit atoll, as part of the Kimmel plan to relieve Wake, for that island atoll was under almost daily bombardment by the Japanese.

McMorris had suggested that the seaplane tender *Tangier* be taken to Wake to evacuate the civilians, and that she carry ammunition, supplies, and radar sets for the defense of the island. This plan was now approved, and orders were prepared to dispatch the *Saratoga*. She arrived on December 13 and became the nucleus of Task Force 14. Rear Admiral Aubrey W. Fitch was in command when the *Saratoga* came in, but Rear Admiral Frank Jack Fletcher was selected to lead the task force. Fletcher and Fitch had been classmates at the Academy (1906), but Fletcher was senior in terms of the date of his admiral's commission.

On December 15 the *Tangier* and the tanker assigned to the Task Force 14 sailed from Pearl Harbor. *Saratoga* and the rest of the force were held up, for the carrier had to fuel. Wake was being bombed almost daily by two- and four-engine bombers, and when Admiral Kimmel reported his plans for relief, Admiral Stark radioed his concurrence. Next day the rest of Task Force 14 set out for Wake, and it was decided that when Halsey arrived with Task Force 8, he would receive the word that as soon as possible he would go out to join the others in this vigorous if risky operation.

Admiral Kimmel's plans were thorough. Halsey and Brown were to seek out the enemy and divert or destroy them if possible, while Fletcher moved in to relieve Wake.

All the way home, however, Secretary Knox had fumed over what he had seen at Pearl Harbor, and by the time he reached Washington on December 14 he was prepared to report to President Roosevelt that the fleet needed a complete changeover at the top. Halsey's task force was still in harbor as the machine began to grind back in Main Navy. Kimmel was informed that he would be relieved. Admiral Draemel, who had been out with his destroyers, came into port on December 17 and made his way quickly to the office of the commander in chief. He had a bone to pick. Some time earlier Kimmel had planned the relief of destroyer captains over the age of forty-five. (President Roosevelt had the same idea.) Draemel did not like the idea, particularly in wartime, because it meant he would have to relieve the captains of nearly all his force. He came to argue on this afternoon of December 17.

Draemel found Kimmel sitting quietly at his desk, and they talked. The destroyer commander suggested in some heat that Kimmel had no business concerning himself with such details, and that if he did not approve Draemel's conduct of his command, he should relieve him. Kimmel agreed in a very mild tone that he had overstepped and then looked at the clock. It was a few moments before three in the afternoon.

"I am being relieved at three," he said.

Draemel was taken aback. He offered to leave the room, but Kimmel told him to stay. Then, at 1500, Vice Admiral W. S. Pye came into the room. Pye was comander of the Battle Force, one of those admirals who had been passed over when Kimmel was promoted to head the fleet. The two senior admirals read their orders, while Draemel looked on. Then Kimmel left the building, and his command.

Draemel went back to his ship, conscious of having seen the destruction of a fine career. He had scarcely regained his cabin on the *Detroit* when word came that the commander in chief wished to see him. Back at headquarters, he learned that he was to become the new operational chief of staff of Pye, thus stepping in front of

Captain Smith. Orders were orders. Draemel went to his desk, and his flag lieutenant went to the *Detroit* and packed the admiral's gear.

Admiral Pye was simply the interim commander of the Pacific Fleet. President Roosevelt and Secretary Knox had decided for reasons of high policy that Kimmel must immediately be relieved. It was perhaps not totally coincidental that on December 15 Knox had announced some of the losses in the Japanese attack—the sinking of the *Arizona*, the capsizing of the *Oklahoma*, the damage to the *Utah*, the *Oglala*, and three destroyers. In any event, the political leaders took an action that seemed necessary to them and appointed Pye, although the real commander of the Pacific was to be Chester W. Nimitz. The younger admiral could not reach Pearl Harbor for several days, so Pye was put in to hold the line.

Younger is a relative term. Nimitz was born in 1885, Pye in 1880, and by the time a man reaches middle age a five-year difference seldom amounts to much. And perhaps age was not the difference in this case either, so much as a manner of thinking. Admiral Richardson's prescription for the achievement of flag rank in the Navy went just so far—it did not consider how the admiral would comport himself once he achieved those two stars. Particularly, the Richardson formula did not delve into the most important of all conditions: what was required of a naval leader in that period for which all of them trained all their lives, the time of war.

Seemingly, Pye was admirably suited for command of the Pacific Fleet. He had completed the four-year course at the Naval Academy in 1901, spent two years at sea as a passed midshipman, as required then, and was commissioned ensign in 1903. He had served as an engineering officer, ordnance officer, aide, and staff officer in his early years. In 1916 he commanded his own destroyer, but his particular abilities as a staff officer brought him to the Atlantic Fleet in World War I, and there he served with distinction as fleet intelligence officer and later as war plans officer. He had commanded a destroyer division in the Pacific Fleet. He had commanded a battleship, the USS *Nevada*, the destroyer flotilla of the Pacific, and eventually the entire battle force of the Pacific Fleet. Between these assignments were tours in the office of the Chief of Naval Operations, a course at the War College, a tour teaching at the War College, and various special assignments. He was a successful and admirable officer. He was noted as a strategist, and some of his subordinates felt he was eminently suited for the command of the fleet, permanently, in this time of crisis.

Wanting a man of his own general tenor of thought, Pye had chosen Draemel as his chief of staff for this brief interim period. Together, then, they began a reassessment of the war situation. Draemel's job was to pull together the facts for his superior and make his recommendation, which would be considered along with other recommendations of the senior staff, before Pye made the ultimate decision as commander in chief.

As Draemel examined the messages and intelligence reports, he became more uneasy by the hour. Samoa must be reinforced, that was apparent. But Wake was a different matter. Intercepted messages indicated that the Japanese were moving around the Pacific. Guam had fallen on December 10 to forces from Truk. The three American task forces were widely spread. The difficulties of the *Lexington* in fueling were known. The tankers supplying the three task forces did not have enough oil to keep all the tanks topped off, and as Draemel contemplated the sharp upswing of the graphical curve of fuel consumption in a warship at top speed, he was dismayed. A ship traveling at 30 knots might consume five times as much fuel as the same ship traveling at 10 knots. If the American vessels were to go into battle, how would they get home, even if they sank every Japanese ship in sight?

On December 19 Admiral Wilson Brown's Task Force 11 and Admiral Fletcher's Task Force 14 were steaming toward their objectives. On the ships the men were ready for battle, as Brown's message to his force indicated:

> This force is conducting a reconaissance raid in enemy water. The *Lexington* planes will have their first contact with the enemy. We know they will do a grand job. The rest of us must be prepared to deal with enemy carriers, enemy planes, surface ships and submarines. Be on the alert, keep calm, and use your head. Shoot straight when the opportunity offers.

On the ships the battle preparations continued, and the men

were inoculated against tetanus. Task Force 8, refueled, sailed from Pearl Harbor to support the other two. D-Day for the arrival at Wake—relief and possible attack—was December 23.

In Washington the naval authorities were engaged in warm debate over the Wake relief expedition. On December 16 Admiral Towers had gone into the office of Assistant Secretary Gates to urge that Gates do something. (Towers did not then know that Kimmel had evolved his three-prong aggressive plan, for the relief of Wake and possible engagement of the Japanese.) Towers pleaded with Gates to use his influence with Secretary Knox "to break the present defensive attitude in the Pacific fleet, which attitude definitely has the support of Admiral Turner of War Plans." Towers also asked Gates to "recommend most strongly that a heavy force, including at least one carrier, preferably two, be sent to relieve Wake, the carrier to fly off a squadron of fighters and some dive bombers to land on Wake and assist in its defense." Gates said he would try, not knowing that Kimmel's audacious plan called for the use of *all* American carriers in the Pacific—three of them—to the distress of the conservatives who were in control of Washington's naval affairs.

On December 19, as the men of the task forces prepared grimly but eagerly for battle, the command situation of the Navy was thoroughly confused. Nimitz was to be commander of the Pacific Fleet, but he was not in command yet. Secretary Knox, not trusting Admiral Stark's qualities of aggression, had brought Admiral Ernest J. King from the Atlantic Fleet, and asked him to take a new post, that of Commander in Chief of the Navy, which would outrank the Chief of Naval Operations. President Roosevelt concurred on December 18, but on December 19 King was back in Newport, Rhode Island, divesting himself of his old command. In the Pacific, Admiral Pye and his staff were faced with the awful responsibility of supervising the commitment of the entire fighting force of the Pacific Fleet—a commitment Pye had never made, but for which he was now responsible.

Pye sat down in his office and estimated the situation on the morning of December 20. He found evidence of increasing Japanese air activity in the Marshalls, both land and carrier, and indications of naval activity there, too. He feared that the surprise element in the attack of Task Force 11 would be missing, and it was part of his philosophy that carrier operations depended on the element of surprise for effectiveness and safety of the carriers. The admiral feared that the "long delay in initiating the plan" had made it possible for the enemy to know that the move was afoot. He blamed the hiatus on the difficulties of the *Lexington* in fueling in those first days after the Pearl Harbor attack, and this brought his mind, again, to the fuel problem. The enemy would come up full of fuel, and his forces were short.

As Pye saw it, Task Force 14 was relatively safe, at least from enemy air activity, because its operations around Wake would keep the force at least 750 miles from Japanese air bases. But Task Force 11 might be in danger because of the lack of "surprise" and serious loss might be sustained. "Such a loss would have a seriously depressing morale effect on the fleet and country and jeopardize the Hawaiian islands." And then, at the end, either or both task forces might be overtaken by "enemy carrier groups full of fuel" on the long run back to Pearl Harbor, while only Halsey with Task Force 8 would be there to protect the others.

Making this estimate, Admiral Pye issued new orders, changing the operation. Brown's Task Force 11 was called back from the strike on Jaluit, and ordered to move in to protect Fletcher's Task Force 14 at Wake. Halsey would operate as planned with Task Force 8, with emphasis on protection. Fletcher would go about his relief business, and stick close to Wake, not looking for the enemy.

Wake Island was bombed on December 20 and again on December 21. At least one Japanese carrier was involved—radio intelligence indicated it was the *Soryu*—and two-engine planes were identified, as well as dive bombers. Because of the number of planes, Admiral Draemel suspected that two or more carriers were in the area. (He was right. *Soryu* and *Hiryu* were both there.)

Communication with Wake was spotty, but the staff at Pearl Harbor relied on reports from the submarine *Triton*, which was patrolling the area. On December 20 the *Triton* developed "material troubles" and was recalled to Pearl, leaving Pye without his "eyes." *

---

* CINCPAC Gray Book, December 20. In his *History of United States Naval Operations in World War II*, Vol. III, Samuel Eliot Morison notes that in January, 1947, Vice Admiral McMorris told him the *Triton* was withdrawn by Pye lest she mistake the approaching Task Force 14 for the enemy.

The fueling problem disturbed Admiral Fletcher as much as it did Admiral Pye. On December 21 Fletcher decided to fuel his destroyers from the tanker *Neches*, and in the process slowed his force, which was about 600 miles from Wake. He did not complete his fueling that day, either, and during the day he was disturbed by several conflicting dispatches from Pearl Harbor which indicated the confusion at headquarters. One said he was to move to a point 200 miles from Wake and launch search planes. Another canceled that and told him to send the seaplane tender *Tangier* in, unescorted, to evacuate the civilians.

At headquarters Pye and Draemel were worried. They now believed there was a sizable Japanese force operating off the island. The three American task forces were widely separated—Draemel did not believe they could close on each other enough to offer mutual support.

At 0520 on the morning of December 22, the communications officer at Pearl Harbor received a report from the Wake Island commander announcing a Japanese landing attack on the island. Pye and Draemel began to consider the problem. Pye asked Draemel to prepare a situation estimate, and said he would do the same. At seven o'clock that morning, Draemel wrote out his estimate.

Can the forces at sea, *in fact*, relieve Wake? [it began].

Even if the *Tangier* lands everything—the best that can be said—is—it affords a temporary relief. Further operations must be conducted—a series of them to hold Wake. If this proves impossible, Wake eventually must capitulate. Wake was very weak prior to this attack.

Is the condition of Wake *after this attack* such—that the aid on the *Tangier* will be—can be landed? We must not overlook the fact that this effort of the Japs—*may be successful*. Marine planes must have information before taking off.

Wake—*now*—becomes of secondary importance. The important issue now—is—action with Jap forces attacking Wake.

If Japan is unaware of, or has not deduced that our forces at sea may attempt to relieve Wake—he may have inferior forces.

On the other hand—if he knows or estimates our strength at sea—and deduces—their mission as a relief of Wake—he may be fully prepared and set for action. If so—his forces are undoubtedly—strong—or what he considers strong enough to do the job.

Task Forces 11–14—evidently plan to fuel en route returning—in event of an action—such fueling may not be possible. This is a definite weakness.

In event of an engagement with Jap forces is accepted—as attempting to support Wake—the possibility of the action developing into a major engagement cannot be overlooked. Are we willing to accept a major engagement—at this distance from our base—with an uncertainty in the fuel situation?

There are no reserves—*all* our forces are in the area of possible operations.

The General Situation—dictates caution—extreme caution. We must decide—either

(1) To abandon Wake—or (2) accept the risk of a major engagement.

An hour later, Captain McMorris presented his estimate.

McMorris' analysis was much more detailed than Draemel's. He noted the attacks by shore-based horizontal bombers and carrier dive bombers. He noted that the size and constitution of the enemy force was uncertain. "Only one carrier is *known* to be present. Others may be. *If* there be additional carriers they *may* not participate in the attack but be disposed to prevent interference with the landing and to attack any of our own forces going to relief of Wake. No real evidence of this."

He, too, said that the position of Wake now was secondary, "even though there continue to be strong reasons for relieving that place at an early date." "The point is," McMorris said, "there is an enemy force (possibly weaker) that we can get at."

As for the fuel problem:

The exact situation as to fuel is not known but there are strong reasons for feeling that the cruisers and DD [destroyers] of TF 11 and 14 have recently fueled and that the CV's [fleet carriers] of these two forces still have ⅔ or more of their capacity. TF 8 has thus far steamed only about 1500 miles. The carrier of that force is a long range one. The DDs of TF 8 are probably the units least well off in fuel and they can steam a long way at high speed.

McMorris agreed that the American forces were widely scattered, but he also said they were "converging."

The way to clear the situation, said McMorris, "is to get at the enemy."

He offered four courses of action:

A. Withdraw.

B. Attack with Task Force 14 and bring up Task Force 8 and 11 for support.

C. Search wide area for enemy units and delay a decision until the results of the search are known.

D. Concentrate the three task forces and drive the enemy from Wake.

McMorris rejected course A as "unduly cautious," an action that would "tend to destroy service and public confidence." He rejected course C as a temporizing and delaying action, and course D as also delaying, and giving the enemy a chance to escape. He advocated attack, because "this course offers great chance of success against enemy forces off Wake and added possibility of damaging or destroying the enemy forces piecemeal if they are in the vicinity. Even though the enemy be encountered in superior strength the chances of falling back without serious losses are excellent. It is an opportunity unlikely to come again soon." And, he noted, "we are in great need of a victory."

Admiral Pye had to make the decision. Pye's own estimate was dated at seven o'clock in the morning, and McMorris', apparently coming in an hour later, did not change his views. Pye reasoned that the enemy knew the American relief forces were coming, and thus timed their attack.

The danger to damaged ships at 2000 miles from base must

not be underestimated. A loss of a large part of our forces would make possible a major operation against the Hawaiian Islands. We cannot afford such losses at present.

The decision therefore appears to lie between two courses of action:

(a) Direct Task Force 14 to attack enemy forces, Task Forces 8 and 11 to become involved only in covering the retirement of Task Force 14, or

(b) Retiring all forces without any attempt to attack enemy concentrated near Wake.

In deciding, Admiral Pye was assisted by a message from Admiral Stark, who said that he and Admiral King both then considered Wake Island to be more trouble than it was worth.

"OPNAV dispatch just received states Wake will continue to be a liability and authorizes evacuation. *Evacuation is impossible*; it will eventually be forced to capitulate. The real question at issue is, shall we take the chance of the loss of a carrier group to attempt to attack the enemy forces in the vicinity of Wake."

Admiral Pye's answer was no. Task Forces 8, 11, and 14 were ordered to retire immediately to the northeast, then come back to Pearl Harbor. Thus the decision was made to avoid the first chance the United States had to avenge the destruction at Pearl Harbor.

When the official orders flashed through the air, and arrived at the task forces, they were greeted with anger and dismay. On Admiral Fletcher's flagship the talk was so mutinous that he left the bridge, and Admiral Fitch left his bridge for the same reason. Halsey was furious.

But Admirals Halsey, Fletcher, Brown, and Fitch were disciplined to obey the orders of higher authority. It has been suggested that Fletcher might have turned off his radios and gone in to attack in spite of Pye's recall, but to do so without sufficient intelligence and without the support of the others could have been suicidal, and had he won any less than a clear-cut victory over the Japanese, Fletcher would undoubtedly have been court-martialed. Such decisions were made only by Horatio Nelsons, and even Nelson had the advantage of seeing his enemy before deciding on an engagement. Also, despite the need for a victory, the war plans since at least 1939 had assumed conflict in both east and west, and the primary mission of the United States Navy in the Pacific was the defense of Hawaii and the west coast until decision was achieved in Europe, whereupon the resources of the United States and possible allies could be turned to the Pacific.

Right or wrong, the decision was the responsibility of Admiral Pye, a decision made in those first wretched days of the Pacific war. It could be argued, and was, that Pye's primary responsibility under the American war plan was to protect the continental United States and Hawaii. The conservatives among the admirals believed he had done just right; the more daring believed he had missed one of the great opportunities of war.

Chapter
Two

ENTER NIMITZ

December 7–December 25, 1941

Like millions of other Americans, Rear Admiral Chester W. Nimitz was at home on Sunday, December 7, when the first word of the Pearl Harbor attack was broadcast over the radio. Nimitz happened to be listening to a concert by the New York Philharmonic Orchestra, when the music was interrupted by a scarcely contained announcer who brought the bad news. Unlike millions of other Americans, however, Nimitz did not take the report of the disaster as a signal for despair or shock, but as a call to action. The admiral rose from his chair, telephoned his assistant, Captain John F. Shafroth, and when Shafroth arrived at the Nimitz home, the two headed for the Main Navy building in downtown Washington.

Nimitz went to the Bureau of Navigation, his own office, to consult the war plan. Like Artemus Gates in Pensacola, Nimitz discovered that the plans were carefully protected against mishap—

locked in a safe, secured by a time lock that was set to open on Monday morning.

Nimitz was joined by others who came drifting in as they learned the news, admirals and lesser officers and civilians. Rear Admiral Jack Towers came and immediately plunged into the preparation of despatches and memos about the disposition of Army and Navy aviation forces.

Most of the admirals and others of this privileged group had no such clear-cut responsibilities, however. They drifted into the office of Secretary Knox, who had come hurrying to the Department when he heard the reports. Undersecretary Forrestal arrived, and then Assistant Secretary Bard. Admiral Stark, Chief of Naval Operations, came with his flag secretary, and along came Nimitz's own flag secretary, Lieutenant (jg) H. Arthur Lamar. The conferences began.

There was no talk of responsibility—no recrimination. The decision to remove Admiral Kimmel from command of the Pacific Fleet was not made in these meetings; such a course was not even considered. But Secretary Knox was in Pearl Harbor during the week. When he returned from Pearl Harbor a week later, the Secretary was determined to make a change. As military historian Fletcher Pratt put it: "A fleet commander in any navy holds office on much the same terms as a heavyweight champion. It is neither punishment nor fear that he will repeat his mistake that causes him to be removed when he is once knocked out. Confidence has been lost, and with it full control of the medium."

Poor Kimmel. Nimitz said it could have happened to anyone, and of course it could have. There was no way Kimmel could help, he had been denied by Pye his brave gesture in trying to relieve Wake and close with the enemy. Kimmel was facing the Roberts commission, which that week began meeting in Hawaii. And that commission represented the thinking of Knox and President Roosevelt, as Knox indicated in a letter to Paul Scott Mowrer at the *Chicago Daily News.*

That trip of mine to Hawaii was an inspiration that came to me just as I heard the President read his message. Immediately the air was filled with rumors. There was a prospect ahead of a nasty congressional investigation, and I made up my mind in a flash to go out there and get the actual facts, and if the facts warranted it, to initiate the investigation myself . . . . When I found out what the facts were, it didn't take long to start the investigation, and I think the President was pretty happy in the men he chose to conduct it.

Kimmel was to be sacrificed to public opinion, and every admiral in the fleet knew it by this time. The fact that in *November* a fleet exercise had presupposed a Japanese air attack on Oahu meant nothing.* There was no excuse for Kimmel, in the public eye, and that view was shared by many younger officers in the fleet. Commander Arthur Radford was strong in his denunciation of Kimmel. Captain Charles Lockwood was equally furious. "Someone should burn for this," he wrote.

Admiral Kimmel had been brought to the Pacific Fleet to snap up the fleet and install in it an aggressive attitude. The Pearl Harbor disaster destroyed him, no matter what he might do, because he no longer had Knox's confidence. A change had to be made. Moreover, Congress was clamoring for someone's scalp. It was inconceivable to the members of Congress that their policies and those of previous administrations had brought the United States to so low a military state that one blow, smashing half a dozen battleships and a few cruisers and destroyers, could emasculate the nation's

---

* Task Force 3 operational order 11-41 for exercise set up the following hypothetical plan in the fall of 1941:

White controls the Hawaiian islands and Palmyra Island. Pearl Harbor is an advanced White fleet base with limited repair facilities, which is defended by a defense battalion of approximately 1,000 marines, numerous guns up to 10 inch in caliber and about 24 short range shore based aircraft. Maui, a nearby atoll, contains an emergency landing field, but otherwise has no facilities. All the Hawaiian islands except Oahu represent undefended atolls. Palmyra Island is an outlying White patrol plane base. The White homeland is approximately 2,000 miles to the east of Oahu.

Black has established an advance base at Midway, which is the easternmost of a chain of atolls under the sovereignty of Black. The Black homeland is approximately 2,000 miles west of Midway. On December 7 White learns from intelligence sources that a Black force of 2 heavy cruisers, a carrier, and several destroyers are at Midway. . . . By December 10, relations are so strained that war is expected. At 1200 December 11, war is declared by Black. . . .

defenses. Had Kimmel been retained until a successor could arrive, a victory might have been achieved at Wake. The President and Knox would have none of it; on December 17 Nimitz was told that he would become commander of the Pacific Fleet as soon as he could reach Pearl Harbor. He demurred, since there were many admirals senior to him on the list, but his superiors insisted, and he accepted the orders with good grace. Nimitz was, if anything, the epitome of the successful officer by Admiral Richardson's exacting standards.

The qualities of the Nimitz character were apparent in his face, in his career, and in his heritage; combined, these factors made him precisely the man he was and placed him in this particular situation at this moment in history.

Nimitz was a medium-sized man, but with such broad shoulders and erect carriage that he seemed taller than his five feet nine inches, more slender than his 180 pounds. He was a physical fitness advocate. He played tennis whenever the weather would allow it, walked long miles to keep his figure trim. But the telling characteristic of Nimitz in this winter of 1941–42 was his mouth, usually carried in a thin straight line. He was not a cold man, or a bad-tempered man—quite the contrary—to the world he presented a figure of almost total complacency; he seldom lost his temper or raised his voice. His light-blue eyes peered quizzically from beneath a beetling brow that was robbed of fierceness by the light hair of the eyebrows, and his fine white hair gave him the air of an elder statesman. But the month told more, it indicated an almost con-tinuous—and victorious—struggle for self-control.

In the Navy, of course, this view did not prevail. In his job as chief of personnel (Bunav), to juniors he had appeared stern and completely dispassionate. The word "sundowner"—descriptive of the spit-and-polish officer—had sometimes been used to describe him, as it was often used to describe Admiral King, the new Commander in Chief. But if King might be able to say that when the going got tough, they brought in the tough officers (the word was sons-of-bitches), Nimitz would not have thought of putting the case that way. It could be said that King was a driver who knew how to lead; it could also be said that Nimitz was a leader who conquered any personal urge to drive, and achieved his ends more by persuasion and inspiration to men under his command. Not that he was a weak disciplinarian. Flag Secretary Lamar had always found his boss "tough" in the past, and so had countless other officers. But the Nimitz who was moving to take control of the Pacific Fleet was a man very conscious of a destiny and of his part in the war to be won, as a leader of men.

The Nimitzes were an old military family. Chester's half-brother Otto was a Naval Academy graduate, too, a commander, serving in the Bureau of Ordnance. The admiral's son, Chester, Jr., was a lieutenant, junior grade, assigned to a submarine. But these represented only the current generations—the Nimitz family claimed direct descent from an honored major, Ernst Freiherr von Nimitz, who lived in the seventeenth century in the German states. He had a coat of arms, featuring a crown. The Freiherr claimed descent from military forebears who went back to the twelfth century.

Charles Henry Nimitz, Chester's grandfather, had been a merchant seaman, not a profession inclined to gather a man much fortune. Charles Henry, attracted by the New World, had left Bremen in 1844 on one last voyage, which carried him and his few belongings to Charleston, South Carolina. He made his way down to Texas, arriving in the spring, and there he settled in the little town of Fredericksburg. He served for a time with the Texas Rangers, and two years after coming to Texas Charles Henry Nimitz married Sophie Dorothe Muller. He decided to become an innkeeper, which meant then a dancehall proprietor and saloon keeper as well, and he erected a building of sundried brick. In the process, Charles Henry's love of the sea overcame him, and the building turned out to be a replica of a ship, a land-bound ship whose balconies were decks ensconced inside railings.

Captain Nimitz (for he kept his seagoing title when he came to Texas) was the father of twelve children. They grew up working around the Nimitz Hotel, a landmark quite close to the Pedernales River, and eventually they married and had families of their own. Chester Bernard Nimitz married a Fredericksburg girl named Anna Henke, then died five months later. In February, 1885, Chester William Nimitz was born to the widow, who took refuge with her father-in-law at the hotel. For the next six years Anna and her son lived there, the boy falling under the influence of his grandfather. Yet the real father figure in Chester William Nimitz's life was his stepfather, William Nimitz, for when the boy was six years old Anna married her youngest brother-in-law. William and Anna had two children, Otto and Dora, but the three youngsters were brought up as brothers and sister, and the man who was to become commander in chief of the Pacific Fleet always regarded Otto as his brother.

The Nimitz family in America was anything but wealthy. In centuries past in Germany, the family had the privilege of using *von* before the name, but along the way this branch of the family descended from a "younger son" and the *von* was dropped as too expensive to maintain, in terms of social obligation. It was thus in the New World as well. The hotel on the Pedernales was a haven, and Captain Nimitz was always able to meet any emergency needs among his many children. But by and large they had to make their own way in life, and William Nimitz chose to do something he knew well—he went into hotel management as assistant manager of the St. Charles Hotel in Kerrville, a few miles from Fredericksburg.

As a youth Chester was a towhead. His mother insisted that he wear his hair long—even past the time when a boy began to realize that long hair was for girls. (This was the nineteenth century, remember.) Young Chester pondered a means of escaping his torture, and hit upon a brilliant idea: he painted his long hair green. Then it had to come off, to his intense satisfaction.

Chester Nimitz might well have gone into hotel keeping, for he was so trained from his early years. His mother ran the kitchen at the St. Charles Hotel, and Chester and Otto did the boy's chores while little Dora helped her mother. The boys also found outside jobs to earn their spending money, and when Chester was twelve years old he earned a dollar a week delivering meat around the town for a local butcher. When he was a little older his stepfather gave him a regular job as hotel handyman. Chester was paid fifteen dollars a month and his board and room, like any handyman. For this he was to light the fires early in the morning and call the early risers at the hotel, do the morning janitorial chores, and then he was free to go to school. After school he must return for more work. As a teenager, then, Chester began a routine of arising at three in the morning, studying until five-thirty, then tending his dozen stoves and fireplaces. After school let out at four each afternoon he would return to the hotel, chop wood and split kindling, rake leaves, sweep up, and carry out trash. Then came supper, and after supper he worked as desk clerk until ten, when he retired for the night to a cot in the ladies' parlor of the hotel.

Chester did well enough in school, although the course was not terribly demanding. He was known there as "Cottonhead," and was as popular as a working boy might be, in the little time he had to spare for amusement. William, his stepfather, was a stern employer but he was also a very decent man. Even so, there was no hope in the family that Chester would be able to pursue his education beyond high school. There just was not the money for college. With the grace of youth, Chester accepted this condition and made tentative plans to join a surveying crew when he graduated from high school, and thus learn a useful trade that might lead him into engineering.

In the summer of 1900, however, young Nimitz's plans changed completely. One day a pair of new second lieutenants of the United States Army Field Artillery stopped off at the St. Charles Hotel for the night, on their way to duty at a summer artillery camp maintained by Fort Sam Houston, near Kerrville. The young lieutenants were William M. Cruikshank and William I. Westerveldt, and both, Nimitz discovered, had attended the United States Military Academy at West Point, New York.

Suddenly, a whole new world was opened to Chester William Nimitz. If he could only secure an appointment to the military academy, and bone up to pass the examinations, he could have the education he wanted, and a dashing career as well. He applied to Congressman James L. Slayden, but was told that all the appointments to the miiltary academy had already been made. Slayden said that he did have one appointment left for the Naval Academy, and that he would make his choice on the basis of the outcome of competitive examinations to be held in the spring of 1901. Was young Mr. Nimitz interested?

Mr. Nimitz was interested, and began setting his academic house in order. His mother helped him as much as she could. His high school principal tutored him in algebra and geometry. A teacher, Miss Susan Moore, helped him with history and English. Nimitz studied very hard, and when the Congressional district examinations were held in April, 1901, he was high man and secured the appointment. He was still not in, however, and would not be until he passed the physical and academic examinations given by the Naval Academy itself. In July Chester Nimitz came north, and Congressman Slayden accompanied him to Annapolis, where he entered the Werntz Preparatory School to study with masters who knew precisely what the Academy demanded. After two months of brushing up, Nimitz passed the Naval Academy examinations in August and was sworn in on September 7, 1901, as a naval cadet. He was one of the younger members of his class, having foregone the last year of Texas high school in order to secure the appointment. Other members of this class of 1905 were Royall Ingersoll and Herbert Fairfax Leary, Walter B. Woodson, Ormond Lee Cox, William Rea Furlong, Arthur B. Cook, Harold G. Bowen, William O. Spears, Stanford C. Hooper, John H. Newton, Jr., Andrew F. Carter, Wilhelm L. Friedell, Laurence N. McNair, John W. Wilcox, Jr., John M. Smeallie. These men shared one attribute: all fifteen of them, along with Nimitz, rose to flag rank before their careers were ended—sixteen admirals from a class of 158 plebes.

Nimitz, even as a fourth classman, took very well to the Navy way, and the Navy took to him. He was poor, but money made no difference in the equality of these young men. The government paid each fourth classman a dollar and a half a month as spending money, and to make up whatever else was needed, Grandfather Nimitz sent the rest. During the first month, Chester Nimitz feared that he was "bilging" (failing) in mathematics, but later he found he stood tenth in his class.

Life was hard and demanding at the Academy. The fourth classmen took artillery instruction, for example, and there were no horses to move the big pieces around. The cadets moved them. One blustery day in that fall of 1901, Cadet Nimitz and several others hauled a heavy field piece from one spot to another and immediately afterward were called into formation, to stand in a drafty hallway. Nimitz came down with pneumonia after that adventure, but recovered and was soon up and around again, back at the "grind." He did well in the military sciences and mathematics, and was good in Spanish but poor in French. In athletics he distinguished himself in crew—a team sport—working up from stroke of the fourth crew to become stroke of the first. His coxswain on the first crew was John Howard Hoover of the class of 1907. Eventually their roles were virtually reversed. Hoover became one of Nimitz's trusted if little known admirals in the Pacific war.

In his first-class year, Nimitz was a three-striper, commander of the Eighth Company, which indicated his adherence to the strictures of discipline. He was also seventh in his class academically. Yet he was also an adventurous young man who was not at all afraid to flout the Academy's rules and regulations for a "good cause." One such cause was a beer party—illegal, of course—but that only made it more enjoyable. In his first-class year Bancroft Hall was ready for occupancy (one wing) and the first classmen moved in. Part of the hall was still under construction, and the roof of the new building could be reached by climbing from Nimitz's room. He and his friends climbed there from time to time to drink beer and contemplate the future, throwing the empty beer bottles over the side, where they crashed down among the building materials, to the discomfiture of the established authority.

The trick of a beer party in 1904 was to smuggle the beer into Bancroft Hall without getting caught, dire punishment awaiting even the first man in the class, were he apprehended in the crime.

Nimitz had a way. The favorite tailor of the cadets in those days was a gentleman named Schmidt who kept a shop on Maryland Avenue, a few blocks from the Academy gates. Tailor Schmidt's popularity arose and was maintained, in part, because of his willingness in the matter of buying beer for the cadets. One weekend First Classman Nimitz walked out of the Academy grounds with a suitcase in hand and headed directly for tailor Schmidt's. Inside the shop he saw his tailor, busily talking to a swarthy man in a dark suit. Cadet Nimitz waiting politely for a few moments. The tailor broke off the conversation to ask what the cadet wanted. Nimitz ordered his beer, and tailor Schmidt nodded, but told the cadet to come back in half an hour and pick up the suitcase. Nimitz walked out onto the sidewalk, and spent the next half hour idling along the crooked ways of old Annapolis. He returned, to find tailor Schmidt and the swarthy man still talking. There was a moment of concern—Schmidt might not have got the beer after all—but a look at the tailor, catching his grin and nod, a heft of the suitcase, and all was well. Beer bottles rained down among the bricks and stones again that Saturady night.

Among his other duties—honors—Cadet Nimitz served as a section leader, which meant he marched his felow cadets into class. On Monday morning, after the beery weekend, Nimitz marched his fellow cadets to the science building and smartly led them into their chemistry class, where they were to have a new instructor. Sitting behind the desk at the front of the room was tailor Schmidt's swarthy friend. To make matters worse, the man was not wearing his dark civilian suit, but a suit of Navy blue, its sleeves encircled by two and a half stripes. The mystery man of Saturday was Monday's Lieutenant Commander Levi Calvin Bertolette.

Chemistry could not command First Classman Nimitz's attention that day or the next. For a week he lived in fear lest he be called up and charged with a very serious breach of Academy discipline. Fortunately for Nimitz, Bertolette was an understanding man, and an old beer drinker himself from the class of 1887. No call-up came. But Cadet Nimitz learned something for the future.

"This escapade taught me a lesson on how to behave for the remainder of my stay at the Academy. It also taught me to look with a lenient and tolerant eye on first offenders when in later years they appeared before me as a commanding officer holding mast."

Nimitz's class was graduated ahead of schedule to meet the needs of an expanding fleet, by this time culled down to a total of 114 passed midshipmen, with Nimitz still seventh in his class. In the *Lucky Bag*, the class annual, Nimitz was characterized as Wordsworth's man of "cheerful yesterdays and confident tomorow," and he was said to possess "that calm and steady-going Dutch way that gets at the bottom of things." He was also "mixer of famous punches" and, most significantly, in light of what was to come, a man who always played to win.

"You always play to win," he later told an interviewer. "That's the only way."

Years later the *New Yorker* magazine would report: "A man who used to box with young Nimitz at Annapolis told us about the time he gave Nimitz a bloody nose. 'When I saw what I had done, I took off my gloves and walked out of the gym,' he said. 'I could see he'd kill me if he could, so I just broke off the action.'" And now, in 1941, speaking figuratively, the Japanese had again bloodied Admiral Nimitz's nose.

From the very beginning of his naval career, Nimitz showed a nice balance of fighting toughness, brilliance in his work, steadfastness, respect for discipline, and audacity. He was a humble man of humble beginnings. His family was too poor to come to Annapolis for his graduation from the Academy, and he never forgot that fact. (Ten years later he paid the expenses of his mother and half sister to come and see half brother Otto graduate, for otherwise, he knew, they still could not make the trip.) Chester Nimitz was glad to be out of the Academy, pleased to have what he called the "grueling course" behind him. He resented nothing, he was immensely grateful for the education, and as for the rest, he recalled the philosophy of his sea-captain grandfather:

"The sea—like life itself—is a stern taskmaster," old Captain Nimitz had said. "The best way to get along with either is to learn all you can, then do your best and don't worry—especially about things over which you have no control."

His grandfather's words, such encounters as that with Lieutenant Commander Bertolette, and the other residue of the stiff discipline of Academy life brought Nimitz to accept that philosophy wholeheartedly and to cling to it. Asked what he had liked least about his Academy education, Nimitz refused to consider the question.

"What is behind is behind," he said. "It never pays to worry about those things over which you have no control."

This refusal to look back (at least in anguish) was to mark Nimitz's career and grant him many good nights' sleep in situations when other men stayed up late worrying. Nimitz left the Academy with a month's leave, which he spent in Texas, and then reported to the USS *Ohio*, flagship-designate of the Asiatic Fleet, which was lying in San Francisco Bay. As a lowly passed midshipman he went to the Orient. He showed his audacity one day in

Japan. He and five other midshipmen from the *Ohio* were invited to a garden party given by the Japanese emperor in his gardens, in honor of the victory of the Japanese army and navy over Russia in the Russo-Japanese war. The major architect of that victory, Admiral Heihachiro Togo, was at the party, and the youngsters wanted to meet him. Nimitz was the one pushed forward by his friends to invite the admiral to the table.

In 1907 Nimitz was given command of a tiny gunboat taken from the Spanish in the late war, the original *Panay*, whose namesake would become so famous in the Yangtze River later on. Nimitz, twenty-one years old, was also commander of a miniature naval base at Polloc on Mindanao island in the Philippines. Tiny as the *Panay* was, Nimitz held a responsible job: he had fifty sailors and marines under his orders.

Polloc was so isolated a place that there was not much to do except hunt and fish; Nimitz amused himself by hunting wild pigs with a Datu (chief) named Pyang Datu.

Even as a youngster, Nimitz was calm and always seemed to be on top of the situation. The *Panay* was anything but prepossessing, scarcely seaworthy, and when her crew went aboard they cast caution to the four corners of the universe. One day, traveling up the Rio Grande de Mindanao, the chief engineer called up to the bridge, excitedly. "We've sprung a leak. She's going to sink. What shall I do?"

Nimitz had no idea. But he knew how to find out. "Look on page 84 of Barton's Engineering Manual," he shouted back. "It tells you what to do."

Whatever was done that day, *Panay* remained afloat, and carried her young sea dog of a commander for several more months. In 1907 came a change when President Theodore Roosevelt became incensed against the Japanese and threatened war. The *Panay* was ordered to Cavite, and when she limped into port there, Nimitz learned why.

Ensign Nimitz arrived at Cavite on July 8, 1907, and promptly reported in his best summer whites to Captain Uriah R. Harris, the commandant. Captain Harris handed the young ensign his new orders: he was to report at once to place the USS *Decatur* in service, and to be in Olongapo to drydock in the Dewey floating dock on July 10. Ensign Nimitz rose to leave. Captain Harris asked him where he was going.

"Back to the *Panay* to get my gear."

"No, you don't," said the commandant. "You go straight to the *Decatur*. I will send your gear to the *Decatur*—and some of your *Panay* crew."

Nimitz arose and made his way out, got into a launch, and found his new vessel at a buoy in the small bay off Cavite. She was Torpedo Boat Destroyer No. 5, built by the William R. Trigg Company of Richmond, launched by the great-grandniece of Stephen Decatur himself. She was 250 feet overall, with a beam of 23 feet 7 inches, a displacement of 420 tons, and a mean draft of 6 feet 6 inches. Her trial speed had been 28.1 knots. She was built to be armed with Whitehead torpedoes (two tubes), five six-pounder guns, and two three-inch, .50-caliber rapid-fire guns. *Decatur* had been launched in the fall of 1900 and had served as flagship of the First Torpedo Flotilla on the Asiatic Station until 1905, when she was placed "in reserve"—or "in mothballs" as a later generation would put it. Ensign Nimitz found a ship encased in red lead from stem to stern, completely stripped of guns and stores. There was not a drop of fresh water or a pound of coal on board. He was greeted pleasantly by two Filipino watchmen, who did not know or much care that this young man was supposed to have that ship in drydock many miles away within seventy-two hours.

Nimitz looked around the harbor. Two miles away he saw a cluster of ships, and from them came two boats, heading toward the *Decatur*. They came alongside; in one was Ensign J. M. Smeallie, a classmate of Nimitz's, with two or three men. In the other was Ensign Hugh Allen, class of 1906, with three or four men. They boarded, and he read them his orders.

All hands worked every hour [Nimitz said], to get equipment on board—supplies, guns, torpedoes, ammunition, etc. About 1400 on 10 July the Flotilla Commander, Frank McCrary, Lt. USN, in the *Chauncey*, approached and ordered me to clear the buoy and follow him to Olongapo. We had lighters full of heavy gear on each side and our compass and binnacle was still on the lighter. We got everything on deck by 1600 and got rid of our Filipino working party. In the meantime, the boilers had been lighted, steam raised, engines tested, and at 1600 I was on the bridge ordering, "Cast loose."

I rang ¼ speed astern on both engines . . . and we began to drift *ahead* slowly. I ordered ½ speed astern and we moved ahead faster. As the wind had drifted us away from the buoy by this time, it was convenient to keep moving ahead. Then "full speed astern" and we went ahead at about 12 knots and took position astern *Chauncey* headed for Olongapo. Our engine telegraphs had been reversed . . . .

Eventually the *Decatur* was pushed, limping, to Olongapo dry-dock, and after ministrations by the dockyard there, she was declared fit for sea service.

Nimitz then proceeded to run his second command aground. It happened one night in Batangas Bay. Nimitz was moving in, on this southern end of Bataan island, and he was more or less following prescribed procedure. But instead of checking his speed precisely, he ordered the patent log brought in, for they were in shallow water and near their destination, and he made a few rough estimates as to course, speed, and the navigation guides in the bay. They had been traveling at about ten knots. Suddenly the *Decatur* shuddered and stopped. They were aground on a mudbank.

In peacetime running a ship aground has cost many an officer his career. The Navy brass has always taken a dim view of officers who are negligent in their navigation. Nimitz might well have spent a sleepless night on *Decatur*, as the tropical dark crept down around his shoulders. But he remembered his grandfather's words of wisdom. Having tried to back off and slide off, and seeing that there was nothing to be done to move his ship, Nimitz had a cot brought up on deck and went to sleep.

Next morning an island steamer came by their mudbank and towed the *Decatur* off. Since they had stuck in mud, there was no damage to the ship, and it was just possible that Nimitz could get away without even mentioning the affair. (In later years he remarked that if he had it to do over again he would do just that.) But he reported himself as having gone aground.

Had he known that Rear Admiral J. N. Hemphill was smarting from an official rebuke at the moment, he would not have been so gallant, perhaps. A short time before, two of Nimitz's classmates had gone "out on the town" in Manila. In the course of a riotous evening, they had boarded the Navy ferry that ran up the Pasig River, and there had engaged in altercation with the ferry boat captain, a Filipino. The disagreement had become violent, and the two young ensigns had resolved the difficulty by throwing the captain overboard, into the river. Hemphill had heard of the incident, but had decided it was a case of high spirits and had done nothing. Higher authority had not approved, and Hemphill was simply waiting for another one of the young bloods to step out of line.

Unknowing, Nimitz reported his grounding, and on July 28, 1908, Ensign Chester W. Nimitz was brought to trial before a general court-martial. The charges were long and very specific, involving excessive speed, lack of caution, failure to observe the normal running procedures, and failure to use navigational aides. Nimitz's defense was spirited—his major point being that the type of ship he was commanding demanded a devil-may-care attitude and that was what he had exhibited. Perhaps Commander Walter McLean, president of the court, was impressed by this daring—if not strictly regulation—argument. Perhaps Nimitz's general demeanor and his quiet confidence impressed the court. Perhaps the members of the court realized that no damage had been done, the ship was a rust-bucket at best, and the young officer had turned himself in. Young officers were often grounding destroyers and other ships, or hanging them onto docks. The attitude of boards of inquiry and courts-martial was to accept the fact that inexperienced men were commanding ships. Whatever went through their minds, the officers of the court treated Nimitz very gently. He was convicted of a lesser charge, that of hazarding a ship of the United States Navy, and given a reprimand that Rear Admiral Hemphill delivered simply by publishing the results of the court-martial and making a copy a part of Nimitz's service record.

When he was sent back to the United States, Nimitz asked for battleship duty. He got submarines. It was the policy of the Navy in those years to place officers where they were needed, without much consideration of junior officers' preferences. Nimitz's court-martial probably did not help very much either. The admirals in Washington confined him to the bottom. Cheerfully, as usual, Nimitz accepted the decision of his superiors and set out to rebuild a shaky career. The Navy was not then very high on submarines, and Nimitz was made executive officer of his "pigboat," the USS *Plunger*, even though he was very junior and very inexperienced. He enjoyed the assignment.

As he said later: "I have enjoyed every one of my assignments and I believe that it has been so because of my making a point to become as deeply immersed and as interested in each activity as it was possible for me to become."

In his service in submarines, Nimitz gained much respect for two qualities, mental stability and physical fitness. It was essential that an officer be quiet, contained, and thoroughly confident of himself and his crew in these highly imperfect early submarines, with their cranky diving gear and foul air. Officers and men had to be physically fit to withstand the tensions, the pressures, and the discomforts of life in a dripping tube. The A-1, his first submarine, was sixty-one feet long and had her engine at one end and her torpedo tubes at the other. The men lived on top of the storage battery in the knowledge that it would certainly produce deadly chlorine gas if water got in. Nimitz was then the only officer, and he spent nearly all his time on the bridge or in the conning tower.

He rose rapidly in this stepchild service, and became commander of the *Snapper* in 1910, when she was commissioned. He was also a brand new lieutenant that year. By November he was transferred to the *Narwhal* and given duty as commander of Submarine Division 3. In 1912 he took the *Skipjack*.

By then Nimitz was one of the most knowledgeable men in the Navy on the subject of undersea warfare. In December, 1912, his article, "Military Value and Tactics of Modern Submarines," appeared as the lead in the *United States Naval Institute Proceedings*, the trade journal of the Navy officer corps.

To appreciate Nimitz's views, one must remember that in 1912 the Germans had not yet shown how deadly a submarine can be. Nimitz felt impelled to argue the complete case of the submarine, in terms of its communications ability, mobility, invulnerability to attack, and offensive strength. He predicted that the mobility of submarines would advance more rapidly than that of surface craft. He argued the case of the spindle-shaped submersible against the ship-shaped submarine, and indicated that the future of the submersible was greater than that of the other, in the long run. He made his case with a little quiet humor, unusual in articles in the *Proceedings*, as when he discussed the "gasoline jag" from which men suffered before the gasoline engines were replaced by diesels in the submarines. "The aid of several men is sometimes necessary to control the struggles of the 'jag' and thus prevent self-injury before he loses consciousness [from the fumes of the engine]. The after effect of such a case is usually a violent nausea and headache, and an extreme distrust of the gasoline engine. . . ."

The argument in *Proceedings* did not immediately change the fleet's employment of the submarine, but Nimitz continued to fight for the service, and when at twenty-seven he was put in command of the Atlantic Fleet submarine force, he was much more effective. His career had completely recovered and was moving ahead by this time. In 1912 he had distinguished himself by leaping overboard to save a fireman from drowning, and had earned a silver life-saving medal. In the spring of 1913 he had married and settled down—as much as a Navy man can—to raise a family. He was very lucky in one sense. He and Mrs. Nimitz, the former Catherine Vance Freeman of Wallaston, Massachusetts, had a sort of honeymoon ashore. Nimitz, having regained the confidence of the Bureau of Navigation, was given a dream assignment. In the summer of 1913 the Navy sent the young officer to Nuremburg and Ghent to study developments in diesel engines. He then came home to build and install the first U.S. Navy diesel engines in the tanker *Maumee*, working at the Brooklyn Navy Yard. Here the years of discipline, training, and a way of life were put to the crisis.

Nimitz then shared an office in the Machinery Division of the Navy Yard with Lieutenant W. S. Anderson, the ordnance superintendent. Both men were receiving the Navy's lordly pay—$240 a month plus $48 a month in lieu of quarters, a sum that did not pay the monthly rent in Brooklyn. And they commiserated with one another over this fact, at their adjoining desks.

One day in 1915 a civilian came into the office to talk to Nimitz, and Anderson could not help overhearing the conversation. The civilian represented a company in St. Louis that wanted to manufacture diesel engines. They were having problems, and they had heard of the *Maumee* and of Nimitz. They wanted to hire Nimitz to solve their problems, and they would offer him $25,000 a year and a five-year contract if he would resign from the Navy and join the firm.

"No thank you," said Nimitz. "I do not want to leave the Navy."

The man continued to argue. "Money is no obstacle. Write your own ticket," he said.

Nimitz thought that one over for a moment, but shook his head again. "No," he said, "I don't want to leave the Navy." And he did not.

Nimitz then went to duty as chief engineer of the *Maumee*, where he certainly learned something about machinery—to keep his hands out of it. While demonstrating the engines one day, he became so immersed in what he was saying that he did not watch his hands, and the cotton glove of his left hand caught in a gear. Before he could escape, the third finger of his left hand was badly mangled, and later was partly amputated. There were no other unpleasantnesses, however. It was a time of intense satisfaction; he was doing his work well, and the Navy recognized his worth. At about this time Nimitz was tabbed by his fellow officers as one lieutenant who was bound to make admiral if he did not shoot the Secretary of the Navy or commit some other heinous crime. He had adapted himself perfectly to the Navy life, understanding and appreciating its discipline, and throwing every effort into his career. Later, when he was a fleet commander, his personal physician was to say that Nimitz typified the mercurial character, and the doctor indicated that the easy-going quietness of the admiral was the result of years of total self-control by the man as he rose through the ranks.

In 1916 that career was furthered by promotion to lieutenant commander. When war came in 1917 Nimitz went to duty as aide to Rear Admiral Samuel S. Robison, commander of submarines in the Atlantic Fleet. In February, 1918, he was promoted to commander, and five days later he was made chief of staff to Robison.

The end of World War I found Nimitz moving from job to job, as the Navy tested his capabilities. He was now in the upper reaches, the gold-braid category. He served as executive officer of the USS *South Carolina* (finally getting his battleship duty), but not until he had taken a tour of duty ashore in the office of the Chief of Naval Operations, where he was concerned with submarine design.

In 1920 Nimitz had his first large ship command, the USS *Chicago* in the Pacific. He also built the submarine base at Pearl Harbor, as commander of Submarine Division 14 in addition to his other duty. (The Navy, in these postwar years of cutback, put a great deal of responsibility on a few shoulders.) In 1922 he gained an appointment to the Naval War College, a course almost necessary for an officer who wanted to be an admiral, at least in those days before World War II. At the War College, Nimitz learned fleet command. "I was asked once how we were able to fight the war in the Pacific," he said years later, "and I said that we fought it just as we had fought it all on paper in the naval war college. I fought the whole war of the Pacific when I was there in 1923."

At the commander level, officers did well to have a friend among the admirals, and Nimitz was fortunate enough to have Admiral Robison as his friend and backer. Robison asked for him again, and in 1923 Nimitz served him as aide and chief of staff, Admiral Robison then being commander of the United States Battle Fleet which was in the Pacific. Later Robison was made Commander in Chief of the United States Fleet, and Nimitz was still with him, as aide and chief of staff.

Nimitz was ordered to duty in 1926 to organize a Naval Reserve Officers Training Corps at the University of California in Berkeley, and he was later immensely proud of the fact that two of his young men of that day made rear admiral. "My chief satisfaction," he said, "came in getting in touch with up and going young men—working with young and extremely independent young men with untrammeled minds—and trying to introduce a little discipline into their thinking and actions."

June, 1929, saw Nimitz relieved from his teaching assignment and placed in charge of Submarine Division 20. At San Diego Nimitz gained a reputation as a strong, quiet officer, but also one who was notable for his hilarious and pointed wardroom stories. His associates, in the submarine and destroyer forces, were inclined to believe then and later that he not only collected stories, but made them up himself to suit the occasion if necessary.

Two years after taking the submarine division, he was transferred to command the USS *Rigel* and the destroyers out of commission at the destroyer base in San Diego, and in October, 1933, he took over the cruiser *Augusta* and cruised her to the Far East, where she became flagship of the Asiatic Fleet.

Thereafter his responsibilities grew: 1935, assistant chief in the Bureau of Navigation; 1938, commander, Cruiser Division 2, Battle Force; September, 1938, commander, Battleship Division 1, Battle Force; 1939, chief of the Bureau of Navigation, a staff job he considered subordinate only to that of Chief of Naval Operations.

All this time, Nimitz was raising a family. His first child was a girl, Catherine Vance. Next came a son, Chester, Jr., who entered the Naval Academy and graduated in the class of 1936. Third and fourth were daughters Anne Elizabeth and Mary Manson. On December 7, 1941, Nimitz counted himself a very happy man; he admired the Navy, he was totally happy in his job and at home, and his health was excellent. The future looked bright. Then, within a matter of hours, Nimitz's career was catapulted into a new crisis— not one of his own making this time, but one on which the safety of his nation might depend.

Nimitz had been under consideration for command of the Pacific Fleet when Kimmel was chosen, but Nimitz had then a four-year assignment as chief of the Bureau of Navigation, and so Kimmel got the fleet job. But when Kimmel failed in the eyes of Knox and the public, Knox thought immediately of Nimitz, and the appointment was made on December 17.

Nimitz did not then know that Roosevelt and Knox were determined to shake up the entire Navy Department. He established his lines of communication with Admiral Stark, the Chief of Naval Operations, to whom he expected to report from Pearl Harbor. From then on they would have to rely on the very frank, basic lines of communication that members of the naval establishment had been using since the beginnings of the nation. It was well known among the admirals that no man achieved flag rank without also making a record of excellence and brilliance in the Navy. There were differences among admirals—they were human—but the admirals had usually managed to present a united front against civilian outsiders, and except for some squabbles, usually over such new weapons as destroyers, submarines, and airplanes, the admirals got on remarkably well together. It was largely a matter of the limitations and definitions of the jobs to be done, and the disciplined willingness of all officers to accept the hands that fate dealt them in the matter of command. In the case of Kimmel, for example, the admirals realized that his brilliant career had been blasted because he had failed. In essence it was as simple as that. At the admiral's level there was no room for failure, and there was no justification for it.

Three days after his appointment Nimitz was on his way. The endless meetings and the immense volume of work that had piled up since December 7 had taken their toll on Nimitz. He scarcely had time to sleep, and he seldom thought of food. Captain Shafroth and others insisted that Nimitz take Lieutenant Lamar with him on the journey across the country, and that he go by train to get a little rest.

On December 19, Nimitz packed a bag and stopped in at the Navy Department to see Admiral Stark and Secretary Knox for a few moments. Knox was very emotional, and had difficulty in controlling his voice. After a few words, Nimitz was gone, he and Lamar heading for the railroad station to board the Capitol Limited. Stark wanted to take Nimitz to the train, but refrained because he was too well known. They both knew that tongues would begin to wag if the Chief of Naval Operations was seen putting someone on a train headed west, even if that someone was a "Mr. Freeman," traveling in civilian clothes.

The new commander was extremely conscious of security, and wanted to go unrecognized. Fortunately in this regard, the Washington station was bustling in this Christmas season, and as the pair arrived, so did several trainloads of girls who had been let out of boarding schools and colleges. The two men made their way unnoticed to the first section of the Capitol Limited and got on the train. There they had adjoining compartments with a door between, which made Nimitz a little more comfortable, for they were carrying secret papers: the first report of damage at Pearl Harbor, and various estimates and studies of the fleet and the situation, all in an old canvas sewing bag Nimitz had borrowed at the last moment from his wife. They locked one outer door, and the door between the compartments, and Nimitz settled down to do his homework.

Lamar was the perfect aide. He produced a bottle of Scotch, and they each had two highballs, then went into the diner. Afterward, Nimitz went to bed and slept well for the first time since the Japanese attack. "I awoke at seven A.M. really refreshed and *feeling* that I could cope with the situation," he said. At breakfast in the diner, they were unlucky. A man began staring at them, and when the man left the car he stopped by their table and addressed Nimitz by name and rank. The man was a college professor who had been at Lincoln, Nebraska, in October when Nimitz had spoken before the Association of American Colleges and Universities. But Nimitz was gruff, not wanting to discuss anything with anyone, and the professor went away. As they passed through the lounge car on the way back to their compartments, though, they saw him again, and in their wake Nimitz could hear himself being identified as "the admiral."

Lamar also told Nimitz that just behind them in the diner was a former naval reserve officer who had lost his commission and had been in the Navy Department just the day before trying to regain it. Was there no end to the bad luck and the potential breaches of security?

During the layover at Chicago, Nimitz got his hair cut, visited the Navy pier and the Naval Reserve Midshipman's school, and talked to old friends, including a fat old chief petty officer he recalled from the days at the destroyer base in San Diego. Then back to midtown to take the Santa Fe Chief, bound for San Francisco. The admiral spent a couple of hours on his papers, and then tried to teach Lamar to play cribbage, without much success. Nimitz had been preoccupied and silent for most of the journey; in fact he was worried about his ability to cope with the new job. But as he napped and read on the long trip, his confidence rose. "As I get more sleep and rest," he wrote Mrs. Nimitz, "things are looking up and I am sure that by the time I reach Pearl Harbor I will be able to meet the requirements of the situation."

But the more Nimitz plunged into the papers, the more dismal the future seemed. Next day he confessed he found it hard to remain cheerful, but hoped that when he got over the first shock at the sight of Pearl Harbor, he would adjust.

On December 21 Nimitz learned that Admiral King was made commander in chief, and that King was replacing Stark in charge of operations too. He got this information from the newspapers. Nimitz's classmate, Royall Ingersoll, would become the new commander in chief of the Atlantic Fleet. Comparing, as he was bound to do, Nimitz wrote home that he expected there would be far more action in the Pacific than anywhere else.

In San Francisco Nimitz went to the house of Rear Admiral Ernest Gunther, commander of the air station, and Lieutenant Lamar turned around to return to Washington. The flight to Pearl Harbor was delayed until Christmas Eve. Nimitz hated to take away the pilots of the big flying boat assigned to him on this day of all days, but there was no choice. His orders were to get to Pearl Harbor immediately, and not even Christmas could interfere. Still worried and feeling insecure, he wrote Mrs. Nimitz: "I only hope I can live up to the high expectations of you and the President and the Department. I will faithfully promise to do my best." And on this eve of departure he was very restless, upset because he could not have gotten to Pearl Harbor ahead of the Roberts investigation commission, which had been formed in Washington as a result of the angry reaction of Congress to the "surprise." President Roosevelt had been concerned about the Congressional reaction, and in order to ward off what seemed to be an imminent threat of a full-dress Congressional probe, he had appointed the Roberts commission to look into the problem.

The flight across the ocean was uneventful if cold, and at seven o'clock on Christmas morning, Nimitz arrived at Pearl Harbor to be met by Admiral Pye and several other officers. He was installed in the new four-bedroom house on Makalapa Hill that was reserved for the commander in chief. Rear Admiral Nimitz was now to become the full four-star admiral in charge of the Pacific war. Admiral Kimmel had now been reduced to his permanent rank of rear admiral. Sometime in the last few days Kimmel had quietly moved out of the house on Makalapa, and gone to bunk with the Pyes across the street.

Chapter Three

TO CARRY THE WAR

December 24, 1941–March 4, 1942

On Christmas Eve, a few hours before Admiral Nimitz arrived at Pearl Harbor, Vice Admiral Pye and his staff made a new estimate of the situation the United States faced in the Pacific:

It is sufficient to say here that Japan has: twice as many battleships as we have available, even counting our reenforcement (3 battleships from the East Coast); over twice as many carriers, counting our reenforcement of one [*Yorktown*]. In other types, the comparison is not so unfavorable if we include our Asiatic fleet and allies in the western Pacific.

The mission of the fleet was almost entirely defensive: "While protecting the territory and sea communications of the Associated Powers east of 180° and raiding enemy communications and forces,

49

to reenforce and defend Oahu and outlying bases; in order to retain and make secure, a fleet base for further operations when the fleet is strong enough to take the strategic offensive."

Defense—defense—defense. Pye proposed to strengthen the defenses of Oahu base; increase the Army defenses of Oahu; increase local naval defenses by more antisubmarine patrols, surface air warning net, mine defense, and so forth; improve shore defenses, bomb shelters, and communications; and increase the forces at outlying bases.

He proposed to "cover" Oahu and outlying bases by operating task forces at sea and using submarines, but said: " 'Cover' is a broad term and its application in this case will be discussed later." As to covering the outlying bases, Samoa, for example, could be covered only occasionally and the Aleutians practically never.

Pye and his staff were very much concerned about protection of shipping between the west coast and Hawaii and, to a lesser extent, along the New Zealand–Australia line. As far as raids were concerned, Pye proposed to use the submarine force heavily. As to the surface and air forces, he was much more conservative.

We have forces available—carriers and cruisers—well suited for this work, and a judicious choice of objectives and timing will do much to make our defensive effective and should help to improve our relative strength. We cannot afford to accept losses on a ship for ship basis, but will have to take some risks in order to strike the enemy a blow from time to time. The morale of the Fleet and of the nation demands it, and it is only in this way that we can keep some of the enery diverted to the defensive instead of permitting him to take offensive measures against us at will. Aside from raids on positions we should make sweeps in force (not less than two carrier groups) in areas where inferior enemy forces and supply ships are likely to be. As our battleships become available they can be advanced as supporting "strong points" on which the fast groups could retire.

As Admiral Draemel put it, "We were to fight a *holding* war—but there was little to do the holding with." They had written off the Philippines and the South Pacific. "The crucial and critical time of the Pacific War would be when the Japanese attempted to take the North Pacific—and it was necessary to husband every ounce of strength to meet that challenge. If we should fail in that challenge, the whole Pacific—and our West Coast—would be open to them."

Nimitz knew that a holding war was *not* what was wanted, but this was not the time for him to step in. He planned to take a week to discover exactly what he had to work with. On the hill at Makalapa Drive he met Admiral Kimmel, and those who were there said Nimitz kept turning back to look at the ships sunk in the harbor. The shock had set in.

Christmas dinner was spent with the Pyes and with Kimmel. Nimitz, again preoccupied with the immense task before him, went to bed early, but did not sleep well that night. In his humility, he even wondered if it was proper for him to take over Kimmel's house, but was reluctant to take the alternative: to move to the submarine base and push some senior officer out of the bachelor officers' quarters there.

In the morning Nimitz began a schedule he was to follow for some time. He got up at 6:30, did setting-up exercises, had breakfast alone at 7:15, and then went down the hill to the office. He lunched at the bachelor officers' quarters and went to the office until 6 o'clock, then back to the house, where he was joined by the Pyes and Kimmel, who dined with him each evening. After dinner the group played four-handed cribbage and talked. Nimitz then returned to the office for a short visit or went to bed.

In the beginning Nimitz did not sleep well at all. "To me it seems like I am on a treadmill—whirling around actively but not getting anywhere very fast," he said. But he was not discouraged, or at least he refused to admit that he was discouraged. Soon he had a letter from his son Chester, Jr., congratulating him on the new job, and urging him to be aggressive. He was touched because Pye and Wilson Brown showed so sincerely that they would do anything to help him, although they were much senior to him, and because he could see Kimmel straining to help, too.

The relationships among the three admirals—Nimitz, Pye, and Kimmel—at this moment told a great deal about the Navy and the

Navy way. All were vitally concerned with the Pacific Fleet Command. Nimitz was very distressed to arrive at Pearl Harbor and discover that the Wake Island relief expedition had been abandoned. But he did not voice a single word of criticism to Pye or about him, nor did he mention the matters to others. Kimmel—had the Wake relief gone through and the Japanese been met and defeated—might have saved his career, but Pye had destroyed Kimmel's last chance. Kimmel's resentment, if there was any, was so controlled by his self-discipline that he found it amenable to live in the Pyes' house and eat with Nimitz while waiting for the President and the Navy Department to decide his future. Pye, patiently holding the negative responsibility of a caretaker command, made no attempt to push Nimitz into taking over, and expressed his willingness to serve under the younger man. And each evening these three men ate together and played cribbage.

In the working hours, Nimitz was absorbing information as quickly as he could; it was essential that in the next few days he learn *all* about the Pacific Fleet, something he had no chance to do in Washington in the demanding job of chief of the Bureau of Navigation. Each division of the command had prepared or was preparing summary memos, such as that of Captain W. A. Lee, Jr., on fleet readiness. It was important, of course, that Nimitz have all the weapons that his country could give him. It was equally important that he know precisely the degree of proficiency of the men who would use the weapons. As of December, 1941, the picture was only fair. Lee reported that the general gunnery of the fleet was good. The six-inch, ten-thousand ton cruisers had a very high degree of proficency; the eight-inch cruisers were not quite as good. The carriers shot fairly well by day. The destroyers' gunnery and torpedo proficiency was very good, the submarines were very good, and the battleships had been good to very good.

The fleet was very short of rapid-fire automatic machine guns, such as the Orleikon and Bofors 20 mm and 40 mm. The attack at Pearl Harbor had indicated a distressing lack of ability to break up a torpedo plane attack because of this shortage, although the bigger antiaircraft guns could operate effectively against horizontal bombing.

As for the men who would fly the planes—here was a sad story that lent strength to the charges of fleet unreadiness, and more, American unreadiness. Experienced personnel had been withdrawn from the fleet in the expansion of the air arm of the Navy. The torpedo squadrons were particularly short of trained pilots, and this deficiency could not be rectified before the spring of 1942. There were *no* spare planes in reserve for the carriers in the Hawaiian area. Replacement groups were needed for all three carriers, and the only chance that seemed realistic at all was that they might get one air group of Marines, if the Marines were allowed to fly from carriers. The carriers all had radar—but radar was still experimental, having been introduced only late in the 1930's. The planes had no identification-friend-or-foe (IFF) equipment. The carrier men were fine flyers, and in a good state of training, but they were not proficient with their guns and bombs and torpedoes, because they had not been given enough practice.

There was a shortage of .50-caliber ammunition, a shortage of bombs, and a shortage of torpedoes. Only 15 percent of the fleet (including the carriers) had radar warning equipment, and there were not enough patrol planes in the islands to carry out proper combat air patrol, tactical security measures, or to locate enemy attack units. Just now 20 mm guns were being installed, 16 to a battleship, 12 to a cruiser, 24 to a carrier, and four to a destroyer.

Such deficiency could hardly be blamed on Admiral Kimmel, or on Admiral Stark at the top of the ladder. No, the blame was on the level of policy. It was not that the Navy men did not know that these pieces of armament and equipment were needed. In the case of torpedoes, for example, no one really knew the effectiveness of the torpedoes, because they were never fired, they were only test-fired with dummy warheads so they could be used over and over again. The carrier pilots were not good gunners, because ammunition could not be wasted on practice. Radar was short, because the budget did not have enough money in it for rapid production. After all, in these years just past, the Navy budget had usually been well under $500 million a year, and a $10,000 torpedo was not something to be wasted.

Within the fleet, the *Saratoga* task force was out this Christmas week. The transport *Wright* left to reinforce Midway and the *Tangier* returned to port, with its supplies for Wake intact. A group left to reinforce Johnston Island, and the decision on reinforcing Samoa was left to the commander of the Pacific Fleet, with Admiral Stark's strong hint that it ought to be done.

On December 27 Washington began asking some rather pointed questions about the abandonment of the Wake and Jaluit expeditions. That day, Task Force 14 entered Pearl Harbor for resupply, and that day also Admiral Pye decided to reduce the strength of the task forces and keep them in the Hawaiian area instead of out raiding. "We cannot afford at this time to subject our forces to losses from shore-base air and superior carrier strength, particularly while 2000 miles from base." *

Admiral Stark's urging finally forced Admiral Pye into a positive action: on December 28 he sent the full reinforcement group to Samoa, with the *Yorktown* to form up Task Force 17 and escort the Marines and the supplies. Stark was again after Pye for stronger measures, calling for covering or diversionary operations against the enemy in connection with the Samoan reinforcement.

This turbid state of affairs ended on December 30, however, when Admiral King took command of the United States Fleet. King's first official action was to send a new statement of the task of the Pacific Fleet.

The dispatch to Pearl Harbor, King's first official act, showed what Washington thought of the state of affairs, especially because it was addressed to Nimitz, although he had not yet assumed command.

The new job was to cover and hold the Hawaii-Midway line and maintain communications with the west coast, and to maintain communications between the west coast and Australia by covering, securing, and holding the Hawaii-Samoa line, which, King said, should be extended to include Fiji at the earliest possible moment.

There was to be no more "pussyfooting"—no more pulling back carrier task forces to sail them around Hawaii.

---

* It is interesting to note that earlier the Naval high command in Washington had suggested that Wake might be a liability. When it was abandoned, the same commander, apparently, asked a lot of questions about the abandonment. It was almost as if the command in Washington was in two different hands.

The sense of urgency in this message brooked no further delay by Nimitz in assuming command, and at ten o'clock on the morning of December 31, Admiral Nimitz put on the four-star boards given him by the submariners of the Pearl Harbor base in honor of his establishment of that base so many years earlier, and went to Pye's office, where he relieved the admiral. Mrs. Pye was about to leave for the United States, breaking up the admirals' conclave, and when she left, Nimitz would take other officers in to live with him.

In turn, one of Admiral Nimitz's first acts was to call the staff together. For weeks the staff of the commander in chief, Pacific Fleet, had lived in a sort of limbo, made bearable only by the furious activity demanded of every staff officer. The entire staff consisted of thirty-two officers and men, from Rear Admiral Draemel, whom Pye had brought in as chief of staff, to Boatswain Chester B. Clark, who served as signal officer. Other officers were attached to the staff, but these thirty-two men represented the central core of the Pacific Fleet on December 31, 1941.

Without visible exception, these officers expected to be replaced, following an old Navy custom. It was the practice for an admiral to choose his own staff, and the practice of the Bureau of Navigation to give flag officers the greatest leeway in choosing the juniors they wanted. For example, when Nimitz wanted to switch Captain McMorris from Kimmel's staff in the spring of 1941, Kimmel had objected. "I sincerely believe that McMorris is the one officer of the Navy best fitted for the preparation of War Plans for the Pacific Fleet," Kimmel then wrote Nimitz, and he said he was most unwilling to lose him for any purpose. Nimitz, the Navy's personnel expert, had yielded and Kimmel had his way.

Most admirals had very definite preferences among the younger men of the Navy, and the junior officers were constantly looking for seniors whom they might serve, increasing their own chances of "fleeting up" or achieving promotion within one of the fleets. Nimitz, as noted, had attached himself to Admiral S. S. Robison, and had fleeted up with him.

Thus, on the morning of December 31 the members of the Kimmel-Pye staff were ready for any kind of bad news.

But Nimitz had no intention of cutting the slender line of con-

tinuity; he was too new, and he had too many responsibilities, to assemble and train a staff overnight. Quietly, in his most effective soft-
spoken manner, Nimitz spoke to the men about the past few weeks.
He said he had not wanted the job, that he had recommended Pye
be retained permanently in it, but that he had been overruled. He
did not know all of these men intimately, but he knew a number of
them by reputation, for he had been handling their affairs in Washington since 1939, and he was certain that these men represented the
high standard of the Navy, and that he wanted them to stay with
him. He told them just that.

The staff men were grateful, and showed their gratitude by putting forth even greater effort, if that was possible. For weeks they
had been under constant tension. Take Draemel: as chief of staff
to Pye he was responsible for presenting every situation for the commander's consideration. He worked hard all day. But that was not
all. The submarines were the eyes of the fleet, they and the radio
produced the information, such as it was, about the movements of
the Japanese. The submarines came up out of the depths at night
to sit on the surface, recharging their batteries for underseas running
the next day and sending their messages. A nervous Draemel, then,
found it necessary to work day and night, so he could receive the
submarine intelligence, consider it, and have it ready for the commander's desk the next morning.

Draemel was not alone, although his responsibility was great.
Lieutenant Commander Paul C. Crosley had been Kimmel's flag
secretary. From the moment of the Japanese attack, the job had become a seven-day affair. Crosley moved from Honolulu into the base,
so he could be available at all times, and he spent twelve hours or
more a day at his desk, attacking the mountain of paper that was
piled there.

On taking command, Nimitz began a series of conferences with
the senior officers at Pearl Harbor. Roughly speaking, these officers
fell into two groups: those who believed in the overwhelming power
of the battleship, and those who had transferred their faith to the
aircraft carrier. With the situation he faced, Nimitz certainly was
not one of the former, although he had never learned to fly and did
not like flying himself. Furthermore, although he never said this

aloud during the war, Nimitz already saw that the slow American battleships were a liability rather than an asset. December, 1941, was not the time to say so, but Nimitz felt "it was God's divine will that Kimmel did not have his fleet at sea to intercept the Japanese Carrier Task Force . . . ." Years later, when the Pearl Harbor debate was history, Nimitz explained that the Japanese had a fleet speed at least two knots superior to that of the American fleet with its battleships, and so Kimmel could never have forced an action unless the Japanese wanted it. Even if all three American carriers had been in the area and ready for a battle, the Japanese carriers would have outnumbered them two to one—and with the *Saratoga* on the west coast and the *Lexington* probably unable to join up, this left Halsey in the *Enterprise* to provide air cover. Under those circumstances, Nimitz said, the United States might have lost *all* the ships and the trained men of the Battle Force rather than the 3800 who were lost at Pearl Harbor.

Nimitz's problem as 1942 began was to send fighting admirals to sea to carry the war against the Japanese. The war presented an entirely new problem for the Navy, one that must be solved immediately—the problem of discovering and employing the fighting leaders who would be most effective.

In the years just before the war, a number of admirals were working their way to the top. In October, 1939, as the new chief of the Bureau of Navigation, Nimitz had been in correspondence with Admiral C. C. Bloch, then Commander in Chief of the U.S. Fleet, on the subject of flag officers' assignments. He had spoken very highly of Pye, then commander of battleships. "He has an unusual quality for tactical matters, . . . he is an indefatiguable worker and I believe as Commander Battleships will contribute most materially to battleship tactics and doctrines—and there is a lot to be done in that line." In the same letter, Bloch recommended promotions for Draemel, Robert A. Theobald, and Wilson Brown. Among the younger admirals he mentioned Robert L. Ghormley, Herbert F. Leary, William L. Calhoun, Leigh Noyes, and Nimitz as flag officers who ought to be in subordinate positions in the fleet, to prepare them for command after 1942 and 1943 when the older admirals were expected to retire.

That same year Admiral J. O. Richardson, then commander of

the Battle Force but already selected to succeed Bloch, recommended Pye as commander of battleships, and Draemel as commander of Destroyer Flotilla One. He had called Kimmel "one of the best" and Draemel "superior." The next year, Richardson discussed officers' billets again with Nimitz, noting that he believed the best candidates for commander in chief in the future were Kimmel, Ghormley, Draemel, and Nimitz himself, in order of rank.

Now, in December, 1941, most of these officers were in and around Pearl Harbor, and it was Nimitz's job to sort them out and put them to the best use he could. Pye and Draemel were excellent strategists and tacticians, but their training and thinking were geared to a fleet whose most important weapon was the battleship. The others around Nimitz had varying views, partially based on their training and specialties.

The meetings began, and they were frank meetings in which much salty talk was aired. One of the admirable attributes of the professional Navy officer is that he learns in Academy days that he must live and work with men of differing disposition and opinion, and the successful officers adjust. They engage in arguments of such intensity that one might believe the opponents were bitter enemies, until one discovers that their wives all belong to the same bridge club, and they play golf together, drink together, and go to the same parties.

What Nimitz wanted was action, and some ideas.

On December 31 Admiral Fletcher was at San Diego, preparing to take Task Force 17, with the *Yorktown*, to Pago Pago, Samoa. He had the carrier, two cruisers, four destroyers, three transports carrying about five thousand troops, two cargo ships, and the oiler *Kaskaskia*. His orders called for him to take the train in, then return to Pearl Harbor unless otherwise directed. In other words, Admiral Pye had conceived of the Samoan relief as simply a defensive operation, and had no plans for use of the task force once it came into waters adjacent to the enemy.

The residue of the Wake fiasco, Task Force 11, was expected back on January 3. Task Force 8, with Halsey, would leave Pearl on January 3 to relieve Task Force 11, guarding the Oahu-Palmyra-Johnston triangle. The only offensive action under way was that of the submarines: three submarines were working Japanese waters, two were lurking around the Marshalls, scouting, one was at Wake, and one was at Midway, while one other, the *Thresher*, had just departed for the western Marshalls.

Over the objections of his conservative advisers, Nimitz decided to send the carrier task forces to strike the Japanese. His most enthusiastic supporter among the senior officers was Vice Admiral Halsey, who promptly volunteered to take *Enterprise* out and raid the Japanese where it would hurt—in their Marshall Islands base in the Central Pacific.

On December 31, Nimitz ordered Rear Admiral Leary to take Task Force 14, with *Saratoga* as its nucleus, on an offensive patrol in the Midway area, to seek out any Japanese units, sink them, and return to Pearl Harbor on January 13. Leary had been commander of cruisers of the Battle Force since February. Here was his chance to distinguish himself.

Leary sailed. On January 3 Halsey went out in Task Force 8 for practice firing—to improve the weapons performance of his little armada before taking on the enemy. He would go off for gunnery practice south of Oahu, and then move north to practice antiaircraft firing. He was accompanied by a fifty-five-year-old rear admiral whom few in the fleet knew very well, Raymond A. Spruance, commander of Cruiser Division 5, with his flag in the USS *Northampton*. At the same time the first change that represented Nimitz's influence was seen. Rear Admiral Bidwell, the commander of Cruiser Division 3, was not well. He was sent to the naval hospital at San Diego, and in came Rear Admiral Shafroth, Nimitz's assistant from the Bureau of Navigation, who had gotten his flag and now joined the fleet.

Nimitz demanded readiness dates for the battleships that were under repair, and learned that he would soon have six of them. By January 9 the tempo at Pearl Harbor had picked up remarkably. What was needed was leadership, and Nimitz was supplying it. They talked of the task forces, as if the words meant something. Task Force One was the battleships, under Rear Admiral Anderson in *Maryland*. Task Force 7 was the submarines, which had started right out doing their aggressive job under Rear Admiral Robert H. English and were going strong. Task Force 8 was Halsey, ready to head for the Marshalls. Task Force 9 was the patrol planes, given the mission of searching for the enemy. Task Force 11 was Brown in *Lexington*. Task Force 14 was Leary, out searching for the enemy. Task Forces 12 and 15 were convoy forces, using the available cruisers and destroyers. And Task Force 17 was Fletcher, moving toward Samoa. Convoy action was increasing constantly; the Army was moving too, and 30,000 to 50,000 troops were expected to be moved to Hawaii by March.

Leary was steaming home from Midway on the night of January 11, his mission having borne little fruit, when suddenly the *Saratoga* took a torpedo on the port quarter. Three boiler rooms were flooded, but there was no water above the third deck, and she could be brought in. Still, it was scratch one carrier for the next few weeks. That left three.

Leary had been given his chance, and it had not worked out very well. Before the month was out, he was reassigned, given the *Chicago* and two destroyers, and sent to the South Pacific to command a combined force of American–Australian–New Zealand vessels. It could not be called a demotion; the job was a very important one, a transfer to an activity in which Leary was expected to shine more brightly than he had in carrier task force operation.

The fate of the *Saratoga*, so early in the war, seemed to indicate the verisimilitude of the arguments of the battleship proponents— that the carrier was a launching platform that needed utmost protection. But what Nimitz wanted, and asked for on January 15, was two more destroyer squadrons. There was no hesitation; eleven days after *Saratoga* was hit, Nimitz ordered Frank Jack Fletcher to take Task Force 17 and operate under Halsey in the Pacific as soon as he had disembarked his troops at Samoa.

The fleet had a lot to learn about fighting the war, and it was time to begin. One of the early actions of the new task forces occurred on January 10. It was so unimportant and indecisive that it remained unreported except through official channels. It involved an unsuccessful attack by carrier planes on a Japanese submarine.

At 1045 on January 10 the pilot of the scouting plane 2-F-11 zoomed over the deck of the *Lexington* at sea and dropped a message. He had sighted an enemy submarine on the surface about eighty miles from the carrier. The submarine had submerged when he flew over, but the pilot had the course and speed. He confirmed the facts when he landed aboard the carrier a few minutes later. Captain Frederick C. Sherman of the *Lexington* sent off four torpedo planes, each armed with two 325-pound depth charges, the charges set to explode at 50 feet. At 1320 two of the planes sighted the submarine at the approximate position given, and began a down-sun approach at 2000 feet, carrying out a bombsight-controlled run of 3000 yards at 100 knots, coming in abaft the beam of the submarine. The pilot of 2-T-10 dropped too soon, and his charges exploded 125 feet astern and 100 feet astern. On the first pass, 2-T-14's charges would not release and he did not drop. He came back at 1400 feet and dropped, just ahead of the sub. But the submarine had submerged by this time, as 2-F-17 and 2-F-10 came barreling in, .50-caliber machine guns blazing, after the first depth-charging. The second set of depth charges were seen to explode, and one observer said he was sure the bow of the sub jerked to the right just then, and a small oil slick came up. All six of the search planes (the bombers and the regular fighter patrol) remained in the area for an hour and then returned to the carrier as their fuel became low. Other planes replaced them, and the area was patrolled until 2130, but there was no further contact.

Captain Sherman said it was doubtful if the submarine was severely damaged, and it could be called nothing more than a possible sinking. Admiral Wilson Brown said he was pleased, particularly because sailors had been reporting whales as submarines so often that no destroyer had been sent out on this contact, and it was not until the depth-charging reports reached the task force that destroyers were sent. Nimitz was pleased, not so much about the submarine, but because the pilot of 2-T-14 had used his head and led the sub by 50 to 75 feet, something he had not been taught to do in school.

The men were learning, but there was a good deal to be learned. For example, all that difficulty about fueling the *Lexington* just after the Pearl Harbor attack could be laid to inexperience in fueling at sea. The inexperience was due to lack of opportunity—a serious shortage of fleet tankers. A division of tankers had reported for duty at San Diego in the summer of 1941, but was almost immediately ordered to the Atlantic for the occupation of Iceland. The task forces were still not properly trained in fueling, and there were many other problems, some apparent and some not. The aircraft still did not have IFF equipment. Many of them were not equipped with self-sealing gas tanks—a matter of very little importance in peacetime, but in the European war it had proved to be a question of life or death to a carrier pilot when he went into combat. Aircraft production was not up to the schedule that the Bureau of Aeronautics wanted, and cannon, which had proved very effective in Europe, were just beginning to be installed in the Navy planes.

Within a few days after taking command, Nimitz had the Pacific Fleet moving. He was very quiet about it, and he was not nearly so confident as he seemed to his staff, but the struggle was beginning. And even now Nimitz found time, as Rear Admiral Husband E. Kimmel was detached to go back to the United States, for a generous gesture.

He had Kimmel's orders written in a way that would permit the admiral to take his family home at government expense. Kimmel had been asking Nimitz to secure a job of some kind for him, and Nimitz had tried, but Secretary Knox had refused to give Kimmel any assignment until action was taken on the report of the Roberts commission.

"Naturally, none of us here know all the facts connected with the Pearl Harbor incident, and I am doubtful, personally, whether all the facts ever will be known," Nimitz wrote. "Needless to say, I feel deeply for you."

Nimitz's real attention, at this point, was focused on the South Pacific, where the Japanese were massing for something—no one among the Allies knew quite what. The Australians thought the strike would be at the Fiji Islands. Just as Fletcher moved in toward the Samoan archipelago, the Japanese too were on the move. From Washington, King began to put on the pressure. On January 20 he asked for a speedup of the offensive operations of Task Forces 8 and 17, and a raid on Wake as well as the Marshalls. After talking it over with the staff, Nimitz decided to divert Task Force 11 to the Wake job, and sent the tanker *Neches* to join and fuel the force.

Then, at three o'clock on the morning of January 23, the *Ne-*

ches was torpedoed on her way to the rendezvous, throwing a monkey wrench into the plans once again. No other tanker was available except *Neosho*, which was not yet in harbor, and Nimitz had to order Task Force 11 home. Logistics were giving him a bad start.

That day, the Japanese landed at Rabaul and began moving along the coast of New Britain and New Ireland, and heading for the Northern Solomons.

Halsey, meanwhile, was preparing to deliver the first major American attack of the war. He planned to strike Jaluit, Mili, and Makin on January 31. But again the fuel problem haunted the American Navy. Halsey reported on January 30 that unless he could have a tanker, he would have to confine his strike to one day, in order to get home safely. Nimitz then decided to dispatch Task Force 11 with the *Neosho* to meet and fuel Halsey. The oiler *Kaskaskia*, tanks empty, heading back to San Diego, was diverted to Pearl, because Nimitz was very worried about the fueling problem.

Halsey went in to conduct the first offensive combat by American carriers in history, and the first offensive operation of the United States in the war. Following the latest intelligence, which showed the concentrations of Japanese ships and planes, Halsey hit Wotje, Maloelap, and Kwajalein, while Fletcher went after Makin, Mili, and Jaluit. Spruance took two cruisers and a destroyer to bombard Wotje, and one cruiser and a pair of destroyers worked over Maloelap. For two hours Halsey maneuvered the *Enterprise* in a small rectangle just off Wotje, fighting off attacks by bombers, then he decided to get out—and the phrase "haul ass with Halsey" was coined. There were plane losses from antiaircraft fire and Japanese fighters, and the cruiser *Chester* took a bomb through her main deck, but the attack was a success. Several Japanese ships were sunk or damaged, including a light cruiser, and (although the Americans did not then know it) a Japanese admiral was killed. If the raid did nothing else, it vastly assisted the prestige of the Navy and gave Americans the first chance to be a little proud.

Fletcher was not so lucky. As Nimitz noted, heavy rain had interfered with the attack on Jaluit. Still, Nimitz remarked that the whole action "is considered to have been well conceived and planned and brilliantly executed." Halsey got the Distinguished Service

Medal, and his chief of staff, Miles Browning, was promoted to captain.

The difficulties of the task forces in these early days of the war were indicated by the story of Admiral Wilson Brown's Task Force 11, which was sent down from Pearl Harbor on January 31 to escort the *Neosho*. Brown's orders were to refuel Task Force 8, and then "oppose the enemy" before returning to Pearl Harbor on February 16. He had forty-two days' provisions aboard the *Lexington*. Two days out of Pearl, Brown learned that Halsey would not need the fuel after all, so he headed for Canton Island. But on February 6 King ordered the forces down to the Anzac (Australia–New Zealand) waters for a joint operation with Leary's force. They met 300 miles west of Suva, and Brown took over the Anzacs for the moment, while Leary moved down to Melbourne to establish a headquarters. Task Force 11, so augmented, was to make a surprise raid on Rabaul. It was Brown's idea. King approved.

On February 13 the force began refueling from the *Neosho*. *Lexington* and the destroyers filled up, but the cruisers were only 75 percent full, and Brown regarded this as a serious handicap to his operations. He had communications problems too. He wanted surprise—so much so that to communicate with King and Nimitz he flew two officers from his staff over to Suva to send radio messages, and preserve the silence of the task force.

A serious problem developed when the Anzacs fell short of fuel, but Rear Admiral J. G. Crace wanted to get into the fight. Brown assigned him to cover Suva and Nouméa and take on any Japanese who showed up. Rear Admiral Thomas O. Kinkaid was in command of the cruisers of Task Force 11.

The forces parted company, and Brown headed northwest toward the Solomons, intending to approach Rabaul from the northeast. On February 20, about 420 miles out from Rabaul, the force was jumped by enemy scout planes, and then 18 two-engined bombers. Sixteen of these were shot down, Brown said. (One of the problems early in the war was an American tendency to overestimate casualties dealt the enemy, but in this case it seems that most of the attackers were shot down, at least by Samuel Eliot Morison's estimate.)

In his action report Brown then noted some of his observations. They were all short of fuel, which placed an *"absolute* limit" on high-speed operations. (The italics are Brown's.) "A properly planned raid [which he did not consider this one to be] must start from a base near the enemy." The ships must fuel outside the range of shore-based aircraft. At this point, since he had lost the element of surprise, Brown withdrew from the Rabaul operation, to the south, and was met by the Anzacs. Again there was not enough fuel for all ships, and the Anzacs went off to Suva to fuel, while Task Force 11 moved into the Coral Sea to patrol toward New Guinea.

On March 2 Brown received orders to link up with Task Force 17 and carry out an operation against the Japanese. Back at Pearl, Nimitz was having a rare struggle with King by radio, King insisting on fleet action in the Southwest Pacific against the Japanese to slow down that juggernaut advance that seemed aimed at Australia. On February 7 Nimitz had said he did not have the forces to make anything but hit-and-run raids in the southwest. King wanted him to use his battleships, but Nimitz said they simply would not fit. He did not have the destroyers and cruisers to screen them.

King was doing everything he could—he was moving his chessmen here and there, furiously. He promised Nimitz Marine units from Iceland, to form an amphibious unit. Then he asked for twelve B-17's from Hawaii Army forces, to support Task Force 11. King had great hopes for Task Force 11 as a stopper for the Japanese.

Nimitz wanted to hold off other raids for a time, but King disagreed flatly and insisted that Nimitz was not using his battleships properly, and that he must continue offensive operations in the middle Pacific, around Wake and the Marshalls, if he could do nothing else to slow the Japanese advance in the southwest. Nimitz and his staff were testy about the latest development. "This makes the situation particularly difficult as though orders of Cominch . . . Task Force 11, extra light forces, and tankers are being tied up in the Suva area."

To resolve the differences, Nimitz put Admiral Pye on a plane and sent him to Washington to present the Nimitz viewpoint. He and the staff sweated day and night, trying to find some way to use their slender forces to stop the Japanese descending on Australia.

They considered sending Halsey to join Brown and make a big raid on Rabaul, while Fletcher either held in reserve or attacked Wake. They even considered a raid on Tokyo, but gave up the idea because there would be bad weather for fueling. They decided to send Halsey out to attack Wake, now calling his force Task Force 16. He was originally scheduled for Eniwetok, but Japanese activity there was reported to be very limited.

By February 15 Admiral King had apparently cooled down enough to realize the limitations of the Pacific Fleet, and he told Nimitz by message that occasional raids in the mandated islands (Gilberts and Marshalls) would be considered sufficient for the moment. He was happier because of Brown's plans to raid Rabaul.

Nimitz was not very happy. Pye returned from Washington on February 26 with the bad news that King did not have an overall plan for action in the Pacific. Nimitz was being hammered to help Australia, but he did not know what his priorities were to be.

In the Southwest Pacific, the Rabaul raid was coming unraveled. Brown was in the Coral Sea at the beginning of March, worrying because an enemy force might enter the sea without detection. On March 2 he barely avoided a hurricane, then fueled. Admiral Fletcher joined up, and he and his staff from *Yorktown* came aboard *Lexington* for a conference. Fletcher wanted a dawn attack for 125 miles out against Gasmata and Rabaul. Brown wanted to go in at night by moonlight. He did not want to go into the 125-miles point for a dawn attack. It was too risky. Fletcher demurred. His men were not experienced enough in night flying, he said. (Earlier Fletcher had called off a last sweep at Jaluit after the storm clouds blew over, because he would have to recover his planes after dark if he sent them off.) So Brown agreed reluctantly to the dawn attack.

Task Forces 11 and 17 had maintained radio silence since February 20 (sometimes to the annoyance of Nimitz and King, who would have liked to know what they were doing). But on March 8 the two forces were suddenly caught in a squall before Brown, as senior officer, could execute his flag signals. There was very grave danger of collision between the forces, so Brown authorized a breach of radio silence to send a message on the warning net.

"This shows the *urgent* need for TBS [talk between ships, or high-frequency radio which could not be picked up by forces far away]" Brown wrote in his action report. The second violation came when a cruiser scout plant was lost, and the *Lexington* tried to bring it in. (The plane crew was recovered six days later.) This indicated to Brown the urgent need for homing equipment on the planes.

Brown was certain that the Japanese had picked up the signals, and that once again the element of surprise, which he held absolutely essential, had been lost. So he moved away from Rabaul again. Not to break radio silence, he sent officers to Townsville to radio dispatches back to Washington and Pearl Harbor. His force was short of provisions. Since early January the *San Francisco* had been without replenishment. Brown had ninety days' dry stores on the *Lexington* and he began doling them out to destroyers and cruisers—at sea. It was good practice for the men.

Wilson Brown's messages had many recommendations for Nimitz and the others. He pointed out that the senior officer of the force, the officer in tactical command (OTC), had no way of holding conferences and coordinating attacks. They needed a base in the Southwest Pacific, Nouméa or Suva. He had been able to fuel at sea, but they could not always expect such favorable conditions as he had enjoyed.

Brown felt, however, that he could hold the enemy in check unless the Japanese assigned a major fleet to the area. He advocated daily bombing of the ships and bases from the Australian coast and constant submarine harassment from Townsville or Nouméa. And then he headed back to Pearl, with one final warning:

That since carrier planes have shorter radii than shore based planes, carrier attack on enemy shipping in defended ports will be successful only when the attack arrives as a complete surprise to the enemy and even then, when surprise is successful, the carrier will run serious risks of heavy attack by surviving enemy planes. In other words, the ever growing importance and effectiveness of aircraft has not changed the old

truism that ships are at a disadvantage in attacking strongly
defended shore positions.

Halsey, with Spruance again leading the cruisers, went to Wake
on February 24, and then hit Marcus Island on March 4. Not much
came out of these raids, except practice for the officers and men
of the fleet. But at least one thing could be said: the Pacific Fleet
was getting into the war.

Chapter
Four

THE CHANGING
SCENE

March 1–May 8, 1942

The morale of the American public had been boosted by the successful carrier strikes in the Central and Southwest Pacific, but as far as the high command was concerned, March, 1942, marked a new low point. The Japanese were moving ahead, almost at will it seemed. On March 11 General Douglas MacArthur left Bataan for Australia, and it was apparent that sick, abandoned Americans in the Philippines could hold out only for a matter of weeks.

At Pearl Harbor it was a most trying time for Admiral Nimitz and his staff, but few men around him even suspected how tightly knotted were the admiral's nerves, or how badly he slept at night. His establishment of a solid routine belied these facts. He arose, breakfasted around 7:30, went down to the submarine base where his office was located. Almost always he lunched with his officers and then went back to work. Toward the end of the afternoon he would organize a game of tennis with three of the other officers. Forty years older and thirty pounds heavier than in his days at the Academy, he still played a sharp game, although his doctors had long since advised him to give up the violent exertions of singles. He was a placement expert, and could run his younger opponents ragged with nice little shots chopped along the lines. Or Nimitz would take on one officer or a handful in horseshoes, a game that stimulated idle conversation and got one's mind off the vital and sometimes depressing business at hand. Later, when matters became too tense, he was likely to be found on the pistol range; he had a gallery built alongside his office, and those who knew him might suspect what was going on in his mind as he squeezed off one careful shot after another. But they could do no more than suspect, for Nimitz was the perfect command figure; he kept his thoughts thoroughly to himself except as he needed to communicate with his subordinates to further the ends of the war. Of small talk there was plenty, with stories and grins and laughter. But of the grim days that lay ahead there was no talk at all.

Exercise cleared Nimitz's mind, warded off the results of yielding to the temptations of his cook, and helped him sleep at night. A walk of several miles was not unusual, with younger officers puffing along behind; and if the walk was along the shore, Nimitz might slip into the sea and swim for a mile. On days when there was no time for such lengthy relaxation, he was known to organize a health club and stimulate his juniors by smacking a medicine ball into their soft bellies. The other officers were not soft long, for the "old man's" example brought most of the younger ones around, and the submarine base was probably the healthiest major headquarters in the world.

In the daily conferences, when tensions ran high and disagreements threatened to flair into the open, Nimitz exerted his remarkable memory and his precise timing, to carry a discussion to the absolute limit of usefulness, and rescue it from futile argument with a brief, telling story. Sometimes he made up these tales on the spot, but he was forever swapping stories with Secretary Knox by mail, and as the people of the Pacific learned of this interest, they brought him stories from near and far.

Nimitz's patience was tried almost to the limit, for the powers in Washington had not yet formulated an overall approach to the war against Japan. Early in March Admiral King asked Nimitz for comment on the subdivision of the Pacific areas. The Joint Chiefs were trying to work out the relationship between MacArthur and Nimitz. Generally speaking, it was a time of consolidation and regrouping, waiting for whatever strength could be spared to the Pacific from the needs stated by the forces committed to Europe.

Toward the end of the month, Admiral Theobald made another estimate of the situation, and it was taken up in the morning conference by Nimitz. Theobald said the Japanese would probably not move against either India or Australia, but that an attack on Hawaii was probable. He recommended holding strong forces within a thirty-six-hour run of Oahu until the Japanese committed themselves one way or another. Nimitz sought a consensus: and it was that such an attack might come but that it was not coming right away—at least it had best not come, because Nimitz did not have the strong forces to operate as Theobald wished.

Wilson Brown went on to hit Lae and Salamaua, where the Japanese had landed on March 8; and on March 10, 104 planes from the two carriers crossed the Owen Stanley Mountains and attacked, sinking a minesweeper, a transport, and a converted light cruiser. The pilots came back with optimistic accounts of even greater damage, and they were forwarded. When the news reached President Roosevelt, he was so pleased that he sent a special message to Winston Churchill. "It was by all means the best day's work we have had," the President said.

As Brown's forces returned, Vice Admiral Halsey flew to the west coast to make arrangements for a special operation that had been originated by King and his staff. It was to be a raid by B-25 medium bombers from a carrier which would take them as close as possible to the Japanese homeland, so they could hit Tokyo and other targets. When a staff officer from Washington came to Pearl Harbor to present the plan, Admiral Draemel had opposed it as wasteful of America's limited air power. Most of the planes would certainly be lost, Draemel said, and the amount of damage they could do was very limited. The planes would be much better in

Australia or at some advanced base where they could strike the Japanese day after day. But Draemel was overruled, for the admirals and generals in Washington felt the need for some spectacular operation that could raise American morale and retaliate for Pearl Harbor. The Doolittle Tokyo Raid (led by Lieutenant Colonel James Doolittle of the Army Air Corps) was on.

At this same time, as Wilson Brown was coming back, King indicated that he was less than pleased with the return. On March 30 he sent a message questioning Brown's apparent retirement from the enemy. That same day, Nimitz detached Brown from task force duty and made him commander of the new Amphibious Force, to have headquarters at San Diego. King had decided that Brown was not aggressive enough to be a task force commander.

There was much talk about amphibious operations. Rear Admiral Richmond Kelly Turner, head of King's war plans division, was working up a plan which he hoped would persuade King to create the machinery for a naval program. Turner was an able student of amphibious warfare, and was supervising the revision of the Navy's plans for this type of operation. It was apparent to all concerned that if the territory wrested by the Axis powers from the western powers was to be retrieved, it would have to be by amphibious landings. So Wilson Brown would go to establish the Pacific Amphibious Force, which would be called Task Force 3.

By April the lines of command in the Pacific were being sorted out. King informed Nimitz on April 4 that he would have the Pacific Ocean area, that General MacArthur would command the Southwest Pacific, and that MacArthur would have his own navy, with Vice Admiral Leary to command it. Nimitz selected Pye to become his commander in the South Pacific, and to face the new problems. Among them was the fact that New Zealand, Nouméa, and Fiji fell within the Nimitz command, while the area where the Navy had been in operation, around the Solomons and New Guinea, was actually in MacArthur's territory.

On April 8 an exuberant Halsey departed with the famous Task Force 16, which would carry him, the *Enterprise*, and the *Hornet* with its B-25's toward Japan. Ten days later the attack was carried off, but Nimitz and his staff were of two minds about it. It tied up important forces (two carriers, four cruisers, eight destroyers, and two oilers) for a long time, the damage was very slight, and the risk of losing a carrier was very great. It would not be done again.

But the consideration of the Tokyo raid was a minor matter compared to what else was occurring. On April 18 Nimitz was gearing himself for a new offensive by the Japanese in the Southwest Pacific. It was expected to come around the first of May in the Solomons–New Guinea–New Britain area. Nimitz felt that he must support MacArthur with the forces he could use. He could not use battleships because of the difficulty of screening and supporting them. He could use carriers. He was hoping to have two carrier task forces, of two carriers each, to send down to the area.

The admirals were learning how to use task forces, and Halsey was learning faster than any other. Before December 7, 1941, there was no important body of information about carrier warfare. The carrier was a new weapon, developed between the wars, and although the British had some experience, especially at Taranto, American experience was limited to maneuvers over a period of about fourteen years, and maneuvers are not war.

In the Marcus raid of March 4, for example, Halsey for the first time used radar to locate his own air group on their way to the target and to correct their navigation. He learned that his planes needed incendiary bullets to attack land objectives effectively. He spoke again (as had Brown and Fletcher) of the need for leak-proof fuel tanks. ("It is quite possible that the only casualty of this attack, the loss of 6-S-7 which was forced down on fire, was due to this deficiency.") He reported the need for reserve pilots, particularly since the carriers might be at battle stations for twenty hours or more, with the pilots flying a four- or five-hour mission, then coming home to have to fly search-and-patrol missions.

The enemy has a tendency, when part of the attacking surface vessels have been located, to concentrate his air strength upon it and to regard as of secondary importance, for the time, the locating of other forces known or suspected to be in the area. There results a dangerous and heavy attack upon the one but the other may escape detection and attack. Two carriers provide "alternate airports" each of which could accommodate two air groups in an emergency. It should not necessarily follow that because a carrier suffers serious damage it must lose its entire air group. On the other hand, a carrier's underwater body and below deck machinery might remain unimpaired yet two or more well placed bombs or a serious hangar or flight deck fire might make recovery of the air group impossible.

In Washington, the naval high command was planning many changes for the future of carrier operations, and Admiral Towers, chief of the Bureau of Aeronautics, was fretting because these aviators, of whom so much was asked, were not being advanced rapidly enough. Towers prepared for King a memorandum listing the officers under the rank of rear admiral whom he found strongest in "ability, aggressiveness, stamina and modern ideas." They included Marc Mitscher, C. P. Mason, Ralph E. Davison, Gerald F. Bogan, Arthur Radford, J. D. Price, Donald B. Duncan, Forrest P. Sherman, and half a dozen others. Not one of these officers was on Nimitz's staff.

Nimitz, at this time, was preparing for an important meeting. Late in April he boarded the big flying boat that had been placed at his command and headed for San Francisco. There, on April 25 he and his aides would meet with Admiral King to discuss high strategy that neither wished to confide to messages or secret hand-carried letters.

King and Nimitz had agreed to meet at the offices of the commander of the Twelfth Naval District in San Francisco. Beginning April 25, they met for three days. First they discussed the matter of radio intelligence. In the past few months a bright intelligence officer on the staff of the Fourteenth Naval District, Lieutenant Commander Rochefort, had begun to unravel the Japanese naval code, and through application and some intelligent guesswork the Americans were able to tune in on some Japanese plans and operations. It was absolutely essential, the commanders agreed, that all information about Rochefort's work, and the substance and terminology of the radio intelligence be suppressed.

They began, then, to discuss personnel in the Pacific Fleet.

King expressed considerable uneasiness about Frank Jack Fletcher's operations. He was worried that Fletcher was not in control of his carrier task force at all times, that Fletcher was not aggressive enough to carry the war against the enemy. Nimitz expressed his concern on the same matters, but Nimitz had learned something a long time ago in the Philippines—that a good man may find himself in a bad situation. King agreed with Nimitz that they should wait and see how Fletcher comported himself in future operations.

Nimitz was very pleased with Wilson Brown, and King, who was less enthusiastic about Brown, agreed that the other would recommend Brown for the Distinguished Service Medal. They talked about decorations a bit, then more about personnel. Secretary Knox and King wanted to bring youth into command, so admirals who were getting ready to retire would not be employed in future operations. Brown was regarded as one of these admirals. King suggested that Nimitz begin using junior flag officers at sea. Admiral Jacobs, who had replaced Nimitz as chief of personnel, suggested that it might be time for Wilson Brown to retire in favor of a younger man. Nimitz was aware of King's astringent personality and his strong views; he had had experience with King when the latter was commander of the Atlantic Fleet and Nimitz headed the personnel division. King had one important personality trait involving personnel: if he once got down on a man for some failure or apparent failure to perform at the highest standard, that man would never be employed in high position if King could stop it. Admiral John Hoover, who had served as a carrier commander under King, said that when King announced in the evening that he proposed to be under way at 0730 in the morning, he did not mean 0731, and when he said under way, he did not mean casting off. Another officer who enjoyed an extremely distinguished wartime career in the Pacific never achieved flag rank during the war, although his record entitled him to it. The reason: before the war he had been in command of a ship that ran aground, and King simply stopped every effort to promote this officer.

Because of this, because of his own willingness to give a man every chance, because he did not want to become involved in such matters as the replacement of officers he admired, Nimitz suggested that Admiral Jacobs make the assignments of officers to command and flag positions. Obviously it would save him much embarrassment.

King and Nimitz then talked about the carriers, and their major weapons. King had qualified as an aviator and wore those wings. Nimitz's knowledge of aviation was limited to his studies at the Naval War College and his reading since. It was apparent that much was being learned in combat, and King said the combat carrier men must teach the new men, so the principle of "makey learn"—a bit of pidgin to describe the battle education of a rear admiral who was selected to command a task group—was adopted for the fleet. And as for battle, should carrier group commanders be separate from task force commanders? Nimitz and King agreed that the best man to ask was the man who had performed best to date—Admiral Halsey. Pye would not go south; instead Vice Admiral Robert L. Ghormley would become commander of the South Pacific area. Pye would remain with Nimitz for the time being.

The joint command, with Nimitz separated from MacArthur by the equator and the meridian at 160 degrees east, was not a month old, and it was to be expected that there would be some difficulties. The Army had directed MacArthur to bomb more ships, but without much effect. Still Nimitz and King spoke of the need for mutual cooperation in this strained situation. Nor was that the only strain. Nimitz felt that he needed specific authority to direct the movements of Army troops and planes within his area. Furthermore, with this new responsibility, he needed a supply service for the South Pacific.

The meetings ended with discussions of the fleet building program and the assistance Nimitz could expect from home, and he returned to Pearl Harbor.

King had agreed to the assignment of carriers in pairs to the task forces. On Nimitz's return to Pearl Harbor he told Halsey to be ready to take Task Force 16 to the Coral Sea on April 30. Task Force 17 was still there. Nimitz's next move was to send Task Force One, the battleship force, back to the west coast for the moment, under Pye. Ghormley was officially ordered to go south, aided by Rear Admiral J. S. McCain as commander of air forces in the South Pacific. McCain was a tough, wizened aviator, who wrote an indecipherable scrawl, rolled his own cigarettes and left a trail of tobacco bits wherever he went, and was ready to fight like a demon. McCain had come to aviation late in life—he took up flying in 1935 at the age of fifty-one—but he was a pilot and an air admiral, the first in the Pacific to command. Another air admiral was moving south, Rear Admiral Aubrey W. Fitch, commander of the Air Task Force. He was in the *Lexington*, while Frank Jack Fletcher, the senior admiral, was in the *Yorktown*.

The American carriers still had their problems. In the dive bombers the windshields had a tendency to fog up and so did the sight telescopes. The bomb-release solenoids in *Yorktown's* planes were most unreliable. In the Salamaua-Lae raid the *Lexington's* torpedoes did not function very well, and it was suspected there was something seriously wrong with them.

It was intended, obviously, that Halsey was to be in charge of the South Pacific carrier operations, and at Pearl when they spoke of his departure in Task Force 16 for the Coral Sea area, the members of the staff said as much. But as it worked out, Nimitz knew pretty well that Halsey could never reach the Coral Sea before the fireworks began, unless his radio intelligence was much in error. The Japanese were planning to occupy Port Moresby and Tulagi and southeastern New Guinea. Nimitz hoped to break up the occupation with a carrier raid, which, under the circumstances, almost had to be staged under Admiral Fletcher.

Fletcher had been in the South Pacific since March with his Task Force 17, operating directly under the orders of King. Nimitz had sent the transport *Bridge* down to Nouméa with provisions for Fletcher, to arrive around the first of April. The destroyers of the task force were getting low on provisions, and Fletcher sent a dispatch to King, with a copy to Leary in Australia, telling them he would return to Nouméa about April 1 for provisions.

On March 29 Army aviators reported to Leary that they had sighted Task Force 17 228 miles south of Rabaul. What they had seen, apparently, was an enemy force of some kind, which they had mistaken for Fletcher's. The confusion became complete when Fletcher told Leary where he actually was, and sent a copy of the message to King. By that time, King had blown up, and asked Fletcher if he was retiring in the vicinity of the enemy. King did not forget such actions.

Fletcher's policy was to wait in the Coral Sea until the enemy moved south and then attack. Some of his staff wanted him to move in on Rabaul and attack the shipping (as King and Nimitz certainly wanted, too). But Fletcher was certain that to do so would be to expose himself and lose the surprise element, as Wilson Brown was sure he had done earlier.

On March 30 Leary reported from Australia that the Japanese were moving south, and Fletcher said he would attack the Shortland Islands area on April 6. But as Fletcher approached he found the Japanese were gone, and he had no definite information about Japanese concentrations. So again the attack was off, as Fletcher told Leary on April 4.

At about this time, *Yorktown's* leakproof gas tanks began "going sour," Fletcher said, and on April 14, when he was reduced to twelve operational fighters, Fletcher announced that he was retiring to Tongatabu if any more trouble developed. Next day, the command situation was straightened out and Fletcher was placed under Nimitz, who ordered him to Tongatabu for supplies.

On May 1 Fletcher returned to the Coral Sea to meet Admiral Fitch and Admiral Crace of the Anzac force, who had the cruisers. Fueling again took an enormous amount of time. (Morison remarks, in Vol. IV p. 22, "As usual in forces commanded by Admiral Fletcher, fuelling was a very leisurely affair.") Fletcher now was in charge of the whole force as senior officer. His task was to break up the enemy movement by the only means at hand, a hit-and-run raid by the carriers.

Fletcher's force fueled from the oiler *Neosho*. Fitch fueled from the oiler *Tippecanoe*, but before Fitch's own force took fuel, he let the cruiser *Chicago* and the destroyer *Perkins* fill up, so they could go north and join Fletcher; thus Fitch's two carriers and four destroyers did not begin replenishing their oil until May 2. Fitch was told that the fueling could not be completed until noon of

May 4, and Fletcher moved. He had intelligence from the Mac-Arthur headquarters referring to the movement of the Japanese. At 1800 on May 2 Fletcher headed west from his station southwest of Espiritu Santo, with instructions for Fitch to meet him at a rendezvous at daylight on May 4.

At this time, the Japanese invasion force under Vice Admiral Shigeyoshi Inouye was moving very rapidly. At 0800 on the morning of May 3, Rear Admiral Kiyohide Shima landed his amphibious force on Tulagi in the Solomon Islands. Thus the Japanese intended to secure control of the Coral Sea and areas all around it. They would move to Port Moresby too, to Samoa, the Fijis, and New Caledonia.

That plan was the original Japanese war plan for the Pacific. Had King and Nimitz known that the Japanese intended to stop at the Solomons, they might have reacted less vigorously. But the Japanese were as flushed with victory as a schoolboy drinking sake. Initially they had expected it would take five or six months to conquer the Philippines, Malaya, and the Netherlands East Indies, and six months to restore the damage done by the retreating westerners. In fact all this was accomplished by May, 1942.

The Japanese military planners, then, were victimized by their own propaganda, which told them that the westerners were decadent and unable to withstand the Sons of Heaven in equal combat. Their losses until this point had been negligible—no ship larger than a destroyer had gone down—and altogether in taking the Pacific in west and south, and southeast Asia, they had lost only a hundred vessels of all types, a few hundred airplanes, and a few thousand sailors, soldiers, and marines.

As they planned this Operation Mo, the Japanese expected opposition. There would be planes from Australia, and one American carrier, the Saratoga. This task force was expected to steam into the Coral Sea, where it would be caught in a pincers movement by Rear Admiral Aritomo Goto on the one side, with the light carrier Shoho, four heavy cruisers, and a destroyer, and Vice Admiral Takeo Takagi's force of two fleet carriers, two heavy cruisers, and six destroyers.

Nimitz's intelligence had indicated that the Japanese plans

would be finished on May 3, and this intelligence turned out to be precisely correct.

Fletcher was fueling again that day, and so was Fitch. They were about one hundred miles apart. On the evening of May 3, Fletcher received a new intelligence report from MacArthur that announced the Tulagi landings. Fletcher sent *Neosho* to the rendezvous to meet Fitch the next morning, and steamed straight north toward Tulagi at twenty-four knots, ready to strike.

At Tulagi the Japanese were overconfident of success because success had come so easily to them since December 7, 1941. So having landed unopposed, the naval support forces of heavy ships left the area three hours after the landings.

Fletcher steamed all night, increasing his speed to 27 knots, and on the morning of May 4 he was 100 miles southwest of Guadalcanal, at just about the moment that Fitch encountered the *Neosho* and learned of the new developments. Fletcher's orders had been for Fitch to meet him about 300 miles southeast of Guadalcanal. Soon Admiral Crace came up with the *Australia, Hobart,* and *Whipple,* and the two admirals moved away from Fletcher, as ordered.

At 0630 on May 4, Admiral Fletcher began launching 12 torpedo planes and 28 dive bombers, and a combat air patrol of six fighters. The *Yorktown* had only 18 operational fighters, which were to be used in groups of six to protect the carrier. Thus there were no fighters to protect the bombers.

The torpedo planes were off first, and they set out independently to attack. Then came the dive bombers. The dive bombers arrived first (they were faster) and attacked. They wrecked a destroyer which had to be beached, and two small minesweepers. The torpedo bombers sank one minesweeper. Then the planes returned—all safely—and armed for a second strike.

On the second strike 27 dive bombers and 11 torpedo bombers went out. The dive bombers damaged one patrol craft and sank two seaplanes. The torpedo bombers were less effective—12 torpedoes were launched and 12 torpedoes skidded aimlessly into the sea, and sank to the bottom as their motors ran down.

Fighters were sent out, and they destroyed three Japanese seaplanes and strafed a destroyer, kiling her captain and some of the crew. Two fighters were lost in operational accidents, but both pilots were rescued. A third dive bomber attack sank four landing barges.

The Americans had enjoyed the freedom of the air all day long. The Japanese at Tulagi had radioed for help, but Admiral Takagi was fueling north of Bougainville. He rushed southeast, but could not help.

Fletcher moved to the rendezvous point he had announced to Fitch, and they met on the morning of May 5. Fletcher fueled. (With the amount of fueling done here, one is reminded of the worrisome days of the old coal-burning ships.) That evening he headed northwest, expecting the Japanese to come out of Rabaul.

On May 6 the American and Australian forces moved on together. Fletcher indicated that he intended to delegate the tactical command of the carrier force to the short, rugged Fitch, who was the most experienced carrier commander in the United States Navy. But through some failure of communications, Fitch was not informed of this delegation until much later.

By the afternoon of May 6, Fletcher knew of the movement of the Port Moresby invasion group, and at 1930 that night he moved northwest so he could be within striking distance on the morning of May 7. Unfortunately the American information was very scanty. There were not enough land-based search planes to cover the area properly, and so Fletcher knew nothing of the whereabouts of Admiral Takagi's fleet carriers.

Takagi spent about as much time fueling as did Fletcher. On May 5 and 6 he did not even bother to send out search planes—if he had done so he would have caught Fletcher fueling. (At one time Fletcher and Takagi were only seventy miles apart.) The Japanese were having their communications problems too. At 1100 on May 6 a Japanese search plane from Rabaul found Fletcher and reported, but Takagi did not get the word for hours, and when he did, Fletcher was moving in a different direction.

On the afternoon of May 6, Admiral Inouye estimated that Fletcher was moving up, probably about 500 miles from the Japanese at that moment. He ordered the operations to continue on plan, with the Port Moresby invasion force to move in, and Takagi and Goto to close the pincers on the Americans.

On the morning of May 7, Admiral Takagi's search planes from *Shokaku* and *Zuikaku,* the two big fleet carriers, were out on search. Just after 0730 one pilot reported excitedly that he had found the American carrier force and he gave the position, 16 degrees south, 158 degrees east. The Japanese launched a torpedo and bombing attack.

The ships sighted were the unlucky oiler *Neosho* and her destroyer escort *Sims,* which had peeled off to find a "safe" rendezvous well away from the area where battle was to be joined. Scores of torpedo planes, horizontal bombers, and dive bombers hit the two ships. *Sims* was smashed by three 500-pound bombs, two of which exploded in the engine room. She began to sink, and then exploded—only fifteen of her crew were saved. *Neosho* was soon smashed too, but she remained afloat. The navigator made an error in taking a position sight, and it was four days before she was discovered and her survivors rescued; after that she was sunk.

That day Fletcher detached Admiral Crace to attack the Port Moresby invasion force, while Fletcher sought battle with the carriers. Crace then drew the attention of the land-based Japanese bombers.

Because of an error in communications, next morning *Yorktown* and *Lexington* launched a strike of ninety-three planes against a very small force at right angles to the Takagi force, but on flying to the target the attack group of *Lexington* found the Goto force with the carrier *Shoho* and attacked. Within half an hour all ninety-three planes had attacked her, and she was sunk. All but three of the American planes returned to their carriers before noon, and Admiral Goto's half of the pincers retired to the northeast.

In the afternoon the air commanders of *Yorktown* and *Lexington* were raring to go on another strike, but Fletcher held them back. He had *Zuikaku* and *Shokaku* to contend with. The weather was bad, and he decided to rely on shore-based search craft. He steamed west, planning to hit the Port Moresby invasion force the next day. But the Japanese had been frightened off, temporarily, by the Crace move. Admiral Inouye had told the invasion force to stand off and wait until the American carrier force was destroyed.

That evening American and Japanese carrier planes crossed and fought, nine Japanese going down, and two Americans. Several Japanese planes mistook the American carriers for their own, and eventually the Japanese had to turn on their lights to bring back their own planes.

That night each force had a pretty good idea of the location of the other, and both Fletcher and Inouye contemplated night attacks. Fletcher decided against it in the interest of concentrating his force for attack against the carriers next morning. Inouye's position was that he had to protect his invasion force; that was his prime responsibility.

In the morning the forces found one another. At 0830 Fletcher was ready to launch—and only at this time did he tell Fitch that the junior admiral was now in command of the tactical force. Fitch and his force were out in the bright sunlight.

The *Yorktown* planes found *Shokaku* and attacked her first. The torpedoes failed, but two bomb hits were scored on the carrier, one of which made it impossible for her to launch again until repaired. So except for the strike just launched, as an offensive weapon, *Shokaku* was out of the fight. *Zuikaku* was attacked, but escaped unhurt.

The Japanese planes crossed paths with the Americans, and the Japanese air strike was conducted in a far more effective fashion than the American. *Lexington* took two torpedoes and two bombs. *Yorktown* took one 800-pound bomb in the flight deck, but it penetrated four decks and killed or wounded 66 men.

The carrier battle was over before noon on May 8. The Japanese believed they had sunk both American carriers. But with the loss of *Shoho* and the departure of *Shokaku*, Admiral Inouye canceled his invasion. He was afraid of the Army air force bombers that ranged along the shores of Papua. Admiral Yamamoto did not like this decision, and ordered Takagi to take *Zuikaku* and wipe out the American forces, but it was too late, contact was lost.

At the end of the battle of the Coral Sea, *Lexington* was in very bad shape. She was listing and partly flooded, but an hour later she could recover and launch planes. Then an explosion smashed her insides. A generator somewhere below had been left running, and gasoline fumes from leaky tanks had collected, then blasted the ship with more fury than any torpedo. One explosion followed another, until finally Admiral Fitch ordered the ship abandoned, and the orderly retreat began. She was still exploding as the last men went over the side, and then she was sunk by torpedoes.

That afternoon Nimitz ordered Fletcher to leave the Coral Sea, and the battle was over. The Japanese invasion of Port Moresby was turned back.

At Pearl Harbor, Nimitz was very much concerned about the loss of *Neosho* and the *Sims,* for he could not afford to lose either ship. The early reports from the Coral Sea indicated a "red-letter day," however, with one Japanese carrier sunk and another badly damaged. Then came the bad news about the *Lexington.* Still, there was much to rejoice about at Pearl Harbor. For the first time, a Japanese movement had been stopped. The Americans had lost more ships, and more important ships, and could afford to lose them less than the Japanese. But Port Moresby was saved. As far as the *Lexington* was concerned, if it had not been for the carelessness of one man who left an electric motor running, there might not have been any gasoline explosion. With the state of affairs on *Lexington,* her gas tanks leaky from hits and near misses, a match or even a spark from a nail or a dropped tool could have accomplished the same thing. As the Nimitz endorsement on the Task Force 17 action report put it, "Means must be provided for reducing the menace to carriers of the large quantities of gasoline carried."

Nimitz had many comments for the consideration of King and his battle commanders.

In the Tulagi attacks of May 4, 22 torpedoes and 76 1000-pound bombs were released, resulting in five torpedo hits and 11 bomb hits.

Considering that there was practically no air opposition and very little anti-aircraft fire, the ammunition expenditure required to disable the number of enemy ships involved is disappointing. This is particularly true in the instance where 11 torpedoes were fired against a maneuvering aircraft tender without any hits, although fogging of sights and windshields affected accuracy of the first attack, this condition did not apply in subsequent ones begun from lower altitudes.

As for the action on May 8, Nimitz seriously doubted the pilots' claim that both carriers were hit:

The reports of the attacks by the two air groups do not clearly prove that both carriers were attacked and damaged. It is possible that only one enemy carrier was hit on May 8 and that the air groups of the *Lexington* and *Yorktown* attacked the same carriers. The second carrier may have taken advantage of cloud concealment and thereby escaped. If the number of hits is approximately as claimed (8 torpedoes and 8 heavy case 1000 pound bombs fused with Mark 21 and Mark 23 one-hundredth second fuse), both bomb and warhead must be improved. [Sarcasm?]

From the experience, Fletcher had learned that he needed more fighter planes for protection. Nimitz agreed and suggested that fighters be increased to twenty-seven. Also that the torpedo planes be replaced (slow TBD's by faster TBF's).

The action showed bad gunnery. This would have to be corrected. The fogging of sights and windshields had to be corrected. Torpedo and bombing attacks must be closely coordinated. (Thus the success at Coral Sea.) Carriers must have two long-range radar sets. Operations of land-based aircraft and fleet units must be better coordinated. Bombs and torpedoes must be improved. The 1000-pound bomb was not suitable. The torpedo warheads were not large enough. Replacement units for plane crews must be made available. Screening ships against torpedo attacks should be placed in 1500- to 2500-yard circles around the carriers.

The battle was over, and much was learned from it. The problem, however, was that as far as the mechanical aspects were concerned, even when the defects were known, Nimitz could do little about them in time to improve his forces for the next big struggle. For even as the battle report of Coral Sea was being written at Pearl Harbor, the Battle of Midway was upon him.

Chapter
Five

MIDWAY

May 5–June 30, 1942

One day early in May Lieutenant Commander Edwin T. Layton, Pacific Fleet intelligence officer, came into Admiral Nimitz's office to present the admiral with a detailed analysis he had worked up with Lieutenant Commander Rochefort, showing the probable intentions of the Japanese, based on intercepted Japanese naval radio dispatches. Thanks to Rochefort's partial breakdown of the Japanese naval code, the intelligence men were able to read enough of the material to gain important clues.

Nimitz took up Layton's report with his senior staff. What Draemel and Pye had feared from the beginning seemed to be materializing: a Japanese move into the Western and Northern Pacific.

The analysis was imperfect, and there was room for doubt. The Japanese had used a code name for the place they planned to invest, and Nimitz was not absolutely certain this was Midway. He made a test. In the clear he sent a message which indicated that Midway was short of water. A few hours later the Japanese indicated that the place they would attack was short of water.

By May 16 Nimitz was certain that unless the Japanese were using massive radio deception for some reason he could not understand, they were planning a major offensive in the Central or North Pacific. Specifically he feared the attack against Midway, and a raid on Oahu, around the first week in June.

What was to be done? The striking force must be used. That force now was down to three carriers, one of them injured. Perhaps the carriers could be assisted by a battleship covering force—but the prewar battleships were very slow, and although Admiral Pye was a brave and intelligent officer, these battleships would need very strong protection from light ships if it was worthwhile at all to move them out from the west coast.

The problem was to get Halsey into Pearl, and out again, with his two sound carriers, and to bring the *Yorktown* back and get her repaired in time.

King, perhaps sensing that if the forces at Pearl Harbor were lost he would have nothing else for west coast protection, decided against the use of the battleships in the coming struggle. Layton was queried and queried again, and he said he would stake his reputation on the accuracy of his reports. So Nimitz decided to lay it out in one piece—to make the supreme effort, hazarding the American forces, as Pye had been unwilling to do in the Wake confrontation.

On May 18 Nimitz held a final planning conference. He decided then to reinforce Midway with a part of a raider battalion, station four submarines off the islands, use Midway to stage Army bombers, use a dozen PBY's for searching, and employ Task Force 16 plus the *Yorktown*, if it could be repaired in time. He would also send out a North Pacific force, under Admiral Theobald, to move to an Alaskan rendezvous.

Admiral Yamamoto, the commander in chief of the Japanese combined fleet, proposed to take Midway, occupy the Aleutians, and raid Oahu. But through the efforts of Rochefort and his associates, the Americans had a very good idea of what the Japanese planned to do—and when and where.

The seven old battleships were to sail east to the Pacific coast. Task Force 16, arriving at Pearl Harbor about May 26, would be turned around in two days and sent to Midway by June 1. Task Force 17 would arrive at Pearl Harbor on May 28, and if the *Yorktown* could be repaired there in four days, it would be done. That was the key to the whole defense, for *Saratoga*, at San Diego, could not be ready for sea until June 5, and *Wasp*, headed for the Pacific, could not arrive in time.

In mid-May, estimating the enemy courses of action, Nimitz and his staff erred slightly in assessing Admiral Yamamoto's strategy. He wrote:

> The enemy knows our building program—and that in time —our forces will be sufficiently strong to take the offensive. He further knows our defenses are inadequate now—but gradually being strengthened. Hence, from the time factor alone, such operation should be conducted at the earliest possible time. While he is "extended," he is able to assemble a considerable force—as most of the occupied territory is unable to make any real effort. He knows that Australia is being heavily reinforced from the United States and would undoubtedly desire to cut that supply line. But he may also consider MIDWAY to be just another WAKE and ALASKA undefended. Regardless of our ideas of his strategic possibilities, the purpose here is to discuss immediate possibilities.

Japanese Admiral Isoroku Yamamoto had become so worried about the increasing activity of the American fleet in the south that he proposed an action that should destroy that fleet. His worries were based on what Halsey, Fletcher, Brown, and Fitch had accomplished in their raids, and on Yamamoto's knowledge of the United States industrial potential. He had opposed war against the United States, in the first place, because he knew that potential, and was only too well aware of Japan's slender resources in steel and oil. While the rest of the Empire, and much of the naval high command, basked in the happy glory of success, Yamamoto warned that unless he could knock out the American fleet there was going to be trouble. Within two years, he said, the balance of naval power would shift to the United States unless the American fleet could be put out of action in 1942.

Yamamoto proposed, then, to occupy Midway Island, and also the Aleutians, and thus pose the double-barreled threat to the United States of enemy forces in their very back yard. He suggested that such occupation, along with the destruction of the American fleet, would make the government of the United States negotiate a peace that would leave Japan free to expand in China and the waters of the Pacific Ocean.

One of the deciding factors in persuading the naval general staff to Yamamoto's view was the Doolittle Tokyo Raid in April. The General Staff agreed to a four point plan for 1942: June—capture Midway, Adak, and Kiska; July—invade New Caledonia and Fiji; July—stage carrier strikes on Australia; August—send the combined fleet to strike Johnston and the Hawaiian Islands.

Perhaps it was just as well that the real intentions of Yamamoto and his men were unknown, and that the Japanese striking power was underestimated. The Japanese were bringing to Midway four carriers, two battleships, three cruisers, fourteen destroyers, and five oilers in the striking force. To cover the actual occupation of Midway they would have two battleships, nine cruisers, one light carrier, eleven destroyers, and various other ships. To screen the transports would come another eleven destroyers, plus seaplane carriers, minesweepers, and a dozen transports in the train. Then there was the main body, with three more battleships, a light carrier and two seaplane carriers, a cruiser, and thirteen more destroyers, which could either accompany the Aleutian invasion force or the Midway force, or attack the American fleet.

As for intentions, certainly Admiral Yamamoto wanted to occupy Midway. Having done so, and having created a Japanese air base there, he proposed to challenge the remnants of the American fleet and destroy them, thus making the Pacific Ocean into a Japanese lake.

Radio intelligence indicated that the Japanese left Saipan on

May 26 for Midway. Having set the wheels in motion, Nimitz's task was to sit, wait, and take advantage of opportunity.

Nimitz received a serious blow that day. Admiral Halsey brought Task Force 16 into port. One look at Halsey, and Nimitz knew that his favorite fighting commander could not be available for Midway. The strain of the past few months, plus personal family problems of the most serious nature, had affected Halsey's nerves, and he was suffering from skin eruptions that made sleep impossible and kept him in constant pain. It was off to the hospital for Halsey, and then came the problem of choosing a substitute for him.

At this time, several basic changes were in the offing. Vice Admiral Wilson Brown had fallen ill while on the Pacific coast, and had said something about feeling that he needed a rest. He was now recovered. His statement, however, gave Admirals Jacobs and King the chance they wanted, to remove him for a younger man, and they assigned him to the First Naval District; in essence, as far as the war was concerned, this amounted to deportation to Siberia. Admiral Draemel was severely shaken by events of the past few months and his constant vigil in the nights; also, he was not thinking along Nimitz's lines and was not effective as chief of staff. Draemel, then, was to replace Brown as commander of the Amphibious Force of the Pacific Fleet, still just a potential unit, for the most part. Both men took the change in good part, as admirals almost always did. Brown was disappointed and said as much to Nimitz, who wrote him a very friendly letter assuring the older admiral that he, Nimitz, had nothing to do with the change. It was true, strictly speaking, because Nimitz had abjured the responsibility, and thrown it back on Washington.

For a new chief of staff, Nimitz chose Rear Admiral Raymond Spruance, who had proved himself in his forays with Halsey as an aggressive, fighting admiral, and more, in the sessions on the folding chairs in Nimitz's office, as a shrewd and trained strategist.

Spruance was a small, trim man whose passion for exercise exceeded even that of Nimitz; it was said that Spruance like nothing better than a ten-mile walk to spruce himself up for the day. He was a Baltimore boy, a few years younger than Nimitz, and had graduated from the Naval Academy in the class of 1901. His record at the

Academy had been good: he stood twenty-sixth in a class of 209 graduates. He was two years behind Nimitz, a year behind Ghormley, Fletcher, Towers, Draemel, and Fitch. Spruance was distinguished at the Academy for his studies in electrical engineering, but later he spent six years at the Naval War College, five of them as a member of the staff, which meant that he was more than an apt student of naval tactics and strategy. He was not an airman, but he had a strong respect for the principal weapon at the fleet's disposal in this coming fight. "The carrier," Spruance said, "is a highly mobile, extremely vulnerable airfield from which you can operate short range aircraft and do much more accurate bombing than long range bombers from land airbases can do."

After considering the possible commanders who could move quickly into action, and recalling Halsey's words of high praise for Spruance, Nimitz chose Spruance to lead the Halsey task force into battle. Nimitz was not totally pleased with the actions of his commanders in Task Force 17, at least not at that moment. On May 27 Task Force 17 entered port, and Admiral Fletcher came to headquarters to report himself to Nimitz. There were some searching questions about Fletcher's activities in the past three months in the South Pacific. King might be one to judge in anger, but never Nimitz, and gently he asked Fletcher to explain why his force had been so ineffectual. Fletcher retired to his flagship, then, and wrote a long explanatory letter about his activities.

Nimitz read, and on May 29 he made his decisions and wrote King a letter which indicated the state of affairs at Pearl Harbor on the eve of the Midway battle.

Dear King,

I have finally had an opportunity to discuss with Fletcher during a three day stay in port, his operations in the Coral Sea area, and to clear up what appeared to be a lack of aggressive tactics of his force. I also discussed with him the opportunities for using light forces in night attacks following the aerial attacks from his carriers in early May.

Both these matters have been cleared up to my entire satisfaction, and, I hope, will be to yours . . . .

The long delay and apparent lack of aggressive tactics can be charged partly to lack of sufficiently reliable combat intelligence upon which to base operations, to the necessity for replenishment of fuel and provisions, and to the replacement of defective leak proof tanks in fighter planes.

I hope and believe that . . . you will agree with me that Fletcher did a fine job and exercised superior judgment in his recent cruise in the Coral Sea. He is an excellent sea-going, fighting naval officer, and I wish to retain him as a task force commander in the future.

Nimitz noted that Halsey was sick, but thought it was only a temporary indisposition.

He is in the best of spirits, full of vim and vigor, and anxious to get going again. But he does need a short period of rest. He is neither ill nor on the sick list.

Fletcher with Task Force 17 will leave on the forenoon of May 30 to join Spruance and to take charge of the two task forces which contains three carriers. I have not yet separated Task Force 16 into two task forces, each with a carrier, but expect to do so after these operations are over. At this time it is essential that our organization be stabilized as much as possible.

The *Yorktown* was docked yesterday for inspection and repair of a minor leak. When she leaves tomorrow, 30 May, she will have a full complement of planes and will be in all respects ready to give a good account of herself.

We are very actively preparing to greet our expected visitors with the kind of reception they deserve, and we will do the best we can with what we have. We are thankful for the many contributions now coming in from the army.

To offset the bad news about Halsey, there was good news about *Yorktown*. Although Nimitz had underestimated the damage so as not to worry King, the carrier really was not too badly hurt, and could be put in service by May 29, if drydocked to patch oil leaks and reinforced internally. Some 1400 men poured into her and worked for two days and nights, doing a reconstruction job that Admiral Fitch had estimated would take three months. (Fitch, by the way, backed Fletcher's actions in the South Pacific all the way. Later, Admiral J. J. Clark was to write that *Lexington* could have been saved if only Fletcher had sent off planes he had on deck, which could have intercepted the Japanese attack on the other carrier. Clark, who had once been executive officer of the *Yorktown*, was critical of Fletcher and Captain Elliott Buckmaster. Fitch's comment: "He was not there.")

On May 28 Admiral Spruance left Pearl Harbor with Task Force 16, which consisted of the carriers *Enterprise* and *Hornet*, with six cruisers and nine destroyers. Two days later Admiral Fletcher came out in the reconstituted *Yorktown* with two cruisers and six destroyers. Nimitz had shown his faith in Fletcher by putting him in charge of the operation.

"You will be governed by the principle of calculated risk," Nimitz wrote in his orders to the two commanders, "which you will interpret to mean the avoidance of exposure of your force to attack by superior enemy forces without good prospect of inflicting . . . greater damage on the enemy."

Nimitz had suggested that they move to a point northeast of Midway, where they could flank the Japanese as they came in from the northwest. Spruance and Fletcher agreed. Spruance arrived in the area, about two hundred miles northeast of Midway, on the morning of June 1; Fletcher arrived the next afternoon. Both forces had fueled before meeting, and were probably as ready as they would ever be for action.

They were very careful. Spruance learned that the radio operators on *Enterprise* had picked up a high-frequency TBS (talk between ships) message from Pearl Harbor to the inshore patrol just off the islands. It was a freak—TBS was not supposed to extend more than a few miles—but it spooked Spruance so that he ordered his task force to keep off the TBS unless absolutely necessary. And he gave the pilots grave warning: he would not use the radio to bring back any carrier planes which might get lost while on a mission. Even his message to task force was transmitted by signalmen, not by radio or TBS.

As the Americans converged and began to search and wait, the Japanese moved steadily down on them. Vice Admiral Chuichi Nagumo was moving from the northwest, with a force built around the four carriers *Soryu*, *Hiryu*, *Kaga*, and *Akagi*. Three hundred miles behind was Admiral Yamamoto's main force. The second carrier striking force, and the Attu and Kiska invasion forces, all under Vice Admiral Boshiro Hosogaya, had split off and were coming near the Aleutians from the southwest. Vice Admiral Shiru Takasu led a screening force that would split off and follow the invasion force about five hundred miles behind. And finally, up from Saipan in the southwest came the transports and the minesweepers, and the heavy cruiser from Guam, and from Japan itself the main body of the landing force that would invade Midway and make it part of the Japanese Empire.

The Japanese submarines were to set up two picket lines, about halfway between Hawaii and Midway, for it was the Japanese idea that the American fleet was sitting in Pearl Harbor and would have to be drawn out. The Midway invasion was expected to draw out the Americans, so the striking force that included Admiral Nagumo's four carriers could be alerted by the submarine pickets, make a few calculations, and then polish off the American carriers once and for all as they steamed up into the trap.

The Americans were lucky. The Japanese submarines arrived late on station, and the American task forces were already past them, on their way to Midway. The Japanese had provided for seaplane reconnaissance of Pearl Harbor on May 30. The flying boats were to meet Japanese submarines off French Frigate Shoals, refuel, and carry out their mission. But when the submarines arrived there, they found two American seaplane tenders at anchor, and two American flying boats also there. So the Japanese canceled their plans for a look, which would have warned them that only one American carrier was in harbor. They might even have seen Fletcher's force move out, heading toward the Midway atoll.

At 0904 on June 3 a Midway search plane came upon part of the Japanese minesweeping group, coming up from the southwest, and reported two cargo ships sighted five hundred miles out. Twenty minutes later another patrol plane reported six ships, again coming

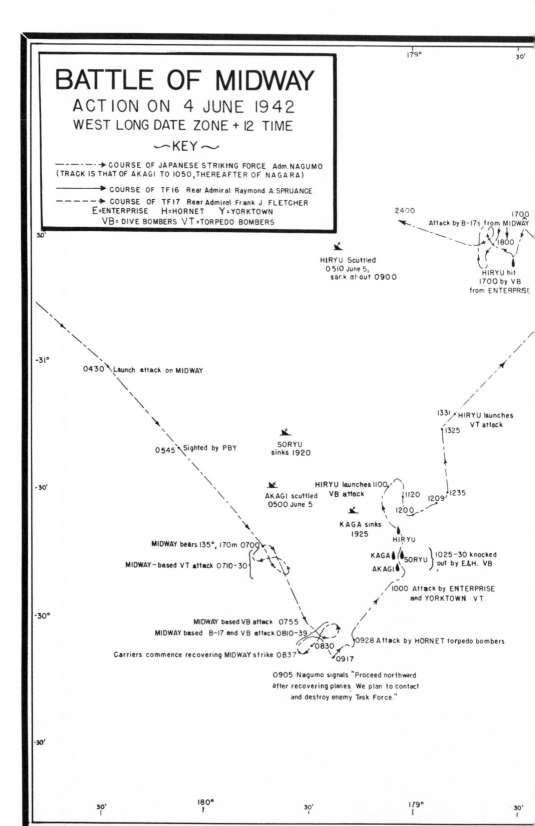

BATTLE OF MIDWAY
ACTION ON 4 JUNE 1942
WEST LONG DATE ZONE + 12 TIME

~KEY~

------→ COURSE OF JAPANESE STRIKING FORCE Adm. NAGUMO
(TRACK IS THAT OF AKAGI TO 1050, THEREAFTER OF NAGARA)

———→ COURSE OF TF 16 Rear Admiral Raymond A. SPRUANCE

-----→ COURSE OF TF 17 Rear Admiral Frank J. FLETCHER
E= ENTERPRISE   H=HORNET   Y=YORKTOWN
VB= DIVE BOMBERS VT=TORPEDO BOMBERS

179°   30'

HIRYU Scuttled
0510 June 5,
sank about 0900

2400   1700
Attack by B-17s from MIDWAY
1800
HIRYU hit
1700 by VB
from ENTERPRISE

30'

-31° 0430 Launch attack on MIDWAY

1331 HIRYU launches
VT attack
1325

0545 Sighted by PBY   SORYU
sinks 1920

-30'   AKAGI scuttled   HIRYU launches 1100
0500 June 5   VB attack
1120 1209 1235
1200

KAGA sinks
1925   HIRYU

MIDWAY bears 135°, 170m. 0700   KAGA   SORYU   } 1025-30 knocked
out by E&H. VB
MIDWAY-based VT attack 0710-30   AKAGI

1000 Attack by ENTERPRISE
and YORKTOWN VT

-30°   MIDWAY based VB attack 0755
MIDWAY based B-17 and VB attack 0810-39
0928 Attack by HORNET torpedo bombers
0830
Carriers commence recovering MIDWAY strike 0837   0917

0905 Nagumo signals "Proceed northward
after recovering planes. We plan to contact
and destroy enemy Task Force."

-30'

30'   180°   30'   179°   30'

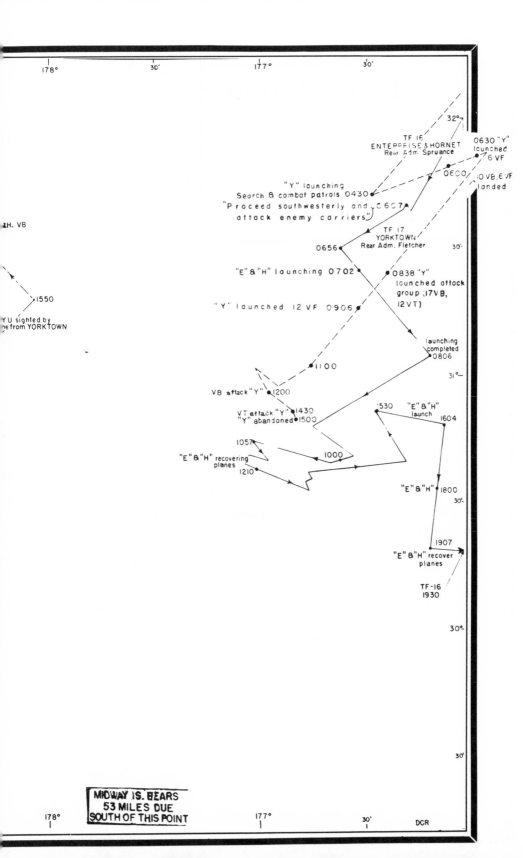

178° 30' 177° 30'

32°

TF 16
ENTERPRISE & HORNET
Rear Adm. Spruance

0630 "Y"
launched
6 VF

0600

10 VB, 6 VF
landed

"Y" launching
Search & combat patrols 0430
"Proceed southwesterly and
attack enemy carriers"

0607

TF 17
YORKTOWN
Rear Adm. Fletcher

30'

2H. VB

0656

"E" & "H" launching 0702

0838 "Y"
launched attack
group (17VB,
12VT)

1550

"Y" launched 12 VF 0906

Y U sighted by
ne from YORKTOWN

launching
completed
0806

1100

31°

VB attack "Y" 1200

VT attack "Y" 1430
"Y" abandoned 1500

1057

1530   "E" & "H"
launch

1604

1000

"E" & "H" recovering
planes
1210

"E" & "H" 1800

30'

1907
"E" & "H" recover
planes

TF-16
1930

30°

30'

MIDWAY IS. BEARS
53 MILES DUE
SOUTH OF THIS POINT

178° 177° 30' DGR

up from the southwest, seven hundred miles out. Later another contact was made with eleven ships.

That afternoon nine B-17's from Midway flew out to intercept the "eleven-ship" force. They dropped bombs but did not hit anything because they came in at extremely high altitude.

At dawn on Thursday, June 4, Admiral Nagumo's four carriers launched 36 horizontal bombers, 36 dive bombers, and 36 fighters against Midway, and brought the second wave of the same type of planes up on deck to ready for another strike. This time, however, the multipurpose horizontal bombers were armed with torpedoes, in case ship targets should appear.

As the Japanese carrier planes flew toward Midway, sixteen B-17's took off to attack the transports which were bringing the invaders from the west. At 0545 in the morning an American patrol bomber caught sight of two enemy carriers. All the planes at Midway that could fly took off, and the torpedo bombers, Army B-26's and Marine dive bombers headed for the carriers. The twenty-seven fighters were kept over Midway for protection.

The assorted bombers went in against heavy antiaircraft fire and zooming Japanese fighters. The B-26's hit nothing, and two of the four were shot down. The TBF's hit nothing, and five of the six were splashed. The Marine dive bomber pilots were inexperienced; instead of dive-bombing they came in to glide-bomb. Twelve were shot down, and they hit nothing. The B-17's, diverted to the carriers, came in at twenty thousand feet and hit nothing. The Japanese antiaircraft guns and the Zero pilots could not reach them, so they lost no planes.

The Japanese carrier planes, meanwhile, slashed across Midway and began bombing and strafing, taking care to save the runways they thought they would be using in a few days.

In the Japanese carrier force, Admiral Nagumo surveyed the situation before him. The Americans still had air power at Midway, which ought to be knocked out. He had no reports of surface shipping anywhere around. So the admiral ordered the bombers of *Akagi* and *Kaga* back down to the hangar decks where the torpedoes would be removed and changed for bombs.

The Japanese were to sight the Americans just before 0730 that morning, but even then the identification was confused and it was an hour later before Admiral Nagumo learned that there were big ships in the area, and concluded, without immediate confirmation that there must be a carrier in the bunch.

The Americans, moving cautiously with their far smaller force, were in action already. Early in the morning, Admiral Fletcher had launched a dawn security search to the north, looking for the Japanese they knew to be in the area, because of the sighting before 0600 of the carrier planes, and the sighting of two of the carriers a few minutes later.

"Two carriers and battleships bearing 320, distance 180, course 135, speed 24," came the message from the flying boat.

When Admiral Spruance was informed, he turned on a course to intercept and raised the speed of Task Force 16 to twenty-five knots. Fletcher instructed Spruance to attack the enemy carriers when they were definitely located.

Miles Browning, the slender, caustic chief of staff of Task Force 16, whose services Spruance had secured from the ailing Halsey, suggested that the timing of the first attack on the Japanese be made as soon as possible. That way, said Browning, there was a good chance of catching the Japanese with their decks foul with newly landed planes that were unready for action.

Spruance's plan had been to launch at 0900, when he estimated that they would be around 100 miles from the enemy. Since the American torpedo bombers had a range of only 175 miles, that distance seemed safe for recovery of the TBD's. But Spruance was quick to see Browning's point, and he undertook the calculated risk. He launched without actual location of the enemy, hoping he knew their position, which he estimated to be about 155 miles away, bearing 239.

Captain Murray in the *Enterprise* and Captain Marc Mitscher in the *Hornet* were ordered to turn south, into the wind, and begin launching, just after 0700.

First the combat air patrol went off and began circling the formation. Next went the dive bombers, some armed with 500-pound and some with 1000-pound bombs. The torpedo planes took off, followed by fighters which were to escort the slow torpedo bombers to the target and protect them.

At this point the inexperience of the Americans influenced the course of events. About twenty minutes before the last planes were launched, the presence of the American ships was apparently discovered by a Japanese search plane. That would account for the turn of the Japanese carriers off the course on which they had been spotted earlier.

Spruance then ordered the dive bombers from *Enterprise* to go ahead of the torpedo planes and fighters, and hit the carriers. This decision put an end to the coordinated attack that had been planned, but Spruance was more interested in surprise.

Task Force 17 was operating independently, and launching its planes as well. But as the planes began to search the expected area, they did not find the Japanese, who had changed course.

First to find the enemy were the planes of Torpedo Squadron 8, which had flown off *Hornet*. In the morning confusion, the *Enterprise* fighters accompanied the *Hornet* torpedo bombers instead of their own, and then lost touch even with these bombers. So Torpedo 8 suddenly found itself in sight of the enemy, with no protection.

Lieutenant Commander John C. Waldron, the leader of Torpedo 8, finally saw the Japanese as he was running low on fuel. He reported the contact, and asked permission to withdraw and refuel before attacking. But Spruance and Browning, aboard the flagship, knew the importance of surprise in a carrier battle. The reply was negative. "Attack at once," was the order.*

Without fighter protection, low on fuel, knowing how the deck was stacked against him, Waldron headed in. The weather was good. The visibility was excellent. The whole approach was made at low altitude, in complete view of the Japanese—and their deadly Zero fighter planes.

The squadron was in two divisions. First came four two-plane sections, then two more two-plane sections and one three-plane section. Lieutenant Commander Waldron headed for the southernmost of the carriers, until he saw the mushrooms of the antiaircraft fire, then he turned to the central carrier. When they were about sixteen thousand yards out, the Zeros came down onto the deck and the slaughter began.

---

* This report is contrary to the legend of Waldron's heroic sacrifice. It is, however, documental. See notes.

Ensign G. H. Gay, a Naval Reserve officer, was flying one of those TBD's, in the last section of the second division. As Gay moved toward the target he heard an anguished voice from his gunner. He had been hit. Gay went on in, dropped his torpedo at eight hundred yards, and it missed, like all the other torpedoes of Torpedo 8. He pulled up over the bow of the carrier and turned sharply into her wake, but then a Zero dived down and an explosive shell carried away his left rudder control. A bullet struck him in the left arm, and a fragment hit him in the left hand, He took the plane down, made a crash landing, but the right wing carried away and the plane began to sink. He had no time to rescue his radioman before the plane went down, leaving the ensign treading water.

The rubber boat in its bag had floated clear, and so had a black cushion from the bomber compartment. Gay inflated his life jacket, grabbed the boat bag and held it, and covered his head with the black cushion, so the Japanese would not see him. Several Zeros zoomed low, but he was not observed.

Ensign Gay then had a ringside seat at the arena where the *Kaga*, the *Akagi*, and the *Soryu* were performing.

At first it was quiet except for the landing of Zeros on the carriers. He noted, with the interest of a professional, how the other fellows did it, coming in on long approaches, from straight astern, with long intervals between planes. And then the action began.

Hornet's dive bombers had found nothing, and went empty-handed to their carrier when they ran low on gas. *Enterprise's* torpedo planes found the Japanese at about 0930, but their attack was more successful than that of Torpedo 8 only in that four of the fourteen TBD's managed to get back to their carrier. There were no hits.

But the very ineptness of the American attack worked in its favor this day, for the Japanese grew careless, and their fighter cover was pulled down low above the sea by the chase for the lumbering torpedo bombers.

As the TBD's flamed into the sea, *Enterprise's* dive bombers were searching for the enemy. They did not find the Japanese where they expected them, but an accommodating Japanese destroyer led them to the carrier force, and they sighted the enemy at 1005.

The torpedo bombers had accomplished two other useful feats

in their sacrifice: they had caused the carriers to maneuver constantly during this critical period, and their brave gestures against the impossible odds they faced had given the Japanese a certain contempt for the American weapons, if a definite respect for American willingness to die. The Japanese had watched the B-17's come in like little specks in the stratosphere and drop their hopeless bombs. They had watched the clumsy tactics of the ill-trained Marine bombers, and the misses of the B-26's, too. Suddenly, however, down screamed the dive bombers of the *Enterprise*. Ensign Gay, who was watching from his wet ringside seat, said that most of them did not even seem to be using their dive flaps, for they came in at very high speed, dropped their bombs, pulled out just above the water, and sped away.

Kaga and *Akagi* were just getting ready to launch their planes for a strike, when the bombers began scoring hits. In a moment Gay saw flames arising from the flight decks, and billowing black clouds of smoke dirtied the blue sky.

Soon *Akagi* was a wreck, and Admiral Nagumo transferred his flag to the cruiser *Nagara*. Then the *Yorktown* dive bombers found the carriers, and attacked *Soryu*. The torpedo planes suffered the fate of the squadrons of the *Hornet* and the *Enterprise*; only two of a dozen returned to the *Yorktown*; but the dive bombers started several fires on *Soryu*, and not one dive bomber from *Yorktown* was even damaged, so thorough was the confusion of the Japanese.

Spruance was elated with the performance of *Enterprise* and *Yorktown*, but much less pleased with that of the men of *Hornet*. He wanted that fourth carrier, and had *Hornet*'s planes done their job, *Hiryu* might have been found that morning. Instead, *Hiryu*'s planes found *Yorktown* at 1205, and the dive bombers put three holes in her, stopping her, starting fires, and damaging the flight deck. In two hours the damage was partly repaired. *Yorktown* could operate her planes, and make nineteen knots. But a few minutes after she launched her second strike, *Hiryu*'s torpedo bombers came in and put two torpedoes into the carrier, jamming the left rudder and giving her a list that soon stood at 23 degrees. Admiral Fletcher moved his flag to the cruiser *Astoria*. Soon Captain Buckmaster ordered the *Yorktown* abandoned (for which he was later criticized severely by some of Young Turks, especially the fighting admiral J. J. Clark).

But in turn, the planes of *Enterprise* had found the *Hiryu* by 1700 that afternoon, and sped in to attack. Four dive bombers scored hits on this fourth carrier, and soon she was dead in the water. "*Hornet* and *Enterprise* groups now attacking fourth carrier located by your search planes," was the message Admiral Spruance sent to Fletcher, who was in overall command still. "*Hornet* about twenty miles east of me. Have you any instructions for future operations?"

Fletcher replied: "Negative. Will conform to your movements." Thus a gallant Admiral Fletcher, knowing the battle was virtually won, turned tactical command, and the chance for glory, into the hands of his subordinate, because Spruance's primary weapons—the carriers—were intact and ready to fight while Fletcher's own major weapon was out of action. He detached the two cruisers from the task force and sent them to Spruance. He would keep the destroyers, and attempt to salvage the *Yorktown*.

After the first attack on *Yorktown* her planes began landing on the *Hornet* and the *Enterprise*, and served, in fact, as replacements for the many that had been lost in the day's action. Some of these were lost to enemy action, many to force landings when their fuel ran out. After recovering all the aircraft from the attack on *Hiryu*, Spruance headed east, away from the enemy. He knew that out to the west was the enemy, a powerful force, more powerful than his own, perhaps. Here is the way Spruance spoke of his decision immediately after the battle:

> After recovering our air groups following their second attack, Task Force 16 stood to the eastward, southward and back to the westward during the night. I did not feel justified in risking a night encounter with possibly superior enemy forces, but on the other hand, I did not want to be too far away from Midway the next morning. I wished to have a position from which either to follow up retreating enemy forces or break up a landing attack on Midway. At this time the possibility of the enemy having a fifth CV [fleet carrier] somewhere in the area, possibly with his Occupation Force or else to the northwestward, still existed.

In fact, Admiral Yamamoto wanted a surface engagement. He believed there was only one American carrier and that it was out of action. When Admiral Nagumo began to withdraw, Yamamoto relieved him and put Vice Admiral Kondo in charge of the striking force. Kondo moved toward Midway to make a night bombardment, but later that mission was canceled and the Japanese retired to the northwest.

At daybreak Task Force 16 was moving west at fifteen knots. The weather was very bad. The submarine *Tambor* made the first report of the Japanese, sighted ninety miles west of Midway. Early that morning, trying to avoid the *Tambor,* the Japanese cruisers *Mikuma* and *Mogami* collided, and then headed slowly away from the action toward the repair station at Truk.

Spruance was looking for the enemy. As the weather cleared, he learned that one group was west of Midway and the other group was northwest. He chose the northwest group to chase; it contained, he understood, the crippled carrier and two battleships, one damaged. All he found that day were two small ships, apparently destroyers. The planes took a night landing, and one crashed in the water astern of *Enterprise,* because of the pilot's unfamiliarity with the technique. The crew was saved, and all other planes made it aboard the two carriers, although sometimes landing on the wrong one.

That second night Spruance headed west. "I figured the enemy DDs [destroyers] would report our attack and that he might either get the protection of bad weather ahead or else change course to the westward to head for Japan and to throw us off."

Next morning the search planes found two groups of Japanese ships southwest of the task force, about forty miles apart. They had found *Mogami* and *Mikuma,* and dive bombers sank *Mikuma* that day and damaged *Mogami* so badly that it took one year to repair her when she reached Truk.

Identification by the pilots was so faulty that they believed *Mikuma* was a battleship. But what difference? The victory was completely glorious. The reason, Spruance indicated, was the uncertainty of American knowledge about the dimensions of these Japanese ships. Before nightfall he questioned the pilots of two photographic planes, and came to the conclusion that the sunk ship was a cruiser of the *Mogami* class (a pretty good guess). "She was definitely larger than the other cruiser accompanying her," Spruance said. (*Mogami*'s bow had been torn off in the collision with *Mikuma*, and that was the reason for the wrong conclusion in her case.) Meanwhile, on Saturday, June 6, a Japanese submarine torpedoed the *Yorktown*, sinking her and the destroyer *Hammann*, which was alongside, taking away some of the glory.

Admiral Yamamoto, still hoping to salvage some shred of victory from his inglorious defeat, attempted to lure Spruance into the range of the shore-based Japanese aircraft at Wake Island. By the end of the day, Spruance's force was running low on fuel, and he also felt that he had pushed his luck about as far as was sensible. The Japanese shore-based planes had a range of six hundred miles from Wake, and he was determined to stay outside the seven-hundred-mile circle. He sent back destroyers, and found himself with only four, not enough to screen his carriers against the Japanese submarines known to be in the area. So Spruance turned east, and the battle of Midway came to a close.

At Pearl Harbor, Nimitz and his officers had been waiting eagerly for the bits of news as they came in. On June 4 Nimitz said, "It may be the greatest sea battle since Jutland." If the outcome was as unfavorable to the Japanese as he hoped, it might end their expansion in the Pacific. Nimitz was worried, however, because the total destruction of Torpedo 8 symbolized what had happened to the American fleet that day: the United States had lost a large percentage of highly trained pilots who would be hard to replace. (The Japanese, of course, had lost far more, the pilots and aircrews of nearly every plane of the four carriers. The bite of Midway would be felt by the Japanese naval air force throughout the rest of the war.) On the second day, Nimitz issued a conservative communiqué about the victory. The staff was jubilant, terming the battle a major defeat for the enemy.

"This was a great day for the American Navy," said the Gray Book of the Commander in Chief of the Pacific Fleet that day. The Cincpac gray book was the unofficial war diary—very secret and sometimes more informative as to attitudes at Pearl Harbor than any other documents to come out of the war. The nation was not to know the Navy's real role in that battle for a considerable length of time. At Midway, Army B-17 bombers had the first crack at the Japanese—and did not score *a single hit*, yet that failure did not keep the Army Air Corps from claiming it had won the battle of Midway. Nimitz was constrained by security to forbear from reply —the Japanese would have liked nothing better than to know precisely what had happened to them at Midway and what American dispositions and losses had been. Secretary Knox was aware of the facts and concerned about them, as he indicated to Nimitz, at the same time sending out a new public relations officer, perhaps rather pointedly.

> Confidentially [the Secretary wrote], there is a great deal of feeling here and, I understand, also in the Fleet, on account of the obvious attempt of the Army Air Corps to play up their part in the Midway battle. It is most unfortunate that they have this disposition and I have a memorandum on my desk together with a copy of the Honolulu paper which contains a statement by General Arnold which I propose to discuss with Secretary Stimson at the first opportunity. He feels as strongly as I do about anything likely to produce friction between the two services and I feel sure that he will take the necessary measures to prevent this sort of thing happening again. . . .

This incident was the occasion for deep-seated resentment of the Army by Navy airmen during the Pacific war.

Knox did what he could. He was, in private life, publisher of the *Chicago Daily News*, and he arranged to have war correspondent Robert J. Casey write a series of articles explaining the facts of Midway. But by and large the Army had the first publicity, and many people went through the war believing the B-17's had smashed the Japanese navy.

That navy was not smashed, but the power of its air force was very definitely curtailed, with the sinking of four of her carriers (*Kaga, Akagi, Soryu,* and *Hiryu*) and the loss of 250 planes and more than two thousand men.

Having sunk four carriers and a Japanese cruiser and destroyed an invasion before it ever got started, Spruance's reaction was typical and terse. In writing to Nimitz, he was primarily interested in what had been learned.

> The operations during this period have been most interesting and instructive. We must, I think, improve our identification of types from the air . . . . Another point is that emphasis should be placed on continued tracking of enemy forces by shorebased planes whenever conditions permit. It would have been of great assistance if the damaged CV [fleet carrier] had been tracked down on Friday . . . . For use against CVs, particularly those caught with planes on deck, our present bombs are perfect. For use against tough ships with armored decks, we must have an armor piercing 1000 lb bomb. Against such targets I would use about half of each. The present type works terrible destruction on the unarmored portion of the ship, but it does not disable except after many more hits than should be necessary. We have a 1600 lb AP bomb now, but to use it our present dive bombers have to reduce their gas carried, which is not a satisfactory solution.

Regarding Fletcher, Spruance was most generous.

> I cannot close . . . without expressing my admiration for the part that Fletcher in the *Yorktown* played in this campaign. We had a fine and smoothly working coordination between the two Task Forces before the fighting commenced. When the battle started, the *Yorktown*'s attack and the information her planes furnished were of vital importance to our success, which for some time was hanging in the balance. The *Yorktown* happened to be between the *Hornet* and *Enterprise* and the enemy's fourth and still functioning carrier, so she took his blows.
>
> Halsey's splendid staff have made my job easy. I appreciate more than I can tell you the fact that you had sufficient confidence in me to let me take this fine Task Force to sea during this critical period. It has been a pleasure to have such a well-trained fighting force to throw against the enemy.

The reason for the letter was that Spruance had been ordered to move north in the vicinity of the Aleutians, meet with Fitch and the *Saratoga* group, and then go after the enemy again. This was just what Yamamoto wanted, and he was attempting to lay a trap for Spruance, going so far as to make a plain-language radio broadcast that was supposed to come from a disabled battleship—bait for the Americans. But since Nimitz had begun to suspect the existence of a trap and ordered Spruance back to Pearl Harbor, the effort came to nothing.

In a way, the Midway battle had been a "makey-learn cruise" of the first order, for two commanders had learned a great deal about carrier operations. Admiral Marc Mitscher came home in the *Hornet* with a number of ideas. America needed something to compete with the Japanese Zero fighter, he said. American fighters should have the same fuel capacity as the planes they escorted. Radio silence had been broken on the fighter director circuit. Again, he added a plea for IFF equipment, along with other advice. In his official report, Spruance added that ships unsupported by fighters are easy prey to carrier air attack, which seemed obvious, and that a carrier air group which had suffered heavy losses in action should go ashore to train and receive replacements—meaning the supply of replacement air groups, which was not nearly so obvious.

When the action report of the Battle of Midway—some three inches of single-spaced typed paper, with diagrams and photos— was completed, Nimitz studied it and made some comments for the eyes of Admiral King, matters of gravest importance to the future of naval operations in the war.

He advocated the procurement of B-17's and B-24's for the Navy, as better planes than the PBY's for continuous tracking under conditions where enemy air is present.

He noted how ineffectual high-altitude horizontal bombing had proved, and recommended that island and coastal base planes be torpedo bombers and dive bombers.

He recommended the supply of the Marines with Army-type planes for use from shore bases, instead of the carrier-type planes with their built-in limitations.

He noted the lack of coordination of dive-bombing and torpedo-plane attacks, which cost most of the American torpedo planes. He also noted that the TBD planes in use "are fatally inadequate for their purpose. The loss of the brave men who unhesitatingly went to their death in them is grievous." He asked for long-range carrier fighters to protect the better TBF's.

Nimitz agreed with Mitscher and Spruance about the superiority in speed, maneuverability, and climb of the Zero. "These characteristics must be improved," he said, "but not at the cost of reducing our *present overall superiority* that in the battle of Midway enabled our carrier fighter squadrons to shoot down about 3 Zero fighters for each of our own lost."

Since in most engagements the American fighters were outnumbered, he suggested the increase in the number of fighters in each carrier from eighteen to twenty-seven. He endorsed Spruance's view on the need for replacement air groups.

Nimitz called for sharper, more thorough air training, better, quicker launching and attack, better tracking of enemy formations, and superfrequency voice sets for voice communication. He called attention to improved communications, improved gunnery ("Some crews have been in enough battles to consider themselves seasoned veterans"), better aircraft torpedoes with larger warheads designed for high-speed drops, and the thousand-pound armor-piercing bomb.

At the Battle of the Coral Sea, King had been critical of Fletcher for not using cruisers and destroyers in night attacks against the Japanese, and the Commander in Chief reiterated that criticism of the Midway action. Nimitz had to be prepared to explain. At the same time, he was preparing for his next meeting with King in San Francisco, watching the Aleutian situation, where the Japanese had landed and occupied two islands, and preparing for offensive action that was coming later in the South Pacific.

On June 29 Nimitz decided to send Task Force 11, Task Force 18, and the Second Marine Division to the South Pacific, where they would report to Ghormley. Fletcher was in charge of the force. Cincpac's plans section was ready with an estimate for an offensive in the Bismarck-Solomons area.

Then Nimitz took off, in the big flying boat, accompanied by

Flag Secretary Commander Preston Mercer and Assistant War Plans Officer Captain Lynde McCormick, for Alameda air station. Just before 0900 on June 30 the big plane moved down over San Francisco Bay and prepared to land on the water. Swooping in, she moved low, and as she landed, struck an unnoticed telegraph pole floating in the bay, with such force that the bottom was slashed and the plane nosed over. Immediately, the shocked officers in the greeting contingent ashore sent the launch out for rescue. Nimitz carefully picked himself up, in the upside-down plane, and clambered out a hatchway.

"I'm all right," he shouted to Mercer, "but for God's sake save that briefcase." (The briefcase contained the three-inch report of the Battle of Midway.)

The copilot, Lt. Thomas M. Roscoe of Oakland, was killed in the crash, and several of the other survivors were injured. When the launch reached them, Nimitz climbed in with the others, and then stood up.

"Sit down, you" bellowed the coxswain.

Nimitz obeyed. A few moments later the sailor recognized his Pacific Fleet commander, and was horrified. He tried to apologize.

"Stick to your guns, sailor," Nimitz said. "You were quite right."

At the air station, all the survivors were rushed to the hospital for checkup. Nimitz, who hated hospitals and confinement, struggled free shortly and made his way home to Berkeley, where Mrs. Nimitz was spending the war, and found a change of clothes. Mercer, who was as sopping wet as the rest of them, had to put on a loud checked summer suit he had bought in San Diego before the war, and appear in that rig, much to his chagrin, when he met Commander in Chief King.

Among the exhibits for discussion at the meetings in Vice Admiral D. W. Bagley's office in the federal building was a discussion of the role of the battleship by Admiral Pye.

Pye suggested that the Japanese loss of five carriers in recent weeks had changed the situation so that the battleships might be used for the first time in the war. Still, Pye recognized that

the war to date, both here and in Europe, has proven without doubt that even battleships are more vulnerable to torpedoes and bombs than had been previously estimated. This increased vulnerability has been due in large part to higher explosive charges than were considered probable heretofore, and in a large part also to the increased number of hits made by the greatly increased use of the torpedo plane, and by the increased proportion of dive bombers.

Battleships, then said Pye, should be employed only where their fire power could be used against ship or shore defense with enemy air and submarine defenses neutralized, or at least anticipated, and the losses discounted.

Specifically, Pye considered and discarded the use of battleships against Kiska or Attu in the Aleutians, unless Nimitz proposed to recapture these islands, with the battleships providing support.

In the Central Pacific, battleships might be useful against Wake—if accompanied by at least one carrier, Pye said.

If the Japanese tried to invade Australia, Pye saw the battleships as useful—"any and all possible naval strength would be of value." But unless logistics could be improved, the operation of Task Force One (the battleships) would be impracticable for any extended period.

In minor amphibious operations, cruiser and carrier support seemed to him enough. When the Japanese hold on important islands was threatened, and the Japanese main fleet might come out, then the battleships should be used to engage the Japanese main fleet.

But most practically, the old battleships could be used to prevent invasion of Midway or the Hawaiian Islands.

For a battleship man, this acceptance of limitations seemed very progressive, but Pye was always progressive. King agreed with just about everything Pye said, and they discussed the continuing need for development of tactics for large forces.

At this meeting, Nimitz and King, and the other officers who were present—going in and out to give information on specific subjects—were vitally concerned with the coming offensive to be launched in the South Pacific. Looking ahead, King suggested that the future would mean movement to Truk, then Guam, then Saipan.

Rear Admiral Richmond Kelly Turner, the planner whose eye had always been on amphibious operations, had been selected to supervise the landings on Guadalcanal island, and now Nimitz was ready to send him to Melbourne to discuss the whole operation with Ghormley and General MacArthur. The problem involved some change in the line of Cincpac-CincSoWesPac responsibility, because the Solomons fell within MacArthur's area, but this would be a Navy show.

Turner sat in on the discussions for a time. Nimitz wanted a promotion for Fletcher to vice admiral, and King agreed: he had accepted Nimitz's appraisal of Fletcher's actions at Coral Sea. Nimitz also wanted the authority to appoint task force commanders regardless of seniority, an authority he did not then have. They discussed other aspects of the coming operation for a time, and then Turner withdrew. Nimitz and King talked about Alaska and then about personnel. Mitscher's name came up, and Nimitz spoke highly of him. (King and the others had not always spoken so highly of Mitscher.) Halsey was still sick, and if he did not come back, Nimitz said, he wanted Aubrey Fitch to become the senior air flag officer of the fleet. Several officers of the Pacific Fleet had been indiscreetly involved in a leak to the press on the breaking of the Japanese naval code, and their fates were discussed.

Nimitz broke from the seriousness for a moment to report that he had rented a small house on Oahu for the rest and rehabilitation of senior officers. (It came to be called Prostate Rest.) Then they got down to the tiresome but vital business of logistics for the expanding naval operations in the South Pacific. They talked about medical storehouses, a fleet anchorage in New Caledonia, and the effective life of a submarine captain. (A captain could be expected to hold up for three or four full patrols—about a year—before needing a prolonged rest.)

Nimitz asked for more tankers, and this request was discussed in full. The problem as always these days, was balancing the absolute needs of the Pacific Fleet against the growing demands of the war in Europe.

Chapter
Six

NEXT STEP

June 6–July 26, 1942

"It has been a fearful period of anxiety for us all," Secretary of the Navy Frank Knox wrote to Mrs. Knox on June 6, as the Battle of Midway ended victoriously for the Americans. "The outcome will seriously affect the whole war situation in the Pacific."

Midway *was* the turning point. Before Midway, Admiral Nimitz kept away from the press as much as possible; he issued few communiqués, and none that could be considered expansive. After Midway, he was convinced that the United States would win the war—he did not predict when it would end, but he did say he believed it would end much earlier than the gloomy prediction, then common, of 1949.

Midway also seemed to be the catalyst for another development not nearly so pleasant to contemplate: the divisive and sometimes vitriolic three-way argument over air power. The argument had been nascent for many years, since the days of General Billy Mitchell and his plea for a separate air force. Alexander P. De-Seversky had come out with a persuasive program of strategic bombing which he called Victory Through Air Power, and he was busy writing and lecturing very effectively. General Arnold and the top officers of the Army Air Corps wanted to make a separate air force—which would also take over the Navy's air functions. And within the Navy itself the airmen, led by Admiral Towers, were agitating for greater responsibility and more control of naval operations. The work of hitting the enemy had so far been done by the submarines, by surface ships in the East Indies, but most gloriously by the carriers. The first two great battles, Coral Sea and Midway, had involved carriers and no gun duels. The aviators were grumbling that they ought to have a greater voice. Halsey was still sick, and the aviators did not regard him as one of them anyhow. Admiral McCain was working as commander of aircraft in the South Pacific, and the aviators did not regard him as one of them either, because he, too, was in his fifties when he had learned to fly. Nimitz had inherited an aviation officer, Captain Arthur C. Davis, but the aviators did not consider this nearly enough recognition.

Actually, Nimitz was alive to the problem and was already working toward solution. In June, before he had gone to meet with King in San Francisco, Nimitz had made that request to the Commander in Chief for the authority to assign force commanders regardless of relative rank. It could be argued (and was by the aviators) that Admiral Fitch should have been in command of the task forces at the Wake relief expedition and at Coral Sea, when he was subordinate to Fletcher. Fitch was more acceptable to the young aviators than any other Pacific admiral, for he had taken air cadet training in 1929, when he was forty-six years old, and had commanded the seaplane tender *Wright*, the aircraft carrier *Langley*, the naval air station at Hampton Roads, Patrol Wing Two, the *Lexington*, Carrier Division One, and finally the Air Task Force in the Pacific. Fitch was also thoroughly acceptable to nonaviators, for he had served in battleships, destroyers, minelayers, in the Navy Department, and he had taken the senior course at the Naval War College. He had not been in command at either battle because he was junior by a few numbers to his classmate Fletcher, and it was Navy rule to make the senior officer the OTC—officer in tactical command.

"I foresee that such a situation may arise in which I will desire to designate a task force commander who is junior in rank to the commander of the cruisers in the force," Nimitz had written King. And he was pressing for this concession.

McCain had written Nimitz from the South Pacific about the air situation he faced. He wanted an Air Corps brigadier general, if he could get one, to assist him in air operations. He was planning bases at Efate and Espiritu Santo, and waiting for Army bombers to come in to assist his force. He and Nimitz were agreed to having a carrier replacement group stationed on every island—McCain said the entire Pacific, to the Philippines. In a letter to Nimitz he said, "Jove never hurled a thunderbolt as destructive as a split-second-trained carrier group—vide Lexington pilots." McCain complained about the supply and administrative problem. He had been asking for three months, he said, for base personnel, and was still using combat men to do base jobs.

The letter came in during the Midway operations. By the time Nimitz was able to answer it, the victory had been won. "I regard the entire operation as a wonderful example of coordination and utmost determination by all concerned," Nimitz said. "Our aviators bore the brunt, but decidedly not in vain."

Nimitz was concerned with overall air policy, agreeing with McCain that Army aircraft in the South Pacific should be permanently assigned to various bases. "It is most fallacious to expect in emergency, except with rare good luck, to have time to move aircraft to threatened points and get them organized for effective employment." He wanted to get naval aircraft down to McCain as soon as possible, but the shortage of pilots and planes was still dogging him. "The situation should soon improve but the demands for new aircraft, combined with losses of carrier aircraft in action, still have us operating on not much more than a shoestring."

It was a serious letter, but Nimitz found time to include a poem, one that he said "was slipped under the cabin door of one of our cruiser captains during the last phase of the battle of Midway." It purported to be a dispatch from the Japanese commander in chief, second fleet, to the commander in chief, first fleet. It read:

Send aid,
Send it fast.
Have lost face,
Am losing ass.

Nimitz was very much concerned about air, obviously. In July he wrote to Secretary Knox, calling for new and better planes both for the carriers and for the land-based Marine pilots.

We have learned many lessons in *particular* that all our planes do not fill the bill "best in the world" at least in the Pacific. In our development of airplane types we have probably been heavily influenced by the picture in Europe. The little Japs, however, got down to cases, and planned specifically for their local problems. Thus they have long range landplane fighters for escort, and seaplane fighters for work among the atolls, both of which have shown marked usefulness (and superiority) for the job at hand. In these categories we are decidedly lacking.

Again, in the case of the Zero fighter, the Jap has sacrificed various qualities in order to obtain the highest performance and maneuverability. In this case, since I am positive that we must retain such features as tank and armor protection, we can only out-do the enemy by very superior designing.

At this time, Nimitz was also concerned about a cloud he saw shaping up on the aerial horizon. Just after Midway, Captain Logan Ramsey of Patrol Wing 2 wrote a secret letter to Nimitz, supplementing the official report of air operations by Midway-based forces during the battle.

"Broadly speaking," Ramsey said, "Army air units operating from Midway were distinctly below Navy standards in efficiency, resolution, initiative, and devotion to duty." There was an exception, the squadron led by Lieutenant Colonel Walter Sweeney—

and Ramsey suggested that Sweeney's performance was good because he had been working with the Navy during the six months just past, at Oahu.

One Army failure cited by Ramsey was bad navigation. (Nimitz found, however, that this was a problem of communications: the Army used a different grid system from the Navy's.) Much more serious was the problem of bombing from high altitudes—as high as thirty thousand feet. Only Colonel Sweeney's planes had come close enough to the enemy ships even to be damaged by antiaircraft fire. On June 6, despite the known lack of enemy air opposition, some B-17 squadron commanders would not take off until they had replenished their oxygen stocks, which would not have been needed below fifteen thousand feet.

Ramsey said he was convinced that "had the B-17s operating from Midway on June 5 and 6, been manned by personnel up to the standard of the navy patrol plane crews, few, if any enemy ships within 600 miles of Midway would have been able to escape." Ramsey had given no hint of these opinions to Army people, and the Navy officers had tried hard to smooth over many difficulties. Brigadier General Willis Hale had left Midway on June 3 stating that he intended to make the strongest representations to Nimitz and others about the excessive demands being made on the B-17 crews during the battle. His departure, said Ramsey, averted the great danger of rupture of interservice relations.

As if the problem of Army-Navy air relations were not thorny enough, the Navy aviators now began kicking up their heels. Someone in Navy air planted a story in the Washington *Post* criticizing the Navy for sending out task force commanders who were not experienced in carrier operations. The criticism obviously referred to the use of Spruance at Midway, and Fletcher at Coral Sea and Midway, for neither was an aviator. Secretary Knox was very much annoyed by this article, and called Admiral Towers on the carpet, saying he would have no more of it. The most ebullient and ambitious of the aviators, however, continued in their contentious ways.

Nimitz had greater worries in the air department, with the South Pacific offensive very definitely on. In June the Pacific Fleet received its first reinforcements. They included the carrier *Wasp*, the new fast battleship *North Carolina,* the heavy cruiser *Quincy,* and seven destroyers. Nimitz was then able to reorganize his carrier task forces. Fitch had Task Force 11, and if Halsey did not come back, he would soon be made senior air officer. Fletcher had Task Force 16, Marc Mitscher had Task Force 17, with the *Hornet,* and Rear Admiral Leigh Noyes, a classmate of Fitch and Fletcher, had Task Force 18, with the *Wasp.*

General MacArthur had said that if the Navy would give him the ships, a couple of carriers, a task force, an amphibious division, and a handful of bombers, he would capture Rabaul. King had opposed the idea and remained steadfast for the Solomons invasion, and that was where the offensive was going.

On July 5 Nimitz received a piece of intelligence that put the whole program in high gear: the Japanese were beginning to build an airfield on Guadalcanal. Its completion would seriously hamper all of King's plans. And so King made one of the major decisions of the war—ordering the seizure of Tulagi, Guadalcanal, and Santa Cruz islands.

Nimitz had the operation order out and in Ghormley's hands by July 10. By this time, MacArthur had his own navy, under Vice Admiral Arthur S. Carpender, chief of what would become the Seventh Fleet, but would not be involved in this operation.

Here is how the command would stack up: Ghormley would be in command, in charge of strategy, but would not be in the field. Fletcher, who had just been made a vice admiral, would be the officer in tactical command. Rear Admiral Richmond Kelly Turner, who had been agitating for a sea command since the beginning of the war, would supervise the amphibious operations against the islands. Major General A. A. Vandegrift of the Marines would head the troops ashore. McCain's planes would operate from landing bases in his area; MacArthur would offer aerial and submarine support from the Southwest Pacific.

By July 7 three of the four task forces were committed to the Tulagi operation, as the Japanese continued to land troops and workmen on Guadalcanal for their air field. Nimitz was as busy as a midshipman on his first cruise, occupied with logistical problems, command problems, and the responsibility of shoring up all his other defenses so the Japanese could not sneak in and attack him when he was not looking. He felt particularly exposed at Midway, and moved to strengthen that position. The problem was still that there was so little to work with, and it was needed in so many places. McCain needed bombers, so Nimitz sent him thirty-five B-17's from Hawaii—then learned that the War Department would not or could not replace the defenses for Hawaii. Nimitz told McCain this sad truth: "Therefore I think we must face an indefinite period during which calls for help will get little response from home."

Nimitz had some bad news for McCain. There had been delay in forming and training four Marine squadrons, and only one fighter and one dive bomber squadron would be ready to move in August. The other two squadrons would come two weeks later, after the operation began.

The good news: Nimitz had talked to Major General Harmon, the Army air man, when he came through Pearl Harbor, and Harmon understood that McCain was to be in charge of the air components in the South Pacific. "I feel sure you will work *harmon*iously together," wrote Nimitz, making one of his typical bad puns. Yes, even when harried by a thousand details Nimitz was able to keep his sense of humor.

On July 26, for example, Nimitz spent a regular day at the office. He dealt with his staff meeting in the morning, and absorbed the depressing news that Halsey would not be back with him before the middle of September. He made the decision to fleet Fitch up to vice admiral and make him commander of carriers in the Pacific, and eventually commander of all air activities. Murray, the carrier captain, would become rear admiral in charge of Task Force 17.

Nimitz held several discussions with Spruance, his chief of staff, and then got into the big black Buick sedan that was his staff car, and went off to Honolulu to attend a wedding. He returned just as his dinner guests arrived: Lieutenant (jg) James E. Bassett, Jr., and two young intelligence officers. They stalled, to give him a moment to himself, and then went up the triple flight of stone steps to the house on the edge of the crater. The young officers came in, past the Marine guard, who gave them a smart salute, and were led to the admiral by a Filipino messboy.

"Let me know when 'upstairs' is ready," Nimitz said, and the houseboy nodded. Nimitz then took his young guests outside to "inspect the livestock," which consisted of four mongooses, trapped by the steward for stuffing purposes, and an Island dog of uncertain ancestry.

Nimitz had a tale for them. One evening, not long before, he had invited three flag officers to dinner but had forgotten to tell Perez, his steward, that they were coming. Dinner that night was skimpy, and Perez was upset, but said that he would go out and rustle up something for them. He did.

"We ate it," Nimitz said, with a grin. "Next morning a mongoose, stuffed, appeared on the sideboard in the dining room. We never knew," the admiral said.

As Nimitz finished the tale, in came Perez to announce that "upstairs" was ready, and the admiral asked his juniors if they would like a drink. They walked by the admiral's work table, a drawing board set on sawhorses, where he toyed with Pacific area charts. "Hobby," he laughed, as they passed.

Then they went to the second deck, and to a small blacked-out room at the head of the ladder. In it stood five small straight chairs and a desk. On the desk were a bucket of cracked ice, a bottle of bitters, slices of lemon and orange, and a jar of maraschino cherries, and a tray of canapés. The admiral sat down and looked at his guests keenly from beneath the white brows. "Bourbon or Oke?" he asked.

Bassett asked for bourbon. The others took Oke, which was *okulehou*, a very strong Hawaiian liquor. Nimitz made the drinks, and handed them around.

"Luckily," Bassett said later, "we had been warned about the Boss's cocktails so we hadn't fortified ourselves beyond a small beer base, or mattress, for what followed."

They had a second drink ("strong as a mule's kick") and then Admiral Spruance came in. He picked up a cup of tomato juice which was waiting for him, and added a pinch of salt. Nimitz asked him if he wanted a dash of Oke. "No," Spruance said. "I don't think Oke would be good. Causative and curative in one drink. No. Not good."

With the drinks, they talked and Nimitz proved himself a fine host and commander, talking on the level of his junior officers. The young men opened up enough to discuss the idea of bringing a USO troupe to the islands, and ran into one of Nimitz's prejudices: women in the war zone.

"Well," he growled, "when Emmons [the Army general in command of Hawaii] gives out a signed statement that he figures this place is safe enough so that 'non-essential' people don't have to leave, then I'll okay these movie stars coming out. But not until. . . ."

They talked of the nine thousand young men of Japanese ancestry on the island. Nimitz said he thought they ought to be in uniform—sent to Africa or some other fighting front where they would not fight Japanese. "They're good fighters," he said.

The discussion came to Japanese submarines. There was no reason in the world why a Japanese submarine could not come in some night, surface, throw twenty-five or thirty shells into Pearl Harbor installations, submerge, and get out. "We'd never catch her," Nimitz said, thoughtfully. The others scoffed. "I could do it," Nimitz said.

Spruance again demurred. "We don't know whether the Japs are capable of it," he said.

Nimitz grunted. "Hell, we don't know what their submarine motives are. I think they're more interested in reconnaissance than sinkings."

Just then another Filipino messboy appeared at the head of the ladder and nodded. Nimitz nodded back, and they tossed off the last of their cocktails and went down the ladder. Dinner was beef Stroganoff, Nimitz having just received the recipe from one of his daughters on the mainland. Then came the dessert, which was avocado ice cream. ("I could have done without that," Bassett said.)

After dessert came coffee and cigarettes, and Nimitz began telling stories. He told a story about three Chinese girls who wanted men with dragons on their chests. He told a tale of the young

Marine parachutist who was going to make his first jump. The boy was scared, but his sergeant told him not to worry, just to pull the rip cord and everything would be all right. If the chute didn't open, the Marine was to pull the rip cord on the emergency chute. And then, when he came down, he would be met by a station wagon and taken back to camp. So the marine jumped. He pulled the first cord, and nothing happened. He pulled the second cord. Nothing happened. He looked down. "I'll bet that damned station wagon won't be there, either," he said.

Nimitz laughed at his own stories, and then told the young men confidentially that his wife had warned him when he achieved flag rank that he would have to stop telling those "awful" stories. And he laughed again, at himself.

They talked about race problems; there had been some difficulty with Negro troops in Hawaii. Before the war, as chief of the Bureau of Navigation, Nimitz had been faced with the ticklish problems of Negroes and Negro promotion. He had advocated higher ranks for Negroes, but usually by the formation of all-Negro units, such as Negro bands. For this moment Nimitz was serious. The race problem would grow more difficult after the war, he said.

Then he was on another topic. The young officers had been out driving past Nanakuli, and had seen the soldiers in the field, stationed in the algarroba patches, out in no man's land. They said they were sorry for them. Nimitz frowned.

"Soft. They're soft. They've *got* to learn to be hard. They're not having trouble. Only think they are. We're going to be here a long time; and they'd better get used to it."

They talked shop a bit, Bassett suggesting that the Navy Department in Washington was taking away the play from the Pacific, with its Washington datelines (notes of origin). Nimitz smiled at that.

"We've got bigger things to worry about," he said. "After we sink four more carriers, *then* you can publish anything you damned please."

The talk continued, friendly, frank talk, until nine in the evening. Then Nimitz pushed back his chair. "Let's get a breath of fresh air," he said.

Spruance and the younger men followed the admiral outside. They breathed deeply and looked up at the pale moon for a few moments, and listened to the pumps which were dredging mud from the harbor into Makalapa crater. "Sounds like rain on a tin roof, doesn't it, Ray?" asked Nimitz. Spruance nodded. "We'll sleep well with this going on. Homey." Spruance nodded again. The younger men sensed that it was time to go. As they left, Bassett asked one last question.

"I understand you read a lot at night, sir?"

Nimitz grinned. "Yes I do. I read from three until five every morning."

"When do you sleep, sir?"

"Well, I turn in at ten and sleep till three. Then I catch another wink from five till 0645."

The young men turned, waved, and walked down the drive in the moonlight, Bassett saying to himself that here was his admiral, "a human, likeable, hearty, zestful kindly man, the best of any flag officers I have ever met." And Nimitz went to bed.

Chapter
Seven

SPRUANCE

June–July 1942

With his clear eyes, regular features, athletic figure, and square jaw, Raymond Ames Spruance was almost a motion picture representation of the perfect naval officer. He was saved from caricature by his shyness, his intellectuality, and his immense ability as naval strategist and tactician. This new chief of staff to Admiral Nimitz was precisely what a fleet commander would demand. He was agreeable without being obsequious, shy without being retiring, businesslike to a point of irritating visitors, and totally dedicated to the job at hand. As chief of staff Spruance was responsible for organization of all the detail of the command, and he was on top of it.

He had always been on top of everything, it seemed, from the days of his youth when he had not one but two appointments to the Naval Academy, having won competitive examinations in Indiana where his family lived and in New Jersey where his grandmother lived.

At the Academy they called him "Sprew." He was twenty-sixth in his class academically, and totally undistinguished in the extracurricular activities of the midshipmen. He was so shy that as it came time to characterize him for the *Lucky Bag*, the class yearbook, the editors were hard put to find anything outstanding except that characteristic—and his devotion to duty.

His class of 1907 was divided into three sections, and Spruance was actually graduated in the fall of 1906. He went to the battleship *Iowa* as a passed midshipman, served creditably but without distinction, was promoted to ensign in 1908, and promptly asked for special duty as a postgraduate student of electrical matters at the General Electric Company in Schenectady. Wireless was new and that was what he studied.

For the next few years Spruance served in battleships and cruisers as a junior officer in engineering. His first command was the old *Bainbridge*, DD1, in the Asiatic Fleet at Olongapo, in the Philippines. As the senior officer afloat, he was commander of the Destroyer Division, which included DD's 1, 2, 3, 4, and 5.

The *Bainbridge*, according to a shipmate, Carl Moore, was the first torpedo-boat destroyer in the American fleet, a development from the old torpedo boats. She was 440 tons, with a speed of twenty-eight knots, and she had two three-inch guns and four torpedoes aboard. She was powered by four boilers with reciprocating engines, reciprocating forced-draft blowers. She was also a coal-burning, dirty, "miserable little tub." Five years earlier, Ensign Nimitz had served aboard her sister ship, DD5, the *Decatur*. Matters had not changed very much since, at least not for the better. In the interim the destroyers had earned a reputation as rough, tough ships. "The officers," said Carl Moore, who was an ensign in those days, "were dissolute, drunken, crooked, the darndest bunch of people you've ever seen, and demoralized completely by life in the Asiatic station. Several of them had Chinese boys aboard that weren't enlisted—they'd picked them up in Hong Kong or Canton or someplace—and they brought them down to the Philippines and wouldn't let them off the ship because they'd be arrested immediately if it were known."

Spruance already had a reputation in the fleet as a quiet, solid officer who knew his way around. He was sent in for one task, to straighten out this bunch of roughnecks and bring the Destroyer Division back into the Navy. So bad were affairs that one night when Spruance moved the division to Cavite, the captain of Nimitz's old ship, the *Decatur*, was dead drunk in his bunk, and Spruance had to send Ensign Carl Moore over to move the ship.

He was efficient, and he began whipping the division into line. Socially, in the Philippines, Spruance was a "drag." His younger officers got him invited to picnics and sailing parties and dinners, but he could not shine, he was absolutely incompetent at small talk. Moore and the other junior, Ralph Haxtun, insisted that Spruance accompany them on their jaunts, and little by little they broke him down. The girls called him "Spriscilla Sprudence," but they did it behind his back. It was not too long before Spruance was actually enjoying the company of girls, but there was one difference. The others drank, sometimes to excess. Spruance did so only once. The morning after a big dinner party ashore, Ensign Moore found his commanding officer in bed with his mackintosh and seaboots still on. That was the one time.

At Christmas, 1913, Moore and Spruance went up to Bagio. They visited Igorot villages, and they walked, and walked, and walked. Moore was to remember how much they walked, not very many months after Spruance became Nimitz's chief of staff.

To straighten up his destroyers, Spruance made it a practice while in port to eat each meal on a different ship, and soon had improved the food on all of them. He accompanied the swimming parties to the beaches, and soon had the men getting regular exercise in Subic Bay.

In 1914 Spruance was transferred to a shore job at Newport News. His title was assistant inspector of machinery, but soon he was supervising the electrical work aboard the new USS *Pennsylvania*, and when she was finished, it was not long before he went to her as assistant engineering officer. Here, Lieutenant Commander Spruance met Lieutenant Richmond Kelly Turner, and they became good friends.

Electricity was Spruance's specialty. He went to the New York Navy Yard as electrical superintendent. He was promoted to commander and went to London to supervise installation of electrical fire-control systems on the ships of the Sixth Battle Squadron. There he took transport duty, as executive officer of the *Agamemnon*, and later was commander of the destroyer *Aaron Ward*. His division commander was Commander William F. Halsey, who wrote Spruance's fitness reports. "An able, bright destroyer commander," said Halsey of the younger man.

Each of Halsey's fitness reports on Spruance was equally positive—Halsey called him one of the best naval officers with whom he had ever served—and Halsey could be very tough to please.

Spruance moved back into engineering and electricity after destroyer duty and spent three years in Washington in the Bureau of Engineering. But he escaped typing, and was again a destroyer commander in 1924. While so serving, Spruance received an official reprimand when a chief commissary steward played fast and loose with the naval regulations regarding mess expenditures. As captain of the ship, Spruance was responsible for the steward's peccadilloes. The reprimand went into his service jacket, where it very easily could have sat bleakly for years, to be brought up and examined by the selection board—and keep Raymond Spruance from becoming a flag officer.

Even as a young officer, Spruance was a reader. His friends Moore and Haxtun of the *Bainbridge* preferred to roister at night in Manila; often Spruance could be found reading a book instead. He made a study of Philippine politics and economics in those days, too, quite an unusual activity for a young naval officer in the Asiatic Fleet. And as he grew older, Spruance continued this intellectuality.

He was a family man. In 1914 Spruance married Margaret Vance Dean of Indianapolis, his home town. Two children were born of the marriage. The boy, Edward, attended the Naval Academy and became a captain in the Navy. The girl, Margaret, married a naval officer, Gerard S. Bogart. In 1926 Spruance took the family to Newport, because he had been selected to attend the senior course of the Naval War College. And here he studied strategy. After ten months he was graduated from the course, and went to the Office of Naval Intelligence for a two-year tour. He then became executive officer of the USS *Mississippi* of the Pacific Fleet.

In 1931 Spruance was selected to become head of the tactical section, teaching at the War College. There he rejoined his friend Carl Moore, who became Spruance's assistant. They lived in houses a hundred yards apart, and their families became friends.

During this tour, Richmond Kelly Turner came up to the college to take the course. Turner proved himself a good tactician, but one with a temper. One day they were simulating a battle, and Turner was in command of a squadron of destroyers, fighting another squadron. Carl Moore was the umpire, and he knew how many shots were fired by Turner's destroyers and how many by the enemy, and, according to the board, what damage they had done. Turner and his opponent knew only the damage to their own ships, which they could figure from the position charts. Suddenly Moore turned to Turner.

"All your ships are sunk," he said.

"Oh, for Christ's sake," shouted Turner in disgust, and he refused to believe it. Moore finally had to chase Turner off the board. "Then I indirectly just bawled the hell out of Turner," he said. The next day, Turner came around and apologized.

During this tour, Moore and Spruance decided they would take their wives up to northern New England in the fall to see the autumn leaves at the height of their golden glory. It was raining in Newport, but they thought the weather would be better further north and inland, so they drove to Hanover, New Hampshire. They arrived just as the Dartmouth–Holy Cross football game ended, and discovered that they could not even get up Hanover's main street to ask for accommodations at the Hanover Inn—and then they found that they could not find a place to stay in all the little town. Finally they found tourist rooms at Plymouth, stayed overnight, and went on the next day. They drove up Mt. Washington, where the others froze in their heavy coats, but Spruance seemed comfortable enough in his light raincoat.

As they drove back down the mountain, Moore, Mrs. Moore, and Mrs. Spruance were thinking only of stopping at the bottom for a hot meal and a cup of coffee to assuage the pains of the rain and the sharp winds on top of Mt. Washington. At the bottom of the mountain they found a little restaurant and went in. Moore ordered a warming meal, and so did the ladies. Spruance ordered a cream cheese and olive sandwich and a glass of milk. That was his lunch, a sandwich and a glass of milk, and he was not going to change his routine.

In the house on Makalapa, Spruance developed other routines. He did not care much for liquor but he was a connoisseur of coffee.

When the American forces moved into the New Hebrides and New Caledonia, Spruance learned that those places were celebrated for their coffee. He had several bags of green beans sent up to Pearl Harbor to the house on the hill. There the houseboys took charge, except that Spruance supervised the roasting, the grinding, and the brewing of fresh ground coffee beans for breakfast in the mornings.

The stuff was so strong that some tender souls, such as Admiral Nimitz, tried it once and never again. Spruance scoffed at such flowers, and each time an important visitor turned up he would give him a cup. These attentions resulted in many a burned tongue, and many memories by visitors of their kaffeeklatsches on Makalapa.

Soon the coffee and the walks, and his reputation for integrity began to make the chief of staff a legend, comparable to those of Nimitz and Halsey, among the men of the Pacific Fleet.

Chapter
Eight

THE DESPERATE DAYS
OF GUADALCANAL

August 7–October 1, 1942

It was the time of the *kona* weather at Pearl Harbor. The offices in the submarine base were hot and sticky, the fans scarcely stirring the flies that traced tiny lines in the dust on top of the filing cabinets.

Early in the still morning, the officers trooped down to the headquarters, each to his desk or cubicle. Nimitz moved into his office with the big steam pipe rising next to his chair. Spruance was nearby, in an office where he stood at his desk—a special one rigged for him. There was no chair in the office. Visitors came in, stated their business standing, and were quick to move on to some place more comfortable and congenial. Spruance was all business when he was in his office.

Nimitz had a tendency to amble around headquarters in spare moments, dropping in to chew the fat with his officers. One day he

130

might stop for ten minutes at the operations office, pause in the door, and discuss affairs of the day. Or he might go to the public relations office and stop in the threshold, as if he were waiting for an invitation to come in. Then he would start talking. One day he stopped to talk to Commander Drake and Lieutenant Bassett, and they got to discussing the code names that were used at headquarters in talking about places and objectives in the Pacific.

"Take Truk," said Nimitz, grinning a mild grin. "That should be called *cojones*."

And that, of course, was because *cojones* was what Nimitz proposed to have the Japanese by one of those days in the future.

The staff was still small and homogeneous, most of the staff officers still those holdovers from the Kimmel command who had by now adjusted themselves to the easygoing yet demanding ways of Admiral Nimitz. Without a visible exception these officers admired their "boss." His unruffled disposition, his thoughtfulness, even his stern admonitions when necessary—all endeared Nimitz to his staff.

The war plans officer, his assistants, the aviation officer, gunnery officer, Marine, intelligence, communications, medical, supply, public relations, and all the rest had their separate duties, but in their general level of intense activity they were nearly all the same.

In the morning the staff men came to headquarters to read the dispatches that concerned them, dispatches that had come in during the night. They read the papers, the *Star Bulletin* and the *Advertiser*. Then they got down to the task at hand.

Perhaps a submarine was coming in that morning from patrol. The Submarine Squadron (SubRon) bandsmen then straggled down to the dock, lined up, and struck up their welcoming music; the sub's diesels sputtered and blew off blue smoke, the young captain warped her into the dock. Admiral English trotted down to the water's edge and skipped aboard, grinning from ear to ear, for when a sub came back the patrol was never a failure. The public relations photographers came out and began snapping pictures. English disappeared down into the conning tower, and listened to the stories of the boat's adventures in the loneliness of a Japanese sea.

Or a warship would come in and moor, and the officers concerned would get into the big gray Fleet motorboat and ride out into the harbor, over water still smeared with the oils of defeat. The launch would twist its way through the antitorpedo nets and go alongside. The officer would climb the gangway, ask for the captain, and step into his cabin for a cup of coffee. Then, later that day, the captain would come ashore and pay his duty call on Admiral Nimitz, who would question him gently but thoroughly about his operations, what he had seen and done, and why. Perhaps a visiting captain, and certainly a flag officer, would be invited to attend the morning conference, made to feel a part of the Nimitz war in the Pacific.

There would be lunch. Nimitz might be suffering from waistline trouble, and if so, he would go back to the house on Makalapa and rest for a time without eating, then get up a game of tennis or go back to the office. Or he might take a plunge in the pool beside the BOQ, where the Navy nurses giggled in their powder room.

Nimitz was particularly allergic to the nurses. If he could have had his own way there would have been no women at all in the war zone. Each time a nurse became pregnant and had to be sent home, the Nimitz quarters resounded with his views.

The afternoon would be hot and sticky this August, 1942. Nimitz might be asked for an interview by a correspondent or two—more were coming out almost weekly to join the force and don khaki uniforms with the green and white brassard. Nimitz would see them and tell a few stories, bragging about some of his men. The correspondents would go away pleased by their reception, and glad to have seen the admiral. But when they came to writing their stories, they found that Nimitz had really told them very little.

At the end of the workday there would be a social hour, dinner, and then perhaps a movie in a small theater where the air was like "warm consommé," which Lieutenant Bassett suggested bottling and selling to the Campbell soup company. For Nimitz there might be a small, informal dinner party so that he could get to know some of his staff better and assure them, simply by his presence, of his approval; or he would give a dinner in honor of some visiting flag officer, general, politician, or dignitary.

After the movie it was back to the office to read the dispatches, as the duty yeomen moved from room to room, slamming the black-painted windows, shutting out the tradewind clouds and the little breeze that blew up from the harbor.

Every night it was almost the same, and here is Lieutenant Bassett's description.

So it goes. Every night, seven a week; and every day and every month. It's the nearfront business of fighting a war. Just beyond the horizon, plus or minus a thousand miles or so, the fleet is engaging an enemy, we'll say; back here the clatter of typewriters, the clangor of coding machines, the deep buzz of earnest conversation over plotting boards, the whisper behind partitions in secret chartrooms, the moving of pencils across aerographic maps, the drafting of memos that might mean victory or defeat . . . it's a gravely moving synthesis of activity. I like it, although at night and in the dull gray morning I sometimes curse it. I guess we'd better just wipe the sweat off our foreheads and dig in again. Because (Oh Christ, it's right) it is going to last a long, long time . . . .

That's how it was for the staff. For Nimitz there was the added burden of the terrible responsibility, and as August rolled around, the tension grew by the hour.

As the day of the Tulagi-Guadalcanal invasion drew close, Nimitz half expected a Japanese raid on Hawaii or Midway, or both. He had sent three carrier task forces to the South Pacific, leaving only one to protect the Central Pacific. Task Force One—the battleships—would move to Hawaii during August, but was not really ready for battle because it was short of screening ships and air cover. Air strength in Hawaii was inadequate to stop a raid because of the movement of planes to the South Pacific. Even the submarine offensive was suffering, because the submarines were being employed around Truk and in the Aleutians.

One trouble was that after Midway, those unfortunate remarks by one or two officers about the Japanese code had caused the Japanese navy to change the codes. "We are no longer reading the enemy mail," the staff estimate of the situation on August 1 noted dolefully, "and today (August 1) we must depend almost entirely on traffic analysis to deduce enemy deployment."

The trouble was that Japan had so many possibilities. Her strategic situation was still so strong that Nimitz had no way of knowing what the enemy's next move would be. So like the Ensign Nimitz who had curled up on a cot on the deck of his stranded destroyer in 1908, Admiral Nimitz refused to waste time making wild guesses, and got on with the business at hand.

August 7 was D-day at Tulagi—which was regarded as the key in the Solomons campaign. Again, Nimitz waited.

While he waited he turned considerable attention once again to the problem of naval air power. Hanson W. Baldwin, of the Naval Academy class of 1924, military editor of *The New York Times*, was seeking information for a book Secretary Knox was encouraging him to write on air power in a sea war—for Knox was hopeful that Baldwin would thus counteract the influence of Alexander De-Seversky. But much more immediate, and important, was the appointment of Admiral Fitch as commander of naval air forces, Pacific. His would be the responsibility for logistics, placement, and commands in the coming air war.

How Nimitz felt about the Solomons invasion is only obliquely indicated, for one of his great attributes as a fleet commander and admiral was his total self-discipline. He did as his chiefs ordered, without complaint. By the summer of 1942 Nimitz had a new set of bosses, the Joint Chiefs of Staff. The line of command for the United States Navy, then, was: President of the United States, Joint Chiefs of Staff, Commander in Chief (King), Commander in Chief, Fleet (Nimitz, Pacific).

King had been plumping for a South Pacific invasion since February, and in early July the Joint Chiefs, of which he was a member, had agreed on the Solomons campaign. They called it Operation Watchtower. Nimitz called it Operation Shoestring.

Except for requests to King for all the material and weapons he could get, and frank warnings to Ghormley and McCain that they were going to get very little, Nimitz did not have much to say about the strategy here. Once the decision was made by higher authority, Nimitz followed the old axiom of command and he expected his subordinate commanders to do the same, with every possible bit of bravery and gallantry.

The hurry-up nature of the Solomons operation was indicated in a letter Admiral Draemel wrote Nimitz late in July. The First Marine Division (which actually invaded the islands) was to be in the South Pacific by August. The Second and Third Marine Divisions were to be there by December. Fortunately the First Marine Division had been training for several months and the men were toughened up. The Ninth Marine Regiment was still in Camp Pendleton at that point, and when they cleared out, the Amphibious Command would be practically out of business. But in the meantime, several of these Marine regiments due in the South Pacific in *December* had *not yet begun* amphibious training, and several Army regiments were also waiting. Draemel was confused, and no wonder. It was a matter of too far, too fast; but the war would not wait.

For the invasion and the operations, Vice Admiral Ghormley (as noted) was in overall command. Frank Jack Fletcher was in charge of Task Force 16, the expeditionary force, and Rear Admiral Leigh Noyes was in charge of the air support force, or carriers. Rear Admiral Thomas C. Kinkaid had a task force which included the carrier *Enterprise*, whose captain was Arthur C. Davis, lately Nimitz's air officer, who had finally gotten the sea assignment he wanted. Also in this battle from the Nimitz staff were Captain Charles H. McMorris, commander of the cruiser *San Francisco*, and Captain Walter S. DeLany, commander of the cruiser *New Orleans*. McMorris had been operations officer for Kimmel and war plans officer for Nimitz; DeLany had been operations officer for Nimitz. All were being given the chance every naval officer wants, one that Nimitz had wanted himself—a battle command.

Rear Admiral Richmond Kelly Turner was in command of the Amphibious Force, and Rear Admiral McCain had the land-based air. Submarine support was being given out of MacArthur's navy, the Southwest Pacific Force, headed by Rear Admiral Charles A. Lockwood, Jr., the former naval attaché in London who had so itched to avenge the Pearl Harbor disaster. Lockwood's second in command was Captain Ralph W. Christie at Brisbane, a man most instrumental in development of the torpedo the American Navy was then using.

These were fighting men. One of the least known of them—and perhaps the most aggressive of the lot—was Turner. Richmond Kelly Turner had come originally from Portland, Oregon. He was fifth in his Academy class of 1908. He had commanded a destroyer in 1913 and served in battleships during World War I. He had been ashore in ordnance work for three years and had trained as a naval aviator. He had commanded the aircraft squadron of the Asiatic Fleet in 1928 and had been in the plans section of the Bureau of Aeronautics from 1929 to 1931. After his course at the War College, he had served with Spruance on the staff there in the tactical division. Then he had taken command of the cruiser *Astoria*. In 1940 Kelly Turner had gone to the office of the Chief of Naval Operations as director of the war plans division.

He was rough and tough, as Carl Moore remembered him. Moore had come to the war plans division in the summer of 1939 as head of the plans section, and when Admiral Turner came in in October, 1940, Moore was working on the plan called Rainbow Four, which had been assigned by the Joint Army-Navy Board. Turner looked through the work at hand and ordered Moore to work on Rainbow Five, which was the big Navy plan for the Pacific in particular. Moore agreed, but went back to finish Rainbow Four first.

Two or three days later, Turner had come into Moore's office and "chewed him out" as Moore had never been upbraided before. He ordered Moore to stop work on the Four plan and also never to go to the War Department (where Moore had been working part of the time on his plan).

Moore was shaken, but not so upset that he did not recognize Turner's abilities. Within a matter of weeks, Moore said, Turner had Admiral Stark (his boss) and the whole Joint Army-Navy Board swung around to his idea that the plan for the Pacific war was the most important. He was forceful—also "pigheaded and determined," according to Moore. He was so violent in his arguments that other officers of all services would back down rather than quarrel with him.

Whatever else might be said, Turner got things done, and that is what counted with Admiral King, his boss. Turner's method was to drive his subordinates and demand their best. No one seemed to care how he got the job done.

Physically, he was prepared to work around the clock, and did so. He would beetle his brows, curse, and demand answers on short notice from his subordinates.

This rough personality was not the best suited in the world to negotiations with Army officers, and something had to give. It did give in February, 1942. Turner was fired.

Turner was upset, and King knew it. He did his best for this hot-tongued officer who had so much ability, so much drive, and so little control of his emotions. And thus it was that Turner was selected for the very difficult job of running the Navy's first amphibious assault of the war, into Tulagi and Guadalcanal island.

On July 18 Turner raised his flag in the transport *McCawley* in Wellington. Eight days later—somehow—the expeditionary force was assembled in mid-ocean, seventy-five ships. On August 7 this flotilla came moving around Cape Esperance, and the invasion of Guadalcanal began.

The initial landings were relatively easy: a transport was lost and eleven fighter planes and a dive bomber went down. But Vice Admiral Gunichi Mikawa of the Japanese navy had been caught by surprise, and was only beginning to fight. Turner was having a difficult time unloading his transports on the narrow beaches, and he sensed that time was running short. It was. Admiral Mikawa set out with seven cruisers and a destroyer, supported by the land-based air power of the Japanese-held islands nearby. Mikawa planned to rush in and torpedo the American ships lying north of Guadalcanal island, cross the bay to Tulagi, and smash the American ships lying south of that island, then turn to port and dash northeast to retire behind little Savo Island. It was to be done at night. The Japanese were very confident of their abilities as night fighters at sea, and somewhat contemptuous of the American ability to fight at night.

Turner had sent in landing craft from his fifteen transports at Guadalcanal on the first day, and eleven thousand Marines had gone ashore four miles east of Lunga Point. By the second day the

Marines had fought their way into ownership of the airstrip—the reason they were there. The Japanese had only about two thousand troops on the island, most of them laborers, and they did not put up much resistance.

Tulagi had been tougher. The Japanese had fighting men there in number, and the going was rough. Nevertheless Tulagi was secured on August 8, and it appeared that the invasion was a success. But the Japanese under Admiral Mikawa were ready to dispute the case.

The battle that followed was historic, and so complex that Samuel Eliot Morison devoted forty-eight pages to it in Volume V of his *History of United States Naval Operations in World War II*, and later Commodore R. W. Bates of the Naval War College wrote an entire volume on the subject for the use of senior naval officers. Both studies indicated that Savo Island was an example of how not to fight a battle.

First of all, after the Japanese began plowing down on the force, Admiral Fletcher took his carriers away from the area.* (Morison says he seemed determined to take no risks, having lost *Lexington* at Coral Sea and *Yorktown* at Midway.) Then, the sound between Tulagi and Guadalcanal was divided into three sectors. Australian Rear Admiral V. A. C. Crutchley was in charge of the southern force of cruisers and destroyers; Captain Frederick Riefkohl took the northern force of cruisers and destroyers; Rear Admiral Norman Scott had a force of cruisers at the eastern side; and a pair of destroyers covered the west. Unluckily, Admiral Crutchley was called aboard Admiral Turner's flagship as the Japanese were steaming in at twenty-six knots, and there he was when his mixed Australian-American force was challenged to battle.

The Japanese came in through the destroyers—the weakest point. They passed by the destroyer *Blue*, which did not see them,

---

* *Later (as Vice Admiral George Dyer told the author) Nimitz revealed that he had ordered Fletcher to keep his ships in such position that the enemy could never do more damage to him than he could do to the enemy. In the condition of carrier operations in the summer of 1942, the American carriers were incapable of effective night operations, and so the carriers within range of the enemy would be targets that must be defended, and could not be used offensively during the night. Nimitz's orders, in other words, told Fletcher to do precisely what he did.*

and the *Jarvis*, which did not see them either. (She had been damaged in the air attacks of the day before.) Then the Japanese were in among the Allied fleet, having achieved complete surprise. Above the Allies, float planes dropped flares, and the Japanese began to shoot. The first ship sunk was the *Canberra*, the Australian cruiser, her captain killed. The destroyer *Patterson* was hit next and badly damaged. The cruiser *Chicago* was struck by a torpedo and part of her bow was knocked off. Then the Japanese turned and rushed across the bay to hit Riefkohl's force. The cruiser *Astoria* was next, smashed by shellfire. Then came the cruiser *Quincy*, which capsized, and finally the cruiser *Vincennes*, which also capsized and sank. The destroyer *Ralph Talbot* was badly hit in the fight, but managed to make Tulagi. The Japanese retired, fearing the American aircraft carriers, which were nowhere about, and having suffered only minor damage to their cruisers. When the news of the battle reached Fletcher's force at about 0300, Captain Forrest Sherman of the *Wasp* asked Admiral Noyes for permission to take some destroyers and move in at high speed to protect the Turner force, because Sherman's pilots were trained in night operations. But Noyes would not even transmit the request to Fletcher. At dawn the Japanese fully expected a carrier plane attack, but it never came. The only Japanese loss was that of the cruiser *Kako*, that second day, sunk by the American submarine S-44.

At Pearl Harbor, the dispatches that came in were more confusing than anything else. Nimitz knew he had suffered serious losses. He gathered from Ghormley's requests for more aircraft that there was not enough air cover in the Solomons, but there was nothing he could do about it. He was distressed, too, because at this time the destroyer *Perkins* damaged a propeller in the South Pacific and the *Morris* and *Mustin* collided during night exercises with Task Force One off Hawaii. "Although the damage to these DDs was apparently slight," said the estimate, "it further depletes our DD strength at a time when they cannot be spared without embarrassment."

One problem was the faulty intelligence which existed since the security violation that had caused the Japanese to change their naval code. Nimitz did not know where the Japanese carrier force was located, and this bothered him more than anything else in the days just after Savo Island.

Ten days after the battle, Nimitz still did not know what had happened, but he was beginning to get the idea from Ghormley's dispatches that the outcome was serious. He was not very happy. "Our losses were heavy and there is still no explanation of why. The enemy seems to have suffered little or no damage . . . . The food situation there has not yet been cleared up. In fact since the initial landing not much of anything has been done by our Task Forces. And the air under General MacArthur has been of little help except for reconnaissance."

Now began the long and grueling Battle of Guadalcanal on the ground and at sea.

Despite his own orders, Nimitz was becoming queasy about Frank Jack Fletcher. On August 21 Fletcher sent a message saying he must withdraw to fuel on August 24. Cincpac's comment was succinct: "There is plenty of fuel in the vicinity of his force."

That same day, Nimitz heard that two Japanese forces were descending on the Solomons and he knew that an all-out attempt was going to be made to recapture the area.

Fletcher apparently did not have that word. On August 23 he sent Admiral Noyes and the Wasp to a fueling rendezvous far away. Meanwhile the Japanese carriers were fueling on the run, coming in. So the Americans had two carriers at hand, instead of three.

The Japanese had two fleet carriers, a light carrier, an escort carrier, and a seaplane carrier, plus battleships, cruisers, destroyers, and auxiliary ships. In the action that came, the Americans showed that they were learning new carrier techniques. The carrier planes were for the first time controlled by vectoring—that is, by direction from a combat intelligence center which "saw" the positions of planes and ships on radar. The technique was effective. First the carrier Shokaku was slightly damaged. Then the light carrier Ryujo, offered by the Japanese as bait, was sunk. Enterprise, however, took several bombs and went out of action, to fuel again 175 miles southeast of San Cristobal. Morison concludes (Vol. V, pp. 106–107) that it was an American victory, because the Japanese lost a carrier and the Americans did not, and the Japanese failed to reinforce Guadalcanal, which was part of their objective. But he charged "timidity" on both sides.

In Washington, at this time, there was not too much anxiety over the Solomons, despite the heavy losses. Secretary Knox wrote to Nimitz: "The losses incurred to date, while heavy, are not out of proportion with those we must expect to incur as we pass from the defensive to the offensive."

But as the full extent of the losses at Savo Island sank in, and it became apparent that the Japanese were not evaporating from the Solomons, anxiety began to appear in high places.

In the Solomons during the next few days, land-based Marine planes damaged the light cruiser *Jintsu*, and the transport *Kinryu Maru* was sunk. B-17's sank the destroyer *Mutsuki* on August 25. On August 28 dive bombers stopped another Japanese attempt to resupply the islands, sinking one destroyer and damaging two others. But the Japanese sank the fast transport *Calhoun*, and a destroyer landed troops. *Saratoga* took a torpedo from a submarine on August 31. (Admiral Fletcher was wounded.) The "Tokyo Express" of Japanese destroyers carrying troops was running in and out of the Solomons, resupplying the enemy. Early in September the destroyers *Little* and *Gregory* were sunk in a night action. And the fighting was so fierce, the outcome so uncertain, the problems of command so difficult and sometimes confusing, that strong action was indicated.

Early in September, James V. Forrestal, Undersecretary of the Navy, came out to the Pacific to inform himself about the problem, and then went to see Nimitz. He arrived at Pearl Harbor very quietly: Lieutenant Bassett came into the public relations office at 0800 on September 6 and saw a small fellow with a battered face in an open-necked blue shirt pecking away at a typewriter. Bassett thought he was the typewriter repairman. Forrestal had just come back from the South Pacific, and he made a tough speech to workers at the Navy Yard, telling them that Americans had to kill plenty of Japanese and Germans to win the war, and describing the fierce fighting on Guadalcanal. And when Forrestal returned to Washington, he made strong representations for reinforcements in the South Pacific, and for changes in the air establishment.

Guadalcanal had looked like a pushover until the Battle of Savo

Island. But in the second week of August, General Vandegrift knew the struggle was going to be a long, hard one. Admiral Turner had been forced to retire with the transports, and that meant the Marines were alone, while the Japanese for all practical purposes controlled sea and air around the island. The Marines had to hold the island and complete the airfield for the use of fighters and bombers. The Japanese were determined to reinforce the handful of troops they had left on Guadalcanal, and retake the island. On August 17 troops were landed at Tassafaronga. The next day a thousand troops were landed by destroyer near Taivu Point.

The first brutal action was fought at the Tenaru River, and here the Marines faced a banzai charge led by sword-waving officers. They learned the Japanese tricks: it was a night attack, launched at 0130 on the morning of August 21. The Japanese came in, bayonets fixed, shouting and screaming. They tossed grenades over the heads of the Americans to make them think they were surrounded. They charged into and overran positions. They lay down and pretended to be dead, then rose up behind the Marines who passed them by, with rifle and grenade, to kill.

But the Marines held them off that night, and counterattacked the next morning, closing the Japanese into a palm grove on the east bank of the river. In this battle the Marines learned never to trust a "body" unless it was discernibly dead. Thirty-five Marines were killed and seventy-five were wounded, but the ratio was very low, a thousand Japanese died. The pattern of the Pacific war encounters was set here; the Japanese did not surrender, they fought to the death, and by and large the Marines were satisfied with that arrangement.

The deep jungle and the mud and mosquitoes were as much the enemy as the Japanese. It was a new kind of war, even for the Marines, and they quickly learned to improvise. One night, for example, Vandegrift sent a message to Pearl Harbor asking for a hundred gross of a medical article, stipulating the number. The message arrived at Pearl Harbor around 0300 in the morning and the communications watch officer looked up the number. Then he went rushing to wake up Lieutenant Commander Lamar, Nimitz's aide.

What Vandegrift wanted were contraceptives. Contraceptives in the middle of a battle? What in the devil could Vandegrift be thinking of?

Lamar woke, put on his clothes, and went up to Nimitz's house on Makalapa to the little hall bedroom where Fleet Surgeon Gendreau was sleeping. The surgeon shook himself awake and got up to investigate. He came back to report that there were not a hundred gross of contraceptives (14,400) on all Oahu at that moment.

Perplexed, Lamar awakened Admiral Nimitz and stated the problem to him. To Nimitz the light dawned at once.

"Vandegrift is probably going to use these on the rifles of his Marines to keep out the rain," he said. (Which is part of the reason that Nimitz was an admiral.)

Eventually the Marines got their contraceptives, but it took a little time. One of Kelly Turner's serious problems was the confusion in supply and logistics. The transports came in, and spent their time around the beach trying to unload and dodging attacks; they would move out perhaps still half-loaded, as night fell and the Japanese held the waters, and then come back by day. Two weeks after the Guadalcanal landings, Turner was apologizing to Marine General Vandegrift for what seemed like neglect.

We have been greatly handicapped in fixing up cargoes because we could not find out what material most of the ships still had on board. Transport quartermasters were in most cases landed with you and we had to dig information out by patient ship to ship canvass of cargo. Some of the captains did not even have copies of the loading plan, and did not know what was left, because the transport quartermasters took with them the only lists of the cargoes.

The first order of business when Nimitz next met with King in San Francisco on September 7, 1942, was the matter of aviation. It was apparent that carrier and land-based aviation was assuming an ever more important role in this island war. Forrestal and Artemus Gates had been pressing for a more important position in the Pacific command for aviators than that of aviation officer, and Nimitz had accepted the idea. Rear Admiral Towers, Naval Aviator No. 2, would become commander of aircraft of the Pacific Fleet. Nimitz welcomed this coming of an air officer, which would relieve his staff of some of the detail of managing the airplanes. So it was decided that Towers would become a vice-admiral and take the Pearl Harbor job. Fitch, who held that job, would go down to the South Pacific to run air affairs there; and McCain, who was in the South Pacific, would go to Washington to take Towers' old job as chief of the Bureau of Aeronautics.

Towers was only partially pleased with this program. His move was fine, for he had visions of becoming the super-admiral of the fleet—occupying a job something like Yamamoto's in the Japanese navy, with a bevy of carriers under him, and battleships and cruisers and destroyers to support the air forces. He did not, however, want McCain in Washington in his old job—he wanted one of his own boys there. He recommended Ramsey, Davison, or Radford for the post. McCain was not qualified for administrative air work or procurement, he said. Nonetheless, McCain was chosen.

Halsey was finally recovered from his illness, after a long siege that included many weeks in a Virginia hospital. He was itching to get back into action, and Nimitz was eager to have him, even though there were problems. Halsey had the rank of vice-admiral because he had been the senior air officer in the Pacific when he left in June. But so much had occurred in the days since June, that two other officers were really in superior positions: Ghormley as commander of the South Pacific, and Towers, who was to be chief air officer. It was a tribute to Halsey that King and Nimitz so respected him that they agreed to let him keep his three stars, yet be used as a task force commander.

Another command problem was presented by the strong-willed Admiral Theobald in the Aleutians. He had been quarreling with Generals Buckner and Butler over many matters, and King was so annoyed that he had sent Vice Admiral Freeman up north to make an investigation. Freeman came back with a clean bill of health for Theobald. But that did not change the fact that Theobald was stuck in a backwash of the war, or solve the problems of Army-Navy cooperation in the Aleutians.

A few days earlier, Nimitz had moved into a new headquarters up the hill from Ford Island. (The building and swimming pool cost nearly two million dollars and he ordered his staff to figure that cost out in terms of ships and planes it would have supplied, so they would always remember what the war was all about.)

On moving, Nimitz installed the wartime souvenirs and bric-a-brac he was collecting there, including a sign which warned his callers:

1. Is the proposed operation likely to succeed?
2. What might be the consequences of failure?
3. Is it in the realm of practicability of materiel and supplies?

That sign warded off a lot of foolish ideas, as did another, much gaudier, decoration. Nimitz told King about a visit in August from Lieutenant Colonel Evans Carlson, the head of the Marine Raider battalion, and Major James Roosevelt, his second in command. They had brought Nimitz a bloody samurai sword, which Nimitz promptly hung up on the wall beneath another sword, which had been carried by one of the Japanese pilots shot down in the Pearl Harbor raid. But now, in San Francisco, Nimitz gave the sword to King, who presented it to the Naval Academy Museum. He also gave a captured machine gun which went to the Marine Corps Museum.

King and Nimitz were having troubles with General MacArthur, and they discussed the best methods of getting along. They were having more troubles with logistics. On his return from the Pacific, Forrestal had spoken of this problem, and Nimitz asked that Admiral Calhoun, his service corps officer, should have a representative in Washington. It was agreed, but King did note that the supply situation in general was a matter for the desk of the paymaster general who was supposed to be fleet supply officer.

In the talk about personnel, the name of Fletcher came up, and King said he wanted him in Washington for a couple of weeks of temporary duty (which meant he wanted to look Fletcher over). They talked very seriously about the problems at Guadalcanal. The day dispositions, they said, were all right. The night dispositions looked bad. And King asked questions which could not then be answered.

Was the best use made of forces available? Specifically in the question of Savo Island, why were flag officers absent from both groups of cruisers? When Crutchley, Turner, and Vandegrift had met on Turner's flagship that night, all three officers were half sick with fatigue. Why had no consideration been given to this problem of fatigue? And what about Turner's retirement to cover under Ghormley during the Japanese raids, leaving Vandegrift to hold out by himself? Was the surprise attack at Savo Island the result of inefficiency? Anyhow, why were not steps taken to keep the Japanese from getting in?

Nimitz talked about the tactical decisions made, and at the end of the discussion the two admirals agreed on one general thesis: the overall responsibility was Ghormley's. Turner was Ghormley's immediate representative. Final judgment on the fault would be withheld until receipt of completed reports.

On the second day of this King-Nimitz meeting the two admirals got down to the problems of public relations and press dispatches. They were not very happy with General MacArthur's treatment of press matters because it was obvious to them both that he was releasing as news some materials from secret dispatches. Nimitz complained that he was bedeviled by reporters at Pearl Harbor, and that he wanted Elmer Davis, the director of the Office of War Information, to know that he considered any release of war news to the press meant he was giving it directly to the enemy. King was brusque: he fought that battle every day, he said.

They came back, again, to the problems in the South Pacific, the looseness of the operations, the bad planning in refueling, the delay in setting up a new cruiser task force (Task Force 64), and the surprise attack at Savo Island.

With this problem pressing on his mind, Nimitz returned to Pearl Harbor to learn that the Japanese were building up to another major effort to capture Guadalcanal. Major General Kiyotake Kawaguchi staged such an assault on September 12, and it gave Vandegrift some anxious hours. Three days later the carrier *Wasp* was sunk by a Japanese submarine, the battleship *North Carolina* took a torpedo which forced her out of action for the moment, and so did the destroyer *O'Brien*.

At this time came another mild harassment. Lieutenant General Delos Emmons of the Army was commander of Hawaii, and Nimitz got on very well with him. Emmons had just returned from a trip to Brisbane, where MacArthur had his headquarters, and had come back full of MacArthur strategy which he was eager to pass on to Nimitz, "as he is a thorough student of strategy and has been in direct contact for months with the Japanese."

So Emmons wrote Nimitz a letter of good advice. MacArthur was very pessimistic about Guadalcanal, Emmons said. Emmons had asked him what could be done. The best thing, MacArthur had said, was to base the British Indian Fleet in Australia (where it would come under MacArthur's command). The British fleet would then be able to reinforce Ghormley and "carry out its own mission."

Nimitz had best look out, too, said MacArthur, because the Japanese were certain to attack Hawaii in great strength in the near future. It was possible that the attack would come while there was little naval protection there, before the Solomons could be won. On the other hand, MacArthur had soothed, he thought the Japanese would wait until they had isolated the Marine division in the Solomons before taking on Hawaii.

With an almost straight face, Nimitz sent a copy of the letter to King. "While I cannot accept MacArthur's estimate of the Pacific situation, nor Emmons' estimate of MacArthur and the Pacific situation, I believe that you should know what is in the minds of our high army command."

As to himself: "We are far from being downhearted," Nimitz added. "On the contrary, we view the future with optimism and anticipation."

But if Nimitz was optimistic, the same could not be said of all the men of the ships that were fighting the attrition and disease in the South Pacific, or the Navy and Marine fliers who risked their necks hour after hour. Morale was low in the South Pacific, and Nimitz was not quite sure what must be done to set it right and get the operation there moving more quickly.

As Nimitz pondered this problem, he was cheered by Halsey's coming to Pearl Harbor a few days later. The grinning, bouncing Halsey stepped in to help out with the air commander's duties until Towers arrived. "In a most energetic manner"—that's how Nimitz described Halsey's work.

Towers was spending his last few days in Washington, trying desperately to get to see King and have his air captains promoted to flag rank before he moved away from the seat of power. But he was unsuccessful, he noted ruefully. He was more successful in another request. He asked that Forrest Sherman be made available to him as chief of staff when he took over as commander of aircraft in the Pacific. Lucky for Sherman, for the captain who loses his ship (the carrier *Wasp*) no matter the gallantry or the cause, runs the serious risk of being put on the beach and far away from the action. Sherman was being moved up, instead, to a job of great importance even if it was a staff job.

Nimitz was agreeable. He had more important things on his mind at that juncture—for he was just getting ready to make an inspection trip to the South Pacific, to see if he could get to the bottom of the fleet's troubles there. Had he seen the current issue of *Collier's*, he might not have been so happy with Towers or his coming. *Collier's* had long prided itself on its "air-mindedness"; it had offered the Collier air trophy and supported aviation actively for many years. At this point *Collier's* lamented editorially that it had taken Towers so long to move into a command post. "It shows in the experience of one man why we are not winning the war faster."

There was a very definite tendency on the part of some air enthusiasts to believe the airplane and its auxiliaries were the only weapons that counted.

Not all airmen were so single-minded. McCain and Fitch, for example, were naval officers first, then airmen, and they did not belong to the group of Young Turks, led by Towers, who hoped to take over the Navy.

On September 24 Nimitz and members of his staff left Pearl Harbor and flew to Palmyra to confer with the returning McCain. Also present at the meeting were Colonel Pfeiffer, the Marine officer, and Captain Ralph Ofstie, the aviation officer of Cincpac.

Nimitz talked about various air problems. He wanted McCain's advice on the use of the New Zealand air force, which was itching for action. Nimitz wanted to feed their pilots into American squadrons, because he did not have the planes to provide them with their own materiel. Then, knowing he was going south, he asked McCain: "What shall I look into down there?"

McCain: The first thing is to get as many reserve planes up

to BUTTON [Espiritu Santo] as you can. CACTUS [Guadalcanal] cannot handle any more planes right now but you have to be ready to feed them in all the time. Aviation gasoline supply at CACTUS is the present most critical question.

They talked of other problems of logistics. Then Nimitz got down to personnel.

NIMITZ: How is Noyes?

McCAIN: All right, just suffering a little from the blast. [Noyes was nearly killed in the torpedoing of the *Wasp*.]

NIMITZ: How about Fletcher? We are going to give him a blow [rest] on the mainland.

McCAIN: I was going to write you about him but I didn't. Two or three of these fights are enough for any one man. A rest will do him good.

NIMITZ: Is there anything else?

McCAIN: I want to emphasize the aviation gas supply and relief for pilots at CACTUS. We can fly VF [fighters] up but not back. It is a one way wind. The Marine VF pilots are very tired. A relief for them is there now and the SBD [dive bomber] pilots will be next. They have had no rest; they are just tired. They had to work during the day and could get no sleep at night.

The Marines are not worried about holding what they have on CACTUS but you have got to stop the Japs coming in. On these moonlight nights we will try torpedoes but we haven't many of them. We lost two SBDs trying to bomb ships at night. Harmon has been working on a new method for the B-17. He is going to have them come in "weaving" at low altitude and then straightening out just before the drop. Harmon says a new field of employment for B-17s is necessary because of the big investment in material and personnel that has been put in them. We are developing a new night sight.

NIMITZ: How about the Norden sight?

OFSTIE: It is a high altitude bomb sight for above 6000 feet.

McCAIN: The B-17 pilots are good. They will come down but doctrine keeps them up. I saw the pictures of REKATA BAY where they strafed and destroyed five seaplanes on the water.

Another one strafed a combatant ship. I saw the pictures and you could see the Japs falling right over on the deck. He made two passes before the ship fired at him. During the third they opened up on him and he left with about 20 or 30 holes in him but he got back all right . . . .

In trying to discover what was wrong with Fletcher, Nimitz had asked McCain to make some inquiries. On his way back to Washington McCain saw Fletcher at San Diego and did just that. He reported, in a letter:

My Dear Nimitz:

I talked with Fletcher. He said he was very concerned and very apprehensive as to the location and character of service of his Task Group, both before the hit [Saratoga] and until arrival at Pearl. Also very tired. He added that he was in good shape and rested now and after a little leave would be ready to go in again. He did appear to be in good shape except for a slightly strained expression about the eyes, which you have become so accustomed to seeing in the eyes of others returning from active operations. I told him that he should not ask to go on another detail unless he felt at his best; that he owed that both to himself and to the job. He thought this over for a while and said, "You are right, I will take as long a leave as I can get, and if I feel my best will ask to go again and I am sure I will." I feel he should be taken at his word.

So Fletcher was to have a blow. For how long would depend on what King saw and what King thought in those two weeks of temporary duty in Washington—for that was why Fletcher was being ordered back. Somehow he seemed to be the unluckiest of admirals; he had participated in more major operations than any other carrier admiral (although he was not an aviator); every one of them except Midway had gone a little sour; and in the case of Midway Spruance came out with the glory.

McCain also had a sense of humor, which he revealed in the next paragraph of his letter to Nimitz.

I talked with Admiral King by telephone and asked him to find 50 high altitude VF [fighters] and put them on board ship bound for the South right away. He yelled into the phone, "That's your business—that is why I brought you back." If he meant that, which I doubt, I will surely get them.

My very best to you.

It was a friendly little ending—they both knew their commander in chief—whose propensity for shouting transcended Main Navy, for King, stern taskmaster with himself, was equally stern with all about him. Indeed, it was said around Main Navy yard that you always knew when you were doing a good job if you worked for King, because he only grunted at you.

On his way south, then, Nimitz knew that one of his problems was solved. Fletcher would not be back soon, which opened a nice, big hole for Halsey to step into with no complications. It was enough to make a commander in chief sigh with relief.

On September 28 Nimitz was aboard Ghormley's flagship, the USS *Argonne*, in Nouméa harbor. With Nimitz were Captain Ofstie, his aviation officer, and Colonel Pfeiffer, his Marine officer. Ghormley was present with Captain Callaghan, his chief of staff, and Turner was there. So were Generals Arnold, Harmon, Sutherland, Street, and Kenny, representing various aspects of the Army, from MacArthur to the Air Corps.

Nimitz opened the meeting: "The purpose of my visit is to inform myself and members of my staff with conditions in the Sopac area; and to inform myself on the problems of Admiral Ghormley and General MacArthur. We will begin the conference by having Ghormley or Harmon outline the situation in this area. . . ."

GHORMLEY: As you know, we are now occupying the CACTUS and RINGBOLT area [Guadalcanal and Tulagi] with one division plus a regiment. On CACTUS we are holding only a small area which Turner or Harmon can describe for you. Our forces and position there is under constant pressure. Logistic supply is most difficult. We can send in only one ship at a time and from the eastward there is only one channel. Most of the Japs in the area are on CACTUS, but Vandegrift reports that most of those previously to the east and south are now gone. By recent report he has surrounded a group to the westward, but he has not yet reported how many he has caught in his bag. The Japs are still getting in despite our air activity. Nobody knows exactly how many are on CACTUS right now.

We have lost 3 APDs [converted destroyer transports] and one, the *Stringham*, has to go to the yard. We have no craft for raids on enemy positions since we lost those APDs.

At RINGBOLT [Tulagi] there have been no enemy raids but there have been several bombings and bombardments. Our dive bombing against enemy night attacks by surface vessels has not been successful. There is a tricky 45 knot wind and although our aircraft have turned back their destroyers on some nights, no hits have been made . . . .

. . . One AK [naval cargo vessel] can go into RINGBOLT harbor, but the Japs know the area perfectly and are able to bombard from close to the foul area. One time they had only 10,000 gallons of aviation gas left."

TURNER: 5,000.

NIMITZ: Is that the time you turned back and later went in?

TURNER: Yes.

GHORMLEY: McCain sent in a tender with aviation gasoline. One ship could spend only six hours unloading in the two days it was there. The rest of the time it was dodging bombers . . . .

So it went—Nimitz asking his pointed questions, and not stopping until he got answers.

There was another meeting on October 2, concerned first with amphibious operations. In the interim, Draemel had been sent back from San Diego to Washington for temporary duty with King—and he had been sent to the Fourth Naval District in Philadelphia. For all practical purposes the Pacific Fleet Amphibious Force was dissolved, left in the hands of a captain on Draemel's staff. In October Admiral Turner proposed to establish an amphibious training group in the Southwest Pacific area. Nimitz told his admirals what he wanted: all-weather airfields, plenty of storage for aviation gas, good housing for pilots (Quonset huts, not tents).

He addressed himself to Ghormley: "I want you to go up and see conditions for yourself. Callaghan can take care of things here while you are away. I am going to ask Holcomb to go up there and I want you to go up there not later than the time he does."

He snapped out more directions.

Improve cargo handling facilities.

Complete all-weather roads.

Provide good repair services for planes. "Planes are too expensive and too hard to get to let only minor damage render them permanently unserviceable."

At Guadalcanal Turner was to have at least two heavy ships, bow and stern moorings, with nets around them for torpedo protection. They would also move PT boats into the area.

He wanted a salvage tug in the area.

He wanted good communications, and he would send Captain John Redman, Cincpac communications officer, to help put it in.

Nimitz said he wanted to talk about the future, after consolidation in the Solomons. Originally the operations plan had called for the building of airfields on adjacent islands and consolidation of port facilities—but Nimitz and King had junked the old Task Two and Task Three, and were reworking the operational plan. But first, Nimitz said, Colonel Pfeiffer had some matters to take up.

Pfeiffer spoke about the need for labor battalions for Guadalcanal. Turner did not want to use CB's (men of the construction battalions). Nimitz asked if they could get natives from Malaita. Ghormley said it sounded like "blackbirding." Nimitz asked if the Army had labor battalions. Pfeiffer said yes, and Pfeiffer and Turner went off into a technical discussion about getting and using labor.

Nimitz put a stop to it. "That is enough discussion on that question. We must get our own labor battalions out here. I think we can get some good material down south."

PFEIFFER: The next question is to reduce weight of landing mat bundles from 5000 to 2000 pounds.

TURNER: The only way to do that is to have it done in the States where they are first bundled. To repack here would take too much time and labor and would ruin lots of mat. Arnold said he would arrange that.

NIMITZ: Perhaps we should remind him of it. What else do you have, Pfeiffer?

They went on to discuss radio and coast watchers, unloading procedures, and IFF equipment. Captain Ofstie said the problem was to get the technicians to keep the IFF equipment operable.

NIMITZ: Ghormley, you tell Harmon to get the necessary qualified personnel out to the bases.

Next question was the mail, Pfeiffer said.

NIMITZ: Yes, that is an important and serious question. If we can get mail to the men, it boosts morale. What is the situation?

The problem was maintaining secrecy about ship movements.

NIMITZ: . . . I realize the need for secrecy of ship movements. I suggest you get one man from each ship and have him look out for his ship's mail. He will find out how to get it to his ship or they will find out why. Every ship can afford one man for this important duty. Ofstie, you look into the mail situation further and let me know what should be done.

They talked about Ghormley's communications officer. Ghormley said he was fine. Nimitz indicated he thought the officer was a technician and not a man of broad view. Ghormley was stubbornly loyal to his officer. Turner broke in to say *he* certainly wanted an experienced communications officer on his staff, and asked Nimitz to send him one (which made Ghormley look foolish, since Nimitz had earlier indicated that Ghormley's man was inexperienced).

The others began a technical discussion of fuel and storage.

CALLAGHAN: . . . so called Spooner projects about which we know little . . . .

NIMITZ: Those are details I can't and don't intend to settle . . . . I want now to hear about future operations.

GHORMLEY: First, we must get CACTUS stabilized. That will be a big job and will take time. Then we are going to occupy Ndeni where we will build airfields. That will extend our search 325 miles and will be a great help. We are now going into the Ellice group at Funafuti.

The next step will be to Rabaul. How this is to be done is an open question. MacArthur wants to take a lot of airfields and bomb out Rabaul. I think he should go ahead and clean out New Guinea first. He has not filled in for us his plan for getting from his present position to Rabaul.

We have to neutralize the Solomons. We have to go up that chain of islands. If the Japs make a maximum effort there, we can't stop them. The purpose of the Japs going into the Gilberts I first did not know whether was for the offensive or the defensive. I now think it was for a defensive purpose. They might try to make a diversion for us down here by going against Hawaii. I think they have in the Rabaul area from 15,000 to 60,000 troops.

TURNER: Five divisions.

Ghormley was miring himself deeper and deeper as the conversation continued. He had accepted MacArthur's estimate, which Nimitz refused; he was indicating defeatism, which Nimitz could not bear; he did not have such details as the realistic appraisal of the Japanese situation. Turner did.

GHORMLEY: A Jap division has about 15,000 men, so that would make about 75,000 there. In Bougainville they have many troops at both ends of the island but I don't know exactly how many.

NIMITZ: How many ships does it take to move a Jap division?

TURNER: About two-thirds of what it takes us.

GHORMLEY: I think they would use large landing boats to make a move against CACTUS. If they use larger ships, Turner's estimate of two-thirds of ours is about correct . . . .

NIMITZ: But their movements by small boats have not been successful.

[Deeper and deeper and deeper.]

TURNER [obviously trying to pull Ghormley out of it]: They lost about 20 percent but they are still fighting offensively on CACTUS.

NIMITZ: I know that, but they still have the momentum of unchecked offensive, they have the morale, and they have the bases from which to operate.

Turner now began to speak very strongly and forthrightly to his fleet commander.

TURNER: They are better trained.

NIMITZ: Yes, but there certainly are reasons why they have not come against CACTUS in greater strength.

TURNER: I haven't changed my mind since what I told you when I saw you in San Francisco [at the summer King-Nimitz conference]. I said then that Guadalcanal could be easily taken but that it would be costly. It has been costly. We have not made further progress on CACTUS due to our ignorance and lack of skill.

The previous schemes were to pull the Marines and go ahead. But they only have a five mile square area now. The troops there have to clean up the place and extend their lines so we can get another airfield area. They want relief by the Army and to go back for reorganization, rest and replacements. I want enough forces there, and light forces, and more iron to throw out the Japs. I want to get another trained outfit with boats, to build up the air strength, and to go ahead with new troops.

We can't go ahead with a single line because it could be too easily cut off. We must have supporting positions to keep it going. We must have the situation in hand at CACTUS to use it for a spring board. The Marines now there must stay there.

They are veterans and a valuable force. We must get our other forces trained. Many of our losses came from lack of training.

Nimitz asked about the Army forces coming.

It would be the 43rd Division, but except for one regimental combat team which was ready, the others were going to Auckland for training.

Nimitz asked about Patch's troops, but Ghormley said only one regiment was trained for combat. Nimitz asked Ghormley if he had authority to move Army troops where he wanted, and Ghormley said he would take that authority—the first statement he had made of which Nimitz thoroughly approved. But when Nimitz asked about New Zealand troops, Ghormley bogged down in a discussion about the problems.

NIMITZ: If we can't find a formula for using them, it is Japan's gain. We should use all resources that are available to us.

Ghormley was not sure that all the leadership of New Zealand was agreed to fight under American control.

NIMITZ: Well, let's get it into the record. Ask them, and if they refuse it will be in the record for the peace conference. They know that. We must overcome the obstacles in the way of how and where to employ them.

Ghormley was not sure the New Zealanders were well enough trained to hold.

NIMITZ: Well, don't put them in a place where they can lose the war for us. But there must be some place where we can use them. However, that is a detail I won't go into. That is your job to find out. I repeat again that to win this war, we must use every resource we have.

I agree that no change is to be made in the troops at CAC-TUS until the position there is secure. No other thought has ever been in my mind. I have a high regard for the Marines up there and I can't agree that they are so inexperienced. They have handled everything the Japs had. Now they are not able to spread their influence very far because of lack of means of communications such as roads and trails to move troops and tanks. They have to cut roads through the jungle to move their tanks . . . .

How about the Raiders? he asked.

TURNER: The Raiders and the parachute troops of the 1st Division are shot. They will have to come out to rebuild. I am against the use of the 2nd Raiders on Guadalcanal.

NIMITZ: Well, you see about using New Zealand and Army troops.

Ghormley broke in to discuss a dispatch he had received in *August* from King, speaking for the Joint Chiefs of Staff. The Joint Chiefs had wanted Ghormley to supply a plan and schedule for further operations against the Japanese south and east of Rabaul. Ghormley had not answered.

"I feel that our present operations have not yet reached a point where such plan and schedule would be worthwhile," he said.

This omission represented a command failure of the most serious type. King and the Joint Chiefs were not unaware of the difficulties at Guadalcanal, but they still wanted ideas from Ghormley, who was on the scene, to compare with ideas being generated at MacArthur's headquarters. Ghormley's indecision, his fumbling, was becoming a serious problem.

Nimitz asked Ofstie what he knew, and Ofstie had a proposed directive on the subject for issue by Cincpac.

NIMITZ: We can't consider that proposal in the five minutes we have left. Ofstie, give Ghormley a copy of the proposal and Ghormley, you send us your comments and recommendations on it.

I repeat again—if we can't use our allies, we are Goddamned fools.

Chapter
Nine

THE COMING OF
HALSEY

October 5–31, 1942

Nimitz returned tired and troubled from the South Pacific. The twelve-day trip had been grueling, in many ways. They had left Pearl Harbor on Thursday, September 24, in a Coronado flying boat. One engine of the plane had failed, and after they limped into Palmyra the plane was sent back to Pearl and another was substituted for the next leg of the trip. They had flown to Canton Island on Saturday, September 26, and Nimitz had inspected the installations and conferred with the British resident. There were meetings as described, especially that of September 28, when they flew to Nouméa, where the vital meeting with Ghormley had lasted from 1615 in the afternoon until 2015 that night. On Tuesday Nimitz had inspected the facilities in the Nouméa area along with Major General Patch, the commander of the Army forces in New Caledonia, and others. He had visited the Ile Nou naval air base. Rear

Admiral Murray, commander of Task Force 17, had called. Nimitz had made a presentation of the Navy Cross to Admiral Turner, and at 1320 in the afternoon had flown to Espiritu Santo, arriving at 1700. There he had talked to Admiral Fitch and given out medals, a Distinguished Service Medal to Fitch, two Navy Crosses to marines, two Distinguished Flying Crosses for naval pilots.

Next day there was another inspection trip, and then the party went to the Army air field. A young captain met them there, and discovered that he was to take this distinguished party to Guadalcanal. He did not know there was a four-star admiral in the area, for the security of Nimitz's trip had been carefully maintained.

They took off in a B-17 at about 1630 that afternoon. An hour out, the plane encountered heavy weather, and soon the pilot admitted he was quite lost.

Captain Ofstie was riding up front with the aircrew. He went back to find Lieutenant Commander Lamar, because he remembered that Lamar, a born aide, had brought along a National Geographic map of the South Pacific. Lamar dug into his bag and found it, and with this guide, Ofstie navigated the B-17 into Henderson field. That night a rather shaken party spent the evening with General Vandegrift and his officers.

At 0630 the next morning Nimitz was up and about, awarding medals at an assembly in the bamboo grove in front of Vandegrift's quarters. Navy Crosses were awarded to Vandegrift, General Rupertus, Colonel Edson, and Lieutenant Colonel Carlson of the Raiders, and three young Marine officers, including Marion Carl, the pilot.

Then came the moment when Nimitz gave a Navy Cross to a hulking sergeant, who might have weighed 250 pounds. Lamar read the citation, for bravery, far beyond the call of duty, and Nimitz reached up to pin on the medal—whereupon the sergeant fell over in a dead faint. Vandegrift was very upset. When the Marine came to he said he was sorry but he had never seen a four-star admiral before and he was scared to death.

Nimitz was the "Jonah" again. Trying to take off from Guadalcanal, the big plane skidded and slid to the end of the runway. Nimitz and party were forced to wait several hours until the part of the field not covered by Marston netting dried out. (Obviously, first-hand experience caused him next day to start talking about the need for all-weather airfields.) The Nimitz party was further delayed that day when a coast watcher on another island reported Japanese bombers heading their way. The bombers never arrived but Nimitz took the extra hours to go forward and visit the Marine lines and finally got away at 1300, returning to Espiritu Santo, where he presented another Navy Cross, to Major James Roosevelt of Carlson's Raiders.

The next day he flew back to Nouméa for what became the fateful talk with Ghormley, then on October 3 went to Fiji (Suva) making aerial reconnaissance of the Nandi area, and later of Wallis and Hull islands. He was back in Pearl Harbor at noon on October 5, Monday, and at his desk.

Nimitz was troubled because he was worried about morale in the South Pacific and particularly about Ghormley, who seemed to Nimitz to be unable to face the obstacles and enemy strength.

But worried as he was about Ghormley's performance, Nimitz hoped for the best. He had indicated to Ghormley what he must do, and in his thoughtful way, he was rooting for the man to do it.

On October 8 he sent Captain Redman to the South Pacific, bearing a letter to Ghormley. Halsey, accompanied by Admiral Calhoun, the service force commander, and Spruance, would be coming down to Nouméa, he said. Halsey would visit the area first, and then join Task Force 16 as commander, and also as senior Pacific Fleet task force commander in the area. Halsey, Nimitz, said, would be subject to Ghormley's operational control as long as he was in the South Pacific. Kinkaid was to relieve Murray in command of Task Force 16, and new captains would be coming for other ships. Fletcher was supposed to come back in November with Task Force 11, but if he did not, then Frederick Sherman would take the task force.

Nimitz spoke a little bit about ships and task force deployment, gently critical of Murray, who was staying too far away from Guadalcanal to take advantage of opportunities in the Solomons. He also wanted the battleship *Washington* moved closer to the fighting area. And he disapproved of the plan of keeping another task force south and southeast of Guadalcanal, too far away. He wanted this force moved west and south of Cape Esperance, which might be open to air attack, but he wanted Ghormley to accept the risk so he could strike the enemy.

Ghormley had indicated that he would reinforce Guadalcanal with an Army regiment, and Nimitz approved. He was not sure King would approve of his, Nimitz's, advice—King might think Nimitz too reckless—so he sent a copy of the letter to King. He promised Ghormley every assistance, urged him to visit Guadalcanal (which he had not done) and see for himself.

"In closing," Nimitz said, "let me again urge you to take such calculated risks as may be warranted in order to continue the attrition which we are now inflicting on the enemy's sea and air force."

Nimitz was very understanding of Ghormley's problems. He said he was pleased with the accord between Army, Navy, and Marines in the area, and he cautioned Ghormley to do everything possible to maintain the accord. "Tempers worn thin by fatigue and loss of sleep break out easily. Patience and tolerance on the part of all hands will help preserve that unity of purpose and good will that is so essential to success."

But Nimitz was not soft. The steel fist was there in the velvet glove. "I wish you to include in your final report on the Savo Island Battle of 8–9 August your opinion as to the responsibility for the dispositions and actions of that night. Such a blow cannot be passed over, and we owe it to the country to do our best to fix the responsibility for that disaster, and to take the action necessary to prevent a recurrence." Which, in simple English, meant that some head was going to roll.

On October 11 Admiral Scott was patrolling not far from Cape Esperance, with orders from Ghormley to seek offensive action against the enemy. (Nimitz's letter had apparently reached home.) That night Scott engaged the Japanese in the Battle of Cape Esperance. The Americans lost the destroyer *Duncan*, the cruiser *Boise* was badly damaged, and the *Salt Lake City* was damaged. The Japanese lost the heavy cruiser *Furutaka* and the destroyer *Fubuki*, and two more destroyers were sunk the next day. The cruiser *Aoba* was badly hit and the commander of the Japanese force, Admiral Goto, was mortally wounded.

The victory was excellent for American morale, but it did not prevent the Japanese from achieving their end: the Japanese force was escorting ships loaded with troops and guns to throw at the Marines in the Solomons.

Two days later the Japanese began their monthly attempt to recapture Guadalcanal. It opened with bombardment of Henderson field by the battleships *Kongo* and *Haruna*, knocking out forty-eight of the ninety American planes on the field. On October 14, the Japanese sent six transports down the slot, escorted by destroyers and fighter planes, and they unloaded in the full light of the next day, while nothing could be done for several hours until gas was found (even by siphoning it out of B-17's on the island) and fighters managed to destroy three of the transports and drive the others away.

By October 15 Nimitz had this to say: "It now appears that we are unable to control the sea in the Guadalcanal area. Thus our supply of the position will only be done at great expense to us. The situation is not hopeless but it is certainly critical." The next day even that old optimist Secretary Knox was not sure the Americans could hold on, and said so to a reporter from *The New York Times*.

The trouble was that the problems were just not being solved, and Nimitz had the feeling that time was running out. On October 15 he conferred with various members of his staff on the question of Ghormley. They believed—and he did too—that Ghormley was simply not aggressive enough. Nimitz sent King a dispatch asking for permission to relieve Ghormley, and received permission that night. Next morning he made the decision, and on October 18, when Admiral Halsey arrived at Nouméa to look over the area where he expected to operate a task force, he was suddenly informed that he was taking over the whole South Pacific.

Halsey had flown to Nouméa accompanied by Captain Miles Browning, his chief of staff, and Colonel Julian Brown of the Marine Corps, his intelligence officer. The plane settled down on Nouméa harbor at 1400, and a whaleboat came alongside. Halsey stepped aboard and an officer handed him a sealed envelope. Halsey opened it. Inside was another sealed envelope, marked SECRET, and inside that were his orders.

"Jesus Christ and General Jackson!" Halsey exclaimed. "This is the hottest potato they ever handed me!"

In a way, the choice of Halsey to command the South Pacific

seemed odd, for he was known in the fleet as a hard-fighting, hard-playing, devil-may-care commander, who was at his best under conditions that another admiral might have called desperate.

Halsey was a Navy man from a seagoing family of at least five generations, starting with Captain Eliphalet Halsey, who sailed the first Sag Harbor whaler around Cape Horn. Halsey's father had entered the United States Naval Academy in 1869, and retired finally with the rank of captain. His son, William F. Halsey, Jr., was a member of the class of 1904 at the Academy, a year ahead of Nimitz. This class was also the class of Kimmel and David Bagley, two other distinguished Navy men. Halsey was very active in Academy life, and stood about the middle of his class academically —which indicated his personality and interests. He held more class offices before he was finished than any but one other man, and he was, without a doubt, the most popular man in the class. "A real old salt . . . . Looks like a figurehead of Neptune . . . . Everybody's friend. . . ."—so the class yearbook described him.

As an ensign he served on the battleship *Kansas* when she went on the famous round-the-world cruise as one of twenty-one ships of the Great White Fleet. He was promoted very quickly to full lieutenant, and then spent most of the next twenty-three years in torpedo boats and destroyers. A real old salt, indeed. But in those twenty-three years there were other experiences, a hitch in naval intelligence in Washington, and another in the sensitive post of naval attaché to the American embassy in Berlin. He had been commander of the receiving ship *Reina Mercedes* at the Naval Academy, and when that ship was made headquarters for the little aviation detachment at Annapolis, Halsey became an aviation enthusiast. In the spring of 1930 Admiral Richardson, then chief of the Bureau of Navigation, had learned of Halsey's interest and offered him a chance at flight training. But Halsey could not pass the physical examination. Instead he went to the Naval War College at Newport, and the next year to the Army War College at Washington. At the one institution, Halsey studied naval campaigns; at the other he studied high strategy of wars. And then, in 1934, Admiral King, who was chief of the Bureau of Aeronautics, offered Halsey command of the carrier *Saratoga* if he would take the aviation observers' course at Pensacola. Halsey was then fifty-one years old.

Halsey did better than that, he took the pilot's course, having sneaked in under the wire in another guise. The stratagem worked, and somehow without passing the physical examination, Halsey was qualified as a pilot. How good a pilot—well—his instructor, later Admiral Bromfield Nichol, recalled the mysteries of Halsey's flying: "The worse the weather, the better he flew." But he could fly and he did fly.

After two years in *Saratoga*, Halsey was made commander of the Pensacola school and base. He was made rear admiral in 1936, and two years later became commander of Carrier Division 2, which included the carriers *Yorktown* and *Enterprise*.

Then and later, in command of Carrier Division One, Halsey was instrumental in the development of carrier techniques. One, for example, was the use of a single wavelength for all scout planes of a carrier force, so that all carriers would be told when the enemy was sighted.

When war came, he had been in charge of Task Force 2, when he split off from Milo Draemel, calling his carrier *Enterprise*, three cruisers, and nine destroyers Task Force 8.

Halsey had been sent with this force to support the Wake relief operation, and he never did learn why the task was called off. But then came the Marshalls raid, and Halsey was in the thick of the war.

From the beginning of the war, Halsey had endeared himself to the men of his task force and to the sailors of the whole fleet by his flamboyant gestures. On the last day of January, 1942, Halsey was fueling *Enterprise*, preparatory to the attack on the Marshalls, when a Japanese patrol plane came by. He watched on the radar screen as the blip closed on the force—then moved away without sending an alarm. Immediately Halsey called his Japanese language officer and prepared a message of defiance: "From the American admiral in charge of the striking force, to the Japanese admiral on the Marshall islands. It is a pleasure to thank you for having your patrol plane not sight my force."

Next day, planes from the *Enterprise* dropped copies of this leaflet on the islands, and of course the men who prepared, printed, and delivered it spread the word throughout the fleet.

Halsey was the fighting admiral. He was the one chosen to lead the carriers *Enterprise* and *Hornet* on the ticklish and dangerous Tokyo raid. He came back to Pearl Harbor just too late to make the Battle of the Coral Sea, and then returned sick with nervous dermatitis, to go into the hospital.

Now he had been handed what he called the "hot potato" of the Pacific war.

There was little doubt about the difficulties ahead. Back in Pearl Harbor, Nimitz was preparing for action. He wanted Kinkaid to relieve Murray in Task Force 17, and Frederick Sherman to command another task force. He would have Fletcher back, if Fletcher was ready "in all respects" to return to sea. "If you feel that Fletcher needs a longer period of rest," he wrote King, "I suggest that he be trained ashore in some capacity . . . ."

Leigh Noyes was holding the fort for Towers as commander of aircraft in the Pacific, but would then be a spare flag officer, and Nimitz suggested Noyes might be sent elsewhere since he would have C. P. Mason and Dewitt Ramsey as spare flag officers.

In the South Pacific the coming of Halsey was greeted on the decks of the ships and in the mud of Guadalcanal with cheers. Now, said the Americans fighting there, they would go someplace. What Halsey did was bring a new morale to dispirited men, and immediately he began to change the atmosphere from the gray of defeatism to the brightness of hope. The change was electric.

"I early placed emphasis on the principle of unity of command," he said. "I insisted that each commander of a task force must have full authority over all components of his force, regardless of service or nationality. I believe the wholehearted efforts of all hands to create one South Pacific fighting team prove the key to success in overcoming the many obstacles in the conduct of later operations, involving the use of Task Forces of varied composition."

Halsey set out to unify. His slogan was "Kill Japs, Kill Japs, Kill More Japs," and no one in the South Pacific forgot it. The slogan was painted on buildings, and hung over the fleet landing at Tulagi. In his correspondence he usually closed with the remark.

He set about establishing relations with MacArthur in the south, and with Admiral Thierry D'Argenlieu, the French governor, up on the hill of Nouméa. There was much difficulty with the French, because the New Caledonian colonials were divided between adherence to Vichy and DeGaulle, and DeGaulle insisted that the French forces on the island retain their independence and aloofness. There was, after all, a strange relationship between France and Japan that affected Indochina, where the Japanese were garrisoned but the French still ruled in theory. Except for some matters concerning supply and housing, however, the French of New Caledonia were only an irritant—or social companions.

Halsey set up shop in the Japanese consulate and began building confidence. Part of his formula, "though not exactly good copy, was the principle of a bottle of Scotch on the table always bore fruit in our dealings with other commands." It was not just the whiskey—Halsey charmed his guests, and soon after beginning to listen, they learned that he knew what he was talking about. Halsey had never considered this type of command for himself. In the winter of 1941, when Admiral Nimitz in the Bureau of Navigation had written him about his next assignment, and asked how he would like to command the Norfolk Navy Yard, Halsey had replied that he was completely skeptical about his ability to handle an industrial establishment. What he wanted was a sea command. Now he had everything: diplomatic relations, interservice relations, supply stations, repair stations, camps, clubs, hospitals, an entire military establishment. All this was thrown at Halsey on October 18.

Two days later, Nimitz was writing new instructions. He intended to send to the South Pacific for each carrier one battleship, two heavy cruisers, one light cruiser, one antiaircraft cruiser, and a full squadron of destroyers, Nimitz said. But Halsey could use these forces otherwise. Nimitz suggested the employment of two carriers and four antiaircraft cruisers in one force. Two days after that Nimitz was writing again, asking for reports on the loss of the destroyer *Meredith* on October 15, and the failure of the *Portland* and the *Porter* to "complete destruction" of Japanese forces they encountered in actions of October 15 and 22.

Nimitz wanted to be sure that Halsey was *fighting*. There was a feeling in the Navy Department that commands and commanders must be very carefully looked over. "I am tremendously pleased over the results of your quick trip of inspection to the Solomons area," Secretary Knox wrote Nimitz. He went on:

> While I have the highest possible regard for Admiral Ghormley, I had repeated reports of his physical condition, which gave me a great deal of anxiety and I am satisfied that you acted most wisely and with the most admirable initiative in ordering Halsey to relieve him. It was most unfortunate that the brilliant success which attended the initiation of the Solomons Island expedition was followed by a period of what, at this distance, looked like indecision in employing the forces at our disposal and the complete lack of offensive use of our surface craft until Norman Scott's very successful raid north of Savo Island.

Knox said he knew one could not gauge an officer's battle competence and personal courage until he had been tested. He could understand the feeling of fair play that would prompt Nimitz or others to give an untried man a chance. But, said the Secretary, "in a war on so vast a scale as this, and with such vital issues concerned, just treatment of an individual must yield to higher considerations, even at the expense of doing what may appear to be an injustice. Men of the aggressive fighting type must be preferred over men of more judicial, thoughtful, but less aggressive characteristics." Knox recalled Lincoln's problems in the Civil War: "I presume most of us, if we had been required to choose at the beginning of the war between the brilliant, polished, socially attractive McClellan and the rough, rather uncouth, unsocial Grant, would have chosen McClellan, just as Lincoln did."

But the mistake was not to be repeated. So the lineup was being changed in many places. Pye was relieved as commander of the battleships—Task Force One—and appointed president of the Naval War College. Here his celebrated strategical abilities could be used fully, without any nagging doubts as to his aggressiveness. Training of future admirals was still a very important part of the Navy mission. Vice Admiral Leary was called back to the Pacific

Fleet from his job with MacArthur to take over Task Force One. Admiral Carpender replaced Leary. Ghormley showed up in Pearl Harbor, very upset about the manner in which he had been relieved, and Nimitz had to tell Ghormley very frankly that he was not the man for the job at the time. It was some, if little, solace to Ghormley that Nimitz interceded and secured his appointment as commander of the Fourteenth Naval District in Hawaii. He, at least, did not go to Siberia.

Frank Jack Fletcher had hoped to come back to sea, but after his leave he did not pass muster with King. So instead of returning to task force duty he went to Seattle, where he would be commandant of the Thirteenth Naval District. It was not quite so much of a "Shanghaiing" as in the cases of Draemel and Brown, although his duties were similar. Fletcher's duties also included command of the northwestern sea frontier, which meant an active defense job against possible Japanese attack. Yet it was a comedown for a man who had been thick in the action, and hard for Fletcher to take.

Brown was later able to solve his problem, in part by securing a third term of duty as naval aide to the President of the United States. At the White House he would run the Map Room and keep President Roosevelt informed about the progress of the Pacific war, with the prescience of one who had held a command post at the beginning of the conflict.

To the front came the fighting men, and leader of them all was Halsey. Later the British Royal Navy's liaison officer, Commander Harold Hopkins, went to visit Halsey one day when he was ashore. He came at about sundown, and found Halsey sitting on a veranda, in shorts, a khaki shirt without insignia, and no stockings. Halsey mixed a drink for his guest, and sat and swatted mosquitoes as they talked, yarning for half an hour. "I remember thinking that he might well have been a parson, a jolly one, an old time farmer, or Long John Silver. But when I left him and thought of what he had said, I realized that I had been listening to one of the great admirals of the war."

Halsey had arrived just as the Japanese were mounting their mid-monthly attempt to recapture Guadalcanal. On the night of October 20 he held a meeting aboard the *Argonne*. Vandegrift came up, as did Major General Patch, the Army commander, and Major General Harmon, the senior Army officer in the South Pacific. Vandegrift and Harmon told of their difficulties.

"Are we going to evacuate or hold?" Halsey asked.

The generals said they would hold if they got enough help. Kelly Turner said the Navy was doing all it could. Halsey told the generals to go on back, and he promised them every resource he had available. Then Halsey made two quick decisions. He called off the building of an airfield at Ndeni, in the Santa Cruz islands, and diverted the troops being sent there to Guadalcanal to shore up the defenses. Then he ordered an airfield built at Aola Bay on Guadalcanal—and ran smack into the flat opposition of Aubrey Fitch and Marine General Roy Geiger, who had been in the area and knew the territory was totally unsuited. As a result the Second Marine Raider Battalion was marooned, went overland, and ended up making a thirty-day march behind the Japanese lines which resulted in a brilliant victory. (A successful admiral had to have luck, in addition to everything else, and Halsey had it; even his mistakes turned out well.)

The Japanese were growing restive. Admiral Yamamoto was in the area with four carriers, five battleships, 14 cruisers, and 44 destroyers, to Halsey's two carriers, two battleships, nine cruisers, and 24 destroyers. Kinkaid had Task Force 16 with the *Enterprise*. Murray had Task Force 17 with the *Hornet*. Rear Admiral W. A. Lee had Task Force 64, a group of battleships and cruisers.

On October 24 Halsey sent the two carrier groups on a sweep north of the Santa Cruz islands, thence to move southwest, to be **able to intercept** the Japanese if they tried to approach Guadalcanal. This they were almost certain to do, for on the island the Japanese land forces were making another desperate attempt to capture Henderson field, the disputed air field.

Early on the morning of October 26, Admiral Halsey noted from the dispatch stack that patrol planes were in contact with an enemy force about two hundred miles northwest of the *Hornet*. He ordered Admiral Murray to attack, and at the same time Admiral Kinkaid's men were coming into contact with the enemy. A pair of planes from the *Enterprise* hit the Japanese carrier *Zuiho*, damaging her seriously and putting her flight deck out of action.

Her planes had already flown off, but they could not come back.

Hornet was hit that morning, by bombs, torpedoes, and a suicide plane crashed by the Japanese squadron commander; before 0930 she was dead in the water. Her planes closed on the Japanese and smashed carrier *Shokaku* so that she was put out of the war for nine months, and the cruiser *Chikuma* was also put out of action temporarily. Trying to pick up an air crew, the destroyer *Porter* was sunk. Then *Enterprise* was hit and so was the battleship *South Dakota*. *Hornet* was abandoned and finally sunk by the Japanese. The battleship *Washington* was very nearly sunk by another Japanese submarine.

Nimitz had been ready for some such news. On October 22 he had suggested that major elements of the Japanese fleet were in the Solomons area, and that they might be expected to attack, with superior force, any time in the next few weeks, when they would be stronger than the Americans. "Having inferior forces, we must count heavily on attrition, but losing no chance to come to grips with the enemy under the principle of calculated risk." By October 31 the situation in the South Pacific was still cloudy to Nimitz and his men, but that day Halsey was writing to his chief, to explain.

Halsey was anything but downhearted. He promised Nimitz that "it will be my utmost endeavor to patch up what we have and go with them. In other words I will not send any ship back to Pearl Harbor unless it is absolutely necessary." He hoped to get the *Enterprise* back in action. He knew he could repair the *South Dakota* locally.

Without a whimper, Halsey took the responsibility for one poor aspect of the American show: the fighter control of the carriers. He had brought the communications officer of the *Enterprise* to his headquarters to be a member of the staff, and since the head of the fighter director school was on the *Enterprise* he had not felt badly about it. But in his letter to Nimitz he offered the facts and took the responsibility. Halsey paused for a moment to bring Nimitz up to date on strategy.

As you may well imagine, I was completely taken aback when I received your orders on my arrival here. I took over a strange job with a strange staff and I had to begin throwing punches almost immediately. As a consequence quick decisions had to be made. Since the action, I have about reached the conclusion that the yellow bastards have been playing us for suckers. Their pattern of attack has been practically the same on the four occasions they have come down. The scouting force of submarines probably on the surface, backed up by cruisers and possibly battleships and behind that their carriers, two together and one separated some forty or fifty miles with accompanying battleships, cruisers and destroyers. These are placed generally to the northward of the Santa Cruz islands. To the westward and generally to the northward of the Solomons-Guadalcanal area, their covering force. With the transports again to the westward of this force. I think they have sucked us out beyond the easy reach of our shore based aircraft and are willing to play attrition tactics with us . . . .

Halsey had several ideas. "The question of keeping battleships and carriers continuously at sea in the submarine infested waters, I believe to be a mistake." He intended to use his heavy ships more sparingly, and he doubted if a battleship or cruiser surprise attack of the kind made by Norman Scott would be made again, but if he had a chance, he assured Nimitz he would certainly take it.

The big problem, as both admirals knew, was logistics. There was practically no fuel at Nouméa. "We need tankers and more tankers and more tankers." He needed repair ships, and men who could repair. "The biggest and best thing is the army. They have made available to us various mechanics, electricians and welders, and I would like to see it widely advertised that the army is helping us here. I have never seen anything like the spirit there is in this neck of the woods. It is a real United States service."

It was a long letter, eight single-spaced typewriten pages, and it discussed many aspects of the war. Halsey had spoken to Captain Christie, second in command of the submarine force in the area, and they were going to cover Ironbottom Sound to catch the Japanese coming down with the Tokyo Express. "I trust this may help him in securing more monkey meat."

We are in need of everything we can get, planes, ships, escort vessels, men, and so on ad nauseum. You are well aware of our needs and this is not offered in complaint or as an excuse but just to keep the pot boiling. We are not in the least downhearted or upset by our difficulties, but obsessed with one idea only, to kill the yellow bastards and we shall do it. My admiration for the officers and men of all the services down here who are doing the actual fighting is beyond all expression. They are superb . . . we are going to continue to give them hell.

He closed, for the plane was due to leave early the next day, and of course such a revealing letter could only be sent by special courier. He promised, however, to write "home" once a week.

Chapter
Ten

HALSEY'S TRIUMPH

November 1–December 9, 1942

Assessing the American situation in the Solomons on the first of November, Nimitz's staff found that the pressure there was doing what King had wanted, stopping the Japanese and keeping them from undertaking any other sizable operations. At Pearl Harbor the command was under no illusions: the Japanese would continue to try to capture Guadalcanal until they suffered a major setback, which had not yet occurred.

And when might a real American victory come?

When the men and weapons could get down to Halsey.

At the moment, the old battleships were still stationed at Pearl as a last line of defense against possible Japanese landings there. Task Force 11 was at Pearl, and could be sent south in mid-November when the repairs to *Saratoga* and *North Carolina* were finished. Task Force 17 was finished—the force had been broken up on the loss of *Hornet* and injury to *South Dakota*. Task Force 16 was not ready for battle and would not be until *Enterprise* was repaired. What Halsey had, then, besides unlimited courage, was a force of cruisers and destroyers, the battleship *Washington*, and Admiral Fitch's land-based airplanes with which to fight. There were also twenty-four submarines available.

There could be no offensive until more planes came down, until Henderson field was ready for all-weather operation, and supporting fields were built. On the island the Marines were tired and needed to be pulled out, but this could not happen until reinforcements could be brought in, which would probably not be in November.

Logistics was the problem of most importance. It was hard to get food and fuel, ammunition and equipment into Guadalcanal.

So the same problems existed that had existed before Halsey arrived, with one great difference.

The situation was critical, said Nimitz, "but the determination, efficiency, and morale of our people there is so fine that even the most pessimistic critics must concede that we will win out in the end."

There it was—Halsey's infectious grin and tough words had reached even back to Pearl. It was no accident that Halsey was building morale, and building it fast. Before the ships damaged in the Battle of Santa Cruz arrived back at Nouméa, Halsey had called in the senior officers of all branches of the services and directed them to pool their forces. "Our shoestring had held . . . but it had been badly frayed, and it had to be patched up . . . ." Halsey then headed for Guadalcanal, where he held his famous press conference ("Kill Japs, kill Japs, and keep on killing Japs") and then visited the hospital at Efate. The word got around—the boys on Guadalcanal had a boss who *cared*. The word was slower getting home, because the correspondents' stories had to go back to Pearl Harbor or Washington for censorship and transmission home. Secretary Knox was concerned about this aspect of the war—realizing, as the admirals tended to forget, that the whole nation was involved in this war, and winning it was a job at home as well as in the theaters of operations. Knox asked for—and got—Nimitz's concurrence in handling press copy at Nouméa. Knox also wanted to use Navy communications facilities for transmission, but here Nimitz balked. He knew the enemy monitored his radio, and he feared that the sending of press copy would give the enemy a basis for breaking the American codes.

In comparison to the Army, the Navy's public relations were rudimentary. King and Nimitz, and even Halsey, considered the press a nuisance—whether necessary or not depended on the admiral's point of view at any given moment.

But in operations, Halsey was snapping the boys to, as the Marines would say. An example of the manner in which the Americans were learning in this war could be seen in the report and comment of various officers on the fighting of Fighting Squadron 5, which went into action on Guadalcanal in September.

Shortly after Halsey took command at Nouméa, the commanding officer of Fighting 5, Lieutenant Commander L. C. Simpler, made an operational report which was destined for Nimitz. The squadron of twenty-four F-4-F's and twenty-four pilots had come ashore at Guadalcanal to operate with the First Marine Air Wing. Later eight more pilots had joined up. Between September 11 and October 16 two pilots were known to have been killed in action, three others were missing, and four were wounded. They lost eight planes from enemy aerial action, five planes in operations, and seven planes because of enemy bombardment of Henderson field. They destroyed forty-five enemy planes and another six probables.

Here is the way Fighting 5 operated in those hard days. One pilot for each operational plane stood by in the ready tent, and the planes were dispersed around the field with the captains standing by as soon as word came of an enemy air strike headed their way. The guns were charged by the ordnance crew and everything was ready.

The commanding officer issued his order—SCRAMBLE.

And the pilots rushed to man their planes, taking off as quickly as possible, in no special order.

First plane off acted as leader until the assigned leader got into position. Section leaders were assigned, but it was really up to them to take over a two-plane section, and everyone flew wing from time to time. The climb was made as quickly as possible, to 26,000 feet or more. It took 35 to 40 minutes to hit 30,000 feet.

The flight leader led the attack then, using the steep high side, with full deflection, then coming down to half deflection aim. The attackers fired just ahead of the enemy planes, letting them fly into the fire. If they were attacking Mitsubishi navy bombers, they aimed just behind either engine, hoping to "flame one." After attacking, each plane joined up on the first fighter in sight, for mutual protection.

When escorting, the pilots learned to keep together, never to be diverted by a chance to strafe a surface craft, and to stick with the bombers all the way. On strafing missions they had learned to make a steep sweeping dive from ten to twelve thousand feet against any ship that could put up a heavy barrage of antiaircraft fire. With each plane's attack, they discovered, the fire from a ship like a cruiser would decrease. No sweeping—the pilots were to pick out a fixed point and aim at it. The fliers of Fighting 5 were proud of their strafing record: in many attacks they had still not lost a plane. They had learned about men as well as flying. Commander Simpler said they needed two pilots for every plane, pilot relief every two weeks, oftener during heavy action. A pilot was as good as his physical condition, and one exposed to too much combat might be out of the war for good. Older pilots were as good as younger ones, and even better as flight leaders.

A pilot's offensive spirit was measurable directly in relationship to his equipment. As for fighters generally, a plane should be measured not by the number of Japanese who were shot down, but by the number of Japanese who *escaped*. And the F-4-F had its faults, these pilots said. The rate of climb was too slow, the speed was too much slower than that of the Zero, and the range of the F-4-F was too short. That meant that half the Japanese bombing attempts on Guadalcanal made the target because the F-4-F's could not climb fast enough to intercept, and that the Japanese base at Buka was beyond the range of Fighting 5.

As for the engine, the Pratt and Whitney 1830–86, the pilots were generally pleased. There were minor problems, but they knew that under combat conditions the planes were "abused." Prolonged climbs were made at full horsepower output, with cylinder head and oil temperatures exceeding maximum limits. Dives were made with full throttle and in high blower. Under such conditions, said Fighting 5's commander, the engine life was about ninety hours, but he was not complaining. "This, however, usually exceeds that of the plane," he said drily.

One problem was the oxygen equipment: four pilots had died under conditions that indicated oxygen failure, and no one knew why. The masks were troublesome, and interfered with goggles and with microphones. But they did not know *why*; one pilot was killed thus who had been up to high altitude several times. One day he checked his oxygen equipment and took off. At 22,000 feet the flight leader saw his plane maneuvering strangely, and called him on the radio. But the pilot did not respond, his plane nosed over, and after a long dive crashed into the water.

The radio the flight leader used was unreliable for plane-to-plane talk. The throat microphones were a dangerous nuisance. What was needed was a radio giving instant transmission, frequency selection, and positive tuning without giving the pilot much trouble.

The guns gave trouble—too—but in this the commander indicated one of the problems that Nimitz had already recognized, even as he sent these carrier planes ashore for service. Carrier planes were not fitted for land-based air operations. "Maintenance at an advanced base is far more difficult than on a carrier," said Simpler. And what he wanted, if his pilots came ashore to fight, was land fighters. "Had P-38s been available at Guadalcanal at least 80 percent of all enemy aircraft appearing in the area would have been destroyed." But of course the P-38's just were not available. Operation Shoestring again.

Fighting 5's report went to Admiral Fitch first of all. It was written on November 11, and he got to it on December 1. He liked and appreciated the report—"an excellent presentation of the problems encountered by land plane squadrons shore based in a combat area."

As for operations and tactics, Fitch was satisfied that they were sound. He congratulated Simpler on learning fast and collating the information for others. Fitch noted the sharpness of Japanese tactics, and suggested that the use of P-38's would solve many problems. He agreed that each plane should have two pilots where the fighting was heavy. "Under these conditions it is necessary to 'scramble' all planes when bombing is imminent and the physical condition and effectiveness of pilots deteriorate rapidly if they are maintained indefinitely on call."

In the future, Fitch warned, the Navy simply had to make adequate provision for ground echelons, including enough mechanics. "The situation on Guadalcanal has been far from satisfactory in this respect and is only now, three months after the invasion, showing improvement."

Halsey had the report and Fitch's endorsement on December 20. He, too, approved of Simpler's succinct report and agreed with Fitch's comments. He noted that more training was needed in aerial gunnery, to ready the pilots for the difficulties of full- and half-deflection shooting, and that the Japanese shooting had dropped in effectiveness. He recalled for the minds of higher authority that Japanese strafing at Pearl Harbor had been "masterly," but at Guadalcanal it was ineffectual. He was concerned about the oxygen matter, and about the radio deficiency—which was already being corrected by supply of pushbutton sets.

Next the report and the endorsements appeared on the desk of Admiral Towers, who had arrived at Pearl Harbor and begun to function as commander of the air force, Pacific Fleet. By now it was January 17. Towers agreed with all that was said, but added his own spice. He lamented the fact that it had been necessary to use Fighting 5 ashore at all. The need for trained carrier pilots was such that they should be assigned to carriers. True—at the moment that Towers wrote—and it would become ever more true as the promised carriers came off the ways and were fitted out for the Pacific war, but in those grim days at Guadalcanal, when *Saratoga* had been crippled, and every man and weapon had been needed, it was much more sensible to send Fighting 5 ashore than to return the squadron to Pearl Harbor, where the planes would be out of action.

On February 22 Spruance, the chief of staff to Nimitz, had the report and passed it along to Admiral King, agreeing that it was best to keep carrier pilots on carriers. It seems a long time between the writing of Simpler's report and its arrival at King's desk, but the fact was that the people who needed the details were getting them all the way along. Fitch had read about, and was fighting for, land-based planes and better radio. Halsey had read and was talking about training. Towers was urging the recall of these men to their carrier duty. Spruance and Nimitz were comparing the needs of the moment with the best of plans.

The attrition continued in November. After Santa Cruz, Halsey sent the destroyer *Smith* back to Pearl. She had been hard hit in the last stages of the battle, but was still going. The *Mahan* had also been hurt, much of her bow torn away, but she could be repaired in Australia, as could the *San Juan*, the antiaircraft cruiser, which had taken an armor-piercing bomb. *Enterprise* was under local repair, and on November 6 Halsey had her ready for sea on thirty-six hours notice, capable of operating sixty-nine planes.

In his letter to Nimitz, Halsey went into great detail about the damage done the Big E and the others. He was showing the stuff of wartime command, precision of detail, aggressiveness, leadership of the men: "If we get away with it, and I fully believe we shall, I think a splendid job has been done under the conditions pertaining here."

Halsey was firing things up. They canted the *South Dakota* and repaired her at Nouméa. One of her turrets was not very strong, but he was not going to complain. She was ready to fight again.

The *San Diego* developed a bulge in one gun, but instead of sending her back to Pearl, Halsey's men found a spare five-inch gun and set about making the change themselves.

More guns, that was what Halsey wanted. "I am having prepared a list of our minimum requirements of destroyers, supported by the reasons therefore, I will forward this to you by dispatch. You probably will not be able to meet it, but do the best you can and bring all the pressure to bear possible. Escort and more escort vessels are a crying need. That is where the shoe pinches."

Halsey was also feeling the pinches of command. Rear Admiral H. H. Good, who had been commanding Task Force 17, fell sick with the flu and had to be evacuated to Australia. Halsey wanted to fleet up Captain McMorris, but Nimitz had other ideas—McMorris was slated for a task force in the Aleutians. So Admiral Dan Callaghan was sent out with a task force. "He was delighted to get into things and with his good Irish name and splendid character, I feel sure he will make good."

Every time Halsey sent something or someone to Australia, Nimitz was concerned lest MacArthur swallow it or him up. But Halsey was not letting go. He kept tight control of Christie's submarines and of some B-24's he sent to Australia at General Harmon's request.

Halsey could be critical of methods, and at the same time supremely generous about people. He was upset about the air corps's bad bombing record. At Santa Cruz the B-17's dropped eighty-eight bombs and secured two hits on a destroyer. He talked to Harmon about it, and kept asking that the bombers be brought down. But as for Harmon, "I do not understand why he has not been given three stars commensurate with the important command he is holding . . . . I would be delighted if anything could be done to get the additional star for him. . . ."

He groused about the Bureau of Personnel. He had wanted a specific officer who was an ROTC instructor at the University of North Carolina, and had been turned down. "I wish someone would tell some of the people in Washington that we have a little war on our hands out here," he complained. And immediately he was contrite: "As you may rightly interpret, my growls and grouches are the privilege of an old sailorman. We are not in the least downhearted and are going to continue to lick the hell out of the yellow bastards. . . .

"As Ever, Cheerfully yours—"

That was Admiral Bill Halsey, November, 1942. Nimitz was very pleased with Halsey and so was King. Secretary Knox had not been so sure of Halsey's abilities in overall command as had Nimitz, but he was convinced by this time. It was fortunate that this confidence was established before the second week in November, for with the middle of the month coming up, the Japanese were again ready to launch an effort to recapture Guadalcanal. Admiral Yamamoto was a very determined man.

The Americans brought in 155 mm artillery pieces, and the Japanese brought in 1500 new troops to Koli Point, where they were hard hit by ship bombardment and the Marines. But the Japanese kept coming down the slot, and in eight days brought sixty-seven shiploads of troops to western Guadalcanal.

On November 9 Nimitz predicted a major enemy attempt to capture Guadalcanal, with the thirteenth as the target date. He had a new task force, 61, ready to sail for Nouméa, and it was on one-hour notice for departure.

At Nouméa, Halsey returned from an inspection trip that day to find an anxious Captain Miles Browning waiting for him, Browning's thin face screwed up as if he had bad news. He did. The Japanese were coming in with great force to reinforce the island of Guadalcanal, the force including two carriers, four battleships, five heavy cruisers, some light cruisers, and thirty-six destroyers. That was Halsey's initial information. To oppose this force he had Norman Scott's force, a light cruiser and four destroyers, Turner with a heavy cruiser, a light cruiser, and four destroyers, Callaghan with two heavy cruisers, a light cruiser, and six destroyers, Kinkaid with the *Enterprise* (which was still under repair at Nouméa), a heavy cruiser, a light cruiser, and several destroyers. Then there was a force of two battleships and a pair of destroyers under Rear Admiral Willis Augustus Lee, which were actually part of the *Enterprise* force.

One trouble, however, was that these forces were all over the lot. Scott was at Espiritu Santo on November 9. Turner was at sea, en route from Nouméa to Lunga Point, escorting several transports. Callaghan was at sea.

On November 10 Turner, who was in charge of tactical operations, wrote Callaghan a letter. "It looks this time like the enemy is finally about to make an allout effort against CACTUS," he said. "Whether we will be there in time or not I can't say. I do wish we were a day earlier, but that was impossible. In any case I fear we can't turn back this time and still have the chance to go in later."

Turner discussed the enemy strength, and then closed. "In any case, you have under your own control your own tactical operations. If we can *really* strike the enemy hard, it will be more important for you to do that than to protect my transports.

"Good Luck to you Dan. God bless all of you and give you strength."

On November 12, while unloading at Guadalcanal, Turner's force was attacked from the air, but drove off the Japanese. On the night of November 12 Callaghan led his ships and those of Scott, his junior, into Ironbottom Sound, and early on the morning of Friday the thirteenth, Vice Admiral Hiroaki Abe led a raiding group of two battleships, a light cruiser, and fourteen destroyers to bombard the Americans ashore on Guadalcanal. The two forces met. Almost at the opening of the action Admiral Scott and most of the others on his bridge were killed by a shell that struck there. In a few moments the ship, the *Atlanta*, was dead in the water. Next down was the destroyer *Cushing*, which had just fired half a dozen torpedoes at the battleship *Hiei*. But the torpedoes missed. *Laffey* came up and fired torpedoes too soon, which bounced off the battleship's sides without exploding. She was hit at point-blank range and destroyed. Destroyer *Sterett* was hit but kept fighting. Admiral Callaghan and most on the bridge of the *San Francisco* were killed by a shell from the battleship *Kirishima*. The *Portland* was hit by a torpedo. The *Juneau* took a torpedo. The *Barton* was sunk by a torpedo.

On the Japanese side, the destroyer *Yudachi* was sunk, so was *Akatsuki*, and the destroyers *Ikazuchi*, *Murasame*, and *Amatsukaze* were hit. The big battleship *Hiei* was also badly hit, and her rudder destroyed.

Next day, *Atlanta* sank, and *Juneau* blew up when she was torpedoed again, this time by a Japanese submarine.

That was the end of the first phase of the battle, the Japanese having dealt out tremendous punishment, but having failed to achieve their objective, the bombardment of Guadalcanal. Next day, bombers sank *Hiei*, which helped even the score. And then Halsey ordered out Admiral Lee with the battleships, and Admiral Kinkaid to protect the hurt American vessels.

The orders to Kinkaid and Lee came late (Morison later said *very* late) and another Japanese bombardment group came into the sound and hit Henderson field before Kinkaid could arrive. The Japanese seemed to be in control, and their transports were moving in.

But in the morning of November 14, Henderson field was still operational, seventeen fighter planes and one bomber had been destroyed, but there were still planes to fly. Northwest of Guadalcanal the planes found the Japanese second bombardment force and attacked. They started fires on the heavy cruiser *Kinugasa* and the light cruiser *Izuzu*. Later planes from *Enterprise* found the force and sank *Kinugasa*. They damaged heavy cruisers *Chokai* and *Maya* and the destroyer *Michishio*.

Meanwhile the Japanese transports were heading for Guadalcanal. They were attacked repeatedly by planes from *Enterprise* and Henderson field, holing some and sinking one. All morning and afternoon the fighting went on, and seven transports were sunk but four remained, escorted by eleven destroyers—and they were steaming straight for Guadalcanal.

South of Savo Island Admiral Lee came up with his six-ship column, four destroyers and the battleships *Washington* and *South Dakota*. The Japanese had re-formed and were coming in, the Tokyo Express in spades, with one section that included a light cruiser and three destroyers, a screen section of a light cruiser and six destroyers, and the big group with the heavy cruisers *Ataka* and *Takao* and the battleship *Kirishima*. They spotted the Americans and moved to attack, in four different sections.

The destroyers *Walke*, *Gwin*, and *Benham* were hit. *Preston* was put out of action. In a very short time all were out of action, *Walke* was sinking, *Preston* was abandoned, *Gwin* and *Benham* were limping away. They had accomplished very little.

South Dakota was plagued by power failures and fires, and came under the guns of three heavy Japanese ships. But Admiral Lee then found the enemy, and *Washington* began to open up. In a few minutes she lobbed nine 16-inch shells into *Kirishima*, plus about forty 5-inch projectiles, and that battleship was out of the fight, blazing furiously. Soon *Atago* and *Takao* were hit by both American battleships, and they retired. *Kirishima* sank before dawn. The Japanese did succeed in landing their four transports, beaching them, and putting another two thousand soldiers ashore. They had dealt out fearful damage, especially with their torpedoes, but they had not succeeded in really reinforcing their garrison, while Admiral Turner had put all his men and materiel ashore. In terms of the fleet, the Japanese had inflicted great damage, but the object was to win the war and in this instance to win and maintain control of the island of Guadalcanal. The Japanese had lost control, and they would not regain it again. Three months after landing in the Solomons—three very shaky months—the Americans had seized the initiative in the Pacific war. The Japanese had sunk three light cruisers and seven destroyers; the Americans had sunk two Japanese battleships, one heavy cruiser, and three destroyers.

From Washington and Pearl Harbor came messages of congratulation to Halsey, and he passed the accolade along to the troops. "Your names have been written in golden letters upon the pages of history and you have won the everlasting gratitude of your countrymen."

On November 15 General Vandegrift could write Nimitz gleefully of sitting on an observation hill and watching planes drop bombs on four Japanese transports, which went up in flames. "It was indeed a glorious sight."

He could also see the future:

> Things have happened very rapidly . . . we have not only been able to hold on to what we had, but pushed out some three and one half to four miles to the west and an equal distance to the east. Our offensive to the west was gaining ground slowly through a jungle literally infested with these Japs when certain news that we received caused us to halt the advance in order to be prepared to repel boarders . . . . Today we are fortunate that . . . this whole push has been neutralized . . . .

Vandegrift was so moved that he sent a dispatch to Turner, praising the Navy, lamenting the loss of Scott and Callaghan, and referring to the "hopeless odds" they had faced. Turner, to be known in naval history as Terrible Turner, thanked Vandegrift, but called him down for using the term. "The phrase is emphatic, but all of us, and most of you, refuse to believe that the odds are hopeless."

There was time now for such little irritations, time to pick up the pieces of the battle, and that was the job of the commanders.

Halsey was not pretending false modesty when he told the men of his command that the victory was theirs, not his. "I accept them in all humility for myself and as representing the splendid body of fighting men who did the actual job," he wrote Nimitz. And when he was promoted to full admiral for having supervised the victory, Halsey sent his old three-star pins to the widows of Scott and Callaghan, with the messages that their husbands' bravery' had won him the new stars.

Then it was back to business, for there were decisions to be made and plans for the future. One of the decisions was a sad one, to relieve the captain of the cruiser *Helena* for dereliction of duty. On November 14 Captain Gilbert Hoover was steaming southeast down Indispensable Strait after the action with the Japanese. He was senior officer present, following the death of Admiral Callaghan in the *San Francisco*, and so was in charge of a flotilla that included three cruisers and two destroyers. Suddenly the *Juneau* exploded. Captain Hoover saw a B-17 overhead, and notified the plane—asking that the message be transmitted to Halsey's headquarters. Then he moved on out with his four remaining ships, not stopping to help possible survivors. As it turned out there were 120 survivors, and the B-17's messsage never got through to Halsey. Of the men of the *Juneau* only ten were finally saved. At Nouméa, Captain Hoover told his story to Halsey, Admiral Fitch, Admiral Turner, and Admiral Calhoun, commander of the service force. The latter three recommended the relief, and Halsey sent Hoover back to Pearl Harbor. Later, however, he regretted this action, and tried to make amends by recommending Hoover's restoration to combat command.

With the lull that followed the Battle of Guadalcanal, Halsey began planning. He moved his headquarters from the *Argonne* to a house ashore in Nouméa—the Japanese consul's house. There he reveled in using the enemy's silverware and china, and when his Filipino houseboy broke the china, he had no complaint. ("The hell with it. It's Japanese.")

He complained because the furniture was so short they had to "sit on the back of our necks," but the brick house, high atop a hill overlooking the harbor, was very comfortable. He commandeered another house and built two quonset huts for the staff.

Halsey took advantage of the confusion of the enemy to better his logistics. Gasoline storage tanks were brought in to Guadalcanal, thus ending the perennial aviation gas problem. Turkeys were brought in for Thanksgiving dinner, and other luxuries began to appear on the island.

The first part of the Solomons campaign was over, Halsey said on November 29, and at that point he began thinking of the next move. "A tempting thought, we have toyed with, is to bypass everything up the line and hit directly at Rabaul . . . . I believe with Rabaul in our hands the war in the Pacific is approaching an end . . . ."

If the view seemed overly optimistic, at least Halsey was showing a spirit that had not existed six weeks earlier in the South Pacific. And he was laying the groundwork for the island-passing campaign. The idea was so logical that it has been claimed for Forrest Sherman, Admiral Towers, MacArthur, and for Halsey. Whoever might have said the first word about bypassing certain Japanese strongholds, the idea soon gained momentum and was most thoroughly discussed among the Navy men. The attitude of the fighting force was entirely changed. "Everyone here is working like a beaver," Halsey wrote Nimitz, "and we have received a tremendous uplift from the confidence that you have shown in us. We shall lick hell out of the yellow bastards every time an opportunity presents."

Opportunity presented itself very quickly, but the American force was not quite ready for it. Halsey was very proud of Admiral Lee's showing with the battleships at the Battle of Guadalcanal; it proved to him that the day of the big capital ship was far from past. "How are all the experts going to comment now?" he asked. "The use we made of them defied all conventions, narrow waters, submarine menace, and destroyers at night. Despite that, the books, and the learned and ponderous words of the highbrows it worked." A few days later, the general approach would be tried again, with different results.

Admiral Kinkaid was ordered by Halsey to take command of the cruiser force at Espiritu Santo. The force included the cruisers *Minneapolis, New Orleans, Pensacola, Northampton,* and *Honolulu,* plus four destroyers. But those orders were countermanded by Admiral King, who had decided that Kinkaid was to take command of the North Pacific force. Rear Admiral Carleton H. Wright of the class of 1912 succeeded Kinkaid to the cruiser command.

On the night of November 29, Halsey discovered that the Japanese were not finished, but were sending down a force of eight destroyers and six transports to reinforce Guadalcanal. Wright was ordered to intercept. He set out at twenty-eight knots for the trip of nearly six hundred miles to Guadalcanal. On the way he picked up two more destroyers. Actually the Japanese force consisted of only eight destroyers, with several loaded as transports, with drums of supplies that would be shoved off into the shallow water. There small Japanese boats would come out and get them.

On the evening of November 30 the Americans came in to intercept—the Japanese were already moving along the shoreline of Guadalcanal. The Americans caught the Japanese by surprise, the American destroyers launched torpedoes, and the American cruisers opened up on the enemy ships. The torpedoes missed; they were fired too late. The gunfire destroyed the destroyer *Takanami*. But the other Japanese destroyers struck back. Two Japanese torpedoes hit *Minneapolis*. *New Orleans* took a torpedo which knocked off the bow of the ship, back to no. 2 turret. *Pensacola* was hit and set afire. *Northampton* took two torpedoes and went to the bottom before morning, although 773 men were rescued, and only 58 crewmen were drowned or killed in action.

More than a week later, Halsey still did not know how many Japanese ships had been sunk, or how the action had ended. He did know, however, that *Northampton* was gone, and three other cruisers were damaged. *Pensacola* was least hurt, and he hoped to repair her at Tulagi. *New Orleans* had her bow cut off, but was being shored up so she might be moved. *Minneapolis* was in the worst shape: her bow had been blown off, but was still attached to the hull, and had to be cut loose before anything else could be done. Soon all three were sent to Australia for repair.

Admiral Wright's action report must have been dismal to prepare. He took full responsibility for the delay of his destroyers in moving into action, although the senior destroyer commander might have taken some of it. Nimitz was very understanding. He felt that Wright had been unlucky to take command just before a battle and be forced, as he was, to use another admiral's battle plan.

Poor Wright was returned to Pearl Harbor, and there Nimitz had the unfortunate duty to inform him that he would be sent back to the Navy Department on the orders of Admiral King.

"Reading between the lines of your postscript in your December 11 letter," Nimitz wrote Halsey, "I judge that this will be satisfactory to you. In this connection—please be utterly frank with me regarding flag officers. We are out to win a war, and not to please individuals. Those not in line for the first team must be sent ashore."

It was a hard war, with no place for sentimentality. Fond as Nimitz was of his favorite admiral, he would have relieved Halsey, too, had he not done the job that was necessary. There was, however, no need to consider such a course. On December 9 the First Marines were relieved and sent to Australia. The Japanese never again mounted a major attempt to reinforce Guadalcanal. Two months after Halsey's arrival on the South Pacific scene, the battle was won.

Chapter
Eleven

SOUTH PACIFIC VICTORY

December 7, 1942–February 8, 1943

On the first anniversary of the Pacific war, Admiral Nimitz could look at his command with a certain amount of satisfaction. As a result of the last two sea and air battles—costly as they were—the Americans controlled the sea and air in the southern Solomons, and Guadalcanal and Tulagi were safe.

Task One of the broad directive for the campaign had, by and large, been accomplished. Task Two called for the seizure and occupation of the rest of the Solomons, Lae, Salamaua, and the north coast of New Guinea. Task Three called for expulsion of the Japanese from the Bismarck Archipelago.

But these tasks were to be changed; Task Two would now be to capture and occupy the remainder of the Solomons, and hold New Guinea. Nimitz's area was to be extended to the equator at 145 degrees east, then to the center of Vitiaz Strait, to Woodlark Island, Rossel Island, and then south.

In November King had suggested that Halsey and Nimitz threatened to bog down in the Solomons, when perhaps they would best cut off the Japanese by seizing the base from which the Solomons were supplied.

On December 8, Nimitz wrote King a long letter suggesting that there would be considerable delay. The reason was to allow for buildup of American land and sea forces in the South Pacific. Sea forces could not be expected to be superior to the Japanese until the spring of 1943. Air equality had been achieved, more planes could be diverted to the area quickly, but more bases were needed and this would take some time.

As for troops, who must take and hold territory, the First Marine Division would need until March to recuperate. The Second Marine Division could be ready in February, and the Third Marine Division in March. No Army divisions were yet in training, and it would take three months to train them for amphibious operations.

Taking a hard look at Japanese and American capabilities, Nimitz offered this summation:

(a) The Jap is our equal in his willingness to fight.

(b) Surface units must be considered of equal ability except that our fire control radar seems to give us a considerable advantage in low visibility, and our AA batteries are superior. We have no evidence for comparison in day surface action.

(c) Our air forces are definitely superior in quality.

(d) U.S. land forces in the Solomons have proved themselves better armed and more skillful than the Japs, but we could hardly expect a continuation of the disproportionate personnel losses we have been able to inflict, and must realize that we will still require a superiority in numbers at our point of attack.

(e) Our submarines have proved themselves to be more effective units than those of the Japs.

(f) Our great inferiority is in the use and performance of torpedoes.

Nimitz here considered the "bypass" idea, "even to the point of making Rabaul the first objective." It was a strong temptation, he said, but he inclined toward conservatism, because the system of bases the Japanese held outside New Guinea were mutually supporting, and the communication line of any base seized would be flanked by the enemy bases bypassed. To bypass, he thought, would require a strength which was not in sight for the near future.

At that moment, he was considering taking Buin, 300 miles from Guadalcanal, or Munda, New Georgia, 180 miles from Guadalcanal, where the Japanese were starting to build an airfield.

What was necessary—vital—was to build up strength, always planning two moves ahead, so there would be no future delays like the one they were suffering at the end of 1942.

Armed with this summary, Nimitz left Pearl Harbor on December 8 for San Francisco to confer with King again. Admiral Kinkaid was also there, for the North Pacific force which he would command was about to go into action against the Japanese. Theobald, who had been in charge in the Alaskan area, would go to Boston to command the First Naval District, for Wilson Brown was then to become President Roosevelt's naval aide.

They talked personnel for a time. The Navy needed thirty more flag officers to handle the ships that were coming off the ways, and Nimitz supplied a list. He also plumped for the appointment of Aubrey Fitch as a vice admiral, but King felt there were too many vice admirals at the moment, and no decision was made. Nimitz also tried to soften the blow for Admiral Wright by keeping him on the staff, but King felt that bringing in another admiral would overload the Nimitz staff with flag officers, and Nimitz had to agree with him.

On the first day, King, Nimitz, Rear Admiral Cooke, Kinkaid, Captain McCormick, and Captain Fechteler were in the room, as they talked about the Aleutians operation and set a target date for the invasion of Kiska as March 1.

For several months King and Nimitz had been bedevilled by difficulties in the intelligence establishment. It had been decided to establish a Pacific Ocean Intelligence Center in Honolulu. The idea was originally germinated in the Office of Naval Intelligence (ONI), which envisioned a center of five hundred people or more. This center would swallow up the old radio intelligence unit which had been operating in Hawaii—meaning particularly that Commander

Rochefort's operations would come under the new center. Apparently Rochefort had resisted being swallowed up by the new organization, and in the fall of 1942 he had summarily been transferred back to Washington, without Nimitz's knowledge.

Theoretically, of course, there was no need for ONI or anyone else to inform Nimitz of the Rochefort transfer, but in practice Rochefort had been responsible for the intelligence that set up the Midway victory, and Nimitz was distressed when he learned the facts. He admired Rochefort's useful work, and had recommended Rochefort for a Distinguished Service Medal after Midway.

Nimitz stepped into a hornet's nest. He objected in writing to Admiral Train, director of ONI, and to Admiral Horne of the Bureau of Personnel, and finally to King. "I have no information other than that you have furnished, of bickerings and jealousy between the Washington and Pearl Harbor RI [radio intelligence] units, but I observed enough out here to know that Rochefort's sin was probably one of doing too much rather than too little—a hard thing for which to condemn a man."

Nimitz's worry was that the Naval intelligence people were trying to build a bureaucracy; he did not want such a huge intelligence operation around him, and he questioned whether it could bring the information to him *in time*, the way the old setup had done.

King was having none of it. The Rochefort transfer stood, and Nimitz was told, not particularly gently, to mind his own business.

There was even more to it, which they took up at this meeting. Army and Navy intelligence units would be combined if such were possible, King said. And in the discussion it came out that when this horde of intelligence people had begun to descend on Pearl Harbor, Nimitz had turned some of them over to Admiral Towers, the air commander. King was very disapproving; he regarded this act as "the wrong kind of decentralization."

Nimitz asked for submarines—from the Atlantic waters—and King told him he could not have them. He asked for airplanes for the South Pacific, and King said he would take up the matter in Washington.

Next day, they did more planning for the Aleutians operation.

Nimitz again brought up the matter of Fitch's promotion, and King grunted that he would look into it. His mind, closed the day before, was open, he said.

They began talking about strategy, and movement into the Central Pacific, perhaps through the Marshall Islands. They talked about the Marianas.

Nimitz was pleased to learn that King was thinking in terms of giving the Pacific war a given percentage of American war supplies and people—somewhere between 20 and 35 percent. Compared to the earliest days, when Nimitz was told to hold with what he had, this was remarkable improvement.

They talked about the future of the South Pacific campaign that day: first stabilize Guadalcanal, then move to Buin-Faisi, then to Rabaul. They were assuming that MacArthur would soon move into New Guinea and the Papuan peninsula.

This conference demonstrated the relationship between King and Nimitz, and something of the character of each. King was perhaps the most "strong-minded" man in the Navy of his day, and that can be understood to mean stubborn as well as opinionated. He was a highly trained, thoughtful, and ingenious naval officer, noted for his cold, tough attitude at all times. He was also stern, and unforgiving, but these particular qualities, to be exhibited later in relations with the Pacific command, had not led to the Rochefort matter. King's reasoning was obviously of another sort: he was not going to have little kingdoms and little arguments impinge upon the war effort, and if he had to take a man who was doing an excellent job, even an "irreplaceable" man, and change him around, he would do so for the overall good of the service. Whether Rochefort was right or wrong in his quarrel with others was unimportant at that moment; what was important was that the quarrel was fraying the nerves of too many people in the intelligence service and in the places of high command. It was taking too much time and too much effort and it must be stopped.

Nimitz's reaction showed the controlled nature of the commander of the Pacific Fleet. He spoke forthrightly and even with an edge in his voice when he complained about what was being done within his command without his knowledge. But when King said loudly and clearly that it *was* being done, and *would* be done, then

Nimitz simply put the matter from his mind, showed King that he had done so, and did not let the matter affect any other aspect of their relationship. It was a remarkable performance, one that could not be accomplished by many men. King's control of the American naval effort was complete and sure, and the forcefulness of his responses lent strength to his commanders, who could be sure of their own power in their own spheres.

Never did Nimitz question a King decision in any conversation or any letter to a subordinate. Sometimes his officers pressed him to right some "grave injustice" or to stop the operation of some plan they found wanting, but Nimitz's complete answer to them was that they had orders from higher authority, which meant King and the Joint Chiefs of Staff, and above, and there was no questioning. What his officers may or may not have known is that if Nimitz shared their worries, he would already have exhausted every reasonable line of argument in his talks or messages to King, and that Nimitz knew precisely the length to which he could go without beginning the erosion of confidence that would eventually lead to Nimitz's own replacement and self-defeat.

Both men had the faculty of going from some knotty problem with personality overtones that might wreck a relationship, to "nuts and bolts," and then ranging the whole field of the war. They discussed bases, antiaircraft, and the torpedo situation.

King remarked that he was not at all satisfied with the Navy supply system. It simply was *not* properly organized, he said, and he wanted to look into the Army system.

They talked about ships, the old battleships in particular, how to modernize them and how to use them in this war. They discussed the Savo Island battle and the loss of the *Wasp*. King regarded both as unfinished business; he wanted to know who was responsible for the Savo Island disaster, and if there was fault in the operation of the *Wasp*.

Earlier, Admiral Towers had begun a campaign to secure the appointment of aviators as task force commanders, where carriers were involved. Nimitz and King now agreed that a task force commander did not necessarily have to be an aviator and, furthermore, it was not Towers' business to raise the point.

It was agreed that in future amphibious campaigns the Marines would be the shock troops, and that eventually Nimitz would have four divisions of Marines. As for Army units, Nimitz was to feel free to move units around without consulting King at every turn. All he had to do was explain, so King could explain to the Joint Chiefs of Staff.

On the last day they recapitulated, and looked ahead. They considered moving through the Marshalls, or taking Truk. King said that anything would be better than making a frontal attack on the Malay Barrier. Eventually, they agreed, they would go up the China coast to strike Japan. No decisions were made about the future, but King was sure of one thing: they must not nibble around the edges.

In the South Pacific, on December 9, the First Marine Division was relieved and sent to Brisbane for rest and recuperation. To replace them, General MacArthur diverted to Halsey the Army's 25th Infantry Division. Nimitz knew, and he reported to Halsey, that he was getting (excluding the Marines) "the best division west of the Mississippi." Nimitz was also very high on Major General Joseph Lawton Collins, commander of the division. "He has brought his division to a high peak of efficiency and has imbued them with a will to kill Japs."

So the First Marines went to Brisbane. It turned out to be a sort of horror story, through a comedy of errors and misinformation. When looking for a place to rest his Marines, Vandegrift had gone to Brisbane, where MacArthur kept his headquarters. The outlying area of Brisbane itself had been suggested, because it was high on the Australian continent, and the Marines could be deployed back into action quickly if they were needed. It was assumed that Brisbane would be satisfactory in all respects; Vandegrift went to the trouble to inquire about health problems, and there did not seem to be any.

The First Marines had scarcely arrived at Brisbane, however, when their medical officers discovered they were moved from one malarial area to another. The camp was swarming with anopheles mosquitoes, which the Marines were trying to escape, and the luckless leathernecks were infecting one another all over again.

Vandegrift felt that he had been betrayed. He went scouting, and discovered that Melbourne, on the southeast coast, was temperate and comfortable. (It was also far more civilized, and full of girls, motion picture houses, and even had a zoo.)

Vandegrift tried to get in touch with MacArthur, the Supreme Commander of the area, to secure a change. He did not get very far. After pussyfooting for some time, Vandegrift wrote to Halsey about the problem, and then was in touch with Colonel B. M. Fitch, MacArthur's adjutant general, asking that his men be moved south.

On January 1 Vandegrift received a reply to his request. Colonel Fitch wrote him:

> The Commander in Chief directs I advise you as follows:
>
> His recommendations regarding location of Marine Division in Melbourne are approved. This approval is given because of the interjection into the situation of Admirals King and Halsey, which might indicate some inhibition with reference to the Marine division which is not known to the commander in chief and upon General Vandegrift's strong recommendation, although based upon divided medical opinion and despite his personal discussion with the commander in chief of the tactical and strategic inadvisability of such action. No transportation facilities are available in the Southwest Pacific area to effect the move, which will have to be carried out by shipping made available from the South Pacific area. General Vandegrift is authorized to communicate directly with naval authorities to make the necessary arrangements. The already overburdened railroad facilities of Australia cannot cope with such a movement without jeopardizing operations upon which our forces are now engaged.

So there it was: MacArthur would let the First Marine Division move, but Vandegrift would have to get Halsey to move him. Vandegrift was chagrined and embarrassed, but he approached Halsey and laid it out for him. Halsey swore, as was his fashion, and made uncomplimentary noises about Army Generals, but he supplied the transports, and the First Marines went south.

Halsey could be brash, and sometimes Nimitz had to hold him in check. Nimitz had argued the case of task force commanders, securing Washington's permission specifically to choose any officers he wished to command task forces. Halsey was short of aggressive admirals and captains. ("We are almost continuously under pressure here for want of Rear Admirals and Senior Captains in the pool.") He chose Rear Admiral C. P. Mason, an aviator, to command a task force, which included Rear Admiral Harry Hill. Since Hill was senior to Mason, some eyebrows were raised, including those of Nimitz. He wrote Halsey:

I have approved your placing Mason in command of a Task Force which has a senior [Hill] in it, but I desire to control the use of this authority in accordance with Secnav's letter of July 18, 1942. I am sure you agree with me that there are many line officers thoroughly capable of taking command of a task force which has in it aircraft carriers, and that nothing would be more harmful to the morale of our senior officers than to create the impression that only aviators may command task forces which have carriers included.

Early in January, while the Tokyo Express was still running, it was apparent that Guadalcanal was under control. On January 10 destroyers carrying supplies for the beleaguered Japanese moved down onto Savo Island, where they were intercepted by PT boats. A few days earlier they had sent down eight destroyers, and the PT boats got one of them, and kept them from landing supplies. This night two PT boats were lost, but the enemy supply mission was harried, and that was the object.

With such control, Nimitz could begin casting his eyes ahead without much worry. On January 10 he and his staff at Pearl Harbor decided it would be a good idea to meet with General MacArthur, to consult on the next steps the Navy would take, in conjunction with MacArthur's efforts. Nimitz offered to meet MacArthur in Nouméa, on January 17, a date he chose because Secretary Knox was coming to Pearl Harbor on January 12. If MacArthur bridled at going to Nouméa, Nimitz was willing to pick up Halsey and take him to Brisbane to meet on MacArthur's ground.

Nimitz made the offer. MacArthur replied that he was awaiting word from the Joint Chiefs of Staff with reference to the overall plan. He did not want to talk operations at this point.

MacArthur was obviously very chary of any dealings with Nimitz or the Navy, and not without reason. Halsey had growled about the limitation on his activities at the 159th meridian, and Nimitz had told him not to worry. Already the Navy had "invaded" the general's assigned territory, and he wanted to be sure it did not happen again.

At this same time Halsey was fretting. "I have been seriously toying with the idea of a carrier plus bombardment strike at Rabaul," he wrote Nimitz. "It is very tempting, the only thing that holds me back is my lack of knowledge of Phase Two (the second stage of the Solomons operation). I imagine that when that takes place we are going to need all the combatant ships that we can lay our hands on."

Halsey had many problems. He was establishing an offensive force of destroyers, the first purely offensive force of its kind in this war. He was trying to follow Nimitz's directive and bring the New Zealanders more into the war. (New Zealand was part of his responsibility, Australia was MacArthur's.) Early in January Halsey was in Auckland, making a visit of state, so to speak. He comported himself very well, and was immediately a popular figure. He got on well with the New Zealanders, and seemed to be making progress in the difficult job of integrating New Zealand fighting men into his command. He was having more trouble integrating the constant flow of Very Important People who wanted to go out and have a ten-minute war.

Please stop the flow of Washington experts and sight seers to this area [he wrote Nimitz]. Each expert means 200 pounds less of mail. I'll trade an expert for 200 pounds of mail any time. The straw that is about to break the camel's back are the three members of the Economic War Board [Board of Economic Warfare] who arrived yesterday. I cannot imagine a more useless outfit. I am thinking about inducting them into the service, putting them in uniform, sending them to CACTUS —let them do a little stevedore work (they won't be fit for fighting) and after teaching them something about the war, then send them home to economize.

After the Ghormley affair, Nimitz realized that he must keep close watch on so important a command as the South Pacific, which was actually his major fighting front. He had decided to keep one of his senior staff officers in the South Pacific at all times, and to make an inspection trip to the area himself at least once every three months. In the interim Captain Redman had been down south organizing communications, and Admiral Calhoun had been there, energetically helping Halsey set up the supply system for the future.

On January 23 Nimitz was in Nouméa with two members of his staff, meeting with Halsey; Marine Brigadier General Dewitt Peck, Halsey's war plans officer; Captain Browning, Halsey's chief of staff; and Rear Admiral McCain, chief of the Bureau of Aeronautics, who had flown out from Washington.

Nimitz began briskly with that wonderful way of his, in a few words outlining what the conference was going to cover and—equally important—what the conference was not going to cover.

"The object of this conference is to review the situation in the South Pacific and to exchange views," he said. "No decision will be reached. Indeed, we may not agree on all points."

Then he led them into it. "First, as to Guadalcanal. What is Comsopac's [Halsey's] view as to progress, approximate date Japs will be eliminated? Shall we need more troops? What number should be left as a garrison on completion of the operation?"

General Peck suggested a target date of April 1. The Second Marine Division could be withdrawn, and the Army forces could take over, two divisions plus service troops. Peck estimated there were eight thousand Japanse still on the island, with four thousand of them effective as fighting troops. He and Halsey did not expect the Japanese to make a further effort to take Guadalcanal.

"Peck has not been there for two weeks," said Halsey, indicating that there was some possibility of change in that situation. (It was a great change from Nimitz's last visit, for then he found that Ghormley and his people had not been there *at all*.)

Nimitz then sketched out the coming land operation by General Patch and his forces, and they discussed timing. They moved on.

NIMITZ: What is Comsopac's ideas on future operations from CACTUS-RINGBOLT [Guadalcanal-Tulagi] at the end of February with what you have, or on April 1st when planes will increase in number?

McCAIN [Chief of the Navy Bureau of Aeronautics, (cautiously)]: Promised increase in supply of planes.

NIMITZ: Is the increase of planes proceeding?

BROWNING: Yes as regards Navy planes, not as regards Army planes.

NIMITZ [vigorously]: Will Comsopac originate a dispatch to Cominch [King] info Cincpac requesting Army to carry out army replacement and upkeep program?

McCain noted that he would raise this issue on his return, armed with the dispatch, which King would automatically hand over to him. McCain would actually get after the Army.

At this point Nimitz called for General Harmon, the senior Army officer in the command, and messengers were sent to bring him into the meeting.

As they waited, they discussed minor operations, seizure of Russell Island, eighty miles from Guadalcanal, which would make a fighter field. General Patch's staff men discussed the coming ground operations in Guadalcanal, and Nimitz kept pressing for schedules and dates.

"How will CACTUS [Guadalcanal] be used next?" he asked.

General Peck suggested as a supporting base.

But not a permanent one, said Nimitz. "Everything should be based on a forward movement."

When General Harmon arrived, Nimitz restated the purpose of the meeting. "It is our understanding that the Army is behind in fulfilling its plane requirements," Nimitz said.

Harmon agreed. Nimitz asked for a copy of the Army plans, and Harmon promised to get it for him. He then told the conference that when the Japanese were eliminated from Guadalcanal they could begin work on Phase Two. He proposed that Halsey retain command of operations in the Solomons, even though he might impinge on MacArthur's geography, and asked if there were objections. General Harmon did not object and neither did anyone else. So the plans were to proceed.

This visit to the South Pacific included Secretary Knox, who was making his first trip out since the hurried flight to Pearl Harbor on the heels of the Japanese attack.

Knox came to Pearl Harbor, along with Adlai Stevenson, his administrative assistant, and two other aides. The big flying boat was loaded down with steaks and china and silver, so the entourage would not suffer from the rigors of the South Pacific. But they suffered nonetheless. The old "jinx" was along, was he not? The plane took off, and was just circling the cane fields outside Pearl Harbor when pilot McLeod announced that two engines had gone dead and he proposed to make either a deadstick landing on the water or a crash landing in the canefields after dumping the gas. Which did the Admiral want? Nimitz opted for the deadstick landing, and the pilot brought the plane down. But a hole was torn in the bottom, and the flying boat began to sink.

The party began moving up the hatch. Secretary Knox, who was broad in the bottom, got stuck, and the people below had to push him through. Then the others clambered out, in order of rank. They moved onto the wing and floated until Admiral Towers sent boats out from Ford Island to rescue them.

Towers found a PB-4-Y for the party and in a little over an hour they were off again, heading for Midway. Several hours out, Nimitz took off his cap for the first time, and asked his aide to look at his head. Lieutenant Commander Lamar was aghast: the snow-white hair was blotched and stuck with black blood. Nimitz had suffered a cut about an inch and a half long on his scalp.

Lamar found the medical kit. He did not want to put straight iodine on the admiral's cut, so he diluted it with water—not knowing that iodine and water did not mix very well. Nimitz nearly hit the roof.

On they went. At Midway they were greeted and dined by the officers of the command. While they were eating, their plane was refueled—and Nimitz's jinx worked overtime. The fueling boat collided with the plane and tore a hole in a pontoon. They could not take off for another day.

"The next twenty four hours were literally hell," said Lieutenant Commander Lamar. "Midway Island was too small to contain the Secretary of the Navy and the Commander in Chief of the Pacific Fleet and the Pacific Ocean Areas, both helpless and unable to get off the Island. Even the goonie birds ceased to be amusing after a few hours."

On the trip, Adlai Stevenson was initiated into the Ancient Order of Shellbacks of the Kingdom of Neptune by being fed a "cocktail" whose principal ingredient seemed to be fuel oil. Stevenson spent the remainder of that day being quietly but devastatingly sick.

They visited Fitch's headquarters at Espiritu Santo, Nouméa, and then Guadalcanal island. On Guadalcanal it was almost as if the Japanese knew they were coming, for their housing area was bombed sporadically from 2030 in the evening until morning. Halsey, along with Knox and McCain, dived for cover, but Nimitz said he was more afraid of mosquitoes than bombs, and slept in the hut in a mosquito bar.

Knox had a real taste of the new spirit that was developing in the South Pacific, and he told a story that symbolized it when he returned. One day two enlisted men were walking along the deck of the *Argonne*, talking about Halsey.

"I'd go through hell for that old son of a bitch," said one of them.

Just then someone poked the sailor in the back. He turned. It was Halsey.

"Young man," said the admiral, "I'm not so old."

Nor was he a son of a bitch, except perhaps in the eyes of the Japanese. Tokyo Rose delighted in these days in listing the tortures that would be heaped upon Admiral Halsey when the Japanese captured him. There was reason for the Japanese annoyance. Halsey at the end of 1942 had made a New Year's prediction—that the Americans would be in Tokyo before 1943 was out. He did not believe it, but he did not realize, either, what a symbol of the American fighting man he had become, or that his words would be taken as gospel back home. But with the victories in Guadalcanal, that is how it was. One day, Representative Melvin J. Maas of Minnesota wrote President Roosevelt a memorandum, suggesting that Roosevelt discard MacArthur and put Halsey in charge of the whole war in the Pacific.

On Halsey's recent trip to Auckland, he had given an interview to the press predicting Japanese retreat, and one newspaperman had summed up Halsey's public appeal:

> His confidence was clearly immense, but the expression of it was even and not in declamatory statements. It was so great and so obviously no bigger than his conviction that it was infectious, and as statement succeeded statement, it became very clear why it is said of Admiral William "Pudge" Halsey by his officers and men that they would follow him to Hell. He is a man whose confidence could clearly win battles.

That confidence did not entirely account for Halsey's hold on his men. Another reason was his own intense loyalty to them. Months earlier, as we have seen, he had asked for a specific officer, to discover that the officer was teaching ROTC at the University of North Carolina, and the Bureau of Personnel was loath to release him. The officer was Commander Oliver Owen Kessing, a graduate of the Academy's class of 1914, and an old friend of Halsey's. After much complaint to Nimitz and many ill-tempered exchanges with Admiral Horne, Kessing came to the South Pacific, where Halsey proposed to make him a base commander. But he came without promotion.

Halsey went to bat again with Nimitz:

> Kessing, despite my request, came out here a commander. I do not know why he was passed over nor do I care. I know him well personally and officially. He is a fighting man. Peace time and war time standards have small relationship. He will make good in any man's war, and this *is* every man's war. In order to further the war effort, in his dealings with the Army, Navy and Marines, he should be a captain. The fact that he is not is a distinct handicap. I shall officially recommend him.

If the Bupers still insists that peacetime standards are more important than furthering the war effort I am hogtied. Come what may, unless I get orders from higher authority, I shall keep him in command of RINGBOLT [Tulagi]. I consider him ideally suited for that job, which, in my estimation is the most critical in this area for future operations.

On this trip Halsey again brought up "Scrappy" Kessing. Nimitz said he had approved Halsey's request for the promotion.

Halsey announced that if the promotion had not come through by the time they returned to Nouméa he was going to send Kessing a dispatch, with a copy to Bupers: "You will assume rank, uniform, and title, of Captain, U.S. Navy."

"Chester had a fit," Halsey said.

Nimitz pleaded: "No for God's sakes don't do it. You'll foul up everything."

"You wait and see," said Halsey.

When they returned to Nouméa, Kessing's promotion had come through, and the incident was resolved. But again it had served to create impressions of Halsey—an impression that here was a commander of great loyalty to his men, which permeated the staff; an impression of a fighting admiral, which came across to Nimitz; an impression of an interfering revolutionary, which was very definitely in the dark thoughts of the bureaus of the Navy in Washington; an impression of hot-headedness that Secretary Knox took away with him.

By the end of January, Halsey could put five task forces into action—so much had the situation of the ships improved. As Nimitz and his party headed back for Pearl Harbor, Halsey sent these forces into the waters around Guadalcanal, to escort troops that were relieving the Second Marine Division at Guadalcanal. Task Force 18 was one of these groups of ships. It included three heavy cruisers, three light cruisers, two escort carriers carrying 29 fighters, eight dive bombers, and 24 torpedo bombers, and eight destroyers. (The coming of the escort carriers indicated what was happening as America's war potential was translated into ships and planes and men.)

The escort carrier was developed partly as a result of British and American studies of the war in the Atlantic, where the German submarines operated in wolf packs and harried the supply forces and merchant shipping, sometimes beyond the ability of destroyers and corvettes to put up effective defense. As ships became more readily available with the huge growth of the American shipping industry in the war, it became possible to divert some merchant ship hulls to conversion to aircraft carriers. These carriers did not of course, anything like fleet carriers or light carriers. They did not have complete machine shops of that kind; they carried a relative "handful" of planes. But they could be built quickly, they had adequate flight decks for operations, and they could carry fighters and bombers into battle. A half dozen escort carriers could bring a strong influence to bear, and by 1944 they were playing a role in Atlantic and in Pacific warfare in protection of shipping. In the Pacific they would be used for a new job, the covering of invasion forces from the Japanese land-based air, thus supplementing their responsibility to protect invasion fronts.

In this deployment of escort or "jeep" carriers, Halsey was rather hoping that Admiral Yamamoto would send down a major force. Yamamoto was in no position to do so; already the Japanese were beginning to feel the hardening of their oil arteries, and Tokyo had interdicted Yamamoto from any major excursions. But the Tokyo Express was still running—beginning to evacuate Japanese soldiers from Guadalcanal although the Americans were not yet aware of this change—and the Japanese still came in with determination, on the sea and in the air.

On the night of January 29, Japanese torpedo bombers found Task Force 18, and attacked. At a cost of three Bettys, they put a torpedo into the heavy cruiser *Chicago*. She was taken in tow by the *Louisville* that night, and all seemed well. But next day, the Japanese planes were out again, and a dozen of them found the force. Planes from *Enterprise* shot down three of them, but the other nine launched an attack on *Chicago* and the destroyer *Lavallette*. Seven of the Bettys were shot down, but the two ships were hit, and *Chicago* sank.

King was displeased. He was far more displeased with the general tenor of operations in the South Pacific. Because Halsey and Vandegrift, Patch and Harmon, Fitch and Lockwood and Christie had accomplished so much with so little, Washington found it hard to understand why the shortage of supplies was holding up the clearing-out of Guadalcanal, or why anything was holding up this operation. King had already suggested that "wait, delay, and linger" were the watchwords of the South Pacific force.

While Nimitz had been visiting the South Pacific, King was in North Africa, attending the Casablanca conference. There he had made the point that only 15 percent of all Allied war effort was being turned against the Japanese, and had suggested it was time for everyone to push harder in the Pacific. Sir Alan Brooke, the chief of the Imperial General Staff, had suggested that the Japanese were already on the defensive (which Halsey and Nimitz believed, but King did not).

The other members of the Combined Chiefs of Staff had wanted to talk about Europe, but King kept bringing the conversation back to the Pacific. If Japan was not to consolidate her gains, he said, more effort must be made. With his resources he could do nothing more than hold. He pushed for the British to move in Burma, thus to put a new pressure on the Japanese in another area.

King wanted to seize Truk, and move into the Marianas. "Keep moving" was his philosophy.

In the end, at Casablanca the guidelines were laid down for the campaign in the Pacific, until the defeat of Germany, which the President and Prime Minister hoped to accomplish in 1943.

King's biographer summarizes:

> Subject to this, and in addition to the maintenance of vital lines of communication and the continuance of submarine attacks against Japanese shipping, various operations in the Pacific were contemplated. These included an advance from Guadalcanal and New Guinea, leading to the capture of Rabaul, an advance westward in the Central Pacific toward Truk and the Marianas, a movement along the New Guinea-Mindanao axis as far as Timor, the establishment of the security of the Aleutian islands and steps toward the recapture of Burma . . . .

On February 2 King met with President Roosevelt and the others of the Joint Chiefs of Staff. Two days later he wrote Nimitz, complaining about the lack of progress in Guadalcanal. King seldom complained without offering specific remedies. In this instance he had several suggestions, which amounted to commands.

First, Secretary Knox had been up to his usual snap judgments. Coming back from the South Pacific, Knox had decided that the "failure" lay in Halsey's inability to plan movements ahead. His solution: replace Captain Browning as chief of staff with someone who knew more "about the capabilities of certain ships, amphibious forces, etc." There was much more to it than that—Browning had obviously antagonized Secretary Knox, just as he had sometimes antagonized King himself. Browning did have a sharp tongue, Halsey admitted it. But the saturnine and hard-living Browning also was a master tactician: he was given credit for choosing the moment of strike against the Japanese at Midway which resulted in the Japanese carriers being caught rearming their planes, and was a major factor in the stunning defeat administered by Spruance. It was no less Spruance's victory for all that—a commander takes the risks and the rap for any advice from staff members—but Spruance had nothing but praise for Browning's capabilities, as did Halsey. For both commanders, Browning's brains more than compensated for any personality deficiencies. Still, such are the fortunes of the military; even in wartime careers were made and wrecked by a snarl or the absence of a pleasant smile. Browning was to be replaced.

The second point, one of King's own, was that Fitch would need some help in planning and managing air bases in the Pacific as they moved along. King wanted to bring Rear Admiral Richard E. Byrd into that position. "I suggest Dick Byrd for this job because he is a 'driver,' but more than that, he has a vast fund of experience in planning and carrying out expeditions as well as a very considerable first hand knowledge of Naval Aviation." Byrd had already made a survey of islands suitable for air bases, in behalf of the Bureau of Aeronautics, visiting Palmyra, Tutuila, Upolu, Wallis, Tongatabu, Efate, Nouméa, and Bora Bora. King also requested a progress report on the Solomons campaign. "I am still 'unhappy' about the lack of progress," he said, ". . . and would like to hear from you (and from Halsey) some definite plan for getting on with the job. At present as for some months past, it seems to me that we merely continue to 'swap punches' with the enemy—to our advantage, to be sure—but without working to any plan that is apparent here."

King was irritated by MacArthur's continued failure to "state what his plans—not views—are . . . ." He wanted the ideas of Nimitz and Halsey as to what they would do if they were given a free hand in the Solomons.

Nimitz had known precisely how to handle the Army's failure to supply its airplane requirements when he had asked Halsey to send a hot message to King. On his return from Africa, King had found the message, and McCain had not had to do anything—King had taken the Army's failure up with General Marshall posthaste. He did not think there would be any more trouble, he told Nimitz. He also said, with some pride, that "the U.S. Chiefs of Staff insisted on recognition of the fact that there is a war going on in the Pacific, and that it had to be adequately implemented even though the major part continues to be in the European theater."

Four days later, Nimitz and Halsey gave King the answer they had been preparing for him for four months. The Japanese withdrew all the forces they could from Guadalcanal. There was the answer to King's charges of "punch swapping."

Chapter
Twelve

THE SECOND PHASE

February 9–August 1943

"Now that the enemy on Guadalcanal has been defeated decision must be made regarding our next moves," said the entry in Admiral Nimitz's daily war summary for February 9, 1943. "Cominch [King] . . . requests comments on an operation to seize, occupy, and hold Gilbert and Ellice Islands."

The war had taken a new turn. From the beginning, American submarines had been carrying out a bold and very successful fight against Japanese shipping. Until now they were the only American weapon that could reach into Japanese-controlled waters through which most of that shipping traveled.

The blockade of Japan was beginning, and it would never let up. So effective was Admiral Lockwood's force that Nimitz literally could pay less attention to it than to any other aspect of his war effort.

At this time it began to appear that sufficient resources would be available to continue the offensive in the Solomons and New Guinea area, and also to open up a front in the Central Pacific.

Spruance and Nimitz looked at the Central Pacific. They wanted to take control of that great area which lay west of longitude 180 degrees and north of latitude 5 degrees south. The area was controlled by the Japanese fleet, based on Truk in the Carolines. That is why Nimitz referred to Truk as the Japanese *cojones* and why he often talked of the day when his flag would fly above that base in a way that indicated he felt the occupation of Truk would be his greatest accomplishment to that date. Truk was connected to Japan by a series of air bases located strategically on islands throughout the area. Japan to the Bonins, to the Marianas, to Truk, and then out east and west was the way the line went. The bases were largely mutually supporting, and the air pipeline extended all the way back to Japan. Reinforcements of all kinds of planes could be flown down to Truk, a very great advantage the Japanese held at this point in the war.

But that was longer-range planning than King was requesting at this very moment, and Nimitz knew it. Nimitz was looking toward the Aleutians, hoping to move quickly to clean out the nest of Japanese who had moved in there at the time of the Midway battle.

With the change in command from Theobald to Kinkaid in the north, all the old difficulties that had bothered Theobald seemed to have evaporated. Perhaps both Army and Navy had learned to be a bit more forbearing with one another. In any event, Admiral Fletcher had made an inspection trip to Alaska, and he returned to Seattle to report to Nimitz that all was well. The Army people were learning to bomb at low level—and to operate under difficult conditions.

Nimitz confided his thinking to Kinkaid. He and his staff were considering a push toward Paramushiru and the Kurils. What he really wanted, however, was an estimate from Kinkaid about the difficulties of taking Kiska.

Late in February, Nimitz flew to San Francisco again to meet with King. This meeting marked a major change in the discussions between these two admirals. Before, the problems had been immediate, demanding answers and action. Now the two sat down to plan for a long and complicated war.

The major items for discussion involved logistics. There was the matter of dredges needed for Midway. When one is engaged in a life or death struggle for islands that control a continent, dredges do not seem very important. But Midway needed dredging, and the Pacific Fleet needed Midway as a staging area for ships and submarines on the offensive.

There was the matter of airplanes. Captain Ofstie, Nimitz's air officer, was to go to Washington to confer with McCain and the Joint Chiefs on air matters. Airplanes were beginning to come through for the Pacific, and it took some new bookkeeping to keep track of them. There would be reports from Washington about the number of airplanes sent. There would be reports from Halsey and other headquarters on the number of planes actually received; for some ships might be torpedoed, and some might deliver their cargoes to the wrong places. The war was becoming complicated, and more controls were being devised.

Much as Nimitz hated to consider the idea of increasing his staff, he was forced to do so. The old figure of thirty-two had long since been given the deep six. There were forty-eight senior staff members now, plus thirty young officers attached to Cincpac for training in communications, seven on bathythermograph duty, and four on the operations plotting board. It was still a small staff, but how much longer it could so continue was debatable: at this meeting there was talk of setting up a whole new section to deal with technical matters and analysis.

But it kept coming back to logistics. An aircraft assembly plant for Bora Bora? Joint information centers for the ports? Basic logistic plans for theaters involved in joint Army-Navy operations? Army services of supply officers for Navy service forces? Should there be 1620-ton destroyers, or 2100-ton destroyers for the Pacific? (Six months before *any* destroyers would have been welcome.) A fleet inspector general? As for Henry Kaiser's ships—eight of them were in various ports with cracks in their hulls and one tanker had broken in two at dockside. What was to be done? A floating battleship drydock for the South Pacific? Where?

For some time Nimitz and Halsey and King had been troubled by the demands of correspondents to cover the war, and the provision of transportation and press facilities for them. Actually, none of these commanders really liked having the press about. Nimitz and King agreed here that Admiral Jacobs would conduct a survey looking toward *reduction* of photographic, public relations, and intelligence personnel wherever possible. The press simply was not going to be allowed to be a nuisance in the war effort. Although radio intelligence had been very valuable already, sometimes the intelligence men seemed to disturb Nimitz and the others. In the early days of the war, before Midway, Captain E. M. Zacharias had been in Pearl as commander of a cruiser, and he had spent several hours telling Admiral Draemel of the dangers of an uprising of people of Japanese ancestry in the islands. Draemel had come away from the encounter with the feeling of clutching a ghost, a feeling that many line officers shared when confronted by specialists in intelligence.

It was not all logistics and annoyances, however.

King laid out the war plan for 1943. "Limited operations" was the term for it, protection of the allied lines of communications, while attacks were made on the Japanese. The American submarines were already proving to be a formidable weapon against Japan, and were whittling very satisfactorily at the long Japanese supply lines. But there must be more action.

Halsey would carry it. In the absence of any concrete statements from MacArthur, King said that Halsey would have to continue to work his way up the Solomons, for political reasons if none other. The test would be: "The operation should cut the Japanese supply lines, while protecting our own."

In one way, the American position was reversed, and not favorably. Earlier the Japanese had air superiority, but in the Solomons campaign the Americans had attained air superiority on a defensive basis. The haul for the Japanese to attack was a long one. But now the haul for the Americans to attack the Japanese bases would be a long one, and would temporarily preclude the use of torpedo planes and dive bombers against their shipping. It would be unwise, said King, to bypass their land-based air positions until their air strength had been whittled down considerably.

Air fields at Tarawa, a seaplane base at Makin, a succession of air fields in the Marshalls, fields and seaplane bases at Jaluit, Maloe-lap, Wotje—all these demanded attention before the advance could be carried on. So the action was to be "attrition" while concentrating on building up American air strength, pushing the Army into meeting its commitments, and building air bases.

King, of course, wanted action—which meant the seizure of territory. But Nimitz argued against frittering away American strength in seizing territories which he might not be able to hold. They agreed that the Japanese fleet was, at that moment, still stronger than anything the Americans could put together to oppose it.

Nimitz argued for caution. The new *Essex*-class carriers were on the ways, but it would be months before they were ready for action. In the meantime, the Japanese had this strong interior air supply line by which they could ferry planes and equipment through the islands from Japan to the South Pacific without use of ships, while the Americans simply had to depend on shipping. Nimitz was in favor of attrition, knocking out all the Japanese planes possible and waiting until the fleet strength could be ready with the fleet air power that was needed.

The move at this point, said Nimitz, was to be economical in the use of American forces, concentrating on attack by submarines and aircraft against Japanese shipping. He would undertake any operation that had a reasonable prospect of success, and whose failure would not be disastrous, but he did not want to go too far. (Here was the slogan that hung by his desk again.)

King argued back. It was a question of initiative. The Americans had it, they must keep it, even take "very considerable calculated risks" to retain that initiative. Otherwise Nimitz might find himself in a position where he would be ordered (by the political leaders) to undertake operations which might not be sound.

Nimitz must not forget, either, said the Commander in Chief of the Navy, that King had been through considerable difficulty in obtaining allocation of more forces for the Pacific at this time. They must be used, or he could not justify asking again at the Combined Chiefs of Staff meetings. In other words, Nimitz had to honor the promissory notes King had given at Casablanca, if King was to be able to help Nimitz further in the matter of supplies and men.

Nimitz said Japan would never give up just because her fleet might be decimated. King agreed, and added that China must be kept in the war, if for no other reason than to provide necessary bases for the later stages of the campaign against Japan. Operations would eventually move to the China coast, the admirals agreed.

The meeting on February 23 was devoted to review of the military situation in the South Pacific. Nimitz noted that he now had about 250,000 men in the area. A move would be made, using the Samoa–Fiji–New Caledonia line as the basis for operations.

Now began a period of building and consolidating. Halsey was hard at it; in spite of Secretary Knox's low estimate of Halsey's abilities as commander (as opposed to fighter) Halsey saw precisely what had to be done, and began to do it. The problem was to get the ships a place to come to, to bring them in, to get them unloaded in the right places, turned around, and out of the South Pacific. Halsey had asked Nimitz for more destroyers—but there were no more destroyers. Nimitz had suggested that Halsey let the ships move about in the area without escort. Halsey refused, even though the days when Ironbottom Sound seemed to be a Japanese lake had ended. "I do not feel justified in sending ships into the CACTUS-RINGBOLT area, particularly troop ships, without an escort," Halsey told his chief.

The supply and logistics problems were extremely complicated, even here, because the Navy was not geared to a long-line logistics approach. In order to help things along, Nimitz had sent Admiral Calhoun down to Halsey numerous times, and Calhoun had established a service squadron (ServonSopac). But in the tactical area, logistics were the responsibility of Admiral Turner, the Amphibious Force commander—and that specifically meant Tulagi and Guadalcanal, where bases had to be built up.

Thus there were two commands involved. Nimitz had suggested that the whole supply organization be put under Rear Admiral Cobb, the service squadron commander. Halsey had both commanders working, separately, for him, and they liked it.

For example, when ships arrived at Nouméa consigned to the

Navy, Cobb worked out the details of unloading with the Army, for the Army had charge of unloading at Nouméa. General Williamson, the Army base commander, had Army, Navy, Marine, and native laborers as stevedores, working on a sixteen-hour basis, with no distinctions among them. On arrival at shore, the Navy hauled off its own supplies, the Army did likewise, and so did the Marines, and put them in their own dumps. (Warehouses were being built.)

In the meantime Captain Nick Carter, the advanced bases supply man, was free to travel around to various bases and worry about their special problems. He was directly subordinate to Halsey, and Halsey felt it ought to stay that way. So did Carter. So did Cobb.

Supply in the forward areas was also difficult and complicated, because it involved Army, Navy, and Marines. Cobb would allocate vessels to all forward areas except Tulagi and Guadalcanal. The commanding general (Army) on Guadalcanal would submit a requisition for all the forces there and in Tulagi, and these would go to the commanding general of the services of supply (Army) who parceled them out to the various services. The stores were then allocated and assembled on ships moving forward. Kelly Turner would appoint a convoy commander, and the ships would move out. The commanding general on Guadalcanal would then supervise the unloading.

Halsey wanted to keep the organization that way. "However," he said, "I am not bull headed, at least I do not think I am, and I am perfectly willing to change at any time."

Soon enough, he would have to change. During all these months when Nimitz had been directing the war in the Central and South Pacific, General MacArthur had been fighting in the Southwest Pacific. After Bataan, MacArthur had been completely on the defensive for several months. The Japanese had cleaned up the Philippines and the Netherlands East Indies. They had moved into Timor and Ceram, and then Dutch New Guinea. They had moved into Lae and Salamaua. In May, 1942, they had started to invade Port Moresby—this was the invasion stopped by the equivocal victory of the Americans at the Battle of the Coral Sea.

All this time, MacArthur was getting practically nothing from America. The forces allocated to the Pacific went to Nimitz, to fight the Battle of the Solomons. In the autumn of 1942, when

Vice Admiral Arthur Carpender had relieved Leary, MacArthur's naval forces consisted of five cruisers, eight destroyers, twenty submarines, and seven smaller craft. The once-proud, though small, Asiatic fleet of the United States had been practically wiped out in the battles of the Philippines and the East Indies. Admiral Thomas C. Hart had come home. What was left of the fleet had been put in the hands of a Dutch admiral, and that was soon dissipated.

The first offensive action had been the capture of Milne Bay, New Guinea, using Australian and American troops, and Australian and American naval forces. The Japanese had tried to take Milne Bay, launching an amphibious operation, but the Australians and the Americans had fought them off. General MacArthur then set out to push the Japanese out of Papua. After months of almost unbelievable jungle fighting in mountains and swamps, the Australians and the Americans concluded the Papuan campaign just two weeks before Guadalcanal fell. The Japanese then decided to reinforce Lae with a convoy and naval force from Rabaul. Eight transports and eight destroyers set out. They sailed at midnight on the last day of February.

On March 2, B-17's of General Kenny's command caught the convoy north of Cape Gloucester and sank one transport. The B-17's came in at medium altitude, and the Japanese ignored them. But then along came several flights of A-20's and B-25's, medium bombers whose pilots had trained for low-level attack by skip-bombing. They moved in and devastated the convoy. Most of the ships were stopped or sunk. Four undamaged destroyers rescued survivors as they saw them, and fled north to escape the allied planes. Then, on March 3, the PT boats found the Japanese. Together, PT boats and bombers did away with twelve of the sixteen ships of the convoy—only those four destroyers escaped.

This Battle of the Bismarck Sea set the stage. A new offensive and a plan were wanted, within the framework of the 15 to 20 percent of men and material that the Combined Chiefs had estimated they could spare to the Pacific during 1943. What was needed was more correlation of effort between MacArthur's and Nimitz's commands. In March the efforts began.

On March 7 Miles Browning and other staff officers from

Halsey's South Pacific force went to Pearl Harbor, where they met with MacArthur's representatives. Halsey wanted to move against Munda in April. MacArthur proposed to move against the Huon Gulf, and suggested that Halsey delay until May. Nimitz agreed with Halsey, and since the argument could not be settled, the Halsey men and the MacArthur men went to Washington, accompanied by Admiral Spruance and Captain Ernest G. Small, Nimitz's war plans officer. They would take their cases before the Joint Chiefs of Staff. One point was that MacArthur had always felt the Solomons fell within his bailiwick, but now the Navy had so built up the area that it had a vested interest.

The Joint Chiefs decided that Halsey should wait until MacArthur moved. Furthermore, they issued a directive throwing command into a very difficult situation. MacArthur would be in charge of the next operations. Halsey would be in charge of the Solomons campaign, but he would be responsible to MacArthur, except that any ships, planes, and ground forces of the Pacific Fleet that were not specifically assigned to the operations under MacArthur by the Joint Chiefs would remain under Nimitz. There, obviously, was a formula under which a minor tactical defeat could be turned into a strategic disaster by a failure in communications, or a clash of egos. What was needed was total cooperation between the commands.

In the past Halsey had been extremely critical of MacArthur; not the least of this attitude had stemmed from MacArthur's highly developed sense of public relations. He gave newsmen very thorough access to the facts of the war. Having such material available, the correspondents wrote many stories about the MacArthur command, and its activities were dominating the newspapers.

The Navy's sense of public relations was embryonic. Traditionally the Navy liked to mind its own business. In the case of the Pacific Fleet—and the Navy at large—there was another indefinable factor. During the Spanish-American War (which came during the formative years of most of the men who were admirals in World War II) Rear Admiral William T. Sampson had been assigned to blockade the Spanish along the northern shore of Cuba. Commodore Winfield Scott Schley had been assigned the southern coast. Sampson had set out at once to hunt for the Spanish, Schley had delayed, and the Spanish fleet had gotten by him and into Santiago de Cuba, where it lay under the protective guns of land batteries. Admiral Sampson had arrived off Santiago de Cuba on June 1, and assumed command of the blockade, since he was senior officer present. There was a certain friction between the two men and their adherents because of the manner in which the Spanish fleet had made its flight to safety.

Admiral Cervera, the Spanish commander, was under orders from his king to fight to the death, and on the morning of July 3, 1898, he brought his little fleet of four cruisers and three destroyers out of Santiago harbor. At that moment, Admiral Sampson was absent, and Commodore Schley took tactical command. Sampson rushed back to the scene, but by the time he got there the battle was virtually history: the Spanish naval might was destroyed.

Then came a dingy page in American naval history: the two commanders began to quarrel about the honor of the victory. The quarrel lasted until their deaths, and divided the naval service; many hot arguments were waged and many friendships destroyed by adherence to one or the other of these men.

King, Nimitz, Halsey—all the senior admirals—could remember this disgraceful period only too well. They blamed the press, by and large, for keeping the struggle alive. Nimitz had vowed "that if ever I reached a position of high command, I would do my best to stifle any such family controversies before they reached the attention of the public." But more than that, Nimitz, like King, Richardson, Bloch, and others, had become exceedingly shy of publicity.

One reason for the Sampson-Schley controversy to have become as important as it did, was the taking of sides by various members of a new breed—the war correspondents. Greatest of all these was Richard Harding Davis, but the war correspondents of the Spanish-American War were all romanticized figures, and their words carried much weight. In World War I the Americans entered late and the Navy's work was largely unromantic. World War II brought an entirely different picture, and yet the Navy was not attuned to the changes.

The American press had been too well informed for too long to accept censorship without a struggle. The Navy had a very good argument: fleet operations must be treated with far more secrecy than land military operations. Take a simple case of identification, which proved all-important. The Japanese believed that they had sunk *Yorktown* in the Battle of the Coral Sea. Had they known the truth, Admiral Yamamoto's planning for Midway might have taken quite a different turn, and the whole balance of the battle might have been changed. The Japanese did not know the truth about the *Yorktown* because naval censorship concealed the facts about the movements of ships and damages. In other cases the Japanese might think they had sunk a cruiser when actually they had sunk a destroyer—and the difference in fleet power was very great indeed.

Such was the legitimate argument for special public relations practices in the Navy that differed from those of the Army. But censorship can also be used to cloak idiocies. Furthermore, the people at home in the United States were vitally concerned with the progress of the war, their production efforts depended on their morale, and this effect of the military upon the civilians was a factor the Navy professional officer corps was not yet ready to appreciate. America had never been involved in an all-out war before.

When Nimitz took command of the Pacific Fleet he inherited his public relations officer, Lieutenant Commander Waldo Drake, of the Naval Reserve, who had been shipping editor of the *Los Angeles Times*. Drake was a conscientious and extremely loyal man, inclined to hot temper and sometimes injudicious use of language, but he knew precisely how Nimitz wanted the press handled, and he did as he was told.

In the beginning, a handful of newspaper correspondents was assigned to cover the war. Foster Hailey came for *The New York Times*, James Kilgallen for *International News Service*, Keith Wheeler for the Chicago *Times*, Robert Casey for the Chicago *Daily News*, Robert Trumbull for the Honolulu *Star Bulletin*, Frank Tremaine for *United Press Associations*, Jack Rice and Wendell Webb for *Associated Press*.

Wheeler, for example, had flown out to Pearl Harbor by clipper, with Hailey and Kilgallen, on Christmas Day, 1941. He had secured his press credentials, and the Navy had let him interview a handful of fliers who had shot down some Japanese planes. The wreckage of the battleships was in plain view for all to see, but the correspondents' questions were not answered. A few days later Wheeler, Rice, Robert Landry of *Life*, H. R. Knickerbocker of the Chicago *Sun*, and Joseph C. Harsch of the *Christian Science Monitor* and Casey went to sea with Task Force 8. They were to be involved in the first big Halsey raid.

As the war progressed, more correspondents came to join the fleet. Waldo Drake was promoted to commander, and his assistant, Lieutenant James Bassett, was sent down to the South Pacific to work for Halsey. Guadalcanal brought a new flock of correspondents into action, and in those desperate early days the correspondents seemed to be a terrible nuisance. They wanted plane space. They wanted to get their stories out. Some of them, fresh from civilian life, complained about their foxholes and other accommodations, and sometimes the naval officers became furious with these complaints. But by and large, the difficulties came about because Halsey, Nimitz, King, and the others took the position that two hundred pounds of mail was of more value to the fleet than two hundred pounds of correspondent. With Japanese bombs raining overhead, it was easy to forget that back home the people needed to know, independently, how the war was going along, and they needed nonsecurity details, which only writers and reporters could give them.

The difficulties of public relations came to light in this period of lull. The New Zealand minister to the United States asked Nimitz for permission to stop off in Guadalcanal on his way home, and Nimitz granted it, so informing Halsey. Halsey bleated:

I'm afraid I have been placed in a position that may well be embarrassing by your gang. When the fighting was still in progress in Guadalcanal I refused permission for any civilians to go even to BUTTON. Mr. Coates, a very fine gentleman, also a member of the New Zealand war cabinet, requested authority in November to visit both BUTTON and Guadalcanal. I turned him down. Your order for Mr. Nash, the New Zealand Minister to the U.S., to be permitted to go to Guadalcanal will, of

course, be carried out. However, it will give Mr. Coates a real
reason for kicking if he chooses to make use of it. As a member
of the New Zealand war cabinet he will naturally feel he has
more right to visit his own fliers than has an accredited minister . . . .

Nimitz replied soothingly. Halsey had been quite right, he said,
but matters had changed.

As a matter of policy in dealing with New Zealand officials,
I believe we should accord them as much opportunity as is
practicable to visit the areas in which they have an interest.
New Zealand has made, is making, and will continue to make
a very vital effort to participate in the South Pacific War. Their
willingness to participate has won for them a very friendly
feeling in Washington with our high military and naval
authorities.

Nimitz had another matter in mind that day. The fact was, he
told Halsey confidentially, "during my incumbency in my present
job, I have been slowly but surely pushed into the position of
lending all facilities to newsmen which will not prejudice operations,
and of releasing factual material which is of no assistance to the
enemy."

"In doing the above," he added, "I have kept just one jump
ahead of Col. Knox, who has almost taken the matter out of my
hands once or twice."

And thus Nimitz announced a basic change in Pacific public
relations policy, based on recommendations made by Waldo Drake,
who had just returned from the South Pacific. Newsmen had been
denied the use of the airplanes traveling between the South Pacific
and almost anywhere. They traveled by surface ship, and sometimes
their dispatches did too. Nimitz now told Halsey to give the newsmen rides on planes, and to send their press copy out by plane as
well. He sent to the South Pacific Lieutenant (JG) Frank Rounds,
who would go with Fitch and thus handle news copy in the
forward area.

The matter had come to a head just then, because Robert C. Miller, a United Press correspondent, had written a "hot" article about press censorship in the South Pacific. Halsey's censor had refused to pass it and sent it along to Nimitz's staff. Nimitz was releasing it, "without question, because I do not object to honest criticism." He suggested that Halsey read a copy of the article and note the complaints. "While I do not propose to countenance releases which will be of benefit to the enemy, I believe that we should do everything in our power to avoid getting a bad press—which articles like Miller's will certainly bring about."

And as for Drake's recommendations, Halsey had best carry them out quickly: "The above suggested steps should be taken by you at once to obviate remedial directives from Col. Knox."

Another cloud on the horizon was an intraservice rivalry that threatened to become serious. In the first year of the war, it had become crystal clear that the most spectacular weapons against Japan were submarines and airplanes. As far as submarines were concerned there was no difficulty. The "silent service" had proved itself long since. In Nimitz's early days officers were assigned to the submarine service willy-nilly, but no longer. It was a volunteer service now, a highly honored branch of the Navy. Captain Christie had recently fleeted up to rear admiral and was commanding the submarines of the Southwest Pacific, for Rear Admiral Lockwood had just moved to Pearl Harbor to become a vice admiral and commander of submarines in the Pacific Fleet, on the death in an airplane crash of Admiral English. All three of these officers were professional submariners.

The cloud that was growing darker concerned the air service. Where the submariners "ran their own show," and could claim that even Nimitz was one of them, the airmen were disconsolate because they wanted more seniority and more control of their own affairs. There was a big difference, however. A submarine operated alone or in a pack with other submarines. Airplanes operated from land bases or from carriers, and in the case of carriers, these highly vulnerable "portable airfields" demanded support from heavy ships, cruisers at least, and preferably fast battleships, antiaircraft cruisers, and many, many destroyers to protect them from enemy submarines.

That was the rub. The aviators contended that since the central core of the task force was the carrier, the task force should be commanded by an aviator. The "line officers" contended that an aviator *might* command a task force, but not solely because he was an aviator. Actually, aviators *were* line officers, but there was a difference between aviators and other line officers—a difference that had existed for many years. In the years before the war, the aviators had green flying uniforms and khaki uniforms, with black stripes on the sleeves to denote rank, and brown shoes. Sometimes, also they wore the line officer's blue uniforms with gold braid or their resplendent whites with gold braid, and black shoes.

After the war began, and in the southern seas it was a matter of wearing whites, it soon came to Admiral King's attention that whites were really not cut out for warfare—the officers in their white uniforms stood out starkly on the decks of the gray battleships at night.

King then authorized "that" uniform, the gray, which was to be worn by all services. And also there were khakis and whites and blues.

Neither Nimitz nor Halsey liked the grays. Some officers came into the fleet from stateside or from the Atlantic wearing the new uniforms, but they quickly stowed them in their seabags or sent them home, and adopted the khaki that was universal in the Pacific. The difference, then, between the various services seemed to be diminished, but in fact the terms "black shoe" and "brown shoe" now developed. The aviators had been wearing brown shoes with their greens and khakis, the line officers wore black shoes with their blues and whites. The aviators kept their brown shoes and the line officers their black shoes.

The shoes were only symbolic, what was important was the attack by the most fervent of the aviators against the very structure of naval command. The "line officers" feared that if the aviators had their way, then none but the airmen would succeed to major command in the future. And in the development of the war and of air power, the fear was growing month by month. The aviators chafed.

Halsey, an aviator himself, was chafing during the lull in

fighting, but for a different reason. To get things going again, he made a trip in April to Brisbane to see MacArthur, whom he had never met.

"Five minutes after I reported," he said, "I felt as if we were lifelong friends."

MacArthur received Halsey in his office, rose from his bare desk, and paced back and forth between desk and the wall, where hung a picture of George Washington. The general was sixty-three, but Halsey said he did not look more than fifty years old; his hair was jet black, his eyes were clear and piercing, and he carried himself firmly erect. As they talked, MacArthur paced, poking the air with his corncob pipe and orating. Halsey was impressed and admitted it. His unkind thoughts of the past vanished, and were replaced by a deep respect for the general—which obviously facilitated the unlikely relationship between their commands.

Halsey returned with agreement on their combined operations, which were to begin May 15. Just after he came back, naval intelligence scored a new coup. Breaking the Japanese naval code again, the radio intelligence men deduced that Admiral Yamamoto was moving out on an inspection trip and would arrive at Ballale island near Bougainville on the morning of April 18. P-38's of the Army 339th Fighter Squadron moved out that morning to intercept, and shot down the Japanese admiral's plane in flames. Halsey and his people were delighted—Yamamoto had been a formidable enemy. His loss cost the Japanese dear in the months to come.

Plans continued for MacArthur's Operation Elkton, which was to include the invasion of New Georgia by Halsey, combined with MacArthur's moves in New Guinea and occupation of Woodlark and Trobriand islands. The operation was delayed until June, however—logistics and training problems. Halsey continued to be occupied with bombardment and bombing of the Japanese. One day the Japanese mounted a furious air attack on Guadalcanal, and when it was over Halsey claimed 107 Japanese planes shot down, against loss of only six American planes.

When the invasion was finally launched at the end of June, it proved a much more formidable task than expected, and New Georgia was not finally secured until August 5. Then Halsey sent

Major General Oscar W. Griswold a victory message: "This is a custody receipt for Munda and for a gratifying number of enemy dead. Such teamwork and unrelenting offensive spirit assures the success of future drives and the implacable extermination of the enemy wherever we can bring him to grips. Keep 'em dying."

Bloodthirsty, to be sure, but it was this very bloodthirstiness, apparently shared by most Americans in 1943, that endeared Halsey to his countrymen and made him a symbol of the war against Japan comparable only to MacArthur himself.

Such messages kept Halsey in the Amercan public eye while Nimitz, his commander, was scarcely known to the vast majority of Americans. But Nimitz would have it no other way. He was not particularly pleased at Halsey's personal glory—he simply did not care for any for himself.

Chapter
Thirteen

THE ALEUTIANS

January 1–May 20, 1943

As 1942 drew to a close, the complexion of the war was immensely changed from what it had been just a few months before. The Americans could not in any way become overconfident, but they could see, for the first time, a victory ahead if they fought courageously and well.

Since Midway, the Japanese had held a small but bitter thorn against the side of the Americans in the continued occupation of portions of the Aleutian islands, very close to home. King and Nimitz had begun serious discussions of offensive action in the North Pacific in 1942, and much of the King-Nimitz meeting of December that year was devoted to specific problems of mounting such an offensive.

They talked of occupying Amchitka and of launching an invasion of Kiska, the major Japanese stronghold. What had to be done was train Army troops for the job—two divisions, Nimitz said. And the commander of the Pacific Fleet also spoke of one of his favorite projects: operations in the Bering Sea against Japanese fishing, which would hit the enemy where it hurt. King listened rather impatiently to Nimitz's talk about defeating Japan by starvation. He was much more interested in operations against Kiska— and right away.

The man in charge was Rear Admiral Thomas C. Kinkaid of the Naval Academy class of 1908, who had distinguished himself already in the South Pacific under Halsey in cruiser warfare, and had thus become a candidate for a prime command. This command was given him in November, 1942, just before the Battle of Tassafaronga, when Kinkaid had planned an excursion against the Japanese. Instead, his battle plan was adopted by Admiral Wright, and had brought that unlucky admiral to disaster.

Kinkaid moved off to Seattle and Alaska. When Nimitz decided to launch an attack in the Aleutians as quickly as possible, Rear Admiral Francis W. Rockwell was called in as commander of Amphibious Forces in the Pacific Fleet, at San Diego. He would supervise the training of those Army divisions, and then deliver them into battle.

In January, 1943, Rockwell began his work. The Army's 7th Infantry Division began amphibious training in California. Kinkaid, meanwhile, was preparing for overall operations. In correspondence, Nimitz kept pushing for his little project of interfering with Japanese fishing, a little wistfully.

> As you know [Nimitz wrote], this industry plays an important part in their food economy. I believe that up to 30 percent of their fishing craft operate in the Sea of Okhotsk. If we could throw a scare into the boats by occasional forays with our S class submarines, I feel sure we could cripple production to some extent. The operation would have to be executed carefully, for there is always the possibility of shooting up a Russian boat by mistake. In this connection, boarding officers at Seattle have obtained information on the differences between Russian and Japanese fishing craft. This is available to you. This project has been attempted before but always, at the last minute, an

imperative need for the necessary ships elsewhere forced abandonment.

The ship situation was still critical. Nimitz had recently inspected one of the new landing ships-tank (LST). The ugly, flat-nosed LST's represented something new in amphibious warfare. He liked them, he told Kinkaid, but the real problem was the need for skill in handling these ships in rough seas. He did not tell Kinkaid, who had just asked for six of the new LST's for his Aleutians operations, that Kinkaid would get only two. The American forces were still spread very thinly. The new LST's were too scarce to apportion as any commander would like, in good weather or in storm.

Very soon another storm blew up in the North Pacific. Perhaps it was the cold climate and foul weather that brought commanders to one anothers' throats. Just as Admiral Theobald and Generals Butler and Buckner had argued earlier, now Admirals Kinkaid and Rockwell disputed over questions of command, until the Army commander of the Pacific coast, Lieutenant General J. L. DeWitt, was thoroughly confused as to who was running what.

Nimitz felt impelled to explain, which he did in a letter to DeWitt. Kinkaid was to be in command of the North Pacific for the Navy, and Rockwell was to be subordinate to him as amphibious commander. In January the Army had occupied Amchitka, which was uninhabited, but no amphibious commander had been involved. Thus, said Nimitz,

Kinkaid retains command and control until [Brigadier General] Jones advises that the status of the occupation warrants incorporation in the Alaskan Defense Command. In the case of Attu, where opposition will be present, the ground force commander must have tactical command ashore from the time of landing. Rockwell will remain present as the Naval Commander while the landing phase of the operation continues, which will probably be until all opposition on shore has been destroyed. Thereafter, Rockwell's presence and some of his forces will no longer be required and he will revert to my direct command and control. Naval support, however, will still

be required for a considerable period and, upon departure of
Rockwell, the naval responsibility and command for continuing
support operations will be exercised directly by Kinkaid . . . .

Such were the confusing responsibilities of Nimitz's command
that he would have to resolve such questions from a distance of
thousands of miles. They were not very easily resolved. Rockwell
continued to agitate and Kinkaid continued to fret, until Nimitz
was forced to send no fewer than three separate dispatches reiterat-
ing Kinkaid's power, and a soothing letter to Kinkaid besides.

By that time much had happened and much more was committed. At the end of 1942, when Nimitz had decided to remove
Admiral Theobald in the North Pacific because of frictions with
the Army and air force commanders, he had also removed Rear
Admiral H. H. Smith as commander of the task group there, and
substituted Rear Admiral Charles H. McMorris, once a member of
the Nimitz staff.

On March 26, just off the Komandorskie Islands in the North
Pacific, Admiral McMorris was looking for Japanese reinforcements, to harry them, in view of the impending invasion of Attu.
He had the light cruiser *Richmond*, flagship, the heavy cruiser
Salt Lake City, and four destroyers. Just after breakfast that morning, the force made radar contact with five vessels and prepared to
fight. But when the vessels appeared out of the murk, they were
not five, but ten, and although McMorris did not know it, two
more ships were in the area. The Japanese—for this is what the
other force turned out to be—were two heavy cruisers, two light
cruisers, four destroyers, and two transports. The odds were greater
than two to one, but McMorris attacked.

The Japanese, under Vice Admiral Boshiro Hosogaya, came at
them very fast, guns blazing and torpedoes racing. As the action
continued, *Salt Lake City* was struck repeatedly and went dead in
the water when salt sea snuffed out her burners. Fortunately, she
was hidden by a smokescreen at the time.

To save her, Admiral McMorris launched a destroyer attack
on the Japanese column, and as the destroyers came up, the Japanese
turned away. Later it was learned that Hosogaya was low on fuel,
low on ammunition, had not seen the damage done to *Salt Lake*

City, and was disgusted with the performance of his own destroyers, which had been less than aggressive. The Americans were very, very fortunate.

As the Japanese turned, the engineers aboard *Salt Lake City* managed to clear the fuel lines of salt water and get the cruiser under way again, and the force went home to Dutch Harbor, having by bold aggressiveness turned disaster into victory.

Then came the invasion of Attu. Late in April the 7th Army Division embarked at San Francisco, and met the protective force at sea. All the naval forces rendezvoused at Cold Bay, on the end of the Alaskan peninsula. On May 29 ships set out for the invasion, and on May 31 they were ready to land. Fog had closed in that morning, and the landings were delayed until mid-afternoon. But the landings were unopposed by the Japanese garrison, which had retreated into the long valley known as Massacre Valley, and by 2000 hours that evening some 2000 troops were established on the beaches. Eventually a landing force of 11,000 men went ashore, to meet some 2600 Japanese defenders who were badly armed and badly supplied, thanks to Admiral McMorris' attack at the Komandorskies, which had persuaded the Japanese against resupplying Attu.

The terrain was terrible: mud under muskeg, which caused the soldiers to slip and the trucks and tractors to bog down in slime. The ships stood offshore and bombarded the areas where the Japanese were supposed to be, with great vigor but little effect, even though they exhausted all their ammunition. Fog and confusion slowed the American advance, and in forty-eight hours they had gone approximately nowhere—not even a mile inland. General A. E. Brown, the Army commander, was so discouraged that he muttered about needing reinforcements and road-building equipment to get across this land, and so unwise that he growled that it would take him six months to capture Attu. Unfortunately, the growl was issued in the presence of an officer of the USS *Pennsylvania* who took the word back to Admiral Kinkaid; and the admiral, who was in charge of the whole operation, decided to relieve the general. On the evening of May 16 Major General Eugene Landrum relieved General Brown.

The Americans then began to move. The Japanese resisted fiercely, staging a banzai attack by a thousand hopped-up warriors on the early morning of May 29. They overran command posts, and the forward medical station, stabbing a chaplain and several wounded soldiers, but eventually were stopped—whereupon some five hundred of them committed suicide rather than surrender.

Then abruptly, the battle was over. Nearly all the Japanese defenders were dead, either killed by the soldiers or by their own hands.

One of the strong points of the American commanders in the Pacific war was their willingness to admit mistakes and profit from them. At the King-Nimitz meeting in San Francisco on June 1, Rockwell made a thorough presentation of the pluses and minuses of the operation.

Intelligence had led him to expect that there were 300 Japanese on Attu—in which case a landing force of 11,000 men would seem adequate. There turned out to be 1500, he said. (Even after the battle, intelligence still missed the total by over a thousand.) The training had been inadequate: only one ten-day exercise for each army battalion and no training at all on the beach. In the landings they lost nine boats of a total 110. Rockwell blamed this on the lack of an attack cargo ship, which could unload supplies into boats much more handily than attack transports, which he had.

The hydrographic information about the area was totally inadequate, based entirely on photographs. The bombardment had not taught them very much, really: "Now we have learned that this type of bombardment can be done but it should be done more intelligently." But no one went into any detail about the effectivenss or lack of it, and the reasons. Not until after Iwo Jima would the admirals accept the limitations of naval bombardment against deep, strong Japanese-type fortifications.

Major General Holland Smith, the Marine amphibious expert, delivered a critique of the land operations. The assault was good enough (especially since there was no opposition), but the troops did not push ahead when they could have. On one occasion, he said, the troops could have moved ahead a thousand yards more than they did, which would have put them on top of a ridge. They stopped, however, at nightfall, and thus gave the Japanese a chance to regroup. Next morning it took them until noon to take the ridge.

The inexperience of the Army in amphibious operations showed badly. When the colonel in Massacre Valley was killed, and General Brown took over, the advance bogged down immediately, because the scouts were way ahead of the troops, and he did not know they were out.

Smith was extremely critical of the American military philosophy that we must outnumber the Japanese by seven to one or more. He called for development of a fighting spirit. But by and large, Nimitz was satisfied with the performance in the capture of Attu, and he sent an enthusiastic "Well Done" to Rockwell in behalf of the the whole team. He did warn however, that "no commander is ever going to have everything he wants, or feels he needs, for any operation he has to conduct. The manner in which he disposes his means to obtain the best possible results is the real test of his ability to command."

Nimitz also wrote Kinkaid, and showed his appreciation of that commander's work more forcibly: he told Kinkaid he was recommending him for promotion to vice admiral. Nimitz also admitted gracefully that the problems between Kinkaid and Rockwell had been occasioned by Nimitz's failure to have Rockwell report to Kinkaid in the north before undertaking the amphibious operation from the south. The remainder of that letter, however, was devoted to a businesslike discussion of the planned operation against Kiska, which would be next. As for Admiral McMorris, his conduct at the Battle of the Komandorskies won him the job of chief of staff to Nimitz, who wanted aggressive thinkers around him.

As always, after this operation there were some problems and ruffled feathers to be smoothed. The situation of Vice Admiral Frank Jack Fletcher was particularly difficult. Fletcher had been a key figure in the early days of the war, sidetracked because of King's suspicion that he was not sufficiently aggressive. In the Aleutians operations King had directed Fletcher to place himself and his forces at the disposal of Nimitz. Fletcher had placed the resources of his northwest sea frontier at Nimitz's disposal, but not himself, for it was awkward for him to consider taking orders from Rear Admiral Kinkaid. Nimitz had to assure King that Fletcher's action had caused him no trouble, and he also had to soothe Fletcher's feelings, because that admiral was disconsolate at being left out of the action. He did so, with marvelous aplomb. He told King that Fletcher had been most cooperative, and he told Fletcher that he would make more use of his services in the planned operation against Kiska. He indicated to King that this situation would resolve itself after Kiska, since no more operations near a sea frontier would be contemplated. But Fletcher could continue to hope that operations against Japanese possessions in the North Pacific might bring his reinvolvement in naval action.

Although Nimitz was thousands of miles away from the scene of the Aleutians action, the tight hand of his control was here. For example, the transport *Middleton* had gone aground in heavy seas months before, and after an inquiry, Kinkaid disciplined the captain of the ship. His action and his report had come in time to Nimitz's desk, and late in June, Nimitz wrote Kinkaid about the affair:

> The *Middleton* record is at hand. To put it briefly, your action, in the light of the record, puzzled me. A review of the testimony shows no evidence of culpable inefficiency on the part of the captain and no lack of training on the part of his ship's company as would contribute to the grounding. As I see it, the captain knew the risks involved but, required by the Army to accept them he took all the precautions that prudence and good seamanship demanded. Curtis, who is here, spoke of the fine work done by the captain of the *Middleton* in support of the army during the entire time that the salvage operations were in progress.
>
> There may be some background to this that I do not know. Your interpretation of the testimony probably differs from mine. Prior to disapproving your action, as I must on the record, I desire your comment.

Kinkaid replied that the captain *had* made a reasonable plan, but had not followed it, and had shown bad seamanship. He supported his argument with details; Nimitz then, and only then, approved Kinkaid's punitive action. The commander in chief of the Pacific Fleet never missed a trick.

Chapter
Fourteen

PREPARATIONS FOR ATTACK

January 1–May 25, 1943

If the Japanese threat against the American continental territory was to be ended, it must be done in several ways. For as long as anyone could remember the Naval War College studies had indicated that a war against Japan would be fought in the Central Pacific. Still, there were many considerations, and while Nimitz recalled very well his studies at the War College, and later was to say with some exaggeration that everything he did in the Pacific was the application of those studies, the basic naval plan was very much in his mind.

At this point in the spring of 1943, there were many delicate balances for Admiral Nimitz to consider in laying his plans. They were, also, *his* plans. Much earlier the strategy of the Pacific war had been laid down in meetings among the personalities: the Joint Chiefs of Staff entrusted general supervision to Admiral King, and Admiral Nimitz presented his plans to Admiral King, who then approved, embroidered, or disapproved. Usually he approved the major part of the plan, but made some alterations of his own.

In the early months of 1943, and particularly in the spring, Nimitz began "stepping out." With a little more materiel to use, a steady flow of officers and men from the west coast, and some feeling of jubilation in a few hard-won and very important victories, Nimitz's planning could be cautiously aggressive.

When the Joint Chiefs of Staff set up the combined operations between Halsey's South Pacific command and General MacArthur's Southwest Pacific command, Nimitz was quick to see how the wind in Washington was blowing. He recognized a preference by the Joint Chiefs for giving the Army general strategic command of such big land operations as New Guinea would involve. He also saw something else.

"Under MacArthur's plan," Nimitz wrote King, "there will be little real need for major surface forces of the Pacific Fleet in the Sopac area until well into the summer. On the other hand, the presence of the bulk of our forces in Sopac area during this period of waiting will offer incentive to the Jap fleet (which is definitely *not* pinned to the Solomons–New Guinea area) to strike elsewhere in the Pacific."

What Nimitz proposed was the establishment of a huge new task force—Task Force 50—and the promotion of Raymond Spruance to vice admiral to take charge of this force. He would draw from the South Pacific and from the North Pacific to create this striking force. Actually Task Force 50 had been put together from Battleship Division 3 "and some odds and ends of cruisers and destroyers" some time earlier. But Nimitz had come down with malaria, following his exposure in the Solomons weeks earlier, and matters had been delayed a bit.

In that spring Rear Admiral Charles H. McMorris distinguished himself in a cruiser battle in the North Pacific, and thus won first place on Nimitz's list of those who might succeed Spruance. In May, Attu was invaded successfully and on May 18, the day that Holtz Bay was brought under American control and the northern and southern invasion forces of Attu linked up, McMorris was detached and ordered to Pearl Harbor. He came with the highest recommenda-

Chester W. Nimitz (second from right) as a commander and staff officer. The other officers are unidentified.

December 7, 1941—early morning. The USS *Shaw* explodes at Pearl Harbor.

Admiral Halsey speaks up in the South Pacific.

Admirals John F. Shafroth, Raymond A. Spruance, and Arthur W. Radford.

Nimitz pitches horseshoes at an enlisted men's get-together.

Rear Admiral Milo Draemel with President Franklin D. Roosevelt.

Top: Marc Mitscher in a pensive mood.
Left: Admirals J. S. McCain and Aubrey Fitch.
Bottom: Nimitz, front seat, and Secretary of the Navy Frank Knox, rear seat, in Espiritu Santo during the Secretary's tour of the South Pacific. Admiral Fitch is barely visible in the rear.

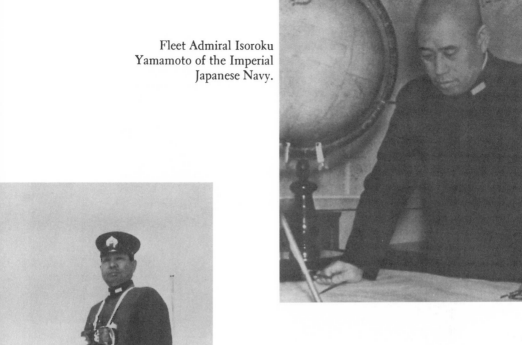

Fleet Admiral Isoroku Yamamoto of the Imperial Japanese Navy.

Admiral Soemu Toyoda.

Admiral Chuichi Nagumo.

Left to right: Admirals John H. Towers and William L. Calhoun, and Secretary James Forrestal at Pearl Harbor.

Left to right: Admirals Spruance, Ernest J. King, and Nimitz, and Major General Sandeford Jarman.

General George C. Marshall and Admiral Nimitz.

Nimitz in his Pearl Harbor office with Captain Preston Mercer and his schnauzer Makalapa.

Admiral John Hoover, standing, with Nimitz and King as they tour the Saipan battlefield.

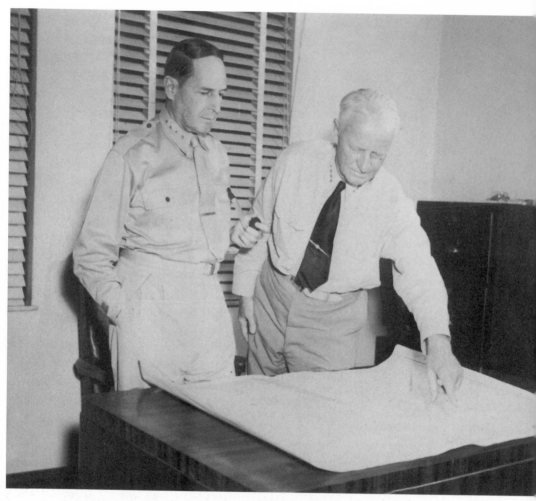

Nimitz and General Douglas MacArthur on the occasion of the celebrated visit to Brisbane when "the mountain went to Mahomet."

The participants in one of the King-Nimitz conferences (left to right): Admirals Spruance, King, and Cook, Secretary Forrestal, Admirals Jacobs, Nimitz, and Fitch.

TOP: Admiral Nimitz in the Pacific with Artemus
Gates, Assistant Secretary of the Navy for Air.
BOTTOM: (left to right) Admirals Kauffman and
Towers, and Generals Douglas and Hale.

Top: Nimitz, aboard plane, rereads one of his
letters home.
Bottom: Admiral Nimitz and Admiral C. A.
McMorris hold the Texas flag on the eve of the
celebrated Texas picnic. Lieutenant H. S. Smith
of the Nimitz staff is behind the flag.

Top: Nimitz with Admiral Sir Bruce Frazer on HMS *Duke of York* on the occasion of Nimitz's receiving the Knight of the Bath medal and ribbon from the British admiral. General Carl Spaatz is at right.

Bottom: Marine Lieutenant General Holland M. Smith, Admiral Richmond Turner, and Admiral Harry W. Hill.

Nimitz decorates his son, Lieutenant Chester Nimitz Jr., for distinguished service with submarines in the South Pacific.

Admiral Nimitz signs the Japanese surrender document. Directly behind him are General MacArthur, Admiral Halsey, and Admiral Sherman.

tions: Secretary Knox called him "a fighting man of the first water" and expected McMorris to "bring a vigorous pushing force into our Pacific command." When he arrived, he found the headquarters very much changed from the place he had left a few months earlier. He moved into Nimitz's house, along with Spruance, and they settled down to make the transition.

An indication of the degree of change that had come to Pearl Harbor in 1943 might be found in the situation of Commander Wilfred B. Goulett, Nimitz's radio officer. Goulett had been on duty at the Naval Research laboratory at Anacostia, when he was chosen to replace Commander Donald O. Beard. He had not wanted more electronics duty, but a sea command. That was too bad: officers were moved where they were needed, and communications officers were in short supply.

Goulett came to Pearl by clipper in January, 1943. He found the small staff, his new skipper with the china blue eyes and soft voice, the demand for loyalty and long and hard hours that all the staffmen accepted as part of their job. He soon discovered that the war was outpacing them there at Pearl—he discovered it when senior officers came to him as electronics specialist, and demanded supplies that he did not have. Then Goulett became aware of the word "logistics."

Until the Pacific war, the Navy's demands for supplies had been reasonable—something that could be handled by the paymaster and supply officer. But no more. By that summer of 1943 the change was in the air. Or was it? That summer, as the pressures grew, a rear admiral showed up with an investigating team, sent out by the Navy Department to find ways and means to *cut down* the admiral's staff and Cincpac's requirements.

When Goulett arrived, really to be electronics officer, he took over the Cincpac Pool, which consisted of thousands of spare parts for electronics equipment. The details of management were handled by the commander of the service force, whose office was next door to Goulett's in the dun-colored building. The system had just grown, from the early days, and Goulett found that he was personally authorizing the release of nearly every item. Spruance talked to him about this one day, and finally they came to the conclusion that the right to release electronics equipment belonged to the people who managed it, the service forces, so the change was made. What they were talking about was radar sets, sonar sets, and all the special electronics equipment that provided so much of a jump for the American forces against the Japanese navy. But Goulett kept control, and soon they were calling the electronics department "Goulett's Empire."

He moved into quarters with Admiral Calhoun's house on one side of him and Admiral Nimitz on the other. Nimitz's house was very quiet, but Calhoun could be seen striding across the lawn, cutting across from headquarters to his house, talking to himself in very loud tones, and sometimes swearing so loudly that he could be heard a block away, as he considered the supply problems of his Pacific Fleet.

Nimitz was unbelievably patient with his young men. One day when Lieutenant Commander Francis Duborg had the staff night duty, the commander brought Nimitz the night dispatches early in the morning when the admiral came to the office. Nimitz went through them quickly with Spruance, and came upon one that had been put out by a junior staff member without authority. He did not approve of the action.

"I'll call the young man on the carpet and see that he never pulls another boner like this," said Spruance.

Nimitz looked up mildly. "Well," he said, "there's no real damage done and perhaps the idea has some merit. It isn't what you or I would have done, but at least he showed initiative and took positive action. Let's not kill his fire. Keep your eye on him and insure that he is kept informed of command policy."

But Nimitz could also be very, very tough. As McMorris gradually took over from Spruance that summer, the office of chief of staff quickly became known as "Bottleneck Bay," and the situation indicated by this title posed some interesting problems for members of the staff. One day the assistant public relations officer, Lieutenant Commander Kenneth McArdle, was asked to prepare a list of questions the correspondents wanted to ask the admiral.

McArdle did his job—fourteen questions it was—and passed them on to Admiral McMorris. Now, Soc (for Socrates) McMorris was a strategic thinker of renown, but he had very little use for the press. Consequently the questions went into Bottleneck Bay. And there they stayed.

Next morning, the correspondents gathered in the public relations office and McArdle took them down to see Nimitz. He welcomed them individually by name, and they sat down in the folding chairs in front of the desk and he began to talk. He covered the situation of current operations—he answered all fourteen questions and more—and when it was over McArdle was delighted.

At 1600 that afternoon McArdle was called to the admiral's office, and there he found Nimitz sitting behind the desk with that half-smile which meant nothing at all.

"McArdle," said the admiral, "do you see what time it is?"

"Yes, sir," said McArdle.

"It's four o'clock," said Nimitz, "and that list of questions I asked you for came in just this minute. This is a hell of a time to get questions here for a ten o'clock press conference."

McArdle gulped and stammered. "Sir," he said, "I thought—I mean I gave it to Admiral McMorris at this time yesterday."

"Hereafter," said Nimitz, as though his junior had not spoken, "when I ask you for a communication, give it to me direct. If anybody else wants a copy, send them a copy. But send the original down here to me. That's all."

McArdle, feeling like a seven-year-old boy with his hand caught in the jampot, slunk out. He did not even have the strength to blame old Soc McMorris for his troubles.

Another of Nimitz's great attributes as a commander was his ability to keep on learning even when he had reached the top of the Navy ladder. Gradually he was leavening his attitude toward public relations. His greatest fault, from the standpoint of his public relations men, was that he failed to see the difference between information and personal press agentry, and he shunned the limelight for himself and was forever warning his Public Relations officers (PROs) that they must not build him up.

Spruance was an entirely different personality from Halsey, for example, and although on the surface he seemed to be much more like Nimitz, he was sterner, more intellectual perhaps, and far more introverted. If he had his way, the correspondents would not have been allowed hammock room on his ships, and he very seldom would meet with the press. Spruance expressed his attitude:

> Personal publicity in a war can be a drawback because it may affect a man's thinking. A commander may not have sought it; it may have been forced upon him by zealous subordinates or imaginative war correspondents. Once started, however, it is hard to keep in check. In the early days of a war, when little about the various commanders is known to the public, and some Admiral or General does a good and perhaps spectacular job, he gets a head start in publicity. Anything he does thereafter tends towards greater headline value than the same thing done by others, following the journalistic rule that "names make news." Thus his reputation snowballs, and soon, probably against his will, he has become a colorful figure, credited with fabulous characteristics over and above the competence in war command for which he has been conditioning himself all his life.
>
> His fame may not have gone to his head, but there is nevertheless danger in this. Should he get to identifying himself with the figure as publicized, he may subconsciously start thinking in terms of what his reputation calls for, rather than of how best to meet the actual problem confronting him. A man's judgment is best when he can forget himself and any reputation he may have acquired, and can concentrate wholly on making the right decisions. Hence, if he seems to give interviewers and publicity men the brushoff, it is not through ungraciousness, but rather to keep his thinking impersonal and realistic.

Spruance *did* give reporters the impression that he was brushing them off. Yet he could be surprisingly cordial. Frank D. Morris of *Collier's* sought an interview with him after Spruance was appointed to his new job, and Waldo Drake said, in that high, scratchy record voice of his, that it would probably be impossible but that he would try. Surprisingly to all in public relations, Spruance granted the interview, and could not have been more cordial in discussing the progress of the war. Yet he made several points that indicate why

Spruance has come down in history as the prototype (along with Nimitz) of the Navy officer living the Navy way.

> This job we have to do out here in the Pacific can't be handled by any one branch of the service. It requires complete coordination of surface and air forces, troops and submarines . . . .
>
> There's one thing you have to remember about making war—the breaks, good and bad . . . . Luck plays an important part in any of these operations . . . .

Characteristics that would not have made Spruance President of the Baltimore Rotary Club were held in high esteem by his fellow admirals. "I consider him one of the most competent men I have ever met," said Vice Admiral Calhoun, ". . . a cold-blooded fighting fool. If he possesses one fault it is that he believes too much in work and doesn't get enough play."

As a personality, that allegiance to efficiency was one of his problems. The mind that conceived of saving time by having a stand-up desk to drive away visitors also had little use for popular vices. Spruance found no time to drink, except to taste cocktails, in a crowd often given to hard drinking while ashore. Perhaps it was because by this time he had only one kidney. He did not smoke. One time, while walking with Goulett at Kailua, he led the younger officer at a fast pace until Goulett was virtually panting. They stopped to rest, and Goulett lit up a cigarette.

"There," said Spruance. "You've had some good exercise and now you go and spoil it all."

In the house at Makalapa, McMorris soon found his place, along with Nimitz and Captain E. A. M. Gendreau, who was fleet physician and the one man—outside his chief of staff—whom Nimitz felt he could allow into his confidence to a certain extent. But the degree of "confidence" was never really great: even as chief of staff, Spruance did not know until Nimitz actually relieved Ghormley and put in Halsey that Nimitz was going to take this action, and Spruance was surprised. Spruance was with Halsey at Nouméa, having started on an inspection trip—but obviously Nimitz had never discussed Ghormley's command performance with him in this case.

Always, with all his subordinates, Nimitz kept at arm's length. He was extremely fond of Halsey, but when Halsey sent Captain Browning back to the United States for a "blow" and Browning did not present orders, Nimitz put on his Cincpac cap and dressed Halsey down, reminding him that Nimitz was still in charge. Yet even as he chided, Nimitz did it gently. The same day that Halsey was apologizing thoroughly for having overstepped the mark in the matter of Browning's orders, Nimitz opened a letter to Halsey by enclosing a clipping from the Honolulu *Advertiser* which praised Halsey and MacArthur as "kindred souls."

As Nimitz prepared for Central Pacific operations, he made assessments. In May he sent Admirals Calhoun and Callaghan down to Halsey, with orders to make a complete survey of the logistics, situation, and plan for the future. The bottlenecks were ships, aircraft, and amphibious troops, in that order, he said. As for ships, Halsey was doing a fine job of turning them around at Nouméa, but it was still not enough for the type of operations they would be facing in the future.

All this effort was preparatory to travel to San Francisco at the end of May for one of the most vital of the King-Nimitz meetings, at which the course of the offensive war in the Pacific would be shaped.

Chapter
Fifteen

PUTTING THE TEAM TOGETHER

May–July 1943

Nimitz had recommended a plan to King in the spring of 1943. It called for the first big move in the Central Pacific, the capture of the Marshall Islands. The Joint Chiefs had ordered this capture, the order had come down through King to Nimitz, and at the San Francisco conference in May, Nimitz was to give King the detailed plan for operations, the strategy all filled in, the tactics to be left to the man who commanded the battle force.

Nimitz took the matter up with Spruance, his chief of staff. How would they take the Marshalls? The problem became a matter for discussion in the staff meetings.

The first plan, advocated by many, called for the division of the Marshalls group into four or five atoll targets—those which were needed by the Americans to control the islands. American strength was to be divided into four or five forces to take the islands. Admiral

Spruance objected. He said his fellow admirals were looking upon this operation as far too easy. "I proposed an approach from the southward, tying it into our lines of communications between Pearl Harbor and New Zealand–Australia. Forrest Sherman, who was then chief of staff to Comairpac [Towers] was the only officer at these conferences who recommended a preliminary operation prior to going into the Marshalls." He favored taking Wake first.

Nimitz listened to all his admirals. He finally decided on the southern approach—which meant taking the Gilberts first, as Spruance wanted to do. That plan was submitted to Admiral King. He approved, but he ordered the simultaneous capture of Tarawa and Nauru, about 380 miles away, in the general direction of Truk. Spruance did not like it; the Japanese fleet, which was as strong as the American fleet at that moment, was based on Truk. "We had no land-based aircraft that could observe Truk, and were dependent on our submarines for information of Truk." Nauru was a phosphate island, which the Japanese had taken from the British and used as an airbase to search the southern sector of the Marshalls and Gilberts. It would have been of very little use to the Americans.

Spruance ordered his planners to come up with alternatives. In this atmosphere Nimitz went to the King-Nimitz meetings of May. Most of the talk was about plans and the changing needs of the fleet for offensive operations. The building program had caused troubles— training was needed for ships and men coming into the fleet—for several destroyers had recently arrived which showed very low ratings in gunnery. The trouble, of course, was that the ship-building program was getting ahead of the manning and training. King was complaining about the slowness of the fleet in sending men back to man the new ships, Nimitz was pushing his admirals and captains to let good men go to new jobs, but the whole performance was ragged.

The opening day of this King-Nimitz conference was devoted to a first-hand report on the recent Aleutians operations by Army General DeWitt.

The second day was devoted to personnel problems. As the number of commands increased in the Pacific war—ships and shore —so did the complications of command. King and Nimitz talked over the question of making some commodores, an old Navy rank long since abandoned except for such circumstances as the Navy now found itself in. An officer might find himself in a position, as a captain, where he directed the activities of a number of other captains senior to himself. It would be useful to make him a commodore, settling the matter of rank, yet not creating another flag post with all its complications. Halsey wanted at least eight commodores (including Browning, who was still his chief of staff). Towers wanted Forrest Sherman made a commodore as chief of staff to the commander of air forces, Pacific. Calhoun wanted his commander of service squadrons made a commodore.

Browning was really in trouble. Nimitz and King discussed again the need for replacing him as chief of staff to Halsey. Nimitz said that the practice of giving temporary duty with leave (to get expenses) had been abused and he was cutting it out. Unlucky Browning was the cause.

Nimitz did not forget the people who were doing good jobs for him. Captain Small, the war plans officer, wanted a sea command. Nimitz recommended him for rear admiral and a cruiser division. He also recommended that Kinkaid be promoted to vice admiral, on the basis of the victory at Attu.

His memory was long. Milo Draemel was long gone from the Pacific command, but Nimitz wanted a Distinguished Service Medal for Draemel, in honor of his unstinting service as chief of staff in those first dark days before Midway.

Nimitz was not above reveling in a small triumph, either. Back in the days before the war, when the clouds were darkening, Nimitz, as the Navy's personnel man, had stuffed the ships of the fleet with enlisted men, to train them at sea. At the time, indignant Congressmen (spurred by angry letters) had brought the practice to the attention of President Roosevelt. The President had charged the Navy with maintaining unhealthy and unreasonable conditions on the ships and had demanded that the complements be reduced below 100 percent, as established by the uniform standards. The finger was pointed at Nimitz and he had been in trouble. But before long came the Japanese attack at Pearl Harbor, and this matter was forgotten. At this meeting, however, Nimitz could not resist reminding King of the dispute, and the benefits the training was now bringing to a fleet short of enlisted men.

Assessing the commanders in the southern reaches of the Pacific, the shrewd King and Nimitz agreed that sooner or later MacArthur and Halsey were going to come to blows over publicity matters. Nimitz said that was all right—he had already instructed Halsey to let MacArthur have it.

On the third day the two admirals talked about troop disposition in the South Pacific, and Halsey's forthcoming operations there. Then they got down to the future.

The Navy's freedom of action was in the Central Pacific, they agreed, and the most promising point was the Marshall Islands. Or was it the Gilberts? Both were considered.

Nimitz assessed the Japanese situation. Their striking force had been the third fleet, consisting of fleet carriers and fast battleships, with screen ships. Now the Japanese had only four fleet carriers, *Junyo, Hiyo, Shokaku* and *Zuikaku,* plus several converted carriers which were suitable for ferrying and not much else. He did not believe the Japanese would fight on the fringes of their empire, with the bulk of their fleet. We would have to move in closer to the Philippines and the China coast first. He also believed Truk had been eliminated as a major naval base.

On the next day, May 31, Nimitz and King had a long discussion (with King doing most of the talking) on various moves to reorganize the Navy. King said he was willing to let the specialists reign in their own areas, but he insisted on preserving the principle that line officers constituted the command corps of the Navy. (The day before, from Pearl Harbor, Admiral Towers had written to Artemus Gates suggesting to the Assistant Secretary that the job of Commander in Chief of the Navy be dropped, and the old Chief of Naval Operations reign supreme—with his principal deputy an aviator.

It was always essential for these two men to be looking far ahead. Talk of the Central Pacific operations led to more talk about South Pacific operations. Just what was going to happen down there, King wondered. MacArthur was supreme in his area; how would that affect Halsey's status?

Among other titles, Halsey held the command of the Third

Fleet. Would it be a good idea to relieve him as South Pacific commander and let him take the ships to sea as a fleet? Nimitz thought it was a bit too soon to consider a major change, and King agreed. But maybe Halsey should be given to MacArthur as a task force commander, thus letting him move about where he might be needed.

Admiral C. M. Cooke, Jr., of King's staff, suggested that it might not be a bad idea to keep a running check on what MacArthur was getting down in the Southwest Pacific, in ships and planes and men. The problem was to give MacArthur what he needed for his operations and keep him happy, and still keep his supply geared to actual plans.

The meetings continued on June 1, with a first-hand report of the Aleutians affair by Admiral Rockwell, the amphibious commander. The reports were of unusual interest because everything said was adding to the body of knowledge on amphibious warfare. At this moment, everyone assembled there expected that they would have to put up a much stiffer battle to take Kiska than had been the case with Attu.

One item for discussion at this meeting, as at previous meetings of these admirals, was the submarine campaign. Nimitz was very pleased with the operation of the Pacific submarines. He wrote Halsey:

Our submarines continue to turn in a fine performance of duty. With a gradual increase in the number of submarines in the Western Pacific, the Japs' ability to keep their far-flung island Empire supplied will gradually wane, and the time will come when they will have to make tough decisions regarding the abandonment of this, that, or the other distant island base, simply because it cannot be kept supplied.

At the May conference King had assured Nimitz that the submarine building program was going to continue, unabated, and that he could expect a gradual increase in submarines in the Pacific. Earlier the admirals had discussed the problems of the submarine torpedoes, which had dogged the American Navy since the outbreak of the war.

When war had begun, torpedoes were manufactured by the

Naval arsenals, and it was impossible for them to meet the demand. Industrial firms were asked to begin building torpedoes. Their first big change was to fabricate torpedo casings from bent sheet steel.

Another problem of the submariners could be tracked back to the prewar budgets. Congress was not very generous with the Navy, and so the Navy parceled out its dollars very carefully. Although there were hundreds of submariners in the service, most of them had never seen a torpedo explode, because torpedoes were fired with dummy warheads, so they could be picked up and used over and over again. A hit was supposed to mean an explosion.

When war began, and Admiral English's submarine captains came back to Pearl Harbor with reports of torpedoes that porpoised, or ran deep, or exploded prematurely, or hit the target and did not explode at all, in the beginning the naval authorities were inclined to be suspicious. But the reports continued, and they came from the Asiatic fleet, from the Southwest Pacific, and from the submarines that ranged out from Pearl Harbor itself. Something was wrong. When Admiral Lockwood appeared at Pearl Harbor early in 1943 to take command of the fleet's submarines, one of his first concerns was the poor performance of the torpedoes. He stated, in a letter to Rear Admiral W. H. P. Blandy, chief of the Bureau of Ordnance:

> The percentage of hits has in many cases been low, and the average is still below my hopes and desires. Some of this is due to bad shooting, lack of knowledge of the T.D.C., buck fever, jitters, etc. and we are trying to correct that part by a T.D.C. school here with Dusty Dornin, our best operator, doing the instructing. Also, our training by actual attacks and torpedo shooting prior to patrol is being needled.

Yet Lockwood knew that more was wrong. Stocks of torpedoes were low, and Lockwood was talking to Nimitz about undertaking extensive mining operations to make up for the poor torpedo performance. His torpedo officer suggested that they deactivate the magnetic exploder on the Mark 6 torpedo. "There is much of interest and much food for thought in this memo," Lockwood added.

By June, Lockwood was definitely displeased. The Bureau of

Ordnance had made some changes in the Mark 6 exploders, but they had not yet come to Pearl Harbor.

The fact that so many of our prematures have occurred in torpedoes fired against aircraft carriers is to me most significant. If the Japanese have a means of creating a magnetic field which will explode our torpedoes at a point beyond the dangerous range, certainly they would apply this system to their most valuable ships first, i.e. to CV's. Naturally I am loath to inactivate the magnetic feature because it produces such splendid results when it does perform properly, but unless we get an aircraft carrier soon, I feel that we must cut out the magnetic feature. We have shot at 4 with prematures in every case, in the last two months, and I await only news of the results of Mr. Bayh's conversions before taking this step.

At this time the Bureau of Ordnance was working on a new Mark 18 torpedo, but it was far from perfected. In the spring of 1942, Westinghouse Electric Corporation was given a contract to produce the Mark 18, an electric torpedo, although the faster Mark 14 torpedo was already being built. The idea was to put through a rush program. But with a new weapon a "rush" is relative. By June the Bureau had five handmade torpedoes to begin experiments. A year later the experiments had not gone very far. As far as the Mark 14 was concerned, four to six hundred were being produced each month. The struggle, then, continued. Nimitz was aware of the torpedo problem, but since it was only one of so very, very many that faced him, he left it in the hands of Lockwood.

One of Nimitz's pressing problems was the organization of Halsey's command. He and King were certain that many of the problems that appeared came from faulty organization, and this, they felt, could be traced to his chief of staff: Browning. Nimitz went to Nouméa in June and looked over the situation. He returned, satisfied for the moment, and ready to turn his attention to the Central Pacific.

One of Nimitz's command faculties was the ability to stretch to its limits the principle of command for the commander, yet keep total responsibility in his own hands and make sure that he knew everything that was going on in the planning of an operation. He did not want the details, but he insisted that he know the broad outlines, and more—how the outlines would be sketched in.

Equally important, when Nimitz picked his men, he stuck with the "first team" (his own word) and he brought to his senior commanders the same feeling that only "best" men need apply for top jobs. Without overdoing it, Nimitz made command in the Pacific as important as it could be anywhere, and he engendered a pride in his commanders that was unmatched in the war—or at least unsurpassed. What happened, logically, was that Nimitz's top commanders then picked up some of the attitudes of "the boss."

A case in point is that of Admiral Spruance. In his behavior and his planning, he followed Nimitz's course. It was sometimes said by members of the staff of Cincpac that Nimitz had brought Spruance in as chief of staff, kept him in the Nimitz presence by day at the office and by night in the house on Makalapa, and reshaped Spruance's thinking until it matched his own, then sent Spruance out, confident that the junior admiral would act just like Nimitz himself in all conditions.

One of Admiral Spruance's assignments as commander of the new offensive force of the Pacific Fleet was to gather the men who would work closely with him. Over the years, in command positions and as teacher at the Naval War College, Spruance had learned as well as any senior officer in the Navy how to pick men and give them the authority and responsibility to do the jobs demanded. In that tenor he began to choose.

Spruance's first task was to assemble his *personal* staff. Most admirals had specific people in mind for all jobs. Not Spruance: he chose Captain Charles J. Moore as his chief of staff—for he had served years earlier with Moore when Spruance was a lieutenant commanding the destroyer *Bainbridge* and Moore was a young ensign under his command—and then he directed Moore to choose the remainder of his staff, with the injunction that Moore keep the staff to a minimum.

Getting Moore was not entirely easy, for this particular captain was serving as a member of the war plans division of the Office of Naval Operations and senior member of the Joint War Plans

Committee of the Joint Chiefs of Staff. In other words, he was in a key job in the top command. At the May meeting of Nimitz and King, Nimitz had asked for Moore's service in behalf of Spruance, and King had growled that he was not at all sure Moore could be spared. But the old Navy principle of giving an admiral the men he asked for stood Spruance in good part, and King let it be known that Moore would be made available.

Spruance's second task was to pick the senior commanders who would transport the troops to the area attacked, and to get them ashore, lead them once they were placed ashore, and protect them from the air during the battle.

For the first, he chose Rear Admiral Richmond Kelly Turner, the man who had put the troops ashore at Guadalcanal and had supplied them under almost impossible conditions. Spruance had made a trip to the south during the tough days at Guadalcanal and he was impressed with "Terrible" Turner's tenacity and fighting spirit. He wanted no other. Nimitz quite agreed, and that was vital because Nimitz would make the decisions. In June Nimitz ordered Halsey to release Turner.

In June, also, Nimitz had taken Major General Holland M. Smith of the Marine Corps to the Pacific to see how his troops were managing. Smith was commander of amphibious training on the west coast, and was itching to get into battle. He was also the leading student of amphibious warfare in the Marine Corps; he had visited Attu during the fighting there, had undergone a *banzai* charge which caused heavy casualties, and had gone back to California to puzzle out countermeasures against such suicide attempts.

On the trip to the South Pacific, Nimitz observed Smith and they talked about offensive operations. But the more he talked about the war, the more depressed Smith grew because he was stuck in a training command. Smith recalled later:

> Seated by the window in the Coronado, watching the immensely thick and fantastically molded banks of clouds that form the perpetual Pacific ceiling, I was lost in this depressing speculation, when Nimitz called me to the other end of the cabin, where he had been reading a magazine.
>
> "Holland," he said gravely, "I am going to bring you out to

the Pacific this fall. You will command all Marines in the Central Pacific area. I think you will find your new job very interesting."

Spruance agreed with Nimitz that Holland Smith was the man for the command of the Marines who would carry the assaults. It was established, through the King-Nimitz conferences, that the Marines would be used in the Central Pacific as the shock troops, although Army units were also under training and had shown in the assault of the Seventh Army Division on Attu that they could absorb the training. (Nimitz, by the way, was far more aware of the similarities among the men of the services than many of his officers, and fond of reminding them. When confronted by a complaint about Army infantry ignorance or Army Air Corps failures, he often noted that it was a matter of education and information. All these American boys had approximately the same background prior to basic training, he said.)

These discussions between King and Nimitz had centered over an invasion of the Marshall Islands, but Spruance, the strategist, suggested that it would be best to move first into the Gilberts. These islands were vital to control of the Central Pacific, because they lie north and west of islands held by the Americans, and south and east of the major Japanese bases in the Carolines and Marshalls. Going straight into the Marshalls would be far more difficult because so little was known of them. The Gilberts had been held by the British until 1941, but the Marshalls had been held by the Japanese since they were taken away from Germany in World War I. What the Japanese had been doing in either place was only sketchily known, but aerial reconnaissance must be made of either island. In the Marshalls, it would have to be done from carriers, very expensively and dangerously, or from bases. The logical base was the Gilberts. And as for the Gilberts, the reconnaissance could be done from a base at Funafuti in the Ellice Islands, which was already in operation.

Thus Nimitz decided that the Gilberts should come first—in the late fall of 1943—and then the more important Marshalls would be invaded early in 1944.

Nimitz and Spruance spent many, many hours together every

day. They worked nearly side by side in the new headquarters. They took long walks and swam together, sometimes with Dr. Gendreau. The doctor was a good listener and an absolutely perfect companion for senior officers, because he was sympathetic and never talked about what he learned; no conversation need be hushed in his presence. It was sometimes said that Nimitz, during all this time spent together, was remaking Spruance in his own mold—a nonsense statement, but one that did call to attention the intrinsic similarities between the two men. It might be said that Nimitz was the bolder, but both men had one constant aim: to bring the war to a successful conclusion. There was the major difference between the men who would be Nimitz's two arms: Halsey and Spruance. Halsey wanted to fight, to "kill Japs and more Japs." He would do almost anything for a chance to hit the Japanese fleet. But Spruance was not interested in the Japanese fleet, except to the extent that knocking it out would further the general war effort. In this he followed the Nimitz philosophy, a far gentler and more thoughtful one than Halsey's. One day, for example, there was a report of an earthquake in Japan. One young officer of the Halsey persuasion remarked that it was too bad the earthquake had not submerged the Japanese islands.

"Oh, I don't know," Nimitz said quietly. "When the war is over, we may well be glad to have a strong, although defeated, Japan between us and Russia."

During that summer of 1943, an armada was being assembled on the west coast and at Pearl Harbor that was more powerful than the entire Pacific Fleet had been two years earlier. The essence of this fleet was different; its center was no longer the battleship and had not been since December 7, 1941, but the aircraft carrier. In this force there would be six fleet carriers, five light carriers, and eight escort carriers. There would also be battleships (four new fast ones that could keep up with the carriers and seven old slow ones that could not), nine heavy cruisers, five light cruisers, and assorted destroyers, plus the transports, cargo ships, and lesser vessels; but the carriers were the heart of the covering force. To command the force, Task Force 50, Nimitz chose Rear Admiral C. A. Pownall, a naval aviator of the class of 1910 at the Naval Academy.

By this summer of 1943, the entire thinking about the carrier had changed remarkably. The task force was known as the Fast Carrier Task Force. The new battleships were attached to this force, the old ones would stick with the invasion fleet and bombard the invaded islands. The Fast Carrier Task Force was ready to take on anything but the whole Japanese fleet, it seemed. Besides the carrier, this force was to be augmented by land-based air forces, which would be headed by Rear Admiral John Hoover, the coxswain on Nimitz's Academy crew. For nearly two years Nimitz had been trying to utilize Hoover's services in the Pacific, and now he had found a spot for his old friend.

With this change had come a strong surge of activity by the Young Turks of the Navy's air arm, prompted partly by the successes of the carriers, partly by the carrier building program, partly by the general enthusiasm for air power, and partly by specific activity in behalf of air power then in progress in the Navy.

When the Army Air Corps's successors to Billy Mitchell began once again to struggle for a separate air force, naval aviators became concerned. Admiral William Yarnell, diplomat, aviation enthusiast, and one-time fleet commander, was asked to come from retirement and study the Navy's special problems of aviation. His study, in a way, became a catalyst for the complaints and ambitions of the naval aviators.

In 1942 one of the Young Turks, Captain J. J. Clark, suggested that the United States needed 150 aircraft carriers to win the Pacific war. Admiral Towers agreed with him, and Clark was sent around the country on a speaking tour, even as Halsey took command in the South Pacific. Clark distinguished himself in the landings in North Africa, and was given command of the new *Yorktown*, a carrier of the *Essex* class, one of three 27,100-ton ships, carrying a crew of nearly 3500 officers and men, 36 fighters, 36 dive bombers, and 18 torpedo bombers. By midsummer she was in Pearl Harbor training, along with *Essex*, and the light carriers *Independence*, *Monterey*, and *Princeton*. Soon the new *Lexington* arrived.

With so many carriers in and out of port, Pearl Harbor became very aviation-conscious. Aviation had not taken over the Navy. Gunnery Officer Tom B. Hill was one of the busiest men at

Pearl Harbor, for among other things, he was responsible for weapons training of *all* the Navy there, including the aviators. Captain Hill and his assistant, Commander E. M. Eller, began a school of fire control. They sharpened up the use of radar, and saw that operations sent destroyers out into the Pacific on training missions before they went to war. They established gunnery schools in the South Pacific and at Pearl Harbor. The aviators did their own training under these officers' careful eyes, but some of them resented the advice of line officers. Admiral Towers, for example, wrote often in his diaries about the "defensive" attitude of some of the senior staff and senior officers at Pearl Harbor. When Admiral Ghormley, for example, began building a bomb shelter for 400 men at Pearl Harbor, Towers totted up the figures, 42,000 bags of cement and sixty tons of steel, and $400,000. "I often wonder if Hitler's secret weapon isn't our defensive attitude," he said.

Towers was chafing in his job, which was largely a matter of logistics. He wanted a combat command, but Nimitz was firmly resisting him, telling Towers of his responsibilities as commander of the air forces in the Pacific. Towers and his junior commanders took the position that the fast carriers should be used extensively as offensive weapons, and should not be tied down to the invasion forces. He was now backed fully by several officers: his chief of staff, Forrest Sherman, Clark, Arthur Radford, Frederick Sherman, and Alfred E. Montgomery, all experienced task group commanders or carrier commanders.

By midsummer Towers was writing to his friend Undersecretary Forrestal, very dejectedly. "I must confess," he said, "that those of us out here who are in a position to have a reasonably good idea of not only what is going on, but also what is planned, have a feeling approaching utter hopelessness, and when I say this I am referring to major plans and major policies."

The basic problem, Towers believed, was that aviators were not given sufficient responsibility in either the planning or the execution of major policies. It was hard to say more by letter, but Towers said Sherman was on his way to Washington, and that perhaps Forrestal could find some time to see him.

In this period of planning the first big Central Pacific offensive,

Towers was trying to make the power of the air force felt. On August 21 he wrote a long memo to Nimitz about carrier application.

Now, said Towers, there were three ways to use the carrier forces at Nimitz's disposal. First and foremost was to send carriers in air attacks against ship and shore. Second was to use carriers in direct support of amphibious operations. Third was air support of other ships in the task force

The expanding carrier force, Towers said emphatically, demanded new skill and imagination in use. It would mean the difference between a short war and a long one, if the carrier force were used properly or improperly. The carrier force would be able to attack Truk, the Marianas, Bonin, and the Japanese homeland.

"To be air minded," said Towers, "is no substitute for long aviation experience." What he wanted was aviators in charge, and if they could not be in charge, then these senior commanders responsible for coordinating carrier striking forces with surface and amphibious operations should have seconds in command who were aviators.

The discontent of some of the aviators was growing very serious that summer. Towers wrote an anguished letter to Admiral Horne summing up all the complaints of the aviators.

He first cited the failure of the Navy to publicize the naval air force victory—"which has never been forgiven." His second grievance was the slowness of awarding decorations or commendations to naval airmen. It seemed that Army aviators had only to get up in a combat zone to win a medal, whereas naval fliers were very seldom honored.

Towers complained about the failure of the Navy to make spot promotions for gallantry, or to give rank commensurate with position. The Navy officers were always comparing, they saw Army Air Corps officers of the same length of service who were colonels or brigadier generals, while most of the Navy men were still lieutenant commanders. And finally he mentioned "the failure of the high commands to give senior aviation officers, of long experience and proved professional ability, a real voice in strategic plans."

What Towers wanted was Spruance's job. If he could not have that, he wanted to command the task force that would support the invasion. He went to Nimitz, pleading for this chance to go into combat, but Nimitz again said that Towers should stick to his job as commander of the air force. Towers put his plea in writing, but still Nimitz refused.

To Towers it seemed that Nimitz was simply being obfuscatory, but the Towers view of the picture was more limited than that of his commander in chief. Towers did not know, for example, that Nimitz was also being harried by Admiral Lockwood, who itched to take a submarine out on patrol. Nimitz wrote Lockwood, too, saying he appreciated Lockwood's emotions and shared them, but that both must stick with their commands. Frank Jack Fletcher offered to take a demotion to rear admiral if he could get back to sea. But Nimitz could not take cognizance of individual pleas, and he did not.

The Towers-Nimitz discussion grew more animated. On August 22 Towers presented a long memo to Admiral Horne, repeating much of what he had said earlier and emphasizing his unhappiness because so few senior air officers had "real voice" in overall policies. He had read in the newspapers of the reorganization of the Navy Department in Washington—and that the chief of the Bureau of Aeronautics, who had been directly under the Secretary, was now deprived of most of his authority. (This was also true of all bureau chiefs in the reorganization, and none of them liked making the Chief of Naval Operations supreme in fact.)

The next day, Towers went to confront Nimitz. McMorris was in the room, but said nothing. Towers made his case, and Nimitz disagreed. They had a long discussion of the subject, and at the end of it Nimitz said simply that Towers had "the wrong picture." Later Towers wrote to Admiral Yarnell. "To put it bluntly," he said of Nimitz, "his reaction was to the effect that I did not know what I was talking about." And Nimitz apparently came as close to losing his temper as he ever had. ("Rather violent," said Towers, of Nimitz's reactions.)

Towers was shaken by the result of his boat-rocking, but in fact he was more effective than he might have believed. Nimitz was about to relieve Captain Ralph Ofstie as aviation officer on his staff, because Ofstie was eager for a command of his own, and when this came about, Nimitz said, he proposed to upgrade the job to that of assistant chief of staff for aviation.

Pearl Harbor was busy with plans and operations. In July Turner arrived to begin working up his Amphibious Force. The war was very personally brought home to Nimitz just two days later.

As fleet medical officer, it was Captain Gendreau's duty to be sure that conditions for the treatment of the wounded and the sick were all they ought to be. He was noted throughout the fleet for his genial disposition and his willingness to go anywhere and do anything in performance of his duty. One stormy night in the Hawaiian Islands he had ridden out from Pearl in a whaleboat at considerable risk to consult with the ship's surgeon of the *Mississippi* about a young man who had suffered an accident in a turret on the battleship.

In July Captain Gendreau went to the South Pacific to make an inspection of the hospitals there. The New Georgia operation had begun and was successful enough, quickly enough to please all concerned. The fighting was continuing on Rendova, and Captain Gendreau went there, with the intention of riding an LST (landing ship, tank) back to Guadalcanal so that he might make a complete report to Nimitz on the line of evacuation of the wounded from the fighting front.

At 1600 on July 21 Captain Gendreau boarded LST 343 at Rendova to make the voyage back to Guadalcanal. Captain J. S. Crenshaw put him in his own cabin, and they talked for a while about the evacuation of the wounded. At 1630 they went to supper, because they intended to get under way an hour later.

A few minutes after they sat down in the wardroom, the ship was called to general quarters. Bogies (enemy planes) were coming in. Captain Crenshaw gave Gendreau a helmet and a life jacket, and invited him to the bridge, but Gendreau said he would stay down out of the way.

Five dive bombers came swooping down moments later. Four missed with their bombs, but the fifth let his bomb go and it made a direct hit on the LST deck house—just as Dr. Gendreau stepped out on deck. He was killed instantly.

So there was a vacancy in the four-bedroom house overlooking Makalapa crater, but not for long. Into the little hall bedroom without a closet, where Dr. Gendreau had been living, came Captain Moore when he arrived to take up his duties as Spruance's chief of staff.

In the mornings Spruance and Moore made plans for the coming operations. In the afternoon they went walking, and talking. One day they walked eight miles in the foothills. Next day, Spruance slowed the pace and let Moore off with four miles, but the day after that they covered ten miles in three hours. In the evenings, it was quiet in the house. Captain Moore wrote to his wife: "I have just spent the evening stretched out on a davenport in our big living room in the dark, listening to the radio . . . . Soc was on one other davenport and Raymond in a distant corner. Each was oblivious of the others. Very pleasant . . . ."

Moore was very pleased to be so close to his commander, although a little uneasy at living with "four, three, and two stars," as he put it. It *was* unusual. A friend who had a vacancy in his house asked Moore to come there and live, but a captain did not tell four, three, and two stars that he did not want to live with them, so Captain Moore remained where he was.

He and McMorris sneaked out in the later afternoons to practice up on their horseshoes—as newcomers they needed practice if they were to join the Spruance-Nimitz league. Life in the house was very pleasant. In the afternoons they might visit the senior officers' beach house ("Prostate Rest") from which they would walk a few miles along the beach and then go swimming. At night there would be cocktails (Spruance's special was a drink he made with orange juice, rum, sherry, ice, and water) and then dinner, often graced with such unusual things as mango ice cream, and evenings spent listening to music, symphonies for the most part, in deference to the taste of Nimitz and Spruance.

It could not last forever, and it did not. A captain, unless an aide, had no place in the house of a four-star admiral, and Moore was shoved out one day when a flag officer came to visit Pearl Harbor. He moved down the hill to live with Admiral Calhoun. He was piqued at having been pushed out, but glad to be away from Spruance and the grueling hikes.

That summer of 1943 was notable for many changes, not the least of them the fulfillment of a policy dream, the coming of the island bypass technique. For a long time various officers in the Pacific had been talking about bypassing some Japanese garrisons. King and Nimitz had discussed it in principle in their meetings. Admiral Towers had talked about it in the South Pacific at the end of 1942. Halsey's staff members had suggested the idea too. Physically, the first bypass came with Attu, which was attacked before Kiska because it was regarded as an easier objective. Attu was taken in the spring, and then the Americans and Canadians launched an offensive against Kiska in August—and found that the Japanese had evacuated the island, forced out by their inability to supply it.

Nimitz had spoken of the day when Japan would have to face the unpleasant decision of evacuating positions she could not supply. Now it was coming to pass. Halsey came up against another such situation in the middle of the summer. New Georgia was taken, but the Japanese on the island continued to resist. The plan called for him to move on against Kolombangara, an island north of New Georgia, which had a fighter strip and ten thousand Japanese defenders. Again, Halsey's staff brought up the question of island-hopping, and on looking at the map, Halsey saw that Vella Lavella island, above Kolombangara, was thirty-five miles nearer the Shortlands, was suitable for an airstrip, and had only 250 Japanese in garrison.

Thereupon, Halsey sent Admiral Fitch down to Brisbane to see General MacArthur and convince him that they ought to change the plan and bypass Kolombangara. Fitch knew that he had a big selling job ahead. He took with him senior officers from submarines, surface ships, and service forces, so that all questions might be answered quickly. The Navy group was greeted in MacArthur's outer office and escorted into the general's presence, where he was the soul of courtesy. But they had scarcely settled down, and Fitch proposed the question, when MacArthur began a peroration about the grand strategy of the war—not in the Pacific—but in Europe. He walked up and down the office, in his brown leather flight jacket with ribbons extending from clavicle to floating rib, and he jabbed his corncob pipe out in front of him as he spoke. After fifteen minutes, General MacArthur stopped, smiled, and said, "Thank you, gentlemen."

They were dismissed. Fitch did not know what to do. He had

no answer to his question. He could not return to face Halsey without an answer. He called MacArthur's office, and was told that MacArthur was very busy. He called again, and spoke to various colonels and generals, until finally, with great reluctance on the part of the MacArthur staff, he was granted another short interview.

This time Fitch went alone. ("The first time, we provided MacArthur with an audience," he said.) He went in quickly, sat down, made his case in a very few brief sentences. MacArthur looked up and nodded. He was in perfect agreement. "Work it out with General Sutherland," he said. "I agree with anything you and Halsey want to do."

So the bypass was on. Vella Lavella became the new target, the invasion was swift and successful, and in the months and years that passed, many men took credit for inventing the process. But as Fitch indicated, and as the papers of many others have indicated, it was a general idea, an idea that had come into its time, and it was possible, as were so many other developments of the Pacific war, only because of the cooperation of men of many services and many nationalities.

Chapter
Sixteen

THE COMMANDS
SHAPE UP

June 1–October 15, 1943

If it had been noticeable at the last meeting or two between King and Nimitz that the Pacific theater of operations was growing so rapidly in men, materiel, and ships as to become unwieldly, the change became unmistakable in the summer of 1943. The logistics problem bedeviled Nimitz increasingly. In a spirit of helpfulness, the Army sent General E. H. Leavey on a trip through the South Pacific to examine Halsey's supply system. Leavey returned to Washington in July and reported to Lieutenant General Somervell, the chief of the Army system of supply, and to Admiral Calhoun in Pearl Harbor. The changing nature of the war made it essential that Nimitz accept ideas that were completely foreign to the Navy way of doing things in the past. Leavey and his ideas were a case in point.

Leavey had come to the conclusion that Nimitz did not have a theater staff at all, but a fleet staff, concerned primarily with operations in the Central Pacific. Actually, he said, there was no logistics section in the Cincpac headquarters; Admiral Calhoun was in charge of fleet supply only and was not a chief of staff for supply, as he had earlier believed. In other words, there was no one capable of controlling supply activities in the whole Pacific.

Nimitz kept control over everything in the Central Pacific, including the Army. He had decentralized the operation in the South Pacific so that Halsey had almost complete control. (Leavey did not know how closely Nimitz supervised Halsey's activities.)

"From my observations so far," wrote Leavey, "I am convinced that in order to have a complete and coordinated operation in the Pacific theater, it will be necessary for Admiral Nimitz to set up a GHQ type of theater headquarters with a combined army, navy and Marine corps staff, including Air officers, for both operational and service functions."

When King and Nimitz met at the end of July, one of the problems was a growing pressure from the Army for Nimitz to adopt an Army-type organization. It had been suggested that Nimitz abandon his title as commander in chief of the Pacific Fleet, perhaps to Halsey, and that Nimitz become supreme commander of the Pacific Ocean areas—which meant an exact counterpart to MacArthur or Eisenhower. Admiral Jacobs noted that Eisenhower had nine hundred officers on his staff.

The Army, like the Navy airmen, was pressing for a greater voice in the Pacific planning. Nimitz and King did not like the comparisons with the Southwest Pacific command of General MacArthur, but they were being made constantly. And one reason for it was that there were so many thousands of people moving in and out of the Pacific each month; more ships, more troops, more planes were coming in.

There certainly was truth in the Army charge that Nimitz was an active fleet commander. He took interest in everything regarding his fleet. Dr. Gendreau had been killed because he wanted to be able to give the most complete report possible to his chief; he knew Nimitz would want that. One day while walking on the beach, wearing informal clothes with no insignia of rank, Nimitz fell in with a young sailor who told him of the difficulties of life on his ship. After some discussion, Nimitz asked why the youngster did not report these conditions to his commanding officer or the executive officer. "No officer would care," said the young man. Then Nimitz identified himself.

On another occasion, Nimitz's office door was open and a young sailor from the fleet looked in, saw that no one was in there, and walked in, just to look around. Nimitz came in and trapped him. The flustered young man began to apologize. Nimitz cut him off. "You have as much right to see this office as anybody in the fleet," he said gently. Thus Nimitz kept his appearance of a close relationship between the commander of the Pacific Fleet and his lowest apprentice seaman. It was a vital demonstration of morale-building.

On another occasion a young sailor came into the concrete "fortress" of Makalapa and into the admiral's corridor. He was stopped by Lieutenant Commander Lamar outside the office. Inside, Nimitz happened to hear the conversation, and he learned that the sailor was from Texas. He had gotten into an argument with his shipmates the day before, contending that one Texan would always respond to another Texan, and that, by God, if he wanted to go up and see Admiral Nimitz he could walk right in.

The sailor's mates had given him the raspberry, and he had gotten his dander up and bet twenty dollars that he could do it. So there he was.

Lamar was explaining to the sailor that gobs do not call on four-star admirals, when Nimitz opened the door, grinned benignly, and invited the Texas sailor in for a visit. Furthermore, he ordered Lamar down to public relations to pick up a photographer and come back to take their picture.

That day the Texas sailor had a chat with his commander in chief about affairs of the fleet, and went back to his ship with a photograph to prove it.

For reasons of his own, too, Nimitz liked to feel that he was in touch with the men of his command at every level. As the fleet grew, and ships were constantly on the move, it was no longer possible for Nimitz to know every commander of every vessel that steamed out of west coast ports. He felt that he was getting out of touch, and one day he told an aide to tell the type commanders (battleships, cruisers, and so on) that in future, when a ship touched Pearl Harbor, the captain was to pay a duty call on the admiral. Each day at eleven o'clock, after the morning staff meeting, Nimitz held open house for his captains.

He was careful each day to make sure that the enlisted men who served him had their meals, and he would enquire about chow of the Marine guards at the house on Makalapa and his driver. He knew he could count on them to sample the corps's morale.

One night, while coming back to Pearl from Honolulu, Nimitz saw an extremely intoxicated sailor standing beside the road. Nimitz told the driver to stop and they picked up the sailor, who turned out to be a Seabee. He did not recognize the admiral, but under questioning he told a story of unhappy conditions in his Seabee camp. That night the sailor was dropped off just outside his camp's gate. Next morning, Nimitz announced that he was going to inspect that Seabee battalion at eleven o'clock. He made the announcement at ten, which gave Lamar time to call the commander and warn him, but did not give the commander time to do anything to spruce up the camp. Just as Nimitz wanted it, the camp would be "as is."

It turned out to be as the sailor had said it was. But not for long. Soon there was another story making the rounds about "the old man's" omniscience in all matters that affected the good of the fleet.

Nimitz's concerns in this regard were not confined to the rather artificial matter of maintaining the semblance of personal relations with the enlisted men. He realized very well the isolation of the commander, and was constantly on guard lest necessary solitude cause him to miss a basic change in the nature of his command, something which could easily come about through mistakes in judging people.

In the spring of 1943, Nimitz learned from his staff members that there were unhappy rumors going around about conditions aboard the *New Orleans* which had been down in the South and Southwest Pacific. It was said, for example, that in Sydney seventy-four summary courts-martial had been handed out to the crew, and that the captain had been very severe on liberty.

Nimitz said gently that the captain had been under great strain in battle, and that his ship had been hit at Tassafaronga. These were all rumors, he said, but there were too many of them. So he wrote to Admiral Jacobs and asked him to look into the affair.

Another incident proved how strongly Nimitz felt that the good of the naval service came before personalities.

If Halsey had a fault as a commander, it was one tied to his virtues: his willingness to make quick judgments and take action. After Admiral Wright's failure to create greater havoc among the Japanese in Ironbottom Sound, Halsey had relieved the commander of the destroyer *Fletcher* for not being aggressive enough. A few days later he learned that the commander had acted absolutely properly, and he tried to make amends. Halsey had removed Captain G. C. Hoover from command of the *Helena* for failing to pick up survivors of the *Juneau*, and he was later sorry for that action. In the summer of 1943 he removed another senior officer, using an old Navy formula —"lack of confidence"—and was chided by Nimitz:

> My long experience in handling naval personnel both as assistant chief of bureau and later as chief of bureau, leads me to believe that ———'s case had not been correctly handled and that there is danger of doing him an unwarranted injustice . . . . If in your explanation of the detachment you use the "lack of confidence" formula, your explanation must satisfactorily offset your strong recommendation for his temporary promotion which passed through my hands some time ago, and which at that time received only my lukewarm endorsement.

Nimitz suspected that something from the man's past had been the cause—for he knew that another officer who had quarreled with this one was also in Halsey's command.

> . . . I was reminded of the fable of the Pot and the Kettle [Nimitz continued]—one calling the other black, etc. As this case has developed over the years, I find myself in the position of urgently recommending for temporary promotion both the Pot and the Kettle. Both had been passed over for promotion by the usually constituted selection boards.

I have been able to see the professional merits of both the Pot and Kettle, and curiously enough, I was the agent who finally secured orders for the Kettle to report to you in response to your urgent appeals for his services in your area. Also, I was the agency that finally secured temporary promotion for the Kettle. To top it off, I now find myself having recently recommended the Pot for promotion, based partly on your written recommendation and partly on my observation just at the time you detach him, presumably for cause.

We have already spent far more time on this case than is warranted by the importance of the individual. My efforts are based on principles and the desire to avoid injustice by hasty action. In this connection, I am not sure that we did not make a mistake to sanction the hasty detachment of Captain G. C. Hoover from his command [*Helena*] last year. His courage was certainly not in question because we knew of his previous battle record. However that is all water over the dam—and my only desire is to safeguard the interests of our personnel and to give even the lowest his day in court.

Halsey was adamant. He wrote back in reply:

War is a cruel thing at the best, and individuals must be subordinated for the good of the country. I am in thorough agreement with your idea that every man's interests should be safeguarded in every possible way. However, I also feel that we have leaned over backwards too often in safeguarding individual interests, and have forgotten the interests of the Navy. I am presuming my official dispatch to you regarding ———'s detachment was all the necessary official correspondence you desired on this subject. If not, please inform me and I will write an official letter.

At this time Halsey was also still defending his detachment of Captain Hoover. Only later did he come to see it in another light and try to make amends.

But if there were difficulties between Nimitz and Halsey over

personnel in this period of regrouping at Pearl Harbor, they were as
nothing compared to the command difficulties between Admiral
Lockwood's submarine command and the Bureau of Ordnance over
the matter of the faulty torpedoes.

Lockwood was very seriously hampered in his struggle to solve
the torpedo problem by Rear Admiral R. W. Christie, who had succeeded Lockwood in command of the submarines of the Southwest
Pacific, at Fremantle. Christie had been instrumental in the development of the Mark 14 torpedo with its magnetic warhead, and
he did not believe what the submarine captains were saying about
the weapon. He wrote thus to Lockwood:

> Torpedo performance here is steadily improving and we are
> definitely not in accord with the opinions expressed in various
> patrol report endorsements such as—I quote—"Kingfish Third
> Patrol, endorsement of CSD-102: 2 prematures, 1 observed dud,
> and 1 probable dud in 17 torpedoes fired do not tend to improve
> waning confidence in the weapon!"
>
> What conceivable good such a remark can do is beyond me
> but it is not beyond me to appreciate the very definite harm
> that can be done and has been done by such endorsements . . . .
>
> Difficulties with torpedoes should be put up squarely to the
> Bureau of Ordnance with all possible definite evidence so that
> they will have something to work on beside indefinite ill-con-
> sidered and ill-mannered criticism.

It was, indicated Admiral Christie, the submariners and not the
torpedo that caused the trouble.

Lockwood was certain that the torpedo was at fault, and he took
exception to Christie's remarks which blamed the submarine captains, and himself, in a sense, for sympathizing with them. He was
making experiments with the Mark 14 torpedo, firing some against
cliffs that jutted up from the sea on Oahu, and discovering that,
aside from the magnetic exploder's faults, the firing pin was troublesome. He said as much to Christie.

Christie apologized. "The shortcomings of the submarine torpedo can be laid to me very properly for, for 2½ years I had charge

of the design of the 14 and for three tours at Naval Torpedo Station was concerned directly with the magnetic exploder. I meant to emphasize the harm done in anything which lessens the confidence of the submariners in their weapon."

That autumn Nimitz stuck his nose into the torpedo business because Lockwood was not as successful as he had hoped to be in hurrying change.

"I am very much concerned about the torpedo exploder situation," Nimitz wrote Admiral Blandy of the Bureau of Ordnance, "in spite of the progress which is being made by Comsubpac in his local experiments here. I should like to hear from you on this subject, giving me your prognostication of what we can expect in the way of improvement both in the mechanical and magnetic exploders."

What was needed was time. Later Lockwood deactivated the magnetic feature of the torpedoes, the defective firing pin was corrected, and the slower electrical Mark 18 torpedo came into use. Eventually Christie was persuaded that the magnetic feature was faulty, but it took a few more months.

Nimitz, meanwhile, was moving in several directions, as always. He was trying to work out the logistical setup for a greatly expanded Pacific Fleet operation, without yielding to the Army's continual pressure to undertake Army-type organization. The Army command in the Pacific had changed, and Lieutenant General Robert C. Richardson had become the new commander in Hawaii. Richardson was a pleasant officer, and he and Nimitz got on well personally, although officially there was a considerable amount of friction, which Nimitz was at great pains to try to lubricate.

Lieutenant General Somervell, commander of the Army service forces, hoped to persuade Nimitz to exercise his command function as Pacific Ocean area commander, and then bring in Army and Navy commanders on equal bases under him. But Nimitz insisted on keeping direct command of all operations in his theater. Spruance was now commander of the Fifth Fleet, and for operations he was a task force commander, with the aviation and troop commands also under his supervision. That was the way it would continue to be.

In the forthcoming operations, most of the troops ashore would be Marines, but the 27th Army Division would also participate in the Central Pacific campaign.

With the development of plans, another difficulty began to present itself. Nimitz had chosen Admiral John Hoover to head the land-based air forces, and the defense of all land areas. What this meant, in essence, was that the Fifth Fleet would move into its objective, with Admiral Spruance in charge. The Amphibious Force, under Admiral Turner, would land the troops and their supplies. The Marines, under General Holland Smith, and the Army forces, under General Ralph Smith, would capture control of the islands. Holland Smith was in overall charge on land. Once the islands were secured, the control would be passed to Admiral Hoover, who would be responsible for their defense, the use of the islands as air bases for attack on other enemy positions, construction of air bases and port facilities.

Hoover's job was comparable to that of Fitch in the South Pacific. Initially, he was to have two lines of approach for his land-based air attacks into enemy territory: up from Samoa through Wallis and the Ellice islands, and from Canton through Baker.

Hoover went down to Nouméa to serve under Halsey for a while and learn the ropes from Fitch.

Again that summer, Nimitz had occasion to worry about Halsey and personnel problems. During the New Georgia operation General Hester had suddenly been removed from command of a division. Nothing was said about it, and Nimitz heard rumors a few days later. He wondered.

But as it turned out, there was nothing to worry about. Major General Hester had gone into action suffering from stomach ulcers (about which he said nothing) and had nearly broken down. ("He was traveling on his nerve," said Halsey.) He had been relieved by Major General Oscar W. Griswold of the XIV Corps, and sent back to hospital. It was a relief to Nimitz, but as he informed Halsey, he would really like to know about these things as they happened.

By late summer Operation Galvanic, the invasion of the Gilbert Islands, was assuming shape. Spruance and Moore and several others made a quick trip to the South Pacific in August to look over atolls that would be similar to the Gilberts, and to study the Guadalcanal story and Halsey's South Pacific operations. They were fortunate, obviously, in having as amphibious commander Admiral Turner, who had been through the whole Guadalcanal battle in the same capacity. He had been replaced in Halsey's command by Rear Admiral T. S. Wilkinson.

Soon Rear Admiral Harry W. Hill joined the Central Pacific team. He had been "Terrible" Turner's assistant in the war plans division in Washington, and had spent the past year in the South Pacific in command of a division of the old battleships. His specific detail would be the landing on Tarawa, and he would report directly to Turner.

There were problems to be worked out. Turner wanted to remain in command of the amphibious operation until the end, but Holland Smith insisted that he assume command once the men and equipment were ashore and in control of the situation. Captain Moore, after refereeing the argument day after day, called upon Spruance to make a decision. Spruance simply would not lay down a dictum. "I have chosen these men because they are intelligent and reasonable," he told Moore. "Let them work it out." Whereupon he left the office, and went out for a long walk.

The task force that was being assembled under Admiral Pownall was the biggest yet seen in the Pacific, and it needed a good deal of training.

Late in August, Pownall took his force out for a raid on Marcus which would also be a practice for the coming operation. This raid was conducted by *Yorktown*, *Independence*, and *Essex*. Pownall had expected a wind of eight knots, but faced a dead calm, needing thirty knots speed for launching. At 0422 on September 1 all was ready, the carriers were speeding along in the dark, and the forward screening ships turned on their searchlights so the pilots could see to take off and orient themselves for rendezvous. Some of the planes carried flares and incendiaries, and these were dropped first to light up the target. No Japanese planes got off the ground. The planes delivered five attacks, two from *Yorktown*, two from *Essex*, and one from *Independence*, along with continuous combat air patrols and inner air patrols. The formation stuck together well at a speed of twenty-five to twenty-eight knots and there was absolutely no trouble.

There was trouble over the target, from antiaircraft fire. On the first attack *Yorktown* lost a TBF and a fighter. On the second attack she lost another fighter. No one saw the planes go in. One pilot thought he saw a man swimming, and the submarine *Snook*, on patrol in the area, was asked to take a look. But no one was found.

Several other planes were hit, and one pilot in a dive bomber received a facial flesh wound from antiaircraft fire.

On completing the attack plan, Pownall noticed that the pilots were getting tired and landings were becoming ragged, so he collected the planes and cleared out. One of his Young Turks, Captain J. J. Clark, was very critical of Pownall's operations.

To put it flatly, Clark thought Pownall was an old woman in his extreme caution. Clark later wrote:

> One day while *Yorktown* was recovering her combat air patrol by steaming into the wind, we reached a position far ahead of our station in the formation. The other ships were zigzagging to dodge possible submarines. I turned toward the group of ships at 25 knots. They were steaming toward me. By using my "seaman's eye" I passed the first line of ships, made a sharp turn in the middle of the formation and landed my ship squarely on station in the ring of cruisers and behind the guide in *Essex*. I fishtailed the rudder to kill the ship's speed. On the flight deck, *Yorktown*'s crew, who had been holding their breath during the tight maneuver, broke out in cheers. But the next instant Admiral Pownall came running to my bridge, scolding me, "Clark, *Clark*. Don't ever do that again. It's too dangerous." On the other hand, Captain Donald Duncan, skipper of *Essex*, sent me his congratulations on my smart seamanship.

Clark was also critical of Pownall that day for not taking the carrier force out to pick up the men of the TBF, a pilot and his two crewmen. In a letter to Nimitz, Pownall reported that "a message drop was received on the *Yorktown* stating he saw three men in a rubber boat, Lat 25° 35′, Long 154° 32′. The [cruiser] *Nashville* sent two planes to work rescue. Negative results. From 1200 to 1600 eight TBFs from *Yorktown* made an extensive search of this same area. Negative results. Nevertheless in my official dispatch I requested Lockwood to have any submarine east or west bound to take a look north of Marcus."

Clark had pleaded with Pownall to take the task force 70 miles west to find the men. Pownall thought the risk was too great, Clark said, but he let Clark organize that air search. On the search the pilot who was to cover the area of the last known position of the raft stopped to strafe a Japanese patrol boat. (The carrier pilots had not learned very well the lesson of the Fighting 5 about not stopping to strafe.) Clark's theory was that he got off course and missed the rubber raft. That night a Japanese submarine found the raft, and the three men spent the rest of the war in a prison camp.

"At 6:49 P.M. that night," Clark said, "the last of the planes landed on board and Pownall raced the force away from Marcus as quickly as possible. The Japanese airfield on Marcus had been rendered unusable, and as there was no air opposition, I could see no reason for leaving our men without a better effort to recover them. I was deeply distressed at their loss."

Clark also gave bad marks to Frank Jack Fletcher for leaving three men in a rubber raft afloat during the *Yorktown*'s raid on the Gilberts in February, 1942. Fletcher had then said the risk was too great. Clark had told the story to Admiral Towers and Admiral King in Washington. Now he would begin telling the story of Pownall's decision in the same critical manner.

The return of the task force to port was the signal for an argument to break out between opposing philosophers in the Pacific Fleet organization. Pownall represented the fleet thinking of Nimitz and Spruance. Towers represented the Young Turk thinking of many of the officers who were primarily air officers.

On September 8 Pownall came to Towers' office to report, and said that Spruance had said Pownall would be commander of carriers in the Central Pacific force. Towers said that was a ridiculous idea—he saw no place for a commander of carriers. The carriers were distributed among the task forces, he said. All Pownall would end up doing, he said, was aviation staff work which should be done by the task force commander's staff.

The next day Towers had a long talk with Ralph Ofstie, Nimitz's air officer, who promised to take up the matter of task force operations with Nimitz after the morning conference the next day.

At this point there was tremendous disagreement among the senior members of the Pacific Fleet organization over the coming course of the war, and most of it centered around the use of carriers and air power.

The divergences of opinion showed themselves in every way, from petty arguments to real basic differences in operations.

For example, Generals Somervell, Richardson, Hale, Gross, Franklin, and Leavey came into Nimitz's office one morning to talk about logistics for the coming Central Pacific campaign. The talk turned to air logistics. Nimitz said Hoover would handle all this as commander of shore-based air. Somervell questioned the idea, still plumping for his theater-command principle. Towers said that whatever happened, the deputy commander ought to be an air man. So no conclusion was reached that day. Nimitz tried to resolve the air-fleet argument by sending Towers on an inspection trip to the south, but Towers came back to take up the battles just where he had left off. He was asked to recommend staff for Hoover; he said he could not until he knew what Hoover was going to do. He was asked to recommend staff for Pownall; he said Pownall ought to have one of several task forces.

Towers was constantly on the defensive. He felt that he was fighting a losing battle against "black shoes." Captain Steele of the Nimitz staff one day suggested that the carrier *Lexington* be sent to Alaska to ferry over some engineers who were badly needed in the Pacific. Towers was aghast. (Nimitz turned that one down very quickly.)

On September 24 the morning staff conference dealt with command for operations, and particularly the command of task forces which involved carriers. For days this problem had been under discussion, and it was discussed again.

Then Admiral King arrived for his next meeting with Nimitz.

The King-Nimitz meetings of late September, 1943, included Halsey, for there were important matters to be discussed. MacArthur wanted to move on into Bougainville by the end of the year, and King wanted to be sure that the Gilberts operation was all set and ready to move out. These matters were discussed. Admiral Towers wanted to talk about task forces and the use of air power. There were administrative matters: whether the commander of the air forces in the South Pacific should be under Halsey or under Towers, and similar problems. Towers, however, wanted to talk about *use* of air power. He had recommended the use of one fleet carrier and a light carrier in a task force. King turned him down until there should be more experience with the new abundance of carriers available.

All summer, Spruance and his planners had applied themselves to the problems of the Gilberts. Spruance did not like the Nauru expedition at all, so he put Turner and Holland Smith to considering Makin, the closest Gilbert atoll to the Marshalls. They all agreed that Makin was a much better choice than Nauru, which was useless and too far from the other objectives. Spruance urged Nimitz to secure a change from King and the Joint Chiefs, but Nimitz would not start crying out at long distance, and nothing happened.

Finally, one day Holland Smith came to Turner and said he did not have enough troops to take Nauru, and there were no transports ready to bring in other troops if they could be made available. They went to Spruance, who asked Smith for a letter to that effect.*

Spruance recalls:

As the conference assembled in Cincpac's office, Admiral Turner handed me General Holland Smith's letter about taking Nauru together with his own endorsement. I read this and gave it to Admiral Nimitz. The latter in turn read it and passed it

---

* In his letter of April 25, 1966, to Admiral Eller, Admiral Spruance recalls all this as happening in the spring. Actually Turner and Smith were not assigned to Pearl Harbor until after the King-Nimitz conference of May, 1943, so the events obviously occurred in the summer of 1943.

to Admiral King. After Admiral King had read it, he turned
to me and asked what I preferred to take instead of Nauru.
My reply was Makin. After a little discussion of the value of
Makin over Nauru, Admiral Cooke said that one of the reasons
they had selected Nauru was to "broaden the front." The up-
shot of the conference was that Admiral King soon agreed to
the change in objectives, and said that he would recommend
it to the joint chiefs of staff for approval.

The second item of business was the matter of hydrography,
or the navigational mapping, of the Central Pacific. The charts in
the hands of the Navy could hardly be called scientific instruments,
as indeed the Gilberts operation was to prove so conclusively. The
Japanese had been in control of the old German possessions for a
quarter of a century, and some other Central Pacific waters had never
been charted by anyone. As areas were taken and secured, the
hydrographic teams were brought in. Already they were working in
the South Pacific.

The third item for discussion was the use of pontoon causeways
in the Central Pacific operations. So important did King consider
this that he ordered Rear Admiral Alan G. Kirk to come to the
Pacific on temporary duty. Kirk was to bring assistants and films
of operations involving pontoon causeways and instruct Turner and
his officers in their use.

On the second day of that series of meetings, Nimitz opened
by noting that he was preaching to the British on the advisability
of establishing air bases in the Cocos Islands.

The second item concerned old ships in General Somervell's
possession which he was willing to give Nimitz. But it would not
work that way—Somervell must give the ships to King, who would
decide on their disposal, east or west.

Third, Nimitz brought up the troublesome problem of the
torpedoes and exploders. He suggested that King "build a fire" under
the Bureau of Ordnance, and reported on Admiral Lockwood's tests.

—They discussed antisubmarine operations.

—Night training for carriers came up. Nimitz reported that
Towers was working on it.

—Nimitz questioned Halsey's tactics in running up the slot in the Solomons. Halsey promised a memo on the subject.

—Towers had asked earlier for a separate supply system for his air forces. Nimitz posed the question. King vetoed it.

—Nimitz suggested that captured Italian submarines be brought to the Pacific to ferry men and supplies among the island. King took it under advisement.

—Nimitz worked out a command arrangement for the Pacific Ocean areas, which meant rear areas.

—Nimitz brought up radio intelligence and wanted to know if anyone was decoding Japanese army traffic. King authorized a study of the whole problem by Rear Admiral R. E. Schuirmann, the director of naval intelligence.

—They discussed the naval organization in the Marshalls and Carolines, once they were taken. Ticklish problems: the Gilberts, for example, had to be turned over to the British (as a British possession), but the administration of property and population could not be allowed to interfere with the war effort. At least, in the Marshalls and Carolines, the administration would be American— but now Nimitz had to think ahead and order up administrative officers for areas not yet captured. Four officers, he said, was about what he would need at the moment.

—They discussed the coming Marshalls campaign, and Spruance raised the question of seizing Mili and Jaluit first. (In these meetings, only Nimitz, King, and selected members of their staffs would remain during the entire discussion. If Halsey's opinions or report were wanted, he would be brought in, as would Spruance and Turner, or any other officer.) Nimitz said his staff was talking in terms of Wotje, Kwajalein, Maloelap, and Roi, leaping over Jaluit and Mili. Photo reconnaissance was about to begin. As soon as more facts were in, Nimitz would discuss the matter with Spruance, and make a proposal to King, who would then take the matter to the Joint Chiefs for a directive. All right, said King, but Nimitz must remember that it would be best to avoid two steps in the Marshalls operations if possible.

—Rear Admiral R. B. Carney, who had replaced Captain Browning as Halsey's chief of staff, had made a report on the coming Bougainville operation, then moved on to planning for the next step, which in September would seem to be the taking of Kavieng and Manus. Nimitz, then, had to consider the timing. They would need carriers, which he would have to supply from the fast carrier forces of the Pacific. Halsey was talking about March 1, 1944.

—The unwieldy relationship with MacArthur came up, as it almost always did at these conferences. Carney remarked that Comsopac (Halsey) had obligations to MacArthur and to Nimitz, and that it was not clear whether Halsey was at liberty to commit himself to MacArthur as questions arose. (He was not, without Nimitz's understanding and permission.)

—Nimitz and King talked about the possible seizure of Paramushiru, which would give a base for operations against the Japanese islands. One of Nimitz's favorite programs was the harassment of Japanese fishing, which he felt would help immeasurably in shortening the war by denying the enemy a major source of food. Thus would the North Pacific operations become offensive instead of defensive.

—They discussed the Army's contributions to Central Pacific operations. Captain Steele remarked that the Army was establishing three defense battalions which were similar to Marine organizations.

—Halsey, King, and Nimitz talked about logistics. The Ellice Islands, where Admiral Hoover and his land-based air command would operate, would be supplied from Samoa. The Gilberts would be supplied from Pearl Harbor. As the Gilberts operation began, Samoa and the Ellice Islands would fall under Spruance's command. When they were secured, they would revert to Halsey.

—Nimitz had to plan, and plan, and plan ahead—as with the next item: Admiral McMorris noted that after the Gilberts operation, the Second Marine Division, which would do the fighting, would be rehabilitated at Pearl Harbor. A small item—but what it meant was that Nimitz and his staff had to make every plan, for housing, supply, recreation, medication, and replacements, all to be directed at Pearl Harbor.

—For the Marshalls, the amphibious operation would be

mounted half from Pearl Harbor and half from the west coast. The specific plans must be made.

—Base commanders had to be found for the moment the Marshalls were taken. Hoover would again command shore-based air, but again this matter had to be hashed out with the Army, and Nimitz was already involved in negotiations with General Richardson, the Army commander in the Pacific.

—They talked about a floating dock, which Nimitz wanted.

—Nimitz spoke of his plans for deceptive measures: his radio men would launch a campaign to convince the Japanese that the invasion of Paramushiru was imminent as the Gilberts operation began.

—King informed Nimitz of Winston Churchill's plan to send a fleet of four or five battleships, five or six cruisers, and about fifteen destroyers through the Panama Canal to operate with the United States Navy for a time before going on to the Bay of Bengal. Nimitz remarked that the logistics problems of supporting such a force—a foreign navy—would be tremendous. King remarked that he was aware of this, but that the idea had caught President Roosevelt's fancy, and it might be forced on them. (The problem was enough to make a supply officer shudder: different food, different uniforms, different calibration of guns, different ammunition, even different systems of measurement. When Nimitz said coolly that the logistic problem would be "serious," it was an understatement. And he had not mentioned the operational problems this force would cause him.)

—Halsey again brought up the question of the Fijis, as a fleet logistics base for operations against the Marshalls or the Bismarck Archipelago.

—Admiral Cooke, King's deputy, had been studying the patrol report of the submarine *Flying Fish*, whose skipper had suggested submarine operations against Japanese escort vessels. Nimitz said he would investigate—another little burden heaped upon him.

—King noted that there was danger of tipping off the enemy to American knowledge by giving merchant vessels enemy positions by radio direction finder fixes. This was not to be done; someone must be put in charge of merchant vessel routing, and rerouting, without telling the merchant vessels why they were being moved around.

The third day of the conference indicated how quickly matters had to be considered and decided. It was reported that Admiral Kirk was on his way, with his films on pontoon causeways and the invasion of Sicily. Nimitz had talked to Lockwood and had a report for King on the torpedo tests. (The exploder problem was solved as long as they used contact exploders and stayed away from the magnetic feature.) The minutes were checksed and revised, and the commanders went back to their various spheres of activity, King to his overall supervision of the Navy, Nimitz to the direction of the Pacific war.

Several of the subordinate commanders knew something of what had been discussed, but only King and Nimitz knew all, and even their staff members were not in position to understand the full extent of the responsibility these officers carried.

On a smaller scale, this was also true of Spruance's command of the Central Pacific forces, and it explained why he could agree with Pownall and Towers that the carriers ought to be accorded more latitude, and yet refuse to give them the latitude they wished. Here at the verge of Operation Galvanic—the Gilberts invasion— Spruance had to weigh every decision as it affected his overall responsibility, which was not to knock out Japanese airpower in the Central Pacific, not to destroy the Japanese fleet, but to take the Gilberts. It was true that Nimitz accorded Spruance the greatest of latitude, and in the orders for this and other operations Nimitz always noted that if he had a chance to strike the enemy fleet he might take it.

Spruance was ready for such action, too. "If a major portion of the Jap Fleet were to attempt to interfere with Galvanic," he wrote his admirals, "it is obvious that the defeat of the enemy fleet would at once become paramount." He warned them to be prepared at all times to engage the Japanese fleet.

All this while, ships were coming into Pearl Harbor and being assigned immediately to the "type commanders" for training. This meant the destroyers went out with the fleet destroyer commander, the cruisers with the cruiser admiral, and the carriers with Pownall.

On September 29, with the King-Nimitz meetings over, Admiral Nimitz held his regular morning conference and then called a special meeting afterward to discuss Central and South Pacific strategy. Halsey was there. So were Towers, Spruance, Hoover, Turner, Soc McMorris, Rear Admiral Robert B. Carney, Captain Steele, Captain Redman, and Captain Sherman.

The discussion soon became an argument, with Spruance taking the view of fleet operations with carriers as a part of them, and Halsey, Towers, and Carney arguing that air was paramount. Towers said at the moment they were using an elephant gun to kill gnats, and suggested that the *Saratoga* and the *Monterey* be sent off to the South Pacific to harry the Japanese until needed. He also recommended a combined battleship carrier attack on Nauru to keep the Japanese off balance. And Towers spoke out very strongly against the classic fleet training which demanded overwhelming gun force with carriers.

These conferences were becoming very testy. Next day there was an argument about air logistics, with Towers on one side, and Nimitz's nonair staffmen on the other. Nimitz finally called a halt to it, assuring Towers that the necessary means for supplying the air needs would be provided.

"But who is to coordinate it?" asked Towers.

There was no answer.

Towers did not lose all the battles, by far. Nimitz said the *Monterey* and *Saratoga* would be available in the South Pacific and not hauled out to the Gilberts. Nimitz also placed Hoover under Towers for administration. On September 30 there was a long discussion in the meeting: Spruance wanted to talk about training for fleet action; Halsey wanted to talk about operations against the Japanese.

October opened with the same kind of argument. Towers wanted the carrier forces to go out on raids against Japanese targets —to train them for the coming operation. Spruance said these raids would interfere with his fleet training program, the tactical training, and the upkeep of the carriers.

Towers argued that they needed photo reconnaissance of the Gilberts anyhow—they had overhead shots but no obliques. Spruance and Turner agreed to get along without obliques; he wanted all possible carriers to protect his convoys, and none to go out shooting alone.

At the meeting on October 5, a general melee seemed to threaten. It began with the argument about carriers and training as opposed to operations. Towers remarked again that they were sending a huge force against the Gilberts. "I felt that unless a more offensive attitude is taken and our great carrier strength employed to the limit we might all lose our jobs and justly so." Then Towers threw the dirt into the fan. He did not believe the Galvanic operation was even justified, he said. It should be abandoned in favor of a direct move into the Marshalls "which if successful would automatically reduce to unimportance the objectives set up in the first step." (He noted that he had told Nimitz this even in the spring.)

Nimitz said it was a little late. The operation against the Gilberts had been ordered by the Joint Chiefs of Staff and had to be carried out. (Nimitz had recommended it to the Joint Chiefs, Towers reminded himself bitterly.)

All right, said Towers, but why not stage a major carrier raid on the Marshalls or elsewhere before the Gilberts operation?

Pownall broke in, much to Towers' disgust, to talk about night carrier operations. Towers said impatiently that there was no use talking about night operations without night fighters, and they had no night fighters to speak of.

Turner on the one side, and Sherman and Towers on the other, got into an argument about the value of indirect support during an amphibious operation, when the carriers went against adjacent air bases. Turner said he wanted the planes overhead or available. Towers said the best defense was a good offense, wiping out the enemy air before it could get off the ground.

McMorris got into the argument, supporting big air operations before the Gilberts landings.

Nimitz broke it up, by asking for specific time and space schedules.

On October 6 Towers went to the west coast on business and Sherman, his chief of staff, held up the arguments for him. Spruance did not want to make strikes in the Marshalls before the Gilberts operation. Turner wanted all carriers on defensive activity at all times. On October 7 Nimitz decided that was how it would be: he was guided by the shortage of destroyers at the moment (a destroyer had just been lost off New Guinea and three had been damaged in the Solomons). As for the Gilberts, Turner again argued that he must have the direct support of all aircraft for the landings. Forrest Sherman argued that they ought to hit Mili and other bases to neutralize them.

Later that day they talked about Nauru, which was potentially very dangerous to the Gilbert operation because the Japanese maintained an air base there. Admiral Fitch suggested that Central Pacific carriers move in and hit Nauru. Spruance did not want his carriers moved around before the Gilberts operation. It would interfere with their upkeep, he said, and besides the strike would not accomplish anything.

Fitch, who was very outspoken when he was aroused, said he thought things would be better all around in the fleet if Nimitz would make some new efforts. First, the aviators needed a better promotion schedule and more liberal awards policy. Also, Fitch added, there should be less of that "damned aviator" philosophy around Pearl Harbor. Nimitz listened.

On October 11 Towers returned from the United States mainland, and the arguments were renewed. Towers again said too much was being thrown against the Gilberts. He was supported by Captains Keliher, Ofstie, Redman, and Admiral Hoover. Nimitz listened and said he would reexamine the plans and perhaps make drastic reductions in personnel and material committed to the Gilberts.

After the arguments had ended for the day, Nimitz decided he had heard just about all he wanted to hear from the airmen for the moment. Towers had written several letters in the last few weeks, concerning his own wishes to become a task force commander. Nimitz now suggested that maybe Towers would like to have Fitch's job down at Espiritu Santo. He could go and retain his rank of vice admiral. "Please let me hear from you at an early date on this matter," Nimitz said. Towers realized he had gone too far.

There, in the summer and early autumn of 1943, as the first big independent Central Pacific operation shaped up, was a picture of the complexities of Nimitz's command. In that summer he had begun to adapt a foreign concept of supply to the old naval idea of a fleet traveling on its own with base support. The Army system, which was basically the one adopted, called for a constant infusion of supply, and a planning and delivery network as complex as the fighting system itself. In this new kind of war, Nimitz saw that the Army way was superior to his own, and he accepted it. In 1943 Nimitz began to become a legend in the fleet—no accident, since his customary comportment, as has been shown, created tales that would travel across every mess deck. He laid down the law for Halsey in matters of personnel, because he saw, quite correctly, that Halsey's weakest point as commander lay in his inability to judge men as dispassionately as Nimitz could do himself.

In the matter of responsibility, Nimitz was showing his reliance on those who could accept almost total responsibility themselves. Lockwood and his submarine men could take that load, and Nimitz gladly gave it up to them. One seldom heard of Lockwood being called to the office or the house on Makalapa for one of those long, searching, private conferences during which Nimitz probed his admirals when he felt they were showing weaknesses. Lockwood was doing everything Nimitz would have done himself, so he was let alone.

Nimitz saw that the Army, once it got its foot in the door with the logistics changes, would try to exert even more influence, but he fought that struggle with Somervell, as shown, and won it. At the same time, he was able to oversee the addition of more and more fighting officers: Hoover, Hill, Wilkinson, for example. He was much troubled by the groping of the naval air forces as they prepared for the first big carrier operation. The Navy in 1926 had agreed to the recommendations of the Morrow Board that only aviators should command carriers, seaplane tenders, and air stations. Thus, in 1943, the United States Navy had a backlog of command experience in aviation work that was greater than the number of carriers in the prewar fleet would indicate. Forrest Sherman and J. J. Clark were young but thoroughly experienced carrier commanders. Frederick Sherman, A. E. Montgomery, and Pownall were experienced task group commanders. Yet the burgeoning of the air forces of the Navy had been so rapid that the edges were still very rough, and it was also indicative of Nimitz's understanding of the problem that he spent so much of his time concerned with air affairs, so little with the submarines which were equally vital to victory. And finally, in these months of summer and fall of the second year of war, Nimitz was faced with an anomaly: his aviators had a very good point, strategically, when they wanted to bypass the Gilberts entirely and go on to the Marshalls. But Nimitz saw more, from his vantage point as comamnder in chief of the Pacific forces. The carriers might have been ready, but the rest of the American Pacific force was not. There were too many new ship captains, too many reserve officers in the ships, too many young sailors from the farm, and too many marines who had just begun to learn about amphibious operation. The airmen could see, from their point of view, precisely how they would handle the job, but they did not have to contend with Nimitz's problems. It was a mark of his stature as a commander that most of those aviators never knew what the problems were.

Chapter
Seventeen

OPERATION GALVANIC

October 7–December 1, 1943

For two days Towers pondered the quiet but very firm letter he had received from Admiral Nimitz about his future. Then Admiral Towers sat down and wrote a secret personal memo to his commander in chief, stating that he was not unhappy with his job, and that he did not want to relieve Fitch. He felt that his job was more important than Fitch's and that as more carriers came to the Pacific it would become increasingly important. His struggle to strengthen the position of the airmen in the Cincpac staff, he said, was simply for the best interests of the fleet and the Navy.

The arguments continued, but on a markedly less emotional plane where Towers was concerned.

This leavening was working both ways. Although Towers did not know it, the fight he had been waging for so long was extremely effective. Assistant Secretary Gates and Undersecretary Forrestal were both naval airmen and they were no mean allies. Forrestal had written encouragingly to Towers a few weeks earlier. "Don't give up the battle yet on Naval Air," the Undersecretary had said. "It may seem slow from out there, but I think we are making progress."

The progress was immense, and it was, in effect, changing the entire nature of naval operations. But one could not expect that change to come overnight, nor expect commanders trained in conventional naval methods of the past to embrace a developing weapon before they understood its potential. The Navy shipbuilding program was emphasizing carriers, because of the struggles of the naval airmen and the strategists' realization that the airmen were conceptually correct. Twenty-four large *Essex*-class carriers were being built—some, as noted, were already in the Pacific, 27,000-ton ships that seemed to be monsters. Nine light carriers, built on hulls originally intended to be cruisers, were in the water or on the ways. New planes had been built to fly from these carriers—planes that were, to a very large extent, the result of the sweat and argument of Towers, McCain, Radford, and the other airmen in the Bureau of Aeronautics. The F-6-F Hellcat and the F-4-U Corsair were the new fighters, built with an eye on recommendations such as those of Fighting 5, with all those endorsements from Admirals Fitch, Halsey, Towers, and Nimitz. These new planes were armed with .50 caliber machines guns, but carried twice as much sting as the old F-4-U's. Their top speed was at least 100 miles faster than the F-4-U's 300 miles an hour. They could climb faster and maneuver more quickly. They did what Nimitz and the others demanded, they outclassed the Zero in performance without abandoning the safety factors such as armor for the pilots.

In hindsight, one can spell out the course of the war in the matter of airplane types. All the American planes were improved, while the Japanese fought the entire war with only slight modifications to the fighters and bombers and torpedo planes that had attacked Pearl Harbor. It was a matter of raw materials, tooling, and industrial capacity, not brains; the Japanese simply could not meet the challenge of an awakened American behemoth whose submarines were smashing their empire.

And if the carrier fighters were more improved over the old than the dive bombers and torpedo bombers over their predecessors, then the fighters were converted to fighter bombers. Soon the carrier planes began sporting five-inch rockets. The carriers had the Oerlikon 20's and the Bofors 40 types plus improved five-inch anti-aircraft guns with improved controls and rate of fire. The development of radar had brought about the combat information center (CIC), in which the directors could "see" all around the carrier task force for many miles, identify friend and foe, and send combat patrol planes out to destroy the enemy long before he could come within range.

With the coming of the new fast carriers, training for the fall operations was speeded up. On October 9 Towers conferred with Pownall, Montgomery, and Sherman regarding training operations.

In September Nimitz had written Admiral Harold Bowen, chief of the Bureau of Ships, discussing radar:

> You are quite right about the importance of radar: It runs like a thread through just about all of our operational activities. Its impact on the Navy is nearly as heavy as the advent of steam or of modern shooting weapons. We have agreed out here that a Radar officer solely for the Operational end of Radar is desirable for my staff, and have taken steps to obtain one, realizing that he will be most active in gunnery, aviation, identification, and navigational matters. (I only mention the CIC problems, largely concerned with the most effective uses of Radar. The CIC, now experiencing growing pains, has taken on new importance in the last six months.)

On October 5 in the combat information center (CIC) of the carrier *Yorktown* Lieutenant (JG) Charles Ridgway, acting as fighter director, spotted on the radar screen two flights of Japanese planes coming in from the north Marshalls as the carrier moved to attack Wake. Each formation consisted of six fighters and six bombers. The American fighters were vectored out to attack, and shot down ten of the Japanese planes. The others turned away from the fight and the carrier, and landed on Wake. So the ability of the carrier to protect itself was indicated very strongly, and this was part of the argument in the conferences in Nimitz's office. In a meeting on October 9 the merits of long-range strikes versus close amphibious support were discussed fully. Captain Forrest Sherman showed the group films taken of the Wake and Marcus attacks, which showed the great power of carrier aircraft.

Three days later came irrefutable proof of the growing importance the Navy attached to aviation: after the morning conference in Nimitz's office, the admiral kept McMorris, Lockwood, Towers, Steele, and Ofstie to discuss staff changes. Principal among these was the upgrading of air officers on Nimitz's staff.

Nimitz asked Towers to nominate an officer for the job. Towers named Radford, Forrest Sherman, and Donald B. Duncan. Nimitz said to put them in order of preference, and Towers said he was listing them in order of seniority.

Nimitz insisted on preference. Towers said the Commander in Chief of the fleet knew more about these men than he, Towers, did.

"If you were Cincpac, which would you take?" Nimitz asked, again feeling out his air commander.

"Sherman," said Towers, reluctantly, but if Sherman was taken, then one of the others ought to be Towers' new chief of staff.

That same day Nimitz brought Sherman to the Cincpac staff, and Arthur Radford became Towers' chief of staff. Here, obviously was a victory for the aviators who had felt suppressed for so long.

Sensing this victory, the airmen pressed on. Operation Galvanic, the invasion of the Gilberts, represented an entirely new approach in the Pacific war, and for the first time the United States Navy had a heavy concentration of carriers and aircraft to devote to the sweeping of the skies.

The airmen wanted to take the carriers to strike every possible Japanese air base within range of the Gilberts, on the principle that it was best to knock out all the enemy air power before the operation began. Thus the landings would be opposed only by the Japanese ground forces in the Gilberts, and the fleet would be opposed only by Japanese submarines, and whatever sea strength Japan might choose to send forward.

On the evening of October 14 Pownall and Radford came to

see Towers. They really disagreed with the plans Admiral Spruance and Captain Moore had worked out with Admiral Turner and General Smith for the Gilberts operation. Their main point of disagreement involved the use of the carriers in the operation. They wanted to strike the enemy and strike him hard. Towers heard them out, and found that he agreed completely with their viewpoint. He sent them over to see Spruance. At 1900 that evening a dejected pair came back to Towers' quarters. They had seen Spruance and the interview had been most unsatisfactory: Spruance would not change his plan to free the carriers. The objective was to *take* the Gilberts, Spruance said, and the carrier men's program involved too wide a separation of the carrier strength from the attack and support groups.

Towers asked if they wanted him to go to Nimitz with the problem. Under the circumstances, Pownall said, it hardly seemed desirable. Pownall was right for one reason, at least, that he did not suspect. Nimitz would not have been found in any case—he had come down sick and had reluctantly allowed himself to be ordered into the hospital, where he would be stranded until October 22.

The discussions continued without Nimitz. On October 17 Chief of Staff McMorris presided over the morning staff meeting, which became a tactical conference dealing with the coming Gilberts operation. In this meeting Towers doggedly brought up the arguments advanced by his airmen: it was improper use of carriers to hold them in a landing area for defensive purposes. Carrier strength should be used to make repeated strikes against the enemy's principal bases, he said.

Surprisingly, perhaps, Spruance quite agreed with Towers. The rub was that Kelly Turner did not agree at all, and said so very volubly. He wanted those carriers kept right alongside his ships to defend them against attack.

It was possible, then, to see what Spruance was up against. The airmen were thinking one way, the amphibious men were thinking another. (Historians have tended to blame Spruance for holding an *idée fixe* regarding carrier use. Towers, in his papers, indicates the contrary, and when one realizes that Spruance always felt that

Towers was inimical to him, the discovery seems even more important.)

Nimitz had quite gone beyond this tactical matter in his character as commander in chief, as was shown when he returned to duty on October 22. He wanted to talk then about Operation Flintlock —which was the invasion *after* the Gilberts, the occupation of the Marshalls. As far as Nimitz was concerned, the Gilberts matter was wrapped up, it was in the hands of Spruance and the subordinate commanders and, except under the most extraordinary conditions, not his tactical concern. Towers, Pownall, and the others had sensed this, and kept the argument among themselves.

Furthermore, Nimitz's allocation of ships and aircraft for the Central Pacific operations had to be made in consideration of the needs of Halsey and of MacArthur's Southwest Pacific command. In the fall of 1943 Halsey and MacArthur agreed that Halsey should move on Bougainville, the largest of the Solomon Islands, by December 1. November 1 was set as L-Day, or landing day, with General Vandegrift to lead the Marines ashore.

At Pearl Harbor, Nimitz and his staff were discussing two kinds of futures during the last days of October. First were such matters as Flintlock. Should the Marshalls be invaded in January or February? (Spruance was told to stop his consideration of his forthcoming Gilberts raid and concentrate on this future for a bit.) Second was the immediate future. Halsey wanted some carrier raids down south. He had Rear Admiral Frederick C. Sherman and his task force, but Towers wanted to give him some more help. Sherman struck the area, and then went back south of Guadalcanal to refuel. On the night of November 1 the Japanese came in against Halsey's landing in force, and Admiral Merrill's cruiser task force repelled them, sinking a light cruiser and a destroyer without losing a ship. Next day the Japanese began sending in air strikes, and air and surface reinforcements from Truk. Sherman hit back at Rabaul and drove the Japanese back to Truk.

All this was very much touch and go, because part of the Pacific Fleet's fast carrier forces had been sent south to give Halsey a hand: Admiral Montgomery in *Essex*, with *Bunker Hill* and *Independence*, as Task Group 50.3, and Sherman in *Saratoga* with

Princeton, as Task Group 50.4. The problem was to use them as fully as possible in the south and then get them up to Spruance by November 19, ready to go on the Gilberts operation.

The organization of this new striking force was as complex as it was large. It included 200 ships, more than 35,000 troops, 6000 vehicles, and 117,000 tons of cargo. Part of the difficulty at Pearl Harbor's endless meetings among strategists was that only Admiral Nimitz saw the whole picture of the Pacific war. For example, when the airmen cried out for the opportunity to take their carriers afield and smash the Japanese at their bases—Nimitz could quite see their point. The evidence of Marcus and Wake was clear: the United States Navy now possessed a remarkably effective striking weapon in the fast carrier. When Kelly Turner and Holland Smith insisted stridently that they must have full support of the landings on the beaches—Nimitz could see their point as well. But what Turner, from his vantage point, and Towers, from his, could not see, was the war as it looked to Nimitz, who was responsible for the defeat of Japan. At the September meetings of Nimitz and King it had been made quite clear that the Gilberts operation was to be a dress rehearsal for the Marshalls. The organization of such an effort had never before been attempted. The Gilberts operation was to be the testing ground, and that is why Nimitz could really pay no heed to Towers' suggestion that the Gilberts operation be dropped as unnecessary.

Admiral Spruance was in charge of this complex effort, although, as noted, much of his personal attention was already being focused on the Marshalls—just as much of Nimitz's personal attention was focused on operations that would not take place for many months. But there were problems even here. The facilities at Pearl Harbor were not adequate for the training of the units as a fleet, so the ships would have to concentrate somewhere else on the way to their objective—a new problem for Spruance.

Another problem was the coordination of land-based aircraft, including naval, Army, and Marine units. This task had been assigned to Admiral Hoover, who moved into port at Funafuti on November 7. The *Curtiss*, his flagship, was quickly moored, antitorpedo net was run out around the ship, and telephone lines were run ashore. The command problem was raised immediately, for General Willis Hale, who was the Seventh Army Air Force commander, refused to live in secondary splendor on Hoover's ship, as invited, preferring to live in a tent ashore. A telephone line was run from the *Curtiss* to Hale's headquarters, and the work began.

By November 13 the air strikes on the Gilberts and other islands had begun. The flights were long—the longest thus far made in the Pacific, and the strikes were not as effective as they might have been. The Army crews, who manned the one hundred Liberators (B-24's), were green, but at this moment one of their prime responsibilities was gathering pictures of the various atolls, and this work went on apace. They dropped seventy-five tons of bombs in the Gilberts, and also struck in the Marshalls.

The striking force assembled for the Gilberts operation was called Task Force 50, and Spruance put it under Admiral Pownall.

Before the operation, Nimitz called the senior commanders present into his office for a talk. He laid down the law—told them what he expected of them—for nearly an hour. "If I hear of one case of a naval officer not giving required help to the Army ashore, I will immediately relieve him," he said.

Then he was finished. And in his usual way he broke the tension: "By the way, have you heard the one about the two male squirrels that were racing around the chestnut tree?"

The task force was divided into four groups. Pownall, in the *Yorktown,* led the *Lexington* and the light carrier *Cowpens,* in what was called the Carrier Interceptor Group (Task Group 50.1). The Northern Carrier Group (Task Group 50.2) was led by Rear Admiral Arthur W. Redford in the *Enterprise.* He also had the light carriers *Belleau Wood* and *Monterey.* The Southern Carrier Group (Task Group 50.3) was under Rear Admiral Alfred E. Montgomery in *Essex.* He had the carriers *Bunker Hill* and *Independence.* The Relief Carrier Group (Task Group 50.4) was Admiral Sherman's, *Saratoga* and *Princeton.*

The Southern Attack Force (Task Force 53), which would drive against Tarawa atoll, was commanded by Rear Admiral Harry Hill, and it included 16 transports, three battleships, and five cruisers, five escort carriers, 21 destroyers and one LSD which carried tanks for the landing. Hill would command until General Julian Smith of the Second Marine Division indicated that he was ready to assume command. This force would be augmented, too, by a number of destroyers and LST's carrying amphtracs, or amphibious vehicles.

The Northern Attack Force (Task Force 52) was commanded by Admiral Turner. It would take Makin. This force included six transports, carry the 27th Army Division, under Army General Ralph Smith, four battleships, four cruisers, three escort carriers, one LSD with tanks, and three LST's carrying amphtracs.

Turner's organization of the amphibious forces had been carried out under very difficult conditions. He had been brought up from Halsey's command, with the understanding that he would be given the staff of Admiral Rockwell—officers who had been involved in the planning and execution of the Aleutians operations. But this plan did not work out, and he found himself without experienced men. He asked Halsey for some of his old officers, and Halsey said they could not be spared from South Pacific amphibious operations. Turner went to Nimitz, who ordered up three of the officers. The problems continued, however, and a month before the invasion of the Gilberts, Turner asked Marine headquarters in Washington for a new Marine officer to be assistant chief of staff in the amphibious command. This request came eight days *after* Nimitz had issued Cincpac Op. Plan No. 13-43, which was the fleet order for the capture of the Gilberts.

The assembling of the invasion force was quite a feat. The Second Marines were in New Zealand, so Admiral Hill flew down to Auckland and joined General Julian Smith. They came north on November 1 in the transports, to rendezvous with the battleships, cruisers, and destroyers at Efate in the New Hebrides, held a practice landing operation there, and sailed for Tarawa on November 13.

Montgomery's Task Group 50.3 and Sherman's Task Group 50.4 had been in the south, on loan to Halsey. They fueled at Espiritu Santo about November 12, and sailed for the Gilberts on November 14, having mauled Rabaul on several strikes earlier in the month—so effectively that the Japanese in Rabaul were unable to help the Gilberts.

Pownall in overall command, and operating Task Group 50.1, and Radford in Task Group 50.2 sailed from Pearl Harbor on November 10. So did the Northern Attack Force. Admiral Spruance accompanied that force, in the cruiser *Indianapolis*, having chosen the smallest ship that would accommodate his staff. Admiral Turner's flagship, the battleship *Pennsylvania*, was far more impressive, but that is how Spruance wanted it. He had placed Turner in command of the Northern Attack Force and he was merely riding with the force. He spent his time pacing the decks, listening to music, reading, and relaxing. He had planned the operation and written lucid orders for his subordinates. He would not step in unless a command decision was in order: and that would mean either disaster, or an opportunity to smash the Japanese fleet.

The ships were coming in, from Pearl Harbor, Efate, Samoa, Funafuti, and San Diego, following tracks preset by the planners, so that all would converge in the Gilberts area in time to meet the D-Day schedules on November 20.

Part of the mission of Spruance's force was to "deny Nauru" to the Japanese. In days before, the enemy had used Nauru as a staging base for air strikes. But on October 18, planes of Admiral Hoover's land-based force hit Nauru. On October 19 Admiral Sherman's Task Group 50.4 hit Nauru again—and thereafter it was out of action. The first part of the mission was accomplished.

On that same day Pownall's force hit Jaluit and Mili, the two Marshall atolls nearest the Gilberts, and began knocking them out. That same day the Northern and Southern Attack Forces made visual contact at sea four hundred miles southeast of the Gilberts. Spruance left Turner's force, because he wanted to be on hand at the Tarawa landing, where there was more possibility of trouble than in Turner's area.

On Makin the Japanese had a handful of guns and eight hundred troops in the area of principal fortification, Butaritari Island, and nearly three hundred of these were construction workers. All their float planes but one had escaped, and the crew of that plane committed suicide as the attack began. Against this force came four battleships, four cruisers, thirteen destroyers, and five carriers of various sizes.

At 0500 on the morning of November 20, the atoll was visible from Kelly Turner's flagship. Forty minutes later the ships began launching spotting planes and by 0600 the transports were ready to disembark the 6400 soldiers who would assault the beach. Carrier planes swooped down on the flat beaches. The whumpf-whumpf of 14-inch guns roiled the air and for nearly two hours the guns barked and growled until a pall of smoke hung above the island.

First blood was drawn then—a turret exploded in the battleship *Mississippi*, killing forty-three men and wounding nineteen others. As for the Japanese, they sat silently in their bunkers and took the battering—they had nothing with which to fight, and not even a patrol ship was in the harbor.

The remarkable fact of the Battle of Makin Atoll is that it took the Americans three days to secure the area, in spite of the tremendous armada, the air power, the eight-to-one ratio of American fighting soldiers to Japanese—of whom only three hundred were really fighting men.

The Japanese did oppose the landings. Their small-caliber machine guns began popping like firecrackers. But only sporadically. The amphibious waves began coming in, the first amphtracs touched shore at 0832. But then the beaches began piling up with men and machinery, and to add to the confusion the native Gilbert Islanders came down to Red Beach to see the fun, and offer the "liberators" coconuts. It was quite a job to wrest them away from the beach; they were lured by K-rations and other "luxuries."

By mid-morning the western beachhead of the island was secured and troops began moving eastward. They were slowed by a shell crater in the road, and stopped by fifteen Japanese riflemen with a machine gun. Obviously the men of the 27th Division, a National Guard Division, were not proving to be fire-eaters.

The trouble on the beaches was partly because of the reef, which extended out a quarter of a mile from the beach. Under normal conditions, the reef was covered by perhaps four feet of water, which would make it possible for amphtracs, and also landing craft, to land easily. But this day was haunted by an extremely low tide, and only the amphtracs could come in. They shuttled men back and forth from the regular landing craft.

By mid-day the beaches were in good shape, except for the pile-up of supplies. But the troops were just not moving. As night fell on D-Day, the American troops were firing at everything that moved, including each other. Next day, as progress did not improve, General Holland Smith came ashore from Turner's flagship. He was raging, for as he watched the lazy popping of a few Japanese guns on this island, he was aware of a desperate battle being fought for the other objective, Tarawa, 450 miles away.

Holland Smith had harsh words for nearly everyone on that island of Butaritari, and one tale shows why:

Accompanied by my aides, Major Woodrum and Captain Asbill, I was driving along the beach where hundreds of troops were unloading supplies. A company came through, firing indiscriminately right and left and forcing the unloading party to take cover in the belief it was enemy fire. Jumping from my jeep, I located the lieutenant in command and asked what he was firing at.

"I'm trying to clean out snipers in this area," he replied.

"Can't you see there aren't any Japs around here?" I shouted. "Our men are working all over the area and you come shooting at tree tops when any damn fool can see there aren't any Japs up there. Why, the enemy is thousands of yards up front."

"I was given orders to clean out this area," the lieutenant persisted. "And I think there still may be Japs around here. I'm shooting at everything so we won't be taking any chances."

This did make me howling mad. "If I hear one more shot from your men in this area, I'll take your damn weapons and all your ammunition away from you," I said, revealing my identity. I was wearing my utility suit, without insignia. The shooting stopped and unloading was resumed.

Holland Smith was never one to pull punches, and he did not now. He blamed the Makin fiasco on the Army's General Smith and his officers, and he later told Nimitz that if Ralph Smith had been a marine he would have relieved him on the spot. But since there was no question about the taking of the island eventually, Holland Smith left, and headed for Tarawa, where there *was* trouble. (A short time after he left, Ralph Smith announced that Makin had fallen.)

Tarawa was indeed a different story. Here is how it looked to Admiral Hill, who wrote to Nimitz at 0600 on the morning of D-3, hours before the issue was resolved: "Our preliminary studies gave us a fine looking tide table which indicated that our H hour was within approximately a foot of high water on a rising tide. As it turned out the table was practically 100% in error with the reef almost bare out to 500–700 yards off shore."

Aboard the flagship, the battleship *Maryland*, there was a feeling of wonder and confidence. As one witness saw it:

> The destroyers were out wide in a protective screen; the three battleships—*Maryland*, *Colorado* and *Tennessee*—leading the van within the circle; cruisers bringing up the rear; escort carriers far off our port quarter; the APAs and an LSD—big, humpbacked landing ship which served as drydock for small craft—clustered in the middle for maximum protection. You felt the muscle, the pent-up power, ready to be hurled against that spit of land which was our target, and you felt that nothing on earth could resist the momentum of this vast sea-going war machine.

Two days earlier the feeling of going into battle had come to the men. The loudspeakers on the ships boomed: "Now hear this . . . . We are now entering enemy waters. You are directed to exercise every precaution not to disclose our position. There will be nothing thrown over the side. The smoking lamp is out at sunset. . . ."

On D-1 a submarine contact was reported to Admiral Hill, and he left two destroyers behind. All day long they played cat and mouse with the sub, and in the end came back to the force to announce that they thought they might have damaged him. That day, also, planes from the carrier force shot down a big Mavis four-engined flying boat "before he knew what hit him." "I do not think that this force was ever detected, although there was a possibility

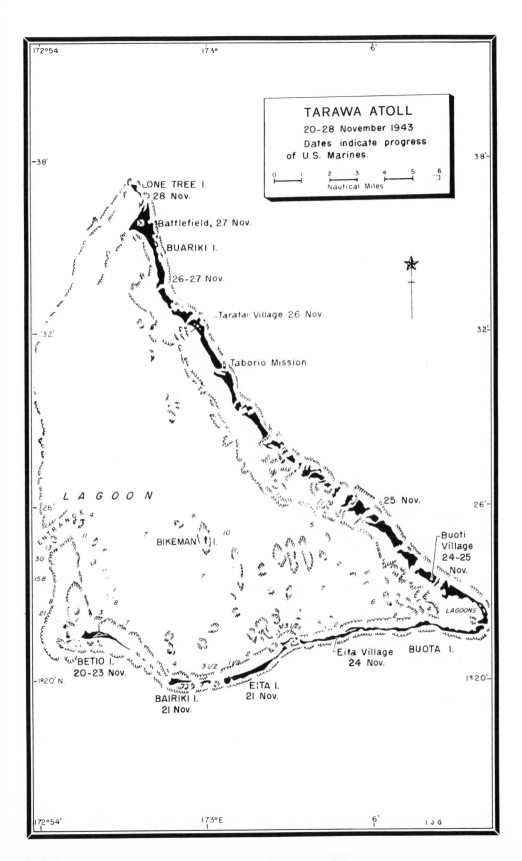

TARAWA ATOLL
20-28 November 1943
Dates indicate progress
of U.S. Marines.

0   1   2   3   4   5   6
Nautical Miles

LONE TREE I.
28 Nov.

Battlefield, 27 Nov.

BUARIKI I.

26-27 Nov.

Taratai Village 26 Nov.

Taborio Mission

25 Nov.

Buoti
Village
24-25
Nov.

LAGOON

ENTRANCE

BIKEMAN I.

LAGOONS

Eita Village
24 Nov.

BUOTA I.

BETIO I.
20-23 Nov.

BAIRIKI I.
21 Nov.

EITA I.
21 Nov.

I J G

that Turner's force, slightly to the north of us, had been reported," Admiral Hill said. (Morison noted that a scout plane *had* sighted Turner's force that day, according to Japanese sources discovered at the end of the war.)

Then came another adventure, which Hill reported in these terms to Nimitz:

> As we were sneaking through the pass south of Tarawa, trying to keep out of radar range we got a surface contact which we assumed to be a picket boat patrolling the passage. My picket reported it and I sent Dubose out to develop the contact. [Rear Admiral L. T. DuBose, commander of Fire Support Group Section 2 in the light cruiser *Santa Fe*.] They closed to about 8000 yards and opened fire together with my destroyer picket and after a few salvos it disappeared off the screen. They asked me on TBS if they should challenge and I replied in the negative, as this was a very critical part of our approach and it was vital that we remain undetected if possible. It now appears that this contact may have been the *Nautilus* and if so please tell Charlie Lockwood that I am sorry to hurt one of his fine subs but under the circumstances there was no alternative.

(It *was* the *Nautilus*. The picket destroyer *Ringgold* sent a five-inch shell through the base of the *Nautilus'* conning tower rupturing her main induction value, but not exploding. Her commander took her down, and she hid for two hours while a sweating damage control party put her together again so well that she could move on and complete her mission, then return to base.)

> My direction and time of approach was well known to all hands and I had to assume that no friendly vessels would be placed in my way at that period.

At dusk the ships were just out of sight of the atoll, and they crept in quietly, until from the *Maryland* Admiral Hill could see the lights of the island.

Three decks down in the *Maryland*, aft on the starboard side of the ship, Lieutenant Commanders Kenneth McArdle and E. A. MacPherson made themselves ready for the next day. McArdle, the public relations officer in charge, was posted on the flag bridge; his job would really begin when the first phase of the action was completed and his dozen correspondents began flocking back from the beaches or wherever they had assigned themselves to cover the story.* MacPherson's job was one of the most dangerous on the ship. He was a pilot, and he was to fly one of the *Maryland's* catapult planes out to spot for the bombardment. MacPherson was a methodical man, he spent several hours tidying up his gear in the cabin that night, so that in case he did not come back it would be easy to send home. Then he settled down with his favorite records, playing them *seriatim* on his portable record player.

McArdle, a citizen-sailor, knew he should sleep with his clothes on that night, but he was too tired. When General Quarters sounded at 0330 MacPherson was up immediately, and ready. McArdle was still dead to the world. Just before he went out of the cabin, the aviator shook his roommate awake.

Then McArdle began to race, for he knew very well that in a few moments the ship would begin to shut down below decks, the watertight doors would be closed and latched, and any man not at his action station had very small chance of getting there.

Godamighty. I fumbled in the darkness for my shoes, socks, shirt, life-belt, helmet, canteen—and the minutes rolled mercilessly by. I really made fair time, but not quite good enough. I managed to dash up two decks to wardroom level before the watertight doors began swinging ponderously shut. I almost got trapped in the wardroom, but managed to squeeze into a passageway before that door was closed. I found myself next to a ladder leading to the main deck, ran up it, and bumped my head on the dogged-down hatch, but no one heard. Then,

---

* *McArdle's correspondents were some of the most distinguished of the reporters of the Pacific war, and they produced some of that war's most vivid and telling reportage. They included William Hipple of the Associated Press, Richard W. Johnston of United Press, Robert Sherrod of* Time, *Keith Wheeler of the Chicago* Times, *John Henry of International News Services, Gilbert Bundy of King Features Syndicate, and Henry Keys of the London* Daily Express.

fumbling, I found I could unscrew the twelve-inch center panel, and finally got it open. Somehow I squeezed through, battened it down again, and breathed the fresh night air of the main deck.

With the help of a sailor who led him up top, McArdle made his way to his battle station, flag plot. There he learned why the call to battle had come an hour earlier than expected and caught him unawares: a Japanese searchlight, sweeping the horizon from the island, had caught one ship fully, hesitated on the ship, and then blinked out. Since that time, there had been silence from the island.

It was about 0530 when the enemy began firing from the beach, at the transports twelve thousand yards away.

"Shall we go ahead, sir?" Captain Ryan asked Admiral Hill.

The admiral said yes, and Captain Ryan turned to the TBS. "Commence firing," he told the ships. "The war is on." McArdle describes what happened next:

"Stand by for main battery," came the bark over the ship's p.a. system. Then a warning buzz—and moments later, the after four sixteen-inchers let go. The big ship flinched as though a giant had struck her with a hammer. Old trouper that she was, she quivered in every corner, and dust filtered down from the overhead fixtures in flag plot. Several lighters were jarred out in that first blast, and I thought several of my teeth had been harred out. Then the forward two turrets let go in unison, and then they alternated, forward four and after four, wham! wham!

At dawn the smoke was curling above Tarawa as it had plumed above Makin, but there was a difference: as the planes dived down, they came under fire, and McArdle saw one shot down before his eyes. One moment there was a plane—the next moment a stick of fire blazed down toward the ground, and he hoped the pilot had been killed by the antiaircraft shell, for there was no parachute.

Admiral Hill seemed calm and collected to those on the bridge. Actually, he was watching the development of the battle with more than a little worry, as he later told Nimitz:

The air strike, scheduled for 0545, failed to arrive until about 0620, which disrupted our plans a little but we went right ahead with gunfire, holding up only for a few minutes after the planes arrived and took over. Fortunately we had enough flexibility in our fire support plan to accommodate this change without too much difficulty.

The bombardment really was terrific and I don't see how any personnel, except those in bombproof shelters and dugouts, could have taken it. Everything above ground on that island was demolished, houses, trees, planes, etc. My aviator tells me there is one house left standing. During the preliminary period we took battleships in as close to the reef as we could get them, which ran from 4000 to 5000 yards. Cruisers went in closer still and we sent destroyers in onto the south shore to where they could use their automatic weapons. There were a few shots fired our way but they were wild and very quickly silenced. For the H minus 45 to H minus 5 firing, as I think I told you, we lined up three battleships and three cruisers in the arc of a circle close to the reef at the west end of that island and poured over 700 tons of metal into the landing beaches, an area of less than a mile long and 250 yards wide, just prior to the landing. It really was terrific and will give you an idea of the strength of some of those concrete dugouts and block houses they had prepared.

Hill sent Nimitz pictures taken two days later which showed that Tarawa was covered with dugouts, pillboxes, blockhouses, and other fortifications so strong that thirty-six hours after being overrun the Japanese were still holding out in some of them. Reports had it that some four thousand workmen had been preparing Tarawa against invasion in the weeks prior to the operation.

The island in the Tarawa atoll that they were actually attacking was Betio, some 291 acres. The defenses included mined boat obstacles, barbed wire, and logs, outside the beaches, to divert landing boats into lanes covered by the Japanese shore guns.

Behind the beach was a barricade, which stood three to five feet high, made of coconut logs wired together. Behind this, commanding it, stood blockhouses and dugouts, connected by trenches, in which machine guns were set up with crossing fields of fire. Spotted at points of vantage were fourteen coast defense guns, with underground storage vaults for ammunition and bombproof shelters for crew. Along the beach were some twenty-five 37 mm and 75 mm field guns, most of them in pillboxes, some armor-plated, and 13 mm and 5.1-inch antiaircraft guns, and fourteen tanks that had been locked in position for use of their 37 mm guns. For the Japanese defenders, here was a system of bombproof shelters so built that only armor-piercing or delayed-action shells could break them down.

As the big fighting ships blasted the island with shells, the six transports which carried the landing force began disgorging boats, which scurried about to find amphtracs in the LST's and put the marines aboard, or circled, waiting. As the Japanese continued to return fire, the transports were ordered out of range, and they moved back, but their men were already out and in the smaller craft.

The air strikes began just before 0630 and lasted seven minutes. Then came more gunfire from the ships, at random, really, laid down on the beaches.

Betio resembled a Malay kriis, and at the butt end of the kriis was Green Beach. Moving along the north shore of the island from there were Red Beaches One, Two, and Three. The naval guns swept all of them repeatedly.

Minesweepers were also doing their work, making a safe channel into the lagoon. Above them flew Lieutenant Commander MacPherson, dropping smoke-pots to indicate shoal water.

Hill's letter to Nimitz went on:

> Our plans had provided for sending two destroyers into the lagoon. We got them in safely, having marked turns in the channel by buoys marked by my flag aviator. We covered their entrance with smoke and the plane also guided them through coral heads from overhead as we could not go close enough to the beach to use the main channel. Those destroyers inside the lagoon, I believe, proved to be the decisive factor in getting the troops ashore.

MacPherson came back that day with a wounded rear-seat gunner and holes in the fuselage of his plane, but he came back.

The LSD *Ashland* also moved into the lagoon, and the amphtracs began surging forward toward the beach, from the rendezvous area. They were delayed by a choppy sea and current they had not expected and H-Hour was postponed to 0845 in the morning, then to 0900. The troops actually began moving ashore at 0913 on beaches Red One, Red Two, and Red Three.

"They'll go in standing up. There aren't fifty Japs left alive on that island," someone on the flag bridge shouted. But the shout did not come from General Julian Smith or Colonel Merritt A. Edson, his chief of staff, who stood at the rail, watching silently through their field glasses.

As the boats approached the beaches, the trouble began, and from the flag bridge of the *Maryland* it could be seen. In the water, a long way from the shore, the boats began to stop, apparently without reason. Then little green-clad figures climbed over the sides and started to wade in. "At that distance they seemed hardly to be moving at all," said McArdle, "they would be waist-deep now, and suddenly just their heads would be sticking out, and their arms with rifles clutched high overhead. Now and then one would slip down into the water and not appear again . . . ."

The Japanese shore defenses caused the amphtracs to bunch up on the beaches, and the landing teams began to suffer heavy casualties.

Wave followed wave. By the time the fourth wave began to move in, the tide was so low that the LCVPs (landing craft, vehicles, personnel) could not pass the reef, and the 37 mm guns had to wait for nightfall to get to the beach. The fifth wave, tanks from the LSD, were put off in three feet of water. Some were quickly disabled, others moved inshore, but the tanks on the Red beaches were not to be decisive; only two of them remained intact throughout the battle.

Around noon, word came to flag plot from the beach that the Marines had established a beachhead. General Smith rushed over to Colonel Edson and thrust out his hand.

"They've done it!" he shouted.

Edson did not take the hand. "I'd rather wait, sir," he said.

How right Edson was! The bloody beachhead was there, but the Marines were moving forward inch by inch under devastating fire.

This was no Makin, not at all. On beaches Red Two and Red Three, some twenty amphtracs were stuck on the reef, under cross fire and shellfire from the island's big guns. There was a beachhead—yes, some 1500 Marines were pinned down on a narrow beach before the coconut log barricades. The tide was so low that the landing craft could not get in. On Beach Red Two the Marines held a two-hundred-yard front, tenuously. Their commander, Colonel Amey, had been killed in the water as he stepped off his amphtrac. Colonel David Shoup, commander of the assault force, knew his landing was in deep trouble.

Early in the afternoon, Colonel Shoup sent Lieutenant Colonel Evans Carlson, the raider leader, back to the *Maryland* to make a report. So bad were conditions, off the beaches as well as on, that Carlson did not reach the flagship until late evening, and there McArdle encountered him.

> . . . a boat pulled up alongside [McArdle recalls], and I looked down to see the weatherbeaten face of a middle-aged marine looking up at me. He had no insignia. He came clambering up the side on a rope ladder and asked me the way to the signal bridge. Having learned it myself the hard way, I was more than glad to give him a lift. On the way he introduced himself. . . .
>
> "You been to the beach?" I asked incredulously.
>
> "Just got back," he told me, grinning. He displayed a hole in his pants leg. "Lucky," he said, "just got a nick."

Carlson's report to Admiral Hill was anything but encouraging. Unless reinforcements and ammunition could be brought in to the beaches, they could not be held. The bombardment had simply not knocked out the Japanese as those aboard the ships had expected. Later General Holland Smith would complain that the bombardment was ineffectual, and still later Admiral Hill would remind Smith that his staff participated in the planning. At this moment, however, there was no room for recrimination.

General Holland Smith at this moment was aboard the *Pennsylvania,* watching the sluggish movement of the 27th Division troops across Makin against light opposition. The first messages from General Julian Smith on the *Maryland* came an hour and a half after the landings on Tarawa.

"Successful landings on Beaches Red 2 and 3. Toe hold on Red 1. Am committing one LT [Landing Team] from division reserve. Still encountering strong resistance."

Seeing Makin, it was impossible for Holland Smith to visualize Tarawa. But by afternoon, he learned how dreadful the situation was on the other atoll. Julian Smith sent another message, reporting heavy casualties, and asking permission to commit the Second Division's Sixth Regiment, which was held in reserve. The battle was only a few hours old, and Holland Smith was immediately aware of the desperation on Tarawa—he knew Julian Smith and he knew that this officer would not overstate his troubles. The last words of Julian Smith's message—"the situation is in doubt"— sent Holland Smith to Kelly Turner's cabin, and together they agreed to commit the reserves on Tarawa.

That night, at Tarawa, Admiral Hill's ships retired twenty or thirty miles off the island. On the first day the ships had been able to deliver fire to help the troops, but as the Marines moved inland it became very dangreous, and less and less fire support was called for. The carrier planes came overhead, on request, and bombed and strafed, but the Japanese defenses were extremely strong. McArdle, for example, went into the beach on the morning of D-1, was stranded in his boat on the reef three hundred yards offshore, and thus had an excellent view of a duel between a destroyer and a coastal gun in a pillbox—because his boat was caught in the middle. Eventually the pillbox must have caught one, for its fire stopped.

By the end of the first day, 5000 Marines had gone ashore and 1500 were killed or wounded. On D-1 the reserves were committed. General Julian Smith went ashore (his boat was hit by a shell, he was dunked and had to wade in). He did not know it, but the Japanese were in serious difficulties, even by this time. Half the 4500 troops in defense had been killed, and the other half were cut up into little units in pillboxes and blockhouses. Rear Admiral Keiji Shibasaki's communications were cut off and he was out of touch with his men, marooned in his own command post.

During the night some heroic Japanese had swum out to an abandoned freighter wreck off the beach. Others had occupied stranded tanks and amphtracs. They set up sniper posts and kept a devastating fire on the beaches and the approaches.

That day, McArdle rounded up press copy from Richard W. Johnston of United Press, Robert Sherrod of *Time*, Henry Keys of the London *Daily Express*, pictures by a press photographer and Marine photographers, and artists' sketches by Bundy, and headed back for Pearl Harbor with the first reports of the battle.

The reef and the tides were the worst enemies of the Navy and the Marines. The ships and planes kept up the fire support, and overhead the carrier fighters flew combat air patrol. But very little patrol was needed: so effective had been the strikes on Nauru and the other islands that the Japanese were unable to throw any serious air threat against the landings.

The fighting was furious, and many men fell, killed or wounded. Even on the second day, Colonel Shoup was not at all certain of the outcome, at least not until late in the afternoon when he was able to report back, "We are winning." That welcome news came to General Holland Smith even as he was wriggling with the frustrations of watching an inept Army force bogged down by its own weight on Makin.

As noted, on the third day, the news came from Makin that the island was in American hands, and a few hours later word came from Tarawa that it had come into the hands of the Marines. But what a difference. The Army on Makin lost 64 men killed and 150 wounded. The marines on Tarawa had casualties of nearly 2900, nearly a third of them killed or dead of wounds. And yet both islands were secured within a few hours of each other.

When King and Nimitz had spoken of the Gilberts as a dress rehearsal for the Marshalls, they had been wiser than their subordinates could have dreamed. So many were the mistakes made in this action that Captain James Steele back at Pearl Harbor prepared a report called "A Hundred Mistakes Made at Tarawa," and even before the island was secured, Admiral Hill was writing Nimitz about some of them.

More LVT's (landing vehicle tracked) must be provided to

carry in tanks, Hill said. He and Julian Smith had agreed that at least three hundred should be made available for an operation the size of Tarawa. More LSD's should also be provided. The Marines should have amphibious tanks, so that in case they were stuck in deep water they could extricate themselves. More escort vessels should be provided.

But these comments were mild, compared to those of General Holland Smith, when he came ashore and saw the signs of battle a few days later:

No words of mine can reproduce the picture I saw when the plane landed after circling that wracked and battered island. The sight of our dead floating in the waters of the lagoon and lying along the blood soaked beaches is one I will never forget. Over the pitted, blasted island, hung a miasma of coral dust and death, nauseating and horrifying. Chaplains, corpsmen and troops were carrying away the wounded and burying the dead. We had about a thousand killed and added to this nightmare of mangled bodies, were the four to five thousand Japanese. The marines took 146 prisoners, but only 17 were Japanese. The others were Korean laborers.

Holland Smith knew, instinctively, that he and the Marines would be severely criticized at home for the heavy casualties of this operation. Almost in a state of shock, he toured the island.

"I don't see how they ever took Tarawa," he said. "It's the most completely defended island I have ever seen."

In his tour of the island, General Holland Smith began to draw conclusions. He visited every pillbox and blockhouse on the western end of the island—and discovered how ineffective had been the naval and aerial bombardments. Only one of the fortlets, said Smith, was destroyed by naval gunfire. All the rest had been taken by Marines with explosives and hand grenades.

As the battle closed, the Navy suffered a severe loss. A Japanese submarine penetrated the American screen south of Makin and torpedoed the escort carrier *Liscome Bay*, which blew up, and then sank, taking 644 lives, including that of Rear Admiral Henry Mullinix, the commander. Earlier the *Independence* had taken a torpedo.

For the next few days there was a bit of mopping up in these islands, and in others of the Gilbert group. Admiral Spruance remained in the area.

Back at Pearl Harbor, the Nimitz staff meetings had been involved in very heavy argument on the eve of this action. Towers had opposed the entire Operation Galvanic until three days before Spruance's sailing. Then, for the next few days, Nimitz and his advisors had been completely wound up in the planning for the Marshalls invasion, which was next on the calendar. The Joint Chiefs of Staff were pushing Nimitz as early as November 7 for a date for Operation Flintlock, and on November 8 he had sent them a date of January 17. Before the sailing of the fleet to the Gilberts, Pownall had suggested a carrier attack on the Marshalls as soon as the Gilberts were secured, one that would involve the carriers and the fast battleships.

A few hours after the invasion of the Gilberts began, Towers asked in the morning meeting at Pearl Harbor that Spruance modify his orders and let the carriers move out to attack the Marshalls. Nimitz asked why Spruance had planned, as he did, to keep the carriers close by.

Towers replied that Spruance was half expecting a strong Japanese naval force to move out from Truk and was ready to fight a fleet engagement. McMorris concurred.

But Towers thought it would be better to put the carriers to use against the Marshalls bases, rather than leave them sitting ducks outside the Gilberts.

Nimitz told McMorris and Sherman to draft such a dispatch to Spruance. On November 24 the strikes began, with one at Mili in the southern Marshalls, but it was not until November 26 that the carriers were released. Some of the carrier men claimed that the loss of the *Liscome Bay* and the torpedoing of the *Independence* were the direct result of keeping the carriers as "sitting ducks." But that was the job of escort carriers, as would be shown beyond doubt at Leyte.

That day Nimitz and several members of the staff took off in the X PB2Y-I, which was the staff plane, and flew nonstop from

Pearl Harbor to Funafuti. A message came in from Spruance pro-
testing the aircraft disposition, and McMorris showed it to Nimitz.
The admiral simply said to ignore it, and went on, bound for
Tarawa to look over the results of the action.

Spruance remained in the Gilberts. Most of the naval forces
were sent away, the carriers under Pownall and Montgomery to hit
Kwajalein and Wotje, and make aerial reconnaisance of the Marshalls for the future. Rear Admiral Lee with five battleships, two
carriers, and twelve destroyers, was sent back to the South Pacific,
stopping at Nauru to bombard and smash the defenses with carrier
strikes. Early in December, the postmortems on the Gilberts operation began.

The public was involved, to some extent. For Lieutenant Commander McArdle had taken dispatches for the press with him
back to Pearl Harbor on D-3, and Richard W. Johnston's United
Press story was pooled among the three American wire services (not
without bitter remarks by UP manager William Tyree in Honolulu).
The story of the bloody, bitter battle was out. Some correspondents
and many editorial writers said Tarawa was a terrible mistake, and so
did some of Nimitz's commanders, particularly Holland Smith and
Admiral Towers.*

In December Nimitz supervised the picking up of the pieces,
the discussions of the learning process at the Gilberts.

Spruance came back to recommend in his report that air and
surface bombardment should be measured in terms of days rather
than hours. He also said that "flat trajectory fire support ammunition
proved ineffective against many shore targets. Greater angle of fall
required." That remark might have suggested to the airmen a need
for the prolonged aerial bombardment of landing targets, using
armor-piercing and delayed-action bombs. The airmen, however, were
much more interested in fighting the battle of command and influence, it seemed, than in studying the uses to which their weapons
might be put in such tactical situations. Or perhaps it could be said
another way: the needs for naval bombardment, as shown at Tarawa,
were still not really totally accepted.

---

* Rear Admiral E. M. Eller noted that Smith did *not* say this before the Tarawa
landing.

There were other recommendations, arising from specific problems. Spruance wanted control boats to guide landing forces to favorable landing spots—a result of the pile-up of forces on the edges of the beaches. He wanted LVT's for assault waves and amphibious craft or DUKW's for succeeding waves—a result of the wrecking of many of the amphtracs in the Tarawa operation. Other recommendations were for protection of the bomb stowage compartments of the escort carriers (a result of the explosion of *Liscome Bay's* bombs when she was torpedoed), the development of night fighters for carriers (the result of a night attack on Radford's task group, which Radford was able to drive off because he had trained three pilots in night-fighting), and flagships *designed* as headquarters ships for attack force commanders (the result of communications failures aboard the *Maryland,* because that old battleship's wiring could not stand the strain of the firing of those sixteen-inch guns).

General Holland Smith had some suggestions of his own. For one thing, he wanted no more Marine Raider attacks on invasion objectives. Evans Carlson had raided Makin in August, 1942, and made a name for himself and his battalion. But the fact was, Smith said, that the Japanese buildup of defenses on Tarawa dated from that Makin raid—for the Japanese were astute enough to realize there was a purpose in the operation.

There was no question about the mistakes, and everyone knew it, but it had been Nimitz and King who knew, before the fact, that the mistakes would be made, and that they would *have to* be made sooner or later. For, even as Spruance and his armada were sailing for the Gilberts in the middle of November, Nimitz was holding special planning meetings with Vice Admiral John H. Newton, his new deputy; Rear Admiral McMorris, his chief of staff; Rear Admiral Forrest Sherman, his new plans officer; and Vice Admiral Towers. The purpose: closing in on Japan, with a foothold gained on the China coast. They talked about possible attacks on the Kurils, and the seizure of Hokkaido as an air base. Such operations would mean far greater armadas and far more extensive amphibious operations than Tarawa.

Tarawa had been a bloody, costly victory, but in essence it had been absolutely necessary training for the Americans in the Pacific.

Chapter
Eighteen

ON TO THE
MARSHALLS

December 1–25, 1943

Life was not all beer and skittles among the staff at Pearl Harbor. Holland Smith came back from the Gilberts operation to justify the name hung on him by his Marines—Howlin' Mad Smith—and he was very, very critical of the Navy's gun and air support of his boys when they went ashore on Tarawa. He gave an interview to the press, and although he said much of it was garbled by Navy censorship, the gist was plain enough: he was not pleased with events. This displeasure included Spruance's insistence that command of the expedition be in the hands of the naval amphibious officer until the beachhead was secured.

Other frictions were exposed. The Army commander, General Richardson, complained that the shore-based airplanes had accomplished practically nothing during the Gilberts operation, and he blamed the naval command for this failure. Hoover blamed the Army training, and Army directives that kept the bombers up too high. Towers blamed Spruance, because, he said, Spruance had no experience in directing shore-based aircraft. The discussion became heated. On December 4, after Richardson complained about the subordinate position of Army ground and air forces in the Gilberts operation, Nimitz held a special conference in his office, and at the end of it asked Admiral Towers to undertake an investigation.

On December 5, while Spruance was still clearing up details in the Gilberts, he proposed to Nimitz that he appoint a flag officer to be deputy to Admiral Hoover, taking direct charge of the American bases in the British Gilbert Islands. Towers was bitterly aware that Spruance proposed to use a nonaviator for this task, and he and Sherman pointed out that it would also foul up Army relationships to do so. So Spruance's plan was disapproved.

The next day, "Terrible" Turner was back in Pearl Harbor, and he presented to the staff a report on the Gilberts operation. Holland Smith and Turner agreed on one thing: the plans for the Marshalls now appeared far too ambitious, after what they had learned at Tarawa. They could not take Kwajalein, Maloelap, and Wotje all at once, as planned. Holland Smith wanted to take Maloelap and Wotje first. Nimitz and Sherman wanted Kwajalein. Other officers had other ideas. Nothing would be decided until Spruance returned.

Admiral Spruance did return to Pearl Harbor on December 8, 1943, and the discussions began again. Towers went off to Canton Island on his mission. The others met each morning to talk.

Towers was absent, then, when Admiral Pownall brought Task Force 50 back to Pearl on December 9. Pownall had been given permission to strike the Marshalls after the Gilberts operation, because Nimitz and Spruance wanted to know what was there, and wanted some of that Japanese power knocked out. Six carriers went in on December 4 to hit the group, in one day of air strikes. The Japanese air opposition was very strong, but many planes were destroyed on Kwajalein and Wotje. Planes on the airfields at Roi were not destroyed; Admiral Pownall had grown restless in hanging about the edges of this Japanese strong point, and had decided to head home even though those planes were still capable of inflicting much damage. One aspect of the strike had been to take pictures of the islands, and the pictures had shown the Roi bombers, and a bomber strip that was more than half finished on Kwajalein.

Captain J. J. Clark of the *Yorktown* was furious with Admiral Pownall for refusing to stay in the area and hit the islands again, and when the task group arrived at Pearl Harbor, Clark went looking for his superiors. Towers, of course, was gone. Clark then saw Forrest Sherman, and showed him the undestroyed planes on the ground. Sherman opened the door to the next room and called Soc McMorris in to see the pictures—"You want to see the fish that got away?" But he was equally interested in the airfield, and took the picture in to Colonel Ralph Robinson, Marine officer and assistant plans officer.

"What do you think of that, Robby?" he said.

"Jesus, this is it," said Robinson. And the photo of the half-built airstrip was taken to Admiral Nimitz, who saw better than any other the importance of Kwajalein.

As for his subordinate commanders, they had other worries, and thus other viewpoints. Admiral Spruance had been informed that as soon as the Marshalls were taken, the fleet must be released for use in the Southwest Pacific to support MacArthur's coming operations. The idea of losing his fleet worried Spruance greatly—particularly the thought of losing his fast carriers. The Japanese defense of the Marshalls was built about garrisons and fortified atolls protected by a series of airstrips which extended in hopping distance all the way back to Japan. Thus the Japanese could funnel aircraft into the Marshalls remaining in their hands and continue to strike the Americans after the fleet had left the new conquest. The way to stop this, said Spruance, was to take the outer islands first—such as Eniwetok, the westernmost atoll of the Marshalls. By taking the outer islands and cutting off the airfield chains, the Americans could destroy the Japanese hopping technique of defense. Eniwetok, for example, was a thousand miles from the Marianas and the key position for air supply of the Marshalls.

"I was strongly opposed to capturing Kwajalein and then to leaving it without fleet support when the fleet went to the South Pacific," Spruance said. "A considerable amount of shipping would be required for the buildup of Kwajalein, and it would be moving by a route within the Marshalls which we did not control."

In the second week of December, with all the principals in attendance, Nimitz got down to cases. When should they go in the Marshalls, he asked. Then, as was sometimes his practice, he started around the room, asking each of the officers squatting on a folding chair just what he thought.

"Raymond, what do you think now?" he asked.

"Outer islands," said Spruance.

"Kelly?"

"Outer islands," said Turner.

"Holland?"

"Outer islands," said Smith.

And so it went with all the others except Nimitz and Forrest Sherman.

Nimitz looked calmly about the room, his white brows steady, and his mouth set in that typical straight line. Then he spoke, quietly.

"Well, gentlemen," he said, "our next target will be Kwajalein."

The final plan called for the first attack to be made on Majuro, an undefended atoll whose lagoon would give a good anchorage for the service squadron. Kwajalein was to be assaulted from two ends simultaneously, and if the troops could manage it they would move on to take Eniwetok.

Spruance, Turner, and Smith still had misgivings. Smith came around quickly like a good soldier. The others acceded to Nimitz's orders, like good flag officers, even against their judgment. But Nimitz had deduced that the fast carriers and land-based air from the Gilberts could knock out Japanese airpower in the eastern Marshalls before the landings.

In a way it was unfortunate that Admiral Towers was off on his mission when Captain Clark came in from battle steaming with indignation. By the time he returned, Clark and his navigator, George Anderson, had prepared a "White Paper" complaining about Pownall's lack of aggressiveness and making the case for stronger use of the fast carriers. As often happens with such affairs, once the document was written, it began to assume a life of its own.

Clark took his paper to Admiral Radford, chief of staff now to

Admiral Towers, and to Towers himself. Not satisfied with their re-action, Clark decided to go even higher. He detached his no. 2 combat air intelligence officer, Herman Rosenblatt, and got him a ride back to Bremerton aboard the *Lexington* (which was going home for an overhaul, having taken that torpedo on the way back from the Marshalls). Clark told Felix Stump of the *Lexington* that Rosenblatt was going back on an air combat intelligence matter.

In Seattle, Herman Rosenblatt got a ride to Washington in an airplane, and took the paper to his brother Sol Rosenblatt, who was a lawyer and intimate of the Roosevelt family. Sol Rosenblatt said the paper should be seen by the President himself. Herman Rosenblatt then sought out Franklin D. Roosevelt, Jr. Two days before Christmas he saw young Roosevelt and said he had a story for the President. That was fine, said FDR, Jr. "Let's go up to Hyde Park for Christmas Dinner."

The young men went to Hyde Park.

After dinner in the comfortable old dining room, FDR pushed back his chair and spoke.

"Young man," he said to Herman Rosenblatt, "how is the war in the Pacific?"

"Father," said FDR, Jr., "this man has a story to tell you."

So Herman Rosenblatt handed over his paper, and Roosevelt read it carefully. Then he told Rosenblatt to go back to Washington and to report to Artemus Gates on Monday morning.

Rosenblatt went back to Washington and did report to Gates. He was told that he could go back to his ship. The matter was taken care of. Rosenblatt returned. By that time changes had been made.

And Captain Clark was sure that he had caused them, with his action.

"Insubordinate? Obviously," said Clark. "But I wanted to win the war. I felt it was a patriotic duty," he said years later in the oral history he prepared for the Columbia University Oral History Project and the Navy.

"I think I did right," he said, "because I did not think we were being properly led and I don't think I could have talked to anybody out there. It was the wrong place to talk. I think once in a life-time something like that happens—it has to be done."

The fact was, however, that Clark's insubordinate action had no meaning whatsoever. Indeed, had Nimitz or King known about it, there is good reason to believe that Clark's career would have come to an ignominious end right there—for neither commander would stomach such disloyalty.

No, what had actually happened was that Towers, also upset by Pownall's failure to make what he considered to be the most aggressive use of the carrier weapon, had asked that Marc Mitscher be put in charge of the fast carrier force of the Pacific. Mitscher was, like Towers, an airman's airman. He was thin and wizened and brown, with the squint of a man who looks much at the sun. He had been in command of the *Hornet* when she ferried the B-25's to raid Japan. He had commanded her again during the battle of Midway, and even though the *Hornet* had not distinguished herself in that battle, Mitscher had not been accused of lack of aggressiveness.

Towers brought the matter up with Nimitz in a special meeting on December 23, as Herman Rosenblatt was moving around Washington, trying to get access to the President. Towers began the discussion by asking for a more aggressive use of the carrier forces, and then went into some detail. Forrest Sherman backed him to the hilt. Nimitz was impressed, and he agreed to send a dispatch to Admiral King with that recommendation.

On Christmas Day, as Herman Rosenblatt journeyed to Hyde Park, Nimitz told Towers that Mitscher could be brought in as commander of the fast carrier force, but that it must not be done until after the Marshalls invasion.

One reason for this delay was Spruance's reluctance to take Mitscher at all. The relations between Spruance and Mitscher went back a long way, to the days of the 1930's when Spruance had been chief of staff to Rear Admiral A. E. Watson, commander of destroyers of the Scouting Force, and Mitscher had been commander of Patrol Wing 2. One day at San Diego, when Mitscher was flying a scouting mission out of the base, the weather began to turn foul, and the big patrol planes bucked and shivered in the sky. Mitscher headed straight out for some time, but as the turbulence grew more severe he began to fear for his scouting planes, and requested permission to return to base.

The skies above San Diego were clear and blue.

"Permission denied," said Admiral Watson.

Mitscher flew on, the buffeting growing ever more severe, the rain pelting down so harshly that it distorted the view of the windshield of the plane and the wipers could not keep up.

A few minutes passed. Mitscher again radioed back. "Request permission to return to base."

"Permission denied," came the answer.

Mitscher squinted and grimaced and his face grew hard. A few more moments convinced him that the weather was ever worsening and growing dangerous.

"Am returning to base unless specifically ordered otherwise," he said into the radio transmitter. And then he pulled out the plug.

Such incidents gave rise to the term "damned aviator" among nonflying senior officers who had no sympathy for the sometimes unorthodox views of their flying companions.

And then there was Midway.

That Christmas Day, 1943, Admiral Sherman suggested that Mitscher go out with Spruance on the Marshalls invasion, riding as a "makey learn" admiral, who would become a force commander. Nimitz liked the idea, but he refused to commit himself at that moment. But since the question of Pownall's aggressiveness had been raised by Towers, Nimitz now also wanted an appraisal of the other air officers who might be available for important commands.

Towers came back with the requested appraisals:

Vice Admiral Aubrey Fitch, commander of the air force in the South Pacific: "All around experience. Physically tough. Aggressive. Popular. Fine qualities of leadership."

Rear Admiral John Hoover, commander of the air force in the Central Pacific: "An Enigma. Physically fit. A positive character. Not popular. Standoffish. Lack of close relationships between him and his staff. Hostility to [General] Hale. Tough job. Not accomplished too well. Ability as commander carrier task force, untried."

Rear Admiral Bernhard, prospective commander of an atoll. He was talkative, he was reported to do a good job at sea, but he had a bad leg.

Rear Admiral Pownall, commander of Carrier Division 3: "Over-cautious in plans and operations. He worries intensely before and during operations. Lack of aggressiveness—resented by sub-ordinates." Towers recommended Pownall be replaced by a more aggressive admiral, but said he would be pleased to have Pownall in any administrative capacity.

Rear Admiral Mitscher: "Tops for carrier force command."

Rear Admiral Frederick C. Sherman, commander, Carrier Division One: "Self-interest. Very unpopular with aviators because of intolerance. Able but not for high command because personality absolutely precludes establishment of wholehearted loyalty."

Rear Admiral R. F. Wood: "Unpopular."

Rear Admiral John W. Reeves, commander of the air forces in the Aleutians: "Efficient, determined."

Rear Admiral A. E. Montgomery: "Energetic, courageous and determined."

These recommendations were submitted, and Nimitz read them very seriously. Two days later, Nimitz called a special conference. Admiral Newton was there, along with Spruance, McMorris, Sherman, Towers, and Pownall.

Nimitz was very frank, as he could be without being in the slightest bit offensive. He told Pownall that he had been criticized by his subordinates and others as being too cautious and mentioned the official reports of the carrier commanders. He was disappointed, he said, in the lack of effectiveness of the Kwajalein raid.

Carriers were always "at risk," said Nimitz, when brought against enemy positions, but they should be used to do the utmost damage. The purpose of the discussion, Nimitz said, was to impress on Pownall the need for aggressive action in the forthcoming operations, not to abuse him.

Nimitz then said that he wanted an air operations plan from Pownall and Spruance immediately so he could study it. He would give Pownall entree to anyone on the staff that he might need. To soften these blows, Nimitz said gently that Pownall had performed very well as far as Spruance was concerned in the Gilberts operation —Spruance had said as much.

Pownall emerged from the meeting surprised and hurt. That afternoon he went to see Towers to discuss the problem.

Towers, while he lent a sympathetic ear, was not really very sympathetic to Pownall's position. But the result of the furore raised by the airmen over these last weeks was not long in coming. Mitscher was to replace Pownall—and Pownall was to replace Towers, who would become Deputy Cincpac and Cincpoa—commander of the fleet and of the Pacific Ocean areas. It was far from what Towers wanted—he would much rather have had Mitscher's combat job any time. But the aviators had been complaining for many months that they did not have sufficient representation in high places, and now the complaint could be made no longer.

Chapter
Nineteen

OPERATION
FLINTLOCK

December 25, 1943–March 1, 1944

Admiral McMorris was a very tough hombre, and that is precisely why Nimitz had brought him in to replace Spruance as chief of staff. He was called Soc for Socrates, because of his prowess as a strategist (and a hangover from Academy days). He was also called other names not quite so complimentary, for other reasons. One day, for example, a brand new Army colonel came to Fort Shafter and demanded a private jeep to take him between the fort and Honolulu. The people at the motor pool advised the colonel that they would be glad to give him a jeep, but first they needed a chit from the chief of the joint staff—which meant McMorris.

So the colonel came to Makalapa, found his way to Admiral McMorris' office, and stated his case.

McMorris, who had a face like a fried egg and was sometimes called the ugliest man in the Navy, screwed up his lips and said one word.

"No."

Why not? asked the colonel. What skin off McMorris' nose was it if the Army wanted to give the colonel a jeep for his own use? It was not a Cincpac jeep. It was not a Navy jeep. It was an Army jeep out of an Army motor pool.

"No," said McMorris.

"And why not?" repeated the colonel.

"Because I'm a born sonofabitch and I'm going to stay one," said McMorris.

The situation at Pearl Harbor at the end of 1943 demanded similar treatment for the hundreds of self-serving requests that came to Nimitz's staff. And indeed that staff had become something of a nightmare to an admiral who liked, as Nimitz did, to have a handful of trusted men around him, all of them to be called by their first names, all willing to work day and night for "the boss." At the beginning of the year, the entire staff numbered forty-nine, from four star admiral Nimitz down to Ship's Clerk Fred H. Haas, who was his personal stenographer, or *writer* as the Navy has it. By the end of the year, the staff numbered 126, plus sixty-seven communications watch officers, five operations plotting officers, and fifteen officers assigned to the staff for various temporary duties. It took a very tough man to keep even the staff under control.

That was McMorris. McArdle came to the conclusion that McMorris liked to eat public relations officers for breakfast. He was not alone.

McMorris was shrewd, outspoken, and thoroughly loyal to Nimitz. He was also as contemptuous of many of the airmen around him as he was of public relations. And with the growth of the carrier force, the airmen were making themselves heard, ever more loudly.

At the end of 1943, as Nimitz prepared to meet again with Admiral King, one of the primary items on their agenda was the agitation of the aviators for more prominence in command. McMorris had some ideas about those demands.

"Promotion among naval aviators has been so rapid that nearly all who have had reasonably wide experience are flag officers," McMorris said.

What the aviators were asking for, specifically, was that they be put in command of forces, or where they were not in command, that an aviator be designated as chief of staff or deputy. But aviation officers were not necessarily very good at surface-ship tactics and strategy. McMorris continued:

Aviation Admirals are at times so inexperienced in such matters that they do not even know of their weakness in that regard. Flag officers such as King, Halsey, Fitch, Pownall, to name a few, have had considerable experience in the employment of both ships and aircraft. Some of the younger aviation flag officers have devoted nearly all of their careers to matters exclusively and directly connected with aviation. The added proficiency gained in that regard has mitigated against their gaining the experience, knowledge, and some of the broader aspects of warfare.

McMorris, obviously, was not going to win any popularity contests, even at Pearl Harbor.

By the end of the Gilberts operation, the matter of the press had begun to get out of hand, for several reasons. One was the reluctance of the Navy men to give out information about battles. They argued, quite rightly, that even to name a ship, under certain conditions even to name a type of ship, could be of great assistance to the enemy. Submarine operations, for example, were so secret that they simply were not discussed at all anywhere. But after Midway, the Naval airmen found a ploy of their own: they sent such men as Lieutenant Joseph Bryan III and Commander "Spig" Wead out to the Pacific, where these officers rounded up information, and then went back to Washington to write their articles and release them outside the Pacific commander's purview, through the Bureau of Aeronautics. On the side of the Navy public relations men at Pearl were Forrest Sherman and Preston Mercer, the admiral's flag secretary; and creating the most trouble for them were McMorris and Howell Lamar, Nimitz's flag lieutenant, sometimes known as Little Rollo, who controlled transportation and small boats, and felt it necessary to outdo the regulars in his devotion to standards of the Naval Academy he had never attended.

The casualties at the Gilberts made the matter of public relations very important. Undersecretary Forrestal had a very strong sense of public relations, and he did not at all approve of the way things were going.

The correspondents who came back from Tarawa used the words "bloody" and "slaughter" in their dispatches, and for a time Commander Drake, McArdle, and Commander Murray Ward, the censor, carefully cut out the words. But eventually they gave up—because it *was* a bloody battle, and that impression had leaked out from a dozen sources in spite of censorship. They could conceal the number of casualties—but only until the press conferences of Evans Carlson and Holland Smith. Then the story was out, and the press at home was very angry because of the attempts that had been made to suppress it. The public relations men, representing the Navy, could argue that it helped the Japanese to learn how effective their defenses were. The press would have none of it, because the press was certain the "admirals" were simply sitting on the information to avoid criticism. And so it went, with the Navy only gradually yielding. The Case of the Japanese Snooper became a celebrated issue, of this type.

One day a Japanese submarine launched a scout plane which followed an American plane back to Hawaii. The snooper was detected at the shoreline, but not before, and there it drew so much antiaircraft fire that the pilot, if not planning to turn back there, changed his mind and hightailed it out of the area. In a matter of hours the story was common knowledge in Honolulu, and the facts were released.

The newspaper correspondents came to public relations to ask why the plane was not picked up out at sea by radar. The answer was that the American plane had screened the Japanese plane behind it. The correspondents asked for permission to write this explanation into their stories, noting that unless they did so, the American public would have a very poor opinion of the Pearl Harbor defenses. The answer was no.

"It's been said before," said Barney McQuade of the Chicago *Daily News.*

"True, but just the same it can't be said now," said Commander Drake.

Soon the irascible correspondent and the irascible public relations officer were standing toe to toe tapping each other on the chest and shouting.

The discussion was taken to Captain Mercer, who calmed both men and said that McQuade could use the phrase "detection devices similar to those used before Pearl Harbor" but could not mention RADAR.

McQuade snorted. He threatened to take his case to Frank Knox, who was his publisher as well as Secretary of the Navy.

"Go ahead," said Drake. "I'm still talking for C. W. Nimitz."

And of course he was. And of course the word got back to Knox that Navy public relations was the worst in the world, and the kettle continued to simmer in Washington.

Part of the cause of the short tempers around Pearl Harbor at the end of 1943 was the lacing the Navy took on Tarawa, but part of it was physical: with the huge increase in staff, and more coming almost day by day, the headquarters building had to be enlarged, which meant building on more stories. First a breastworks around the top of the building had to come off—which was done by air hammers during working hours.

Public relations was on the top deck, and one of the machine gun nests that was being removed was directly above the public relations offices. It took three weeks to hammer off the stone.

"All day long the hammering came down through the walls and shook our teeth," said McArdle, "filling the air with a din so palpable you could crack walnuts on it. At these times, even if you could hear the telephones ring, it didn't do any good to answer them—the conversation was strictly one-way."

It was a period of respite—but somehow there never seemed to be peace and quiet at Pearl Harbor. "Perhaps the bedlam at headquarters," said McArdle, " . . . was chiefly responsible for the popularity of combat operations. There was not an officer in the public relations staff who would not have preferred being out forward where the shooting was than back at headquarters where the headaches were."

And that applied to other officers too, such as Admiral Lockwood, who kept petitioning to go out on a submarine patrol, Admiral Towers, who wanted eagerly to have a task force, and Admiral

Nimitz himself. As 1943 came to an end, the pressures grew much heavier on Nimitz. Although he possessed control over the "most powerful naval force ever assembled," the assault shipping was already inadequate. There was a serious shortage of attack transports and all other kinds of assault and commercial shipping. The Joint Chiefs of Staff were calling for concurrent thrusts in the South Pacific (including the Southwest Pacific, of course) and in the Central Pacific. Nimitz was trying to make his plans so he could move the transports from Central to South Pacific and back again, using one ship to do two jobs.

Preparing for the new year, Nimitz called Halsey to come up from the South Pacific for meetings, to determine the course of action in that region. Halsey came up just before the end of the year and then went on to the west coast.

Nimitz and King were now thinking in terms of the next step—not the Marshalls, which had been placed in the hands of Spruance as an operational matter, with planning completed. Spruance was to move into Kwajalein at the end of the month, and then mop up the Marshalls as quickly as possible. He would have assistance from Admiral Hoover's land-based air and everything Nimitz could give him.

What the planners were interested in at the end of 1943 was the way to go next. Halsey proposed to move into Green Island on February 15. He wanted to bypass the stronghold of Kavieng and seize Manus island, then build airstrips on the two islands for future moves ahead. At the King-Nimitz meetings early in January, this plan was explored thoroughly. Admiral King had some questions, and so did Nimitz. King pointed out that Green Island was no good for a naval base. Neither was Kavieng, said Nimitz.

Halsey had argued for Green Island from the beginning, and he was the man on the scene. It was about time to put an end to the South Pacific operations; the plan had been to knock out the big Japanese base at Rabaul. Halsey had shown rather conclusively that the offensive strength of these two bases, Rabaul and Kavieng, had been knocked out by his air raids of recent weeks. But those places could still put up a wicked defense. With Tarawa fresh in mind, Halsey's superiors were quick to see his point. Green Island,

120 miles away, commanded the approaches to Rabaul. Emirau commanded the approaches to Kavieng. Manus, 220 miles from Kavieng, commanded the western approaches to both Rabaul and Kavieng.

So it was decided at San Francisco that Kavieng and Rabaul would be bypassed. Halsey would take Green Island, and MacArthur would take Manus. Halsey would also take Emirau. A tentative date of April 1 was set for both operations, and the word was sent to MacArthur to see if he would agree. Green Island would be taken by Halsey much earlier, on February 15.

Thus the schedule was set up:

1. Flintlock (Kwajalein), 31 January, Spruance.
2. Green Island, 15 February, Halsey.
3. Emirau Island, 1 April, Halsey.
4. Manus Island, 1 April, MacArthur.
5. Eniwetok, 1 May, Spruance.

The last of these, Eniwetok, would represent the wiping up of Japanese resistance in the Marshalls and the beginning of a new phase of the Pacific war, with the Japanese being driven back inside the holdings they had obtained at the end of World War I in the Central Pacific. The key to the Pacific, said King, was the Marianas, which ought to come next.

The great Japanese base at Truk had been a thorn in the side of the Allies since the beginning of the war, and at various times plans had been presented to Nimitz to knock out the base. Knockout was fine, at this point, and a major air strike was to be made before April. It was then believed that the Japanese would move their fleet units out of Truk and make it possible to bypass that heavily defended position. A great deal, indeed, had been learned at the Gilberts.

At this meeting, Forrest Sherman suggested that it might be possible to bypass Truk by taking Saipan, Tinian, and Guam.

King was agreeable. Simply let it not be forgotten, he said, that all operations of the United States Navy were aimed at a drive through the Pacific to China, in order to make use of China's strategic position and her manpower in the final assault against

Japan. To move along, suggested Halsey, they should seize Palau at about the same time as Saipan. They must also establish a base in the Bismarcks, said King.

And once the South Pacific operations ended, the forces would be split up between MacArthur and Nimitz.

Until this point in the Pacific war, any quarrels between Mac-Arthur and Nimitz over the direction of the advance on Japan had been submerged in the demands of day-to-day operations. But the Navy had always held to a plan for operations against Japan, and successive generations of students at the Naval War College had followed it, working out the details time and again. Indeed, in September, 1942, the tall, dark Hanson Baldwin, military editor of *The New York Times*, had visited Pearl Harbor and looked at the big war maps.

"Why the hell are we started *up* from the Solomons when for ten years we've planned a frontal movement *west* through the Mandates?" he growled to the young public relations man who was showing him around.

The Americans had found themselves in the Solomons then because King insisted that the Japanese drive must be stopped before they could make use of Henderson field on Guadalcanal. But the essential plan mentioned by Baldwin remained the same.

Not so MacArthur's plan for victory. His plan called for a return to the Philippines, with him in charge. He would move up through the Bismarcks, up New Guinea into the Sulu Sea, and there he would be joined by the forces of Admiral Nimitz, which would have taken the Marshalls and the Carolines. At that time, Nimitz would become MacArthur's admiral, securing Truk and wiping out the Japanese flank, while the general moved into the Philippines. The British, meanwhile, would move their fleet east through the Malacca straits and seize Hong Kong. A combined Chinese-British-American force would reopen the Burma road from India to China and move southward, smothering the Japanese.

This plan had been regarded with favor by the Combined Chiefs of Staff in its incipient stages and MacArthur was moderately pleased. But the vicissitudes of war eroded the thinking of the Combined Chiefs by December, 1943. The war in the Mediterranean was so vigorous that the British could not spare fleet units for a move to the west. And new developments in naval and aerial warfare had also changed matters. First, the Gilberts operation had shown the tremendous strength of the amphibious forces working with the fast carrier forces. Second, the Army air forces wanted a Pacific base for the new B-29 bombers with which General Arnold hoped to devastate Japan.

So King's unchanged plan for the move across the Pacific had more appeal in January, 1944, than it had shown a few months earlier.

The war brought an amalgam of ironies: the Navy had never wanted to fight a war in the South Pacific, as Hanson Baldwin had so shrewdly indicated in his surprise when he saw it happening. The entire Southwest Pacific approach to the war was foreign to Navy thinking; it was the result of General MacArthur's vanity and the shortage of military leaders in 1941 who knew the Orient, plus the desperate need to stop the Japanese at Guadalcanal, that had produced this first irony. The whole Central Pacific campaign, as it developed, was keyed to the rapid development of "hardware," the fast carriers, and then along in the middle came the Air Force's B-29's, which changed the strategy and made the Marianas into a key target.

The basic differences in strategy between the Army and the Navy brought frequent mutual irritations. In December General MacArthur sent representatives to the Cairo conference, where the Combined Chiefs of Staff were in session, and King was fully aware of the attempts by MacArthur's men to bring about a change in the plans. Some of the Southwest Pacific air generals were taking exception to calls for their aircraft to bomb ships and shipping. Since Nimitz had been pushed into forming a joint Army and Navy staff, a huge and growing combined staff operation which he cordially disliked in principle, it was an annoyance to him that neither MacArthur nor Eisenhower had joint staffs.

Certain other Army practices were annoying to the Navy men. For one thing, the Army air forces had only thirty-five air crews per heavy bombardment group, which was not enough to do the job properly. General Marshall, on a recent visit, had agreed. But the Army had refused to raise the number of crews for the Seventh Air Force, which was detailed to the Central Pacific, and General Richardson was unwilling to reopen the question. Halsey was particularly upset because the Army was awarding medals in such large numbers that the effect was terrible on the Navy flyers who got medals only for distinguishing themselves. And Halsey suggested that he would like to move his headquarters from Nouméa up to Manus island when that area was taken.

The two matters—aviators and interservice relations—were to be serious problems in the months to come.

For some time it had rankled Captain J. J. Clark that a TBF (torpedo bomber) flight crew had been lost during the Marcus raid. Now someone at Pearl Harbor was saying that Pownall had *deliberately* left the crew to perish. Pownall asked the commander of Torpedo Squadron 5, Commander R. Upson, to make a statement, and Upson stated in writing that on August 31 cruiser planes had searched for the TBF crew reported down, and then Torpedo 5 had sent eight TBF's out to search 175 miles under conditions of excellent visibility. They had not found the life raft.

"The personnel participating in this search, who were shipmates of the missing crew, were all satisfied that a thorough search had been made."

The letter was forwarded through Captain Clark, who had been quite voluble in his previous (and later) complaints about Pownall's refusal to take the task force in search of the life raft. Clark also wrote a letter stating that he was "satisfied that a thorough and efficient search had been made by Torpedo Squadron 5."

But Pownall's fate was sealed, and had been for some time in the sense that he lost the fighting command. Although changes had been ordered, Nimitz had been talking to King about moving Pownall to the west coast as air commander, to take the place of Mitscher—for Mitscher had definitely been selected as new head of the fast carrier forces of the Central Pacific. Spruance was not at all pleased with the changes, and he insisted that Pownall come along on the Marshalls operation, riding on Spruance's flagship and acting as Spruance's unofficial air adviser. Pownall was thus kept in action for a time, but no longer as commander of the first carriers.

Spruance's valiant defense of Pownall helped, for Nimitz respected Spruance's judgment, certainly more than he did that of Towers. It was arranged, then, that Newton would become available for other command, Towers would be the new deputy, and Pownall would become air commander in the Pacific. Since the job was basically administrative, no one could complain—except Pownall, and like most Academy graduates he had been so long disciplined and self-disciplined that he accepted his lot with the best grace he could muster.

Operation Flintlock was even bigger than Galvanic. Nimitz was in charge. Spruance was in command of the overall force, which was now called the Fifth Fleet. Turner was in charge of the Joint Expeditionary Force, with Holland Smith on his flagship, the *Rocky Mount*, as overall commander of ground forces. Smith claimed that Kelly Turner "always had suppressed ambitions to be a general" and had tried to euchre him out of the command. Smith said that a week before sailing date, he had seen a directive which omitted his name, and that only by going to Spruance had he managed to secure places for himself and his staff in the actual operation.

Perhaps. Spruance's chief of staff, Captain Moore, spent a good deal of his time refereeing arguments between the strong-minded Turner and the equally opinionated Smith. Sometimes, Moore said, Smith was a "crybaby," so great was his affection for his Marines, and so deep his suspicion of the Navy in relation to the Marine Corps.

Turner himself commanded the Southern Attack Force. Rear Admiral R. L. Conolly led the Northern Attack Force. Rear Admiral Harry Hill led the Majuro Attack Force. And so powerful was the American fleet participating here that it was possible to keep a task group in reserve, under Captain D. W. Loomis.

On the ground on Kwajalein, the troops of the southern force would be led by Major General H. C. Corlett, and the troops were the Seventh Infantry Division of the Aleutians. The Northern Attack Force would be the Fourth Marine Division, with Major General Harry Schmidt in command. Harry Hill's smaller Majuro landing would be accomplished by the 2nd Battalion of the 106th Infantry Division.

Again the operation came from diffuse sources. The Northern Attack Force sailed from San Diego, where the Fourth Marines had trained, stopping at Pearl Harbor and picking up the Southern Attack Force. Harry Hill's Majuro force sailed the next day.

On January 19, four days before Turner, Admiral Spruance had sailed in the *Indianapolis* for Tarawa because he wanted a few days to consult with Admiral Hoover about the land-based air support the invasion would have.

Nimitz had informed Hoover of the coming Marshalls operation on December 18, and called on Hoover to reduce the Japanese air forces at Wotje, Maloelap, and Mili. Affairs were improving; Nimitz could say casually that "it will be possible for Towers to send you additional dive bombers if you need them and have facilities for their operation."

Nimitz expected a great deal, as a message to Hoover indicated:

Reports from recent visitors to your area indicate that there will be no insurmountable difficulty in basing your heavy bombers in the Gilberts. With the shorter distances to their targets and the additional two weeks [the date had been postponed] in which to work, we hope for a successful demonstration of their effectiveness under conditions where they can carry a full bomb load. The deferment of the target date by fourteen days should contribute to their success.

That was Nimitz's quiet way of laying it on the line for a commander. He told the officer what he expected and why, and usually in plenty of time to let the officer explain his difficulties. Then, when the chips were down, Nimitz expected high performance.

Hoover came back on December 24 with a report of difficulties. The building of camps for the heavy bombers was proceeding very slowly because the materials had not arrived in time, but Hoover hoped to move up four heavy squadrons by the middle of January which would cut down the consumption of gasoline. As for himself, he hoped to move to Tarawa very soon.

Hoover was busy. Like Nimitz he believed in physical fitness and he still played tennis energetically. Indeed, as one of his officers

remarked, his flagship would no sooner moor in a harbor than someone was out building the tennis court. He was Towers' "enigma,"
and some of his ideas amused Nimitz, too. For example, Hoover
had a yen to "trade with the natives" and had asked Nimitz for a
barrelful of trade jewelry and knickknacks of the kind so prized in
the Pacific of earlier days. He had already tried half a dozen times
to get over to the native villages of the Ellice Islands for a trading
expedition, but duty or the weather had so far kept him from it.
On December 24, as Hoover wrote to Nimitz, he was waiting eagerly
for his trade goods to arrive, and planning a little Christmas party
on the beach, for "some of the nurses and all the Admirals and
Generals in the vicinity."

By the end of January Hoover had about 350 planes working.
They dropped several hundred tons of bombs on Mili, Wotje, Roi-
Namur, and Maloelap. They drove Japanese shipping out of Jaluit.
But Wotje and Maloelap were heavily defended, and after three
B-24's were shot down by antiaircraft fire over Maloelap in one daylight raid, the big bombers were limited to night attacks, which were
not very effective. They had problems hitting these targets. Maloelap,
for example, was out of range of fighters, so the B-24's had to go in
alone, knowing they would have to run home pursued half the way
by Japanese Zeros. On January 26, however, Admiral Hoover gave
the Japanese a good lesson. When the Zeros came back harrying the
B-24's as usual, a squadron of P-40's lay in wait at the optimum distance they could achieve, and shot down six of the Japanese planes.

Even so, the distances were too great and the interservice organization not perfect either, and when Spruance arrived at Tarawa on
January 24, there was still plenty of Japanese air power left in and
around the Marshalls.

On the eve of the operation, Nimitz held his usual meeting of
commanders, and again reminded them of what was expected.

"That's all, gentlemen," he said then. "By the way, have you
heard the one about the gob who was marooned with six nurses on
a desert island?" The building tension was relieved—just as Nimitz
knew it would be.

A picnic was held just before that Marshalls operation. On Sunday afternoon all Texans in uniform who were in Hawaii were invited to a giant Texas picnic in one of the city's big parks. General

Richardson came from the Army, and Nimitz came from the Navy. He played horseshoes and laughed and joked with the soldiers, sailors, and Marines who were there. It was a long, busy, gay, exciting afternoon, with an estimated forty thousand servicemen in attendance at one time or another. Next day the Honolulu police and sanitation departments cleaned up the mess. They picked up 120,000 beer bottles from the bushes, and lunch cartons, K-rations, C-ration cans, pop bottles, used leis, a scattering of khaki shirts, and other jetsam. The servicemen called it the greatest picnic ever. But to the police and sanitation men it was a pure disaster.

Two days later, Spruance sailed to make rendezvous with Carrier Task Group 58.2 which was Admiral Montgomery's force with the *Essex*, the *Intrepid*, and the light carrier *Cabot*.

The fast carrier force was the most rapidly developing weapon. Halsey had learned a good deal about carrier tactics in the early days of the war, how to steam along under a protective overcast, and then launch aircraft to break into clear skies for quick strikes at the enemy. He had learned and taught others to make maximum use of antiaircraft fire.

But as the new battleships were coming off the ways, and the new cruisers, and the fast destroyers, the fast carrier force was changing and its methods were altered, as well. The fast carrier force still had all the speed of a long-distance runner—and now it had the muscle of a fullback. The fast battleships made the force a fast fleet that could take on the Japanese fleet and need not run from anyone. No longer was the carrier force a raiding outfit. If Fletcher and Brown had been right in their deep-seated belief that the carrier forces of 1942 must have surprise or risk annihilation, the same considerations did not apply in January, 1944.

The fleet now had the escort carriers to protect the beaches, and the old battleships to give the necessary firepower against the fortifications. The old battleships were not suitable for command ships —but they had been replaced by special command ships, such as the *Rocky Mount*, which were floating wireless offices.

So the fast carrier forces were able to range outside the beaches now. The question was simply how much and how far, and the answers to that still rested with Admiral Spruance.

For a rear admiral, Marc Mitscher had a tremendous responsibility on the eve of the Marshalls invasion. He had four carrier task groups, six fleet carriers, and six light carriers under his command, plus the fast battleships under Admiral Lee, eight of them, and a huge flotilla of heavy cruisers, light cruisers, and destroyers all of which shared one characteristic: they could keep up with the thirty-knot speed of the fast carriers.

What had made the task force into this the important striking arm was the huge train of oilers, ammunition ships, supply ships, and their attendant protectors, the escort carriers and destroyers. For instance, in the combined force that went to attack the Marshalls there were 103 destroyers and escorts. To carry the 84,000 troops who would seize and occupy the islands there were vessels that most officers of the United States Navy had not even dreamed of three years earlier: landing ships tank, landing ships dock, landing craft tank, landing vehicle tracked. Nearly all of these were the result of studies by men like Major General Holland Smith and Rear Admiral Richmond Kelly Turner in the arts of amphibious warfare.

On January 29 the fast carrier force hit the Marshalls. One of the four task groups went to Maloelap, one took Kwajalein, one Roi, and one moved against Wotje. Mitscher's admirals were Rear Admirals Reeves, Montgomery, Frederick Sherman, and S. P. Ginder—who had replaced Radford when that admiral first became chief of staff to Towers, then moved on back to Washington for staff work.

The Marshalls air strikes were a triumph for the fast carrier forces, showing conclusively that four task groups could do in a few hours what land-based air had been unable to do in two weeks: knock out the Japanese air power that might threaten the invasion. On Roi alone they smashed nearly a hundred planes, in the air and on the ground. The cost of the pre-invasion effort was twenty-seven fighter planes and twenty-two bombers, with most, but not all of the crews—losses due to fighters, antiaircraft fire, collisions, and other accidents. In ships, the cost was equally bearable: the destroyer *Anderson* was hit by shells from a shore gun, and her captain was killed, along with two other officers and three enlisted men; the battleship *Indiana* missed her turn in maneuvering and smashed the battleship *Washington*, putting both out of action. (This failure cost Captain J. M. Steele, lately of the Nimitz staff, his command and his chance for glory in the war.) But the price was not high for what was secured. During the invasion that was to come, only one air strike of any significance would be made by the Japanese, from a long distance, and not one ship would be hurt by Japanese air.

As for the Japanese, Nimitz did not know it, but they had decided against making a major stand at the Marshalls. The garrisons were, for all practical purposes, abandoned to their fate, with the understanding that they would fight to the end. Admiral Koga, charged with the defense, had guessed with Spruance, Turner, and Smith—that the Americans would attack the near Marshalls, Wotje, Maloelap, and Mili, and had shifted his defense forces to these

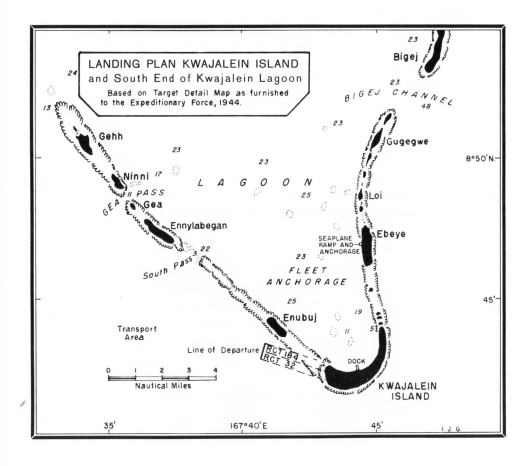

LANDING PLAN KWAJALEIN ISLAND and South End of Kwajalein Lagoon
Based on Target Detail Map as furnished to the Expeditionary Force, 1944.

islands that faced the expected line of attack from the east. The reinforcements he did get from headquarters went to these islands,
leaving some nine thousand Japanese troops on Kwajalein, and none
at all on Majuro atoll, whose major island was Darrit. A Marine
scouting force that searched Dalap, Uliga, and Darrit islands found
that the Japanese had pulled out, but the force was unable to get
the word to Admiral Hill before the bombardment of Darrit began.
The Japanese had left many buildings intact, or unfinished, and the
cruiser *Portland* and the destroyer *Bullard* began throwing in shells.
Fortunately for the service forces they did not hit anything important.

At Kwajalein atoll the Americans began the assault of the
northern and southern islands of the winding chain that surrounds
the great lagoon—Kwajalein and Roi-Namur.

Rear Admiral Richard Conolly led the force against the northern
bases on Roi and Namur islands. His previous experience had been
at Sicily, where he had distinguished himself and come to the attention of King, who had chosen him for the Pacific job, even as the
planning was under way for the Gilberts operation. He was an
Academy graduate, with War College experience, Naval Academy
teaching, and Washington staff duty—all the indications of a comer
in the officer corps. He and Kelly Turner did not agree on methods
and tactics, but Conolly had been able to train his men independently, since Turner was engaged in operations during the fall while
Conolly was bringing his Amphibious Force into being on the west
coast of the United States.

Early on the morning of January 31, the force moved in northeast of Roi. There were the problems of unfamiliarity and inexperience: not enough amphtracs to land all the assault troops on
schedule, delays because of miscalculations of wind and currents. For
two days the naval forces had stood off shore, battleships, cruisers,
the island was declared secured, after some heavy fighting. On Namur
This day, Conolly's forces first took five little islets around Roi and
Namur, at a cost of twenty-four killed and forty wounded. These
islands would become bases for field artillery which would assist in
the pulverization of Japanese fortifications on Roi and Namur.
Conolly took his battleships in to a point two thousand yards from

shore for bombardment, and for this won the acclaim of the Marines and the cognomen "Close In" Conolly, a real term of endearment considering the Marine attitude toward the Navy. In spite of the failures in communications and the slipups of green troops, the islands were secured by nightfall and the artillery was put ashore. Bombardment and harassment of the main islands continued until the morning of February 1, when the major invasion of Roi and Namur was launched. "The magnitude of the Kwajalein bombardment was historic," said Holland Smith. For once he was completely pleased with his Navy cousins.

Again there was confusion in getting ashore, but at noon on February 1 the assault waves landed on both islands. On Roi some three hundred Japanese defenders were left alive, and by 1700 hours the island was declared secured, after some heavy fighting. On Namur the resistance was heavier, but about forty-five minutes after the landing an ammunition dump blew up—killing some twenty Marines, but God knew how many Japanese. Then two more ammunition dumps blew up on the island. The Japanese defenders resisted stoutly and usually killed themselves rather than be captured. By nightfall most objectives had been secured, but the island had not. During the night the green Marine troops fired in all directions, endangering themselves more than the enemy. In the morning various small Japanese units staged suicide charges and were wiped out. By the afternoon of February 2, Namur was secured.

In the south, Admiral Turner and General Corlett moved against Kwajalein island. "Never in the history of human conflict has so much been thrown by so many at so few," announced a joker aboard Turner's flagship *Rocky Mount*.

This time, the Navy was to be criticized for using a sledgehammer to smash an ant, but it was a criticism that no responsible officers, from King and Nimitz on down the line, would honor. There was friction again. Naval historian Samuel Eliot Morison wrote with some indication of glee that General Corlett (Army) threatened to put General Smith (Marines) under arrest if he came ashore and interfered with Corlett's operations with the 7th Army Division. Smith did not go ashore, but he was critical of the slowness with which the Army division moved ahead on Kwajalein when the assault began on February 1. It was called a "beautiful" assault, and if this was true, Holland Smith deserved much of the credit in more ways than one, because the 7th Division had been his baby in the beginning, back in the days when he trained those troops for the Adak invasion.

The landing moved more slowly than that in the north. "In contrast to the Marines," Morison wrote, "the Army was taught not to advance until all possible fire had been brought to bear on the path ahead of the troops." Consequently Holland Smith fretted for four long days and waited. Then, at the end of February 4, Kwajalein fell and the basic islands of the atoll were secured. There would be another twenty little islands to take, in minor amphibious assaults, but Kwajalein was in American hands.

The statistics leave room for argument about the techniques of Army and Marines. In the north, where 20,104 troops were committed, 195 Americans were killed and 545 wounded, while 3472 of 3563 Japanese were killed. That was the Marine operation. In the south, where 21,342 troops were committed, 177 Americans were killed and 1037 wounded, while of 5112 Japanese 4398 were counted as killed. That was the Army operation. It would seem, then, that the Marine way, of moving ahead rapidly was not only quicker, but brought proportionately fewer casualties—and that was Holland Smith's stout contention.

Yet, in the total picture these were quibbles. The fact was that bombing and bombardment had kept the casualty figures of the Americans very low, and the operation was a great success.

Kwajalein had been taken so quickly and with so few casualties that Spruance's team decided to move in on Eniwetok. It had been planned back at Pearl to let a month or two go by before launching an assault against this northwestern bastion, but all the commanders were flushed with victory. Spruance had spoken to Nimitz about this possibility before he left Pearl Harbor, and it was Spruance's opportunity as well as responsibility. As for the planning for Eniwetok, which became known as Operation Catchpole, Holland Smith claimed that he handed Kelly Turner a plan he had made out earlier. Morison says the planning began at a conference aboard Turner's flagship among Turner, Admiral Hill, and Marine Brigadier General

Thomas E. Watson. He does not mention Holland Smith at all in this connection.

Hill took charge of the operation. The first task was to knock out enemy air that might strike the landing force, and this was done in massive carrier strikes on Truk on February 16 and 17 and on Saipan the next week. Here Mitscher's fast carriers inaugurated a new technique: the night attack. At Truk, in two days and one night, the fast carriers flew 1250 individual combat missions or sorties, dropping 500 tons of bombs and torpedoes on installations and shipping in the lagoon, knocking out 200,000 tons of shipping, including two auxiliary cruisers and a destroyer, to reduce the Japanese fleet. Actually, the air commanders did not consider this an optimum job; the carrier pilots did not do as well as they might have. Next day, Spruance took the surface forces on a sweep, looking for Japanese ships that might have fled Truk. With carrier support, he sank the *Katori*, a light cruiser, the destroyer *Maikaze*, and a trawler. The net result of the strike on Truk was to damage the Japanese navy sorely, and to knock out the base as a threat to Eniwetok, particularly when the fast carriers destroyed some 250 Japanese planes here.

During those same two days, Admiral Hill's plans were complete and he moved out of Kwajalein lagoon with Task Group 51.1, the Eniwetok expeditionary group. One of the reasons for the tremendous success of the operation against Kwajalein had been the utter secrecy maintained, so that surprise was a major factor. For the first time in the Pacific operations Tokyo Rose had not come on the radio to announce where the Americans were going, threatening them with terrible death and unheard-of tortures. But such was not the case with the Eniwetok operation. The cause: Chester W. Nimitz.

On February 17, Eniwetok D-Day, Admiral King wrote to Nimitz, cautioning him against talking to the press. "You may be surprised to know how widely you are quoted as the basis for comment and speculation as to what we are going to do next in the Pacific Ocean Areas," King remarked.

Referring to a recent Nimitz encounter with the press, King said:

In fact you said nothing much but what would be obvious
to military men of high status—but—the use of it has, I fear,
verged on "giving aid and comfort to the enemy." You must
watch your step in dealing with the press, etc.—basically, they
care for nothing except their own "kudos" and the news—or
interpretation of news—that will enable them to peddle more
papers! . . . Press and radio here can have left no doubt in the
minds of the enemy that our next objectives were Eniwetok and
Ponape.

Hill was excited with the prospects of this new operation, for his
Majuro invasion had been so simple as to leave him half frustrated.
The "luck" that he had felt with him at Tarawa had been strained.
Oddly, the choice of Hill as an amphibious commander was due
to much more than his work for Turner in Washington in earlier
days. Indeed, he was not at all sure that Turner had anything to do
with it. Much earlier in the war, Hill had been on the Murmansk
run in the cruiser *Wichita*. He had been selected for flag rank and
while waiting for reassignment in Washington had asked Admiral
Jacobs, the chief of personnel, for temporary duty in Norfolk, where
he could see the new specialized landing craft that would be used
in amphibious operations. Much later in the war, Hill encountered
Admiral King on one of the latter's visits to the Pacific, and King
asked him how he liked his job.
"I love it," Hill said. "Amphibious command is where the
action is."
Then King asked Hill wryly if he knew how he got the job.
Hill professed ignorance, and King told him that it was because of
that request for temporary duty to Norfolk just to see the new
developments in amphibious warfare. As luck would have it, Jacobs
had told King about the young admiral's request, it had stuck in
King's mind, and when Nimitz had requested a new amphibious
commander, King had designated Hill, who by that time was running old battleships down in the South Pacific.
Hill's luck had stayed with him at Tarawa. Why should he have
had Tarawa anyhow, with his senior, "Terrible" Turner, taking the
much less exciting and much less challenging Makin operation?
There was no mistake or guess involved: it was known that Makin

was much less of a nut to crack than Tarawa. Hill once asked Turner why, and Turner turned him off with a wisecrack: the only way to see if a kid could swim, he said, was to throw him in head first. But that was not Turner's real reason; tough as he was, and argumentative, and stickler for detail, and overbearing, he recognized ability, and he was a thorough officer. Hill had been chosen for the more interesting and more demanding task because Turner was bogged down in detail at the time of the Gilberts and something had to give, and because he took the position where he hoped the enemy fleet and air might strike.

Now, going into Engebi and Eniwetok, Hill's luck was to be

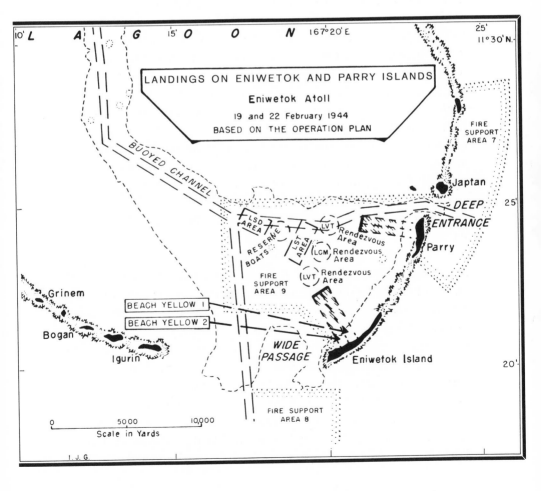

LANDINGS ON ENIWETOK AND PARRY ISLANDS
Eniwetok Atoll
19 and 22 February 1944
BASED ON THE OPERATION PLAN

tried again. Already it was in the works: the Japanese had been ready to reinforce this Marshalls outpost, but had not yet done so. Hill was in the communications command ship *Cambria,* a far cry from the old *Maryland* whose communications broke down and whose lights went out every time a gun fired. He had nine transports, eight thousand men, Marines and Army, tanks and guns in LST's and other landing vehicles. His fire support group, led by Rear Admiral J. B. Oldendorf in *Pennsylvania,* consisted of three battleships and three heavy cruisers. He had fifteen destroyers and a group of escort carriers.

Eniwetok provided a difficult problem of entry which might not have been solved very easily except for a chart of the area captured from a beached Japanese patrol boat. Still, the invaders found a mine field and it had to be swept, so the invasion was off schedule. There were confusions, the transports made some wrong moves, a sub chaser captain was relieved of command and so was an artillery commander. But two little islands next to Engebi were captured that day, and the artillery was moved ashore. Next day the bombardment began. First the guns spoke for an hour and a half, then the landing began, against a Japanese force of some 1200 defenders. This time 3500 American troops landed, and took the island in that first day, with only 85 killed and 166 wounded. It was estimated that a third of the Japanese died in the bombing and bombardment before the landings.

Next were Eniwetok and Parry islands. Admiral Hill had been led to believe that these islands were vacant, but documents captured on Engebi showed that they were defended by shock troops of the Japanese first amphibious brigade. The news came late, shortly before the scheduled landings, and no aerial bombing had been planned, nor was there a sustained bombardment of the islands. There was no time for it, nor had the fire-support ships brought the ammunition to do a thorough job. The lack of fire support was very definitely felt on the shore, where the resistance was the strongest yet encountered in the Marshalls. The landing force consisted of Marines and troops of the 27th Division, which had fought at Makin. Again the Marines were far more adept than their Army companions, and Admiral Hill said it was a question of poor command.

Consequently, when the island was taken on the third day, Hill and General Watson decided to use the Marines alone to take Parry. On February 22 they landed there against very tough opposition which included antitank mines. The marines took the island in one day, killing most of the 1350 Japanese defenders. At the end of that day, for all practical purposes the Marshalls were under American control. To be sure, the Japanese still held important islands; Jaluit, Maloelap, Mili, Nauru, and Wotje. These were heavily fortified and the Japanese were dug in. The Americans bombed them often, the Japanese resupplied the islands occasionally by submarine, and they remained Japanese until the end of the war, but offered very little trouble.

Operation Flintlock was the most successful amphibious attempt to date, and its success quieted many lingering doubts in Washington as to the usefulness of amphibious undertakings.

The Truk bombardment started C. J. Moore to thinking. Moore had been active in those last days before the war in preparing the war plan for the defeat of Japan. But in the months since, Nimitz had done a lot of talking about flying his flag on Truk, although the war plans called for the move to the China coast. In January, before they had set out for Kwajalein, Moore knew that the Joint Chiefs had decided on the Marianas campaign, but he did not know why. (The reason was that the Joint Chiefs wanted bases for the B-29's, although that was not the Navy's only reason.)

So Moore suggested to Spruance that they bypass both Truk and the Marianas, and head into the Celebes Sea. Spruance saw the memo, and grunted. Admiral Pownall, who was riding the *New Jersey* as Spruance's air adviser on the operation, took a copy back to Nimitz, who took it with him to his next conference with King.

Chapter
Twenty

INTERLUDE

January–March 1944

Some commanders, such as "Close In" Conolly, considered the Marshalls another turning point in the war. It was, they said, the point at which the inner defenses of Japan were first breached and the war assumed an entirely different aspect. For a number of reasons this statement was true, not all of them concerned with the geographical position of the Marshalls, the end of the legendary "invincibility" of Truk in the Carolines, or the coming offensive that the Japanese and everyone else expected in the Marianas.

One reason for the change was that if the Gilberts operation showed how strong the armada of the Fifth Fleet had become, and tested the Amphibious Force, then the Marshalls proved the amphibious force's abilities and showed beyond doubt the massive strength that could be launched from Spruance's "floating airfields."

The air power of the Pacific was becoming overwhelming. Even

346

in January came harbingers of things to come: on January 17 Nimitz called a special conference in his office to deal with a dispatch that had come in from General Arnold in Washington. Foreseeing the defeat of Germany in the last months of 1944, General Arnold was thinking about redeployment of Army Air Forces in the spring of 1945. How would the Pacific command like forty-one air groups in March or April of that year? Forty-one groups, that meant about seventy-five fighters and fighter bombers per group, or forty-eight medium and heavy bombers. Forty-one? Admiral Towers shuddered a little when he considered the logistics. How would they employ so many planes?

Two growing problems gave Nimitz a very good indication of worries yet to come in the prosecution of this war against the Japanese. Perhaps it was inevitable that success brought with it jealousies and struggles for power within the ranks of the victorious; this was certainly occurring in the United States effort against Japan, as ambitious men, certain they were right, pressed their own cases as strongly as they dared. Not many were so ambitious or so convinced that (like J. J. Clark) they subverted authority openly. Fewer yet were as lucky as Clark. (Thanks to King's personal intervention, Clark got his flag and assignment as a carrier task group commander just after Eniwetok.) But other flag officers, particularly the air officers, were nearly trembling with ill-concealed ambition, and sometimes with ambition that was not concealed at all.

About a year earlier, Retired Admiral Harry E. Yarnell had been asked by King and others in the Navy Department to make a thorough study of the problems and opportunities of naval aviation in a changing military scene. Included in Yarnell's exhaustive report were the written opinions of as many senior naval officers as he could persuade to comment on the needs of naval aviation, and the opinions of not a few brave juniors as well.

In this January the report was in and under consideration. Admiral Yarnell had recommended that the commander in chief of the Pacific Fleet be an aviator. Which would mean exit Nimitz, if the report were accepted in the highest places. Yarnell's view and his support for it were spread throughout the aviation circle of the Navy. Rear Admiral H. F. Kingman, commander of Battleship Division 2, suggested that naval air was taking the best young men of the Navy. He suggested a separate naval air force. Admiral Halsey, who was first a ship sailor and then an aviator, suggested that all Navy officers be familiar with air matters. Admiral Kinkaid said that while Navy air had played an important part in the war in the Pacific in particular, it had been "conducted generally along the lines visualized before the war." Kinkaid, in other words, saw no basic need for change in the present state of affairs. Nimitz himself had replied candidly that he was not really intimately associated in the past with naval air over any extended period, and that was about all he said. Spruance said:

> To begin with I think there can be no doubt that aviation is required as an integral and essential part of our fleet. This aviation may be operated from carriers, it may be operated from shore bases; it may contain all types of aircraft from heavy bombers down to fighters. This was the case during Galvanic, where available planes of all suitable types were used most effectively. Without them, as without the supporting combatant ships, the transports, and cargo vessels, and the assault troops, the operation would not have been carried out.

Marc Mitscher, who would rather fight than write, and who had what he wanted anyhow, said nothing at all. Aubrey Fitch, who was a man of long experience in surface craft and airplanes, like Halsey, felt that air and sea and submarine instruments were all to be welded into a team. The Young Turks of the air service accounted for the outrageous and demanding statements, except for one of the more senior admirals, Frederick Sherman. Admiral Sherman was as ambitious as any admiral in the Navy, and had once aroused the ire of brother officers by admitting at a dinner party that he was tying his future to the carrier because that was the place to be for advancement, not because he had any particular commitment to naval aviation. Now Admiral Sherman wrote the most outrageous letter of all.

War at sea would be dominated by air in the future, said Sherman.

Our present organization and methods of conducting sea warfare are antiquated . . . . Naval aviators . . . should have the
dominant voice in determining all naval policy and not just
naval aviation policy. One highranking officer remarked that
naval aviation has an adviser in every office in the navy department but authority in none. This situation is not satisfactory and
all questions of policy should be passed on if not initiated by
naval aviators and should be satisfactory from all angles to that
branch . . . . I prefer to consider naval aviation as the navy
rather than a subordinate part of the navy.

Admiral Frederick Sherman then recommended that the following officers of the fleet be naval aviators at all times:

Commander in Chief of the Fleet
Chief of Naval Operations
Chief of Naval Personnel
Half the members of the General Board
Commanders in Chief, all fleets
Commanders, all mixed forces

Also, on all staffs of all forces, aviators should hold the offices
of chief of staff, operations, and plans.

Reading Admiral Sherman's recommendations, an admiral from
any other service might have grounds to wonder how anyone but
naval aviators would ever achieve flag rank, if those recommendations were followed, or how the Navy would be held together.

Admiral Forrest Sherman, Nimitz's plans officer, who was every
day gaining more and more of "the boss's" confidence, wrote very
clearly that the job was "to see that aviation units are operated by
competent commanders with aviation experience, or with staffs
which include sufficient competent senior officers with air experience." He placed importance on the fact that naval aviation was still
of naval character. He knew the frustration of the younger pilots,
and their discontent, but he said there were other considerations.

Forrest Sherman's view endeared him to King and Nimitz, as
much as another Sherman's would make any senior commander (except an aviator) shudder.

Admiral King was forced to take this matter very seriously. On January 29 he wrote Yarnell, saying he did not concur that the Pacific Fleet commander be an aviator:

I cannot subscribe to any rule which would result in the removal on such grounds of Admiral Nimitz or any other admiral who has demonstrated the qualifications for high command. The question of air representation on the Pacific Fleet staff has been left to Admiral Nimitz's discretion. An officer who bears the responsibilities which he does should not be circumscribed in selecting the members of his staff.

King also noted, however, that it was current policy to assign a naval aviator to command each carrier.

As this controversy bubbled, and the public relations controversy simmered, Undersecretary Forrestal arrived in Pearl Harbor. He was vitally interested in air matters and in public relations matters, and what he saw did not much please him, as was to become apparent later.

Admiral Turner was assembling his attack transports and supply ships in Lahaina Roads these days. Admiral Nimitz thought it would be a good idea to show Forrestal the fleet from the sea, and he took him over on a destroyer.

When they arrived and saw the fleet assembled, the destroyer skipper asked Nimitz what he wanted to do. Nimitz said he would like to go up and down the line of anchored ships so that the Undersecretary might get a good look at them.

They did, but a destroyer moving past a line of anchored vessels at twenty-five knots or so creates a bit of fuss, and some of the anchored vessels began to roll in the wake.

The commodore of the transport squadron took exception to the destroyer's speed and sent a message: "I do not like your sea manners."

The signalman showed the message to Nimitz's aide, who showed it to the admiral. Nimitz smiled and ordered his four-star flag broken out over the destroyer. Then came another message, an apology from the transport squadron commodore.

Nimitz decided that he would take the Undersecretary to inspect this ship, so the destroyer was stopped and a boat put over the side to take them to the transport flagship.

All the way across, the enlisted men and the admiral's aide tried to signal to the transport that the Undersecretary of the Navy and the commander of the fleet were coming. But no one paid any attention. They arrived at the gangway, with no recognition at all. The young ensign who was officer of the deck was simply oblivious.

On the quarter deck, the admiral was not pleased. The captain and the commodore were roused quickly enough, and came struggling into their uniform jackets as men who had been awakened from their afternoon naps. Nimitz then made a thorough inspection of the ship, and what he saw did not please him very much. He said so, and the officers blanched.

Then, in thoroughly good humor, Nimitz returned to the destroyer. Forrestal's flag was broken out at the peak, and the ship raced back to Pearl at thirty knots.

These little excursions did not get Nimitz away from his real worries for long. He was almost immediately plunged into other difficulties. The Joint Chiefs of Staff had directed Nimitz and MacArthur to get together on plans for future operation in the South and Southwest Pacific and submit joint recommendations. Getting together with MacArthur was not easy unless one was willing to take second seat. Halsey knew this from experience, despite his admiration for MacArthur. In the matter of public relations, for months Lieutenant Commander Bassett had been trying to get the right to release news of South Pacific operations from the South Pacific. But MacArthur had insisted that nothing be said from Nouméa until MacArthur's communiqué from Brisbane had first been sent out. Thus the public had a hazy idea that everything that went on in southern climes was MacArthur's doing, and it was never established that MacArthur's headquarters did anything to correct this misinterpretation.

This pettiness rankled. It bothered the officers, it bothered the public relations officers, it bothered commanders in Halsey's command who were aware of it, and it bothered the newsmen in the South Pacific who lived with it. But the public relations problem was as nothing compared to the command problem. In December General Sutherland, MacArthur's chief of staff, had been on the road, trying to convince higher authority that the Navy's Central Pacific operations ought to be wiped out. Even as the amphibious forces were moving against the Marshalls, Sutherland was in Pearl Harbor, ostensibly to listen. Sutherland came to the morning Nimitz meeting on January 25, along with Generals Richardson, Harmon, Kenney, and Chamberlain. Nimitz was there, of course, along with McMorris, Newton, Lockwood, Calhoun, Ghormley, Kinkaid, Towers, and Forrest Sherman. The last-named was asked to discuss the overall operations plan for 1944 which the Nimitz staff had drawn up, and Sherman unfolded it. Operation Granite was the name.

It was the first time he had ever been able to get anyone in the Navy to make a definite statement, said Sutherland, as Sherman gave target dates—such as June 15 for the invasion of Truk.

For several days the representatives of the two basic commands exchanged views, with the understanding that the Central Pacific operations would continue, while MacArthur moved up New Guinea. There was perfect agreement. Sutherland presented a plan for co-ordinated operations, and everyone thought it was fine. Kinney, Harmon, Richardson, and Towers lunched together on January 28, and by that time everything was "all settled."

But was it all settled?

Early in February, Sutherland was in Washington again, presenting quite different views to the Joint Chiefs of Staff, the old MacArthur views that MacArthur must lead the show up the New Guinea trail to the Philippines.

By February 8 the fat was definitely back in the fire, and Admiral King in Washington was furious. On that day he wrote to Nimitz, having received and read the minutes of the meetings at Pearl Harbor, and having been subjected to the new pressures applied in Washington by Sutherland.

"Indignant dismay" was King's term for his emotions. The reason: all that agreement at Pearl Harbor that the proper method of conducting the campaign against Japan was to accept MacArthur's view of moving up the Philippines. He was particularly upset because Towers and Calhoun seemed to have joined the MacArthur camp. "This view does not appear to have been refuted by any other members of the conference. The other Pacific Ocean Areas Members of the conference expressed the view that there was a possibility of bypassing the Marianas and the Carolines."

Apparently, said King, no one had bothered to consider when the Marianas and Carolines would be wrested from Japan. "I assume that even the Southwest Pacific advocates will admit that sometime or other this thorn in the side of our communications to the western Pacific must be removed."

King was furious because Towers had stated (and was unrefuted) that the object of taking the Marianas was to provide a base for B-29's to bomb Japan. That may have been the airmen's object; to King it was only a useful corollary. The Marianas were to be taken to dry up the Carolines and to speed up the clearing of the line of communications to the Philippines.

King was holding for the Marianas and the Carolines. If the Japanese fleet was too strong, they must take Truk. If the Japanese fleet was weakened enough, they could bypass Truk and take the Marianas. King went on:

The idea of rolling up the Japanese along the New Guinea coast, throughout Halmahera and Mindanao, and up through the Philippines to Luzon, as our major strategic concept, to the exclusion of clearing our Central Pacific line of communications to the Philippines is to me absurd. Further, it is not in accordance with the decisions of the Joint Chiefs of Staff who made their decisions after hearing all of the points of view expressed in the minutes of your conference.

The Commander in Chief was at some pains (he always wrote a very clear letter) to show that he was not merely piqued. The letter began with fulsome praise for Nimitz's "brilliant and accurate concept for the Marshall Islands campaign" and the "energy with which everyone concerned has grabbed the ball in exploiting the favorably developing situation."

King realized that Nimitz, McMorris, and Sherman accepted the need for taking Japan from the Korea-China side, but he was critical of Nimitz for not maintaining these views strongly vis-a-vis MacArthur's officers. He was also upset because so many of Nimitz's officers presented views so divergent from his.

The admiral ended the letter with a restatement of his strategy for the defeat of Japan: the enemy would be forced eventually into the "inner ring" of Japan, Korea, Manchuria, and Shantung Peninsula. Everything must be related to that forcing. China must be used as a base with Chinese manpower securing it.

The Japanese should be cleared from the Carolines, Marianas, and Palaus, then take Luzon, which would open sea routes to the China coast. Then Chinese ports would be taken, and the linkup made with the Chinese land forces which could move up the coast. The occupation and use of Mindanao, which MacArthur wanted, would require "rollup against tremendous difficulties," King said.

Until the very successful raid on Truk, by the fast carriers, Nimitz had considered an assault on that base as necessary. By February 17, King was so concerned about this apparent plan that he wrote again, advocating the taking of the Marianas next. By this time, however, Nimitz had made a trip to the Marshalls to see what had been accomplished there. Nimitz wrote King on February 22, still not having made up his mind finally, but leaning toward the Marianas on the basis of what he had learned of the disposition of the Japanese fleet. He was still awaiting news of the strikes Mitscher was then making against the Carolines.

By February 29 all was settled in Nimitz's mind. The tremendous success of the fast carriers against Truk, the damage they had done, and the flight of the remains of the Japanese fleet from that once powerful base had led him to embrace the Marianas attack wholeheartedly. Cincpac's plans division that day presented Operation Forager to the assembled staff—the operation for the capture of the Marianas.

King was still uneasy about the direction of affairs in the Pacific, with so much of Nimitz's staff apparently falling down before the onslaught of the MacArthur mystique. He brought Nimitz to Washington for conferences early in March.

The aviator issue was still before them. They discussed the question of making commanders who were line officers take aviators as chiefs of staff, and making aviator-commanders take line officers as chiefs of staff. The Navy was also having problems with the air forces; the Army did not like working under Admiral Hoover, and

Army officers had suggested to Nimitz that they come directly under him as commander in chief of Pacific Ocean areas, or under Spruance as commander of the Central Pacific. Nimitz, however, stood stoutly behind Hoover.

King and Nimitz reviewed their strategy for the Pacific, in light of the highly successful Marshalls operation. They had many problems regarding MacArthur's Southwest Pacific command, and they did not seem very close to solving them. Halsey wanted to move into Emirau island, but Nimitz doubted if MacArthur would agree. They talked again about Truk, and Nimitz said he was now certain the Japanese would never again use Truk as a naval base, except perhaps as a staging area in connection with some particular mission. He wanted to move against the Marianas.

Admiral King wondered why Nimitz wanted to use the Marianas as a fleet base—why not Eniwetok as the big naval base? The question, however, kept coming back to Truk and whether they should take it. And that question hinged on the acceptance of the Navy plan or the MacArthur plan for operations in 1944.

The trip to Washington came at a fortuitous time: Nimitz's daughter Catherine was getting married that week and he was able to attend her wedding to James T. Lay, a graduate of the Naval Academy class of 1931. He was also the subject of something of a plot on the part of the Waves and the lady Marines. The commanders of these two august organizations had long been wanting to infiltrate the Pacific theater of war. But Nimitz had a "thing" about women in the war theaters. He simply did not want women around, and the Navy nurses were the one exception that he could not control. He would not accredit women correspondents to the fleet, and when one lady, Peggy Duell, managed to secure a card, he had it revoked. Nor would he allow the ladies to come to Pacific Fleet headquarters, although the Waves and the lady Marines tantalized him in Washington with the fairest flowers of their respective corps.

Nimitz was back in Pearl Harbor by March 21, with solid commitments for the continuation of the Central Pacific amphibious offensive. That day he wrote Admiral McCain, chief of the Bureau of Aeronautics in Washington:

Our problem in the Pacific is one of moving rapidly over great distances with limited logistic resources. Accordingly we must ruthlessly reduce base developments and garrisons, both land and air, to the minimum which will suffice. As long as we maintain the offensive and keep rolling westward our essential needs at advanced air bases are fighters for aid defense and heavy and medium bombers for long range attack and for search. Short range striking aircraft are of little value except where there are active enemy bases within their reach, unless the enemy resumes offensive operations and thereby presents ship targets.

He did not expect that to happen in the Marshalls.

Nimitz believed the Navy ought to stick very closely to its carrier-type training, and not get into either the field of land-based fighters and light bombers, which the Marines held, or heavy and medium bombardment, which was the province of the Army. He told McCain so in this letter, an indication of his preoccupation with the problems of the new fast carriers.

The matter of military policy still bothered Nimitz, for he must have total agreement with MacArthur on the general plan for 1944, and he did not have it yet. He did, however, have the backing of the Joint Chiefs in the Navy program for the Central Pacific, and so it was not hard for Nimitz to be gracious. He had invited MacArthur to come to Pearl Harbor, but MacArthur had steadfastly refused to move out of his own bailiwick. Now Nimitz decided that he would go to Brisbane, to try to smooth the ruffled feathers of the peacock of the Southwest Pacific. It was easier said than done. According to military protocol Nimitz was junior to General MacArthur, who had been a general officer when Nimitz was still a commander, so Nimitz had to ask permission to go to Australia and MacArthur's command. His pretext was that he wanted to visit the Naval forces in the Southwest Pacific.

MacArthur very graciously invited Nimitz to visit him in Brisbane, as Nimitz hoped he would. Then the admiral began making preparations for the journey.

He sent his aide, Lieutenant Commander Lamar, into Honolulu

to have several silk playsuits made up for little Arthur MacArthur, the general's son. Lamar also laid in a stock of Hawaiian candy for Mrs. MacArthur, and Nimitz collected a flock of orchids to give the lady, preserving them by inserting their stems in little glass tubes filled with water. Then they set off by flying boat to Brisbane.

MacArthur met them at the dock. That first night, he invited Nimitz and his aide to dine with the MacArthurs in their suite in Lennin's Hotel, across the street from the Queensland houses of Parliament. The gifts were delivered, and the general was nearly as pleased, it seemed, as little Arthur in his playsuit.

MacArthur was very mellow. During the visit Nimitz discovered that one of the difficulties between the commands was MacArthur's staff policy. General Sutherland, the chief of staff, simply did not show MacArthur all the dispatches from the Nimitz headquarters, but summarized, and sometimes this led to troubles and misunderstandings. Halsey had the same trouble. He had visited MacArthur a few weeks before to try to settle a misunderstanding about Manus island. Halsey had wanted to make Manus an advanced naval base and had proceeded to send materials there for that purpose, with the agreement of King and Nimitz. But Manus was in MacArthur's territory so Nimitz had suggested by dispatch that MacArthur yield Manus to the Navy. MacArthur's sense of possessiveness was outraged: no one had explained the need to him, and it appeared that the Navy was simply trying to whittle down his command—particularly so in light of the decisions of the Joint Chiefs of Staff regarding operations in 1944. It had taken Halsey two days of persuasion to convince MacArthur to let him have the island.

Now MacArthur was furious because at Nimitz's suggestion in Washington, Emirau had been substituted for Kavieng, and Halsey had moved right ahead, taking the island before Nimitz arrived in Brisbane. MacArthur, meanwhile, had landed forces on New Britain. The twin movements had cut off Rabaul, which no longer threatened the Allies, and had encircled some eighty thousand Japanese in New Britain and New Ireland and the Solomons. The South Pacific campaign was over and so was the interlude.

Chapter
Twenty-One

THE MARIANAS

March 1–June 18, 1944

In the middle of March, 1944, Admiral Spruance was off in Majuro lagoon, conducting training exercises against the Japanese-held islands of the Marshalls. One might say that the Japanese on the islands were perfect foils for the training program—the ships would come in to practice bombardment techniques, and the Japanese on such islands as Mili never failed to shoot back with their shore batteries. The result was that the United States Navy could learn fast, practicing, as it were, with live ammunition against real but not overly dangerous targets.

Spruance was troubled by one decision made in Washington and at Pearl Harbor: by the end of March King and Nimitz had definitely decided that nonaviators in command had to have aviators as chiefs of staff and aviators had to have nonaviators. Thus Hoover was instructed to find a "line officer" for his staff, and Spruance was told that Captain Moore must go. "Ching" Lee, the battleship com-

THE MARIANAS   359

mander of the Fifth Fleet, was also instructed that he had to bring in an aviator to his fast battleship force.

As the war continued and the relationships became more complicated, Nimitz's celebrated diplomacy was sorely tried in many areas.

Dealings with MacArthur remained difficult. When Sutherland and other Southwest Pacific officers had come to see Nimitz early in the year, the Pacific Fleet public relations people had prepared a press release about the meetings, on instructions from the admiral. As a courtesy, Nimitz sent a copy of the release to MacArthur before giving it out, suggesting simultaneous release. Back from MacArthur came a hot message, saying that the general could see no possible reason for issuing a press release. And the matter was dropped right there. But when Nimitz went down to Brisbane to visit MacArthur, the general made sure a press release and pictures were given out immediately. The mountain had come to Mahomet.

And sometimes the war seemed to get completely bogged down in red tape, as on the occasion when Admiral Turner tried to deliver a captured Japanese flag to the Secretary of the Navy. One of Turner's officers, Captain J. H. Doyle, was detached from the Turner team and sent back to Washington to other duty, after the successful invasion of the Marshalls. Turner gave Doyle a battle flag as a souvenir and told him to deliver it to the Secretary of the Navy. Doyle then proceeded to get thoroughly mixed up with the Washington commandos in the Navy Department.

He reported in to Admiral Cooke in Washington, and mentioned the flag. Cooke was only half hearing him, because he and King were about to leave for London that day, so he told Doyle to discuss the matter with Admiral Edwards, Deputy Chief of Naval Operations. Edwards was dubious.

"There's a lot of protocol mixed up in that," he said. "What does Nimitz think about it? Maybe Nimitz should be presenting it to the President."

Doyle explained that Turner had been on the scene at the Marshalls and Nimitz had not. It was a gift from Turner to the Secretary of the Navy, just like the flag from Guadalcanal that Turner had sent the Secretary earlier.

Edwards was still dubious. "Don't do anything," he said, "until I let you know."

Doyle waited. He talked to Admiral Delany in the Navy Department, and Delany was soothing but not solving. Doyle threatened to return the flag to Turner. Delany said he would get answers.

Doyle then sat down and wrote a letter, to be signed by Edwards, to the Vice Chief of Naval Operations, asking for a flagpole to be installed in Doyle's office. "Insofar as practicable . . . all materials used in the construction of the flagstaff should be critical except that the stand must be constructed of hand carved protocol."

The memo went out into the morass of official paper. A week went by, and nothing happened.

In the middle of the second week, Doyle was notified that he could deliver the flag to the Secretary of the Navy but he was not to mention the delay, or try to explain it. So Doyle took the flag to Secretary Knox, who was very pleased to have it, and brought in photographers to have the presentation recorded.

At the beginning of the third week, the picture appeared in the Washington newspapers, with a caption that identified Doyle as the man who hoisted the flag on Kwajalein.

The war was growing infinitely more complex, as anyone could see. One result of the complexity, as detailed here, was the increasingly important lack of understanding between the Nimitz command and the MacArthur command. Each day the differences seemed to mount. Each week the approaches spread further apart. The solution did not lie on the MacArthur–Nimitz level, however, but on the King–Marshall level, and unless it could be resolved in Washington no one could expect it to be settled at all.

By this time, 1944, in spite of the growing administrative troubles of a complex organization, which so often manifested themselves in human pettiness, the fighting team of the Pacific was stronger and more effective than it had been before. In the process of weeding out all but what Nimitz referred to as "the first team" in combat command, some injustices were done, which Nimitz was as quick to recognize as anyone; but like Halsey, Nimitz had taken the position that personal interests could not possibly be considered in wartime. Nimitz might have brought Mrs. Nimitz to Honolulu, he might have engineered leaves for himself, but he lived a sternly spartan life at Pearl Harbor, attending relatively few of the social functions in the busy whirl of civilian life. On one occasion he was eager to get to the west coast, where his daughter was christening a ship, but such a trip did not fit any of King's plans, and so it was immediately abandoned. By 1944, then, there was a feeling in Washington and at Pearl Harbor that the job was being done properly. "You have a good team here now in the Pacific," Undersecretary Forrestal wrote to President Roosevelt on the occasion of a visit to Pearl Harbor early that year. "The contrast between a year and a half ago and today is as between night and day."

That is not to say that all was sweetness and light. Far from it. In the Central Pacific, "Terrible" Turner raged and drove his officers—sometimes nearly to distraction—trying to get them ready for the Marianas landings. Admiral Hoover was in almost constant argument with General Hale, the Army Air Force commander who ran the army's land-based fighters and bombers that supported the Pacific operations of the Navy. In February Hale had made a trip away from his base without consulting Hoover, and Hoover was furious enough to complain to Nimitz, who tried to smooth it over. The relations between Nimitz and Towers were always strained. Both men walked on eggs. Towers was almost constantly frustrated because his aim in life was a combat command, and he was not getting it. Nimitz was well aware of the persistence of the airmen, and he was generally very patient with Towers' constant state of irritation, knowing that the growing weight of logistical worries, which were the burden of the deputy to Cincpac, were a major cause of Towers' troubles.

Even though "Baldy" Pownall had taken over as air commander in the Pacific, the airmen still tended to come to Towers with their troubles, adding to his burdens, but not altogether without reason. Towers still regarded himself primarily as an aviator and interested himself most in the aviation problems. He took a strong dislike to Admiral Hoover, for example, and was very critical of that admiral.

There was, then, friction among what might be called Nimitz's lieutenants—all the more reason that Nimitz was the ideal commander for the Pacific Ocean areas, just as MacArthur was an ideal commander in his region. That there was friction between and within the commands was not surprising; that there was so little damage to the war effort by that friction is somewhat remarkable. Admiral H. B. Sallada, an airman himself, who served part of the war in the Bureau of Aeronautics, part at sea, later contrasted the American war effort with his own studies of that of Germany. "I can't avoid a feeling of pride," he said, "at the friendly and cooperative feeling that prevailed within our naval high command throughout the war . . ."

Most irascible of all the Nimitz lieutenants was Holland Smith. He might have been a very happy general if the amphibious operations had been run his way. That way called for the Navy to provide ships, lots of ships, with big guns, and to transport the Marines to an island, throw the complete weight of naval airpower against the island for several days, bombard the island steadily for perhaps ten days, and then let the Marines walk ashore. Actually, if Holland Smith's plans had ever been worked out to perfection, the way he wanted them, a company of Marines might well have taken Tarawa.

But the Navy was not running amphibious operations in Holland Smith's way, and would not do so. Kelly Turner included Smith in his planning. In fact, despite Smith's complaints about the insufficiency of the Tarawa bombardment, he and his staff had been in on the planning of it. Turner's rule of thumb, an absolute dictum nonetheless, was that no aspect of the landing operations would be put in the master plan until and unless Holland Smith and his staff had approved. The bombardments were subject to the vagaries of war. In the case of Tarawa the invasion fleet had gone in with orders from Nimitz himself to "get the hell in and get the hell out." The Japanese fleet was at large, and for all anybody knew it might sally forth to destroy the American invaders. Of course no one— from King to Nimitz to Spruance—wanted to risk an invasion force that they had worked so hard to prepare.

The conflict between Holland Smith and his Navy friends was largely a matter of different views of the war, from very different vantage points. Just as King and Nimitz saw the war from different positions, so did Admiral Turner and General Smith. Turner was responsible for the landing and protection of the troops, and for the safety of his ships, *as well as* the overall success of the invasion of an island, two islands, or three islands as the case might be. If Admiral Hill, for example, had somehow failed at the Gilberts, Turner would have been responsible (unless the failure could be attributed to some deviation from orders or some immense gaffe), even though he was at Makin while Hill was at Tarawa. Had the Marines been driven off Tarawa, Turner would have been responsible to Spruance.

Holland Smith was with Turner at Makin, and his responsibility went further than his direct presence would indicate: had General Julian Smith's troops been pushed off Tarawa (unless the failure was caused by deviation from plan), Holland Smith would again have been held responsible. But he did not have to worry about the Japanese fleet, or the Japanese submarines, or the Japanese planes (these were Navy worries), and so his criticisms of naval amphibious operations had to be judged within the framework of his responsibility.

It was as at the Marshalls, when Admiral Hill went in to take Eniwetok after the primary target islands had been secured. By the time Hill's force reached the strongly defended Parry island, he did not have sufficient ammunition on his ships to give the kind of bombardment that would have been most effective. Also, because of the failure of command of the Army troops in that expedition, the tired men of the 22nd Marine Regiment had to take Parry directly after their assault on Engebi. Eniwetok, then, was certainly not an example of the best possible manner of staging an amphibious assault, but it *was* an example of what Nimitz and King prized far beyond masses of materiel and fleets of ships and armies of men: the ability of a commander to make the best of what he had, and to *win*.

Nimitz went on to the Marshalls on April 7 for inspection, taking Lockwood, Pownall, Forrest Sherman, and several other officers. There was the usual Nimitz plane trouble. The staff plane had to turn back with engine trouble, but shortly after landing they were off again in a PB-2-Y. At Kwajalein, Nimitz and his admirals looked over the blockhouse area and the "before" and "after" pictures, which showed what a naval bombardment could do. The "before" pictures, taken on January 31, showed forty or fifty buildings nestled among the palm trees, with a system of roads leading around the area. The "after" pictures showed four recognizable buildings still standing, and not a palm tree in the blockhouse area.

Nimitz looked around with grave interest. The correspondents were there that day, in a circle around him.

"What do you think of the island?" came the question, as the reporters raised their pencils.

"Gentlemen," said Nimitz, "it's the worst scene of devastation I have ever witnessed except the Texas picnic."

The impressive victory had been accomplished by planning, hard work, and instant decision, even when the decisions were hard to make.

So it was all the way down the line. General Watson at Eniwetok would remove an artillery commander because, when the chips were down, he was not getting the job done. Admiral Hill would remove a sub-chaser commander *in action*, because that officer had made a serious mistake in taking station in the wrong place and confusing the transport captains, who were told the ship would be elsewhere. On a higher level there was the disappearance from the Pacific scene of Admiral S. P. Ginder of Task Group 58.4. Marc Mitscher came back from a furious round of air strikes in April and complained to Admiral Towers that he did not like the way Ginder was handling his task group. Towers went to Nimitz, who did not hesitate—Mitscher was told to order Ginder back to Pearl Harbor—for there was no time to waste on personalities. Yet Nimitz was never precipitate. When Ginder came back to Pearl Harbor in mid-April, Nimitz conducted a thorough investigation, with Pownall and Towers, into the reasons for his removal. Towers finally said Ginder's services here had been unsatisfactory. Only then did Nimitz indicate to King that Ginder's fate was to be placed back in the hands of the Bureau of Aeronautics, and he was to be removed from the Pacific.

As for Holland Smith, he was unhappy in the spring of 1944 because Spruance was promoted to four-star admiral as a result of the Gilberts and Marshalls victories, and Turner was promoted to vice admiral, while he, Holland Smith, remained a major general.

King was not enthusiastic about promoting Smith, but General Vandegrift, then commandant of Marines, was very firm. As a last resistance, King said Nimitz had not recommended Smith's promotion, whereupon Vandegrift insisted that King ask Nimitz, which he did. Nimitz recommended the promotion.

To move ahead against the Japanese meant growth, and growth was under way throughout the Pacific war effort in 1944. Growth meant change, and apparently change meant almost endless minor conflicts. Admiral McCain, in Washington, wanted to get back into the war, feeling that his friends in the Pacific were seeing all the action while he was flying a desk. With the windup of the South Pacific operations, Fitch would be more or less out of a job, and Halsey and Nimitz suggested that perhaps he go to Washington to replace McCain, who could come out and have the task force he wanted. But Artemus Gates, Assistant Secretary of the Navy for Air, was very much opposed to this change. The Navy was fighting for money and, literally, for its life, in a Washington where the Congress was bombarded by demands for a universal service, and particularly an air force that took over all aspects of air operations. Gates penned a note to Forrestal stating that the change "does not make sense." Gates had no animosity toward Fitch; he did not want to upset the applecart with Congress. McCain had learned his way around, and was effective before Congress; Gates was afraid that Fitch's inexperience in Washington would hurt the Navy cause. But there was another reason, part of the only conflict. Fitch was "recent" in naval aviation, Gates said, and his appointment as Deputy Chief of Naval Operations (air) would not be popular with the young aviators.

With the progress of the war the naval airmen were becoming convinced that *theirs* were the essential factors of victory, just as Holland Smith was convinced that Nimitz was "riding to fame on the shoulders of the Marines."

How very complex the war had become was indicated in May when Nimitz journeyed once again to San Francisco to meet King and settle basic matters of policy for the Pacific. The meetings began on May 5.

First was the problem of the South Pacific, now that operations had slowed down there. Halsey, Nimitz, and King discussed the future, and it was agreed that Admiral Newton, who had been displaced by Towers as Nimitz's deputy (at the insistence of the airmen, working through Forrestal), should become the new commander of the South Pacific. King wanted him also to have a fleet command, under Nimitz. Other personnel changes included the decision that Captain Moore would give way to Rear Admiral Art Davis, following the principle that the nonair Spruance must have an airman as chief of staff. Another change was the replacement of Captain Preston Mercer, Nimitz's flag secretary, who would get a sea command, by Captain B. L. Austin. Mercer, who had been with Nimitz a long time, wanted his chance to win flag rank. The moment was also suitable, because Mercer had antagonized Admiral Towers, who a few weeks earlier had asked Nimitz to get rid of the captain.

Mercer's removal from the staff would be accounted a particular loss by the public relations men, for he was often their interlocutor in disagreements with Naval Academy philosophers. On many occasions Mercer had gone to bat for the correspondents and the public relations men to get information through the censors, bearding Soc McMorris and even Towers and Nimitz at times.

The handling of Negroes had been, and remained, a problem in the Pacific. There had been riots in and around Honolulu as early as 1942. The question of Negro officers was raised, and Nimitz said that he was not eager to have Negroes in his command because of the additional problems. Yet for the future, Nimitz said, the best way of handling the Negro problem in the service was to eliminate segregation.

When the personnel problems were resolved on this first day of meetings, Nimitz and King brought several other officers into the sessions to discuss general strategy and tactics. They included Admiral Cooke, King's deputy; Admiral Carney, Halsey's chief of staff; and Admiral Sherman, Nimitz's plans officer.

With the changes that were coming, Nimitz wanted a clear-cut break with the MacArthur command. MacArthur would assume responsibility for all operations west of the 159th meridian. It had been suggested in the personnel sessions that Admiral Newton would be responsible to MacArthur for bases and to Nimitz for fleet operations. Admiral Cooke agreed with Nimitz that this idea was unsound, and particularly that Halsey should be detached with his Third Fleet from any concern with the South or Southwest Pacific. The South Pacific was to be greatly reduced, and most of the bases and personnel were to pass to MacArthur's navy, now the Seventh Fleet under Admiral Kinkaid.

Following the spring decisions of the Joint Chiefs of Staff in favor of the Central Pacific drive, Admirals King and Nimitz were now talking about the move into Formosa, which would come after the Marianas campaign. The commander, they agreed, would be an Army officer, because Formosa was the largest land mass they had encountered. The Marines were designated as shock troops; their established mission had been to take beachheads and small areas and hold them until garrison troops came along. Formosa was seen as a land operation as soon as the amphibious forces had secured the beachheads and the Navy had guaranteed the safety of the air and seas around the big island. On Formosa, Marines would again storm the beaches, but once the foothold was established, the Army would take over. (Holland Smith, of course, was not aware of this strategy.)

They discussed the Japanese fleet, so badly mauled in its recent encounters with the Americans, such as at Truk. King said he thought it unlikely that the Marianas invasion would bring the fleet out to fight, but that a Formosa operation certainly would. Admiral Cooke had been instructed to prepare a discussion of Pacific strategy after the Marianas, and on the second day of the meetings it was brought out.

In Washington there was much discussion that spring of the MacArthur plan to retake Mindanao. What would happen if the United States bypassed Mindanao? Nimitz and Halsey said there would be hell to pay. (They had been visiting MacArthur recently.) But Cooke's planning was based on King's thinking, and here is how it went:

—CHINA operation appears bigger than FORMOSA in that major Japanese forces (Army) will be met—CHINA Operation similar to Tunis operation.

—If Atlantic War ends by October, 1944, and in keeping with Combined Chiefs of Staff desire to end PACIFIC War twelve months after defeat of GERMANY, we should get to CHINA before 1945.

—Best time to hit FORMOSA is probably November-December, 1944, and, since present plans call for FORMOSA in February, 1945, better check and plan for possibility of speeding up operations.

—If CHINA-FORMOSA operations are speeded up, we may be able to do FORMOSA with less than twelve divisions, as preliminarily planned by Cincpac (say seven divisions).

—Important thing is to investigate possibility of earlier FORMOSA, together with plans for what comes *after* FORMOSA.

After? Admiral Cooke suggested at this meeting that the last step in the defeat of Japan would be to cut the island kingdom off from the mainland, to bombard the Empire, and perhaps even to invade Kyushu. That meant that operations to cut off Korea would be treated as amphibious operations.

As for the work on the China mainland, it would make major use of Chinese manpower. The Navy would take positions along the Chinese coast to supply the Chinese with arms and materiel, and use the Chinese land force to roll up the Japanese army.

The conferees proceeded then to discuss the possible points where they could make entry into China. They did not know, but they did know how to find out, and King directed that General Stilwell in Chungking be asked to provide the information. Nimitz suggested that Stilwell be asked to send someone to Pearl Harbor for conferences, then come on to Washington to report the tentative decisions of the Nimitz command. The man whose advice they really wanted was Commodore M. E. Miles, head of the naval advisory group in China, and more familiarly known as commodore of the Rice Paddy Navy. One of Miles's major responsibilities was naval intelligence. His coast watchers and spy network had been collecting information for just such a purpose for the last two years. So the naval planners, in deadly seriousness, began their preliminary work for the invasion of the China coast that would lead to the bottling up of Japan and the eventual defeat of the enemy.

The admirals turned then to logistical and administrative problems, but the next day, having individually considered the matters at hand, they came back to strategy. Nimitz suggested the substitution of Amoy for Formosa in the initial stages of the operations. The question of Russia came up, and Nimitz suggested that they must assume the USSR would not enter the war. King suggested in turn that the Russians had a score to settle with Japan dating back to 1905, and probably would do so. Cooke suggested the Russians wanted Sakhalin island. This departure led to discussions of the Kurils, the Netherlands East Indies, and the southeastern Asiatic continent.

But it all came back to China. King explained that the Chinese government had agreed at the Cairo conference to provide thirty divisions for the renewed war against Japan, and eventually to put forward ninety divisions. All this demanded supply by the United States, and bases, since so much could not be brought in over the hump of the CBI (China-Burma-India) theater. Nimitz repeated that he believed the best way to go in was up the coast, and to launch major operations from the Shanghai area.

King and Nimitz, then, returned to their respective headquarters —and Nimitz stepped into a hornet's nest. Towers and McMorris had been quarreling while he was away. The aviators of the Pacific Fleet were still restless. One reason was the ease with which Army aviators were receiving medals—air medals for a handful of missions flown, Distinguished Flying Crosses by the score. Navy fliers simply did not get such awards, they were lucky to receive a letter of commendation, except for some unusually gallant or effective action. The pilots were constantly complaining to their commanders, who complained to the carrier captains, who complained to the task group commanders, who complained to Admirals Mitscher, Pownall, and Towers.

In Nimitz's absence a conflict had arisen between Towers and McMorris over awards. The goat of the argument was Lieutenant James E. McNamara, Jr., the unfortunate awards officer of the Pacific Fleet staff. Several members of Towers' staff had recently been on his back, and the result was that almost immediately on his return from the west coast, Nimitz had to step in. He called a special meeting in his office and brought in Captain Mercer, Admiral Towers, and two members of Towers' staff, who had been complaining.

If they had any complaints, Nimitz said, they should bring them to the proper source: Nimitz. He took total responsibility for awards.

That astringent conference ended the argument for the moment. But the aviators went away grumbling, as usual, that Nimitz was unsympathetic to their position, while in fact he had been raising the question of awards and recognition time after time with King. In the meetings just past, the question of awards for aviators, line officers, and staff officers who were doing excellent work outside of combat areas, had been discussed very thoroughly. Nor was King unaware of the problem. But his approach was to keep the bars of the Navy up, so that awards would continue to have special meaning, and persuade the Army and the air forces to stop debasing the whole procedure by giving out medals as though they were chewing gum. Another problem, now that the Central Pacific offensive was moving at full speed, was the demand made on Nimitz's time, and that of his admirals, to keep up the momentum they had created.

"We should have done much better than we did," said Admiral Harry Hill, looking back to a quarter of a century later. "But we simply did not have the time for the paper work." Hill, for example, arose early in the morning and worked far into the night. When the Gilberts operation was ended, he hurried to Pearl Harbor to plan for his part in the Marshalls campaign. There were action reports and a dozen other reports to write, and none of them could take time away from the planning, because in the plans lay the kernels of men's lives. Hill, for one, liked social life and exercise, but during the war he did not go to parties and his recreation was limited to an occasional game of golf when he was in Hawaii. It was the same for the others, except that some wondered if "Terrible" Turner *ever* relaxed.

But as for awards, the captains who rode their ships in these operations did not get medals. (How does one equate four days off a beachhead with air missions?) Certainly there was grumbling through the fleet about the lack of recognition, but that was the way it was.

At the time of the Nimitz-Towers dispute over awards, other issues were in the air. The aviators had been pushing for public relations credit for their activities, and Nimitz had been holding fast to his doctrine of avoiding aid to the enemy at all costs. The Pacific correspondents, quick to catch innuendos, had come to recognize the existence of schism in the command, and at a dinner on Ford Island for the War Correspondents one night while Nimitz was away, a correspondent had asked Preston Mercer: "Which camp do you belong to?" Mercer had reported this question to Nimitz, who was not at all pleased. Today he laid down the law. He did not want Admiral Towers to take any further cognizance of awards or of public relations. He, Nimitz, would take total personal responsibility on these subjects.

"Camp" referred basically to the problem of "black shoe" versus "brown shoe," and officers on both sides had become steamed up enough about the situation as it developed to create many problems for King and Nimitz.

With aviation coming into its own, the line officers were becoming disturbed by what they saw developing around them. Captain C. Moore, Spruance's chief of staff, later expressed the line officers' feeling very cogently when asked about the rapid rise of a certain aviator who had never seen duty on a big ship other than a carrier:

> He was a flier? Well, that's astounding, the way these aviators go. They can command air squadrons based on tenders, and maybe have a tour on a carrier as commander of an air squadron, and then if they're lucky they'll get command of a deep draft ship. It will be the first really seagoing experience of their lives, to command a tanker or a supply ship or a tender, and that will qualify them for command of anything, although they've never been through the process of officer of the deck, division officer, or head of department of a ship at all. They've been aviators all their lives, and then they suddenly come to command rank and they've got to get some seagoing experience. So they put them in a tanker for a year and then they give them command of a 50,000 ton carrier, and they terrify everybody else in the same ocean.

Despite these tensions on the command level, and the grumbling on the operational levels, line officers and aviators generally

worked very cheerfully toward their common goal when specific
tasks were to be accomplished. In the planning for the Marianas
operation, Admiral Hill was eager to try some innovations. One was
the use of mortars on LCT's, which could be used for close-in fire
support on the beaches. When Hill went to Turner with this plan,
the latter was very skeptical, but in his honest, gruff way, he did not
tell Hill to jettison the idea. Turner was difficult at all times with
his subordinates, but he respected independence of thought more
than any other quality, and so Hill had his way: four mortars were
installed port, and four starboard, on three LCT's. Unfortunately,
before they ever got into action two of them blew up in an ammunition explosion, and although the court of inquiry found it to be a
handling accident, with responsibility at the lower echelons, Hill was
shaken by the deaths of a number of enlisted men, and the mortar
experiment was quietly dropped.

All Pearl Harbor was shaken on May 21, when five LST's loaded
with ammunition went up in flames in a series of earth-shaking
explosions. So awesome was the sight that in describing it in his
diary, Admiral Towers wrote with the vivid language of a correspondent relating a military action. For a few hours all Pearl was
very tense, it was not even certain that Operation Forager—the Marianas—would not have to be delayed because of the shortage of
LST's. But in the end, two needed LST's were shanghaied away
from Halsey in the South Pacific, and the schedule was maintained.

On the eve of the Marianas operation, Nimitz was, as usual,
sorting out the multifarious problems of his divided command, and
somehow keeping it relatively homogeneous. The frictions between
Admiral Hoover, Nimitz's land-based air commander, and the Army
Air Forces continued. Hoover was busy building canteens and officers' clubs at Kwajalein and trading his jewelry with the natives.
("Yesterday Bernhard and I paid a visit to the big Marshall chief on
Ailinglapalap Atoll. We exchanged gifts. Theirs consist entirely of
grass mats, baskets, fans, etc.") He was, in a way, the first island administrator in addition to his other duties. But Hoover's other duties
were the ones that caused Nimitz and Generals Richardson and
Arnold considerable difficulty.

The Marianas planning problem was creating difficulties for the
land-based air command, as a reason for taking the Marianas was to

establish bases for the B-29's to bomb Japan. The coming of B-29's meant the bringing of a new air force (the 20th) into the Pacific, and a consequent reorganization of air force setup there. The complications were tremendous.

In May the War Department suggested that General Harmon, the commanding general of Army Air Forces, Pacific Ocean areas, ought to be under General Richardson, the commanding general of the Army for the Pacific Ocean areas, when it came to logistics and administration. But as far as operations were concerned Harmon was to be under command of Nimitz. Harmon wanted to be responsible to Nimitz for operations, to Arnold in Washington for matters in general, and to Richardson for administration and logistics. Nimitz did not want anything of the kind.

The Navy organization made the commander of air forces, Pacific a "type commander." That is, the type commander was an administrative officer, concerned with the administration and logistics of the air forces of the Pacific Fleet, but not actually with operations except in the planning and review of them. The Army had no equivalent organization, and this of course was the problem. Harmon, who was used to exercising command, would not take easily to being a "type commander." Nor would he like the alternative under the Navy system, which would be to place himself under Admiral Spruance, who was commander of the Central Pacific forces.

This problem was the type that Nimitz took to bed with him at night, and in this matter the admiral was as nearly caustic as he ever allowed himself to be:

> While I realize that the ambitions of the Army Air Forces may require that, particularly after the end of the war with Germany, they have complete independence from the Army Ground Forces in the Pacific, I prefer to retain the present system wherein I have only one Commanding General to deal with. I hope that I may be spared the task of coordinating the Army Air Forces and the Army Ground Forces—a task which will be mine if Harmon is set up independent of Richardson.

But in the very next paragraph, lest he be misunderstood by people who dealt in personalities, Nimitz hastened to add that he would be very pleased to have Harmon as commanding general of the Army in his area. He just did not want two coequal Army commanders to deal with.

On the next lower echelon, the Army Air Forces problem was also troublesome this spring. Hoover reported that Hale wanted to set up his headquarters on Saipan, while Hoover intended to set up his headquarters on Guam. McMorris thought they ought both to be on Saipan. Nimitz said no, they should be on Guam, so they could not get mixed up with the 20th Air Force.

These worrisome concerns of the commander in chief of the fleet were scarcely known to commanders other than those directly concerned. One of Nimitz's most important attributes as a successful commander was scarcely observable: the creation of a climate in which his subordinate commanders could operate efficiently.

The most important of these subordinates, at the moment, was Admiral Spruance, whose every faculty was focused on the winning of this war.

Spruance was not an easy man, even for Captain Moore, a friend from the days when they served together in the Philippines on the old *Bainbridge*—DD1. A case in point: After Kwajalein and the successful Truk raid, part of Spruance's force moved to make carrier attacks on Saipan, partially to destroy, partially to secure aerial photographs for the coming invasion planning. But as this force had moved in toward Saipan, they were sighted by the Japanese. Miles away, on the flagship, Spruance and Moore were following the action by radio, and Moore asked if, in view of the sighting, Spruance did not want to call off the Saipan raid—because the surprise element was missing.

"No," said Spruance, indignantly.

That was all he said. Another officer might have been hurt and retired into his shell. Not Moore, who was the perfect chief of staff for Spruance. Moore worked from six o'clock in the morning until midnight every day, preparing the plans and papers for his commander. Moore handled all the detail. And how did Spruance react? Did he appreciate it?

"Yes, I think he did," said Captain Moore. "But under certain circumstances he could be extremely abrupt and extremely disagree-

able. I never let that bother me very much. If I had something to
say to him, I said it . . . . He knew what he was going to do and
there was no fooling."

The "no fooling" came on February 22. That night Mitscher's
force was attacked four times by Japanese planes, without any damage whatsoever, and the raid on Saipan, Tinian, and Guam was immensely successful.

On that same return voyage to Kwajalein, there was another incident. Spruance carried a Japanese-language officer on his staff,
Commander Slonim, who did not stand watches, but spent much
of his nights listening to Japanese intercepts and radio intelligence.
If he found something unusual, he would wake up Captain Moore
to discuss the matter.

On the way back to Kwajalein, the *New Jersey's* radar picked
up an unidentified aircraft. Slonim worried a while with the report,
and then went to Moore and woke him up. Moore worried a while,
and then went in to wake Spruance, who had gone to his cabin at
about eight o'clock as usual.

Spruance did not like to be disturbed at night at sea, unless
something big was up. Moore knew it, but he was troubled this
night, since they had left the task force and were heading back only
with their destroyer screen. So Moore went into Spruance's darkened
cabin, and awakened the admiral.

"Well, is there anything I can do about it?" Spruance asked.

"No."

"Then why wake me up?"

Whereupon Spruance turned over and went back to sleep.

If Spruance was curt, it was because he valued his sleep almost
as much as he valued exercise; he felt both were essential to his well-
being. His point was that as commander of the Fifth Fleet, his basic
task was to make the proper decisions at the proper time, and to do
so he had to be clear-headed and thoroughly alert. This attitude
went back to the days of the old *Bainbridge* in Philippine waters,
when Spruance had been commander of the destroyer, with Ralph
Haxtun as his executive officer and Moore as chief engineer. Haxtun
and Moore were devil-may-care young officers, who liked to go on
parties, and in these days (before the day when Josephus Daniels

dried up the Navy) they drank cocktails, in the wardroom every night before dinner. Every night they would hand the shaker to Spruance, and every night he would sniff it, shudder, and speak up. "I am glad *I* am not a slave to the demon rum," he would say.

Back at Kwajalein, and then at Pearl Harbor, in March, April, and May, Spruance and his staff were almost completely occupied by the planning of the Marianas operation, in spite of Moore's suggestion that the Marianas be bypassed. It was, of course, a truism among the naval officer corps that they might suggest any idea, but when a command came from above, they turned their hands to making the operation successful, without regard to their personal beliefs. Moore's memo on Truk and the Marianas was making its way around among the concerned parties. Spruance made sure that Admiral Turner got a copy of it, although Spruance never commented on the memo himself.

Spruance and his staff spent much of March at Majuro in the Marshalls, an island with a big lagoon and a lovely sandy beach. They walked and swam and worked, and sometimes visited the native villages. Spruance went to Pearl Harbor for conferences and returned with a gaudy pair of swimming trunks. Others of the *New Jersey* swam in the lagoon, but Spruance contented himself with walking the deck in his trunks, and ragging Captain Moore to exercise with him, while Moore quietly bemoaned the fact that Spruance flatly refused to pay any attention to details.

On March 21 Spruance received orders to raid the Palau group, to clear the area of Japanese power so that MacArthur might move handily along the north coast of New Guinea to Hollandia. It was really a carrier raid, but Spruance went along as commander of the Fifth Fleet, to supervise the three carrier groups, and six of Ching Lee's fast battleships, along with thirteen heavy and light cruisers and twenty-six destroyers. To the Japanese the force must have been reminiscent of what they had been able to put forward at Pearl Harbor and at Midway.

Pownall was no longer with them on this raid, but they used a plan he had devised for handling the carrier group. The *New Jersey*, the flagship, ran in the center of the formation, with a carrier group on the port bow, one on the starboard bow, and one astern—all, of course, outside the flagship's destroyer screen. There was only one problem—launch of planes—when the carrier groups would sometimes be completely out of touch as far as visual signaling was concerned, and Spruance was very definite in his insistence that raido silence be maintained.

In his usual fashion, Spruance had his staff work up the orders, looked them over carefully, and issued them, a day before sailing. These were such clear orders, and so explicit that very little else was needed, except to reflect the changes Spruance made in the plans, to fit the changing tactical situation.

Such a change became necessary when they were spotted, three days out, by the Japanese. Then Spruance moved the day for operations against the Palaus up a full day, hoping to catch the Japanese before they moved their ships out. To aid the force, Nimitz had Lockwood send out seven submarines, as life guards for the pilots and to attack any Japanese shipping moving to escape the area. As usual, the submarines performed with skill and gallantry. The *Tullabee* was sunk when one of her own torpedoes made a circular run, but the *Tunny* torpedoed the Japanese battleship *Musashi*, causing her considerable damage. As for the carrier strikes, with the loss of about twenty-five planes, they swept the islands for two days, hitting ships, airfields, installations, and planes on the ground.

Heading back to Majuro, Spruance came flat up against the new public relations policy of the Navy, the one Nimitz had described to Halsey as being forced down his throat. On March 30 the Pacific Fleet command had issued a communiqué announcing the attack on the Palaus. On the way back to Majuro, Spruance began getting requests, then demands, for further information about the success of the strikes.

He ignored them. Spruance's position on such requests was to honor them only under the most exceptional circumstances. Then he would put a dispatch aboard a destroyer, send it out fifty miles on the flank, heading in a different direction, and let the destroyer transmit the message, or put it on a plane and let the plane give it to a shore station. Also, the claims of the Navy and the Army in the first days of the war had been excessive, and Spruance refused to accept his own aviators' claims unless there was proof. It was not a question of dishonesty or even intentional exaggeration. In the heat of battle, the pilots often mistook the nature of the ships they attacked, and the damage they inflicted.

On this homeward trek, as the requests grew ever more insistent, Captain Moore became agitated and asked Spruance if he was not going to do something about the messages.

Spruance simply cocked an eye at him. "No," he said, serenely, "I'm not going to tell them anything."

And he did not. Only when they reached Majuro, and when the aviators' reports had been sifted and compared, and checked by the commanding officers, was the dispatch sent off. Then and only then could Captain Waldo Drake and Lieutenant Commander McArdle prepare the press release that spoke of the raid on the Palaus, Yap, Ulithi, and Wolesi, and told of the two destroyers, the combat ship, two large cargo ships, six medium cargo vessels, eight small cargo vessels, three large, one medium and one small oiler, lesser ships and still lesser ships, ground installations, and planes destroyed.

On the surface, the Palau raid seemed to have been tremendously successful. Captain Moore thought not; he was indignant because Nimitz had sent one of his staff down to Halsey in Nouméa, with instructions to plan for some air reconnaissance over Palau. The plan called for Halsey to send planes up on a night mission, drop flares, photograph the area, and pass on the photos immediately to the Fifth Fleet, en route, so Spruance might have an idea of his targets. But the result was to spook the Japanese, who began to scatter, and to reduce the effectiveness of the raid.

Moore was excited about it. Spruance refused to get excited. (That was what made him such a great man, Moore suggested.)

The result of this raid was that Moore, the "black shoe," came back with enormous respect for the fliers. "We get them to where they want to go and turn them loose, and then bring them home," he wrote his wife. "They do the fighting and beat off the enemy attacks, and they do it thoroughly and well."

Moore, taking his cue from Spruance, was not so sure of the ability of the surface ships to perform as well as the aviators. The ships were suffering from constantly changing personnel as the fleet burgeoned, and from lack of training, "whereas," said Moore, "the

Japs should have reached perfection." The leavening factor seemed to be the overwhelming might that the United States could place in force.

Moore was concerned particularly about the battleships, and two or three time on this voyage he had tried to give "Ching" Lee a chance to move his battleships out as a tactical unit to practice how to stay closed up in column, how to make simultaneous turns, how to concentrate gunfire on a target. He and Spruance were particularly concerned about Lee's readiness for a night fight, for the Japanese could be more than fearsome at night, with their high degree of training.

Early in April Spruance got the word from Admiral Jacobs that he could not continue to delay the change in chief of staff.

Perhaps one reason for Spruance's success as a naval officer was his ability to keep his neck well protected except on those occasions when he felt it was important to stick it out. A case in point was Spruance's failure to push for Captain Moore's promotion. When Spruance received his fourth star, it was obvious to all, including Moore, that a captain could not much longer persist as chief of staff to a full admiral: such things denied the importance of rank and outraged Navy protocol. But Moore could not understand why Spruance, who had chosen him and who was obviously pleased with Moore's performance, would not push for his promotion. Moore was well aware of the personal antipathy of King, dating back to his days in the Atlantic Fleet, but he was not in a position to know that for many months King had been insisting upon the need of a replacement for Moore, and that the argument of the aviators had settled his fate.

It was a difficult problem for Spruance, for he did not like change in the men around him or, for that matter, to have very many men close around him. Moore suited him to a T. Their relationship, bonded by the comradeship of the "Navy club," transcended that of admiral and captain. Moore could write to his wife that one reason he was sorry to leave Spruance was that "he won't get another chief of staff to do all his work for him and give him hell when he needs it." The relationship worked both ways. Moore was slender, even skinny, and since the chairs in the admiral's cabin in the *New Jersey* were huge overstuffed leather club chairs, too big for him, he tended to nestle in them, cuddling his feet under him. He would sit down to talk to Spruance, and pull his feet up. Spruance would wrinkle his nose.

"I wish you wouldn't put your feet on the furniture," he would say.

"Why not? The deck is perfectly clean. Its just as clean as the chairs are."

"I don't want my trousers to get all dirty sitting where you've had your feet," the admiral would rejoin with asperity.

Spruance tried one last time to save his chief of staff, in a message to Admiral Jacobs, although all concerned knew that by the time matters reached the point of official correspondence the decisions had all been made.

On May 25 Spruance and his staff went aboard the *Indianapolis*, which was his flagship for amphibious operations.

This Marianas move was to be, again, the biggest operation yet attempted in the Pacific. Nimitz commanded no fewer than three forces for this move: Spruance's Fifth Fleet, Lockwood's submarines, and Calhoun's service force.

As tactical commander, Spruance had his Joint Expeditionary Force, under Kelly Turner, the fast carrier forces, under Marc Mitscher, and the land-based aircraft under John Hoover.

Turner, of course, had the landing and the protection of the landed forces. Holland Smith would ride with him on his command ship, and would be in overall command of the ground forces.

The attack on Saipan and Tinian would be carried out by the Fifth Amphibious Corps, which consisted of the Second and Fourth Marine Divisions, with reinforcements. It would come partly from Hawaii and partly from the west coast.

The Southern attack, on Guam, would be under Rear Admiral Richard Conolly. The landings would be made by Major General Roy Geiger of the Marines and the Third Amphibious Corps, which consisted of the Third Marine Division and the First Provisional Marine Brigade. This unit was coming up from the Guadalcanal area.

In reserve was Rear Admiral William H. P. Blandy with the 27th Division of the Army under Major General Ralph Smith.

Some indication of the change in Nimitz's war can be gained from the size of this force: 535 ships carrying 127,500 troops, some of the vessels steaming from the United States to go into battle.

As each operation of the past had been different from all the others, so was this Marianas invasion offering something new. It would be the first move in a large land mass, and if an island six miles by fourteen miles did not seem a large land mass to the Army troops, it certainly did to the Navy and the Marines. That was Saipan. All three islands had important air fields. All three were stoutly defended, all three were long-time possessions of Japan, which meant there were new loyalties to consider.

In the planning, Holland Smith and Turner had worked closely together, along with Harry Hill, who was Turner's second in command in the northern force. Once again the speedy planning and execution of the Marianas operation saved many lives, for when Saipan, for example, was invaded, tough as the opposition was, it was still apparent that the Japanese had not been completely ready. Hill's forces found half-finished emplacements, a battery of three 144 mm guns on railroad cars that could have done serious damage if they had been in operation, and three more 120 mm guns still packed in cosmoline.

The five hundred ships were loaded with new weapons and new techniques. Underwater demolition teams of swimmers had been well trained to deal with beach mines and other defenses since the Gilberts. With the tons of munitions and the thousands of men, Holland Smith and Turner hoped to take the Marianas in eight to ten days. Almost up to the eve of departure, Smith was still revising his figures on the Japanese defenders, and he estimated that there were perhaps 15,000 defenders on Saipan. So much for estimates; there were actually about 32,000 troops there.

Spruance's plan was to move in first with the four carrier task groups of Mitscher's fast carrier force and destroy the planes on Saipan, Tinian, Rota, Guam, and Pagan. Next Hoover's land-based planes would hit Truk, Woleai, Palau, and Yap, to prevent these Japanese bases from sending aid to the Marianas. The carriers, meanwhile, would move on up to the Volcanoes, to hit airfields and shipping at Iwo Jima and Chi Chi Jima. Long-range search planes and submarines would watch out for the Japanese fleet, which might be expected to come out and fight, now that the Americans were invading the inner ring of defenses of the Empire.

The first move was to be made against Saipan, after two days of bombardment. Guam would be next. Then would come Tinian, using the troops that had captured Saipan.

While these landings were taking place Spruance would be with the fighting forces of the Fifth Fleet, looking for the Japanese to come out and engage. The Joint Chiefs of Staff had suggested in March that the Marianas operation would cut off the Japanese bases to the south from that air pipeline that had worked so well for so long. It would give the United States Navy an advanced naval base in these islands, bases for the B-29's, and a jumping-off place for any one of several operations next—which would keep the Japanese guessing and their forces deployed over a wide area.

Spruance went to the Marshalls. All the other forces were also in motion or ready to go in motion, to assemble off the Marianas. On June 6 Spruance was steaming out in *Indianapolis* to join Mitscher's Task Force 58, when at dinner he had a radio message announcing that other invasion on the beaches of Normandy. That night he heard part of a broadcast in which President Roosevelt congratulated the generals for capturing Rome.

On June 7 Spruance was at Eniwetok, and he went ashore to stretch his legs. Then it was off to the war. The plan called for the air strikes to begin on the Marianas on June 12, but on the morn- of the eleventh, Japanese "snoopers" spotted the task force and Mitscher asked for permission to send his strikes out that day. Spruance agreed.

The hundreds of planes of the fifteen carriers continued their aerial bombardment on June 12—then the thirteenth—the fourteenth —and the fifteenth, pulverizing Japanese aerial opposition. The only attempts to strike back came from a group of ten bombers that appeared from Truk on June 12 and did no damage, and by two groups from Yap that came in on the fifteenth, and did no damage either.

On June 14 Rear Admiral Clark's Task Group 58.1 and Rear Admiral Harrill's Task Group 58.4 were sent off to the Volcanoes to neutralize those islands. Harrill was not eager to go, but Clark convinced him that they had that job to do.

On June 13 Spruance received word from the submarine *Red-fin* that the Japanese fleet, stationed at Tawi Tawi in the Philippines, had moved out—battleships, carriers, cruisers, and destroyers. Much later on, Spruance had word from a submarine that Japanese battleships had sailed from Batjan in the Netherlands East Indies, bound for the Pacific.

Whatever else might be said about Jocko Clark, commander of Task Group 58.1, he was a fighting admiral. He went after the "Jimas" with a vengeance, charging in at twenty-five knots to be sure he had enough time to knock them cold. His planes shot down twenty-four fighters over the islands, and destroyed the troop-carrying transport *Tatsutakawa Maru*, and worked over the airfields in the area.

Meanwhile two events were taking place. At Saipan, Admiral Turner was conducting his landing. Spruance had gone in to be "where the action was" on June 13, as the bombardment began. Eight old battleships, eleven cruisers, and twenty-six destroyers began hitting Saipan and Tinian at dawn on June 14. Next day the troops went in to Saipan, but the bombardment had not been as successful as the Navy had hoped, and the defenses on Saipan were very tough, so the going ashore was slow. It was so slow, in fact, that the Second and Fourth Marines did not reach their first day's objective until the third day of battle.

The second event was the sortie of the Japanese fleet, moving into action for the first time in months. On June 15 Spruance had word from the submarine *Flying Fish*. Out of San Bernardino Strait the Japanese were moving a force of battleships, carriers, heavy cruisers, and destroyers. The report was made at 1900 hours, the course was 80 degrees, and the speed was 20 knots. An hour later the submarine *Sea Horse* reported a task force east of the Philippines, course 25 degrees, speed 16.5 knots.

On June 16 Spruance and his chief of staff took boat to Turner's flagship for a conference. They agreed that Turner would continue the unloading. On June 17 all transports not urgently required would be withdrawn. The battleships, cruisers, and destroyers of the bombardment group would cover Saipan to the west, but the Southern Attack Force was going to move east. Spruance was also going to take away some of the cruisers and destroyers that belonged to the expeditionary force, and send them out with the fast carrier force.

At the same time, Spruance ordered Hoover to send six patrol planes to Saipan, prepared to make night searches six hundred miles out to the west. He ordered Mitscher to discontinue support operations at Saipan and to restrict the fast carrier air operations on June 17 to searches and to morning and afternoon neutralization strikes on Guam and Rota.

Rear Admiral Reeves in Task Group 58.3 and Rear Admiral Montgomery in Task Group 58.2 were to rendezvous with the reinforcing units of the expeditionary force on the afternoon of June 17.

By the afternoon of June 17, the task force was back together, with Clark and Harrill back from the north. Mitscher and "Ching" Lee, the battleship commander, had the battle plan. The six battleships, along with cruisers and destroyers, constituted a separate task group.

The battle plan was very simple:

> Our air will first attack out enemy carriers as operating carriers, then will attack enemy battleships and cruisers to slow or disable them. Task group 58.7 (Fast Battleships) will destroy enemy fleet, either by fleet action if enemy elects to fight, or by sinking slowed or crippled ships if enemy retreats. Actions against the retreating enemy must be pushed vigorously by all hands, to insure complete destruction of the fleet. Destroyers running short of fuel may be returned to Saipan if necessary for refuelling.

Spruance soon followed these orders with another dispatch to Mitscher and Lee. "Desire you proceed at your discretion selecting dispositions and movements best calculated to meet the enemy under the most advantageous conditions. I shall issue general directions when necessary and leave details to you and Admiral Lee."

In other words, Spruance's admirals were to run the show, unless he decided they were not doing it right. Only then would he step in.

The Japanese were, indeed, moving out for a battle. Ever since Midway, the naval general staff in Tokyo had wanted a chance to fight the American fleet, under conditions that the Japanese would choose. They had a plan, Operation A-Go, which called for bringing the American fleet to bay south of the Palau-Yap-Wolesi line, where the Japanese surface fleet would have plenty of submarines and land-based air to help out. Later the range was extended to include the Marianas.

On June 11, when the first carrier strike was authorized by Spruance, Admiral Toyoda, commander in chief of the combined fleet, realized that the Americans were moving on the Marianas and he put the A-Go plan into operation. On June 12 Admiral Toyoda ordered Admiral Ugaki to move from the Moluccas with the big battleships *Yamato* and *Musashi*, a handful of cruisers, and many destroyers. Ugaki was to go northeast to the Philippine Sea, where he would meet with Admiral Ozawa, who would bring the main body of the mobile fleet. Ugaki's force was the one reported by the submarine *Seahorse*. Ozawa's movement was that reported by the submarines.

The Japanese were moving, and Spruance was tracking them through the reports of the submarines. On the night of June 17 the submarine *Cavalla* reported fifteen or more large combat ships, moving east at twenty knots, some seven hundred miles west of Guam.

And so the enemies were converging. The two Japanese forces had joined and were coming fast, to do battle and avenge Midway. But how different were the odds: this time it was nine Japanese carriers to 15 American carriers; 430 Japanese carrier planes to 819 American planes; five Japanese battleships to seven fast new American battleships; 13 Japanese cruisers to 21 American cruisers; 28 Japanese destroyers to 69 American destroyers.

On the night of June 17 Spruance did not know that the Japanese units had joined. Neither did Jocko Clark, who was just joining up. Clark, however, considered taking Harrill and steaming to the southwest all night, thus placing himself between the Japanese fleet and their base. He called Harrill on the TBS and talked it over, but Harrill said his orders were to stick with the task force, and he moved off without further ado.

Clark had nearly 350 planes of his own, and he considered going it alone. Had he done so, he would have been either the hero of the battle or the goat. He did not. He joined up and contented himself with criticizing Spruance for not understanding how carriers could be used.

Spruance considered the angles. He asked "Ching" Lee if he wanted a night engagement with the battleships. Lee, who was uncertain of the night training of his ships and of their ability to stay in formation under fire, was emphatic in his statement that he did not want a night engagement.

Spruance decided to behave very much as he had at Midway.

"In my opinion," he told Lee and Mitscher by message, "the main attack will come from the west but might be diverted to come from the southwest. Diversionary attacks could come from either flank or from the empire. Task Force 58 must cover Saipan and the forces engaged there and this can be done best by proceeding west in daylight and toward Saipan at night. Consider it unwise to seek a night engagement in view of our superiority but earliest possible strike on enemy carriers is necessary."

As a tactician, Spruance knew that the Japanese tended to split their forces. Their carrier doctrine called for a split in forces, and this had been reaffirmed by a document found in the South Pacific, a plan captured at Hollandia, which he had received just before sailing on this operation. The Japanese plan was to feint at the center with their carriers, then send diversionary forces around the flank to make a pincers movement.

On June 18 the *Cavalla* reported a force of 15 ships zigzagging on a course of 90 degrees at 19 knots. This led Spruance to believe there were still two forces.

That afternoon *Cavalla* again reported that the ships were coming, but still outside the search area. The carriers were operating, and because of the need to head eastward into the wind, they made only 112 miles west between noon and 2000 hours. On that night of the eighteenth, Hoover's shore-based planes began searching six hundred miles out to the west, starting at 2300 hours.

That night, too, Nimitz sent a message reporting a direction finder fix on an enemy transmission at 2023 hours, 585 miles out from Saipan, at 257 degrees—correct within 100 miles.

Mitscher wanted to change course, heading west, in order to be in a position to launch at 0500. Spruance did not believe the fix. He did believe in Japanese strategy, and fully expected an "end run." (Here was the point that was to become the basis for endless argument. Jocko Clark stated one position succinctly. "If carriers are properly utilized," he said, "it is not possible for surface ships to make an end run around them. A great opportunity to smash the Japanese fleet was lost."

Here was Spruance's reasoning:

1. The position of the direction finder fix was not definite, being within one hundred miles.

2. The originator of the transmission was not definitely known.

3. The size and composition of the force was not known.

4. It was important to guard against a circling movement.

5. The transmission could possibly be from a decoy.

6. A *Stingray* (submarine) transmission had been hammed at 2346 hours, indicating that *Stingray* might be in contact 175 miles ESE of the direction finder fix.

The transmission was in fact real, and it was to the Japanese shore-based aircraft, verifying that they were to go into action with the Japanese fleet. But no one in Spruance's fleet knew this.

Spruance really believed there were two forces operating.

To add to this conviction there came a report, from the submarine *Finback*, of searchlights at still another position. Were there three Japanese forces out? It was not inconceivable.

To add to Spruance's problem, the Japanese *knew* who, what, and where he was. The American force had been trailed all day on June 18 by land-based aircraft.

Jocko Clark and many other aviators have since held that "a great opportunity to smash the Japanese fleet was lost." So have a number of naval historians. The difference between the aviators and the historians is that the aviators said it at the time, and the historians have been armed with something neither Spruance, Mitscher, nor anyone else had on June 18—knowledge of the nature and elements of the Japanese forces. Strange things happen in battle. In a sense, the American superiority over the Japanese at this point was analogous to the Japanese superiority over the Americans at Midway, considering skills and outmoded planes. Spruance could be criticized for not going aggressively after the Japanese fleet (Halsey most certainly would have done so) but had he done so and lost, he would have been ruined and the Marianas invasion might have failed.

He took the position that his primary task was to effect the capture of Saipan, Tinian, and Guam. He would wait for the Japanese fleet to come to him. "The way Togo waited at Tsushima for the Russian fleet to come to him has always been in my mind," Spruance wrote later.

Early on the morning of June 19, Nimitz at Pearl Harbor had a report from a PBM based at Saipan (one of those planes of Hoover's that Spruance had ordered out on the six-hundred-mile sweeps), which showed forty ships in two groups about seventy-five miles northeast of that radio direction finder fix that Spruance distrusted. The trouble was that something slipped somewhere, and although Pearl Harbor had the information, Spruance did not get it for eight hours. Nimitz, then, knew more at Pearl Harbor about the movements of the Japanese than Spruance did. Given Nimitz's knowledge. Spruance probably would have moved west at 0130 in the morning, and been in a position to strike the Japanese fleet at dawn. But there was the luck factor: he did not have the information.

At 0715 in the morning, a combat air patrol from the *Belleau Wood* moved toward Guam when the fighter director saw bogies on his radar screen in that direction, and the planes looked down on the island to see enemy airplanes taking off from the fields. Since those fields had been worked over very heavily on June 17 and 18, the planes must have come from somewhere else. They might have been reinforcements flown up from as far away as Truk. They might be carrier planes landing to refuel. Anyhow, Admiral Mitscher then ordered a sweep over Guam, and nearly a dozen Japanese planes were shot down.

Around 0850 on the morning of June 19, that delayed dispatch from the PBM finally reached Spruance, and at long last he had the true picture as of 0130 in the morning. Mitscher immediately recalled the fighters from Guam, and stopped the launch of Harrill's

Task Group 58.4. The fighters were pulled back to the environs of the task groups.

Still there were problems of interpretation. As Moore recalls:

> A supplementary report of the enemy force indicated that it was in two groups, one of about 30 ships and the other of about 10. In trying to analyze this 1:15 report from the patrol plane, with the other contact reports that we'd had earlier in the evening, it was indicated that the force reported by the patrol plane might have been a concentration of all the groups of Japanese vessels that were operating to westward of us, or it might have been (1) the concentration of two or more groups, or it might still have been (2) a single group. So it didn't really mean an awful lot even then, but it didn't preclude the possibility of a flanking movement, either to the north or south, as well as a movement in from the westward.

That second report had come from the same search plane, and had been picked up by Jocko Clark's communications section, then relayed to Mitscher, then to Spruance. At 1000 hours the radar picked up a large bogie bearing 265 degrees about 125 miles away, heading in from the west. It was apparent that this represented a Japanese carrier air strike. Mitscher recalled all fighters to defend their carriers, and sent the dive bombers and torpedo planes off the carriers to orbit east of Guam, thus freeing the decks to launch, land, and service fighters only. At 1004 the carriers sounded General Quarters, and 450 F-6-F Hellcat fighters took off, along with a few F-4-U night fighters, to intercept the Japanese.

Japanese Admiral Ozawa was undertaking a daring operation. On the evening of June 17 Ozawa knew very well what he was up against. He knew that two carrier groups had attacked Chi Chi Jima and Iwo Jima on June 15 and 16. He knew that two other carrier groups were refueling. He knew that the landing force on Saipan had its own escort carriers. He also thought he knew what Spruance would do. The Japanese had captured documents which showed that Mitscher was in command of Task Force 58. The Japanese had interrogated captured aviators and discovered that

Spruance was in command of the whole fleet. Ozawa knew his American admirals, and on Spruance's record Ozawa inferred that the American would behave as he had at Midway, not moving west of the Marianas, but waiting for the Japanese to come to him.

In almost every way the Japanese fleet was inferior to the American—except in one way that might count for very much on this day. All the way along, the Japanese had sacrificed pilot safety for range and maneuverability in their planes; Nimitz and King had steadfastly refused to follow suit, guided by the American concern for personnel. The American planes had self-sealing gas tanks and heavy armor. Consequently their outward range from their carrier was limited to about 350 miles, while the Japanese range was 550 miles. The Japanese, then, could attack at least three hours before the Americans in almost any given situation for, even with bomb loads, the Japanese planes had a range of about a hundred more miles outward than the Americans.

Admiral Ozawa had another advantage. In the days of fighting sail it was called the lee gauge, meaning that Ozawa was traveling against the wind. In steam the lee gauge meant little, but in carrier operations, it was back again to the days of sail, in reverse, for a carrier could launch and recover planes handily while proceeding against the wind, and Ozawa had the eastern trade wind against him.

Ozawa believed he had another vital advantage: the help of five hundred land-based planes. But here Vice Admiral Kakuta, commander of Ozawa's land-based air in the Marianas, had played his superior false by not revealing the damage done by the American air strikes to his forces. Instead of five hundred land-based planes, he had practically none.

On June 18 the Japanese had made a tactical attempt which might go down in Japanese naval history with as much controversy as Spruance's decision to stay close to the Marianas. Rear Admiral Obayashi, commander of a divsion of three carriers, and a Jocko Clark type, decided on his own initiative to launch a strike against Spruance, on the basis of a report from a search plane which had found the American force 420 miles out. He had actually put planes in the air for the strike, when he received a new operations order from Ozawa ordering the mobile fleet to retire temporarily, spend the night, and then hit the Americans first thing in the morning. Admiral Obayashi called his planes back. Had they gone out, with the intention of striking in the evening and then landing at Guam, they might have done very serious damage. Perhaps this was Japan's lost opportunity.

The most interesting aspect to the chess game as of the night of June 18–19 was that the Japanese air operations were so much more successful than those of the Americans, in terms of search and the passage of information to the commander of the force. The superior searching of the Japanese had given them a definite advantage. Jocko Clark, quick to criticize Spruance for caution, might have examined the responsibility of the carrier search forces and how they carried it out. (Morison has suggested [Vol. VIII, p. 245] that the air search might have contributed a good deal more to the American effort on June 18, when the Japanese might have been found.)

But whatever the reasons one might conjure up in retrospect, the result of the maneuvering, up to this moment, was that the battle of the Philippine Sea was joined when that big blip came in on the radar screens at 1000 hours on June 19. The Americans were on the defensive; the Japanese had their position and had launched the first punch. Wave after wave of Japanese planes headed toward the American fleet, and plane after plane was shot down by Mitscher's fighters. Or, if they escaped the American fighters—because there were so many melees in the air—the antiaircraft guns of the fleet splashed them into the sea. Attacks were pressed home on Reeves's and Montgomery's task groups and on the battleship group, but the only ship that got a direct hit from a bomb was the *South Dakota. Minneapolis, Wasp,* and *Bunker Hill* were damaged by near misses, but not enough to interfere seriously with their competence.

Admiral Ozawa sent out four strikes, between 1000 and 1500 hours. They were simply decimated by the highly organized American carrier air force. In the first raid the Japanese sent 69 planes, and 42 did not return to their carriers. In the second, they launched 128 planes, and 97 disappeared. The third strike was more fortunate;

40 of 47 planes returned to their carriers, but most of them did not find the Americans. The fourth raid consisted of 82 planes, and 73 of these were shot down or put out of action on land airstrips.

The Japanese attacks failed because of superior American air organization, superior American planes, and superior American pilots. Take the last as an indicator: the American pilots had two years' training and at least three hundred hours' flying time. The Japanese pilots at this time, most of them, had between six months' and two months' training. The attrition of the carriers and of the land-based air strikes against the Japanese-held islands had shown its effectiveness this day. As for the planes, they were the result of the careful attention to detail and fighting needs by Admiral Towers, Admiral McCain, Admiral Radford, and the other officers who had served in the Bureau of Aeronautics, where the responsibility lay. As for organization, the secret was in communications and the way they were used. The fighter directors sent the planes where they were needed when they were needed. The result was so one-sided a battle that the encounter has become known in history as the Marianas Turkey Shoot: some four hundred Japanese planes from carriers and the islands were put out of action, while the Americans lost about thirty to enemy fire and the accidents of operations.

In the afternoon the submarine *Cavalla* reported that she torpedoed a Japanese carrier of the *Shokaku* class. (It was *Shokaku*.) Shortly afterward *Albacore* torpedoed the carrier *Taiho*. Both sank, but in the confusion of battle Spruance did not know that either was sunk, or that more than one had been hit. The task force was too far away from the enemy to do anything about it at the moment anyhow. All day long the carriers had been heading into the wind to launch and recover planes, then back westward when they might, to close the distance on the enemy. But late afternoon found Task Force 58 only about forty miles from Guam. In the evening Spruance detached Harrill's groups to refuel, making strikes on Guam and Rota on their way to the rendezvous.

Spruance also sent a night message to Mitscher: "Desire to attack enemy tomorrow if we know his position with sufficient accuracy. If our patrol planes give us required information tonight no searches should be necessary. If not we must continue searches tomorrow to insure adequate protection for Saipan. Point Option should be advanced to the westward as much as air operations permit."

But again the searches were not forthcoming from the carriers, although Mitscher had the twenty-four night fighters which could have covered every sector out to four hundred miles (see Morison, Vol. VIII, p. 285). Ozawa might have been found by a night search, and if so, he could have been attacked at dawn. It is not to fault Mitscher, or Spruance either. Morison indicated that Mitscher was concerned about his pilots and not confident of night fighter operations.

But if at this time the American problem was lack of information, it was the same for the Japanese. Admiral Ozawa had lost two carriers (which Spruance did not know but Ozawa did), but he had also lost nearly all the planes he had sent out (which Ozawa did not know but Spruance did). Radio Tokyo was claiming eleven American carriers sunk, and the pilots who did get back from the Turkey Shoot claimed to have downed hundreds of American planes. Ozawa was ready to refuel and rejoin the battle next day.

At Pearl Harbor, Admiral Nimitz was unhappy. Not upset, not distressed, not lacking in confidence of his fleet commander, but unhappy. He sat down late on June 19 to let Spruance know exactly how he felt:

We are following with the closest interest your operations around the Marianas, and we share with you a feeling which I know you must have—that of frustration in our failure to bring our carrier superiority to bear on the Japanese fleet during the last few days. We all understand, of course, that the Japanese had better information of our whereabouts through their shorebased long range search than we had of their locations. It was exasperating to have one of the early reports of the first long range search conducted from Saipan be delayed eight hours in reaching you. Whether or not the situation would have been different had this delay not occurred is of course problematical. It now appears that the Jap fleet is

retiring for replenishment and that following a short period
for this purpose we may have another chance at it. If they
come back, I hope you will be able to bring them into
action. . . .

Spruance was in touch with Mitscher that morning of June 20:

Damaged *Zuikaku* may still be afloat. If so, believe she
will be most likely heading northwest. Desire to push our
searches today as far westward as possible. If no contacts
with the enemy fleet result, consider it an indication fleet is
withdrawing and further pursuit after today will be unprofitable.
If you concur retire tonight toward Saipan. Will order out
tankers of Task Group 58.4 and direct Task Group 58.4 to
remain in the vicinity of Saipan. *Zuikaku* must be sunk if we
can reach her.

It was not until the middle of the afternoon that a search plane
found the Japanese fleet, apparently heading toward Okinawa or
Japan, Spruance believed. Ozawa had been planning to fuel, but
when the Americans were sighted coming toward him, the refueling
was canceled. Ozawa still planned to strike the next day, until he discovered in a check on the fleet how serious the plane losses had been.

If Mitscher's search planes had been out in the morning, they
would perhaps have found the Japanese, and the strikes could have
begun early. As it was, the planes did not begin launching until
after 1600 hours. The planes had a long flight, about 350 miles,
and by the time they arrived over the Japanese fleet, at 1840, they
had little fuel and little time. The report at the time was that one
Hitaka-class carrier was sunk, one damaged and burning, one
Shokaku-class carrier took three or four 1000-pound bomb hits, a
light carrier was hit at least once, a battleship of the *Kongo* class
was hit, a heavy cruiser was damaged, a destroyer was sunk and
two damaged, and three oilers sunk and two burning, and fifteen
or twenty planes were shot down.

Actually, two oilers went first. Then the carrier *Hiyo* was
torpedoed and sunk. *Zuikaku* was hit but managed to reach port.

The carrier *Chiyoda*'s flight deck was wrecked. The battleship *Haruna* was damaged. But by nightfall the Japanese had lost another 65 planes, and of the 430 on the decks of the carriers a day earlier, only 35 were left.

As the carrier planes from the American task force headed home, darkness fell. Jocko Clark takes credit for having been the one to suggest that the carrier lights be turned on. Mitscher ordered the whole force to light up, and Spruance agreed. Twenty planes were lost that day in operations against the enemy, eighty in the confusions of the night recovery. But only sixteen pilots and thirty-three crewmen failed to come back.

So for practical purposes, the battle was over. Questions were later raised. Mitscher, it is said, asked Spruance to release "Ching" Lee's battleships to make a stern chase against the Japanese, and Spruance refused to do so. Next morning the searches began again, but nothing was found. When nothing was found on June 22 either, the battle was at an end.

At Pearl Harbor there were daily meetings of the kibitzers' club. Halsey was there. He, Towers, Calhoun, and others sat around reading the messages and talking. In the beginning Towers was furious. "I told them not to send him out there," he complained to General Leavey, the Army logistics man, after the second day of the operation. But then, after the Marianas Turkey Shoot, when it was obvious that Spruance was seeking out the enemy, Towers' view changed. "I was wrong," he said. "Spruance is a great man."

The carrier task group commanders were uniform in their unhappiness that the enemy had gotten away, and they believed it was the great chance missed.

At Pearl Nimitz was calm. If the tension grew strong, he would go out beside the building to his little shooting gallery and go after the targets with his .22 pistol. Captain Anderson, the fleet medical officer who had replaced Captain Gendreau, had dreamed up the shooting gallery on the principle that target shooting takes total concentration, and Nimitz could not worry while he was squeezing that trigger. It seemed to work, in more than one way. The newspaper correspondents, seeing Nimitz on his shooting

range, would jump to the happy if erroneous conclusion that everything must be fine if the "old man" could play with his popguns.

So the Battle of the Philippine Sea ended in anticlimax, because
so many had expected so much. Yet the fact was that it was a fair
victory by any standards. Three of the Japanese carriers were sunk,
and two were very badly damaged. Never again would Japanese
carrier-based air power play a decisive dole in the Pacific war.

Spruance really had very little time to consider whether or not
he was disappointed; he still carried too much responsibility. The
fighting was going very slowly on Saipan. The invasion of Guam
had been delayed by the Turkey Shoot, and the invasion of Tinian
had still to be accomplished. His primary mission was to take the
Marianas, and he turned back to it.

But he did sum up his views on the fleet action in a letter to
Nimitz a few days later.

To go back to ancient history now—the sortie of the Jap
fleet. To begin with, as you know I doubted if they would
come out after us, particularly in view of their failure to support Biak, where they had a great superiority. When they did
leave the Philippines, I thought that my estimate of their
strategical attitude had been all wrong and that they had decided to risk everything in a determined attack on us while we
were engaged in the early and critical part of a large amphibious
operation.

For the second time it turned out I was wrong. Their
attitude about risking their fleet had not changed. Their
methods of operation had changed, in that they were using
carriers again. They intended to use their fleet to exploit any
advantages that their carrier air might gain. They had no intention of throwing everything at us by coming in to Saipan
at high speed to fight it out.

With the information which we had of their most recent
plans all of which fitted well with what we know of their past
operations, I felt it was necessary to remain with Task Force
58 in air supporting distance of Saipan until we knew definitely
the location of the major portion of the Japanese fleet. We

could not afford to be drawn off to the westward by a diversion created by a portion of their fleet, while the remainder of it was enabled to go around one of our flanks and hit our transports and cargo ships at Saipan or in the areas eastward of Saipan.

He noted how he had sent out 325-mile searches on June 18 at 0530 and 1330, then retired back at night to support Saipan. He noted the failure of the PBM report of that evening to reach him. He noted that next morning he was close enough to Guam and Rota to smash those fields and the planes that landed there, and recalled how they had chased the Japanese fleet. But by this time Spruance's attention was focused on the difficult battle for the Marianas themselves.

Chapter
Twenty-Two

THE PLAN TURNED
UPSIDE DOWN

June 13–September 18, 1944

Almost from the beginning, the fighting on Saipan was desperate. In the first bombardment, on June 13, the fast battleships had not scored at all well. Their crews had never completed training in bombardment procedures, because they had been fully occupied in learning the new techniques of seamanship in working with the fast carriers. The first day's work was pretty miserable. The second day, Spruance was better pleased with the bombardment by the experienced officers and men in the fire-support groups of the old battleships and smaller ships, but any optimism was premature. All the way around, fighting on the bigger island was going to be a different matter from taking those atolls where the ground area could be measured in hundreds of acres.

The Japanese believed they could defend the Marianas against American attack, and so spirits were even stouter there than on other islands. There was no easy time for the first waves here. The assault Marines were fighting for their lives the moment they left the amphtracs.

The landings themselves were accomplished with more skill than before—the amphibious men learned every day. But on the first night, June 15, the landing forces were far from their objective. They did not attain that first day's objective until the third day— June 17. Thus, when Jocko Clark and Marc Mitscher were only worrying about the Japanese fleet, Spruance, even though he had moved away from the beaches, was very much aware that the Saipan invasion was not going according to plan. The Army 27th Division had been held in reserve for Saipan, and it began moving in on June 16 and June 17.

There were anxious moments for Lieutenant General Holland Smith, particularly when Kelly Turner announced that in view of the impending fleet and air battle, he was taking the transport fleet and the supporting forces out to sea. There were anxious moments for Rear Admiral Harry Hill, when he found himself on the *Cambria*, with a handful of destroyers and a few transports and smaller craft, sitting at Saipan feeling all alone. There were 78,000 men ashore then, and everyone who knew what was happening was very nervous, even though the beachhead had been secured on June 17.

On June 19 elements of the 27th Division pushed behind Aslito airfield to the east coast of Saipan. A Japanese plane landed on Aslito that day, its pilot unaware that the strip was in American hands.

Things ashore were going well enough that on the morning of June 20 Holland Smith formally took over control of the ground forces on Saipan from Kelly Turner. Next day, the Battle of the Philippine Sea at an end, Admiral Turner brought the transports and the support ships back to Saipan and the tempo of the invasion stepped up.

On June 22 Holland Smith moved the Army 27th Division in between the Second and Fourth Marine Divisions. He planned a broad sweep across the island. But while the two Marine divisions moved ahead on schedule, the 27th did not, and by nightfall of June 23 it had not moved satisfactorily at all; and instead of a straight line of troops across the island there was a U, with the 27th in the depression of the U. That day Holland Smith spoke to Major General Sandeford Jarman, who was to be island commander of Saipan once it was taken. Holland Smith persuaded Jarman to go up front and talk to Ralph Smith, who promised to move his troops along.

But on June 24 the troops of the 27th were still bogged down, and they were slowing the advance of the Marines on their left and right flanks.

Holland Smith had little patience with the 27th Division by this time. He recalled their slowness at Makin, and their ineffectuality at Engebi, which had caused Harry Hill to employ exhausted Marines to take Parry island. On June 24 Holland Smith took his battle maps and went aboard Kelly Turner's flagship *Rocky Mount*. He had prepared an official letter asking for Ralph Smith's relief. Kelly Turner was a hot-tempered man himself, but this matter was not one in which temper played a part. Holland Smith went into great detail about the operations from the time of landing. "His account," wrote Turner, "closely coincided with my impression of events, which I had carefully followed through troop reports and oral reports given by various staff officers."

Turner indicated that Holland Smith had every right to relieve the other Smith if he wished. But both knew that since Army troops were involved there would be hell to pay between the services. Therefore they agreed to go over to the *Indianapolis* and talk it over with Spruance. Here is Captain Moore's recollection of that meeting:

Admiral Turner and General Smith and Admiral Spruance and I sat around the table in the *Indianapolis* cabin for an hour or more, discussing this situation and what might be done about it. Holland Smith had told us that General Sandeford Jarman who had been designated as the garrison command after Saipan had been captured, was available, and that General Jarman had indicated his disgust also with the performance of the 27th Division and said that by gosh, he could make them fight, and if they'd give him command of the division he'd see that they did fight.

This discussion "bid fair to be rather endless," Moore observed, and he busied himself by drafting a dispatch to Holland Smith, authorizing and directing him to replace Ralph Smith.

Thus Spruance took full responsibility for the relief of Ralph Smith.

Back at Pearl Harbor, the fat began to sputter in the fire. Richard Haller of International News Service came to McArdle.

"When are you going to release the fact that Ralph Smith has been relieved as commander of the 27th Division?"

McArdle replied that officially he knew nothing about the relief. Where had Haller heard the tale?

"It's all over town," Haller said. "I heard it from one of the general's close friends."

McArdle knew there was no point in trying to conceal the scandal, so he included a paragraph on the relief in the communiqué on which he was working, and then took it down to the office of the chief of staff.

Admiral McMorris scanned the communiqué, until he came to the reference to Ralph Smith.

"No!" he shouted. And he scratched out the paragraph with a flourish.

"It's all over Honolulu," said McArdle.

"Who told 'em?" demanded McMorris fiercely (as though McArdle must have done it).

"Fifty thousand men on Saipan know it," said McArdle. "You can't keep a thing like that quiet."

"The answer is NO," said McMorris, and turned back to his papers.

Like Jocko Clark, McArdle was not above defying Navy protocol when he thought he was right. He went to see Captain Austin, the new assistant chief of staff, who had replaced Preston Mercer as "interlocutor" between the public relations men and Admiral Nimitz, in view of McMorris' proclivities for a short, sharp answer.

McArdle argued the public relations point of view, that it was senseless to try to sit on the scandal. Soon, he said, the story would break in the United States and it would sound much worse than if the plain facts had been released.

Austin agreed and took the matter up with Admiral Nimitz. He was gone perhaps ten minutes, while McArdle waited in the office.

"The answer is still no," Austin said when he returned. "The admiral is going to say nothing of the incident; the War Department can make such announcement as it cares to. You see," he added, "the admiral doesn't want to do anything to hurt Ralph Smith."

But if Admiral Nimitz's silence in this matter helped Smith, it did nothing to help Army-Navy relations. A few days after the incident, the news of Ralph Smith's relief broke in Washington. But the implication of the stories was that Holland Smith was the "butcher" he had been declared to be after Tarawa, and that Ralph Smith was relieved because he refused to obey Holland Smith's orders, not wanting to send his men to almost certain slaughter. Another version—certainly less complimentary to the Army than the truth—had it that some of Ralph Smith's soldiers had refused to move into action.

Nor was the bad press the end of the affair. On July 12, Lieutenant General Richardson, commander of Army forces in the Pacific, arrived in Saipan on a visit. He made a display of decorating members of the 27th Division, which was normal enough for a commander. But he did not check in with Spruance or with Kelly Turner, as protocol indicated he should.

Spruance did not care for such protocol, and when Richardson's failure was brought to his attention he quite ignored the fact. But Kelly Turner's quick temper was aroused. Turner had never been noted for his tenderness toward the Army (particularly after General Marshall's complaints about him) and he chose to look upon Richardson's actions as a personal affront.

On July 13 Turner called Captain Moore over to the *Rocky Mount,* and when Moore got there Turner announced that he was going to "bawl out General Richardson" for not reporting either to him or to Holland Smith when he got to Saipan.

"For goodness' sake, Kelly," said Moore, "this seems to me an awful thing to do. It may give you some satisfaction but it isn't going to do a bit of good for the war or the force for you to raise that kind of an issue."

"I'm going to do it anyhow," said Turner.

Moore thought Turner had a hangover. Kelly Turner had a reputation as a two-fisted drinking man. Spruance said that when Turner was finished with an operation there was always a period in which he took a lot of liquor after working hours. Next morning he was always sharp and cool again. As for Nimitz, he, too, knew of Turner's drinking habits, but his answer was that he never saw Turner when he was incapable of doing his duty or thinking straight. And as far as criticism went, Nimitz was wont to cock an eye, grin, and remind his questioner of Lincoln's remarks about Grant. Maybe someone would let Nimitz know what Kelly Turner's brand was so he could feed it to some of his other admirals.

In this particular case, hangover or not, Turner laced Richardson up and down for not checking it. Richardson was furious. He said he had been affronted and left the cabin. He then went to Spruance's flagship and reported on the incident.

"Oh, well," said Spruance, trying to laugh it off. "That's just Kelly Turner. Nobody pays any attention to him."

Obviously this was not one of Turner's best moments. At about this time, also, on learning of the relief of Ralph Smith, Nimitz had asked Turner and Spruance some pointed questions by dispatch, about the use of the forces that would take Guam. Turner had replied snappily—which one did not do to Nimitz under any conditions—and Nimitz informed Spruance that he considered Turner's reply insubordinate.

That Nimitz reaction demanded immediate attention, for as anyone in the command knew, it would take only one word from Nimitz to put Kelly Turner out of a job. The best way to anger Nimitz was through insubordination; he would be almost superhumanly patient with any human error, but he would not bear insubordination for a moment.

Turner was quick to deny any intention of insubordination. Spruance came Turner's aid. "I talked to Turner about his Top Secret dispatch to you," said Spruance. "Turner is overly frank and emphatic at times, very decided in his opinions, sometimes impulsive, but I don't believe he ever has any intention of being insubordinate. In the present case I feel sure he had not. I am sorry that it happened, and I have every expectation that such a thing will not occur in the future."

Nimitz cooled off, as he usually did when reassured by people he trusted.

In the middle of July Nimitz had a chance to come to the Marianas and see for himself what was going on. King had come to Hawaii for an inspection, and Nimitz brought the Commander in Chief out to Saipan for a look.

On the night of July 17, all the brass in the Marianas assembled aboard the *Indianapolis* for dinner. Strategy and tactics were forgotten for the night, but the evening was memorable because of the presence of an infestation of great sluggish flies, nearly an inch long, swarming about the ship.

Next day the fate of Captain Moore was again an issue. His friends suggested that Moore take a job with Admiral McCain as chief of staff (McCain being an aviator). But to Moore this job represented a comedown. He had been chief of staff to the commander of the Fifth Fleet. Now he was being asked to take the job of chief of staff to the commander of the task force—in other words, to step down one whole echelon of command. Actually, Moore should have been a rear admiral to hold the job he had, and need be only a captain to take the job he was offered. It was like saying to a professional Navy officer: "We don't like you, we will not promote you, but we need you, so come and let us rub your nose in the dirt."

At least, that was how Captain Moore regarded the invitation. He turned it down in terms so plain that Spruance spent the evening shushing him up lest King and Nimitz hear. From that moment on, for Moore it was simply a matter of waiting to be detached and sent to other duty, the nature of which he would not know until he got his orders. (Those orders sent him back to Washington in a staff job, where he served the remainder of the war.)

The battle for Saipan was officially over, having ended on July 10 when the flag was raised at Holland Smith's headquarters. On July 12 Major General Harry Schmidt of the Marines relieved Holland Smith in command of the troops on the island. The mopping up continued for three weeks, during which time many Japanese soldiers, civilians, and Chamorros killed themselves, for this was the first thoroughly japanized land the Americans had encountered.

To Holland Smith Saipan was the decisive battle of the Pacific. His point of view is supported by events in Japan: on the day that the loss of Saipan was announced in Tokyo, the Tojo cabinet resigned. For the first time the Americans had breached the inner limits of the Empire.

Tinian was to be taken next. Admiral Turner appointed Rear Admiral Harry Hill to command the Task Force 52 that would attack the island, and Marine General Harry Schmidt was chosen by Holland Smith to lead the ground forces.

From June 14, Tinian had been bombarded by fire-support ships and later by artillery of the XXIV Army Corps from the southern shore of Saipan. The distance across the strait that separated the islands was three miles. Across that water more than thirty thousand rounds of ammunition were delivered in the course of the operation.

Given the assignment of capturing Tinian, Harry Hill began to look over the plans. The Turner plan called for a landing at Tinian Town, but Hill was positive that the Japanese were expecting them there, and he did not like it at all. Studying the aerial photographs, he was drawn to two little white beaches on the northwest shore of the island—"handkerchief size" as far as landings were concerned. Hill went ashore on Saipan then, and looked up Schmidt for a talk. Schmidt called in his chief of staff, William Rogers, and his operations officer, Colonel Robert Hogaboom, and General Erskine, the chief of staff to Holland Smith. They agreed that the white beaches were best for the purposes of surprise if Hill could manage to put the troops in there effectively, and Hill believed he could.

Hill then took his plan, and the indications of Marine backing, and went aboard the *Rocky Mount* to discuss it with Turner. As Hill had half expected, Turner exploded. The answer was no. Hill could damned well stop that planning right that moment and perfect the operations plans for the Tinian Town invasion—as ordered.

Harry Hill went back to the *Cambria* a very unhappy admiral,

which was unusual for him. He was gay and smiling as a rule, free
with his staff and popular with his men. Life aboard the *Cambria*
tended to be light-hearted when there was no desperate work to
be done, for Hill was the exact opposite of his senior admiral. He
was the leader who inspired rather than the driver who manipulated.
His officers all had nicknames and broke themselves up in the
wardroom at dinner recalling their own didoes in operations past—
how "Squeaky" Anderson, the beachmaster, had done this or that
—and even the admiral's actions were not above examination.

But this day there was no levity aboard the *Cambria*, for Harry
Hill was making a vital decision. In the end he stuck with what he
knew to be right, and prepared to lay his career on the line. Turner
had ordered him flatly to stop planning for the white beaches. Instead Hill split his staff in two, half working on the white beaches
plan, half working on the Tinian Town plan.

J-Day—the day to go in—was set for July 12 by Turner. It
would be July 24.

On July 24 Hill went back to Admiral Turner, who refused to
listen to any talk about the white beaches. Then Hill swallowed
hard and began his desperate foray. He took his plan for the white
beaches to Holland Smith. Smith liked it. With that backing, Hill
took the plan over Turner's head to Admiral Spruance. The senior
admiral said he approved. Then Spruance said he would call a
meeting to settle the matter, and Hill agreed.

They met aboard the *Indianapolis*: Major General Schmidt,
Major General Watson of the Second Marines, Major General
Clifton Cates of the Fourth Marines, Vice Admiral Kelly Turner,
and Rear Admiral Hill, all sitting around Spruance's conference
table.

Hill laid out his plan. They discussed it, as he looked sidelong
at Kelly Turner. Then Spruance called for votes.

Watson—For
Cates—For
Schmidt—For
Hill—For
Spruance—For
And what did Turner think, Spruance asked.

"I'm for it," said Turner.

Admiral Hill breathed a long sigh of relief. But he was not out of the woods yet. "Having forced the issue with Turner, it was *imperative* that the plan succeed," said Hill.

He went back to the *Cambria* and redoubled his efforts to make sure there were no holes in the white beaches plan. A few days before the scheduled invasion, Commander Louis W. Mang came to see Hill. Mang was an Academy graduate, and his father was a friend of Hill's from the distant days when Hill had been teaching at the Academy. In 1944 Mang was an aviator, sent out from the states to field-test a new device: the napalm bomb. He showed Admiral Hill how airplane wing tanks could be converted into fire bombs by filing them with napalm and fusing them. Hill was intrigued. In the battle for Saipan the Japanese had contested each yard of territory more ferociously than ever before—one reason Hill wanted to move into the white beaches in the northwest rather than the broad beaches of the south at Tinian Town. Surprise was a weapon of value. So, it seemed, could be this new napalm. The idea of fire was not new; the Marines were using fire from flame throwers to burn Japanese soldiers in their caves and blockhouses. But the use that Mang outlined was staggering in its potential.

Admiral Hill ordered 8500 pounds of napalm from Pearl Harbor by airplane, and the imperturbable men of the service force accepted this recondite demand and fulfilled it without a hitch. Commander Mang began building his bombs at Aslito airfield.

When the first bombs were ready, Hill brought Spruance, Turner, and the Marine generals aboard a destroyer and took them down near Tinian Town for an exhibition. Mang hooked his bombs to a P-51 fighter, and the plane took off, the pilot instructed to come in low and fast and skip-bomb his target, which was on a piece of flat land near the shore.

The run was made, the improvised bomb was dropped, and the field that was the target suddenly erupted in flame as though a gunpowder fuze were being lighted—except that instead of flaming up and going out the napalm burned, and burned, and burned. From the flagship Hill measured the strip burned by the one bomb: it was a hundred yards long and thirty yards wide.

Having convinced the Japanese even more firmly by such activity that Tinian Town was the target, Hill continued to plan for the little beaches. On July 17 the plan was issued; it included the use of portable ramps and floating gas stations, ideas that had been wild dreams a few months earlier.

Meanwhile, on July 21 Rear Admiral Richard Conolly made the long-delayed landing on Guam, marked by the longest sustained bombardment of the war to date—thirteen days—conducted with great skill by Admiral Conolly. It was the most effective naval bombardment of the war, too, knocking out nearly every emplacement that was not either buried or mobile. Marine Major General R. S. Geiger was in charge of the troops, and he comported himself brilliantly in the field against very heavy Japanese opposition. The Marianas represented full-scale fighting: the Japanese staged tank counterattacks and fought with big guns all the way. By the end of the fighting, the Americans had put 54,000 men in the field, to account for 19,000 Japanese. General Geiger said that organized resistance ended on August 10, but resistance never did end; 8500 of those Japanese were killed or captured after August 10, and even at the time of the Japanese surrender in 1945 a lieutenant colonel and 113 officers and men were still at large on the island.

On J-1, or July 23, Admiral Hill divided Tinian into five sectors for bombardment purposes. Very heavy attention was given to Tinian Town, to persuade the Japanese that the Americans were indeed coming into those heavily mined and fortified beaches. A single cruiser worked over the white beach area, but the battleship *Colorado* banged away at Faibus San Hilo Point, destroying a battery of three 140 mm guns which could have played hob with the landing next day. After all, the white beaches were so narrow that not more than eight landing craft could land abreast. Hill sent minesweepers in to comb the area around Tinian Town, again to increase the illusion that this would be the landing place.

Next morning the troops began to land. Transports carrying the Second Marine Division moved off the beaches of Tinian Town, and the Marines climbed down into landing craft which sped in toward shore at 0730 hours. The Japanese opened fire with mortars, and a mile off the beach the landing craft reversed and went back to the transports. The landing had failed!

Indeed it had—just as this fake landing was supposed to fail, further leading the Japanese to believe Tinian Town was the target, and to persuade Admiral Kakuta and Colonel Kiyochi Ogata to concentrate the island's nine thousand defenders in that area. The Japanese were further exhilarated by their own good artillery shooting. Their coastal guns here scored six hits on destroyer *Norman Scott* and 22 hits on the *Colorado*, killing some 60 men, including the captain of the destroyer, and wounding nearly 150 more.

Meanwhile the real landings were beginning on the white beaches to the northwest, the first wave of amphtracs hitting the beach at 0750, and fourteen waves following on their heels. Two amphtracs were knocked out by mines on White 2, but the landings were comparatively easy—only fifteen officers and men were killed on both beaches. Two unhurt pillboxes caused some trouble on White 2, and so did some more mines, but the marines kept coming in and moving on. That evening the portable ramps began to go into place, and next morning loaded trucks could roll directly out of LST's onto the land. By the close of J-day 15,614 Marines, soldiers, and sailors were ashore. It was the beginning of what Admiral Spruance called "the most brilliantly conceived and executed amphibious operation of the war."

On J+1 the Japanese staged a strong counterattack, but it failed. On J+4 the first planes landed on the airstrip. On J+8 Tinian was secured. The cost was 389 Americans killed and 1816 wounded, against more than 5000 Japanese killed and a handful taken prisoner. Even these figures, as always, represented only the American count. There had been 9000 defenders. What happened to the other 4000 Japanese? Some escaped, but most must have committed suicide deep in the caves where they were hidden.

At the end, as the Japanese and their supporters were driven to the high ground that overlooked the sea in the southern part of the island, Harry Hill watched a drama that had been played also on Saipan and on Guam. The Japanese were trying to effect a mass suicide. The Americans brought up a public address system on a jeep, to talk to the crowd on the plateau two hundred feet above the sea, a crowd of Japanese soldiers and thousands of civilian men, women, and children. Japanese-language officers spoke to them, asking them to give up. They would not be hurt. The Japanese answer came when a dozen soldiers threw themselves over the cliff into the sea. The Japanese-language officers spoke again. A Japanese blew himself up with a grenade. Another grenade went off in a crowd of soldiers and civilians, and it seemed to set off some kind of bomb, for dozens of arms, legs, and torsos were suddenly cascaded bloodily into the air. Then the civilians ran for the American line to surrender, the remainder of the Japanese soldiers fled to caves or to leap over the cliff, and the affair was over.

Almost anywhere one looked in the summer of 1944 there was furious activity. Admiral Clark concocted and conducted a brilliant raid on the Volcano Islands (Iwo and Chi Chi Jima), netting scores of planes and a whole convoy of ships before he was finished. At Pearl Harbor, Admiral William Halsey was organizing his Third Fleet, which would employ the same ships and planes as the Fifth Fleet. The difference would be that Halsey and his staff would take out the Third Fleet, with Vice Admiral McCain as commander of the fast carrier task force, which would, under him, be known as Task Force 38. Meanwhile Spruance would come ashore to plan with his staff for his next operation, and Admiral Mitscher would also leave the fleet with Spruance. The plan was to alternate the commands, thus using the same ships for tasks that followed each other like clockwork.

On June 15 Halsey was detached officially from the South Pacific, and Vice Admiral Newton took over. Three days later Halsey was ensconced in offices in the new JICPOA building (Joint Intelligence Center Pacific Ocean Areas), planning for the occupation of the western Caroline islands. The Joint Chiefs of Staff were still talking about the route to Tokyo. Admiral King was committed to the idea of bypassing the Philippines and mounting the next major offensive against Formosa. He ordered Nimitz to draw up such a plan, and reluctantly Nimitz put Forrest Sherman to work on it. Sherman drew up the plan, but he hated it. He said he hoped he had drawn such a bad plan that it would be thrown out, because he believed that to move against Formosa without first taking at least Luzon in the Philippines, with all its available airfields and supplies, would be to court annihilation in Formosa, with attacks from two fronts. But what to do? Everybody seemed to have a different idea. Nimitz wanted to take the western Carolines first, then invade the central Philippines, and Iwo Jima. Halsey wanted to bypass the Carolines, then take the central Philippines, Iwo Jima, Okinawa, and Japan. Spruance wanted to go to the Carolines, but not Yap, and then to Nimrod sound, south of Shanghai. Kelly Turner talked of going directly to Japan with a huge amphibious force.

MacArthur, of course, was steadfast in his plan: to move to Luzon, take the Philippines, reconquer the Netherlands East Indies, and roll up the Japanese empire from the south.

Admiral King was as firm for his plan as MacArthur was for his, and Nimitz as a loyal commander was in the position of having to support the King plan whether he agreed with it or not.*

The result of the pulling and hauling was that in the summer of 1944 President Franklin Roosevelt decided to make a trip to the Pacific and settle the question for himself. It was an election year, to be sure, and there were people who considered Roosevelt's trip a "grandstand play," but the fact of the very basic disagreement among many strategists could not be denied.

The visit was well planned; Secret Service agents came in advance and okayed the mansion on Diamond Head made available to the President. Nimitz sent a message inviting General MacArthur to come to Hawaii. MacArthur replied that he was too busy. King asked MacArthur to come. MacArthur was still too busy. General Marshall then ordered MacArthur to come, and he set out, with five members of his staff.

King came to Pearl Harbor just before the President arrived, but since he was definitely *not* invited to this meeting, King hurriedly left for the Central Pacific on an inspection tour.

MacArthur arrived by plane on July 26, a few minutes before the President's ship, the cruiser *Baltimore*, came in to harbor. Nimitz had asked MacArthur to stay with him in the house on Makalapa, but the messages had somehow been garbled, and Mac-

---

* This point was made very clear in King's letter of February 8, 1944, to Nimitz, in which King berated the Pacific and South Pacific commanders and staff for not uniformly supporting his idea of bypassing the Philippines.

Arthur ended up believing he had only an invitation from General Richardson, which he accepted.

In the meetings that were to follow, Roosevelt apparently intended to discover for himself just what his field commanders planned.

They sat in a big room filled with maps of the Pacific, and Nimitz took up a pointer and stepped to the map to present the Navy plan, to bypass the Philippines and attack Formosa.

MacArthur, feeling that he would be confined to a backwater command if this plan was followed, then presented his old Reno Plan. It was a most forceful presentation, since he knew the plan very well, and had for some time.

When the meetings were over, no one was quite certain what President Roosevelt was thinking about the future. Several decisions were made. The President did favor MacArthur's march into the Philippines, for emotional and high political reasons. MacArthur and Nimitz agreed on one vital aspect of the coming campaigns: MacArthur must have fleet and logistical support from the Pacific Fleet in future operations.

At a special meeting of the Joint Chiefs of Staff (in August) Admiral Leahy outlined the discussions at Pearl Harbor:

"We had a special meeting of the Joint Chiefs in which I gave them a detailed report of the Honolulu conferences. They may have been somewhat surprised to learn that Nimitz and MacArthur said they had no disagreements at the moment and that they could work out their joint plans in harmony." But—and it was a very big but—"the final decision on Pacific operations, especially in the matter of an assault on Japan itself, would have to be made by the Commander in Chief."

Commander in Chief in this sense meant the President, not King as Commander in Chief of the Navy. In fact, there was a basic change of emphasis this summer: although the President had always previously been accompanied on trips abroad by the Joint Chiefs of Staff, he had chosen to go to Pearl Harbor with only Leahy, his aide Wilson Brown, and his military aide General Watson. A bit earlier Leahy had suggested that Admiral King stop using the term Commander in Chief, because Roosevelt, who was by definition

Commander in Chief of all the armed forces, wanted to use that designation. Some writers have since said that the impulse was political, in view of the 1944 Presidential campaign. In any event, Admiral King resisted the idea, demanding an outright order to stop using the title, and nothing more was ever heard of it.

The Presidential visit brought some new problems to Pearl Harbor, to make Nimitz's head spin. Roosevelt announced that he was coming to the Makalapa house for lunch the second day. The Secret Service men rushed up to the house and ordered it virtually rebuilt; doors were to be rehung, bathrooms rebuilt, and even a roadway put behind the house because Roosevelt was sensitive about anyone seeing him get into and out of cars. On the day of the luncheon, five hundred men of a Seabee battalion came to the admiral's house and began taking it apart. They repainted what was necessary and dried the paint with blowtorches. At noon they were gone, and no one would have known they had even been there as Roosevelt sat down to drink a couple of martinis and eat a luncheon of mahimahi, the Hawaiian fish. Lamar, Nimitz's aide, said he counted 136 stars on the collars of the general and flag officers at that lunch that day.

The Navy's strategic plan for 1944 seemed still to be in effect, although nobody was really certain of what had happened. MacArthur went back to the south, feeling that he had won his battle. "He feels that he has the President's and Admiral Leahy's assurances that Luzon will not be bypassed," Artemus Gates wrote James Forrestal (who had become Secretary of the Navy upon Knox's death). But two months after the meetings in Hawaii, MacArthur was still not *certain* that he had won; that was Franklin Roosevelt's way.

Nimitz was extremely busy with new problems. Sparked by Admiral Radford's suggestions, the Navy was planning for a night-operating carrier division. Planes from a night-operating carrier might very well have discovered the Japanese fleet in the Battle of the Philippine Sea. The development of the planes and the techniques was an indication of the rapid movement of the naval science of carrier operation. At the end of July Admiral Pownall left Pearl Harbor, bound for Pensacola and a shore job. He went to see Nimitz before he left, trying to find a place for himself in the Pacific, but there was no room; the younger fighting admirals of the carrier forces had taken over.

On August 8 Nimitz was off to Guam for a tour, accompanied by General Vandegrift, who had come out from Washington, and Forrest Sherman. One reason for the tour was to look over the terrain and harbors, and the possible use of Guam as an advanced fleet headquarters. Nimitz found the buildup of his staff and everything else at Pearl Harbor very trying. So many hundreds of officers had joined his staff that he could not possibly know them all well, as he had known the original group back in 1942. The change was inevitable, with the growth of the fleet and the vigorous prosecution of the war; its proportions can be indicated by the fact that not only was there a complete logistics section of the staff, headed by a rear admiral, but there was an assistant chief of staff for logistics, who in turn (unhappily and unnecessarily) had his own executive assistant, a planning section, a transportation section, a construction section, an ordnance section, an administrative section, and a statistical section.

By this time, an absolutely vital element in the invasion plans was the service force of Vice Admiral Calhoun. Everything the Americans used had to be brought with them, and the responsibility for sorting it out and bringing it was Calhoun's. This meant the finding and use of provision ships, tankers, ammunition ships, and a dozen other types. The big natural base at Eniwetok was used fully, as a staging area, and millions of tons of supplies would pass through there. In the Marianas operation alone, for example, nearly two hundred supply ships were to be employed by the forces of Admiral Spruance. One of the major reasons for the Marianas move was to create a staging area for development of stockpiles within a thousand miles of the scene of the coming 1945 operations. The service squadrons remain largely unsung in the history of the war, like the Quartermaster Corps of the Army, but without them the Navy could never have moved in the conquest of the Pacific.

Nimitz, of course, had his own reason for wanting to go to Guam, besides the huge pile-up of administrative detail: he wanted to be much closer to the scene of operations. In conferences at Pearl Harbor that summer, King had squelched the idea of movement into the Philippines. He did not want to hear any more about

the Philippines (he told Nimitz when he visited Pearl just before
Roosevelt came) until Nimitz and his people had surveyed the pos-
sibility of using Eniwetock and Guam as bases for moving directly to
Formosa.

As Halsey moved out in August to take command of the Third
Fleet, and of the operation against the Western Carolines, the future was still not settled. But it was soon to be settled, and on September 9, Halsey had copies of orders for the invasion of the Philippines.

Halsey went to sea to rendezvous with Marc Mitscher's task
force, because McCain was still ashore at Pearl Harbor trying to
assemble a staff. Admiral Towers was trying to help him. Towers, at
this time, was being pushed into the background in the operations
out of Pearl, although as Nimitz's deputy he had expected to exert
more influence than he had had before as commander of the air
force. Towers put the blame for this state of affairs on Forrest Sherman, whom he had brought to the command in the first place.

New pressures were put on Nimitz. Secretary Forrestal was not
at all happy with Navy public relations. "The public . . . has only a
very inadequate and hazy impression of what the navy has done in
this war," he wrote Nimitz. The failure was the Navy's "own inadequacy in Public Relations . . . part of this stems from the nature
of army and navy training," but not all of it, he said. He also said
of the Army commanders, with obvious reference to Eisenhower and
MacArthur, "They are all pretty good dialecticians."

Nimitz, who had recently experienced in the MacArthur-Roose-
velt visit an exposure to that dialectic expertise, had very little to
say. Nor would it have done him much good to argue, for Forrestal
had long felt strongly about the deficiencies of the Navy's public
relations and was determined to make some basic changes.

In the Guam operation, as an example of this change, Nimitz
had visited the island at the end of the campaign and held a press
conference with General Geiger. It was a friendly affair. Geiger had
recently liberated a number of cases of Suntory whisky, a Japanese
product that tasted almost exactly like Scotch. Robert Trumbull of
The New York Times (formerly of the Honolulu *Star-Bulletin*) asked
with a twinkle what the general had there.

"Don't you think, general," said Nimitz with a grin that proved there was nothing wrong with his public relations, "we could make one case available to the press?"

One case was made available, and the correspondents lugged it over to the tent, where they quaffed and wrote their stories.

Admiral Nimitz's plane was to leave for Pearl Harbor the following morning, and Lamar agreed to take the press copy back to Pearl and give it to Captain Drake for dispatch. Departure was to be at 0700 sharp.

Next morning, however, the plane took off about 0600, and McArdle, the public relations man there, did not even have the copy yet. He put it on the next plane to Pearl, which should have arrived the following day. But it did not. Nimitz reached Pearl Harbor, and the Pearl Harbor commandos came over for a press conference. They got the stories, they were filed, and when the stories of the combat correspondents in the field came in, they were suitable for nothing but the waste basket.

In the forward areas, there was also considerable public relations friction. The Army Air Forces, and particularly the Seventh Air Force, under General Hale, were having their difficulties with the Navy. Admiral Hoover claimed that Hale's boys bombed from too far up and exaggerated their victories. Hoover did not care for their performance at all. Furthermore, he objected to Hale's methods of garnering publicity. McArdle was assigned to Hoover's command at the end of the Marianas operation, and Hoover instructed his new public relations officer.

"I don't care about publicity myself," he said. "There are certain people who have had publicity all out of proportion to their achievements. As long as I am in command here I want to see to it that credit is fairly distributed. I want you to censor all press material originating in this area—and I want to see every line that is written about General Hale."

One of the basic causes of friction in that combined command was opposite attitudes toward publicity. The Air Force made sure that its activities were known in every corner of the United States, and it accomplished this aim by sending out thousands and thousands of personal stories to home-town papers.

The Navy was far behind.

That message was being pounded home in the Navy Department in Washington. Particularly with the expansion of the operations, the correspondents were becoming restless. They did not like the uncertain transportation, the muddled censorship (because there were not enough censors), and the poor communications.

In August Nimitz noted that Captain H. B. Miller was going to come out to Pearl to look over the photographic situation. Miller was an airman, and also a graduate of the Naval Academy of the class of 1924, a former assistant naval attaché in London, and director of training literature for the Bureau of Aeronautics.

He arrived in Pearl Harbor just as the western Carolines operation began, and he took over public relations. Captain Drake was out on the Palau invasion.

Captain Miller moved into Captain Drake's office and moved Lieutenant Commander Allan Bosworth out into the anteroom from behind Waldo Drake's desk. When Drake heard of the change, at Saipan, he took off for Pearl Harbor. He found that his desk had, indeed, been usurped. He moved a new desk in, alongside Captain Miller's. Captain Miller ordered the desk moved out, and Captain Drake ordered it moved back in again.

Then the cold war began.

If someone called for the public relations officer, and Captain Drake answered the phone, he would say, "I am the public relations officer."

If someone called for the public relations officer and Captain Miller answered the phone, he would say, "Speaking."

And so it went, with the callers growing ever more confused.

Captain Drake conferred with Admiral Nimitz, who told him that he, Nimitz, considered Drake the public relations officer, but that Secretary Forrestal, who was in charge, considered that Captain Miller held that title.

Whereupon Captain Drake went back to Washington to straighten out affairs and was never again seen at Pearl Harbor. Forrestal "shanghaied" him, kept him in Washington, and was soon talking of sending him over to the Office of War Information, where they had been asking for someone who knew something about the Pacific.

Captain Miller began moving out the old public relations team and moving in a new one, which would eventually number several hundred officers and men.

In spite of such monumental struggles at Headquarters, the war continued. The operation from which Captain Drake had come back was the successful invasion of the Palaus, 530 miles from the southern Philippines, halfway from Guam to Mindanao.

Vice Admiral McCain was scheduled to be Mitscher's replacement, but he needed some experience in new carrier techniques, so in the summer's operations McCain was given Clark's task group, now called Task Group 38.1. The lineup was changed considerably at this point. Reeves, Clark, Harrill, and Montgomery were all given a rest, and Rear Admiral G. F. Bogan took Reeves's force, Rear Admiral Frederick C. Sherman took Montgomery's force, and Rear Admiral Ralph E. Davison took Harrill's. The force was also changed a bit—two more carriers were added, for a total of seventeen.

On August 28 Halsey sailed from Eniwetok, the big advance fleet base. (Incidentally, and rather more than that as far as the war is concerned, the task forces had been out raiding ever since the capture of the Marianas was assured and their presence was no longer needed offshore.) Halsey went out full of fire and brimstone to hit Yap, the Palaus, and Mindanao. He found that the Japanese air power was so slight as to scarcely constitute a challenge. The task force roamed where it would and bombed and strafed at will. On September 12 and 13 the force flew off 2400 sorties, knocking out an estimated 200 planes, sinking ships from merchantmen to sampans, and blowing up buildings.

The opposition was so slight that on September 13 Halsey suggested that the landings at Morotai, the Palaus, and Mindanao be canceled as not needed to soften up the Philippines (which was their purpose).

It was too late to stop Morotai and the Palaus—the invasion forces were already under way. General MacArthur's landing on Morotai was a direct result of the July conference at Pearl Harbor. It was to be a stepping-off place for the assault on Mindanao that MacArthur proposed to make. Rear Admiral Daniel E. Barbey was the amphibious commander, working under Vice Admiral Kinkaid's

Seventh Fleet. Rear Admiral William M. Fechteler handled part of the invasion. Rear Admiral R. S. Berkey commanded the support group, which consisted of five American and Australian cruisers, and ten American and Australian destroyers. Rear Admiral Thomas L. Sprague had six escort carriers for air support, and Nimitz lent Mc-Cain's Task Group 38.1 to MacArthur for D-Day operations. Some 28,000 troops under Major General Charles P. Hall of the XI Corps were landed. There were difficulties in landing, but they were caused by insufficient knowledge of the beaches. As far as Japanese resistance was concerned, it was a walkaway. At the end of two weeks, only a few Japanese had been killed or captured by the land forces.

At the Palaus, Rear Admiral T. S. Wilkinson was in command of the Amphibious Force, with General Geiger in charge of the land operations. A dozen admirals and general officers were involved in the landings—a reflection of the power that was building up in the Pacific. The fight for Peleliu was very tough, the Marines suffered 3900 casualties in knocking out the 5300 Japanese on the island. At the end of a week the issue was no longer in doubt in any way, but it took the Marines almost until December 1 to wipe out the opposition of the Japanese on Peleliu. On Angaur 1600 Japanese fought fiercely, but their conditions were not the same; the island was secured in a month, and American bombers were operating from the field by October 21.

Ulithi was occupied without opposition, and Vice Admiral Hoover took over the development of an advanced fleet base here. "Scrappy" Kessing, for whom Admiral Halsey had fought so brisk a battle with the personnel people in the Guadalcanal days, became the base commander.

Although the decisions in the Roosevelt-MacArthur-Nimitz meetings in Pearl Harbor had been so fuzzy that the Joint Chiefs of Staff were still arguing about them weeks later, Nimitz and Mac-Arthur did undertake the kind of cooperation Roosevelt wanted.

No one said the Navy accepted MacArthur's Reno V plan, which called for the Navy to throw in the towel in the Central Pacific and support MacArthur in the Philippines and the Netherlands East Indies, any more than the Army would support the Navy's Granite II plan, which called for the Central Pacific drive to forge ahead while MacArthur took the back seat. What they had agreed upon was that MacArthur would take Morotai on September 15, and Nimitz would take Peleliu; MacArthur would move in to Mindanao on November 15 and Leyte on December 20. *Then* would come the big question mark—would the Central Pacific drive be followed to Formosa and Amoy, by March 1, 1945, or would MacArthur lead the way to Manila by February 20?

Roosevelt, Churchill, and the Combined Chiefs of Staff met at Quebec on September 11, 1944, as the Morotai and Peleliu operations were already committed and the forces rode at sea. These military leaders discussed the opposing Army and Navy views. The British took no position, regarding the matter as an American problem; their concern was with Churchill's request that Britain be made a full partner in the war against Japan, and when that was granted, they made no comments on the strategy.

The Combined Chiefs recommended that the target date for the end of the war with Japan be set for eighteen months after the defeat of Germany, and that once the Germans had surrendered "in cooperation with other Pacific powers and with Russia, all available resources be thrown into the struggle to crush Japan."

The American Joint Chiefs agreed to this, but it was not the Navy position or Leahy's position.

"The Army did not appear to be able to understand," Leahy wrote later, "that the Navy with some Army air assistance, already had defeated Japan. The Army not only was planning a huge land invasion of Japan, but was convinced that we needed Russian assistance as well to bring the war against Japan to a successful conclusion."

In Halsey's strikes against the Philippines, a young pilot from Task Group 38.1 was shot down off Leyte. He was Ensign Thomas C. Tillar, from the carrier *Hornet*. The lucky pilot was rescued by Filipinos who informed him that there were no Japanese in the Leyte area. When Ensign Tillar was picked up by a PBY and returned to the *Hornet*, he went to see Admiral McCain and Admiral Clark, who was still riding along as adviser while McCain learned the ropes. Clark immediately informed Admiral Halsey of the report.

As the top admirals and generals talked in Quebec, Halsey came to the conclusion that the Japanese had been all but knocked out in the Philippines. (He was wrong: Admiral Ohnishi of the First Air Fleet was saving his strength for the invasion of the Philippines, which was now fully expected.)

Halsey sent messages to Nimitz and to MacArthur, suggesting changes. MacArthur was at sea, but his staff functioned very well in such matters. General Sutherland knew his commander's mind, and agreed almost offhand to the advancement of the Leyte invasion by two months, to October 20, if the Joint Chiefs approved. The Chiefs, advised of this at dinner in Quebec, interrupted the festivities long enough to hold a quick meeting, and agreed to bypass all other targets and move to Leyte on that schedule. The matter, actually, was of so little moment to them, engaged in their problems of high strategy, that Admiral Leahy does not even mention it in his book in connection with the second Quebec conference.

Just after the middle of September, Rear Admiral Forrest Sherman and Brigadier General W. B. Riley of the Marines met at Hollandia to discuss the role the Third Fleet would play in the Leyte operation. (Sherman was Admiral Nimitz's war plans officer; General Riley was Halsey's war plans officer.)

Halsey would have command of the forward area, except the Marshalls-Gilberts area. Plans had been made to turn over a large number of ships to Kinkaid's Seventh Fleet for the coming operations. Some of these, heavy cruisers, light cruisers, and destroyers, were to be returned later. The escort cruisers in the Third Fleet were to be given to the Seventh Fleet, but this order was conditional on need.

The general outline of Nimitz's directive and Halsey's operation plan was laid out.

(a) The Third Fleet will cover and support the occupation of Leyte by destroying enemy naval and air forces in or threatening the Philippines area, and will provide cover for sea and air communications and for newly established bases in the Forward Areas.

(b) The covering and striking forces will remain free to strike targets of opportunity and to conduct such offensive operations as will best exploit initial success in planned operations or will best counter enemy operations.

Then came the details: sortie on D—13, fuel on D—11, carrier strikes D—10 to D—7 on Okinawa, Formosa, or northern Luzon (Halsey to decide), move to refueling zone on D—6, fuel on D—5, then from D—4 to D-Day make carrier strikes on the Luzon-Bicol area, and the Leyte-Cebu-Negros area in support of the landing in the Leyte area.

"Western Task Force (Third Fleet) beginning on D plus 1 day and thereafter will operate in strategic support of the operation, effecting strikes as the situation at that time requires."

Finally, the memo indicated Halsey would "effect necessary measures of details in coordination with MacArthur, Kinkaid, and the commanding general of the Far East Air Forces."

The plan was settled. MacArthur's navy—Admiral Kinkaid and the Seventh Fleet—was to support the landings on Leyte. In previous landings in which the Central Pacific Forces were involved, Admiral Spruance had been in charge of the entire operation. But this case was more like the old system under which Halsey had operated with MacArthur in the past. The Central Pacific force had no responsibility for the landings, but was in strategic and tactical support of those landings. It would be a very important difference, for the result was to create a divided command, in which Admiral Halsey and Admiral Kinkaid each believed himself in a position to make independent judgments, a very dangerous situation indeed in the face of a brave and determined enemy.

Chapter
Twenty-Three

LEYTE

September 15–October 25, 1944

"Thank heavens Halsey and Mick Carney have stepped into the driver's seat," wrote Admiral Towers in the middle of September. Towers was just back from the Marianas, where he had nearly been shot while riding in a jeep along Guam's dusty roads. He was happy to have even this questionable respite, for the constant warfare within the staff of the Pacific Fleet was getting on Towers' nerves. He was, slowly but surely, being pushed into the background, and he resented it. While Forrest Sherman was off in Hollandia conferring with General Riley, Towers sought the chance to have a long, frank talk with Nimitz about the relationships in the command. He sensed that Sherman had Nimitz's respect and liking, and was occupying the position that Towers had hoped to have himself when he became deputy to the commander of the fleet. But instead of being busy, like Sherman, with the coming operations, Towers found himself concerned about seeds and fertilizer for the natives of the Marianas, or about the development of the Guam forward headquarters, which was to accommodate six hundred officers and two thousand men.

Nimitz was still worrying about the post-Leyte plans, which were very fluid. "It now appears certain that General MacArthur will be ordered to conduct his Luzon operation in December," Nimitz wrote Halsey on September 24. "Plans for subsequent operations are not firm and will unquestionably be affected considerably by the degree of success which you achieve in your first strikes north of the Philippines."

Four days later, Halsey wrote Nimitz a letter about various operations and tactical plans, in which he stated, very completely, his philosophy of battle. Halsey had sat restlessly in Nimitz's headquarters as Spruance had come so near, yet been so far, from engaging the main Japanese fleet in the battle of the Philippine Sea. Halsey had determined then—and it was always his basic point of view—that if he had a chance to destroy the Japanese fleet with his Fast Carrier Task Force, he would move in and do so without fail.

"I . . . feel that every weapon in the Pacific should be brought to bear if and when the enemy fleet sorties," he wrote Nimitz. He was uneasy about strategic considerations, particularly the submarines:

The dispositions outlined in your [messages] appear to leave gaps: Kii Channel and Shimonoseki Strait are unguarded; the subs stationed near Yokosukma and Sasebo are operating so close under enemy shore-based air that their ability to contact and trail is questioned; there appears to be a sizeable gap between the Maru Morgue and the Formosa Boats. Those apparent weaknesses in the disposition might result in the enemy fleet gaining the open sea without my receiving early and vital information.

He gave warning of his plans:

As mentioned in one of my early dispatches, I intend, if possible, to deny the enemy a chance to outrange me in an air duel and also to deny him an opportunity to employ an air shuttle (carrier-to-target-to-land) against me. If I am to prevent his gaining that advantage I must have early information and I must move smartly.

Inasmuch as the destruction of the enemy fleet is the principal task, every weapon should be brought into play and the general coordination of those weapons should be in the hands of the tactical commander responsible for the outcome of the battle.

. . . I hope that you will forgive this lengthy discussion; my goal is the same as yours—to completely annihilate the Jap fleet if the opportunity offers. . . .

As Halsey wrote, Nimitz was on his way to San Francisco for the autumn meeting with King, to determine the strategy of the months to come.

King restated his arguments. He wanted the Formosa operation to support a China invasion (Japanese-held coast). He did not like the Army plan of putting a land force into Kyushu until and unless the Army and Navy were ready to launch a large Tokyo plain operation. But what he really wanted to avoid was huge casualties. Yet King was discouraged, because a study had indicated that until Germany surrendered there simply were not the resources available to launch an attack against Formosa, where the formidable Kwantung army had gone into garrison. Formosa might have to be bypassed.

Nimitz then tentatively offered a new plan, noting that it was based on the nonavailability of resources to do what King wanted (one always had to be very careful with King) and the extremely favorable results of recent carrier operations. The plan called for support of MacArthur's Luzon operation on December 20, and then moves against Nanpo Shoto on January 20 by the Central Pacific forces, and against Nansei Shoto on March 1, 1945.

To quote from the conference minutes:

Admiral Nimitz stated that the proposal for the SWPA forces to work up through the Philippines from Leyte by shore-to-shore operations was discussed with the President and Gen-

eral MacArthur in July. General MacArthur stated that he
could not do these operations. Accordingly, because of insufficient resources for Formosa, he (Admiral Nimitz) came to the
view that the best way to keep pressure on the Japanese was
for him to support the Lingayen Gulf operation proposed by
MacArthur and to take Nanpo Shoto and Nansei Shoto with
POA [Pacific Ocean area] forces.

Admiral Sherman said it would take at least until March to
move on Formosa, even if the supplies could be made available.
Admiral Cooke, who represented King's point of view, said they
really ought not to throw out the Formosa operation.

King asked if it would not be possible to get MacArthur into
Leyte "and hold him there," and then do Formosa by taking over
MacArthur's remaining forces?

Admiral Cooke said that according to the Army there would
still not be enough resources for Formosa.

King asked what they would do if they let MacArthur have his
Luzon operation? Where would the Central Pacific forces go next?

Sherman said the thing to do was eliminate the Japanese air
strength in Formosa by a series of carrier strikes, just as they had
done already in the Philippines. Also, he said, a big carrier strike
against Japan proper was being planned for November 5. Halsey
would range far and wide in support of the Leyte operations. Then
Iwo Jima could be taken with two divisions, the airfields built up
there in a hurry by using a huge Seabee force, and on March 1,
having neutralized Formosan air strength by carrier attacks, the
invasion of Okinawa would begin.

Nimitz said wistfully that he still felt about China just the way
King did. Go to the mouth of the Yangtze. Stay away from Kyushu,
because there the people (Japanese) would oppose them "fanati-
cally," while on the China coast the civilians would be friendly.

King suggested that the Japanese fleet might come out soon,
during these operations.

Nimitz said he hoped so, because this would give the Americans
the chance they had been waiting for. But if the Japanese did not,
they would soon be destroyed without ever coming out.

King wanted to know—why Iwo Jima? Nimitz said possession

would give fighter protection to the B-29's, and the Army Air Force wanted such protection.

Admiral Cooke remarked that in the rest of 1944 they would not have much Japanese air opposition, but if they went into Iwo Jima they would have plenty of it again. Sherman replied that the fast carrier forces would wear down the Japanese air continually. Then, after Okinawa, they could open up the maritime provinces in May.

Again they talked of the Combined Chiefs of Staff and who liked the Kyushu operation. What did they think of China, asked Nimitz. King said they implied that they liked it, but they did not actually say so.

They talked about China, and its future. King said American policy was to support Chiang with all possible lend-lease aid.

Also discussed was the Marine Corps. Sherman said it would be difficult to use all six Marine divisions in forty days for Iwo Jima and Okinawa. They wanted Army replacement troops, and more of them.

When they discussed the uses of the fleet, Nimitz explained that he proposed to use Halsey to cover the Luzon operation and Spruance to handle the Iwo Jima and Okinawa operations.

King very shrewdly remarked that it might be advisable to use Spruance as supporting force commander for Luzon and Halsey as head of the covering force—to stand by for the Japanese fleet. Would that not also work, with Halsey under Spruance, for Iwo Jima, Okinawa, and Formosa? Obviously King was considering the proclivities of Nimitz's two fleet commanders.

Nimitz said he was against such a program at the moment.

A good deal of the meeting was devoted to public relations, because Secretary Forrestal was pressing very hard on that subject. By this time the Miller-Drake feud was raging, and the whole matter was settled by officially placing Captain Drake in Washington.

There was much discussion of logistics and the growing variety of vessels in the fleet, and then the meetings ended, and Nimitz headed back for Pearl Harbor.

Early in October, Halsey had a presentiment that the Japanese were going to move—and he meant the fleet. "I feel sure the Japs will be stung into attempting some sort of counter-measures," he wrote Nimitz. "—He has already made a token raid on Palau and sent some subs out—but that should only result in further by-products of destruction and I welcome it."

A few hours later, Halsey was smarting under a lash from Pearl Harbor—he had arbitrarily relieved Clark of command and put McCain in charge of Task Group 38.1 without consulting Nimitz. The point was not what he did—Clark was destined for leave anyhow and Halsey was showing no feeling against him, which Clark knew—but Nimitz insisted that the rights of command be left to him unless he delegated them. When Halsey was chastened he apologized with the grace and honesty so characteristic of him. Nimitz of course accepted the explanation, and drafted in his own hand a reply for Halsey, which McMorris was to put in the form of a letter. "We must reserve the right to determine operations except that he always acts in emergency situations, etc.," Nimitz noted at the bottom of the Halsey letter.

Here is how those notes were translated by McMorris in a formal letter to Halsey.

You are always free to make local decisions in connection with the handling of the forces placed under your command. Often it will be necessary for you to take action not previously contemplated because of local situations which may develop quickly and in the light of information which has come to you and which may not yet be available to me. My only requirement in such cases is that I be informed as fully and as early as the situation permits.

The letter emphasized what Halsey wanted—power to make decisions, and it certainly was obvious from this correspondence that Halsey intended to take after the Japanese fleet at the very first opportunity. Captain Moore, Spruance's retiring chief of staff, said he was certain that Halsey's attitude was deeply colored by Spruance's experience at the First Battle of the Philippine Sea. Moore explained:

I had been told, much later, that at Pearl Harbor Admiral

Halsey, Admiral Calhoun, Admiral Towers and the others who were around there at the time, after their daily meetings with Admiral Nimitz, would get together during this affair and just pan the whole thing. . . .

. . . The discussions that went on there at that time, I have always thought, and I still believe, had a tremendous effect on Halsey, because in the operation plan that he wrote for the Palau attack and the Leyte Gulf attack he said . . . if a situation arises or can be created for the defeat of the Japanese fleet, that will become the major objective. In other words, the hell with everything else. . . .

Nimitz knew how Halsey felt, and he accepted that fact. In this letter of October 8, setting forth what he expected in matters concerning control, Nimitz was full of praise for Halsey's carrier operations in the Philippines. "They are beyond praise and will be remembered as long as we have a Navy," he said. He noted that Admiral Radford would be coming along in the *Ticonderoga* to join the force, and informed Halsey that in San Francisco it had been decided that the commander of the Third Fleet would remain at sea until the end of the year, handling the Philippines support, and that Spruance would then take over for the invasions of Iwo Jima and Okinawa.

The decision indicated the judgment of Nimitz and King about their commanders. Halsey's task in the Philippines would be almost entirely to hunt the Japanese fleet and knock out Japanese air. Admiral Kinkaid's augmented Seventh Fleet was really given responsibility for the management of the landings, with Rear Admiral Barbey occupying the place that Vice Admiral Turner had if Spruance was running the show with the Fifth Fleet. In other words, while the Fifth Fleet and Third Fleet were called interchangeable commands, they were not totally that; when the Fifth Fleet was used, Spruance was given entire responsibility for the taking and holding of the territory, as well as protection from the incursions of the Japanese fleet. When Halsey was used, his superiors knew that he would concentrate on the enemy navy, and the plans were made accordingly.

As these letters of policy were being exchanged, Halsey was

moving fast. On October 7 he had begun a new offensive. Rear Admiral Allan E. Smith hit Marcus island on October 9 with three cruisers and six destroyers, in a deceptive move to indicate that a landing was planned on Marcus. Next day Mitscher's Task Force 38 hit Okinawa and the Ryukyus, flying nearly 1400 sorties in one day. This particular strike brought the Japanese up short, and Admiral Toyoda, the chief of the combined fleet, made ready Operation Sho-1. This operation was part of an overall Japanese defense plan known euphemistically as Sho-Go or Victory Operation. Sho-1 was to go into effect in case of an American landing in the Philippines; Sho-2 meant Formosa-Ryukyus; Sho-3 meant Honshu-Kyushu; Sho-4 meant Hokkaido-Kurils.

Obviously, if Sho-1 was to be in motion, the Japanese were expecting an invasion of the Philippines. It was a sign of their excellent intelligence.*

To carry out Sho-1, the Japanese would transfer almost all their operational carrier planes to land bases, and this process was begun, stripping the carriers *Zuikaku, Zuiho, Chitose, Chiyoda, Ise,* and *Hyuga.* (The last two were battleships in the process of conversion to carriers.)

On October 11 two of Halsey's groups hit the Philippines. On October 12 the force began a three-day strike on Formosa. The result was destruction of five hundred Japanese planes, the wrecking of hangars and many other installations, sinking of some forty ships of various kinds and sizes. The Americans suffered, however. The cruiser *Canberra* took a torpedo. The light cruiser *Houston* took two torpedoes. Halsey towed them both to safety at Ulithi. In the retirement to protect the cruisers, the American force was attacked by no fewer than a thousand Japanese planes, but beat the attackers off without losing a ship.

---

* *In this instance, Morison notes (Vol. XII, p. 71) that there was a bad leak somewhere in American diplomatic or military mission circles. In October the Japanese ambassador to Moscow learned from the Soviet Foreign Office that the American 14th and 20th Air Forces were to make attacks designed to isolate the Philippines. On October 6 the Japanese naval high command had that word. On October 7, while visiting the Philippines to confer with Army and Navy commanders at Manila, Admiral Toyoda suggested that any day the Third Fleet might launch a massive carrier attack on Okinawa, Formosa, or the Philippines. Imperial General Headquarters predicted a landing on Leyte during the last ten days of October.*

On October 17 Halsey began his support of the Leyte landings which would be staged three days later. The carriers struck repeatedly at various targets in the Philippines, as did Lieutenant General George Kenney's far eastern air forces, coming up from the south.

Somehow, knowing of the desperate air battles fought over the water of Formosa, the Japanese got the idea they had sunk most of the Third Fleet, and Radio Tokyo so announced. Eleven carriers, two battleships, three cruisers, and a destroyer were said to have gone to the bottom, and eight carriers, two battleships, four cruisers, and a destroyer were said to be damaged, plus twenty-five others. The Japanese army believed its own propaganda. The Japanese navy did not. On October 17, when the first ships of the American invading force were sighted off Suluan, the Emperor had issued a special imperial rescript on occasion of the "great naval victory of Taiwan," the press had whooped it up, and the people had literally danced in the streets. But the Japanese navy knew the invasion was about to begin.

Suddenly, on October 19 came a communiqué from Pearl Harbor: "Admiral Nimitz has received from Admiral Halsey the comforting assurance that he is now retiring toward the enemy following the salvage of all the Third Fleet ships recently reported sunk by Radio Tokyo."

The great battle of the Philippines was about to begin.

Some seven hundred ships were to be used in the central Philippines attack force. Most of these came from Nimitz, who "lent" them to MacArthur for the operation. This figure did not count Halsey's Third Fleet, with its 18 carriers, 6 battleships, 17 cruisers, 64 destroyers, and its train of supply ships and oilers. The Leyte invasion was commanded by General MacArthur, with Vice Admiral Kinkaid in the position that Spruance occupied in Fifth Fleet operations. Under Kinkaid, Task Force 78 would hit in the north. This force was commanded by Rear Admiral Daniel Barbey. Task Force 79 would hit the southern area. This force was commanded by Vice Admiral T. S. Wilkinson. In support of Barbey was Rear Admiral G. L. Weyler with three battleships and six destroyers. In support of Wilkinson was Rear Admiral J. B. Oldendorf (in the cruiser

Louisville) with Battleship Division Two, with Rear Admiral T. E. Chandler and three battleships, three heavy cruisers, three light cruisers, and a dozen destroyers. Of course, in the fleet, there were additional dozens of destroyers in the screen.

Near this fleet would be the escort carrier force of Rear Admiral Thomas L. Sprague, the force called Task Group 77.4, consisting of eighteen escort carriers and a destroyer screen. There were other cruisers, torpedo boats, seaplane tenders, minesweepers, and dozens of other kinds of ships in this huge fleet.

On October 17, the Japanese sighted those first ships of the American van. Admiral Toyoda alerted all Japanese naval forces for Operation Sho-1. The next day, as the Americans secured the entrance to Leyte gulf, Admiral Toyoda gave the order to execute.

In October, 1944, Japan's naval power was centered in the First Striking Force. There were no carriers in this force. Since all the carriers had been stripped of their planes to augment the land-based air defenses of the Empire, the carriers had been retired to Japan. Thus one might say that Japanese strategy, of necessity, had reverted to pre-World War II ideas. The First Striking Force consisted of the new battleships *Yamato* and *Musashi*; the old battleships *Nagato, Fuso, Yamashiro, Kongo,* and *Haruna*; the heavy cruisers *Atago, Takao, Maya, Chokai, Haguro, Myoko, Kumano, Suzuya, Tone, Chikuma,* and *Mogami*; the light cruisers *Noshiro* and *Yahagi*; and nineteen destroyers. The two new battleships were the world's largest fighting ships, displacing 68,000 tons each, and carrying 18-inch guns.

This force left Lingga Roads, off Singapore, on October 18 at 0100, and moved into Brunei Bay, in North Borneo, where Admiral Kurita awaited his special instructions.

On October 20 the second move in the Sho-1 plan began. Vice Admiral Jisaburo Ozawa sailed with the northern force from Japan. Part of this force was located in Kure, and part in Beppu Bay. The two parts met in Bungo Suido, and went out together through this southwestern channel entrance into the Inland Sea. They had expected to encounter packs of American submarines, but the submarines were not there. This force consisted of the *Ise* and *Hyuga*, the two battleships that had been converted to carriers;

the fleet carrier *Zuikaku;* and the light carriers *Zuiho, Chitose,* and *Chiyoda.* These carriers were screened by the light criusers *Oyodo, Tama, Isuzu* and by eight destroyers.

This northern force of Admiral Ozawa's was strictly expendable. It was expected, in fact, that the entire force would be lost. The six carriers had only 116 planes aboard—the Japanese factories were working night and day to build planes, but they would be thrown into the air pipeline and delivered by hopping from island to island. The Americans had breached the inner line of defenses of the Empire. Japan's fight now was for a sea empire dotted throughout with island airfields. If any ships could be sacrificed at this stage of the war, it was the carriers.

Admiral Ozawa's unhappy but heroic task was to martyr himself and his force, to move down from the north so that the force would be seen and heard by Admiral Halsey's Third Fleet, and then to decoy Admiral Halsey and that fleet up northeast of Luzon, away from Philippine waters.

On October 20, as Ozawa headed south, Admiral Kurita received his orders. At 0800 on the morning of October 22, Kurita sailed with his force, from which he detatched the old battleships *Fuso* and *Yamashiro,* and the heavy cruiser *Mogami.* Kurita then had two new battleships, three old battleships, ten heavy cruisers, and two light cruisers plus destroyers. Later that day, Vice Admiral Nishimura took the old battleships *Fuso* and *Yamashiro,* the heavy cruiser *Mogami,* and four destroyers, and made a detour to the north. Then he moved toward Balabac strait, into the Sulu Sea, heading for Surigao Strait, the southern entrance into Leyte Gulf. At the same time Vice Admiral Shima was moving down from the north with the heavy cruisers *Nachi* and *Ashigara,* the light cruiser *Abukuma,* and four destroyers.

The plan called for Ozawa to lure Halsey away, and for Kurita to rush through San Bernardino Strait, which runs between Samar and Luzon island. Kurita could then whisk southeast around Samar and surprise the Americans in Leyte Gulf, coming down from the northeast, while Nishimura and Shima would come rushing up from the south, through Surigao Strait, which runs between Leyte and Mindanao, and catch the Americans from the southern side. The

American ships would be unloading their cargoes and their invasion troops, and would be sitting ducks, ready for the slaughter. Meanwhile, Halsey would be hundreds of miles away to the northeast, destroying the carriers which were of relatively little use anyhow. If enough damage were done, the American invasion could be stopped, and the Japanese forces would have time to regroup and even rebuild their air defenses.

At daybreak on October 20, the ships of Admiral Barbey's northern force and Admiral Wilkinson's southern force began to move into Leyte Gulf, Barbey to San Pedro Bay near Tacloban, and Wilkinson eleven miles south of Palo, on Barbey's left flank. The Army forces landed successfully, and the battle for the Philippines land area began. The Japanese began fighting back with artillery and air strikes. The landing plans had been made with the usual thought of getting the ships unloaded and out of the way, in case of Japanese naval attack, and this procedure was followed.

Two days later, Admiral Halsey assessed the situation in a letter to Nimitz.

Mitscher, said Halsey, was certain that Japanese naval air was virtually wiped out. Mitscher based that view on his observations of the result of his operations that summer, and particularly on the results of the last few days of strikes in the Formosa and Luzon areas. Noting the strange assortment of planes that the Japanese threw up from Formosa, Mitscher was sure the enemy would not have risked so many nonfighting types had he not been desperate. He also pointed to the very noticeable lack of skill of many of the pilots who manned these planes.

Halsey, however, was not convinced. "I believe that the prudent view requires withholding judgment, and also requires the assumption that the enemy still has some carrier air strength up his sleeve."

He had no positive information, he said, concerning the Japanese carriers, except the knowledge that some carrier-type planes had come to meet them off Formosa. He wondered where the Japanese carriers were and what they were doing.

Halsey had observed that the Japanese found it impossible to react to an attack in an unexpected quarter in less than a few days —quite unlike the South Pacific period. This inability held true as far as Okinawa; he was ready to test it on the inner Empire.

As for the Japanese fleet, he still felt that it would come out, but only when the chances of success looked very good.

Halsey said he was much impressed with MacArthur's landing, and was then just waiting for MacArthur's men to consolidate enough to justify the Third Fleet's withdrawal to rearm for future operations.

McCain in Task Group 38.1 and Admiral Davison in Task Group 38.4 were off Leyte supporting the escort carriers. Admiral Bogan in Task Group 38.2 and Admiral Frederick Sherman in Task Group 38.3 stood east of Cape San Ildefonso, to hit any Japanese naval forces that might try to break up the landing. The Japanese air situation in the beginning was desperate; it was doubtful if they had one hundred planes in operation on invasion day, so successful had been the strikes of carrier- and land-based aircraft. But within a few hours the call for help was being answered, and planes were in the interisland pipelines, coming from Japan and Formosa.

On October 22, as Halsey wondered about the Japanese fleet, Admiral Kurita was moving northeast through Palawan passage, into the South China Sea that abuts the Philippines. There his force was spotted by the American submarines *Darter* and *Dace*, which sent the word by radio to Australia. Early on the morning of October 23, Halsey had the message too.

Darter and *Dace* attacked. *Darter* put four torpedoes into the heavy cruiser *Atago*, Admiral Kurita's flagship, and two torpedoes into *Takao*. *Atago* sank; *Takao* made her way back to a Japanese base. Meanwhile *Dace* sank the heavy cruiser *Maya*.

On October 23 Halsey's intelligence officers knew that two forces were moving in on Leyte Gulf from the south, while one was coming down from the northwest; Kurita's force had been seen already, and Nishimura and Shima had been spotted; only Ozawa, who wanted to be discovered, had not yet made his presence known.

On October 21, having decided that the MacArthur landings were consolidated enough so that Kinkaid's Seventh Fleet could handle any problems, Halsey had detached Admiral McCain's task group and sent it to Ulithi for resupply. Halsey dispersed his other three task forces so they might make searches fanning out to the west from the islands. Sherman's force was off the Polillo islands. Bogan was off San Bernardino Strait. Davison was off Surigao Strait.

On the morning of October 24, Bogan's search planes found Kurita's force. Within half an hour Halsey had ordered the other two task groups on station to close on Bogan, and McCain to reverse course and prepare to refuel at sea instead of at Ulithi; and all groups were told to strike the enemy.

Halsey did all this, not Mitscher. For with Halsey in command there was no need for a task force commander within the fleet: Halsey was fleet commander and task force commander in one, and Mitscher was very much the patient bystander.

That morning the Japanese had land-based air reinforcements in the Philippines, and they struck at the task groups. They bombed the *Princeton*, in Admiral Sherman's group, and after valiant attempts to save her failed, she had to be sunk by torpedo.

That day the American carrier planes hit the super-battleship *Musashi* with nineteen torpedoes and seventeen bombs—and sank her. *Yamato* and *Nagato* were both damaged, but they could still fight. The heavy cruiser *Myoko* was torpedoed, and had to return to Brunei. These were the results of the Battle of the Sibuyan Sea, in which eighteen planes were lost by the Americans.

The Sho-1 plan called for Kurita to meet with Nishimura and Shima at dawn inside Leyte Gulf, and then in daylight to shoot up the sitting ducks of the American landing force. After this day of strikes by Halsey's planes, Kurita's force was diminished and mauled, and he turned away west, as if retiring. He was simply maneuvering for time, but he was also upsetting the schedule of Sho-1.

Meanwhile that same morning of October 24, Admiral Nishimura's force was spotted by planes from the carriers *Enterprise* and *Franklin* of Admiral Davison's Task Group 38.4, south of Negros island, and Admiral Shima's force was found by an Army Air Force bomber near the Cagayen Islands. Planes hit Nishimura's force, but damaged only the *Fuso* and one destroyer. Davison had to break off the attack because he was ordered north to close on Bogan and hit the Kurita force that day. So Nishimura steamed on.

Admiral Kinkaid was aware of Nishimura's coming, and disposed his forces so the Japanese would have to fight their way through Surigao Strait.

At 1145 Admiral Ozawa's force, coming down from Japan, was

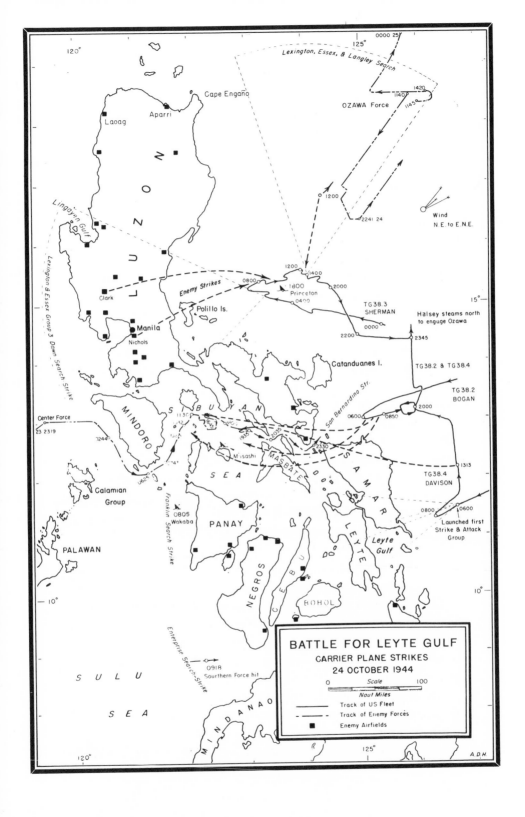

120°

Cape Engaño

Aparri

Laoag

LUZON

Lingayen Gulf

Lexington & Essex Group 3 Dawn Search-Strike

Clark

Enemy Strikes

Polillo Is.

Manila

Nichols

MINDORO

Center Force
23 2319

0244

Calamian
Group

PALAWAN

0625

Franklin Search-Strike

Misashi

S I B U Y A N

MASBATE

1130
0722
1240
1320
1935
2035
0830
2330

0805
Wakaba

PANAY

SEA

NEGROS

C E B U

BOHOL

Enterprise Search-Strike

0918
Southern Force hit

S U L U

SEA

120°

0000 25

125°

Lexington, Essex, & Langley Search

1420
1140
1145

OZAWA Force

1200

2241 24

Wind
N.E. to E.N.E.

1200
1400

0800

1800
Princeton
0400

2000

TG 38.3
SHERMAN

2200

0000

Halsey steams north
to engage Ozawa

2345

Catanduanes I.

TG 38.2 & TG 38.4

San Bernardino Str.

TG 38.2
BOGAN

0600
0850

2000

S A M A R

1313

L E Y T E

Leyte
Gulf

TG 38.4
DAVISON

0800
0600

Launched first
Strike & Attack
Group

15°

10°

10°

125°

BATTLE FOR LEYTE GULF

CARRIER PLANE STRIKES
24 OCTOBER 1944

0   Scale   100
Naut Miles

——————— Track of US Fleet
— — — — Track of Enemy Forces
■ Enemy Airfields

MINDANAO

125°

A.D.H.

210 miles northeast of Sherman's Task Group 38.3, and the Japanese launched a strike of 76 planes. The Japanese admiral then began maneuvering in a rectangle, so the Americans might discover and chase him.

The Ozawa air strike came to nothing. The planes landed on Luzon to join the land-based air. The converted battleships *Ise* and *Hyuga* were detached and sent south to battle the Americans. They carried no planes, but they each still had eight 14-inch guns, which made them formidable enough.

Late in the afternoon, planes of Halsey's force sighted the Ozawa carrier force, four carriers, two light cruisers, and five destroyers. Halsey then had the complete picture. He knew of the existence of all the forces at sea. He assumed that all these forces were planning to rendezvous early in the morning to attack the American ships in Leyte Gulf. He lacked only two bits of essential information: (1) that the Kurita force was the strongest force, and was still coming in, and (2) that the carrier force, apparently the attack force, was a hollow shell, and a diversionary rabbit at that.

Halsey believed in the American carrier doctrine: hit the carriers, and hit them *first*, before they can hit you. He wrote off the southern force: Kinkaid could handle that. He wrote off the central force: his pilots indicated that it was decimated. He decided, then, that he would go after the carriers. He might have left his battleships to guard San Bernardino strait, but he rejected the idea of splitting his fleet.

So Halsey did precisely what the Japanese wanted him to do, he went after the diversionary force, as Admiral Kurita moved into San Bernardino Strait.

The information about the disposition and movement of Kurita and the other forces was available—historian Samuel Eliot Morison indicates that Halsey's own task group commanders knew Kurita was coming in, and tried to warn their commander, but Halsey's staff protected him from the information.

Off went the Third Fleet, like a posse bent on heading off the bad guys at the pass, while the bad guys' confederates steamed on toward the heart of the American invasion fleet.

Rear Admiral "Ching" Lee, the commander of the fast battleships, suggested to Halsey that the northern force was a decoy, and that Kurita would turn around and come through San Bernardino Strait. He received an acknowledgment of that message but no reply. A little later Lee reiterated his worry that Kurita would be coming through. This time there was not even an acknowledgment, and since it was Halsey's show, Lee kept quiet, as a junior admiral is supposed to do.

Aboard the *Lexington* Admiral Mitscher, who knew his Halsey, prepared to turn in for the night, around 2030, expecting to be up at dawn. Before he left his bridge, Commodore Arleigh Burke, his chief of staff, suggested that they check on the whereabouts of the Kurita force. They did check, and found that Kurita was coming through the strait.

Burke suggested that it would be a good idea to detach the battleships and leave them to cover San Bernardino Strait. He woke up Mitscher.

"Does Admiral Halsey have that report?" Mitscher asked.

"Yes," said Commander James Flatley, the operations officer.

"If he wants my advice he'll ask for it," Mitscher said. Then he went back to sleep.

At noon on October 24, Vice Admiral Kinkaid was prepared to fight the Japanese in a night engagement. He expected Admiral Nishimura at Surigao Strait that night. Rear Admiral J. B. Oldendorf, the commander of the bombardment and fire-support group, was told to be ready to meet the enemy there. On the left flank, up to the northeast, would be Oldendorf himself with three heavy cruisers, two light cruisers, and nine destroyers. In the center, across the entrance to San Pedro Bay where the supply ships were anchored, stood the battle line, six old battleships and six destroyers. Behind them were twenty-eight Liberty ships, three amphibious force flagships which were heavy on communications equipment and antiaircraft guns but light on big gun firepower, and the cruiser *Nashville* in which rode General MacArthur. Off to the right flank, against Leyte and looking south, were two light cruisers, a heavy cruiser, and six destroyers. And far out in front was the picket patrol of seven destroyers.

The force was quite adequate for protection against the Japanese who would come up through Surigao Strait. And along the edges and down the Mindanao Sea as far as Camiguin island, were thirty-nine PT boats, strung out. None of these forces knew that Admiral Nishimura and Admiral Shima were both coming in, independently, but there was plenty of power here for both Japanese forces.

The Sho-1 plan called for Nishimura to come through Surigao Strait and arrive off Tacloban at dawn. Kurita would come through San Bernardino and arrive there at the same time. In spite of the attack on Kurita, Admiral Toyoda that night confirmed the fact that the plan was still in effect.

About 2230 that night, Nishimura came in next to Bohol island, and was spotted on radar by PT-131. Twenty minutes later the PT boat sighted the enemy. The PT boat and others attacked, without effect, but just after midnight, Admiral Oldendorf had the word. The Japanese were entering the strait.

Nishimura's force began running the gauntlet of PT boats, which were very effective that night as "eyes of the fleet" although totally ineffective as torpedo boats. Within fifteen minutes, too, Oldendorf learned that he also had the Shima force to contend with.

Out in front of the American forces were the picket destroyers, under Captain J. G. Coward. He planned a destroyer torpedo attack on the Japanese. He left two destroyers on picket duty, took three himself on the eastern side of the strait, and assigned two others on the west under Commander R. H. Phillips. They came in fast, fired twenty-seven torpedoes, swung hard aport, and retired; Japanese shells were falling all about them, but they zigzagged and kept clear of every shot. Explosions were heard, and *Fuso* began to slow down. From the other side, the two destroyers under Commander Phillips, *McDermott* and *Monssen*, dashed in for a second attack. *McDermott*'s torpedoes hit three Japanese destroyers. The first, *Yamagumo*, blew up and sank. The second, *Michishio*, began sinking. The third, *Asagumo*, had her bow blown off, but began limping home. *Monssen* put at least one torpedo into the battleship *Yamashiro*, but did not stop her.

These were only the pickets. Admiral Nishimura steamed on, into the jaws of Oldendorf's battle force. The other destroyers attacked without much effect, except to sink *Michishio*, and to put two torpedoes into *Yamashiro* at the very end of the destroyer rush. The destroyer *Albert W. Grant* was hit, and stopped dead in the water, but later was saved.

Admiral Nishimura's "column" was now one battleship, one heavy cruiser, and one destroyer. The striking power of the heavy American ships was concentrated on *Yamashiro*, already crippled. She began to burn, she turned to retire and then, ten minutes later, capsized and sank, taking down Admiral Nishimura. The cruiser *Mogami* began to retire, with destroyer *Shiguro*. *Mogami* had taken many hits and her commanding officer was killed, but she got away. So, just after 0400 in the morning of October 25, the first phase of the battle was over. The Japanese had lost two battleships; two destroyers, one cruiser, and two damaged destroyers were limping home.

Admiral Shima was coming on behind, unwarned. At 0330 hours PT-137 put a torpedo into the light cruiser *Abukuma*, and she fell out of formation. Shima then had two heavy cruisers and four destroyers. Shima came in, fired eight torpedoes at two small islands seen dimly through the night, and retired. When he retired, *Nachi* collided with *Mogami* of the Nishimura force, adding to the damage and confusion. Then began a chase which lasted much of the next day. The destroyer *Asugumo*, with her broken bow, was sunk by gunfire. *Mogami* was hit by carrier planes from Admiral Sprague's escort carriers, *Abukuma* was hit by Army Air Force planes and sank southwest of Negros. The only survivor of Nishimura's force was the destroyer *Shiguro*, which made Brunei Bay.

That was the end of the battle of Surigao Strait.

All this while, Admiral Kurita was moving through San Bernardino Strait unopposed. Admiral Kinkaid was sure that Admiral Halsey was covering that area for him. At 0645 hours, however, the pagoda masts of the Japanese battleships were seen by the escort carriers off Leyte Gulf, just as the Japanese ships began opening fire, coming down from the north.

Here they came, the destroyer screen, standing off to the east, then four heavy cruisers, two more heavy cruisers, and a destroyer squadron on the west. Behind were battleships *Yamato* and *Nagato*. Then the Battleships *Kongo* and *Haruna*, on the same plane as the other battleships. Out on the flanks were the light cruisers *Noshiro* and *Yahagi*.

At 0645 Kurita had ordered his ships to attack the carriers. He gave no plan, no battle line, no formation of any kind; off they were to go, to shoot up the Americans.

The American force consisted of three escort carrier units. Rear Admiral T. L. Sprague, the overall commander of the carriers, had one, called Taffy 1, which included four escort carriers, three destroyers, and four destroyer escorts. Rear Admiral Felix B. Stump had two escort carriers, plus four more under Rear Admiral W. D. Sample in Stump's Taffy 2, then three destroyers and four escorts for screen. Taffy 3, under Rear Admiral C. A. F. Sprague, consisted of four escort carriers, plus Carrier Division 26 under Rear Admiral Ralph A. Ofstie, Nimitz's old air officer, and three destroyers and four escorts for screen.

The Japanese had come upon Taffy 3. Now the air began to crackle with calls for assistance from the escort carriers, and Kinkaid quickly gave permission to launch all available planes everywhere to repel this surprise attack. Sprague began making smoke in his six carriers, and launched all planes. The carriers moved into a circle, and the destroyers screened them. The Japanese began to find the range and soon were straddling at least two of the escort carriers. Then came a rain squall, and Sprague's carriers ducked inside.

Sprague's destroyers went in to attack with torpedoes. One or more hit the heavy cruiser *Kumano* and knocked her out of the fight. Heavy cruiser *Suzuya* was hit by bombs, and also put out of the fight. Two of the American destroyers were hit.

The battleship *Yamato* began maneuvering to miss torpedoes and maneuvered herself out of the battle.

The American forces did not come through unscathed. The destroyer *Hoel* took some forty shells from Japanese guns, from 16 inch to 5 inch, but she managed to remain afloat until almost 0900, serving as a focal point for the Japanese and, in a manner of speaking, distracting them. They were also distracted by the destroyer torpedo attacks, followed by the destroyer escort torpedo attacks. One of the destroyers, *Johnston*, even took on the battleship *Kongo* in a gun battle and fired thirty shells. The captain said half of them hit, but it was like bouncing paper spitwads off a steel helmet, and as the battleship began firing back at them with 14-inch guns, *Johnston* ducked into its own smoke cloud.

The destroyers and escorts circled about their charges, so many buzzing bees to threaten the Japanese bee-eaters, but all to soon the stings of the bees were drawn. The whole force had been low on ammunition to begin with, because much had been expended on shore targets during the landings. The torpedoes were soon fired, and several destroyers and escorts found themselves almost without any stings at all.

The Japanese moved forward, apparently indomitable. DD *Samuel B. Roberts* was hit by several shells, and then by two 14 inchers together, and completely smashed abaft the smokestack. She sank just after 1000.

Several of the destroyers set out, with smoke and their 5-inch guns, to divert the heavy cruisers from the escort carriers. *Heermann* took several hits from *Chikuma*, but forged on. *Johnston* tore in like a bulldog against a pack, and held a whole destroyer squadron at bay, deflecting a torpedo attack on the escort carriers, but she took the brunt herself. The destroyers closed on her, circled her, and poured shells into the American destroyer, until she capsized and sank at 1010.

All this while, the escort carriers were launching planes to defend themselves by attacking the enemy. *Kalinin Bay* was the first carrier hit, but she was not disabled, until she took one 14-inch or 16-inch shell and about a dozen 8-inch shells, apparently from a battleship. *Fanshaw Bay* was hit four times by 8-inch shells. *White Plains* was hit with 6-inch shells, and *Kitkun Bay* was hurt by several near misses.

The carriers launched as quickly as they could and by 0730 the planes were in the air. For two hours they attacked, some armed with torpedoes, some with bombs, some with 100-pound antipersonnel bombs. When they expended their drops, they came down to strafe or made dry runs, and so did the fighters—anything to divert the Japanese. If the destroyers were bees buzzing about the Japanese force, the planes were angry gnats, but some of them carried real stings. They did divert the Japanese, but not totally. *Gambier Bay* was hit repeatedly by the heavy cruisers, and just after 0900 she sank. But one of her assailants, *Chokai*, was attacked by the bombers, and sank at 0930.

On the day before, Admiral Kinkaid had ordered the escort carriers to load torpedoes, thinking they might be needed in the Surigao Strait battle. So the carriers were ready, or almost ready. *Marcus Island's* TBMS (torpedo bombers) had mostly gone off on a mercy mission, carrying water and food for troops of the 96th Division cut off from their supplies on Leyte.

Knowing in this desperate situation that the Japanese must be turned back, Rear Admiral Stump ordered his Taffy 2 planes to scatter about and hit as many ships as possible (rather than try to destroy a few). In an hour and a half he launched thirty-six fighters and forty-three torpedo bombers. The other escort forces also launched as quickly as they could and kept the gnats moving.

Shortly after 0900 the Japanese attack showed signs of faltering. The heavy cruisers *Haguro* and *Tone* broke off the attack. The other two heavy cruisers, *Chokai* and *Chikuma*, were sunk by the combined attacks of the U.S. destroyers, escorts, and the planes.

Admiral Kurita ordered his fleet north just after 0900, in order to re-form. But he drove north for an hour and a half, then west, then southwest—which indicated he was coming in again—and then back north again. This activity took about three hours, and at the end of it Kurita had passed the latitude of the battle, out at sea, and was heading back for San Bernardino Strait, having decided against hitting Leyte Gulf again. All during that maneuvering Admiral Kurita had been making up his mind. What apparently frightened him off, with his four battleships and his destroyers, was the knowledge that somewhere around was the fearsome Third Fleet, and Kinkaid was calling for it, in messages in the clear.

Still, while the outright danger of disaster from the sea was over, as Admiral Kurita moved away, a new element in the war appeared over Leyte Gulf that morning of October 25. It was the kamikaze, or suicide plane.

A few days before, Vice Admiral Takijiro Ohnishi had come to the Philippines as commander of the Fifth Base Air Force. Ohnishi was a sturdy fighter with an indomitable will to win for the Emperor. He moved about the islands, from air field to air field, and might have been disheartened by what he saw. In comparison to the early days of the war, there were only a handful of planes that could fly, and only a ragtag remnant of the proud naval air force to fly them. Most of his pilots could neither maneuver nor shoot very well. Ohnishi, however, was beyond dismay. He had one major asset with which to work: the intense patriotism and will to fight of the Japanese pilots, no matter how bad their equipment, how weak their physical condition, how poor their training. Immediately Admiral Ohnishi began the preparations to make use of this asset in the Battle of the Philippines. It was a relatively simple job. First, his mechanics had to prepare the planes, putting explosive charges in them, making them into flying bombs. Second, Ohnishi had to create, by speech and mystique, the conditions under which the pilots would sacrifice themselves. But since Japanese folklore was replete with the stories of the self-sacrifice of the old samurai, it was not hard to convince the pilots that their responsibility was to make the supreme sacrifice.

By October 25 all was ready on the airfield where Ohnishi would launch his first attack.

That nightmare, as seen from the receiving end, arrived over the escort carrier *Santee* at about 0745 in the morning. A second kamikaze was splashed by gunfire from the *Suwannee,* and a third barely missed *Petrof Bay*. Then there were many others. Just before 1100, one crashed into *St. Lo* and exploded her torpedoes and bombs. *St. Lo* went down in a few minutes. Then there was a respite, although for the next few days the area would be invaded again by Japanese submarines and more kamikazes would take their toll—in fact, the Americans were not to be free of the kamikaze threat again as long as the war lasted, and could not devise a really satisfactory defense against men who were willing to sacrifice their lives to hit a ship.

The retreat of Admiral Kurita through San Bernardino Strait became a rout. No longer did he have the element of surprise, which had made up for the lack of air power in his force. Running home the heavy cruiser *Suzuya* found herself in trouble, after having taken much punishment off Leyte Gulf. She foundered early on the afternoon of October 25, having been passed over by American bombers seeking unhurt targets.

Those bombers found Kurita off Samar around noon. A bomb hit *Nagato*, doing slight damage. One hit *Tone*, temporarily wrecking the steering gear.

If Admiral Kurita had not made up his mind, this attack made it up for him. He headed home. And just about then, the Third Fleet swung into action.

On the evening of October 23, when Admiral Halsey made the decision to go after Admiral Ozawa's northern force, he ordered Admiral McCain's Task Group 34.1 to close up and join the fleet, Bogan and Davison to head due north at twenty-five knots, and Sherman to hook on as the fleet sped by him. He sent a message to Admiral Kinkaid.

CENTRAL FORCE HEAVILY DAMAGED ACCORDING TO STRIKE REPORTS X AM PROCEEDING NORTH WITH THREE GROUPS TO ATTACK CARRIER FORCE AT DAWN.

This message would seem to be a clear enough indication that Halsey was heading out, leaving San Bernardino Strait. But a lot had gone on beforehand.

First of all, although Halsey had made it plain to Nimitz and all others with whom he corresponded in this period that he was itching to get at the Japanese fleet, and would never let happen to him what had happened to Spruance, still Kinkaid, being in Mac-Arthur's navy, was not really party to Halsey's thinking.

Nor did these two admirals have a specific understanding; both were somewhat confused about what their course would be in the event of a Japanese attack.

And finally an ironic fate played one of its startling cards: Spruance had based his decision at the Marianas on the known fleet tactics of the Japanese, which called for a split of forces and a pincers movement—and the Japanese had actually put all their fish in one barrel that day; Halsey estimated that the big Japanese fish were in the northern barrel, but they actually were not.*

Early on the morning of October 24, Task Force 34 went into action, Halsey used the night carrier *Independence*, and marked a first in naval aviation. Her planes flew out and found the Japanese in the dark, and by 0230 Halsey knew where his enemy was located. At 0630 the planes began to take off from the day carriers.

On the day before, Halsey had laid out a plan of battle which involved the detachment of "Ching" Lee's fast battleships as a striking force to hit the enemy surface fleet. Halsey had meant this as tentative, but when Kinkaid picked up a dispatch noting the plan, Kinkaid put it down as a definite plan of action. And now, on the morning of October 25, with Kurita's force moving down from San Bernardino Strait, Kinkaid asked the question:

AM NOW ENGAGING ENEMY SURFACE FORCES SURIGAO STRAIT X QUESTION IS TF 34 GUARDING SAN BERNARDINO STRAIT

That—TF 34—meant the battleships. Halsey had to answer that Task Force 34 was with the carriers.

The planes were out. The carrier groups were committed. The carriers, at least, could not turn around, without throwing the whole organization into confusion.

Halsey steamed on. A succession of messages caught him as he moved northward. At 0822 he learned that the Kurita force had come through San Bernardino Strait and was firing on the escort carriers. At 0830 Kinkaid said he needed the fast battleships at once at Leyte Gulf.

Just about this time (the pilots said 0800, the Japanese said 0830) the American carrier planes found Admiral Ozawa's force.

---

* *In his book and in his private papers, which are in the possession of the Naval History Division U.S. Navy, there is no evidence to deny that the decisions made this night were all Halsey's and all based on the total information available to him. It has been suggested, however (Morison hints at it—Vol. XII, pp. 195–96), that Halsey was the victim of bad work or carelessness by his personal staff. The facts are not known: they may be clarified to some extent in the future when the papers of Admiral R. B. Carney are made available to historians and writers. Carney, Halsey's chief of staff, was on the bridge with him on the night of this battle. By Carney's wish, his papers are sequestered as of 1970, and this author was unable to secure an interview with him.*

Carrier *Zuiho* launched a few planes, then was hit by a bomb, which damaged but did not sink her. Carrier *Chitose* was bombed, and began to sink. Carrier *Zuikaku*, veteran of so many battles, was hit by a torpedo and listed so badly that Admiral Ozawa shifted his flag off of her. Destroyer *Akatsuki* was sunk, and nine Japanese planes were shot down. Carrier *Chiyoda* was hit (she later sank). Light cruiser *Tama* was hit; she slowed and began trailing oil.

Halsey's reaction, as he awaited the results of Mitscher's air strikes and considered what was occurring back at Leyte, was to wonder why the search planes of the escort carriers had not found the Kurita force before it found them. It was a good question. Later Admiral King investigated and came to the conclusion that Kinkaid's searchers had been remiss. Kinkaid, of course, had been counting on Halsey to take care of everything in that northern sector.

When the call for the battleships came, Halsey would not respond in time to get them there.

"It was not my job to protect the Seventh Fleet," he wrote later.* "My job was offensive, to strike with the Third Fleet and we were even then rushing to intercept a force which gravely threatened not only Kinkaid and myself, but the whole Pacific strategy."

Halsey did send Admiral McCain a message, ordering him to strike the Kurita force, and by afternoon on October 25, McCain's planes were harrying Kurita as he headed home.

At 0900 Kinkaid became more insistent. He asked that Halsey send Lee and the battleships down to Leyte, and that the fast carriers make an immediate strike on Kurita. At 0922 Kinkaid again asked for help, and this time said his old battleships were low on ammunition. (Checking, Halsey found this was an earlier dispatch, but it had somehow been delayed in reaching him.)

Halsey was too far away to send the fast battleships. He so informed Kinkaid, and told him again that McCain was on his way with five carriers and four heavy cruisers.

At 1000 Halsey received two dispatches. One was from Kinkaid:

WHERE IS LEE X SEND LEE

---

* *Certainly that was very clearly outlined, as early as the Sherman-Riley meetings in which the plans officers of the Pacific Fleet and Third Fleet had agreed that Halsey's mission was offensive, not defensive.*

It was sent in the clear, which impressed Halsey more than the message.*

The second message was from Nimitz, asking, in effect, where Halsey was in time of trouble.

Admiral Halsey was first stunned, then furious. At about this same time he had the results of his air strikes: *Chitose* was sunk. *Chiyoda* was dead in the water. Things were going very nicely indeed. He estimated that he and the battleships were about fifty miles from the Japanese, and could finish them off with the big guns. He stopped for a moment to think.

Elsewhere much was being thought about Halsey, too. At headquarters in Pearl Harbor, Nimitz had been aware of developing action since the afternoon of October 24. He had learned with pleasure of the results of the Battle of Surigao Strait. And then, bucketing into headquarters that morning had come that frightful message announcing the attack of Japanese ships on Admiral Sprague's TU [Task Units] 77.4.3 in Leyte Gulf. Worried, Nimitz called Captain Austin, his flag secretary, and asked him what he thought.

The suspense continued, almost unbearably. Finally Nimitz composed a message to Halsey:

WHERE IS TASK FORCE 34

That was all. No chiding, unless the fact that Nimitz had to ask at all was chiding.

Under the communications system established by the American Navy, messages were coded and further protected. It might be possible for a bright Japanese code expert to break a code, given enough repetitions of the same word or the same sequence. One protective device was the padding of messages. It was quite routine.

The message was sent down to the communications center for coding and transmission. The communications officer set it up for coding thus:

TURKEY TROTS TO WATER X WHERE IS TASK FORCE 34 X THE WHOLE WORLD WONDERS

Now the first phrase of the message was obviously meaningless,

* Morison says this message was never sent. The source is Halsey's story.

and it was excised by the receiving communications men on Halsey's *New Jersey* when it came in. The third phrase was also meaningless, and it should also have been excised. But the Halsey communications men were not sure it was meaningless, because it could be construed to be meaningful in connection with the second phrase. And so the third phrase, not so carefully added, was carefully retained, and Halsey was thrown into a swivet.

He turned his flagship around, abandoned the chase, took Bogan's Task Group 38.2 and the fast battleships, and headed south at flank speed, knowing that he could not arrive before 0800 on October 26. Mitscher, with Sherman and Davison and their task groups, was left to do what damage he could to the Ozawa force.

Later Admiral Halsey said that the one aspect of the Battle of the Philippines that he regretted was this decision, made in anger against Nimitz and Kinkaid, to turn south and abandon his chance to destroy Ozawa's force. A newspaper wag, following the action, christened it the Battle of Bull's Run ("Bull" Halsey being the name the correspondents had hung on him because of his ferocious statements about the Japanese and what he was going to do to them). So the Battle of Bull's Run began, and with it, some second guessing by many people.

At Pearl Harbor, where he was planning the invasion of Iwo Jima, Admiral Spruance stood beside the map of the Philippines and put his hand alongside the San Bernardino Strait. "If I were there I would keep my force right there," he said.

Kinkaid's attitude shone through in his messages, and forever afterward Kinkaid took the position that Halsey was supposed to have guarded San Bernardino Strait for him.

In Leyte Gulf the transports and the amphibious forces that morning were not considering the finer points of naval tactics and strategy. Admiral Wilkinson was aboard his amphibious command ship in that gulf, watching the fighting going on around him, and as he wrote Kelly Turner later, "I certainly felt like the heroine shrinkingly watching the hero and the villain fight for her possession."

In Washington, Admiral King was in his office. Rear Admiral Jocko Clark, who happened to be in Washington that day, stopped to pay a call on the Commander in Chief. He found King pacing the office, furious. Halsey had left San Bernardino open for the Japanese to hit the transports at Leyte, said King, and he so far forgot his sense of seniority as to lambaste his absent fleet commander.

But in Nimitz's headquarters thought was much more restrained, and so was conversation. Chester Nimitz, Jr., happened to be visiting his father at Pearl Harbor that day, for the first and only time during the war, since young Nimitz's submarine duty had kept him almost entirely in the South and Southwest Pacific. Mildly, but firmly, Nimitz was blaming Halsey for leaving the strait unguarded, and not keeping Kinkaid informed. His son could dare where others might not, and he asked to see Halsey's orders. When he examined the operational orders issued at Pearl Harbor, young Nimitz spoke up.

"It's your fault," he told his father.

He pointed to the orders, which specifically gave Halsey the right to move out against the Japanese fleet if he had an opportunity to smash major elements. The orders were a reflection of the Sherman-Riley discussions.

"That's your opinion," said Chester Nimitz, Sr., to Chester Nimitz, Jr. And that was the end of the discussion. The rest was left to give the naval historians of the future something to think about: Zuikaku was sunk and the carrier-battleship Ise was hit. Zuiho was hit again and sunk. Cruisers of the task group sank the Chiyoda, which was lying dead in the water, and the destroyer Hatsuzuki. Admiral Lockwood's submarines started closing in on the Japanese force, and Jallao sank the damaged cruiser Tama. But Ise, Hyuga, Oyodo, and five destroyers made it safely home, which they certainly would not have done had Halsey pressed on when he was fifty miles from the Ozawa force with his fast battleships.

Those battleships arrived off San Bernardino Strait and caught the injured destroyer Nowacke of the Kurita force, which was limping far behind Kurita. They smashed Nowacke and picked up some survivors from Suzuya, but otherwise the fast battleships were the victims of faulty communications and changed decision: they left the northern fight and arrived too late for the southern one.

Whose fault was it that Kinkaid was given such a fright? That the escort carrier Gambier Bay was sunk, and the gallant destroyers took their lumps? The facts would seem to indicate that if there is fault to be found it must be distributed.

Admiral King could be faulted for permitting—insisting on—a

divided command, with Halsey retaining his independence of movement, yet "supporting" MacArthur's navy, which was Kinkaid's Seventh Fleet.

Nimitz could be faulted for not making it clear to Halsey that he was responsible for protection of the amphibious forces, tactically, and letting Halsey believe that he was a free agent if he had a chance to hit the Japanese heavy fleet units.

Halsey could be faulted for not knowing or finding out that the Kurita force was as strong as it was and that it was still coming. Of course, like everyone else in the Pacific in 1944, Halsey was super-carrier-conscious, and as the Japanese strategists had figured, the four carriers plus the battleship-carriers were just too much for a carrier admiral to pass up.

Kinkaid could be faulted for not finding the Japanese on the night of October 24 or in the early light of October 25, and bringing up Oldendorf's battleships.

But why fault—except to learn for the future? It was a tremendous victory, even if it might have been more tremendous. The Japanese general staff was more generous to the Americans than they were to themselves: the Japanese said their navy was destroyed at the Philippines.

What the victory meant was very clearly mirrored in Secretary Forrestal's office that day.

On October 25 Kinkaid and Halsey both began sending messages indicating the damage they had caused the Japanese fleet, but these were accompanied by the messages about the attacks on the escort carriers. But at around noon Halsey sent a signal to Nimitz which was intercepted at the Navy Department. "You can say with confidence and assurance," Halsey said, "the Japanese Navy has been beaten, routed, and broken."

King was still angry. He radioed Nimitz to hold up the substance of that message because, King said, Halsey had not had a chance to make a complete evaluation of the situation. Forrestal agreed. "It seemed to me it was wiser to be certain even at the risk of losing two or three hours in announcing the news."

King gave a press conference at 3 p.m. showing great confidence, and indicating that the Japanese fleet was engaged, but not saying much specifically.

Forrestal recalls:

> Just before the Press Conference, I had talked to the President and called his attention to Halsey's message. Just after the conference came the word of the Reuters' story on MacArthur's broadcast of the victory. Harry Hopkins called up and asked what I thought about releasing Halsey's message. I said I was for it, subject to two things: First, a paraphrase to protect the integrity of our codes; second my general superstition about releasing good news until we were absolutely certain of its correctness. However Hopkins said he thought it was worth taking a chance so around six o'clock the President called in the White House reporters and read them a paraphrase of Halsey's dispatch to Nimitz.

And that message is part of the reason why Halsey was a successful admiral. Beyond the immediate problem of the battle—which was really not so humorous as to earn its title: the Battle of Bull's Run—Halsey could see that the Japanese had adopted desperate tactics; with their decimated navy they could only try to achieve a surprise, in a three-pronged attack. Once that failed, and the remnants of the fleet were sent limping back to imperial waters, the navy was no more. To be sure, Halsey, above all American fighters in the Pacific, would have loved to have a straight chance at the traditional Nelsonian battle of fleet-to-fleet, to slug it out with the enemy. But such was not to be; it was never really in the cards. The Japanese knew from the beginning that they would have to win their war by smash-and-grab and then hold the areas they had captured, to create so much trouble that the West would tire of the conflict and come to terms suitable to Japan. Halsey was quick to see, and quick to say, that the Battle of the Philippine Sea represented the last dying gasp of a once-proud fleet. From that moment on the Americans could move anywhere in the Pacific without much worry.

Chapter
Twenty-Four

THE NEW WAR

October 27, 1944–March 23, 1945

If recriminations were in order over the operations of October 24–26, 1944, there was very little time for them in the first days of November. The Japanese fleet was no longer a problem and never would be again in the war, but Japanese air power was very far from finished. Planes could be flown in along the island-hopping route, and they were flown in in large numbers. Many were converted to kamikaze operation, and this suicide club offered the greatest threat to the forces at sea since the days of Guadalcanal.

At the end of October, Marc Mitscher went home for a rest, and Admiral McCain took over as commander of Task Force 38. It was now understood that Mitscher would operate with Spruance and McCain would work with Halsey.

Early in November, Halsey put his finger on the major problem of command in the Philippines. Nimitz had chided him gently for leaving San Bernardino Strait. Said Nimitz in effect, that Halsey must remember that the Leyte operation could not be allowed to fail, and therefore everything must be done to make it a success.

Halsey replied:

> I quite understand that the Leyte operation must not fail, and will be guided accordingly until we are released, but there are factors which I feel that I must report to you—factors that seem to me to be in violation of every sound principle of command'. . . .
>
> In the first place, having two autonomous tactical Fleet Commands supporting the same operation cannot be justified from a naval viewpoint. Cooperation can never be a substitute for command in a naval action, and the further employment of the Seventh Fleet in conjunction with but separate and independent from the Pacific Fleet has all the elements of confusion if not disaster.

Looking ahead, Halsey spoke of the coming operation in which MacArthur would move up the Philippines.

> I don't know what you could do about it, but it would be a great break if a Pacfleet Expeditionary Force could be set up to put the Army ashore at Lingayen and thus keep centralized Naval control of things until the Army says they can take care of themselves ashore.
>
> The last few days at Leyte have been confusing. Under MacArthur's system, the Air, Army, and Navy are three separate commands on the same level; under that system no one agency really runs the show because GHQ is not geared to exercise operational control.

On November 9 Halsey repeated this complaint and amplified it.

"I greatly admire MacArthur's fighting qualities," he said, but he still complained about the command setup. The weakness ". . . showed up at Leyte: Weyler [commander of the North Fire Support Unit] could get no information—there were no properly organized searches—Weyler reported failure by the army to provide the promised CAP [combat air patrol]—Kinkaid reported only 60 fighters at Leyte although more could have been accommodated—the Tokyo Express visited the west coast of Leyte with impunity. And all because neither GHQ nor any other agency coordinates and manages all weapons engaged in the overall operation. Nothing could better demonstrate the need for an expeditionary force under Naval Command."

Halsey was discussing the last few days, which had been most difficult. On October 30 kamikazes hit the carriers *Franklin* and *Belleau Wood*, causing enough damage that they had to retire to Ulithi for repairs. Admiral Weyler's force (he was left as senior officer at Leyte Gulf for the Seventh Fleet) was badly hit because of the air failure on the land. One destroyer was sunk by kamikazes on November 1 and four were damaged. Kinkaid asked MacArthur for land-based air support or more help from Halsey. It had to be help from Halsey. The Army air was not yet much in evidence.

Halsey had plenty of trouble. The cruiser *Reno* was torpedoed by a Japanese submarine, and had to be towed to Ulithi. So Halsey got permission from Nimitz to make a series of air strikes on Luzon, where the kamikazes were originating. On November 5 Task Force 38 hit Luzon hard, claiming 439 planes destroyed in a two-day strike. The carrier planes also sank the heavy cruiser *Nachi*, a survivor of the Battle of Surigao Strait. But *Lexington* (the new one) took a kamikaze on the starboard side of the island, and was hit badly enough that McCain transferred his flag to *Wasp*. Still, the pressure on Leyte was sharply reduced.

Nimitz was pleased. He noted the high cost, but he remarked that Halsey was "inflicting attrition on the enemy at a gratifying rate."

Halsey had wanted very much to hit the Japanese islands in November, and had secured permission from Nimitz for Operation Hotfoot, until the pressure came back on from the renewed Japanese air force. The carriers simply could not be spared until MacArthur could build airfields and get land-based air into Leyte. In the middle of the month the carriers hit Luzon, sinking a light cruiser, five destroyers, and seven transports, at a loss of twenty-five planes for eighty-four Japanese planes. This was, indeed, healthy "attrition." On November 25 planes from Bogan's and Sherman's carriers sank the heavy cruiser *Kumano*. But that day kamikazes hit carriers *Intrepid* and *Cabot* hard, and Admiral Bogan had to go back to Ulithi with his task group for repairs.

At the end of November King and Nimitz met again to discuss the affairs of the fleet. Halsey had been at sea for three months, which was a long time to hold operational command of a fighting fleet without a rest. King suggested at these meetings that Halsey ought to have a two-month rest on the mainland at the earliest opportunity. That thinking accorded with the private plans Nimitz had already discussed with Halsey, to have him come out of battle at the end of the year. But another matter came up—ever so delicately—at these meetings: the composition of Halsey's staff. There was a lingering feeling in Washington and at Pearl Harbor that Halsey's staff was not all it should be. When Halsey went ashore, Nimitz thought, was the time to look into staff changes.

King and Nimitz, along with Leahy, were waiting then for the passage by Congress of a bill creating a new naval rank—Admiral of the Fleet—with the understanding that they would soon be appointed to such posts. If and when that happened, King said, perhaps he ought to make Kinkaid a full admiral, to even up the fleet commands.

On an inspection trip to the Pacific that fall, Towers had been unfavorably impressed by Hoover, who was an outspoken and driving character. Towers had made a firm recommendation that Hoover be replaced, partly on the basis of his impression of Hoover's personality, partly because of the running feud between Hoover and General Hale. The recommendation was heard—and Nimitz squashed the move. He wanted Hoover to continue in his job. The friction between Hoover and Hale, he said, was doubtless due to Hoover's driving qualities and his attempts to make an unwilling Army air force move out on shipping strikes which they believed were a waste of time and talent.

Nimitz was well aware of the animosity between Towers and Hoover. In October Towers had returned to complain about many aspects of the forward areas—too much luxury for Hoover and his staff, too much trouble with Hale, too little attention to civil affairs. Nimitz had called on Hoover to explain, and on October 5 Hoover had written him in detail, naming Towers as the complainant, and answering the complaints.

Of course there was bound to be complaint about Hoover. Lieutenant Commander McArdle, who was assigned to Hoover that fall as public relations officer, described him thus:

> Admiral Hoover was not the most popular admiral in the Pacific. He was harsh and exacting—a perfectionist. If the Seventh AAF's bombing of Iwo Jima didn't suit him (one time he concluded that too many of the Liberators were turning back from engine trouble without reaching their target) he would sit down and write a terse ten word message blistering the pants off the army air force and send it to General Hale. Or he would have an orderly call General Hale's orderly and ask the General to call Admiral Hoover. The Admiral never called a subordinate direct.
>
> And it wasn't always the army air force that caught it. An island commander, a Sea-Bee unit, a navy port director—any of these could become the target of the scathing invective, delivered in a calm, almost silken voice that could send chills down the spines of strong men.

McArdle enjoyed his stay on Saipan with Hoover—or rather on the *Curtiss*, the admiral's flagship. The beds were good and the food was the best in the Pacific. The admiral treated himself well, the ship was the former yacht of millionaire Cyrus Curtis. They had springs in their bunks, always clean linen, ice cream every afternoon, and almost immediately on reaching Saipan an officers club on Maniagassa island. That idea didn't work so well: some officer carelessly threw a cigarette butt, it landed in a Japanese ammunition dump concealed in a cave, and the officer and dump were blown to kingdom come.

But there were always the boats, in which beer could be drunk on the reefs (not on shipboard). And there was the tennis court. The "old man," as his staff called him, was in his fifties, and a bug for tennis. So wherever the *Curtiss* would wander, the Seabees would follow with rollers and equipment to build the admiral's hard-surface tennis court.

Nimitz had heard all the tales. He was very fond of Hoover and intensely loyal to him, and Hoover was doing his best in a most unenjoyable job for a sailor, management of shore facilities and shore people, in addition to shore-based air. Hoover did an excellent job.

This loyalty of Nimitz's was an interesting facet of his character, as has been seen, and a piece with all the rest. As long as an officer did not offend higher authority, and remained in Nimitz's good books by good performance of duty, the admiral would protect him from all the curves thrown by the Army, the Marine Corps, or even the man's peers. Thus Hoover, whose personality and activity offended Admiral Towers and various Army generals, could be safe under the protective mantle of the Pacific command. But a Fletcher or a Brown or a Drake or a Moore who had gotten under the skin of someone higher on the totem pole could not be saved by Nimitz. Even less diplomatic commanders like Halsey and Spruance had learned that personal loyalty in the Navy system had its limitations. Spruance had been forced to transfer Captain Moore, his chief of staff, because of King's dislike for the man. Halsey, the rebel, fought tooth and nail to hold on to Browning, his chief of staff—but to no avail. In sparing himself such useless strain, Nimitz was far more judicious. The admiral was an expert in his own public relations; he never offended higher authority uselessly, and to him uselessly would mean going to bat for someone in serious personal trouble. That was the ancient Navy system. Nimitz had said at the outset of the war that he preferred to let Admiral Jacobs, the personnel director, have the say on senior officers. Thus Nimitz avoided the responsibility for personnel changes throughout the war. It was a wise course, and an effective one.

Halsey was quite the opposite. He would fight like a tiger for his men. True, he would be quick to ship out an officer who "goofed up" or who displayed disloyalty to him, but an officer who was loyal and was doing his job could do no wrong with Halsey. He proved that successfully in the case of "Scrappy" Kessing, who was very nearly a victim of the Navy bureaucracy. And yet the limitations of loyalty are indicated in the cases of both Halsey's and Spruance's personal choices as chief of staff. Halsey had Browning, who fitted him very well. But Browning somehow antagonized the Secretary of the Navy (at Nouméa), and from that point on King put constant pressure on Halsey until Browning was moved out. Spruance liked Captain Moore, who was the ideal chief of staff for him because Moore was hard-working and detail-conscious, so exacting and so able that Spruance could be "lazy" (Moore's word) about detail. But Moore had antagonized King, and thus he had to go. Moore could not even be promoted or have the sop of a Distinguished Service Medal. Spruance and Moore talked over Moore's problem many times, but Spruance was wise enough to refuse to keep butting his head against the stone wall of King's resistance, and thus call down the furies on himself. It was the "Navy way" and if Halsey defied the way from time to time, it did him precious little good, and only his tremendous ability as a commander and a fighting admiral saved him from the wrath of his superiors. Nimitz's course, then, was that of a very judicious man.

At this particular set of King-Nimitz conferences—in November, 1944—there were other personnel matters to be decided, and Nimitz made several recommendations, indicating his manner of dealing with King and with Jacobs, who sat in on this part of the discussion. Rear Admiral George D. Murray, who had taken over Towers' old job as commander of the air forces of the Pacific, was to be advanced to vice admiral—Nimitz's recommendation. Rear Admiral William D. Sample, one of the carrier group commanders in Kinkaid's Seventh Fleet, had been wounded while flying over Leyte. King wanted to know why: was Sample out joy-riding over the Japanese lines (which would have gotten him fired), or was he there to observe the position of the Japanese (which might get him a medal)? Nimitz promised to look into this matter.

So it went, Nimitz exercising restraint on King at times. (King wanted to relieve Fletcher as commander of the North Pacific force, and Nimitz gently demurred. It was not important enough for King to pursue, little was happening in the North Pacific, and in this degree, Nimitz exercised an influence.) Nimitz suggested that Captain Austin, his assistant chief of staff for administration, be made a commodore, and King approved.

They discussed the very ticklish question of the case known as Smith versus Smith—Holland Smith's decision to relieve Major General Ralph Smith of the Army 27th Division at Saipan. The Smith case was still boiling, and the Army had chosen to make a very serious issue of it on the Holland Smith level. General Marshall was very angry. He had already made the flat statement that never again would an Army general serve under the Marines, and now the official buttressing of this position was under way. Marshall had written King on the subject in November, asking King to straighten out the matter between Nimitz and General Richardson. Marshall had also asked that Navy public relations be chided for allowing articles to be published "that will cause friction between the services," quite forgetting the articles the Army had fed the press just after the incident. Marshall was not aware that Nimitz had flatly refused to make any statement, in the interests of Army-Navy amity. Characteristically, Nimitz made no mention of this decision. It was decided earlier and affirmed here, that in the coming operations against Iwo Jima no Army troops would be used, and thus there could be no arguments. Holland Smith would be in charge at Iwo Jima. What would happen after that was yet to be decided.

There were at this time long discussions of the Allies and potential allies in the war against Japan. The British wanted to participate, which would create problems outside the Australia-New Zealand area, as far as logistics was concerned. The Russians were talking about coming into the war, and King noted that "Mr. Stalin had asked for three months stockpiling in Siberia in preparation for their entry into the war against Japan. In addition, Mr. Stalin said that three months after the war with Germany ends would be necessary to build up the 30 to 40 Russian divisions in Siberia to 60 Divisions."

Once again the discussion turned to strategy in the Pacific. Nimitz presented plans for Operation Longtom, which would be an invasion of the Chu Shan archipelago. King liked the idea, as a preliminary to the invasion of Kyushu, which was then tentatively scheduled for mid-September, 1945, followed by a December invasion of the Tokyo plain.

For the first time, serious talk was begun about postwar plans: personnel, bases, sea frontiers, and logistics. It was almost eerie that these top commanders were able to consider the war on so many levels, those of operations, tactics, strategy, postwar planning, and internal administration of the Navy, all in one meeting. Months before, when the news of the casualties at Tarawa had brought Nimitz scores of angry letters from mothers who accused him of sending their sons to their deaths, and wives who called him "murderer," Nimitz had said sorrowfully, "This is one of the responsibilities of command, you have to send some people to their death." With equal aplomb he could now discuss a plan by Halsey "to kill more Japs" in the South China Sea, and the number of Army troops in the Pacific who might be used for operations against the enemy.

In the November meetings King and Nimitz agreed that in future two of the Third Fleet's fast carrier task groups ought to be at rest at Ulithi while the other two were in operation, and late in November Halsey did come into port. Two weeks later he was out in the Pacific again, striking the island of Mindoro in connection with MacArthur's move up the Philippines.

On December 17 Halsey and his force were steaming along in stormy weather, about five hundred miles east of Luzon, standing out from their operations to refuel at sea. It was typhoon season in these waters, and by mid-morning Halsey knew he was facing something more than an ordinary storm. Checking with his aerographer, he decided to move two hundred miles to the northwest. Unfortunately, instead of moving away from the storm, he was moving directly toward its center, because the aerographer took the position that the disturbance center was five hundred miles east of him, and that it would strike a cold front and turn northeast.

Again, communications failures hurt sorely. After Halsey had made his change, he received a delayed dispatch that told him the storm center was not five hundred miles east but two hundred miles southeast. He changed the fueling rendezvous, and changed it again. He ran southwest, and saw the barometer dropping all the way. The destroyers were very low on fuel—some of them took in water ballast, some of them did not. The ships began to struggle under mountains of water in vicious seas, some of them seventy feet high. The mighty *New Jersey* was tossed so that the furniture had to be lashed in place. But the *New Jersey* could and had taken a shell hit from an enemy ship without Halsey even knowing it. On the lesser ships of the fleet, the impact was frightful, and in three cases disastrous. The destroyers *Spence*, *Hull*, and *Monaghan* were turned over and sunk. As a child sinks his toy boats in the bathtub by forcing them under the water, so the storm forced these ships over until the water went gurgling down their stacks, and the weight overwhelmed them. Captain Preston Mercer, Nimitz's old flag secretary, was commander of a destroyer squadron. He managed to save his own ship but could not help some of his others. When the terrible storm was over, twenty-four men from *Spence* had been saved, forty-four from *Hull*, and six from *Monaghan*. Later another ten from *Hull* were found.

The Third Fleet went back to Ulithi, arriving on December 24. Captain Mercer called on Admiral Halsey, and they naturally fell to discussing the typhoon. Halsey asked Mercer for his opinions, straight out, and Mercer gave them: there was fault somewhere.

"You're damned right," said Halsey. "Somebody ought to be court-martialed for this, either me or the Bureau of Ships." Halsey was referring to various modifications made in the sunken destroyers over a period of time since they had been launched—changes that added more and more weight to the ships above decks, and changed their center of gravity. These modifications had made them top-heavy, or at least not as stable as they had been designed to be.

A disaster of the extent of this typhoon demanded an investigation. After all, besides the three ships sunk, the cruiser *Miami* was sorely hurt, so were the light carriers *Monterey*, *Cowpens*, and *San Jacinto*. The escort carriers *Cape Esperance* and *Altamaha* were badly damaged, as were the destroyers *Aylwin*, *Dewey*, and *Hickok*, and nineteen other ships of the fleet. Nearly 150 planes were lost, 790 men were killed, and 80 were injured. "It was the greatest loss that we have taken in the Pacific without compensatory return since the First Battle of Savo," said Admiral Nimitz.

Nimitz came to Ulithi that day bearing a Canadian Christmas tree bedecked with fancy ornaments. He was a little hurt when his thoughtful and generous gesture was not overwhelmingly appreciated by Halsey and the officers of the *New Jersey*; they were really much prouder of the Christmas tree put together by the men of the crew from pipes and nuts and bolts and other items from the machine shop. Nor was it a very happy Christmas, even with the encouraging tenor of the war; Halsey was facing a court of inquiry which Nimitz had to order, reluctant as he might be.

The court of inquiry was headed by Vice Admiral Hoover, who showed his complete impartiality and devotion to duty by taking a very hard line against America's most famous naval hero. Hoover thought Halsey ought to be court-martialed for letting his fleet get into the way of the typhoon. Others said it was bad staff work again.

In the end, Nimitz and King decided that Halsey had been punished enough by the realization that he was responsible, and the matter was resolved by the preparation of a thoroughgoing fleet letter which set out the facts and the responsibilities, and gave the officers of the fleet instructions in the procedures they should follow in tropical storms of the future.

Nimitz went to Ulithi a five-star admiral. So new was the rank that the sailors of the fleet did not even know how a five-star admiral's stars were to be arranged, and it took some puzzling to get him a set. Then, when Nimitz went off to see MacArthur with his five stars, MacArthur was miffed to discover that Nimitz had the insignia and he did not. MacArthur aides were summoned to a summit conference that evening and directed to provide the general with five-star insignia before breakfast.

Such problems of command, and some even more important, often tried Nimitz's patience in his relations with General MacArthur. The whole problem of divided authority could be submerged but it could never be overcome.

In January, for example, Admiral Kinkaid's six old battleships needed some work. Two, in particular, needed major repair of damages suffered in actions since the invasion of Leyte. Nimitz, who "owned" the battleships, as commander of the Pacific Fleet, asked that they be returned to Pearl Harbor. MacArthur refused. He wanted to keep the battleships, he said. He needed them.

Thus was a problem posed for Secretary Forrestal, who wrote:

In exercising his prerogatives of command, if he insists on this order, he will in a sense be overstepping into the broad authority of Fleet Admiral Nimitz. The units MacArthur needs to accomplish his objectives—that is, the protection of Lingayen Gulf area and the integrity of the supply line—is obviously a thing of vital interest to him, but the determination of when ships need overhaul or may be necessary for other operations is obviously the interest of the commander of the Pacific Ocean Areas, Admiral Nimitz.

MacArthur's insistence aroused Nimitz to as strong a letter as he allowed himself to write.

I do not share your opinion as to the ability of the enemy to concentrate a force of six battleships for a quick attack on Kinkaid's forces nor do I consider the Japanese fleet capable of inflicting disaster to our Philippines operations if our fleet is employed offensively. Acceptance of the view that the Philippines must have in addition to your air force a local naval defense force continuously on station capable of meeting all heavy ships left in the Japanese fleet would effectively prevent further major offensive operations in the Pacific for an indefinite period. The best naval protection for the Philippines as well as for the exposed island positions elsewhere in the Pacific is to proceed with offensive operations against Japan.

I therefore repeat my request for the immediate return of the two damaged battleships most in need of repairs in order that their fighting efficiency may be restored and their return to profitable service expedited.

To better meet these new problems of command, Nimitz had decided months before to move to Guam as soon as a headquarters could be readied. Towers had opposed the move strenuously, and why not? He was to be left behind, in a job as deputy commander of the Pacific Fleet which was to become almost entirely administrative and logistical, when all he wanted was a fighting command. At one point Towers' name had been suggested for Calhoun's job as supply admiral, but that idea had fallen by the wayside in the need for someone to keep the Pearl Harbor headquarters going.

In January the Nimitz move began in stages. Guam, in the early days after the capture of the Marianas, had been little but a mudhole. Officers coming in to Orote airstrip often had to hitchhike down to island command headquarters, eight miles away, and the trip might take them two hours. For months there were Japanese loose on the island, roaming about, stealing supplies, taking potshots at the Seabees, being potshotted in turn, and even attending the movies. (One night a Seabee battalion between Island Command and Barrigada flushed a covey of Japanese who were standing on the outskirts of their group, watching their Dorothy Lamour movie, and that night there was a great, noisy "Jap hunt" in the brush.)

By January matters had changed. The Barrigada mud trail was on the way to becoming a paved six-lane highway. At Pacific Fleet advanced headquarters the Seabees were building a town that would have more than 2500 inhabitants. Nimitz had a white clapboard house with four bedrooms and four baths, opening onto a courtyard that was landscaped with grass and flowers. There was a large combination living-dining room and a screened porch with a view of the lights of the harbor at Agana in the evenings. Next door was a staff cottage, where Admiral Sherman and several of the other senior officers were quartered.

Even so, Guam was a dusty place when the sun was hot, and a muddy one when the rains came, which meant nearly every day between January and May. In the beginning, the officers lived in two-storey quonset huts. When it rained, and the lightning flashed and thunder pounded, the staff was miserable. Down below, the water might compete with the heat for most miserable; up on Cincpac's hill it was better. Guam was a forward headquarters, so the uniform in daytime was khaki shirts and trousers or shorts, with no neckties. At night it was tieless khaki.

Immediately the reason for the move to Guam was apparent. Where before the coming and going of officers between Pearl Harbor and Brisbane had been a noteworthy event, now movement between Agana and MacArthur's headquarters became commonplace.

As for Nimitz, he arose early and went walking before breakfast these days, then ate and went to the office, where he observed much the same routine as in the days at Pearl Harbor. He traveled a little more—time was telescoping in this stepped-up war—but he kept open house for visiting ship captains, and was, or gave the appearance of being, very available to officers who needed his counsel. Actually Soc McMorris protected Nimitz from much of the detail these days, and his quick yeses and quicker nos were famous in the fleet. Forrest Sherman spent much time thinking and talking over problems with Nimitz, and as usual the senior staff met every day to keep a running contact with the war.

The public at large scarcely knew Nimitz, in spite of the occasional article that had appeared in one of the big magazines. The war in the Pacific, to this point, was MacArthur's war and, when the Navy was mentioned at all, Halsey's war. Nimitz was happy to have it that way, knowing that his place in the Navy did not depend on public acclaim, and apparently he was also oblivious to his place in history. He kept some memorabilia and a file of correspondence, particularly his admiral-to-admiral correspondence, which was personal but official. The command had its war diary, which described the various daily happenings of note, and the more confidential Gray Book, which included estimates of situations and some comments on personnel, as prepared by the senior members of the staff with Nimitz's approval. (Both, of course, were secret at the time.)

Overall, however, Nimitz was even more shy than Spruance in matters of personal publicity. In January of this year, when the list of five-star officers was published, and Nimitz was among them, his name suddenly leaped out to the American public for almost the first time. Admiral William V. Pratt, one of the oldest and wisest heads in the Navy, who had retired and was writing a weekly column on the war for *Newsweek*, suggested that it was time Nimitz had a little publicity.

"Now I want to tell you something, and it is not hot air," Pratt wrote Nimitz. "I have watched your work, and in my opinion you have displayed all the qualities a top leader should possess. It is about time a few bouquets were given to the Navy for the magnificent work it has done in the Pacific, and I am going to do it. . . ."

Pratt did write a column on Nimitz, but Nimitz scarcely appreciated the honor. At about this time Navy public relations in Washington suggested to Captain Miller at fleet headquarters that Nimitz ought to be built up personally, in view of the pressure from public and Congress that was pointing to MacArthur as the man to lead the invasion of Japan.

"Any plan for a publicity buildup for me is absolutely contrary to my ideas for the conduct of the war in the Pacific and meets with my disapproval," Nimitz said, "as well as the disapproval of Mr. Forrestal, with whom I have discussed this in the last two days."

Forrestal was in the Pacific in February, when the letter was written, for he had determined that he was going to be "in on" one of these amphibious landings, and he had chosen the Iwo Jima operation.

The usual buildup by Kelly Turner had begun months earlier, while Spruance sat in Pearl Harbor and made his plans for the big step forward. Holland Smith looked over the intelligence reports and the statistics, and said Iwo Jima would be the toughest fight his Marines had yet taken on. He would take the island, he said, but his casualties would be high and the fighting would be very fierce.

This warning gave Spruance pause, because he was the principal architect of the Iwo Jima plan. In the floundering that accompanied the basic disagreement between MacArthur, who wanted Philippines-Japan, and the Navy, which wanted Central Pacific–China, King had grasped at Spruance's proposals for Iwo Jima and Okinawa as stepping stones to Asia proper. Now, worried, Spruance began rechecking all the facts that had led to his proposal. What comforted him most was the assurance by Major General Curtis LeMay of the XXI Bombing Command that Iwo Jima would be invaluable to him for his B-29 operations against the Japanese homeland.

Because of the difficulties (the Japanese were heavily dug in), Holland Smith wanted a ten-day bombardment of Iwo Jima. Spruance said it was impossible, there was no time for it. Three days was all he could grant. After all, as they all agreed, Iwo had been bombed intermittently for the last eight months, and as of the day of invasion would have been bombed *daily* for seventy-two days. That should be enough shock and destruction.

It was just a year before the Americans had begun stepping up the pace, and taken the Marshalls. With that loss, and the breach of the Empire's line, the Japanese had begun fortification of the inner line, of which Iwo was a part. For a solid year the Japanese had been rebuilding their fortifications of Iwo Jima. Its strength to resist would be very great, and everyone knew it. The strength of the American Navy had also grown very great in the past year, too.

The Navy had 23 battleships, 89 carriers (13 of the 27,000-ton carriers, 3 pre-1942 carriers, 8 light carriers, and 65 escort carriers), 62 cruisers, 371 destroyers, 378 destroyer escorts, 238 submarines— 1161 fighting ships in all. By the end of 1945 it was projected that the Navy would have 1337 more ships, including 30 more cruisers, and as much of this power as was needed could be turned against Japan. Besides this, the keels were laid in 1944 for three 45,000-ton supercarriers.

The difference between 1944 and 1945 was shown very clearly in the Lingayen Gulf landings on Luzon by General MacArthur's forces. This landing was conducted entirely by Admiral Kinkaid and his Seventh Fleet. He had battleships and cruisers aplenty (mostly from Cincpac, on loan), fifteen escort carriers, six seaplane tenders, and hundreds of planes in support from airfields to the south. It was true that the going was getting tougher all the time, because of the numbers of Japanese troops, and the kamikazes who threatened every ship afloat, and the growing determination of the Japanese to resist; but the numbers of American troops, planes, guns, and ships were increasing every week. It would have to be thus, and so would General MacArthur's force have to increase, for there were nearly 200,000 Japanese troops on Luzon. The war was taking a very different course now that the Americans were nearing Japan.

Nimitz's relationships to the Philippines operation was simply to be "in support," which meant that he supplied the ships and some of the commanders, and the means to sustain them in the battle. He had no say about operations, nor any time to worry about them. In mid-January, when the invasion of Luzon began, Nimitz's concerns were Iwo Jima, Okinawa, and what lay beyond. Neither Nimitz nor Spruance had any taste for invading Japan, but they could see the pressure building up day after day.

Iwo Jima was to be taken by the old team, so to speak. Spruance was in charge. Kelly Turner was commander of the expeditionary force. Holland Smith was commander of the expeditionary troops, and under him came the V Amphibious Corps, with Major General Harry Schmidt in command. Rear Admiral Harry Hill had the attack force, and Rear Admiral W. H. P. Blandy was the support force commander. Marc Mitscher would bring in Task Force 58. Additions, representing the growing power, were a logistic support group and a search and reconnaissance group.

The Japanese buildup of Iwo Jima brought the force to 21,000 defenders, but that figure scarcely told the story. Lieutenant General Tadamichi Kuribayashi had spent many months rebuilding the defenses, and as the Americans flew over the island taking photographs, Kelly Turner's photo interpreters said they could see the positions being strengthened day by day. The shore guns, for example, were placed in position to have protection from naval gunfire, with four to six feet of concrete around them. Antiaircraft guns were placed in fortified pits so that it would take a direct hit to knock one out. The island was tunneled until it became a beehive of caves and passageways under the surface. General Kuribayashi did what he intended to do: transform the island into a fortress.

The Americans knew it would be tough going, yet they did not know how tough.

Spruance's plan called for a strong carrier strike on the Tokyo area just before the landings. The purpose was to take Japanese attention away from a bombardment of Iwo Jima that would begin three days before the landings. Furthermore, the air attack would keep Japanese planes from coming to Iwo until the Marines had a chance to establish themselves there. Holland Smith and his generals really put up a stiff fight to get more bombardment time, but the best they could achieve was Spruance's agreement to give Admiral Blandy the option to bombard for one extra day if he felt it would help. The Spruance-Turner argument against longer bombardment was that it would not be possible because of the limited availability of ships, ammunition, and supplies, and the surprise angle. The ships and ammunition were a real problem; Nimitz was shuttling supply ships and others from Seventh Fleet to Fifth Fleet, so as to support these heavy military undertakings in both quarters.

On January 27 Admiral Halsey turned over command of the fast battleships, the fast carriers, and their supporting ships to Admiral Spruance, and the organization once again became Fifth Fleet. Spruance spent his days planning the next operation (to Okinawa), and making sure of the readiness of various units for the Iwo Jima fight. He was particularly concerned with the coming carrier strike on the Tokyo area, because it was apparent in the battle for the Philippines that the Japanese were still able to turn out airplanes very quickly and very well.

"I could see no object in any longer fighting these aircraft around the perimeter if we could by accurate bombing wreck the factories where they were being produced and so reduce the output." Aircraft factories were strategic targets, and as such they found a new, important place in Spruance's mind, and his thinking about the carrier expanded.

On February 8 Spruance sailed and on February 16 Task Force 58, the fast carriers, hit Japan from a point only sixty miles off the coast of Honshu. The strike was vigorous, but not very successful as far as the aircraft factories were concerned. The force claimed 341 Japanese planes shot down and 190 destroyed on the ground, with losses of 88 planes from all causes. The tactical value of the strike was to delay Japanese air assistance to Iwo Jima. Holland Smith continued to believe it would have been more effective warfare to give longer fire support in the way of preinvasion bombardment. Again it was the problem of an officer's particular view of the war. One reason Spruance was apparently so stubborn in resisting the demands for longer bombardment was the timing of the whole Central Pacific campaign. Originally it had been hoped that Iwo Jima would be invaded on January 20, but logistic problems affecting MacArthur and Nimitz had caused a delay until February 19, and Spruance did not see how he could delay any longer. For after Iwo Jima there must be an interlude, and then the Okinawa operation— and Spruance had to backtime (schedule backwards) from the beginning of the hurricane or typhoon season. He also had to share his ships with MacArthur. Obviously he could not let the Okinawa invasion be caught in a typhoon; Halsey's typhoon had shown just what could happen, and if that damage were multiplied by cargo ships and landing vessels that were not so very seaworthy, there could be the devil to pay.

The Iwo Jima operation had been months in the planning, and ship loading had begun in December. In the last few weeks the worried Marines had asked for many aerial photographs. In studying them, General Schmidt and Admiral Hill and his staff discovered something they had not known, something that brought frowns to their faces. Looking at a Japanese LCI (landing craft infantry) that had been wrecked on the beach, they could see the working of the beach stuff around the vessel, which indicated an extremely soft beach. Later they were to discover that the beach was nothing but dark volcanic sand and cinders which seemed to have no packing quality at all. Hill ordered up some Marston netting, and had it made into pieces ten feet by a foot and a half. Hinged, it could be put together in an accordion pleat and stretched out to fifty-foot lengths. These would be spread out for tractors, and by pulling them along they could quickly set up a 150-foot length. They tried it on an Oahu beach and it worked very nicely.

There were new devices in this operation, as each landing taught the amphibious commanders more about their strange business. They had cranes and fire pumps for the beaches, and seven armored bulldozers.

On January 11 Hill and General Schmidt left Pearl Harbor in the *Auburn*, Hill's flagship. At that moment Admiral Hill was not certain that he was not going to be commander of this force. Turner was laid up with a bad back, and actually had given command to Hill. But on January 27 Turner overcame his personal miseries, struggled into a back brace, and took command. They sailed, Turner with the Fifth Division in the lead, and Hill twenty-five miles astern with the Fourth Marine Division in his ships. On February 5 they were in Eniwetok to take on last-minute supplies. On February 11 they were in Saipan, and there Secretary Forrestal joined Turner and General Holland Smith on the flagship *Eldorado*.

Turner was sick again, and almost from day to day Hill did not know whether he was to command or be second in command.

Three days before the invasion, Admiral Blandy began his bombardment. The weather was not very good, and Blandy did not use up all the ammunition scheduled. Nor did he opt to take the fourth day for bombardment. Later Holland Smith was to say this decision caused many more American casualties than were necessary. Admiral Hill, however, thought quite differently about it. "Based upon my knowledge of the called gunfire over Admiral Turner's circuits which were monitored during the following days by my staff, it is my firm opinion that most of the targets suitable for destruction by naval gunfire had been eliminated." One such was a group of targets masked by the Japanese, very successfully, during the opening hours of the invasion. General Kuribayashi, who would have been an ornament to any nation's army, had ordered his defenders to remain concealed until the troops began to move ashore, then open up. But on D-2, when the underwater demolition teams (UDT) were moving into the beaches of Iwo Jima to check for obstructions and clear the way, the Japanese defenders mistook the UDT men for the invasion force and began firing guns and mortars from the hills. All twelve of the LCI's involved were hit, which gives a good indication of the guns and the marksmanship. But the guns were exposed, and many of them were silenced in the next two days.

The landings went off as scheduled, except that the cinders were far worse than expected, and the vehicles immediately began bogging down. Infantrymen sank in up to their ankles and could only shuffle along. It was going to be a tough fight, that much was obvious.

Tough it was. The Japanese were so well dug in, and their guns so well placed, that they had to be routed out, position by position, with flame throwers, artillery, and grenades. It was the old game of sealing the caves shut once again.

On D+1 the southern airfield was taken. On D+2 the Fifth Fleet met the kamikazes, mixed in with regular fighters and bombers, for the first time; *Saratoga* was hit, the *Bismarck Sea* was sunk, and *Lunga Point* was damaged. Turner, with the Secretary of the Navy aboard, retired from the area for a time.

The fighting was very fierce, but on February 23 Mt. Suribachi was taken and photographer Joe Rosenthal's famous flag-raising picture was made. On D+13 the first B-29 made an emergency landing on the no. 1 airfield, illustrating the value of Iwo Jima to the war effort. By that time the big fleet carriers had gone back to Ulithi to get ready for the Okinawa operation. On March 5 Admiral Spruance decided the critical period on Iwo Jima was over, and he sailed for Ulithi to take up his planning again. On March 8 Turner turned command over to Hill and followed Spruance. Holland Smith moved from the *Eldorado* to Hill's *Auburn*.

Holland Smith, by this time, was a nervous wreck. Whatever else had happened, his relief of Ralph Smith at Saipan had ruined Holland Smith's future in the Pacific war. In title he was in command of the expeditionary troops. In fact he was kept on shipboard all during this operation, only allowed ashore by Turner for "inspections" and *not* allowed to direct "his" Marines. He spent most of his time in his cabin. After he came over to *Auburn*, Hill, who liked Smith and felt sorry for him, would go down to the general's cabin to play cribbage. It was one of Smith's few reliefs from the loneliness in which he now found himself. For Smith had become a victim of the interservice power struggle.

Admiral Hill conceived of a diversionary operation of his own. He sent the destroyers *Dorch* and *Cotton* on a sweep to sink two trawler-type pickets off Japan, and let it be indicated by radio messages that the battle force was out. He called it Operation Sockem. When Nimitz heard of it he approved, and so did King, but King also felt constrained to tap Hill on the wrist for using a code name that forecast the type of operation conducted.

On March 23 Nimitz visited Iwo Jima. He had just come back to the Pacific after a trip to Washington, where he had lunched with President Roosevelt and met with Admiral King to discuss high strategy again. At these meetings Admiral Cooke, King's planner, suggested that after the Okinawa operation the Pacific forces should go into Chu Shan and the Kurils. But Nimitz's basic planning was still awaiting the outcome of the Philippine and Okinawa operations. Iwo Jima fighting lasted until March 26. It was as expensive as Holland Smith and General Schmidt had feared it would be: 6000 Marines and 900 Navy men were killed and 19,000 were wounded in wiping out all but 216 of the 21,000 Japanese fighters on the island. Smith, thoroughly embittered against Navy and Army, soon went home to a training command, never again to return to the Pacific.

In the forthcoming operation against Okinawa, a British task force would work with the Americans. Vice Admiral Sir Bernard Rawlings was bringing four carriers, two battleships, five cruisers, and eleven destroyers to participate in the Pacific war. The manner of their use had occasioned many conferences at Pearl Harbor and Guam, but in the end they were assigned as a special Task Force 57, and given the job of covering the airfields of Sakishima Gunto, the group of islands that lay midway between Okinawa and Formosa, and from which many Japanese aircraft could normally expect to stage to defend Okinawa.

Because of this cooperation, months later Admiral Sir Bruce Fraser, commander in chief of the British Pacific Fleet, came out to Guam to present Nimitz with a new honor, British knighthood in the ancient and honorable Order of the Bath. Originally the Duke of Gloucester had been chosen to do the honors, but he was busy in Australia at the moment and so Sir Bruce had the task.

At 1100 one morning Nimitz and several members of his staff went aboard Sir Bruce's flagship for the ceremony, and after reading from an impressive document the British admiral placed the broad scarlet ribbon of the order about his opposite number's neck. Then grog was issued to the crew and the cheers went up.

The British had an old naval custom for visiting firemen, as Sir Bruce informed Commander Lamar, the admiral's aide.

"Flags," said Sir Bruce. "It is the custom that when your master splices the main brace [issues free grog to the crew in honor of some important occasion] you down a tot of grog bottoms up."

Commander Lamar was not much of a drinker. Nor was he used to drinking black British rum in the heat of the day (125° at noon in the sun). But he manfully downed his tot, then headed below deck, to the first officer's cabin and the head, where he retched up the rum, took a shower, sobered up, and "recomposed" himself. He came back on deck, to find that no one had noticed his absence, and to pull one of the social gaffes of the war. There was another old British custom, which held that if the midshipmen of any ship were able to cozen a flag officer to come into their mess, they were

entitled to free drinks at the expense of the commanding officer
of their ship for the rest of the week. Commander Lamar did not
know of this custom, of course, although all his British counter-
parts did, and no British admiral would go to a midshipman's mess
unless there was some very heroic reason for it. But the young rascals
suspected American ignorance, so they innocently came to Lamar and
asked if Nimitz would come to their mess. Lamar knew that Nimitz
liked to make a show of being friendly to young officers when he
could, so grandly Lamar accepted for his commander. And thus
Admiral Fraser and the captain of his flagship were stuck for a week,
while the young midshipmen drank up everything in sight at their
expense.

Chapter
Twenty-Five

OKINAWA

January 1–August 13, 1945

Life at Guam was always more exciting than life at Pearl Harbor had been. One night the Marine guards were aroused by a Japanese soldier coming up the cliff. They rushed to the Nimitz house, woke up Lieutenant Commander Lamar, and then rushed back to the edge of the cliff to begin blazing away with their rifles. Lamar awakened Nimitz, who came out with his .45 automatic, and joined the shooting. In the morning all that could be found was a worn knapsack, a few fish hooks, and a bloodstained rifle.

Each day Nimitz would hold his meetings, and then go for a swim at his beach, taking along any visitor and a handful of members of his staff. The swims took the place of some of the long walks, and the admiral dispensed with lunch these days, in deference to his expanding waistline. By the time Spruance and the Central Pacific forces began the invasion of Okinawa, the Nimitz life was subtly different from any time in the recent past. He was writing Halsey about fleet public relations, and explaining the efforts that were being made—such as setting up a special press transmission ship, the *Mt. McKinley*. He was corresponding with all his admirals about the postwar fleet. To be sure, Japan was still in the war, and there was a long way to go to defeat her, yet the odor of victory was definitely in the air already.

Spruance had issued his operations plan for the Okinawa invasion on January 3. Okinawa would represent the end of the planning for the moment; from there it would be about equal in mileage to move to China or Japan. Okinawa would be a new kind of operation for Spruance and Nimitz, for although Spruance was to be in charge, with Mitscher running the fast carriers and Turner running the amphibious operation, the Army would be the force to land and take the island. Lieutenant General Simon Bolivar Buckner would bring the Tenth Army into the invasion. Yes, an *army*, for Okinawa, the island that was central to the campaign, was a land mass of nearly five hundred square miles.

The struggle between Army and Navy ways became a little more intense. Nimitz wanted some land-based air support, but Admiral Hoover's planes were too far away to be of any use, and the only planes other than carrier planes that could soften up Okinawa were the B-29 Superfortresses. General LeMay had very definite ideas about the uses of his Superfortresses, and they did not include tactical support of amphibious operations. LeMay and Nimitz argued the point for some time, and according to LeMay's public relations officer, St. Clair McKelway, the irascible LeMay even suggested that Nimitz was impairing the war effort by demanding the B-29's over Okinawa when they preferred to be over Japan.

Perhaps Holland Smith's vigorous complaints about the naval bombardment at Iwo Jima bore some fruit, for Admiral Blandy was to give eight days' bombardment at Okinawa.

It was planned that General Buckner would have Major General Geiger and the First, Second, and Sixth Marine Divisions, four infantry divisions of the Army XXIV Corps, under Major General John R. Hodge, with a fifth division in reserve. It meant there would be more than 170,000 American combat troops on Okinawa to challenge an estimated 77,000 Japanese. To land these troops it would take eight transport squadrons of 57 ships each.

First of all Admiral Mitscher's Task Force 58 began softening up the island. Jocko Clark was back in action, along with Ralph Davison, Ted Sherman, and Arthur Radford, each in command of a task group. It was expected that the Japanese would meet the American force with some two or three thousand planes over Okinawa, and they apparently did. Furthermore, from the moment the task force went into action on March 18, the kamikazes (one-way missions) began coming in, and they proved to be more troublesome at Okinawa than they had ever been before. Radford's Enterprise was hit by a bomb, *Intrepid* was damaged by a near miss, and *Yorktown* was bombed successfully by a non-kamikaze bomber. One bomb blew two big holes in her. Next day Admiral Davison's *Wasp* was bombed so successfully that fires broke out on five decks, and 101 men were killed and 269 wounded. The damage seemed almost as severe as that to old *Lexington* at Coral Sea, but such were the improvements in the new carriers in terms of firefighting and damage control that *Wasp* continued to operate for several days. Davison's flagship, the *Franklin*, was even worse hit. One bomb wrecked the forward elevator and started many fires on the hangar deck. A second bomb hit the flight deck, set fire to planes that were ready to launch, and bathed the ship in flame. Admiral Davison and Admiral Bogan, who was riding as an observer, left the ship to transfer to the *Hancock*, and Davidson told Captain Leslie Gehres to abandon ship. Gehres sent all but his essential officers and men over the side, *Franklin* went dead in the water, but Gehres and his men saved the ship and eventually took her back to the United States under her own power. Those two bombs caused the deaths of 725 men and the wounding of 265 more.

That was the way it went at Okinawa. As the Americans moved into the Ryukyus, of which Okinawa is the largest island, the Japanese defenses stiffened even more than in the past. The Japanese brought out special suicide gliders called Baka bombs. They manned suicide boats, filled with explosives.

On March 25 the bombardment of Okinawa began—and so did the kamikaze attacks. From this point on they would be regular, day by day, coming in groups of one to twenty, or in huge waves. Spruance was on hand in the *Indianapolis* for the bombardment, and on March 31, D—1, his flagship was hit by a kamikaze. Four attacked, three were shot down, and one crashed into the ship's port quarter. Nine men were killed and twenty wounded, but Spruance was untouched.

The landings at Okinawa were fairly easy. General Ushijima, the Japanese commander, had decided to make his stand in the hills around Naha and on the Motobu Peninsula, rather than concentrate his strength to oppose the landings. Spruance was not there; *Indianapolis* had gone to the base at Kerama Retto for repairs. Later Spruance transferred to the *New Mexico*, and *Indianapolis* went back to the United States for overhaul.

The suicide planes demanded new techniques to counter the threat, and Kelly Turner developed them. Sixteen radar picket ships were established around Okinawa to intercept and report on incoming enemy flights. These were strengthened by two ships as the pickets began to take a beating from the kamikazes.

What the Japanese called Operation Ten-Go began on April 6 with a raid of 355 kamikazes. They "got" three destroyers, two ammunition ships, and an LST; they damaged nine destroyers and escorts, a mine layer, and a dozen other ships. Altogether, before Okinawa was taken, the kamikazes sank 26 ships, and damaged 200, including six carriers. Involved in these raids were regular planes and 1900 kamikazes, 250 of them coming from Formosa and the rest from Japan. Roughly, one in ten of these planes got through the American fire.

On April 6 and 7 Spruance and Mitscher found and tracked the Japanese superbattleship *Yamato*, which had come out with a light cruiser and eight destroyers. Spruance was in a position to decide *how* to destroy *Yamato* at this point in the war. Should it be by the fast carriers, which could certainly do the job, or should he let the old battleships have a little fun? Rear Admiral Morton L. Deyo had these battleships, six of them, with seven cruisers and twenty-one destroyers, as a fire-support force. Spruance decided, too, to go along in his flagship.

But on April 7 it appeared that the *Yamato* was not coming direct, and might get away. Mitscher asked Spruance, "Will you take them or shall I?" and Spruance gave up the chance for the gun duel. "You take them," he said.

Mitscher took them. In an hour and a half the planes of his fast carrier force put nine torpedoes and five 1000-pounds bombs into *Yamato*. She capsized, blew up, and sank. The carrier planes also sank the light cruiser and four of the eight destroyers, damaging all four of the others. By this time no more proof of the vast power of the fast carrier forces was needed; what was happening now as far as Japanese naval vessels were concerned was that they had become tidbits for the fast carriers to digest amid the more prosaic but essential tasks of hitting the Japanese at home and protecting the fleet from the dying gasps of Japanese land-based air defense.

Spruance continued in command of what had become a drawn-out and wearing operation. He brought battle repair ships to the area. He worked out new dispositions and ship movements.

Spruance grew impatient with the Army's method of advance. On May 13 he wrote to his old chief of staff, Captain Moore:

> The Jap casualties reported by the 10th Army are pure estimates, not actual counts of dead Japs. I don't take these estimates much more seriously that I do the Japs' figures on our casualties. Since the push started on 19 April we have advanced about 4000 yards. There are times when I get impatient for some of Holland Smith's drive, but there is nothing we can do about it.
>
> Iwo was a very tough job for the Marines, but they finished it up in 26 days. I doubt if the Army's slow, methodical method of fighting really saves any lives in the long run. It merely spreads the casualties over a longer period. The longer period greatly increases the Navy casualties, when Jap air attack on ships is a continuing factor. However, I do not believe the Army is at all allergic to losses of naval ships and personnel.

On May 12 Spruance had a narrow escape. The *New Mexico* had gone over to Kerama Retto to take on ammunition, and left late in the afternoon to return to Okinawa and anchor for the night. Spruance described the event to Moore:

Just about sundown, two low-flying bogies came in through our radar pickets from the westward, presumably from Formosa. A few minutes before we anchored they arrived on the scene, picked out the *New Mexico* [his flagship] and dived on her. One was shot down, landing in the water close aboard on our port quarter. A few moments later the other landed on us, coming in on the starboard side, just about the foremast structure. The bomb went off on the superstructure deck just about the foremast, while the plane crashed in the uptake space on the forward side of the stack. The most curious part of the whole business was that ammunition from the antiaircraft battery was knocked down into the hole made by the plane, and fell through the battle bars into several of the boilers, where it went off, putting three of our four boilers out of commission, probably for several days. The casualties were about 50 killed, mostly in the anti-aircraft batteries but some on the quarterdeck, either from strafing or from fire from other ships. About 80 men seriously wounded and a good many more with minor injuries. Except for several of Slonim's men [Slonim was the Japanese language expert] who were close to the bomb explosion, the staff had no casualties. Slonim had just left there to come aft to tell me the Jap planes were close. Otherwise he would have been killed. Burns [the meteorological officer] was knocked down on our signal bridge. But not hurt. I had just started for the bridge when the AA batteries opened up, so I remained under cover while going forward on the second deck, and we were hit before I got very far, which was fortunate for me, as the two routes to the bridge led right through the area where the plane and bomb hit. This is my second experience with a suicide plane making a hit on board my own ship, and I have seen four other ships hit near me.

The suicide plane is a very effective weapon which we must not underestimate. I don't believe anyone who had not been around within this area of operation can realize its potentialities against ships. It is the opposite extreme from a lot of our Army heavy bombers, who bomb safely and ineffectively from the upper atmosphere.

Spruance grew very restless, as his letter indicated. He liked to go ashore, but General Buckner did not like it at all. Okinawa was hardly safe, and Buckner could not guarantee Spruance's safety. Spruance was delighted, then, to be relieved late in May by Admiral Halsey, who had taken home leave, and then spent the last six weeks in Pearl Harbor planning. One plan called for the invasion of the China coast a hundred miles south of Shanghai. The other, which appealed to Halsey, was an assault on Kyushu.

Nimitz made several changes all at the same time. Spruance was recalled. Turner, promoted to full admiral, was brought back with Spruance, and Harry Hill, promoted to vice admiral, was sent to supervise the remainder of the Okinawa operation, along with Admiral McCain, who relieved Mitscher as commander of the fast carriers. It might appear that the Okinawa operation was over, but such was hardly the case. It had seemed easy. The Marines had done so well in the beginning that Kelly Turner had returned the Second Marine Division which was in reserve, and it had gone to Guam in April. But the Japanese were very tough, and in June Hill had to bring them back.

Spruance had already suggested to Nimitz that the target date for the landing on the Chinese coast be August 15, which meant there was little time if that was to be carried out. He had never liked the idea of a Japan landing. "The question of what operations should be undertaken after Okinawa," Spruance said, "whether to the coast of China or to the main islands of Japan was a most important one. It was my opinion at the time, and I have never had any reason to change it, that landings in Japan proper, such as the planned Kyushu on 1 November 1945 were not necessary and would have been extremely costly."

Nimitz, all this while, was having serious difficulties of his own at Guam. It seemed that General MacArthur was trying to move in on him.

On April 13 Lieutenant General Sutherland and General Kenney arrived at Guam to discuss future command relationships. Sutherland began that evening to lay out MacArthur's ideas.

As soon as possible, Sutherland said, MacArthur intended to take command of all Army forces in the Pacific including the garrisons of the islands under Nimitz. All previous command arrangements had been unsatisfactory to the Army, Sutherland said, and the principle of "unity of command" was an unworkable "shibboleth."

Warming to his idea, Sutherland said further that in the future no Army troops were going to serve under *any* admiral.

Sutherland had apparently been deluded by Nimitz's mild manners into believing that the admiral would take such dicta lying down. He was quickly disabused of the notion.

"He was informed," Nimitz told King in a radio message, "that unity of command in the Pacific Ocean Areas had gotten us through our period of adversity and moved us to the inner approaches of Japan and was the only feasible arrangement for operating and defending an area and coordinating area matters."

Nimitz said he would relinquish the control of troops to MacArthur as they came out of operations.

However, the essential garrison of all positions in the Pacific Ocean areas must remain under my operations control as long as I am responsible for those areas. Abolition of unity of command in the subareas and outlying islands would produce chaos and would retard the prosecution of the war. I shall not therefore accede to his assuming operational control of army forces —ground, air, or service—which are essential to the defense and functions of the Pacific Ocean Areas . . . .

Nimitz informed King that MacArthur was planning to take over the Ryukyus too, and to mount an assault on Kyushu in November.

The next day, the conferences continued. Sutherland and Kenney made detailed proposals to take over the Ryukyus operation, which included Okinawa. MacArthur had told them to do so, because the Ryukyus were his "paramount interest" as the axis of his advance into Japan. Kenney wanted to move the Fifth Air Force into Okinawa—to which Nimitz saw no objection at all, except that of overall command.

They discussed Operation Olympic, which was to be the invasion of Japan. They agreed that MacArthur would draft a plan and send it to Nimitz, who would redraft and revise as he saw fit, and they would meet in Manila for another planning conference. Nimitz informed King that the one difficulty was the matter of command relationships, and, of course, unless he was prepared to take the back seat, this difficulty would continue.

"An interesting sidelight," Nimitz added, "is that Sutherland says MacArthur will land in Kyushu about D plus 3, stay a short time and then return to Manila until time for the Honshu landing."

Later that day, Nimitz quite lost his patience with the Mac-Arthur representatives, when they delivered a paper making the same proposals that had been turned down the day before, adding that Nimitz should take over operational control of naval operations in the Southwest Pacific. The idea was very clearly to push Nimitz into accepting MacArthur as his boss.

"Since these ideas were consuming valuable time and delaying constructive planning," Nimitz told King, "I authorized McMorris to inform Sutherland in writing as follows." Then Nimitz detailed what he would do and would not do.

First, he said it was important to arrange method, time, and place for coordination of the invasion planning and preparations ordered by the Joint Chiefs of Staff. (This was a veiled reminder to MacArthur that the Joint Chiefs of Staff *were* in control.) Such coordination was necessary, Nimitz said, so that he could plan the naval and amphibious operations.

Once and, hopefully, for all, he stipulated what he would and would not do. He would not transfer shore positions to MacArthur. He would not relinquish control of Army forces. He would control all these forces unless the Joint Chiefs ordered him to do otherwise. He would also control logistics in his area unless ordered otherwise. He would not take over MacArthur's naval forces. He would provide naval cover and would provide naval forces to operate under MacArthur.

There was more talk. To give them a carrot as well as the stick, Nimitz finally agreed that he might reconsider giving MacArthur operational control of shore positions after Okinawa was taken "or when a firm directive is received for the Olympic operation."

But as it developed, the MacArthur representatives were in no position to talk about anything except MacArthur's demands, which had been rejected. "It now appears that the SWPA party will leave at 160800 [April 16, 8 A.M.]. Very little useful discussion has taken place concerning invasion plans and preparations and the SWPA party was apparently not prepared for such discussion," Nimitz said wryly to King.

MacArthur was completely unyielding in the matter of control and command. He would not come to Guam to confer with Nimitz. For a time Nimitz attempted to solve their mutual problems by sending emissaries (usually Forrest Sherman) to Manila to talk with MacArthur's staff. MacArthur's sense of protocol was such that Sherman was able to accomplish relatively little. In May Nimitz again went to see MacArthur in the interest of solving their prob-lems. The problems revolved around the concept of the war, but it was becoming apparent that MacArthur was winning the struggle. With the defeat of Germany, General Marshall and the chiefs of the Army and the air force suddenly realized that the Pacific was very heavily a Navy show. The way to make it an Army show was to create the need for employment of huge numbers of troops and military equipment. This meant, and could only mean, the invasion of Japan itself. The Navy's concept of moving into the Chinese coast had always depended on the establishment of bases and the maintenance of naval and air support by the Americans, but the use of Chinese manpower on the continent. These were points that Nimitz had made time and again in the conferences with King.

But by the time of the Okinawa invasion the complexion of the war against Japan had changed. The British definitely had come into the war, and Spruance had very successfully used his British Task Force 57 in the campaign.

"Upon Marshall's insistence," said Admiral King, "which also reflected MacArthur's views, the Joint Chiefs had prepared plans for landings in Kyushu and eventually in the Tokyo plain. King and Leahy did not like the idea, but as unanimous decisions were necessary in the Joint Chiefs meetings, they reluctantly acquiesced, feeling that in the end sea power would accomplish the defeat of Japan, as proved to be the case."

The decision had been that MacArthur would be in charge of

the ground forces in the campaign, while Nimitz would assist Mac-
Arthur in establishing a large beachhead from which the Army
troops could operate, as well as helping with naval gunfire, naval
aviation, logistic support, and antisubmarine operations.

With Franklin Roosevelt's death on April 12, the situation
became even more murky, but by May it was fairly well indicated
that the MacArthur approach was going to be hard to overcome.
The difficulties was readily apparent in the past operations in the
Philippines, where Halsey had complained about the MacArthur
policy of maintaining Army, Air Force, and Navy commands as
separate and equal under his overall leadership. The Navy theory
was precisely opposite. But political and international considerations
now became far more important than before. Congressmen began
coming out to the Pacific for tours, as Senator Tydings of Maryland
did with a party at the end of May. Special representatives of the
State Department showed up for duty at Guam, because diplomatic
considerations were arising. Even the Reconstruction Finance Corporation now became involved in the Pacific, in the islands taken from
the Japanese.

Early in June, as Halsey was getting ready to make more air
strikes in support of the Okinawa operations, he ran into another
storm. The storm was off to the southwest of the fleet, and on the
afternoon of June 4 Admiral Halsey set a course away from the
storm for his fleet, while some of the ships began fueling. On the
evening of June 4, reports began to come in from Guam about the
storm centers to the west and southwest. They were moving east,
but Halsey's advisers convinced him to move to the northwest, and
they did so, right into the track of the storm, which was the recurv-
ing of the typhoon. Admiral Clark suggested that they head away
and so did Admiral Hill, but Halsey refused, guided by his own
aerographer. The result, again, was heavy damage to the ships. In
Clark's task group the *Hornet* and *Bennington* both suffered partial
flight deck collapse when steel girders broke. The heavy cruiser
Pittsburgh lost her bow. *Belleau Wood* lost a man overboard. Altogether 33 ships were damaged, 142 planes were destroyed, and six
men were lost.

Again there was a court of inquiry and again Admiral Hoover

presided. Again he was inclined to recommend the court-martial of
Admiral Halsey for carelessness in this disaster. Admiral Lockwood
was a member of the court, and he summed up the problem pithily.
"The whole matter certainly is a mess, and indicates that nobody
ever heard of a guy named Bowditch." The recommendation of the
court was very strong against Halsey, McCain, and Jocko Clark,
whose force had been hard hit. It went to the Secretary of the Navy,
and for a time there was talk of retiring Halsey. But one did not
court-martial or retire America's favorite and most famous fighting
admiral, particularly if one was Secretary of the Navy with a very
strong bent for public relations.

Nimitz, however, was thoroughly annoyed with Halsey, and their
correspondence from that point on took on a definitely cooler tone.
Actually the coolness had begun with the first typhoon, for Nimitz
had also considered that to be a totally unnecessary disaster. Admiral
Clark had been criticized for not moving independently quickly
enough, in view of the directive from Nimitz after the first typhoon,
which instructed commanders to inform Nimitz directly when they
were in weather trouble. But Clark took the position that as a rear
admiral he could scarcely go over the heads of McCain and Halsey,
and it seemed a reasonable position.

An indication of Nimitz's loss of confidence in Halsey came
in his direct correspondence with Admiral Hill on matters concerning the naval forces around Okinawa that summer. Halsey objected
to Nimitz's dealing directly with Hill. "I would feel a great deal better if my own recommendations were sought rather than one of my
subordinates," he told Nimitz. ". . . I will be much better able to
execute your orders, directives, and policies if you can see your way
clear to working through me . . . ."

There were other complaints. The carrier task group commanders found Halsey extremely difficult to work for. The fact was
that carrier warfare had become so improved and so complicated
when Halsey was managing the South Pacific campaign from Nouméa
that he had gotten out of touch with the techniques as they developed. Instead of starting out afresh, finding himself a new staff of
men who had matured rapidly in these two years of modern carrier
warfare, Halsey had stubbornly, loyally, stuck with his old staff. The
result, as some carrier task group commanders indicated, was very

often near chaos. "When Admiral Spruance was in command," said Admiral Arthur Radford, "you knew precisely what he was going to do." The orders were written clearly and delivered promptly, and except for tactical changes, they stood as written. "But when Admiral Halsey was in command, you never knew what he was going to do." Every night the changes would come in the night orders. And often, as the commanders complained, the changes were so complicated, and referred to so many different messages, that the staffs of the task groups spent hours puzzling over the message board, hoping they knew at the end what Halsey intended to do, and what action they were supposed to take.

Despite technical deficiencies, Halsey never lost his will to fight the war, or his enthusiasm for "killing Japs." And as Nimitz cooled down, the relationship bettered that summer, although it would never again be as close as during those days of desperation in the South Pacific when Halsey was truly carrying the war.

In mid-June the Third Fleet was relieved of its responsibility to cover the Okinawa struggle, and Halsey went to Manila, where Japanese resistance was just being ended. He found MacArthur jubilant and cheerful, understandably. It was becoming an Army war, as far as he was concerned.

By July 1 Admiral Hill's amphibious force was no longer needed at Okinawa and it was dissolved. Admiral Oldendorf was promoted to vice admiral and given a new striking force of cruisers and destroyers to ravage Japanese shipping in the home waters. This task was already being performed handsomely by Admiral Lockwood's submarines, and early in July Halsey was again turned loose, this time to go into Japanese waters and hit Japan itself. His task force, still under McCain, consisted of three groups, under Rear Admirals T. L. Sprague, G. F. Bogan, and Arthur Radford. Admiral Jocko Clark had been relieved, and he was certainly entitled to a rest, after many months of command in the Pacific. His attorney at the court of inquiry had subjected Admiral Halsey to very severe questioning, too, and it took no genius to realize Clark's future relationship with Halsey and McCain could scarcely be very cordial, although in his writing and public statements Halsey never said a word of criticism of his junior.

Halsey struck the Japanese islands repeatedly, against very little opposition, and Admiral Shafroth struck with a bombardment force of battleships and cruisers. From now until the end of the war, the Americans prowled the Japanese waters almost at will, exercising their overwhelming naval and air force.

Meanwhile Nimitz and MacArthur were trying to sort out the elements of command. Perhaps the most helpful person in this series of discussions was Admiral Kinkaid, who had the respect and liking of both men. Nimitz had been disturbed by Sutherland's statements that MacArthur "would not permit a single soldier to be commanded by Admiral Turner or any other Admiral." How could the Navy carry out its amphibious responsibilities? Kinkaid took the matter up with MacArthur, and the general was disturbed. He noted that General Sutherland often got off on the wrong foot. He also corrected the impression Sutherland had given that MacArthur would not remain in command in Kyushu. MacArthur said he saw no reason for disagreement with Nimitz or the Navy. Kinkaid mentioned the Turner-Richardson unpleasantness at Saipan, and MacArthur suggested that Richardson was responsible. Kinkaid spoke of the difficulty of turning over Army forces to MacArthur's command, and MacArthur seemed to be completely reasonable. "The General said of course it is not possible now to turn over to him the control of army forces actually engaged in current operations." What he wanted was to get General Richardson and his staff into the MacArthur command, since they had been transferred to MacArthur and MacArthur's title had been changed to commander in chief of Army forces, Pacific theater.

At the end of June Nimitz went back to the mainland again for meetings with King. Operation Olympic, the invasion of Japan, was very definitely in the schedule, and so tremendous a movement that it would have staggered an officer of the old prewar Navy to consider. For example, no fewer than nine amphibious groups would be employed under Admiral Turner, with four more in reserve.

King and Nimitz talked of demobilization, of reorganization of the Pacific fleet commands, and of relationships with the Russians and with the British. King still kept coming back to the idea of invading the China coast as a possible alternative to the invasion of the Tokyo plain.

By this time in the history of the Pacific war, the Navy had completely reversed itself in the matter of public relations. Captain Miller was to become Rear Admiral H. B. Miller and head of Navy public relations. Kelly Turner, who had refused to have a public relations officer on his ship in the Gilberts operation, showed the change, in a letter to Secretary Forrestal:

> In the Okinawa campaign I think we have had a tremendous success from the public relations viewpoint. I have letters from three of the voice networks and from all of the major wire services thanking us for what has been given to them . . . . Of course this just didn't happen. Admiral Nimitz and his staff have pushed us hard to conform to your ideas as to news. My orders to everyone (as for three years) are that the Navy is owned by the American people and that the owners are entitled to know about us. Then I have had as PRO on my staff for this operation Paul Smith, of the S.F. *Chronicle,* who is about the best newspaperman I know about . . . .

Even Terrible Turner was mellowing.

Turner was busy, as always, planning for the invasion of Japan. He would take charge of the overall amphibious command, and he selected Vice Admiral Wilkinson to be his understudy, "prepared to take over if my ship is hit and I can no longer function."

> This is going to be tough for all of us, and I hope you will give your best advice not only on the major organization but also on the general plans for all parts of it. I do not intend to go into intricate details in my orders, but to decentralize as much as possible. Of course I will issue general orders concerning the screen and various methods of protecting ships, but I do not intend to take charge of them myself, except as to coordination, but to assign responsibility for the various areas to you, Hill, Barbey and Conolly.

The headiness of victory was already in the air at home, and it had begun to create problems for the Pacific forces. Although the submarine force was at a peak in July, 1945, the pressure was on Nimitz to give up the Royal Hawaiian Hotel which the submariners had been using as a base for rest and recuperation between patrols. The civilians wanted their world back.

In July Nimitz and MacArthur were still trying to iron out difficulties in the matching of their commands and responsibilities. Nimitz suggested that MacArthur make his advance headquarters for the coming operations on Guam: "I can make available to you quarters identical with my own." But MacArthur had no intention of coming to a naval sphere of influence, and they continued their discussions by letter, by message, and by visits from members of the staffs. Nimitz's concern was the retention of command when the major responsibility for the Japanese invasion moved to MacArthur. "It will undoubtedly become necessary in the future for fleet units including carriers to attack targets in the Inland Sea and to operate not only in the Philippine Sea west of the 135th meridian but also in the east China sea, later in the sea of Japan, and possibly also in the Yellow Sea," he told MacArthur. "I must retain complete freedom of action in such matters subject to the realities of the strategic and tactical situations as they develop."

By mid-July the command struggle had not been settled. Nimitz insisted on keeping his command of the Pacific Ocean areas and everything in it. MacArthur wanted to take over the Army forces in the Pacific and give Nimitz the Seventh Fleet and all naval forces. But Nimitz would not budge, so MacArthur would not budge either. Nimitz believed MacArthur was trying to take complete control of the operations against Japan, and MacArthur denied it, then complained to the Joint Chiefs of Staff that Nimitz would not cooperate.

On July 17 Kinkaid met with MacArthur and tried to resolve the dispute. "My estimate is that it all adds up to this," Kinkaid wrote Nimitz, "—horse trading. He wants control of all my forces in the Central Pacific and he believes that he will get proper support from the navy by coordinated action."

The matter remained unsettled. Late in July the cruiser *Indianapolis* returned from the west coast where she had been repaired following the kamikaze attack at Okinawa. She brought with her parts for the atomic bombs which were being stockpiled in the Marianas.

She came to Guam briefly, and went out on a mission. She was between Guam and the Philippines when she was torpedoed by a Japanese submarine. Partly because of the split command (Guam was Cincpac; Tacloban, where she was heading, was Seventh Fleet), no one paid any attention to the nonarrival of the cruiser on her stipulated day. Meanwhile, she sank and her survivors floated in the sea for eighty-four hours before the oil slick of the cruiser attracted the attention of a patrol bomber. Only 316 men survived, nearly 900 died. Admiral Nimitz ordered a court of inquiry, and the captain of the *Indianapolis* was court-martialed.

At Guam, in June and July, 1945, Nimitz and Sherman prepared a plan for the occupation of the Tokyo Bay area by the Third Fleet, and the Joint Chiefs of Staff agreed to the idea, since it would be several weeks before the Army forces could be brought into action. MacArthur objected strenuously, however, on the grounds that the Navy could not handle the job—or perhaps because the Army and the Air Corps would be upset if the Navy moved in first.

Now came a series of military-political discussions about the occupation of China, Korea, and Manchuria that are beyond the scope of this book, except to note that in these decisions rested much of the difficulty in which the world was to find itself in Asia for the next quarter-century. Quick decisions, some based on erroneous assumptions, were made at the highest military level—that of the Joint Chiefs of Staff—affecting Korea, Manchuria, North China, and Netherlands East Indies, Malaya, and Indochina. The demand on the Japanese for unconditional surrender, and the total collapse of Japanese power in these areas, with no orderly plan for government, brought about a state of almost unlimited chaos. Such considerations were simply beyond the command scope of the Pacific Fleet.

It was difficult enough for Nimitz and MacArthur, with their differing philosophies of the war, to reach agreement on the occupation. MacArthur, for example, claimed then and thereafter that the Central Pacific campaign was expensive and wasteful in lives. (At Okinawa, he said, the Japanese sank 36 ships, damaged 368, and destroyed 800 American planes. "These figures exceed the entire American losses in the SWPA from Melbourne to Tokyo . . . .")

Again the problem of command had arisen. It would not be

solved in this war, for events began moving much too rapidly. On August 1, Admiral Halsey was busy avoiding a new typhoon, but ready to operate against the Japanese islands as the weather bettered. On August 6 the first atomic bomb was dropped on Hiroshima. Then came the second A-bomb dropped on Nagasaki.

When Nimitz had the news, he was deeply shocked. He had known for some time about the weapon, but no one knew precisely what it could do. Halsey was shocked too. "I am looking forward to seeing you," Halsey wrote on August 9, ". . . and am anxious to hear what you can tell me about this appalling new weapon and about future developments."

The results were still obscure, but the developments came quickly. The Russians declared war an Japan. On August 10 King sent Nimitz a message. "This is a peace warning . . . ," it began, then went on to state that Japan was ready to surrender. A few days later Japan did agree to unconditional surrender.

On August 13 Admiral Sherman was in Manila, conferring with MacArthur. The general's policy had stiffened completely, as Sherman reported to Nimitz.

> He considers that as Supreme Allied Commander he is now fully responsible for, and commands all phases of the occupation of Japan. He desires no communication with Japanese authorities by forces in the Pacific except through his headquarters. He expects to summon Japanese representatives to Manila to make a preliminary arrangement for the surrender. He reiterated in most emphatic terms his disapproval of the use of a fleet landing force prior to the clearance of Japanese forces from the area under armistice arrangements. This disapproval is based both on military grounds and effect on service relationships . . . .

And so the war ended, a very different war from the one that had begun on December 7, 1941. The Japanese, fearing a growing American military power and refusal to accept their expansion in East Asia and the Pacific Ocean, had attacked swiftly to break American naval power. The Japanese intent was to consolidate a Pacific empire before the Americans could move, and to inflict enough defeats on the United States and her allies in this period to cause them to make a peace that gave the Japanese what they wanted in the Pacific. The first part of the Japanese plan had succeeded only too well. American power was destroyed at Pearl Harbor, the Japanese went on to victories in the Philippines and on the shores of the China seas that surprised even the Japanese high command with their ease and swiftness. But there was an element missing: the Japanese had not "gotten" the American carriers. And armed with these weapons, supported by cruisers and destroyers, and manned by determined and angry men, the American Navy set out to avenge the disgrace of Pearl Harbor.

In the South Pacific the Americans and the Australians gained a foothold, when they decided that the Japanese must be stopped at the Solomons. The struggle there was desperate, for the Japanese position was in many ways stronger than the allied; the Japanese had air power at hand through their island chain, and their fleet units were better disposed and better trained in the beginning than the American and the Australian.

From the South Pacific, the real battle against Japan moved to the Central Pacific, and the submarine campaign. General Mac-Arthur took some territory, but his victories in this period served largely to keep the Japanese off balance and to occupy certain forces. The war was being won by submarines and the Central Pacific forces; the casualty figures showed that much; it was the Nimitz command that fought the battles and took the territory essential to the maintenance of the Japanese Empire as it had been planned to exist after 1942.

In 1943 the gallant men of the submarines and the surface fleet, the carriers and the assault forces carried the war. Meanwhile more and better carriers, submarines, and other ships were being built at furious speed on the coasts of America. In 1944 they began coming in force to the Pacific, and along with them came thousands of men who had been civilians a short time before, and were now deep-water sailors. Some of these men sailed directly from American ports into battle, never having been across the sea before—an immense tribute to the American reserve Navy. By 1944 the handwriting was on the wall for any gloomy Japanese admiral to read. There were too many ships, too many planes, too many guns, too many submarines, too many troops coming ashore in too many transports, and the island empire simply could not withstand the pressure for long. No matter how gallant the Japanese, they could not bring their iron and coal and special metals to Japan if the ships were sunk, and the ships were sunk by the dozens and the hundreds. So the gun factories and the shell factories and the airplane factories began to go idle, as the overwhelming American might was brought to crush Japan.

In 1945 Germany was defeated, and then the whole of western allied power could be turned against Japan. Britain was able and eager to bring her fleets to the Pacific to show the Union Jack and recover the prestige lost in the fall of Singapore and the sinking of the great battleships *Repulse* and *Prince of Wales*. By the summer of 1945 scarcely a ship could sail from the far reaches of the Japanese Empire and hope to reach the central islands; American submarines were penetrating the Inland Sea regularly and without fear. When the atomic bomb came, Japan was already virtually defeated; the Navy men said she *was* defeated, and what remained was to pick up the pieces and stage-manage the surrender.

The A-bombs were the spectacular weapons, but it was certain that Japan was beaten by the overwhelming industrial might of the United States, and that the A-bomb simply allowed the Americans to take over Japan and force the debatable policy of unconditional surrender down the Japanese throats without further American bloodshed.

Chapter
Twenty-Six

NIMITZ AND
HIS ADMIRALS

August 1945 . . .

The formal Japanese surrender was signed aboard Admiral Halsey's flagship, the battleship *Missouri*, and nearly every general and admiral alive who had played a significant part in the Pacific war was invited, with the exception of Holland Smith. When the occupation began, Vice Admiral Frank Jack Fletcher had a role to play (Hokkaido), and so did nearly all others. Admiral Harry Hill noted the "oversight" and, in a message to Nimitz, suggested that he would be pleased to have Holland Smith as his guest when Hill moved in to deliver his share of the occupation forces. "Negative" came the answer from Admiral Nimitz.

That was the only really sour note. There was a sad note: four days after the surrender Admiral McCain died of a heart attack, the first of Nimitz's admirals to go since Admiral Henry Mullinix on the *Liscomb Bay* at the Gilberts. (Not counting Willis A. Lee, who died of a heart attack on August 25, 1945, but who was not in the Pacific at the moment.)

So Nimitz and his admirals had come to the natural end of the line without solving the problem of command between Army and Navy. The problem would continue and still be debated between Army and Navy commanders a quarter of a century later: whether the theater command or the unified command system was more workable.

Nimitz continued on as commander in chief of the Pacific Fleet in the summer and fall of 1945. Admiral Halsey, the ebullient fighter, stayed in the public eye. He occupied Yokosuka naval base. Once he had boasted that he would ride Emperor Hirohito's white horse down the streets of Tokyo. Now he was persuaded to board a white horse, and Americans smiled at the didoes of one of their favorite heroes. He came home to a hero's welcome, to receive a gold star in lieu of a fourth Distinguished Service Medal, and to retire, with the rank of fleet admiral. Even at the end Halsey was his old self, outspoken and in trouble; he spoke out flatly against the use of the atomic bomb, blaming the scientists who had worked on it as much as the politicians. The scientists took umbrage. A representative of the Federation of American Scientists demanded a retraction or a disavowal of Halsey's statements. Nimitz replied soothingly, also in character. "I hope that Admiral Halsey's clarifying press statement will inform the public of his real intentions in this matter," said Nimitz, "and that our scientists will continue to accept him as the heroic and indomitable naval leader that he is. It would be most unfortunate for a rift to develop between the personnel of the Navy and the scientists of this country whose work is so essential to our progress."

But as far as the Navy was concerned, Halsey had come to the end of his career. He was a fighting admiral, and the Pacific war had shown him at his finest, with all his faults. He was one of the great naval figures of all time, and his contributions to the Pacific victory in the early days of the war and in the South Pacific campaign endeared him past criticism to Chester W. Nimitz. Halsey knew that the path for him was retirement, and he left the active service with an easy heart.

Spruance relieved Halsey as commander of the fleet, which once again became Fifth Fleet. Kelly Turner retired after some time as U.S. representative to the U.N. Harry Hill organized and commanded a brand-new National War College, which was organized because in the vast expansion of the services Army and Navy war colleges could not handle the task of training officers for command. Admiral Towers finally got his sea command; he replaced McCain as commander of the fast carrier task forces. Mitscher went to Washington to become vice-chief of naval operations (air).

Among the others, Admiral Kimmel never secured the public vindication he sought almost until his death, a sad story of a man whose career was sacrificed; yet it was the Navy way—a captain may not go down with his ship in the twentieth century, but his career usually does. Admiral Pye had been at the Naval War College. He retired. Admiral Fletcher became chairman of the General Board until retirement in 1947. Admiral Draemel continued at the Philadelphia Navy Yard, and retired in 1946. Admiral Brown was relieved as aide to the President after Franklin Roosevelt died, then went to the Bureau of Personnel until he retired shortly after the Japanese surrender.

Admiral Ghormley's career recovered considerably in the last months of the war. He had been the victim of confusion and change, given a huge command and multifarious responsibilities in the South Pacific, from diplomatic to logistic. When the fighting became desperate at Guadalcanal, he was simply overwhelmed, and did not respond quickly enough to suit Nimitz, who nevertheless had great respect for Ghormley's abilities. Those abilities carried him to become commander of American naval forces in Germany in 1944, and to supervise the demilitarization of the German navy and to act as a diplomat. He did an outstanding job, and was awarded the Distinguished Service Medal, then was appointed to the General Board of the Navy.

Admiral Fitch left the office of Chief of Naval Operations to become the first aviator superintendent of the United States Naval Academy. He established the Department of Aeronautics there. He served later in the office of the Undersecretary of the Navy, and then retired in 1947. Hill was superintendent until 1952.

Admiral Hoover replaced Admiral Towers in Pearl Harbor when Towers went to the task force. He served for several months at Pearl Harbor and then returned to the United States.

As for Admiral Nimitz, his postwar career was more difficult than might be imagined. He came home a hero in the fall of 1945, and was feted in Texas and elsewhere. But there were problems. The principal problem was a tension that existed between Nimitz and Secretary Forrestal. Actually Forrestal did not want Nimitz to become Chief of Naval Operations, the one post to which Nimitz aspired. In October the matter came to a head, as the Forrestal diaries indicate.

6 October 1945: Admiral Nimitz came in this morning. He said he hoped to relieve Admiral King. I told him my own view was that he could be of greater use and more effective to the Navy without being tied to the routine of such an exacting job as CNO. He replied that he was fully aware of how exacting it would be in the next two years but in spite of that still wanted to do it and said he was confident that both as regards relations with Congress, knowledge of the Navy, and support of the Service he could do a good job.

. . . I said I thought that might be a mistake and might risk impairing the prestige he now had as a successful commander. I suggested the chairmanship of the General Board or continuing as commander in chief of the U.S. Fleet. He said he would hold to his original preference.

10 October 1945: I spoke to Admiral Nimitz today about our conversation . . . . I said that if he wished to succeed King that I would so recommend to the President with these qualifications: (1) that his staff should be mutually agreeable to the two of us, and (2) that his term be limited to two years, and (3) that he subscribe in general principle to the conception of the Navy Department Organization as expressed in the new chart.

So Nimitz did succeed King as Chief of Naval Operations when Admiral King retired at the end of the year. It was not altogether a happy assignment, for Nimitz and Forrestal did not like one another and on Nimitz rested the problem of moving the Navy into the new Department of Defense single-service concept. There were incidents and there was unhappiness. Nimitz did not really want the

job in some ways; he took it, he said, because he felt that if he was
not given that job it would hurt the morale of the naval officer corps.
Nimitz was relieved as commander of the Pacific Fleet by Admiral
Spruance. Spruance then went on to the presidency of the Naval War
College. Nimitz became relatively inactive after his term as Chief
of Naval Operations, although as a fleet admiral he never retired. At
the end of his Washington stay he moved to San Francisco. In 1949
he was appointed administrator of the planned plebiscite in Kash-
mir, but it never materialized. He did spend some time on United
Nations affairs, and became a regent of the University of California.
He was called upon for much speaking and writing, particularly of
prefaces for books about the Pacific war. Many attempts were made
to persuade him to write his memoirs, but he flatly refused. He had
hoped that his son or one of his daughters would undertake a biography, but Chester Nimitz, Jr., was busy with naval affairs, and then
joined the Perkin-Elmer Company of Norwalk, Connecticut, on his
retirement as rear admiral, and immersed himself in the business
world. The daughters were busy with their own pursuits; one a Navy
wife, one a nun, and one a scholar with the Rand Corporation.
Nimitz lived quietly in a house near the university, and then moved
into naval quarters at the naval station on Treasure Island in San
Francisco Bay, where he lived even more quietly until his death in
1966. Then he was buried in Golden Gate National Cemetery,
next to Kelly Turner. Later Charles Lockwood was buried there.
In 1969, Raymond Spruance joined them, above the wide Pacific
where they had fought so gloriously.

Spruance had retired as president of the Naval War College
after a distinguished tenure, although he never achieved the five-star
rank he wanted and deserved. Nimitz had recommended Spruance
for the honor, but Congress after World War II reverted to its
arms-length treatment of the military. Spruance was honored, however, by an appointment as ambassador to the Philippines, and
served there with distinction until 1955.

As for the other men, they had their ups and downs, as always
happens in the "peacetime" service. Admiral Towers followed
Spruance as commander in chief of the Pacific Fleet, then went to
the General Board for a time, and finally ended his career as a vice-

president of Pan American World Airways. Admiral Lockwood, the submarine commander, enjoyed a very successful postwar career as a popular author of books on submarines. Admiral Jocko Clark, who believed he had engineered the replacement of Admiral Pownall as commander of fast carriers, was subjected to a Jovian revenge: his next assignment was to a training command, under Pownall.

The first years after the war were marred for Nimitz and his admirals by the controversy over unification of the services. Nimitz opposed unification to the point where he, on the one side, and Secretary Forrestal and President Truman were very nearly at an impasse. Nimitz had brought Forrest Sherman in as his Deputy Chief of Naval Operations, and they worked together. Admiral Radford worked with them (he was Deputy Chief of Naval Operations for Air in those days). But the matter degenerated into squabbles that aroused irritations. The Nimitz admirals, old and young, did not have an easy time of it, although several of the younger men went on to very distinguished careers. W. H. Blandy became commander of the Atlantic Fleet, Forrest Sherman became Chief of Naval Operations, Arthur Radford commanded the Pacific Fleet and was later chairman of the Joint Chiefs of Staffs, and Jocko Clark commanded the Seventh Fleet that fought the Korean War.

Such different men. Clark, one might say, was a more modern Halsey, flamboyant and opinionated, but a fighter every inch. Radford, like Sherman, was a thinker. Sherman, somewhat like Spruance, was a strategist and a cool-headed fighter. Each was an individual; sometimes it seemed remarkable that so many individuals of such different temperaments could be welded into a fighting team at all.

There, of course, were the secrets of the principal admirals, Halsey, Spruance, and Nimitz. Halsey instilled in his men a fierce loyalty that was totally reciprocated. He was the favorite of the sailors of the fleet and of the people of the United States. Captain Harold Hopkins, a British liaison officer with the fleet, compared Halsey to Beatty, the British sea dog of World War I who fought at Jutland, or to Horatio Nelson or John Paul Jones. Spruance was the Jellicoe, the thoughtful commander with his eye on the campaign, not the battle.

But finally, when it was said and done, it all came back to Nimitz, the blue-eyed gentle Nimitz, hard as nails underneath, the professional naval officer, who knew best of all how to get optimum performance from his major weapon: men. Nimitz shared with that great soldier Dwight D. Eisenhower a disarming and almost mis-leading appearance of ordinariness and diffidence. Like Eisenhower, Nimitz was a master at delegation of authority. Nimitz had a quality unique to himself, too; there was always a sense of urgency and special responsibility to his delegations of authority. He wanted ac-tion, immediate, appropriate, and resultful action—and he nearly always got it. One can see the tremendous responsibility he gave Hal-sey and Spruance in the operation of the fleets, and the equal responsibility delegated to Lockwood in the submarines. The torpedo question, for example, was vital to the winning of the war. Nimitz and Lockwood conferred on the problem of the erratic performance and "duds," and when Lockwood indicated that he suspected the source, and was working hard at locating the specific areas of diffi-culty and pushing the development of an electric torpedo to sub-stitute for the faulty weapon if need be, then Nimitz, the old sub-marine officer, saw that Lockwood was doing everything he himself might have done, and he relegated the problem to the back of his mind and turned to immediate issues that he alone could resolve.

Or take the matter of amphibious warfare. To be sure, Major General Holland Smith of the Marine Corps knew a great deal about amphibious warfare at the beginning of the war. It had been a specialty of his in the days before, as the art was being worked out. But few others knew much about amphibious warfare, especi-ally top naval officers. It was Nimitz's genius that led him to search out Kelly Turner's mind when Turner was assigned by King to this task, and then to discover that Turner had a special aptitude for the work, and to accept Turner's judgments within the area of his com-petence. He let Turner pick his men, and let Turner have his head. The result was the development of amphibious warfare in the Paci-fic, quickly and efficiently, to reach new dimensions.

Or take carrier warfare. Nimitz knew so little about air affairs and carrier warfare that Rear Admiral Frederick Sherman was cal-lous enough to suggest in a letter that the commander in chief be replaced by an air admiral. And yet Nimitz was the one who shepherded the discussions of air power and use of the air forces in the Pacific. Under his command the modernization of the tactics of carrier warfare took on new dimensions. It was not simply coincidental that the carrier men expanded and perfected their thinking in the Pacific, it was because Admiral Nimitz had the good sense to see that these young, eager specialists could do the job if they were given the responsibility and authority, and he gave it to them.

In the files of the Naval War College there exists a letter from Admiral Nimitz stating that all he knew about strategy he picked up at the college, and of course this was a little bit of icing on the cake, but the fact is that the war college "battles" did give him a basis for his thinking, just as King, Spruance, and Halsey learned their lessons there. But there was a good deal more to command than prefabricated strategy; the Japanese had their equivalent of the war college, too. Nimitz's great strength was his ability to coax the very best from others. In a way his "wardroom stories" summed him up; he told them with the sure knowledge that they would go down the line, and be repeated by the men on the lower decks of the ships of the fleet. One could say that Halsey was the man to win a battle for you, Spruance was the man to win a campaign, but Nimitz was the man to win a war.

NOTES AND SOURCES

Page

PRELUDE

xi   "Let REMEMBER PEARL HARBOR be our battle cry.": Rear Admiral J. H. Newton to Cruisers, Scouting Force, December 13, 1941.

Chapter One: CONFUSION

2   Captain Bruns' repair of drydock and the need for more: 14th Naval District War Diary, December 7, 1941.

3   Battle Force's preparations in war scare: Rear Admiral C. J. Moore, oral history, p. 572.

3   "All those scares": *Ibid.*, p. 573.

3   Harry Hill becomes a "follower" of Admiral King: Admiral Hill to author, fall, 1969.

4   Pearl Harbor fleet's preparations for Japanese attack: Wilson Brown Papers, U.S. Naval Academy.

Page

4   Halsey's readiness: *Admiral Halsey's Story*, p. 75.

4   Armaments of Draemel's destroyers: Rear Admiral Milo F. Draemel, in conversation with author, September, 1969.

4   change in Draemel's orders: Draemel to author.

5   time-locked safe: Artemus Gates to author, September, 1969, in interview.

6   Nimitz's reaction to Admiral Fenner's question about command: Rear Admiral W. G. Lalor, in letter to E. M. Eller, November 3, 1966.

6   Towers' feelings about Nimitz: Mrs. John H. Towers, interviews, June, 1969.

7   "Who is responsible?": U.S. Naval Classified Archives, December, 1941.

7   purpose of Secretary Knox's trip to Pearl Harbor: Knox papers, Library of Congress, undated letter to Mrs. Knox.

7   Admiral Kimmel's orders for ammunition at the guns: Captain P. C. Crosley to author, July 8, 1969.

8   task force searches and air patrols: CINCPAC War Diary, December 7, 1941.

8   Task Force 8's orders: CINCPAC War Diary, December 9, 1941.

9   KNX radio report: CINCPAC War Diary, December 10, 1941.

9   Admiral Stark's advice: CINCPAC War Diary, December 10, 1941.

10   Kimmel's reply to Stark: CINCPAC War Diary, December 11, 1941.

10–11   Kimmel's career: *Admiral Kimmel's Story*, pp. 5–6.

11   "Only the officer who is intelligent": J. O. Richardson to C. W. Nimitz, December 23, 1940.

11   "However, a very powerful striking force": CINCPAC Gray Book, December 10, 1941.

11–12   the fleet's assignment: *Ibid.*

12   Kimmel's planned use of ships: CINCPAC Gray Book, December 10, 1941.

12   *Neosho*'s fueling problems: Log of the *Lexington*, December 11, 1941.

13   "Did you receive": *The Kimmel Story*, p. 3.

13   Knox's assessment of Kimmel: Knox to Mrs. Knox, June 6, 1943.

14   damage to *Neosho*'s fueling apparatus: Log of the *Lexington*, December 12, 1941.

15   preparations for relieving Wake: CINCPAC Gray Book, December 16, 1941.

15   Kimmel's relief: Admiral Draemel in conversation with author, September, 1969.

Page

49 "We were to fight": Admiral Draemel to author, June 8, 1969.

51 Nimitz turning to look at sunk ships: Fletcher Pratt, *Harper's, op. cit.*

51 Nimitz wondering about living in Kimmel's house: Nimitz to Mrs. Nimitz, December 26, 1941.

51 Nimitz's schedule: Nimitz to Mrs. Nimitz, January 4, 1942.

51 "To me it seems like I am on a treadmill": Nimitz to Mrs. Nimitz, December 28, 1941.

52 Nimitz's distress at abandonment of Wake relief expedition: Rear Admiral Chester W. Nimitz, Jr., in conversation with author, September, 1969.

52–53 fleet proficiency and equipment: OP-22-B Fleet Readiness Report, December 19, 1941, Office of the Chief of Naval Operations.

54 Stark and the decision to reinforce Samoa: CINCPAC Gray Book, December 25, 26, 1941.

54 "We cannot afford": CINCPAC Gray Book, December 27, 1941.

54 King's first official act: *Fleet Admiral King*, p. 353.

55 "I sincerely believe": Kimmel to Nimitz, letter, May 8, 1941.

55–56 Nimitz's attitude toward incumbent staff: Fletcher Pratt, *Harper's, op. cit.*, p. 211.

56 Draemel working day and night: Admiral Draemel, interview with author, September, 1969.

56 Crosley's job: Captain P. C. Crosley to author, May 30, 1969.

57 "it was God's divine will": Nimitz to Admiral David McDonald, April 3, 1965, quoted in the *Proceedings of the United States Naval Institute.*

57 "He has an unusual quality": Bloch to Nimitz, October 2, 1939.

58 Richardson on Kimmel and Draemel: Admiral Richardson to Nimitz, November 4, 1939.

58 Richardson's candidates for commander in chief: Richardson to Nimitz, March 4, 1940.

58 Fletcher's orders: CINCPAC Operations Order 48-41.

59 Leary's orders from Nimitz: CINCPAC Operations Order 47-41.

59–60 identity of task forces: CINCPAC War Diary, January 9, 1942.

60 Nimitz's request for two destroyer squadrons: CINCPAC War Diary, January 15, 1942.

61 Nimitz's reaction to sub incident: CINCPAC Report Serial 0311, January 15, 1942.

Page
61–62   tankers from San Diego to Iceland: Wilson Brown papers, U.S. Naval Academy, draft of a review of Samuel Elliot Morison's *History*, Vol. III.

62   aircraft equipment shortages and production schedules: Diaries of Admiral John H. Towers, January 7 and 8, 1942; Admiral E. M. Eller to author.

62   "Naturally, none of us here": Nimitz to Kimmel, January 15, 1942.

63   reasons for ordering Task Force 11 home: CINCPAC Gray Book, January 23, 1942.

63   "is considered": CINCPAC Action Report, February 9, 1942.

65   Nimitz-King disagreement: CINCPAC Gray Book, February 6, 1942.

65   "This makes the situation": CINCPAC Gray Book, February 9, 1942.

66   suggestion for stopping Japanese from reaching Australia: CINCPAC Gray Book, February 10, 1942.

66   Nimitz didn't know priorities: CINCPAC Gray Book, February 26, 1942.

67   "That since carrier planes": Admiral Wilson Brown's action report, Task Force 11, January 21–March 26, 1942. Brown Papers, U.S. Naval Academy.

Chapter Four: THE CHANGING SCENE

71   Joint Chiefs and relationship between MacArthur and Nimitz: CINCPAC Gray Book, March 4, 1942.

71   Consensus on possibility of Japanese attack on India or Australia: CINCPAC Gray Book, March 23, 1942.

71   "It was by all means": Franklin D. Roosevelt quoted in Morison, Vol. III, pp. 387–89, and Brown Papers.

72   Nimitz's action concerning Brown: CINCPAC Gray Book, March 30, 1942.

72   Turner and amphibious warfare: "Naval Amphibious Landmarks" by Vice Admiral George C. Dyer, USN (ret), *U.S. Naval Institute Proceedings*, August 1966.

72   geographical limits of Nimitz's and MacArthur's commands: CINCPAC Gray Book, April 4, 1942.

73   Nimitz's planned support of MacArthur in possible Japanese offensive: CINCPAC Gray Book, Estimate of the Situation, April 22, 1942.

73   Americans' limited experience with carriers: Lieutenant William H. Hessler, USNR, "The Carrier Task Force in World War II," *U.S. Naval Institute Proceedings*, November 1945.

Page
92   Fletcher's response to Nimitz's questioning: Fletcher-Nimitz correspondence, May 1942.
92–93 Nimitz's letter to King: May 29, 1942.
93–94 damage and repair of *Yorktown:* Morison, Vol. IV, p. 81.
94   "He was not there.": Admiral Fitch to author, September 1969.
94   "You will be governed": CINCPAC operation plan, pp. 29–42.
100   detection of American ships by Japanese search plane: Spruance to Nimitz, June 8, 1942.
100   conditions under which Torpedo 8 attacked: Memo from F. A. Ofstie, June 7, 1942, to Nimitz.
101   experience and observation position of Ensign Gay: *Ibid.*
103   "After recovering our air groups": Spruance to Nimitz, June 8, 1942.
104   Admiral Yamamoto wanted a surface engagement: *Admiral Raymond A. Spruance*, pp. 50–52.
104   "I figured the enemy DDs": Spruance to Nimitz, June 8, 1942.
105   "It may be the greatest sea battle since Jutland.": CINCPAC Gray Book, June 4, 1942.
106   "Confidentially, there is a great deal of feeling here": Knox to Nimitz, July 7, 1942.
106   damage to the Japanese navy: Morison, Vol. IV, p. 140.
107   Spruance report on Midway: Spruance memorandum to Nimitz, June 13, 1942.
109   Nimitz's recommendations after Midway: Nimitz endorsement, Midway Action Report.
110   "save that briefcase" anecdote: Stanley High, *Reader's Digest*, April 1943.
110–111 "the war to date": "Estimate of the Most Effective Employment of Units of the Battleship Type in the Near Future." W. S. Pye, July 1942, minutes of the Nimitz/King meetings.

Chapter Six: NEXT STEP

113   "It has been a fearful period": Knox papers, Library of Congress.
113   Nimitz's belief that the war would end before 1949: *Life* magazine, July 10, 1944.
114   request for authority to assign force commanders regardless of relative rank: Nimitz to King, June 24, 1942.
115   "I foresee that such a situation": *Ibid.*
115   "Jove never hurled a thunderbolt": McCain to Nimitz, May 26, 1942.

Page
115   "I regard the entire operation as a wonderful example": Nimitz to McCain, June 24, 1942.

116   "We have learned many lessons": Nimitz to Knox, July 18, 1942.

116–117   Ramsey's secret letter: Captain Ramsey to Nimitz, June 15, 1942.

117   Knox's reaction to Washington *Post* article: Towers diaries, July 20, 1942.

118   King makes major decision of war: Morison, Vol. IV, p. 263.

119–123   details of dinner party: James E. Bassett, diary, July 26, 1942.

124–125   Spruance's early career: *Admiral Raymond A. Spruance*, pp. 3–7.

125   the *Bainbridge* as "miserable little tub": Rear Admiral Carl J. Moore's oral history, p. 78.

125–126   "The officers were dissolute": *Ibid.*, p. 82.

129   Spruance's coffee: Reminiscences of H. Arthur Lamar, Naval History Division, U.S. Navy.

Chapter Eight: THE DESPERATE DAYS OF
GUADALCANAL

131   Nimitz's proposed code name for Truk: James Bassett's diaries, 1942.

133   "So it goes." Lieutenant Bassett's diaries, July 27, 1942.

133–134   "We are no longer reading the enemy mail": CINCPAC Gray Book, August 1, 1942.

134   Knox's hope that Baldwin's book would counteract influence of De Seversky: Knox's letter to Nimitz, August 12, 1942.

134   scope of Fitch's responsibility: CINCPAC Gray Book, July 29, 1942.

135   Draemel's letter to Nimitz: July 27, 1942.

135–136   Christie as instrumental in developing the Navy's torpedo: Christie to Lockwood, June 23, 1943.

139   Nimitz's reaction to Ghormley's requests: CINCPAC Gray Book, August 8–9, 1942.

140   Nimitz's disturbance at not knowing where the Japanese fleet was: CINCPAC Gray Book, August 17 and 18, 1942.

140   "Our losses were heavy": CINCPAC Gray Book, August 19, 1942.

140   "There is plenty of fuel": CINCPAC Gray Book, August 21, 1942.

141   Knox to Nimitz: August 11, 1942.

142   Marine reaction to Japanese fight to death: Morison, Vol. V, Chapter 3.

Page
143 "We have been greatly handicapped": Turner to Vandegrift, August 23, 1942.
144 Towers' reaction to new appointment: Towers diaries, September 12, 1942.
145 disposition of Japanese swords: Minutes, King-Nimitz meeting, September 7, 1942.
147 Emmons letter to Nimitz: September 18, 1942.
147 Nimitz to King: September 18, 1942.
147–148 Towers' lack of success in seeing King: Towers diaries,
September 25, 1942.
148 Towers' request for Sherman as chief of staff: Towers to
Nimitz, September 21, 1942.
153 Nimitz to Ghormley: "Notes on Conference Held Aboard
USS *Argonne* at 1300, October 2, 1942."

Chapter Nine: THE COMING OF HALSEY

160 navigation by National Geographic map: Reminiscences of
H. A. Lamar.
160 Marine fainting: *Ibid*.
161–162 Nimitz to Ghormley: October 8, 1942.
163 "It now appears that we are unable to control": Nimitz
quoted in Morison, Vol. V, p. 178.
163 Halsey given South Pacific command: CINCPAC Gray
Book, October 18, 1942.
163 "Jesus Christ and General Jackson": *Admiral Halsey's
Story*, p. 109.
165 Halsey's message of defiance: *Admiral Halsey's Story*, p. 90.
166 Nimitz to King: October 12, 1942.
166 Halsey's positive effect on morale: Vice Admiral George
Dyer to author, September 1969.
166 "I early placed emphasis": Halsey's South Pacific Command narrative, p. 16ff.
167 "the principle of a bottle of Scotch": Halsey Staff Memo
on Narrative of War, unsigned, pencilled, in Halsey papers,
Naval History Division.
167 Halsey skeptical about ability to handle industrial establishment: Halsey to Nimitz, February 27, 1941.
167 Nimitz's suggestion of two carriers and four antiaircraft
cruisers: Nimitz to Halsey, October 20, 1942.
167 Nimitz asks for report on failure to complete destruction
of Japanese forces: Nimitz to Halsey, October 22, 1942.
168 "I am tremendously pleased": Knox to Nimitz, October
24, 1942.
169 "I remember thinking that he might well have been a
parson": Captain Harold Hopkins, RN, to author, June 8,
1969.

Page
170		"Are we going to evacuate": *Admiral Halsey's Story*, p. 117.
171		Nimitz's suggestion that Japanese might attack in Solomons: CINCPAC Gray Book, October 22, 1942.

Chapter Ten: HALSEY'S TRIUMPH

174		analysis that Japanese would continue to try to capture Guadalcanal: CINCPAC Gray Book, November 1, 1942.
175		"but the determination, efficiency, and morale": *Ibid.*
175		"Our shoestring had held": *Admiral Halsey's Story*, p. 123.
176		Nimitz's refusal to send press copy by Navy communications facilities: Nimitz to Knox, November 2, 1942.
176–178	Report of Fighting Squadron 5: September 11–October 16, 1942.
178		"an excellent presentation": First Endorsement, Fighting Squadron 5 Report of Air Operations, December 1, 1942.
180		ship readiness: Halsey to Nimitz, November 6, 1942.
181		Secretary Knox convinced of Halsey's capabilities: Nimitz to King, November 4, 1942.
182		Numbers of Japanese troops: Morison, Vol. V, p. 226.
182		prediction of imminent Japanese attack and task force 61 readiness: CINCPAC Gray Book, November 9, 1942.
182		Turner to Callaghan: November 10, 1942.
185		"Your names have been written in golden letters": *Admiral Halsey's Story*, p. 132.
185		"Things have happened very rapidly": Vandegrift to Nimitz, November 15, 1942.
185		"The phrase is emphatic": Turner to Vandegrift, November 16, 1942.
186		"I accept them in all humility": Halsey to Nimitz, November 29, 1942.
186		Halsey sends three-star pins to widows: *Admiral Halsey's Story*, p. 132.
186		"The hell with it. It's Japanese.": *Ibid.*, p. 138.
187		"A tempting thought": Halsey to Nimitz, November 29, 1942.
187		"Everyone here is working like a beaver": *Ibid.*
187		"How are all the experts going to comment now?": *Ibid.*
188		damage to American forces: Morison, Vol. V, pp. 298–313.
188		Halsey's knowledge of damage: Halsey to Nimitz, December 8, 1942.
189		Nimitz to Halsey: December 18, 1942.

Chapter Eleven: SOUTH PACIFIC VICTORY

192		Nimitz and King on personnel: King-Nimitz Conference Notes, December 11, 12, 13, 1942.
193		Nimitz to King: November 16, 1942.

Page
196   Nimitz's report to Halsey: November 29, 1942.
198   Halsey's reaction to supplying transports: Halsey-Vande-grift correspondence, January, 1943, in Halsey Papers, U.S. Navy Historical Division.
198   Nimitz's permission from Washington regarding choosing officers: Pacific Fleet Confidential Letter 32CL-42.
198   "We are almost continuously under pressure here": Halsey to Nimitz, December 11, 1942.
198   Nimitz to Halsey: December 18, 1942.
198   PT boats harrying Japanese supply missions: Halsey to Nimitz, December 11, 1942.
199   MacArthur and Nimitz: CINCPAC Gray Book, January 10, 1942. The comments are obviously those of the author of this book.
199   Halsey to Nimitz: January 11, 1943.
199–200 Halsey to Nimitz: January 1, 1943.
200   Nimitz's plan to watch the South Pacific: Nimitz to Knox, November 2, 1942.
200–201 Nouméa conference: "Notes on the Conference Held at Nouméa 1520 to 1700 January 23, 1943.
203   "The next twenty-four hours were literally hell": Lamar reminiscences.
203   Knox's Halsey anecdote: *Admiral Halsey's Story*, p. 146.
204   Maas's recommendation: Roosevelt papers, FDR Library, Hyde Park; memo from Melvin J. Maas to FDR, October 22, 1942.
204–205 Halsey to Nimitz: December 20, 1942.
205   "Chester had a fit": *Admiral Halsey's Story*, p. 146.
207   King's "wait, delay, and linger": Morison, Vol. V., note p. 352.
207   King's philosophy to "keep moving": *Fleet Admiral King*, pp. 414, 427.
207   "Subject to this": *Ibid.*, pp. 423–424.
208   Knox's decision that "failure" was attributable to Halsey: Knox to Mrs. Knox, June 6, 1943, Knox Papers.
208   "about the capabilities": King to Nimitz, February 4, 1943.
208   Byrd's survey: *The Last Explorer*, a biography of Admiral Byrd, p. 350.

Chapter Twelve: THE SECOND PHASE

211   Spruance's and Nimitz's assessment of resources for Solomons and New Guinea offensive and potential for Central Pacific front: "The Victory in the Pacific," address by Admiral Spruance to the Council of the British Royal United Service Institution, October 30, 1946.

Page
211 Fletcher's report to Nimitz: Fletcher to Nimitz, January 22, 1943.
213 "The operation should cut the Japanese supply lines": minutes of King-Nimitz meeting, February 22, 1943.
215 "I do not feel justified": Halsey to Nimitz, January 1, 1943.
217 extent of MacArthur's naval forces in 1942: Morison, Vol. VI, pp. 27–32.
217 efforts to improve correlation between MacArthur's and Nimitz's commands: CINCPAC Gray Book, March 7, 1943.
221–222 Halsey to Nimitz: March 25, 1943.
222 Nimitz to Halsey: April 3, 1943.
222 Nimitz on public relations: *Ibid.*
224 "black shoe" and "brown shoe": Vice Admiral Andrew McB. Jackson to author, October 1969.
225 "Five minutes after I reported": *Admiral Halsey's Story*, pp. 154–155.

Chapter Thirteen: THE ALEUTIANS

228–229 "As you know": Nimitz to Kinkaid, February 5, 1943.
229 Kinkaid not told he would get only two LST's: Nimitz to Fletcher: February 5, 1943.
229–230 Nimitz to DeWitt: March 22, 1943.
230 Nimitz to Kinkaid: April 29, 1943.
232 "Now we have learned that this type of bombardment": minutes of King-Nimitz meetings, June 1, 1943.
233 "enthusiastic Well Done" to Rockwell: June 2, 1943.
233 Nimitz to Kinkaid: June 2, 1943.
234 Nimitz to King concerning Fletcher: June 22, 1943.
234 Nimitz to Kinkaid concerning the *Middleton:* June 26, 1943.

Chapter Fourteen: PREPARATIONS FOR ATTACK

236 Nimitz to King: April 8, 1943.
236 "some odds and ends of cruisers": Nimitz to Jacobs, March 24, 1943.
237 Knox's praise of McMorris: Knox to Mrs. Knox, June 6, 1943.
237–238 Goulett's experience with logistics: Wilfred B. Goulett to author, August 1969.
238 Nimitz's treatment of junior staff member: F. R. Duborg to author, July 1969.
238–239 McArdle and press questions: Kenneth W. McArdle, *I Never Fired a Shot,* unpublished manuscript, pp. 129–31.
240 "Personal publicity in a war": Spruance, quoted in *Admiral Raymond A. Spruance* by E. P. Forrestel.

Page

241   Spruance's one kidney as possible reason for his not drinking: Rear Admiral E. M. Eller to author, October 1969.

241   Spruance uninformed about Nimitz's opinion about Ghormley: *Admiral Raymond A. Spruance*, p. 63.

242   Halsey-Nimitz relationship: Nimitz to Halsey, May 7, 1943; Halsey to Nimitz, May 14, 1943.

242   Nimitz on Halsey and Central Pacific logistics: Nimitz to Halsey, May 7, 1943.

Chapter Fifteen: PUTTING THE TEAM TOGETHER

244   Nimitz's methods of arriving at a decision: Admiral Spruance to Rear Admiral E. M. Eller, April 25, 1966.

246   Admiral Towers' suggestion to reinstate Chief of Naval Operations as supreme commander: Towers diaries, May 30, 1943.

247   Nimitz to Halsey: May 14, 1943.

248   Lockwood to Blandy: March 14, 1943.

251–252 "Seated by the window": *Coral and Brass* by Holland M. Smith, p. 105.

252   Spruance's reasons for suggesting invasion of the Gilberts: Forrestel, *Admiral Raymond A. Spruance*, p. 66.

253   Nimitz on a strong Japan: F. R. Duborg to author, July 1969.

254   Clark and the *Yorktown: Carrier Admiral*, by J. J. Clark with Clark Reynolds, pp. 89–118.

255   Towers on expenses of bomb shelter: Towers to Ghormley, June 9, 1943, Towers papers.

255   Towers to Forrestal: August 18, 1943, Towers papers.

256   Towers' memo to Nimitz: August 21, 1943.

256   Towers to Horne: June 30, 1943.

257   Towers' plea for combat duty: Towers to Nimitz, August 8, 1943.

257   Towers to Yarnell: September 7, 1943.

258   Nimitz's plans to upgrade job of staff aviation officer: Nimitz to McCain, September 2, 1943.

258   death of Dr. Gendreau: Captain Crenshaw to Nimitz, July 25, 1943.

259   Captain C. J. Moore to Mrs. Moore: August 1943.

261   MacArthur's agreement with Fitch and Halsey: Admiral Fitch to author, September 1969, in interview.

Chapter Sixteen: THE COMMANDS SHAPE UP

262–263 Leavey's conclusion that Nimitz had a fleet staff: Leavey to Somervell, July 29, 1943.

264   Nimitz and sailor in his office: Kenneth W. McArdle, unpublished ms.

Page

264 Nimitz and the Texas sailor: Rear Admiral E. M. Eller to author, autumn 1969.

266 Nimitz's request to Admiral Jacobs to investigate rumor of conditions on the *New Orleans*: Nimitz to Jacobs, March 26, 1943.

266 Nimitz to Halsey: July 11, 1943.

267 Halsey to Nimitz: July 16, 1943.

268 Christie to Lockwood: June 23, 1943.

269 Christie to Lockwood: July 23, 1943.

269 "I am very much concerned": Nimitz to Blandy, October 5, 1943.

270 Hoover's original lines of approach: Nimitz to Halsey, September 1943.

270 Nimitz and Halsey personnel problems: Nimitz-Halsey correspondence, August, September 1943.

271 "I have chosen these men": Spruance quoted by C. J. Moore to author, summer 1969 interview.

272 Clark on Pownall: *Carrier Admiral* by J. J. Clark, p. 123.

273 Pownall to Nimitz: September 4, 1943.

273 Clark on Pownall's leaving downed men: *Carrier Admiral*, p. 126.

273–274 Towers on concept of a commander of carriers: Towers diaries, September 8, 9, 10, 1943.

280 Spruance's letter to his admirals: October 29, 1943; quoted in *Admiral Raymond A. Spruance* by E. P. Forrestel, p. 74.

281 argument about air logistics: Towers diaries, September 29, 1943.

282 "I felt that unless a more offensive attitude is taken": Towers diaries, October 5, 1943.

283 discussion about the problem of Nauru: Towers diaries, October 9, 1943.

283 Nimitz to Towers: October 11, 1943.

Chapter Seventeen: OPERATION GALVANIC

287 Forrestal to Towers: August 2, 1943; Forrestal papers, Princeton University Library.

287 improved airplanes and CIC: Commander James C. Shaw, Introduction to Morison, Vol. VII.

288 Towers conference regarding training operations: Towers diaries, October 9, 1943.

288 Nimitz to Bowen: September 12, 1943.

288–289 *Yorktown*'s successful defense as argument for carriers' self-defense abilities: *Carrier Admiral* by J. J. Clark, pp. 128–129.

289 Towers and Nimitz decision on Sherman: Towers diaries, October 12, 1943.

Page
290   Pownall and Radford conference with Towers: Towers diaries, October 14, 1943.

290   Turner's opposition to proposed use of carriers: Towers diaries, October 17, 1943.

292   Gilberts operation as a dress rehearsal: King-Nimitz meeting notes, September 26, 1943, item 12.

293   air strikes on the Gilberts begin: Hoover to Nimitz, November 19, 1943.

293   Nimitz and two male squirrels: S. L. A. Marshall in *U.S. Naval Institute Proceedings*, July 1966.

294   Turner's search for experienced amphibious officers: Turner to Admiral T. S. Wilkinson, November 9, 1943.

294   Turner's request for a new Marine officer: Turner to Lieutenant General T. H. Holcomb, October 13, 1943.

295   Spruance's role in the Northern Attack Force: *Admiral Raymond A. Spruance* by E. P. Forrestel, p. 86.

295   eight hundred Japanese troops at Makin: Morison, Vol. VII, note p. 122.

297   Smith on Butaritari: *Coral and Brass* by Holland M. Smith, p. 127.

298   Hill to Nimitz: November 23, 1943.

298   "The destroyers were out wide": Kenneth McArdle, unpublished ms., pp. 19–20.

298   message over loudspeakers: *Ibid*.

300   Hill to Nimitz: November 23, 1943.

301–302   McArdle's experience: McArdle ms. p. 22ff.

303   Hill's report to Nimitz: November 23, 1943.

303–304   Japanese defenses: Morison, Vol. VII, pp. 147–148.

304   Hill to Nimitz: *Op. cit.*

305   "They'll go in standing up.": McArdle ms.

305   fate of tanks on Red beaches: Morison, Vol. VII, note p. 164.

307   "Successful landings on Beaches Red 2 and 3.": Smith, *Coral and Brass*, p. 122.

308   Hill's statement that more LVT's were needed: Admiral Hill's oral history.

309   General Smith's description of Tarawa: Smith, *Coral and Brass*, p. 129.

309   "I don't see how they ever took Tarawa": *Op. cit.*, p. 130.

310   claim carriers had been lost because they were kept as sitting ducks: Clark, *Carrier Admiral*, p. 137.

311   duties of carriers under Pownall and Montgomery: Forrestel, *Admiral Raymond A. Spruance*, p. 96.

311   Tarawa as a terrible mistake: Smith, *Coral and Brass*, p. 134. Towers papers, November and December, 1943.

311   Spruance on bombardment: Forrestel, *Admiral Raymond A. Spruance*, p. 97.

page

312 purpose of Nimitz's special planning meetings: Towers diaries, November 13–15, 1943.

Chapter Eighteen: ON TO THE MARSHALLS

313 Smith's press interview "garbled" by censorship: Smith, *Coral and Brass*, p. 139.

314 Towers asked to investigate shore-based forces: Towers diaries, December 3, 4, 1943.

315 "You want to see the fish": J. J. Clark, *Carrier Admiral*, p. 142.

315 "What do you think of that": Morison, Vol. VII, p. 206.

315 "I was strongly opposed": Admiral Spruance to Admiral Eller, April 25, 1966.

316 majority vote for outer islands: Admiral Harry Hill to author, fall 1969. The story also appeared as Admiral Hill told it to E. B. Potter, in the *Naval Institute Proceedings* of July 1966.

317 Clark's "patriotic duty": From Reminiscences of Joseph J. Clark, Naval History Project Oral History Research Office, Columbia University, 1963, copy in files of Naval History Division, Washington, D.C.

318 Towers-Nimitz meeting on carrier forces: Towers diaries, December 23, 1943.

318–319 Mitscher incident: Captain James Ogden in conversation with author, summer 1969.

319–320 Towers' appraisals of air officers: Towers diaries, December 25, 1943.

Chapter Nineteen: OPERATION FLINTLOCK

323 McMorris's self-assessment: Carl J. Pritchard, former ship's clerk and assistant to the flag secretary, CINCPAC staff, to author, summer 1969.

323–324 McMorris on naval aviators: McMorris to Nimitz, December 31, 1943.

326 "All day long": Kenneth McArdle, unpublished ms., p. 86.

327 "most powerful naval force ever assembled: Nimitz to Fletcher, November 17, 1943.

327 Nimitz trying to use one ship for two jobs: Nimitz to Halsey, September 16, 1943.

329 "Why the hell": James Bassett diaries, September 6, 1942.

331 Upson's letter on search for downed crew: Upson to Pownall, December 30, 1943.

332 Smith left out of operation Flintlock: Smith, *Coral and Brass*, p. 142.

332 Smith as "crybaby": Admiral Moore to author, summer 1969.

page
333   "it will be possible for Towers": Nimitz to Hoover, December 16, 1943.
333   "Reports from recent visitors": Nimitz to Hoover, December 18, 1943.
334   Hoover tennis court: McArdle ms.
334   Hoover's trade goods: Hoover to Nimitz, December 24, 1943.
334   Nimitz's gob and six nurses story: S. L. A. Marshall, *U. S. Naval Institute Proceedings,* July 1960.
338   Admiral Koga's defenses and bombardment by *Portland* and *Bullard:* Morison, Vol. VII, p. 227.
338   disagreement of Admirals Conolly and Turner: *Ibid.,* p. 233.
339   "The magnitude of the Kwajalein bombardment": Smith, *Coral and Brass,* p. 144.
339   "Never in the history of human conflict": Smith, *Coral and Brass,* p. 144.
339   Morison on Corlett and Smith: Morison, Vol. VII, p. 257.
340   Morison on reason for Army's slow advance: *Ibid.,* p. 265.
341   Tokyo Rose not heard from: Admiral Hill on conversation with author, fall 1969.
343   reasons for Hill's being chosen for Tarawa: Admiral Hill to author, fall 1969.
344   Hill on reason for Army's poor showing compared to Marines': *Ibid.*

Chapter Twenty: INTERLUDE

347   Towers' reaction to logistics: Towers diaries, January 17, 1944.
347–350   opinions on naval aviation: Yarnell File, naval aviation study, 1943–1944.
350–351   Forrestal and Nimitz inspect the fleet: Lamar Reminiscences.
351   MacArthur's headquarters and credit for southern hemisphere activities: Kenneth McArdle, unpublished ms., pp. 105–106.
352   agreement on coordination: Towers diaries, January 25–28, 1944.
352–354   King to Nimitz: February 8, 1944.
356   Nimitz to McCain: March 21, 1944.

Chapter Twenty-One: THE MARIANAS

358   orders for aviators and nonaviators to integrate command staffs: Nimitz to Hoover, March 31, 1944.
359   MacArthur-Nimitz press releases: Kenneth McArdle, unpublished ms., pp. 106–107.

page

359–360 Doyle and Turner's battle flag: Doyle to Turner: February 24, 1944.

361 Forrestal to Roosevelt: February 3, 1944; letter in Roosevelt Library, Hyde Park, New York.

361 Hoover-Hale argument: Hoover-Nimitz correspondence, February 1944.

361 Towers' opinion of Admiral Hoover: Towers papers, April 1944.

362 Sallada's assessment of American cooperative spirit: Admiral Sallada to author, June 1969.

362 Turner's insistence on Smith's approval of landing operations plans: Admiral Hill to author, autumn 1969.

364 Nimitz's comparison of Kwajalein to Texas picnic: S. L. A. Marshall, *U.S. Naval Institute Proceedings*, July 1966.

364 Towers' complaint about Ginder: Towers diaries, April 15, 1944.

365 King's resistance to Smith's promotion: Smith, *Coral and Brass*, pp. 153–154.

365 Gates to Forrestal: May 6, 1944, Forrestal Papers, Princeton University.

365 Smith on Nimitz's "riding to fame on the shoulders of the Marines": Smith, *Coral and Brass*, p. 157.

366 Towers' request that Nimitz get rid of Mercer: Towers diaries, March 21, 1944.

367–368 Cooke's planning: King-Nimitz conference notes, May 6, 1944.

370 Nimitz took total responsibility for awards: Towers diaries, May 13, 1944.

370 Admiral Hill on lack of recreation: Hill to author, fall 1969.

371 Nimitz to Towers on responsibility for awards and public relations: Towers diaries, May 13, 1944.

371 "He was a flier?": C. J. Moore, oral history interviews for Columbia University naval history project, p. 436.

372 reason for Hill's abandoning use of mortars on LCT's: Harry W. Hill, oral history.

373 Harmon's potential as a "type commander": Nimitz to King, June 13, 1944.

373–374 "While I realize": *Ibid.*

374–375 Moore on Spruance: C. J. Moore interview, Columbia oral history project, p. 903.

375 Spruance annoyed at being awakened: C. J. Moore to author, summer 1969.

376 Spruance not a slave to the demon rum: C. J. Moore interviews, Columbia oral history project.

377 success of submarines and carrier strikes in the Palaus: C. J. Moore, oral history.

381 Hill's men find indications of Japanese preparations on Saipan: Admiral Harry Hill to author, autumn 1969.

page

382   Japanese fleet might be expected to come out and fight: C. J. Moore, oral history, pp. 988–990.

382   Spruance and Fifth Fleet's planned operations to keep Japanese guessing: E. P. Forrestel, *Admiral Raymond A. Spruance*, p. 123.

383   Clark convinces Harrill of importance of volcanoes: *Carrier Admiral*, pp. 162–163.

383   Spruance hears that the Japanese fleet has moved out and that battleships have sailed for the Pacific: C. J. Moore, oral history, p. 995.

383–384   Spruance-Turner conference: C. J. Moore, oral history, pp. 996–997.

384   "Our air will first attack": *Ibid.*, p. 908.

385   size of Japanese and American forces: Forrestel, *Admiral Raymond A. Spruance*, p. 36.

386   Clark's actions: Clark, *Carrier Admiral*, pp. 166–167.

387   "If carriers are properly utilized": Clark, *Carrier Admiral*, pp. 168–169.

387   Spruance's reasoning: Forrestel, *Admiral Raymond A. Spruance*, p. 137.

387   Spruance believed there were two forces: C. J. Moore, oral history, p. 1005.

387   *Finback* reports searchlights: *Ibid.*, p. 1006.

389   "A supplementary report of the enemy force": C. J. Moore, oral history, pp. 1007–1008.

389   Admiral Ozawa daring: Morison, Vol. VIII, Chapter 14, is very clear on the Japanese side of the story.

395   Towers on Spruance: C. J. Moore, oral history, p. 1031.

396–397   Spruance to Nimitz: July 4, 1944.

Chapter Twenty-Two: THE PLAN TURNED UPSIDE DOWN

398   lack of training of fast battleship crews: C. J. Moore, oral history, p. 1039.

399   Holland Smith's letter asking for Ralph Smith's relief: Turner to Nimitz, August 18, 1944.

400   "Admiral Turner and General Smith": C. J. Moore, oral history, p. 1044.

401   McArdle and Haller of International News Service: Kenneth McArdle, unpublished ms., p. 134.

402   versions of Ralph Smith story: McArdle ms., pp. 136–137.

402   Turner's plan to "bawl out" General Richardson: C. J. Moore, oral history, p. 1061.

403   Nimitz on Turner's drinking: Vice Admiral George Dyer, in papers lent to author, fall 1969.

403   Spruance tries to laugh off Turner incident: C. J. Moore, oral history, p. 1062.

page

403   "I talked to Turner": Spruance to Nimitz, July 4, 1944.

405   Hill's plan for capturing Tinian: Admiral Hill's oral history.

407   "Having forced the issue with Turner": Admiral Hill's oral history.

408   effectiveness of Conolly's bombardment: Morison, Vol. VIII, p. 382.

409   "the most brilliantly conceived": Spruance in speech to the Council of the Royal United Service Institution, October 30, 1946.

409   Japanese suicides at Tinian: Admiral Hill's oral history.

410   Sherman's disapproval of plan to attack Formosa without the Philippines: C. J. Moore, oral history, p. 1073.

411   Nimitz wanted to take the western Carolines first: *Admiral Halsey's Story*.

411   Halsey's plan: *Admiral Halsey's Story*, p. 195.

411   Spruance's plan: C. J. Moore, oral history, and Halsey, *ibid*.

411   Turner's idea: Admiral Hill to author, fall 1969.

411   MacArthur turns down Nimitz and King: H. A. Lamar, *Reminiscences*.

411   Marshall orders MacArthur to Hawaii: Douglas MacArthur, *Reminiscences*, p. 214; Towers diaries, July 26, 1944.

412   Admiral Leahy on Pearl Harbor discussions: William D. Leahy, *I Was There*, p. 255.

413   King demands order to stop using title Commander in Chief: *Fleet Admiral King*, p. 567.

413   Gates to Forrestal, memo, September 26, 1944, in Defense Department Collection of the James V. Forrestal papers.

413   plans for night-operating carrier division: Towers diaries, July 15, 1944; Admiral Radford to author, summer 1969.

414   number of Spruance's supply ships: Morison, Vol. VIII, chapter 18.

415   Halsey receives orders for the invasion of the Philippines: Halsey to Nimitz, September 9, 1944.

415   Forrestal to Nimitz: September 6, 1944.

415   Forrestal's feelings about Navy public relations: Palmer Hoyt in conversations with author, spring and fall 1969.

415–416   Suntory for the press: McArdle ms.

416   Hoover's claims about Air Force exaggerations: Admiral Hoover to author, summer 1969.

416   Hoover's instructions to McArdle: McArdle ms., p. 182.

417   Nimitz mentions Miller is coming: Towers diaries, August 17, 1944.

417   Forrestal "shanghais" Drake: McArdle ms.; Forrestal to Nimitz, October 10, 1944.

419   Joint Chiefs argue over Roosevelt-MacArthur-Nimitz decisions: Leahy, *I Was There*, p. 254.

420   "The Army did not appear": *Ibid.*, p. 259.

page

420   Clark passes along Tillar's report: Clark, *Carrier Admiral*, p. 195.

421–422   Sherman-Riley plans for Nimitz and Halsey: Sherman-Riley memo, September 20, 1944, p. 2.

422   "Western Task Force (Third Fleet)": *Ibid.*, item (e) (5).

Chapter Twenty-Three: LEYTE

423   Towers' seeds and fertilizers: Towers diaries, September 20, 1944.

424–425   Halsey to Nimitz: September 28, 1944.

425–426   "Admiral Nimitz stated": King-Nimitz meeting minutes, September 29, p. 5.

427–428   "I feel sure the Japs will be stung": Halsey to Nimitz, October 3, 1944.

428   "We must reserve the right": Halsey to Nimitz, letter of October 6, 1944, with Nimitz's scrawled notes on the bottom.

428   "You are always free": Nimitz to Halsey, October 8, 1944.

428–429   "I had been told": C. J. Moore, oral history, pp. 1030 and 1032.

434   "I believe that the prudent view": Halsey to Nimitz, October 22, 1944.

435   Halsey sends McCain's task group to Ulithi: *Admiral Halsey's Story*, Ch. 13.

438   Halsey's decision to go after the carriers: *Ibid.*, pp. 216–217.

439   Lee's message and subsequent silence: Morison, Vol. XII, p. 195.

439   Mitscher on advising Halsey: Theodore Taylor, *The Magnificent Mitscher*, pp. 261–262.

446   Halsey's message to Kinkaid: *Admiral Halsey's Story*, p. 217.

447   Kinkaid's question to Halsey: *Ibid.*, p. 218.

448   "It was not my job . . . my job was offensive": *Ibid.*, p. 219.

450   "If I were there I would keep my force right there": Forrestel, *Admiral Raymond A. Spruance*, p. 167.

450   Wilkinson to Turner: November 7, 1944.

451   King lambastes Halsey: Clark, *Carrier Admiral*, p. 201.

451   Chester Nimitz, Jr., on discussion of Halsey orders with his father: letter to author, September 1969.

452   "You can say with confidence and assurance": quoted in James Forrestal diaries, Department of Defense, October 25, 1944.

453   "Just before the Press Conference": *Ibid.*

Chapter Twenty-Four: THE NEW WAR

455   Halsey to Nimitz: November 4, 1944.

456   Halsey "inflicting attrition": Nimitz to Halsey, November 21, 1944.

page

458 Hoover to Nimitz: October 5, 1944.

458 "Admiral Hoover was not the most popular admiral": Kenneth McArdle, unpublished ms., p. 187.

461 decision not to use Army troops at Iwo Jima, and undecided future policy: King-Nimitz Conference notes, November 24–26, 1944, p. 5.

461 "Mr. Stalin has asked": *Ibid.*, p. 12.

462 "This is one of the responsibilities": quoted in Reminiscences of H. A. Lamar.

463 "Somebody ought to be courtmartialed": Halsey quoted by Preston Mercer to author, fall, 1969.

463 "It was the greatest loss": Pacific Fleet Confidential Letter 14CL 45.

463–464 Nimitz's and Halsey's Christmas trees: Lamar Reminiscences, *op. cit.*

464 Hoover's and others' opinions on responsibility for typhoon damage: Admiral Hoover to author, summer 1969.

464 problem of five-star insignias: Lamar Reminiscences, *op. cit.*

465 "In exercising his prerogatives": Forrestal diaries, Department of Defense, p. 129.

465 "I do not share your opinion": quoted in Forrestal diary, January 19, 1945, p. 130.

466 Japanese watch Dorothy Lamour: McArdle ms., pp. 220–240.

466–467 Nimitz's and staff's activities: Rear Admiral Earl Stone to author, June 24, 1969.

467 Pratt to Nimitz: January 20, 1945.

468 Nimitz on publicity: Nimitz to Rear Admiral Merrill, February 17, 1945.

468 LeMay's desire for Iwo Jima: Forrestel, *Admiral Raymond A. Spruance*, p. 168.

468 Iwo Jima bombed enough: Smith, *Coral and Brass*, p. 237.

469 combat vessel count as of December 31, 1944: Forrestal papers, Princeton University Library.

469 Nimitz and Spruance lacked taste for invading Japan: Admiral Harry Hill to author, autumn 1969.

471 Spruance's timing problems: Admiral Hill's oral history, and discussions with the author, fall 1969.

473 "Based upon my knowledge": Admiral Hill's oral history, p. 603.

474 King criticizes "Sockem" title: Admiral Hill to author, autumn 1969.

Chapter Twenty-Five: OKINAWA

478 McKelway on LeMay's opinion of Nimitz: Morison, Vol. XIV, note p. 88.

page
480–481   Spruance, Mitscher, and *Yamato*: *Admiral Raymond A. Spruance*, p. 204.
481–482   Spruance to Moore: May 13, 1945.
483   "The question of what operations should be undertaken after Okinawa": Forrestel, *Admiral Raymond A. Spruance*, pp. 209–210.
484–485   "He was informed": Nimitz to King, April 14, 1945.
486   "Upon Marshall's insistence": *Fleet Admiral King*, p. 598.
487   increased political visits: Towers diaries, May and June, 1945.
488   Hoover inclined toward court-martial of Halsey: Admiral Hoover to author, summer 1969.
488   "Nobody ever heard of a guy named Bowditch": Lockwood to Rear Admiral Allan R. McCann, June 23, 1945.
488   Clark's position: Clark, *Carrier Admiral*, p. 240.
488   "I would feel a great deal better": Halsey to Nimitz, June 17, 1945.
489   Radford on commands of Spruance and Radford: Admiral Radford to author, summer 1969.
490   "The General said of course": Kinkaid to Nimitz, May 2, 1945.
491   Turner to Forrestal: May 21, 1945.
491   "This is going to be tough": Turner to Wilkinson, June 8, 1945.
492   pressure to relinquish Royal Hawaiian: Lockwood to Merrill, July 11, 1945.
492   "I can make available": Nimitz to MacArthur, July 1, 1945.
492   "It will undoubtedly become necessary": Nimitz to MacArthur, July 10, 1945.
492   "horse trading": Kinkaid to Nimitz, July 17, 1945.
493   "These figures exceed the entire American losses": MacArthur's *Reminiscences*, p. 299.
494   "I am looking forward to seeing you": Halsey to Nimitz, August 9, 1945.
494   "This is a peace warning": quoted in Forrestal diaries, August 10, 1945.
494   Sherman to Nimitz: quoted in Forrestal diaries, August 13, 1945.

Chapter Twenty-Six: NIMITZ AND HIS ADMIRALS

497   Nimitz's refusal to allow Smith to be Hill's guest: Admiral Hill to author, autumn 1969.
498   "I hope that Admiral Halsey's clarifying press statement": Nimitz to Dr. W. C. Michels, September 21, 1946.
500–501   Nimitz's reason for becoming Chief of Naval Operations: Chester Nimitz, Jr., to author, September 1969.

INDEX